The Dog Repair
BOOK

A Do-It-Yourself
Guide for the
Dog Owner
RUTH B. JAMES, D.V.M.

Alpine Press
Mills, Wyoming

Inquiries should be addressed to Alpine Press,
    P.O. Box 1930, Mills, Wyoming 82644

Published by Alpine Press
            P.O. Box 1930
            Mills, Wyoming 82644

Final Editing by Alice Wicks, Dr. Harvel Alishouse, and
    P. J. and Vicki Rose
Cover Photo by Ruth B. James, D.V.M.
Interior Photos by Ruth B. James, D.V.M. and
    Deane M. Stanton
Illustrations by Dean Ingram
Custom photo processing by Norm and Evelyn Grant,
    Grant's Photographic Restoration, Tempe, Arizona, 85281
Printed by Cushing-Malloy, Inc.
    Ann Arbor, Michigan 48107
Printed in the United States of America

Library of Congress Catalog Card Number 89-85758
ISBN 0-9615114-1-9

To

SENSEI PAUL COSCARART
AND JON TAKAGI

Who Died

To

DEANE

Who Lights My World

DISCLAIMER

To help insure the reader's understanding of some of the medical descriptions and techniques in **The Dog Repair Book**, brand names have occasionally been used as examples of particular medications or equipment. However, the use of a particular trademark or brand name is not intended to imply an endorsement of that particular product, or to suggest that similar products offered by others under different names may in any way be inferior. The author has not received any compensation from any of the cited companies which would result in a conflict of interest or bias in the use of any particular product. Nothing contained in this book is to be construed as a suggestion to violate any trademark laws.

Although every effort has been made to present scientifically accurate and up-to-date information based on the best and most reliable sources available, it should be understood that the results of medical treatments depend upon many factors, including proper diagnosis, which are not under the control of the author or the publishers of this book. Therefore, neither Alpine Press nor the author assumes responsibility for and make no warranty with respect to results that may be obtained from the procedures herein. Neither Alpine Press nor Dr. Ruth James shall be liable to any person for damage resulting from reliance on any information contained in **The Dog Repair Book** whether with respect to diagnosis, drug dosages, treatment procedures, or by reason of any misstatement or inadvertent error contained herein.

Also, it should be noted that neither the author nor Alpine Press manufactures, packages, ships, labels, or sells any of the drugs or equipment mentioned in this book. Accordingly, neither can be held responsible for results that may be obtained with products manufactured by others.

The reader is encouraged to carefully read and follow the label directions provided by the manufacturer for any product which may be used. If there is a conflict between instructions contained in the book and those provided by the manufacturer, those provided by the manufacturer should be followed.

ACKNOWLEDGMENTS

So many people have contributed to the writing of this book that I can scarcely hope to thank them all.

Thanks are due to Bob Mills and Ed Arndt who have shepherded me through much of the publishing process. Their suggestions have been invaluable. Thanks also to Dale Hurst, Dave McCabe, Becky See, Margaret Funch, and Jacquelyn Berl who came to my rescue on this book. Thanks to my valued wholesalers and readers, who have demanded that I write this book. Their continuing enthusiasm and support have helped to make my previous book a success; they have my unceasing gratitude.

My thanks to Dr. Harvel Alishouse, without whose careful attention to detail and valuable suggestions, the book would have been much the poorer. Scott Neil also was so kind as to take the time and effort to read the manuscript for me, by the light of a candle lantern in the forest of northern Washington. Meghan and Jessica Sullivan also read it, with technical assistance from "Silver the Wonder Horse." Their comments and corrections have added immeasurably to the book, as have those of P. J. and Vicki Rose.

Thanks to all those who loaned their dogs and themselves for photos. Joan LaMoure, loaned her lovely yellow Labrador Retriever, Sunny. Jill Gorman and Dr. Jim Baldwin graciously modeled for the cover photo. Roger Bramson loaned his Pharoah Hound, Mercury, for some of the photos. Candy Ramirez and her Dachshund, Sally, were also models, as was Dana Cole. Donna Piscopo and Willie (a real character!) also modeled for the book.

Many of my friends have offered love, support, and continuing encouragement through the long process of writing. Deane Stanton contributes his love and suggestions which keep me from going completely crazy during the process of hatching the book. Howard Walworth keeps my head in the stars and my feet on the ground with his ideas and friendship. Keith James provided the quiet hideaway where the book could be finished. Brian Freeman troubleshoots my computers, printers, and programs, mostly by long-distance telephone. He is truly a miracle worker. Jodi Freeman is a continuing friend for whom I am truly grateful. Phill Morrison, Doug and Sue Achenbach, and Jerry Buk offer ongoing encouragement. I am also thankful for the teachers who have helped to shape my thinking, and to the clients and animals who have taught me so much. If perhaps I have omitted someone who has helped me, it has been because of my imperfect memory, not because of any desire to do so.

CONTENTS

INTRODUCTION

My first book, **How To Be Your Own Veterinarian (sometimes)** was written to help horse owners save money on their veterinary bills. It was aimed at helping them tell the difference between problems they could treat themselves, and those which needed the services and expertise of a veterinarian.

Somewhere between the tenth and eleventh printings of that book, customer demand reached a point where it could no longer be ignored. Readers were asking that I write a similar book for the dog owners, telling them how to avoid problems and save money on medical care for their dogs. YOU asked for it! So, here it is.

As with the previous book, I have tried to tell the dog owner how to treat simple problems at home. I have discussed the ailments for which veterinary diagnosis and treatment are essential. And, I have tried to distinguish clearly between the two extremes. Not incidentally, I hope to save you, the dog owner, some money with this knowledge. If I can save each person who buys this book just one veterinary call, it will have paid for itself. If I can also prevent the heartache of losing the dog you love, and save that animal some pain and suffering, the time I have devoted to writing it will have been well spent.

When you get this book, please read it at least lightly from cover to cover. In doing this you will come to know my thinking on treatment of injuries and illnesses, and also which problems are considered minor or which need veterinary help immediately. This first reading will give you an idea of how to begin and where to look for specific information when your dog is ill or injured. It should also point out many ways to keep your dog healthy.

I have tried to emphasize preventive measures which may be taken to keep many problems from occurring so that you may never need to treat them. Many illnesses are in large part preventable, but may be nearly incurable or permanently damaging once they have occurred. Preventive medicine is the cheapest form of veterinary care—and the most effective in the long run!

Chapter 1

HELPING YOUR VETERINARIAN TO HELP YOU

WHAT CAN A VETERINARIAN DO FOR YOU?

What can a veterinarian do for you? He can provide routine care for your dog, including checkups, immunizations and routine surgery such as spaying and neutering. As with your car, maintenance of your dog is much cheaper than repair. Your veterinarian can also serve emergencies such as accidents and illness. He can provide hospitalization for these problems. Because of its cost, hospitalization should be reserved for serious problems or when extensive diagnostic procedures are needed. Some problems can be handled on an outpatient basis much as they are in humans: you bring the dog in first thing in the morning and take him home at night, even if he is still slightly sedated. You provide part of his aftercare in return for a greatly reduced veterinary bill.

Why does veterinary treatment cost what it does? When you or a family member go to a doctor, the hospital provides X-ray machines, nurses and all the other things. All the doctor provides is an office, receptionist and a few routine instruments. On the other hand, the veterinarian provides his or her own hospital and all the equipment, including X-ray machine, anesthetic equipment, pharmacy, and nursing and technical assistants. He has available diagnostic tests, either in-house or from an outside laboratory. He may provide electrocardiograms to examine the heart (EKG's or ECG's), electroencephalograms (the same type of examination, done on the brain) and many other sophisticated tests, depending on your animal's needs. Maybe we should wonder not why veterinary care costs what it does, but how your veterinarian can provide so much value and care for so little cost!

By the same token, you should feel that you are receiving value for your money. Please feel free to discuss fees with your veterinarian. How much will tests or treatment cost? If your vet can't give an exact figure, ask for a high and low range. Some large clinics now ask whether you want minimum, average or no-holds-barred treatment. Give this some thought. What can you afford?

If you can't afford to pay for the treatment all at once, see what arrangements can be made. Does your veterinarian offer charge accounts? Does he take payments or credit cards?

Before you make the final decision, find out what outcome can be expected. Is the cost of treatment consistent with predictions for expectancy and quality of life? If there is only a 30% expectation of the animal living for only three or four months and suffering in pain the whole time, and it's going to cost $2,500, treatment may not be realistic. Even if you can afford it, do you really want to inflict that sort of pain and suffering on your animal to keep him alive for only a short time?

Pet health insurance is available in some areas, but it is too new to know how well it is going to perform. It is your individual decision as to whether projected costs of veterinary care will exceed insurance payments. Most pay only for catastrophic problems such as surgery or severe illness, not for routine care. Would you be better off putting a sum away each month in a savings account? If you never need it for your pet, you still have it for other use. If you watch out for your pet and he never runs loose to get hit by cars or get garbage poisoning, he has much less chance of needing emergency care than a dog who runs freely.

If you can't afford the cost of treatment, what are the alternatives? Can you really not afford it, or do you choose not to? Don't expect free treatment as you drive off in your new car. In some areas, animal welfare groups offer free or low-cost clinical care to those who truly cannot afford surgery or other treatment for their pets. Some of these clinics are not non-profit, nor are they inexpensive. Check and see what their financial policies are. In some areas, one or more veterinarians may do some charitable work. Your own veterinarian may not, but another one in the area might. Some local veterinary societies have programs through which members donate a certain amount of charity work each year. The last choice, if all else fails, is euthanasia to end the animal's suffering (see Euthanasia).

HOSPITALIZATION

In some cases, hospitalization may be needed. If this is the case, you should expect realistic information from the veterinarian, including what treatment will be needed and what it will cost. There should be an evaluation of the dog's prospects for recovery, and a realistic evaluation of what you are or will be putting your dog through. Communication should be open in both directions.

Most dogs with a serious illness or injury will rest well in a veterinary clinic. It is better not to visit your dog at the clinic unless asked to do so by your veterinarian. It is impossible to explain to your dog why you came to see him and then left without taking him with you. Some dogs become extremely upset, and will even paw at the cage until their feet are bloody when the owner leaves without them.

FINDING A VETERINARIAN

Your dog is perfectly healthy. Why do you need a veterinarian now? Because it's easier to find one before you need him. And it's easier to decide whether or not you like the veterinarian and have confidence in him before you need him in the confusion of an emergency. You will want to decide if you can get along with him, and whether he can get along with your animal. Look for a veterinarian before you need him! Take your dog in for a checkup or vaccination.

Some veterinary practices treat small animals only, while others are mixed practices, treating both large and small animals. In many rural areas, the veterinarian who cares for your cow or horse will also take care of your dog. This is a great convenience for the rancher or farmer with several dogs, as one visit from the veterinarian can do double duty. If this is your case, let your veterinarian know that you want him to look at your dogs when you call him so that he can bring the proper vaccine or medication.

In small-animal practices, you have a choice of house-call practice versus a clinical practice. A house-call practice is very convenient if you are homebound, work at home or have small children. The house-call veterinarian may or may not have access to a hospital to provide treatment and hospitalization for more severe ailments.

Veterinarians who practice alone ("solo practice") may fit well with some dog owners. Your animal may get more personal attention from a hard-working solo practitioner. The drawback is that the veterinarian is human, and cannot be on call 365 days a year. You may be referred to an emergency clinic or to another veterinarian who is covering the practice when you have an emergency and your veterinarian takes time off for vacation or is attending a continuing-education seminar.

A group practice is one in which a number of veterinarians work together in the same facility. They may take turns on night and emergency call. Each partner or employee may have a specialty in addition to taking his share of the general calls. Or, some of the members may be full-time specialists who do nothing but work on eyes or bone problems, for instance.

Your veterinarian may refer you to a specialist. This specialist may be on the staff of a group practice, or he may have a small clinic of his own. Expect to pay him substantially more than you would pay a general practitioner. As with any veterinarian, do not hesitate to discuss how much the care will cost. A referral really means that your veterinarian knows his limitations, and is not afraid to send you to an expert on a particular problem to receive the best possible care for your animal. Go back to him after your treatment is finished at the specialist's.

The American Animal Hospital Association (AAHA) is a group of veterinary hospitals which meet certain stated and enforced standards. These hospitals must meet certain facility and equipment, personnel and laboratory standards. The AAHA standards make sure that member hospitals maintain a level of excellence designed to meet the latest standards of veterinary medicine. An "Animal Hospital" or "Animal Medical Center" is a full-service veterinary practice which can provide examination, diagnostic services and treatment, and are equipped to house and nurse patients. These may have "Satellite Clinics," which treat most animals on an outpatient basis, while sending cases needing more intensive care to the main hospital. An AAHA "Central Hospital" has a full range of veterinary services, including 24-hour nursing and specialty consultation. An "Emergency Hospital" takes care of animals when other hospitals are closed. Expect them to refer your animals that they have treated to your regular veterinarian the next morning.

All AAHA hospitals must maintain careful records on all animals they treat. They must provide examination facilities, pharmacies for animal medications, pathology services to do routine laboratory tests, radiology services, anesthetic and surgical facilities, and routine dental services. They must provide nursing care, and maintain certain standards of housekeeping and maintenance. They must have a medical library consisting of basic textbooks and current periodicals. They must either provide adequate emergency services, or have a referral procedure to send after-hours cases to another hospital for care. Some AAHA hospitals offer specialty practices or have veterinarians on staff who are board-certified in specialties such as ophthalmology (eye care), orthopedics (bone and joint care) and many others. An AAHA certification of the hospital assures you that the veterinary clinic and its practitioners are current in their medical knowledge and that the clinic facility meets some rather tough standards.

Many other veterinarians choose not to be members of AAHA, yet still have current medical knowledge, a good facility and provide excellent care. To find one, talk with your friends or neighbors. Ask WHICH veterinarian they use, and WHY they like him or her. Or ask a member of your local kennel club. If you are planning on moving to a new town, ask your current veterinarian to refer you to a veterinarian in your new location. He may know a veterinarian personally in whom he has confidence. While you may not stay with this new veterinarian if your personality does not mesh with his, he is at least a place to start.

If worst comes to worst, you may find a veterinarian through the yellow pages of your phone directory. This has the advantage of telling you if he specializes in certain animals (such as birds or fish). It has the disadvantage of not giving you ANY idea of his qualifications or ability.

GETTING ACQUAINTED

Ask for a clinic tour if you are interested in seeing the facility. Do it at a time convenient for the veterinarian or his staff. This will give you an idea of what the veterinarian can do for you and your animals.

When you call for advice, give the veterinarian as much factual information as you can when first discussing the illness. You are better acquainted with your dog than is your veterinarian. It will be your everyday observations that spot a problem. Don't play down this vital part of the preliminary diagnosis. On the other hand, don't jump to conclusions. Many veterinarians are asked to treat "worms" when the problem is impacted anal sacs or some other problem. Tell your veterinarian what your dog is DOING and how your dog looks, not what you think the problem is. As he becomes more familiar with you and your dogs, he will know whether or not you know what you are talking about and how astute you are in dealing with your animals and their problems. He then will have a better basis to know what questions he needs to ask you in order to sort out the information that you give him. This preliminary information may not seem important to you. However, many times it is essential to an accurate diagnosis of the problem. What may seem minor to you may become meaningful later after further examination and observation, laboratory tests, and watching the course of the disease.

Don't be afraid to give your impressions of change: the dog is acting better or worse, feeling stronger or remaining the same. This is especially important in treating diseases which take some time to heal. If a problem is not responding to one medication, it may be necessary to change to another. Since you are the person seeing the animal several times a day and administering his medicine, you are the one best able to determine progress or lack of progress. Don't be afraid to call the veterinarian and ask him if the animal should be getting well faster. He can then either give you information over the phone, or decide that he needs to re-examine the animal in person.

Wait to give the animal's detailed medical history until you are at the veterinarian's office. Most of us would rather have it then, while we are looking at the animal. If we get the information over the phone, we may have forgotten it by the time we see the animal. Give any information which is pertinent to the problem at hand.

It is important to be honest with your veterinarian. How long has problem been going on? Are there factors contributing to the problem that he should know about? Have you given the animal any medication? Can you administer pills? If you can't, your veterinarian can arrange for another way to treat your dog. He may have you bring your dog in daily for treatment, change from pills to liquid, or show you how to administer pills to your dog.

Is your dog a grouch? Let the veterinarian know so that he can provide assistants who are experienced in holding or treating grouchy dogs. This may save you from being accidentally bitten. Letting him get bitten is not the way to win friends and influence your veterinarian. It's more diplomatic to say something like "My dog sometimes bites" rather than to say "My dog hates veterinarians!" Sometimes this dislike is due to the animal's previous experience. Some of it is because many dogs are sensitive to the smells of other animals or to medication odors present on the veterinarian's hands and clothing despite the best of sanitation procedures. Some dogs probably even dislike the disinfectants which veterinarians use to clean their hands.

A SECOND OPINION

Don't be afraid to get a second opinion on your animal's problem. As with human doctors, veterinarians are not all-knowing. If your veterinarian is secure in his knowledge, he should have no objection to your doing so. If he does object, you probably need to find a new veterinarian anyway.

When should you get a second opinion? Get it when the first opinion doesn't make sense, or when treatment is prescribed which you think is unreasonable in terms of trouble or cost. If you have any question about the first opinion, or if expensive surgery is recommended as the only cure, feel free to consult with another veterinarian. If the two agree, the problem has probably been diagnosed correctly. If the second opinion is different, or perhaps opposite, DO NOT automatically assume that the first one was wrong and the second one is correct. The truth may be the other way around. When the two are significantly different, GET A THIRD ONE!! At this point, it's time to take the dog to a university clinic or specialty hospital. Be prepared to pay for extra tests, and, perhaps, the services of a specialist. If you have a specific problem which you can define, for instance, an eye or orthopedic problem, go directly to an appropriate specialist for your additional opinion. In this case, especially if the specialist is board certified, you can probably trust his recommendations.

A FEW ADDITIONAL HINTS

Please, please, take your dog into the veterinary clinic on a leash. If you don't have one, most clinics will loan you a leash. Go in and get it BEFORE you take your dog out of the car, for the safety of you, your animal and the rest of the clients in the waiting room. And, use it to return the dog to your car. I once saw a client carry her dog back into the clinic after it was run over in front of the clinic. It had dashed out into the street in its excitement and eagerness. There was nothing we could do to save it.

Make sure you understand the veterinarian's instructions regarding treatment and aftercare of your animal BEFORE you leave the clinic. If you are not sure, don't hesitate to ask him to repeat them, or jot them down on paper for you. Most of us would rather go over instructions an extra time than to try to recall every word that we said when you call back two days later. If you don't know how to do the prescribed treatments or techniques, ask for a demonstration.

Carry out treatments as instructed, even if it means getting up in the middle of the night. Correct timing can be important, especially when certain antibiotics are given. Keep a sheet of paper handy and make notes if the veterinarian has asked you to record the animal's temperature, feed consumption, bowel movements, or other information. Also jot down any questions which you would like to ask the next time you call the veterinarian. This will help to make the call brief and more efficient. If your veterinarian has asked you to call him with more information about the animal, or with a progress report, find out what number you should use, and what time of the day it is best to call him. Some veterinarians like to receive incoming calls at one time of the day so they can plan for this important part of their work. It's often worthwhile to call even if you haven't been asked, to tell him that the animal has recovered. We like to hear good news too for a change.

Be sure to keep records of when immunizations are given, and when illnesses or injuries occur. Note what treatments are used and how your dog reacts to them. If your dog has any allergies, be sure to keep track of them. If you change veterinarians or move, be sure to tell your new veterinarian about the allergies.

If your dog does not get well, or at least show improvement within a reasonable length of time, call your veterinarian. He may wish to change the medication, and may be able to do this over the telephone. Or he may wish to have you bring the dog in for re-examination. Don't let the problem go and then complain because the veterinarian didn't "cure" your dog. If you and your veterinarian are functioning as a team, your dog is the winner!

If you call a veterinarian to treat an animal which has been examined or treated by another veterinarian, be sure to give him the details of the first treatment. Some medications can mask symptoms or cause others to develop. If the previous veterinarian has made a diagnosis which is in error (which we can all do), it will save time for the second veterinarian if you tell him as much as you can about what was said and what treatment was given. Discontinue any medication which was given to you by the first veterinarian. Failure to do so may result in a conflict between the old and new medications. In some cases, this may seriously confuse the diagnosis by complicating signs of the disease, while in others it may actually be dangerous.

In some cases, the advice in this book may conflict with that given by your veterinarian. If this occurs, take his advice, because he has the advantage of seeing and examining your animal and working "face to face" with the specific problem.

Chapter 2

THE RIGHT DOG FOR YOU

THE PERFECT PET?

Are you sure you want a dog? Millions of pets are put to death every year because their owners no longer want them. Or, the owners did not have her spayed, and then had to dispose of the offspring.

There are many benefits of pet ownership. Many a dog has provided companionship and even protection for a child, both in the home and in the wide outdoors. A dog can be a very special, non-critical, accepting friend through the difficult teen years. Pets are loving companions for elderly or retired people. Studies have shown that persons who have pets live longer and are healthier. It is thought that in many cases a pet gives a lonely person a feeling of being needed, a reason to live.

Having a dog encourages some people to exercise. Occasionally, people get a dog and lose weight in their dedication to exercising him. Dogs also give adults a chance to relax and play. They can provide the unconditional love, friendship and emotional support which we all need. Research has shown that people who have had heart attacks who own pets survive longer and have lower blood pressure than those without pets.

What are you looking for in a pet? Companionship? Status? A dog to show, to hunt with, to take jogging, to haul your pack up a mountain or to pull a sled? A guard or watchdog? For protection you may want to buy a mature dog that has been professionally trained. For a watchdog, you just need one that can bark. Even a very small dog (toy breed) can do this very well.

What facilities do you have? A large house or small apartment? A farm or ranch? A large yard or none at all? An adequate fence that the dog cannot jump or climb over, or dig under? Storage space for the dog food? A reliable source of clean water?

How much time do you wish to spend with the pet? All dogs will need some of your time. Large dogs need walks or a VERY large yard. Even a large house is not enough space for a Great Dane or Irish Wolfhound. Working-breed dogs are happier with something to do, or at least plenty of exercise.

Will the dog be left alone for long periods of time when you are at work for long days? Two smaller dogs can keep each other company if you are gone long hours. Are you out of town for long periods of time where the animal would have to be boarded, or someone would have to come in to care for him? Will the dog be left alone in the yard to bark and annoy the neighbors?

Will other members of the household help with the dog's care and social needs? It may not be a good idea to get a puppy to "teach the child responsibility," unless it's the child's idea to have a dog. Do you expect a child (or children) to take over ALL care of the dog? This may be an unrealistic bargain which will only make you unhappy when the child does not keep his end of it. Or, the dog may be a pet and toy for a short time, and then be ignored. Do YOU want the dog if the child doesn't? On the other hand, some parents don't want the child taking over ANY of the dog chores. The most happy reality is probably between these two extremes. Do not impose the dog on the child if he is not interested, or loses interest in it.

Do you have small children or infirm persons in the home? A large dog may knock them over and cause injury, just by accident. A small dog may be a better choice for a pet. Do you want a sedate, calm dog or a bouncing, vivacious one? Large dogs may eat 10 lb. or more of food per day. Are you prepared for the cost, and cleanup afterward?

What if you have a baby later? The dog fits into a "pack," and your family is his pack. He must recognize his place in the pack order. Give the dog attention when the baby is present so that he will feel that the baby's presence brings good consequences. Discipline him severely if he growls at or otherwise threatens the baby. If the dog is old and set in its ways, he may be upset when the small child grabs a handful of hair or a tender portion of anatomy. If the dog absolutely will NOT adjust, it may be necessary to get rid of him.

How will the dog fit in with your existing pets? A dominant dog may be gruff about accepting a puppy. Given time, he should come around to at least tolerate the newcomer. A puppy often stimulates an old dog to get up and play and to have a renewed interest in life. A cat may or may not accept a new puppy. Acceptance by a cat could take a while. The cat may sulk and forget that he is housebroken for a time. It is often helpful to feed the two pets separately until they make their peace.

How much grooming are you willing to do yourself or pay to have done? Some dogs, such as Poodles, need grooming every four or five weeks, and the cost may be high. Many long-haired dogs need daily grooming to keep them clean and keep their hair from matting. Do you have the time and desire to do it? If not, get a low-maintenance dog that needs little in the way of combing, trimming or bathing. Other maintenance may be needed, depending on the breed of dog. Ear cropping and tail docking may be needed, depending on the breed and your preference. If you are buying a puppy and want the ears trimmed, make sure it is not too old, and that its ears are suitable for an ear trim. Get a veterinarian's opinion to avoid disappointment.

Some breeds have many medical problems. For instance, we call the English Bulldog "the veterinarian's delight," because it has so many hereditary medical problems. They are very good for our business.

Don't get a dog just because you want your children to witness the "miracle of birth." Dogs rarely have puppies when the children are around to observe. The world doesn't need more little dogs without homes who are just kicked out on their own to be run over by cars or put to death because no one wants them. Don't contribute to the pet overpopulation problem for this lousy reason. Get a videotape and teach them with it, not with a half-dozen helpless newborn puppies.

If you don't have the time to spend with the dog, or if you don't want to be bothered, you might consider a pet that requires less care and social contact: a cat, bird, rodent or reptile. Cats can be left alone for up to a week if absolutely necessary. All it would need would be a couple of clean litter boxes, a large bowl of dry food and a dish of water. They cope better with being left alone for long periods every day and most weekends than do dogs. They adapt well to living their entire lives indoors, in a small house or apartment. Birds need clean food and water every day or two at most, but have even fewer social needs than a cat. A rodent can be left several days with adequate food and water. Their social needs are almost nonexistent, but they can still provide companionship. How about a reptile? A nice boa constrictor, corn snake or similar snake can be left for a week or so with clean water and controlled temperatures. Most snakes need feeding only every couple of weeks, and may go voluntarily for months without eating. They are quiet and don't annoy the neighbors. Your friends, however, may be a little skittish when they first make the snake's acquaintance.

CHOOSING THE INDIVIDUAL

Perhaps your most important decision is whether to get a puppy or an older dog. Do you have the time and patience to train a puppy? Do you have the disposition to put up with mischief, accidents, and to invest the time and effort needed for training? If you are looking for a more sedate, calm, relaxed dog, be careful which the breed you choose, and which specific individual. A mature dog may be better, as you can see what the animal's temperament is going to be. If you are buying an adult dog, be sure you can live with its personality and established habits.

A trained adult dog may be a good bet for a hunting dog. You can see what the dog is and what he can do. The same is true of a guard dog. The animal is ready to do the job you want done, without waiting for over a year to raise and train a puppy and then maybe not have it be suitable for the duties you have in mind. A person who wants breeding stock will often buy a mature dog. Dogs who have been in a kennel all of their lives often are extremely timid and have poorly developed personalities. Do not expect this type of dog to be a good companion. It may, however, be a suitable breeding animal.

Do you want a male or female? Personal preferences are more important here than gender. A male will sniff at everything when you take him for a walk. Some people don't like this. Consider what the urine will do to your yard. Female dogs will leave brown spots on the lawn. Male dogs may damage or kill bushes and flowers if not properly trained to urinate in an acceptable location. They may mark in the house if not trained, and if the owner is not clearly dominant over them. A female can be a nuisance when she comes into heat. She will need to be either closely confined or kenneled if she is not to get pregnant (the abstinence theory of birth control). Neutering or spaying neutralize some of these problems and stop a lot of others, besides. Either sex should be neutered if you're not going to breed it.

What about mongrel versus purebred? A mongrel, mixed breed or mutt can be a good dog. The mongrel may be free or inexpensive. You may be able to make an educated guess about its grown size and appearance if you can see both parents. Dogs are individuals. Registered bloodlines don't have much to do with the ability of the dog to be a companion, although some breeds are more aggressive than others. A purebred dog is the offspring of two registered parents. It may cost a lot, depending on its quality and bloodlines. A purebred may have more predictable characteristics of appearance, personality and adult size than with a mixed breed dog. You may be able to sell its offspring.

A dog registered with the American Kennel Club (AKC) is eligible to compete in AKC dog shows and have registered offspring. AKC (or any other registration) is NO guarantee of quality. It merely means that both of the dog's parents are registered. The address of the AKC is: The American Kennel Club, 51 Madison Avenue, New York, N.Y., 10010. Consult AKC materials to determine what papers you need to get from the breeder to make sure you can register the dog. It would be a big disappointment to pay the price for a registered dog and not have its papers in order. The United Kennel Club of Kalamazoo, Mich., registers Coonhounds and Foxhounds.

Which breed is best for you? This depends on your personality, preference and pocketbook, but most of all what you want the dog to do. There are good dogs and bad dogs in all breeds. Research will allow you to eliminate breeds with high maintenance or hereditary problems, and to determine the positive and negative characteristics of each breed. Much of the dog's personality (when you start with a puppy) is what you make it.

Dogs are grouped into several divisions, about which some broad generalizations can be made. Toy breeds, for instance, are small, convenient and perhaps a bit delicate. Some people find them high-strung and neurotic. Working dogs tend to be more serious, and are often quite energetic. Terriers are somewhat more aloof than some of the others. Hounds tend to be a bit less trainable and more inclined to follow their own noses or eyes rather than listening to their owners. A bit of research at the library will turn up a number of books which will give you general sizes and breed characteristics. The physical descriptions will give you an idea whether a breed will fit your needs. Ignore descriptions such as "extremely loyal." Nearly any dog is loyal to the family with which he is raised if you get him as a puppy. You and your family are the dog's pack.

When choosing any puppy, see both parents if at all possible. This will give you a better idea of what to expect when it is grown, whether it is a purebred or mongrel.

Where do you get a puppy? Humane societies or dog pounds are a common source. Unfortunately, there is a high probability of getting a dog which will become ill with a contagious disease contracted there, especially if it is a young puppy. There is somewhat less chance of illness with an older dog. You may find a good, mature animal who has just been lost and not claimed. You may get an older animal with ears and tail already trimmed. It may already be spayed or neutered. It's easy to tell if a male has been neutered. But, to tell if a female has been spayed may require the assistance of a veterinarian.

If you get a pet that works out, you have the satisfaction of having saved an animal from euthanasia. As many as one-third of pound dogs are purebred. You will, of course, rarely get the registration papers with the dog. On the other hand, you may get a mature animal with unfixably bad habits who ended up there because of them. Plan to try a mature animal and see if it fits you and your family and your situation. At some shelters, a dog may cost as much as if it had been purchased from a breeder.

A pet shop often comes to mind when looking for a puppy. They are often quite expensive. A reputable pet shop may guarantee the puppy's health and allow you to return the puppy for exchange or refund if it is not healthy. Make sure the store is clean and ALL puppies look healthy to help avoid problems. These puppies may not have adequate social contact and play when they are young. This contact is critical for their development. They may not have well-developed personalities when grown because of this lack of early contact. In many cases, the dog may be purebred, but may come from low-quality stock and may not grow up to be a good example of the breed. Above all, don't plan on a pet shop puppy being of show quality. The probability of this happening is extremely remote.

A show breeder or kennel is often a good source for a puppy. Not every puppy, even from champion-to-champion matings, is of show quality. Breeders often sell "pet quality" puppies out of these litters. These are usually excellent individuals, and can be purchased quite reasonably. Young puppies (say under eight-to-ten weeks old) are a good bet. Older kennel dogs, unless they have been kept in the house or yard and had good social contact, will often be shy and have underdeveloped personalities. THEY USUALLY DO NOT COME OUT OF THIS, NO MATTER WHAT THE BREEDER SAYS! If you just want one of these dogs for breeding, it may be OK. If you want it for a pet, it's not a good bet. Keep looking.

A "backyard breeder" is the name given to an individual who breeds one or more dogs and sells the puppies. The quality of the puppies depends strictly on the breeder. Some produce one or two excellent litters of dogs a year, while others turn out mediocre-to-poor dogs as fast as they can breed them. You may be able to see both parents, as well as the environment in which the puppy has been raised from the time it was born. You can get a good idea of the background of the puppy you are planning to buy.

Puppies raised by small or backyard breeders are usually well socialized because they have been handled and given attention during the critical early weeks of their life. The price may be more reasonable than other sources because they don't have the large advertising and store costs of a pet shop.

In general, don't look to this sort of breeder for your next show champion, but if you can look at both parents, you may get an outstanding pet at a reasonable price. These puppies may be more healthy because they have less chance of being exposed to disease than if they come from pet stores or dog pounds. On the other hand, some may be less healthy because of poor sanitation, and because good worming procedures have not been followed—it just depends. You can find backyard breeders through newspaper ads, bulletin boards or through your veterinarian.

How can you find a reputable breeder? Ask your veterinarian to refer you to one who raises the kind of dogs in which you are interested. Attend a dog show and question the owners of dogs you like about where they got their dogs, or if they will be having a litter. Check a specialty magazine which covers the breed that you have in mind. Write to the AKC for a list of breeders in your area. Find someone who has a dog whose looks and disposition you like and ask where he got it.

Swap meets, fairs and auctions are usually poor sources of puppies. You may find a puppy there, but chances are that it may not grow up to be the breed it's said to be. It may also be much older or younger than represented, and of unknown health history. Not a good place to find your companion for the next 15 years!

Regardless of where you get the dog... Make sure that the premises are clean and sanitary. Other animals there should also look healthy and happy. The puppy should be alert, lively and interested in what is going on around him. His eyes should be clear and free of discharge. His nose may be moist or slightly dry, but should not have a discharge or crust on it. His skin should be clean and healthy-looking. There should be no reddened areas or hair loss. Other animals on the premises (dogs or cats) should not show any signs of skin disease. You might buy a dog with fleas or ticks, but be aware that you will have the expense and bother of treating them. Also, their presence may indicate that the overall care of the animal has not been up to par. The gums should be pink rather than pale, and there should not be any coughing. Bowel movements, if observed, should be firm and look normal. There should not be a lump at the belly button area; if there is, this may be an umbilical hernia. It may require surgery if it is large. If small, it can be left untreated, and it will probably go away as the puppy matures.

The puppy or dog should not show hostility or act aggressively toward you. It should be friendly and respond to your attention. It should not mind being held or restrained. A puppy which comes out of the group toward you has a better chance of having a good personality than one that cowers back in the corner. You can administer a quick personality test. Clap your hands loudly, and see if the puppy runs away. An ideal puppy should be curious, and recognize that an unusual sound has occurred. He should not cower. If he barks, that's OK. Drag an empty bleach bottle or similar container past the puppy on the end of a string. Again, the dog should be aware. He should not ignore the object (bad), and he should not run away (worse). This will help you to select an intelligent, easy-to-train dog.

Puppies should be plump but not fat. An older dog should be in reasonable shape and not obese, especially if he is a mature hunting or guard dog.

The dog should have had all shots appropriate for his age. The tail and dewclaws (in some breeds) should have been docked at three days of age. Ears should have been cropped if that is appropriate for the age and breed. It may be impossible to do them if the dog is too old. Check with a veterinarian if you are unsure.

The seller should give you a list of the vaccinations and worming treatments which have been given. It is a good idea to get a written agreement from the seller that you can take the animal to a veterinarian for a health examination, and return it within two to five days if it does not get a clean bill of health or shows behavioral problems.

If the dog is registered, you should get a written bill of sale giving the date of sale, a guarantee of returnability if it is found to be unhealthy within two to five days, the registration number for the litter or individual, the price paid, and the date of birth and description of the individual dog.

You should never have to pay extra for the dog's papers—according to AKC rules, they are not "for sale." A breeder, however, may ask you to sign an agreement that the dog will be spayed or neutered, or not used for breeding. This is within AKC rules, and one copy will be sent to the AKC.

When should you get the puppy? Do you want a puppy in the winter if you live in a cold climate? Christmas is not the best time to get a puppy. There are many things for a puppy to get into. He may not get enough attention because everyone is too busy. Try not to get a puppy just before you go on vacation if you are going to have to send him to a kennel. This can set his housebreaking back rather badly. On the other hand, before a vacation is a good time to get a puppy if you are going to be at home and able to spend time with him. Arrange to have a veterinarian examine the animal, especially if it is expensive.

You must choose the dog which is attractive to you. This is the starting point of your bond with the animal.

WHEN THE PET DOES NOT WORK OUT

A pet is an animal that we keep for our pleasure. Because they are completely dependent on us for food, water, shelter and health care, we have the responsibility to provide these things. Life should be a pleasure for the animal as well. Unfortunately, some pets do not work out as we expect. The dog is too large, too rowdy, untrainable or cannot be housebroken. He has a dispositional or behavioral problem which cannot reasonably be resolved. An example of this is a large dog that bites one of the members of the family. He could perhaps be broken of the habit by behavioral counseling, taking him to a trainer and modifying behavior of family members. But is it worth it? Even if his behavior does change, will he be a suitable pet? Or will he just be a large, unwanted beast that you can never entirely trust?

A pet may have a physical problem which cannot be fixed. This is common in older animals. Chronic problems such as hip dysplasia or chronic heart or kidney disease may reach a point that the dog is no longer comfortable or happy. He is miserable, hurting or ill all the time, and there is no cure for the problem.

When the pet is not satisfactory, it's time to do something about it. If a physical or behavioral problem can be changed or repaired so that the animal is happy and comfortable—and you are, too—you may still have a pleasant pet. If not, why are you still hanging onto the dog? Do you feel guilty about giving him up? If you can find another home for him, he may be far happier than he is now. If not, why continue to have him be miserable? For some reason, many people are much more reluctant to divorce themselves from an unsatisfactory pet than from an unsatisfactory spouse! While we have the responsibility to take care of the animal, we also have the responsibility to ourselves not to be miserable owning him. Some people decide that a puppy isn't working in their home, and then spend the rest of the time they own the dog being miserable because they kept it anyway.

What do you do if the dog doesn't work out? You can see that he isn't suitable for you or your family or your household. If it is a puppy, you may be able to find someone who likes the dog and feels they can get along with him. Give the dog to them and wish them well with it. And make it clear that you will not be hurt if the dog does not fit them and THEY want to get rid of it. After all, they need the same privileges of trial that you had! Don't make THEM live with a dog you didn't want because they feel guilty getting rid of it. There are some dogs, especially older animals who have peculiar personalities, who do not fit in ANYWHERE.

Can't find a home that way? Take the dog to the animal shelter or your humane society. You may be asked for a donation. This helps to keep the doors of the shelter open, and to feed the animals while they are waiting for homes. If you can't afford this, a public animal shelter (the "dog pound") will take any and all unwanted animals. It would be unfair not to warn you that animals that are not adopted after a certain period of time are euthanized (put to death). In Phoenix, Ariz., some 70 to 80 THOUSAND unwanted animals are euthanized annually between the humane society and the county pound. If nothing else, this is a good argument for spaying or neutering your pet.

If the dog is vicious or otherwise unsafe, or if he has injured one or more persons, you owe it to other people to euthanize him. It may just result in more injuries if you pass him on to someone else. In this case, it is your responsibility to have the dog euthanized, and to make sure this is done. Take him to your veterinarian, explain why you are having this done to a dog who is not ill, injured or senile, and then wait until you can view the body. If the dog has bitten anyone, he has to be kept alive for ten days. Otherwise, the person may have to take a series of rabies shots, and you may be in for a lawsuit.

There should be no complaint about euthanizing a dog who is old or ill. Again, just have this done by your veterinarian. We are able to do the final kindness for our pets by ending their misery when there is no solution for their physical or mental problems.

Chapter 3

CANINE CARE AND TRAINING

THE NEW PUPPY

So, you have chosen the perfect puppy to be the new member of your family. If he is between six and seven weeks of age, it will only take about a day for him to form a tight and lasting bond with his new family.

It is a good idea to prepare for the car ride home BEFORE you go puppy shopping. It is helpful to take another person along to hold and reassure the puppy. And be sure to take a towel or blanket along for his lap—it is common for the puppy to be excited, and he may have an accident.

Before you leave with the puppy to go home, get all the information you can about the vaccinations the puppy has had (and when), when he has been wormed (and with what product), his birth date, and any medications, treatments or other products that he has been given. Also get any registration papers or applications for registration that go with the dog. Find out what food he has been eating, and stop at the grocery store on the way home to pick up a sack. If it's late at night, ask the breeder for a couple of cups of food to tide the puppy over until you can get to the store. With all the other changes that are happening in his life, the puppy doesn't need a change of diet at the same time. Ask the breeder for a piece of the puppy's bedding, or something else with the odor of his mother on it. This will help him feel a bit less lost for the first couple of days until he settles into his new home.

When you get home, see that the puppy does not get too much attention all at once. Give him some quiet time to get acquainted with his new home. Let him smell around. Give him small drinks of water and about half a meal until he has had time to settle down. Otherwise, in his excitement, he may overload and vomit. Don't worry if the puppy doesn't eat eagerly for a couple of days as long as he is feeling well otherwise.

Give the puppy a couple of relaxed days to get acquainted with his new environment before you let children play vigorously with him. He may have a few accidents, but it is asking a lot for him to learn about a new home, new people and new rules all at the same time.

Some people wean their puppies onto milk and/or baby cereal. This diet is NOT adequate for a fast-growing puppy, and he will need to be changed to a more efficient diet.

However, continue to feed the puppy this familiar diet for the first two days until he has settled into your home. Then, over a couple of days' time, change him to a regular puppy chow. A very young puppy (not yet of weaning age) can be put on a milk replacer product until he is old enough to eat puppy chow (for further information on puppy feeding, see Weaning).

If you have other pets who are already established in the home, make sure they get plenty of attention so they do not feel left out and become jealous of the new puppy. Introduce the puppy gradually to the older dog or cat, and only with supervision. Put them together for short periods of time when you are there to watch. Feed them separately until you are sure they are getting along VERY well together. A cat may be aloof and unsure of the puppy. If the puppy, wanting to investigate, rushes toward the cat, a swift claw may permanently damage an eyeball. Or a fast, angry bite from a jealous old dog may cripple a tiny puppy. These tragic accidents are rare, but can happen. This is why the animals should be either supervised or separated until you are sure they are compatible.

Make a place for the puppy to call his own from the very first. A small dog will appreciate an animal shipping crate (appropriate to his grown size). This can be a refuge from the hustle of the world, and a place to escape from overeager children. It can become a permanent "den", an indoor dog house. And, it can double as transportation when you travel or ship the dog.

Remove the puppy's collar and tags when you put him in the crate so that they cannot become caught and choke him. Do not put water into the crate, as he will probably spill it, become wet, or need to urinate before you are available to take him outside. You are really doing your dog a favor by keeping him from getting into trouble when you are not home. When you put the puppy into the crate, you can put a piece or two of dog food in the back of it. This way, he gets a reward for going into it.

The puppy's refuge should NOT be a place of punishment. Make it a place of quiet and comfort for him, preferably out of the main traffic patterns of the household. A small or toy dog should be considered an indoor dog, anyway, unless you live in the deep south.

A larger dog may become an outdoor dog. It is easier to be an outdoor dog from the start. If the puppy is six to seven weeks old and the temperature is warm, he can go right outdoors. If it is cold, keep him indoors or in a basement or garage until he is about eight weeks old. A small cozy box will give the puppy a warm place for the night. Or an outdoor dog could have a deep bed of straw in the corner of a tack room or an empty horse stall.

You can use a large cardboard box as a temporary dog house. Cut down one side so that he can get in and out. Line the box with newspapers, and then put in an old blanket, some clean rags or a piece of carpet. Make sure the box is in a draft-free place out of the weather.

If the puppy is very small or it is very cold, put a hot water bottle in his bed. A large puppy will appreciate a gallon milk jug filled with hot water (not TOO hot!) and placed in the box. Do NOT use an electric heating pad, as the puppy may chew the wires and burn his mouth or be electrocuted. An old windup alarm clock will sound a bit like his mother's heart, and will help the puppy settle down and go to sleep.

No matter how sympathetic you are for the "poor little puppy," you need to steel yourself and NOT run to him when he cries. If you do respond to his crying, you will actually train him to whine. He will learn that all he has to do is cry and you will come running. If you can ignore the whining for a couple of nights, the puppy will learn to get through the night by himself. If you talk to him, play with him or even get up to shout at him, you are teaching him that he can get attention by crying. If the crying bothers you, put the puppy farther from where you are sleeping—in the garage, in the shower with the door shut and the bathroom door closed, etc.

If you have decided that the puppy is going to live in a doghouse, start him there as soon as the weather permits. If the weather is warm enough, he can start living in it right away. How large should the doghouse be? In cold climates, it should be just long enough for the dog to stretch out at full length when he is fullgrown. It should be wide enough for his legs to be stretched out straight, at his adult size. It should be just tall enough to clear his withers (the top of his shoulders) when he is fully grown. By having the house just large enough for the dog, his body heat can keep it comfortably warm. A flap of carpet or canvas makes a good door, and you can make a baffle, if you wish, so that he walks down a "hallway" and around the corner into his house. Remember that in the wild, if he wanted shelter, he would just crawl into a hole in a creek bank, or into a hollow log. The space would be just large enough for him to get into it. These housing proportions are also suitable for places such as Arizona where the winters can still be quite cold, particularly in the mountains. The house should be placed where it will be sheltered. Orient its back to the prevailing wind.

In a warmer climate, or where it is continuously hot, the house can be larger. It can be tall, and may have a ventilation area on top. Be sure that the house either has a shade built over it, or is placed under a tree so that it will be shaded during the hot parts of the day, especially from the late afternoon sun.

It is handy to have a removable roof or side so that the dog house can easily be cleaned, and you can replace soiled bedding and treat it for fleas, ticks or other pests without a lot of effort.

If you have decided that your dog will live outdoors, stay with that arrangement. If you bring him inside, and then put him out again, he will be more prone to illness than if he is either in or out ALL the time. Can you imagine how you would feel if you were let in part of the time and then kicked outdoors?

If you have a swimming pool or fish pond, either fence the puppy out of the area or cover it until he is a bit older and you know that he can swim (and is large enough to be able to climb out of it).

Be sure that the puppy has plenty of toys. Rawhide chew toys are good, but often a bit difficult for a puppy to handle. Sponge or foam rubber toys are not a good idea, since pieces can be chewed off and swallowed, causing severe illness. Often, surgery is needed to remove them from the puppy's stomach. Try different toys until you find something that the puppy likes and is safe for him to have.

Make sure that he understands which toys are his. Meanwhile, it may be a good idea to keep your shoes picked up off the floor, and the closet door closed to keep your things out of temptation's way. The puppy may swallow anything small enough to get easily in his mouth. A needle with some thread on it may be swallowed by the puppy, resulting in a fatal injury. The needle stops, while the thread keeps trying to go through the intestine. The thread will cut through the intestine as it moves. Keep pins and needles and small toys like marbles and jacks out of his way until he is large enough (and educated enough) to not eat them. Keep him away from pieces of wood, glass and plastic toys which might splinter. Don't give him turkey or chicken bones, since these bones splinter like wood. Be sure that all medicines and pills are kept out of reach. Keep electric cords out of the way so that the puppy cannot chew on them. A dog who chews through the insulation may suffer mouth burns, or may even be electrocuted.

Don't place your puppy on a bed, sofa or chair. He may break a bone or dislocate a joint if he falls to the floor. This is also a good time to establish ground rules for the future. Do you REALLY want him on the sofa when he weighs 120 lb.? It's better never to let him get on the furniture if you don't want him there when he is an adult.

Give the puppy plenty of exercise and play. Do it in your own yard, away from other dogs who may carry diseases against which he does not yet have immunity. Unless you have absolutely no other place to exercise him, do not take the puppy out onto the streets and to parks until he has completed his series of immunizations, around 16 weeks of age. Give small amounts of exercise, frequently. Two or three short walks a day will help the puppy to grow strong and healthy without overtiring him, and are much better than one daily marathon. Overworking a small puppy may cause joint damage, but adequate exercise helps to develop the bones and muscles to the best of their ability. Moderation is the key!

Avoid bathing a puppy until he is about five months old, unless he is so filthy that you cannot stand him. Bathing him too often can dry the skin and hair and cause him to itch and scratch. It can also lower the puppy's resistance to disease if he is bathed and becomes chilled afterward. If you do need to bathe him, a small puppy can be popped under the kitchen faucet. Hang on to him. He may become frightened, try to get away and fall to the floor. Be sure to dry him thoroughly afterward. If he's just a bit dirty after eating, wash his face and ears with a warm, damp washcloth.

Keep little children from mauling and hauling a small puppy. A small child may accidentally injure a puppy by crushing him in his arms. Many puppies have been permanently crippled when dropped by a child. Teach children to lift the puppy safely with one hand under his chest and the other under his hind end. The puppy will feel more comfortable and safe, and struggle less if he is picked up and held securely. Don't pick him up by the scruff of his neck, or allow him to dangle by the neck or chest. Please teach children not to tease the puppy. This may cause him to become a vicious, untrustworthy adult dog.

Teach your puppy to be confined early in his life. If he becomes accustomed to staying in the yard when he is small, he will not know that there is any other way to live. He will be safe and secure and will not miss the "freedom" to be hit by cars, attacked by other dogs, poisoned by garbage, catch diseases, and be otherwise damaged by the wilds of the city.

HEARTH 'N HOME

We have discussed housing and doghouses; now, let's cover the rest of his environment.

A dog does not have a great deal of logic built into his thinking. Because he cannot always see the consequences of his actions, you have to provide for his safety and help him avoid problems. All dogs should be confined to house or yard if they are not on a leash or directly accompanied by you or a responsible member of your family. This degree of control will keep your pet alive far longer and help to protect him from contact with contagious diseases. It is good preventive medicine with the potential to save a LOT of money on veterinary bills.

A fenced yard should be solid and safe. A wire fence should be tight, and not have any holes that the dog can get his head through (and maybe hang himself), or squeeze through to escape from the yard. This is especially important with a puppy in the yard. A wooden fence should be secure and close enough to the ground that the dog cannot push or dig underneath. Gate latches should catch securely so that the dog does not escape through a gate left open accidentally.

If your yard is not fenced, the dog should be tied securely so that he cannot get loose. Tie pins are available which have a ring to which a chain can be attached. This arrangement allows the dog to run in a complete circle, and will give him more area to play. Or, you can run a HIGH wire from one corner of your house to a post, or from one post to another. Place the wire eight to ten feet above the ground, so that it does not catch you or the meter man across the neck. Put a ring on this wire and let the dog trolley from one end to the other. You can also "trolley" the dog by snapping his chain to a clothesline. Be careful for several weeks about leaving the dog alone until you are sure that he can cope with the chain. After a period of time, most dogs will learn how to unwind their chain when it's wrapped around a post or tree. But, before he learns, the dog may wrap his chain around a post, leaving himself exposed to the sun through a long, hot day while you are gone, or through a cold day in winter. You may end up with a dog with heatstroke or frostbite. Be sure that the dog can reach his house, or other shelter from heat and cold, and that his water is within reach.

You could use a nylon or other rope to tie the dog. This is OK for temporary use until you get something better. But he might chew through the rope and escape. So use a lightweight chain. In many cases, it is best to take the snap off the chain and replace it with a ring, securely fastened to the end. Some snaps are not very sturdy and break easily if the dog lunges against the end of the chain.

If you have the dog tied within a fenced yard, make sure that he cannot reach the fence. A dog who has enough slack to jump over the fence may hang to death if the chain is not long enough for him to touch the ground on the other side. Hanging is also a hazard when you have the dog tied in a pickup or trailer.

Be sure to remove all pesticides and toxic materials from the yard. This includes cans or containers which the dog may chew. Snail baits, ant poisons and rodent poisons may also cause toxicity—use them with care. If the dog is allowed into the garage at all, solvents, paints, acids and other toxic products should be put on high shelves. Swimming pool chemicals also should be stored safely out of the reach of the dog.

Some dogs will swallow small rocks and pebbles. If you notice the dog mouthing them, remove them from the area. Mouthing rocks and pebbles probably starts as a form of play to relieve boredom and then becomes a habit. Broken glass should be picked up to keep the dog from cutting his feet.

Like other carnivores, dogs require an area of their own for hunting. They instinctively take over a territory. A house dog will take your house for that territory; a dog who has a yard will likewise assume ownership of the yard. And a farm dog will define the perimeter of his territory. Within that region, the dog will claim a den for a sleeping area. For a bitch, it serves as a nest for whelping puppies and raising them. In the wild, this would be a cave, hollow log or a tunnel. The den will be vigorously guarded. The house dog may consider your entire house to be his den, or only part of it. If you have a crate for the dog, or a dog house, this will certainly be considered his haven.

A new "fence" on the market allows you to keep your dog within your yard without having to have a tall enclosure. A wire is buried a few inches below the ground, around the periphery of the area where the dog is to be confined. The wire carries a radio signal. The dog wears a collar with a lightweight radio receiver. When the dog comes within the distance you have set, the collar picks up the radio signal. A warning tone sounds. If the dog remains within range of the wire, he then receives a harmless correction from the collar. (Contact: Invisible Fence of San Diego, 1875 Honey Springs Road, Jamul, Calif., 92035).

It is especially important to keep the dog well confined for the first couple of weeks that you own him. An older dog, especially, may not be sure that this is his home until he has lived there for some time, and may run away in an attempt to return to his old home. A puppy that gets loose may wander away and forget, or not know, where home is.

If the dog is inside the house, this area should also be dogproofed. This is even more important when you have just gotten a puppy. Puppies are clumsy. Put valuable glassware high up so the puppy cannot stumble into it. Even an older dog may accidentally damage objects with an eager, wagging tail. Bleach, soaps and other cleaning products should be kept on high shelves or in securely closed cabinets. Nails, screws and thumbtacks should also be kept away from puppies. They are prone to chew and taste everything, and swallow whatever they can. Mature, well-mannered dogs will leave most of these things alone.

Large hunting dogs and breeding animals are often kept in runs. Runs are also useful for dogs who dig, tear up the flower beds or are otherwise destructive. Runs are usually made of chain link fencing. Pre-built kennel panels, complete with gates, are readily available. A dog who climbs should have a wire roof over his run. This feature is also useful to keep males from climbing IN if you are confining a female in heat. The best runs are floored with concrete. The slab can be sloped to one side for easy cleaning or made with one low point, where a drain can be installed. There should be AT LEAST one inch per foot of slope to provide good drainage. This way, you can pick up the solid waste, then easily hose off and disinfect the slab. Pea gravel is sometimes used for the floor in runs. It tends to hold urine and fecal material, and often develops a serious odor problem, not to mention the fact that it cannot be disinfected and is a disease hazard. The dog should have a house or shelter. If the shelter has a flat top, the dog can stand or lie on it for variety. Dogs who are kept in concrete-floored runs often develop calluses on their elbows and/or hocks. These may be unsightly, but they do not cause any problems unless they crack or bleed.

LEASH AND COLLAR

A dog who is walking along a street or road should be on a leash. Even the best-trained dog may run into the street if the temptation is great enough.

In most cities and counties, all dogs over six months of age must be licensed. In some areas this must be done at three months of age. Put the license on a collar which will come off if the dog gets caught on a branch or other object. It is a good idea to put a tag on the collar which has your name and phone number or address. Do not put the dog's name on the collar. If he is lost, the fact that you know his name and he responds to it may be the only real proof you have that he is yours.

An identification tattoo is a good idea, and will prove that you own the dog. Your veterinarian can tattoo your dog with a combination of letters or numbers of your choice. The tattoo may be placed in the dog's flank, on his belly or on the inside of the ear flaps.

HOUSEBREAKING

A housebroken dog is a pleasure to have and to own. A dog who urinates and/or defecates in the house or in other inappropriate places is unpleasant to have around, and not a good pet. Consider that more dogs are taken to dog pounds and animal shelters because they are not or cannot be housebroken than for any other reason. There IS an easy way to housebreak a puppy.

The puppy needs to be around six weeks of age to begin successful housebreaking. Most puppies younger than that do not have enough muscular control to be able to retain their urine and bowel movements for long periods of time.

For the first couple of days you have the puppy, do not be too harsh on him, and do not expect too much in the way of training. He is getting settled in his new home. Put him in a crate or a place in which a mess will not be a problem. Use newspapers on the bottom, along with clean rags, carpet scraps, a blanket or other disposable bedding. A large cardboard box is a good home for the first couple of nights. You can throw it away and fix a new one if he soils it.

On the third day, move the puppy to a crate or cage. Wire cages are available. It should have a waterproof metal pan for the bottom, extending one or two inches up the sides. If you are using a wire crate, you can drape a blanket over the top and sides so that it becomes even more cozy, secure and den-like. Or, you can get an airline-type shipping crate. Again, it should have a waterproof bottom. This crate should be only a couple of inches longer than the puppy when he lies out flat, and only a couple of inches wider than his outstretched legs. It should be high enough that the puppy can stand up comfortably. THE CRATE SHOULD NOT BE TOO LARGE. This is extremely important. If the crate is very large, the puppy can use one end as his "bedroom" and the other end as his "bathroom." The crate should be small enough that all of it is "bedroom," because the puppy will not, if at all possible, make a mess in his bed. If you buy a crate for the mature size of the dog, block off an area appropriate to his current size.

The crate is to be a place of security and comfort. The dog should consider it to be his home or den. His viewpoint is not that he cannot get out but that humans cannot get in. When he is older, you can leave it open so that he can use it as a refuge. Do not let children bother the puppy when he is in the crate, or pull him out of it when he does not want to come out.

For the first several weeks that you have the puppy, he should spend ALL of his time in the crate when he is not directly supervised. Put the puppy there when things are busy around the house (such as a party or guests). He should also spend his nights there. Take him outdoors to play, or let him out to run around the house, but ONLY when someone is with him. In this way, you start developing proper elimination habits from the beginning. You do not have to let the puppy get into bad habits and then figure out how to break or change them.

Plan on spending a few minutes each day with the housebreaking plan. If you can spend about 20 minutes a day on housebreaking, you can have almost any dog housebroken in about two weeks. An intelligent dog will be completely and reliably housebroken (barring accidents such as diarrhea) at the end of this period. Look at this time as an investment in enjoyment of your pet and cleanliness for your house.

The FIRST thing when you get up in the morning, remove the puppy from his crate and TAKE him outdoors. Do not just PUT him out, even if you have a well-fenced yard or large property. Your involvement is the key to this system of housebreaking. If you just put him out, he will not have any idea of what he is supposed to do, or that he is doing anything right. TAKE him outdoors to where you want him to establish his "bathroom." When he does what he is supposed to, praise him LAVISHLY. Pet him and tell him that he's a FANTASTIC dog. Be patient. Walk the dog around a bit if you need to, but don't play with him, or he will likely forget what he is supposed to do. This is potty time, not play time.

For the first week you are doing this, it will be helpful to CARRY the puppy outside, directly from his crate. He will need to go as soon as he gets up and moving, whether the first thing in the morning or after a nap, and carrying him will keep him from squatting and urinating before you can get him out the door. After he gets the hang of what you want from him, you can take the puppy on a leash or let him walk alongside you. If you always go out the same door and to the same place for the first two or three weeks, it will start the puppy on a good routine, likely to last all of his life.

Now, take him back inside and give him his first meal of the day. Keep an eye on him. Between 15 minutes and an hour after he has eaten, the puppy will have the urge to defecate and/or urinate again. Watch for signs that he is ready—restlessness, whining, turning in a circle, squatting or sniffing the floor. Or he may look at you with a slightly anxious expression. When you see any of these signs, IMMEDIATELY take the puppy back out to the designated place. Allow him to take care of his needs, and praise him again. Take him back into the house. If you remain outside to play with him, he may forget why he went outside in the first place. When you take him back into the house, either have someone watch him, or put him in his crate. If you are going to be gone, he should definitely be in the crate. The puppy should also be taken outside after he has a nap, if possible, as this is another natural time to want to urinate and defecate. He will also need to go outside when you return home after having been gone for a while. Be sure to put him in his crate before you leave or you might return to an accident.

Repeat the same process at his lunch and evening feedings. Avoid giving the puppy between-meals tidbits while his toilet training is occurring. They may upset his schedule and cause him to have an accident in the house. Do not give him any table scraps. Do not leave food out for him all the time. Avoid any changes in diet which may cause diarrhea or intestinal upsets and disrupt the housebreaking. Take the puppy out the last thing before you go to bed. Then return the puppy to his crate for the night.

This may seem like a lot of trouble, but it is by far the fastest way to get the puppy housebroken. Basically, you are setting the internal biological clock. Care and precision will pay off for you and the puppy. By the time you have worked the routine for three to five days, you should see definite progress. The dog may soil his bedding in the crate for the first two or three days. Replace the bedding each time it is soiled, but do not make any fuss about it. The dog is living with the discomfort of the mess in his bed, and does not need any comment from you about it. However, if he does make a mess in the house outside his crate, AND you CATCH him doing it, DO make a fuss. In a harsh voice, tell the puppy that that is not the thing to do. You may push his head toward the spot, but there is no need, and nothing is to be gained, by rubbing his

nose in the mess. Then, take him outside to see if he needs to do anything more. If you do not catch the young puppy making the mess, it is not helpful to scold or physically punish him for doing it. His memory span is so short that he does not remember what he has done. Whatever you do, do NOT call the puppy to you and then punish him for making a mess. He will remember only that you have called him and then punished him. He won't associate the punishment with the mess.

If you have the puppy outside and he urinates or defecates, immediately praise him again, and tell him that he is doing a great deed.

If you will ignore the fact that you may feel ridiculous hiking outside in your robe at six in the morning fussing over your puppy, it's almost guaranteed that you will have the dog housebroken within about two weeks, if you start the process when he is six to seven weeks of age.

After you have gone a week or more without an accident in the house, you can begin allowing the dog a little more freedom. Keep up your habit of taking him outside first thing in the morning and after meals, as well as last thing at night. Keep praising him for good performance. Within another week, you can just take him out five to six times a day and get him to do his business. At this point, he is probably housebroken. You can allow him the run of the house, as long as he gets out enough times per day to avoid accidents.

If at any point beyond this, there is more than a rare accident, put the dog right back on the crate-and-supervision program. If there are any medical problems, such as diarrhea, continue to correct the dog, but less severely than you would if he were healthy. And put him outside as much as possible to help keep him from getting into the habit of going in the house. Make sure that the puppy is kept strictly on puppy food, without any milk, and without any table scraps that might upset his digestive tract.

Some breeds are easier to housebreak than others. Dachshunds, for instance, are harder to train and more likely to make mistakes. They seem to need more time to "get it right" than do some other breeds.

DO NOT, as some books suggest, train the dog to urinate or defecate indoors on papers unless that is what you want him to do in the future. It is much harder to "paper train" him and, later, switch him to going outdoors than it is to simply train him to go outdoors in the first place. If you have a small dog, live in an apartment, or for some other reason want him to use paper inside for the rest of his life, paper training is appropriate. Making the conversion from papers to outside will take you a couple of extra weeks (or more) to train him NOT to go on the papers, and to go outside. And, in the future, he might forget and go on a newspaper which someone has left in the middle of the living room floor. It is better just to invest a bit of time in training him to go outside from the very beginning, and save the time and effort of doing the training twice.

If the dog has an accident, clean it up immediately and as completely as you can. If it is urine, it often helps to wipe the area with a mixture of vinegar and water to neutralize the ammonia smell (which will otherwise attract the puppy back to the same spot). Do not use an ammonia-based cleaner, as the odor is related to that of urine, and may encourage the dog to continue to use the spot. First, try the vinegar on a scrap of carpet or in an inconspicuous corner to make sure it will not damage the carpet. If you have an odor-removing or covering product, this can also be sprayed on the carpet. An example of this type of product is called P.O.N.® (Puppy Odor Neutralizer). This product helps to remove the odor from the "mistake" spot.

If the dog has left a stool sample, take it outside and put it in the area where you want him to go. Odor is one of the strongest attractions causing the dog to return to the same spot. You might as well use it in your favor. Until he is completely housebroken, always take the puppy to the same place in the yard, and take advantage of the odor he has left in the area.

At first, the same person should take the dog out all the time, as this makes it easier to establish the habit. Later, have various members of the household take him outside. By the time he is 16-17 weeks old, the dog should have all of his "puppy" immunizations, and should be immune to most of the most serious and common diseases. Now, you can take him out for longer walks. Again, vary the person who takes him for the walk, and the route. Now he can begin to learn the good habits he needs for going out into the world. Also take him out on leash to urinate and defecate in different places from time to time. This will let him know that he can go on grass, dirt or concrete. Otherwise, the dog may become "fixated" on one spot and refuse to urinate or defecate elsewhere.

If you live in a city, do not allow your dog to defecate on someone's lawn, in a park or in a flowerbed. Take along a couple of plastic bags when you are walking him. When he does make a mess, just put one over your hand, inside-out. Pick up the feces and pull the bag back over it; it's now handy to deposit in the nearest trash can. It is both good manners and good sanitation to "curb" your dog. If you notice that he is getting ready to urinate or have a bowel movement, edge him toward the curb. Praise him when he goes there. Soon, it will be a matter of habit for him to seek the edge of the street.

A male dog begins to lift his leg to urinate somewhere between four months and a year or more of age, although it is not abnormal for an older male to squat to urinate. He will usually empty his bladder a bit at a time. If an older male dog urinates in the house right after you have taken him outside to relieve himself, you probably did not give him enough time to finish the job. The female dog will usually empty her bladder at one time and be done with it. She usually squats to urinate, although she may do this at times with one leg lifted. An occasional female may urinate small amounts in a marking manner, similar to a male. If she does not have signs of bladder problems, such as urinating in the house, frequent urination or blood in the urine, this is not abnormal.

Older dogs who make mistakes may do so for a variety of reasons. Urine dribbling, or puddles where the dog sleeps, may be caused by a lack of hormones (especially in the elderly dog) or a urinary infection. Have these animals checked by your veterinarian. Male dogs who urinate on furniture are usually marking their territory. Neutering sometimes helps, as will strict training. Placing the dog's food dish, bedding, or

water in the spot where he is urinating may help if he is marking only one spot. It won't work if he is marking more than one place—he'll just continue with the other spots.

Some dogs urinate when the owner or another person approaches. This may be a gesture of submission to a person that the dog considers to be dominant. This does NOT necessarily indicate that the dog has been abused, beaten or frightened by the person toward whom he is displaying this behavior. For these dogs, ignoring the behavior may be the most effective cure. Do not praise OR scold him. Don't approach the dog directly. Walk slowly and talk quietly. Avoid direct eye contact with the dog when you approach him, as he may take the eye contact as a threat. Handle the dog by rubbing his chest and chin. Do not pat him on the top of the head, back or shoulders, as these are dominant gestures. Don't punish the dog for urinating. Punishment will only aggravate the submissive attitude and urination. You may need to squat down (so that you do not tower so much over the dog) and pet him gently, talking quietly as you greet him. If you can avoid reinforcing the behavior, the dog will probably outgrow it.

Puppies who become very excited (such as when you come home, or play vigorously with them) may urinate because they do not yet have enough control over their bladders. Figure out what is causing the urination. Then, change YOUR behavior. Greet the dog very quietly, or play with him gently. Take him out to urinate before playing with him so that his bladder will be empty. Plan to greet him out on the lawn or at another place where it is OK if he urinates.

Dogs who are startled or frightened by loud noises may urinate, defecate or even empty their anal glands. The dog must be gently and carefully taught to ignore the noise. You can best do this by ignoring him. If you comfort the dog and fuss over him, you are teaching him to react to the noise. Dogs who become upset when separated from their owners (as when left at home alone) may exhibit the same behaviors. The dog who leaves a pile when the owner is gone are often doing so out of spite. He may also become destructive, chewing up clothing, shoes and furniture. This can be a nearly impossible habit to break, although you can try giving him some extra attention before you leave and provide him with something to occupy his time. If nothing works, put him outside or in his crate when you leave.

TRAINING

In the past, trainers have considered that the dog did not learn much until he was at least six months old. With more research and greater knowledge about dogs, we are finding that between six and twelve weeks of age is one of the periods in a dog's life when he is most easily trained. This is the period at which the dog adapts best to a new home. It is the period during which he is most easily housebroken. And it is when imprinting occurs. This is the period in which the dog begins to learn the social rules by which he will live for the rest of his life. It is also easier to teach the puppy the habits you want before he has developed ones that you don't like, so that he doesn't have to unlearn the bad ones and start over. Take advantage of this period of susceptibility when the dog is eager and willing to learn.

It is interesting that, in general, prey species imprint at birth. Animals such as horses are precocious, and learn from the instant they are born. A foal who is born in the wild will run beside his mother within hours of his birth, and imprints from the time of birth onward. In contrast, predators imprint later. The puppy is born with his eyes closed, and is nowhere near ready to face the world. It is a week before his eyes open and he is ready to begin to absorb information from the world around him. It is even later, around seven weeks of age, before he can absorb large amounts of information. At this point, he is ready and eager to learn.

Training is NOT cruel. In the wild, the dog would live in a pack situation. Discipline would be provided by other members of the pack. It is actually unkind to deprive the dog of social structure. He learns how to relate to other dogs, and he learns the signals that will allow him to communicate with them. When you take a dog into your household, you are bringing him into your "pack." He instinctively expects to learn his place just as he would if he were with other dogs. It is your job to be the leader and to teach him his place. If you do not do so, you may end up with a neurotic, vicious or maladjusted dog who will attempt to take over leadership of the "pack." Dogs are insecure without a definite, strong leader. Who the leader is and the ranking of the rest of the family ("pack") must be made clear to the dog. At one time, I had an old, blind cat and a dog in the same household. In our hierarchy, I was "first dog;" the cat was "second dog," because that was how I placed him with respect to the dog, and the dog herself was "third dog." A well-trained dog who knows and is secure in his place is one that you will enjoy owning, and he will enjoy himself with you and your friends.

In the wild, in his "natural" environment, the dog's life would be dangerous and difficult. In contrast, the typical pet dog has a life of love, care and attention. He also has good, nutritious food, exercise, love, attention, and protection against disease and injury. He will have a far healthier and longer life than he would in the wild.

The first and one of the most important "commands" that the dog will learn is his own name. Make it simple—one or two syllables, with a distinct sound. The next command, and nearly as important as his name, is the word "NO!" This word should be spoken sharply and a bit harshly. It should sound like you mean what you say, not like you are pleading with the dog to "please" do what you want.

This is the time that you can begin to train your dog with other commands. It is easy to teach the dog the command "come." One way of doing this is by "naming the action." Instead of trying to explain what you want the dog to do, give a name to what he is doing. When he is heading toward you, say his name and the command: "Waldo, come." When he sits, say, "Waldo, sit." And, so forth. Before long, the dog will be doing what you want because he will associate the word with the action.

Some years ago, I took a Queensland Blue Heeler puppy, at seven weeks of age, on a 2,000-mile trip in an automobile.

By the time we got home a week later, she was housebroken (using the crate method described above), knew her name, would "come" and "sit," and was starting to "heel" and "stay." Granted, she was a very intelligent dog, but it is also a testimonial to the advantages of living closely with the dog for an intense period of training at this critical stage in its life. This stage is so important that you may wish to wait to get a puppy until you have vacation time, or other quality time to spend with him. On the other hand, if vacation is going to mean getting carted all over the country with a batch of relatives and children, the dog is likely to get lost in the confusion. Better in that case to do the training at home in a less harried setting.

Short training sessions are better than long lessons. Small puppies have a short memory and brief attention span. Five or six training periods of 3-5 minutes each will make much faster progress than one 20-minute lesson each day. Better yet, make daily life a training session. When you are in the kitchen and the puppy is heading toward you, say, "Waldo, come!" Take him over to the other side of the room and have him "sit." Then, tell him to "stay," and push your hand at his face. Walk away. When he starts to follow you, put him back in the place where you left him, and say "Stay" again. After you have done this a couple of times, the puppy will begin to get the idea and stay put. Do not leave him for more than a couple of minutes. Go back over to him, and tell him that he is a good dog. Then give him some sort of release command— "OK, can go," or something along that line. For a small puppy, keep it simple. When the dog is older, he can understand longer and more intricate commands.

It is also important not to tell your dog to "come" when you want to discipline him. Whatever he has done, either go after him silently, or say nothing as he comes to you. It is preferable to go after him. That way he is getting punished for what he has done, not for coming to you.

In the beginning, it is easier for one person to do all the training. Consistency is also important. Do not tell the dog to "come" one time and "come here" the next time. When your dog is older, he will probably understand both commands, but for a beginner, it's confusing. Decide what command you want to use and stay with it. Make your instructions as clear as possible, and keep them simple. As the puppy gets older, other members of the family can take part in the training, learning the commands that the person doing the training is using. If you are having trouble getting the dog to understand a command, make sure that you are being clear and understandable. It may not be his fault that he is not understanding what you want him to do.

Reward the puppy often, especially early in his training. You can use pieces of a tasty dog food, and give them, one at a time, as rewards for correct performance. However, treats are not necessary every time you work with the dog. Use plenty of praise after he has done the thing which you have asked. Praise is very important to the dog, and it's easy to have some with you all the time. With a very young puppy, you can be neutral when the puppy does not perform as asked. As he gets older and you are sure that he knows what you want, you can be more harshly disapproving, depending on the type of dog and the situation.

You can, and should, avoid teaching your dog to bite. Dogs chew and bite on each other as a method of determining their order in the pack: who is dominant and who is subordinate. When the puppy begins to chew on your clothing or hands, thump him sharply on the nose with your finger and sharply say, "no!" An older dog who bites must be sharply reprimanded, as one of his packmates would immediately do. The larger the dog is, the more important it is that you react immediately and emphatically. Adjust your reaction to the size of the dog. A small Poodle can be disciplined by a sharp word, or a swat with your hand or a newspaper. An aggressive adult Pit Bull, St. Bernard or other large or potentially dangerous dog may need to be disciplined with a boot or stick. And it is important for such a dog to be securely fenced or chained so that he cannot harm anyone.

By the same token, you can keep your puppy from chewing on furniture and household items that do not belong to him. As pack leader, you have to let him know that it will not be tolerated if he bothers your possessions. Tell him "no!" very sharply when he chews anything that is not "his." Then, give him one of "his" toys. Shake it, push it to his mouth, speak to him in a playful voice, and encourage him to play with it. Do not play with him by pulling on a sock or blanket or anything that may induce him to chew your belongings or clothing. It may also pull his teeth out of alignment, to his lifelong detriment. Do not give him old shoes or similar items unless you want him to chew on the newer ones that you own. He can't tell the difference between old and new. Make sure that he has plenty of chew toys appropriate to his size. If you bring home a toy or two and find that he does not use them, keep trying until you find one or more that he likes. Most puppies are more than willing to chew, because they are at the teething stage, when teeth are coming out through the gums. A bit of tabasco sauce or cayenne pepper will help him to remember not to chew furniture and other items. A product called Chew-Guard® is available, which may also be helpful. Plenty of play and exercise will keep him from being bored. Sometimes puppies chew just to have something to do.

What if your dog gets into a fight? First of all, a dog fight can be a dangerous situation for both you and your dog. Most fights are social in nature, to establish the relative rank between the two dogs, and involve most gesture than anything else. Others, however, are territorial and can get serious. If you try to break up the fight, you might be seriously bitten. Even a small poodle can inflict a lifetime crippling injury on you if he punches a tooth through a tendon or nerve in your hand.

The best and safest way to stop a dog fight is to soak the combatants down with water from a hose or a bucket if it's readily available. If worst comes to worst, and you are unable to stop a dog fight, SIMPLY DO NOTHING. Dogs are rarely killed in dog fights in the street, unless they have tangled with trained fighting dogs. In the latter case, you won't be able to stop the fight anyway, and the fighting dog may turn on you if you try. It seldom does any good to shout at the fighting dogs. They are so excited that they will not hear you,

and, if they do, they may just feel that you are encouraging them.

If you own two male dogs who fight with each other, there are usually only a few choices. Either neuter one or both of them, keep them separated or get rid of one of them. As long as they are both intact (not neutered), their hormones and instincts for male-male competition for dominance will usually keep them fighting.

Having trouble with behavioral problems? A dog's behavior is often a reflection of the relationship between you and him and a response to something you do, or even to your attitude. Don't be too quick to blame the dog. It takes two to tango. One of the best remedies is for you and the dog to attend obedience classes. These are often taught under the auspices of kennel clubs or by community colleges. They are usually inexpensive. The quality, however, will vary with the knowledge and experience of the person who is teaching the class. If possible, watch a class or two before signing up to make sure that you are compatible with the instructor. Another remedy is to ask your veterinarian for assistance. Some veterinarians take an interest in psychological problems and can be of considerable help. If he doesn't know what to do about the problems, he might be able to refer you to someone who can help.

The library is another good source of material on dog training. Check out several books and look them over. Approaches vary from one to another, so find one that fits your way of thinking and your disposition. Begin again with the basics, even if you think that your dog knows part of what he needs. Unless you only have one small, specific problem, there is a good chance that you have missed some of the basics. Most books are written to follow a coherent scheme of training, based on the author's thinking. Going back to the beginning will ensure that your dog has a solid foundation from which to make future progress.

If you have a serious problem with your dog's behavior which you are unable to remedy, a professional trainer may be able to help. If possible, ask your veterinarian or another dog owner to recommend a trainer to you. In some cases, the trainer will coach both you and the dog from the very beginning. In other cases, the trainer may wish to work with the animal separately before he puts you and the dog back together. If you have any questions about the trainer, ask for references of satisfied customers. Call them and ask if they are pleased with the results.

NEW PET OR BABY

What happens when you are getting a new pet, or perhaps a baby in your household? The adjustment is sometimes rather difficult for the dog who has been an "only dog" for a long period of time. He has gotten all your attention and affection. He has even learned to expect and demand it. Now he is going to have to share you with a newcomer.

For about a week before the arrival of the newcomer, have everyone in the family pay slightly less attention to the dog. Give your usual positive, friendly attention. Just give less of it. When the new pet or baby arrives, return to your normal amount of attention. Because he got less during the previous week, this will look like an increase in attention. It will help to compensate for the attention paid to the baby or new pet. If you need to scold or discipline your dog, try to do so away from the newcomer. Otherwise, he may associate the scolding with the newcomer. However, if the dog growls or is otherwise aggressive with the newcomer, your discipline should be swift, sharp and on the spot, letting him know that you, as pack leader, will not tolerate this kind of behavior.

EXERCISE

A dog's exercise can be determined by the activity for which the breed was created. Coursing dogs such as Salukis and Greyhounds will appreciate being run a number of miles. Even a large yard is probably not adequate for one of these breeds, unless you give the animal plenty of extra exercise. These are good dogs to take out into the country to a deserted road, and train to run (safely) beside your vehicle. Hunting dogs, terriers, working breeds and the larger hounds will need similar amounts of exercise. A Basset Hound or a Dachshund is not built to go a long distance, but will appreciate several shorter walks each day.

Be sure to consider the dog's physical condition before you embark on an exercise program. If the dog is out of shape or overweight, once or twice around the block may be all that you can safely do with him. Two or three times around the block at different times of the day are also good for a starting program. Do these walks during cool times of the day to reduce stress on the animal until you get him into shape. Gradually work up to longer and more vigorous walks. If you have any questions, check with your veterinarian before starting an exercise program.

COLD WEATHER

Dogs who live outdoors need adequate shelter to keep them warm and draft-free. A dog house for a cold-weather dog should be small enough that he can heat it with his body heat—more a den than a ballroom. It should be well insulated and placed in a place that is as sheltered from the wind as possible.

If you use a sweater or jacket to help keep your dog warm, put it on him only when you are around. Otherwise, he may become caught on a branch or fence, and could be injured.

Make sure that the dog has lukewarm water available at least twice a day, or put a heater in a bucket so that he will have warmed water at all times. If you feed dry food, make sure that plenty of water is always available.

Dogs are susceptible to respiratory disease and pneumonia, especially if they are worked hard in cold weather when they are not accustomed to it. If you exercise the dog in cold weather, be careful that the exercise is moderate and adjusted to the dog's physical condition. And be sure to cool him down well afterward.

Prevent frostbite by making sure the dog is indoors or has adequate shelter. If an indoor dog is left outdoors for a prolonged period of time, he should be carefully warmed up in a dry, draft-free place. Wiping the dog's toes and footpads when you bring him inside will decrease the risk of frostbite and infection. Wiping his feet off will also help to remove any salt picked up from the street or sidewalk.

Cold is hard on older dogs, and may reduce the efficiency of the animal's immune system, making him susceptible to infection.

Some dogs may urinate more frequently than normal in cold weather. Others may be reluctant to go outdoors as often as they should, and will urinate less than normal. This may cause urine in the bladder to become stale, and may lead to bladder infection. You may need to take the dog out for a walk, or go outside with him to encourage him to urinate.

HOT WEATHER

Hot weather brings extra stress and strain on your dog. Begin by clipping your long-haired dog at the first sign that hot weather is here to stay. Clipping off the extra hair will also help the dog to be more comfortable if he has allergy problems from grass or other plants during the summer. By fall, he will have regrown enough hair to keep warm.

Fleas are a fact of life in many areas in the summer. Begin using flea products on the dog early in the summer. One flea killed in the spring is worth a hundred in the summer. So start treating your dog early in the spring or summer, depending on when the season starts in your area.

Chapter 4

KNOWING YOUR DOG: THE NORMAL ANIMAL

Repairing your dog begins with knowing your own animal, and knowing what is normal for that individual. U.S. Treasury agents are trained to spot counterfeit money by looking at literally thousands of real bills. The same is true of you and your dog. You must know what is normal before you can know what is abnormal. Observe your dog from day to day and note changes that occur. It is extremely valuable to know what is "normal" for dogs in general, and for your breed and individual in particular.

Trust your feelings about your dog. Many times, a dog owner takes his dog to a veterinarian, saying that something is wrong with the dog. The owner knows that the dog is "not quite right." The veterinarian cannot see anything wrong. Whatever is wrong is so subtle that the owner, who lives with the dog every day, is the only one who can see any problem. This does NOT mean that the veterinarian is incompetent, nor does it mean that it is all in your imagination. It only means that the problem is so subtle that it is not obvious at this point. When this happens to you, it means that the dog's problem is not serious, at least not yet. It will either get better or worse. If it gets better, you do not have a problem! If it gets worse, your veterinarian will be able to diagnose the problem and offer a solution for it.

When you see a problem with your dog, take a moment to think before you panic and call the veterinarian or rush the dog in to him. If there is a swelling, see if there is one like it on the other side. A dog owner will occasionally take a dog to the veterinarian to see about a large swelling bulging out between the last rib and the hipbone, just below the back area. In many cases, there is one just like it on the other side. And, the dog is probably significantly overweight, because the bulge is fat! If you have another dog, check that animal to see if he has the same bulges. In many cases, this will give a clue to the reason for them.

This sort of comparison extends to judging the dog's attitude—is he lying down or sleeping more than normal? Does he seem upset or restless? It is useful to know dog conformation (parts of the dog) so that you can discuss where the problem is with your veterinarian.

BEHAVIOR

The dog's behavior will give you many clues to what might be wrong with him. Is your calm, sedate old Basset Hound suddenly grouchy, pushing and chewing at your other dog? Is he snapping at the children? Some bitches (female dogs) become upset when they are coming into heat. This behavior can also be seen with spinal disk problems—the dog is grumpy because he is hurting. Personality changes are also seen with rabies, and other diseases which affect the brain or nervous system. Behavior varies from animal to animal and from breed to breed. Behavior that would be considered outrageous from a Great Dane may be considered normal for a Miniature Poodle, or at least tolerable.

Determine as much as possible how your dog is affected by stress and environmental changes. Some dogs are severely upset by visitors in the household, especially children. Others are disturbed when they have to travel. Make a distinction between those changes which are temporary (an afternoon visitor) and those which are long-term (moving to a new neighborhood, or taking a cross-country vacation). Does the dog settle down after a couple of days of travel, or does he stay in turmoil for the whole of a two-week vacation? Does your dog panic only at storms or loud noises? Is he better with another dog for a companion, or is he a confirmed "only dog?" Not only will knowing the answers to these and other questions help you spot problems, but it will help you to assure an environment in which your pet is comfortable and happy.

POSTURE

Your observation of the dog's posture may be the first clue that something serious is wrong. A dog with a bellyache, for almost any reason, may stand with a humpbacked posture, and have a really "hangdog" look on his face. Or he may lie down, either on his bed or in an unusual place, and roll and stretch his legs forward and back. The same dog may be restless, in contrast to the healthy dog, who stands or lies quietly.

Variations in posture may not indicate a specific disease. If the dog completely refuses to put weight on a foot, this is more serious. It tells you that something is wrong with the leg, but not necessarily WHAT is wrong. The problem may be in the foot, knee, elbow or hock, or as high up as the shoulder or hip. It many be anything from a thorn in the paw to a fractured bone.

Extreme changes in the animal's normal posture often occur with severe disease problems. Tetanus (lockjaw) is an example of an abnormal posture. While this disease is rare in dogs, it is still occasionally seen. The dog may become so stiff and tight with the muscle spasms which accompany the disease that his front legs stick forward and his rear legs push out backward, making the animal resemble a sawhorse. His head will be pulled up and back, his tail may be rigidly extended, and his ears will be stiffly upright. These signs indicate that the condition is nearly terminal, and you are faced with an extreme emergency. Get veterinary help immediately.

MOVEMENT

Movement is closely related to posture. Abnormal movements are often the first sign of injury or disease processes. They can signify that the animal is annoyed or uncomfortable. The dog who has his hackles (the stiff guard hairs over the shoulders and along the spine of the back) stiffly raised is either afraid or defensive. A dog who has his lips drawn back over his teeth in a snarl and his ears laid back along his head is signaling that something is going on that he doesn't like. This is a good time to find out what is bothering him, and change it before either you or another person or dog are recipients of a nip from his teeth, or even an outright attack.

Movements such as pawing at his ears or shaking the head may indicate a serious problem such as ear mites or a hematoma (blood clot) in the ear flap. Or the dog may merely be bored or annoyed. Some dogs routinely lick their paws and wash their faces and ears much as cats do. Other dogs lick their paws out of boredom and keep licking until they cause irritation and sores. It is up to you to compare these movements with your knowledge of your dog's normal actions and decide if what you are seeing is normal or not.

The sequence of movement of the legs is called the gait. These movements can be compared to previous motions of the same animal, or to similar movements of other animals. The term "way of going" is often used to express the combination of movements which make up the gait. In horses this is very important, because imperfections in the way of going can cause the horse to hit one foot on another leg, causing injury. Or, one leg may tangle with another, causing the horse to fall down. Because a dog is not usually expected to carry weight, defects in the way of going are not usually serious, although in a show or field trial they can knock points off the score. They can, however, be an indication of injury in one or more legs. Many breeds of large dogs develop hip dysplasia as they become older. These dogs may show a stumbling gait in the hind end. One or both hind legs may knuckle as the dog travels. This is one of the most severe gait problems seen in dogs. A dog with a fracture or severe injury in one leg may be seen to hold the leg up or drag it. One of the first signs of lameness may be a change in the animal's way of going.

A stiff gait may also be social in nature, as when two dogs meet who are strangers to each other. They often strut the last few steps to the other dog on the tips of their toes with hackles raised and the body somewhat tense and stiff. This maneuver helps the dog to appear larger to the stranger, thus intimidating him.

What is a normal gait or way of going for one breed is often completely abnormal for another. You must know what is normal for your dog. The slight waddle associated with a Dachshund or Basset Hound would be abnormal for a Greyhound. If your Greyhound suddenly starts waddling, look for a problem.

VOICE

The dog's voice is a means of communication, both with other dogs and with humans. Barking warns you of the approach of strangers. Or it may mean that another dog has entered your front yard. After you and your dog have lived together for a while, you will be able to recognize the "language of bark." "I'm glad to see you," "I'm hungry," "Someone's at the door," "There's a stranger in the yard," "There's another dog out there," and other variations are all recognizable with time. Hoarseness may indicate that the dog has been barking for a long time. This is common when the dog has been in a boarding kennel or veterinary clinic for several days. Given a bit of rest and time, he will return to normal.

APPETITE

How well your dog is eating is one of the best indicators of his overall health. When you are feeding the same carefully measured amount of dog food every day, it is easy to tell when your animal is not eating and may have a health problem. Don't panic if your dog eats lightly at one meal occasionally, but look closely for a cause if a hearty eater suddenly lacks an appetite for several meals in a row. Check to see if a neighbor is feeding the dog. Is some member of the household overfeeding him at other meals, or giving him treats between meals which are ruining his appetite? Are there any signs of illness?

The dog's level of activity also has a bearing on his appetite. Moderate exercise may make him ravenous, while unaccustomed heavy exercise may leave him too tired to eat. Loss of appetite is seen with digestive problems, as well as with fever and severe pain from any cause.

A depraved appetite, in which the dog eats dirt or other abnormal substances, may occasionally be seen. Make sure that you are feeding the dog a nutritionally adequate diet, and that he does not have any vitamin or mineral deficiencies. Have a stool sample checked to see that the dog does not have worms. Sometimes odd appetites are caused by boredom. Try to give the dog more exercise and provide plenty of toys for chewing.

Some dogs will eat their own feces. This can become a habit. It can be cured by rigid sanitation in which the dog's environment is kept clean so that the material is not around for him to eat. A medication is available which can be fed to make the feces unpalatable. The disadvantage is that the dog usually starts eating feces the instant the drug is discontinued.

An evaluation of the animal's appetite should also include monitoring his thirst. With some illnesses, the dog may stop eating but continue drinking. Dogs drink more water than normal with fever, diabetes mellitus, and some digestive system and kidney problems. If your dog is sick and you have an automatic waterer, it is a good idea to shut if off and give the dog water from a pan or other container, so you can measure his intake. Make sure the container is heavy enough, or has a bottom wider than the top, so the dog cannot dump it over or otherwise spill it. In this way, you can tell IF the animal is drinking, and how much water he is consuming.

DIGESTIVE SYSTEM

After you have evaluated the animal's appetite, go on to check the digestive system. The mouth should be examined. Check to see that the teeth are normal and that there are no sores, ulcers or foreign bodies present on the tongue or gums. Saliva may drip from the mouth with any of these conditions or when the animal has a bone or other foreign object lodged in the mouth. This may also occur with the administration of certain drugs (especially those that are bitter) or when the animal is unable to swallow. If you are in an area where rabies is present, be aware that dripping saliva may be a sign of

rabies because the animal's throat may be paralyzed and he can't swallow.

SKIN AND COAT

The skin is a good indicator of the dog's health and of the level of care that he is receiving. It should be clean and healthy, free of dirt and parasites. A small amount of scurf ("dandruff") is present near the skin of dogs who are not routinely groomed. Animals who are fed a high level of oil will have shiny, bright-looking coats. Dogs who live in sandy areas or go to the beach frequently may work enough sand into their coats to dull them so the ends of the hairs stick out slightly, giving the animal a rough appearance. Long exposure to sun may dry the dog's coat enough to make it look rough and dull (less shiny). A normal winter coat (on a Husky, for example), should look healthy even though it is long and furry. A well-fed, healthy animal will often have a shine even on his winter coat.

Skin abnormalities may include missing patches of hair, scrapes or bites, sores, or dry, scaly or greasy skin. Contagious disease such as mange, ringworm and lice often involve more than one dog in a household, or more than one dog in the neighborhood if the dogs are running loose and trading diseases. Some of these skin diseases can even be passed on to the dog's human friends. Warts or tumors may be found, and should be examined closely to determine whether they need

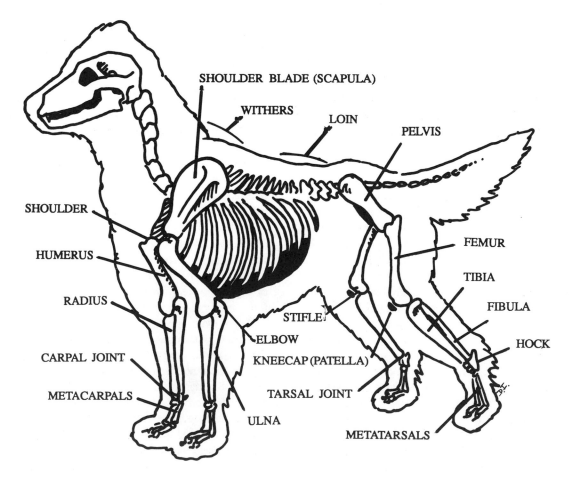

Parts of the Dog.

to be removed or just observed. A foul odor may be noticed with skin infections, seborrhea and some kinds of mange, as well as some other skin diseases.

The leathery end of the nose can be an indicator of health. It does not have to be "moist." It can be either dry or moist, as long as it is not dried, cracked or coated with mucus or dried discharges. The skin just above this area is prone to sunburn and related problems, often described as "Collie nose". This also affects other breeds of dogs (see Collie Nose).

MUCOUS MEMBRANES

These are the membranes which line the body openings: the nostrils, mouth, eyelids, anus, prepuce (sheath) and vagina. The membranes inside the eyelids (also called conjunctivae) and the membranes of the mouth are a good location to evaluate the animal's overall health. This is usually called "checking the animal's color."

A bright red conjunctival sac may merely mean that the dog's eyes have been irritated by dust or it could mean that they are infected. However, if the membranes in the animal's mouth are the same color, this may indicate a serious problem affecting the whole body. A dog with white skin around his eyes, such as a Dalmatian, may be prone to irritation of the conjunctivae by the sun. He may have red eyes much of the time, especially in the summer. Dogs with eyelids that pouch outward, such as many English Bulldogs, collect dirt and are

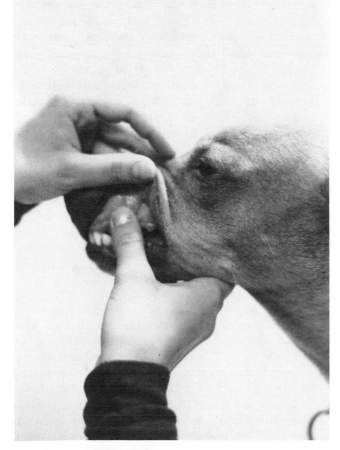

Checking capillary refill time.

exposed to the elements. They will also be red much of the time. This, fortunately, can be helped by surgery. This is another example of needing to know what is normal for your individual dog.

An animal who is short of red blood cells (suffering from anemia) or who has suffered blood loss may have very pale mucous membranes. A dark red (or purplish or bluish) color is called cyanosis, and indicates a lack of oxygen in the blood. It is seen with some heart problems and a few poisonings. A yellow coloration is called jaundice or icterus. It usually indicates a liver problem. With some diseases, small hemorrhages or spots of blood may be seen under the membranes. These may be as small as the head of a pin, or may be large, irregular blotches. Any of these abnormal conditions may indicate a serious illness, and should be checked by your veterinarian.

Dry membranes may indicate a fever, or may be caused by the administration of certain drugs. Note any peculiar odors in the mouth. Gum infections and plaque and tartar on the teeth can cause foul-smelling breath.

A quick indicator of the state of the dog's circulatory system is his "capillary refill time." Lift the dog's upper lip. Press your thumb firmly against the gum area above his upper teeth. Hold it there for six to eight seconds. Remove it and count how long it takes the bleached-out spot to return to the color of the rest of the gums. It should not take more than one second if the dog's circulation is normal. More than two seconds indicates a severe problem.

ABDOMEN

The size and shape of the animal's abdomen depends on a number of factors, including the breed, sex, age and conformation of the animal. It varies with what the dog has been fed and how he is used. A sedate, portly Basset Hound will have a more pendulous abdomen than a Greyhound in racing condition. A sagging, enlarged abdomen may be due to an abdominal tumor or an accumulation of fluid in the abdominal cavity. More commonly, it will indicate that an unspayed female dog is pregnant. It may also show that the dog has had little exercise to help keep the muscles toned up and in shape. The abdomen may suddenly increase in size with a torsion of the stomach in large breeds of dogs. It will be tight and hard and the dog will be in severe distress. This is an immediate medical emergency.

FECES

Feces is the technical name for the waste products of the intestinal tract. Manure, dung, stools or bowel movements refer to the same material. The animal's feces often give important clues to what is going on in his digestive tract. They are normally brownish, depending on the type of food the dog is eating. Puppy feces may be more yellowish, especially when the puppy is still nursing, or fed a milk replacer product.

Normal dog droppings should be well formed but not hard. Hard feces may indicate a lack of water, lack of exercise, or inadequate fiber or bulk in the diet. Very soft feces may be due to food to which the dog is allergic, or to excess fat in the diet. Diarrhea may be due to similar food problems, or to intestinal parasites or bacterial diseases. Eating spoiled food or getting into garbage may also cause diarrhea. Diarrhea which contains blood or large amounts of mucus or does not respond to simple treatment within two days is a signal to have your dog examined by a veterinarian. This is also true if the animal otherwise appears ill in addition to his diarrhea.

Grayish, foamy-appearing feces may be due to pancreatitis or other disease of the pancreas. Black feces may be due to the dog eating a lot of chocolate or blackberries, or due to disease processes. They may also be due to treatment with bismuth subsalicylate products (such as Pepto-Bismol®). Dark, tarry stools may be due to bleeding in the intestinal tract. If you cannot relate it to anything the dog has eaten, have your vet examine him.

Some dog foods produce larger amounts of feces than do others. If you have a Chihuahua, this is not a problem. If you have a St. Bernard, the amount of material which you need to pick up and dispose of may be considerable. If this is your problem, try a dog food with a greater caloric density which will produce less fecal bulk. If the stools become too hard, you've gone too far and need to add some bulk back into his diet.

URINE

Normal canine urine is yellowish and clear. It may be darker yellow if the dog has not had adequate amounts of water. Excessive urination may be due to diabetes or adrenal problems. This urine may be very diluted and almost colorless. It may also be a side effect of treatment with certain corticosteroids. If your dog is on medication and shows excessive urination, call your veterinarian and ask him about it.

The urine of a healthy dog will not usually contain any blood or clots. Small amounts of blood, however, may be seen with a female who is coming into heat. This is coming from the vagina and may merely accompany the urine as it is passed. Dogs who are on high carbohydrate diets and are worked hard may pass dark red or brown urine. Dogs with stones in the kidney or bladder may pass blood or reddish urine. Have the dog examined by your veterinarian as soon as possible if you observe reddish urine.

VAGINAL DISCHARGE

Female dogs usually have a discharge when they are coming into heat. This is reddish to brownish as they come into heat, clear during the estrus period, and cloudy to whitish as they are going out of heat. This whole process takes about three to four weeks, and is accompanied by swelling of the vulva, as well as other signs.

Small amounts of pus or whitish drainage in a bitch that is young or not in heat may indicate an infection of the vulva or vagina. While these are usually not serious, they should still be examined by your veterinarian within a few days.

Large amounts of pus or reddish, tan or brownish vaginal drainage may indicate a severe infection in the uterus. This can be life-threatening. The bitch should be examined by your veterinarian as soon as possible.

After a bitch has had puppies, she may drain material for a week or so. This includes fragments of membranes and fluids which have surrounded the puppies. This may be reddish, brownish or a horribly colored blackish-green. As long as it is not accompanied by a foul odor, this is normal. If it smells bad or the dog does not feel well, she should be examined by a veterinarian.

BRAIN AND CENTRAL NERVOUS SYSTEM

Since we cannot examine the brain drectly, we have to rely on external signs to tell us what is going on inside the animal's head and spinal column. Brain problems may first be seen by attitude and mental changes—the animal becomes dopey or sleepy, or may instead be nervous, upset and excited. Dogs with epilepsy may pass out for a long period of time. Problems in some areas of the brain or spinal cord may be shown by a staggering or uncoordinated gait, or dragging one or more feet as the dog walks.

Nervous signs may be seen from some poisonings, such as strychnine, lead and organophosphate insecticides.

Paralysis of a single limb or one group of muscles is caused by an injury to a motor center in the brain, or, more commonly, to a nerve leading to the involved area. Paralysis of the rear half of the body may result from injury to the spinal cord. This can be due to pressure from material from a ruptured disk oozing into the spinal canal and putting pressure on the spinal cord. It may also occur with spinal fractures or dislocations.

Paralysis of the entire body may be caused by severe damage to the brain. Or it may be due to physical or nutritional exhaustion, where the animal is too weak and too ill to rise. It often occurs shortly before coma and death.

Coma refers to the loss of consciousness. It may be caused by exhaustion of the body's resources by various disease processes, or by certain poisonous plants or other toxins. It is frequently the last stage before the animal dies, reflecting cardio-pulmonary collapse, low blood pressure, and insufficient blood flow and oxygen to the brain and other parts of the central nervous system.

OTHER INDICATORS OF HEALTH

Your observations are extremely important in determining whether your animal is healthy or ill. In addition, you can use some simple tests and measurements to help tell if you have a problem, and to give your veterinarian more information about what is wrong. Use them in addition to examining your dog's overall attitude, behavior and movement to determine whether he has a problem, and, if so, how serious it is. Always check the animal's temperature, pulse and respiration if you think he is ill. Do this before you examine him further or exercise him. If any of these are greatly different from normal (usually higher than normal), do not immediately assume that the animal is ill, but correlate it with other observations on the animal's condition and activity.

BODY TEMPERATURE

This is one of the best indicators of animal health. Use a rectal thermometer. For small dogs, you can use a thermometer made for humans. Very large dogs can handle one made for large animals. These thermometers are stubby and thick so that they are strong and unlikely to break. If you get a thermometer with a ring in the end, it can be equipped with a small alligator clip from an automotive store and a short (10-to-12 inch (25-to-30 cm)) length of heavy nylon thread or fishing line. Anchor the clip onto the hair of the dog's hind end, helping to prevent breakage if the dog swishes his tail and pulls the thermometer from his rectum. Thermometers should be stored in a cool place. Leaving one on the dashboard of a vehicle in summer usually ruins it.

Begin by shaking down the thermometer. The easiest way to do this is to hold it by the upper end between two fingers and the thumb. Shake it downward with a short snapping motion of the wrist. Hold it tightly. Glass thermometers don't bounce when they are flung on the floor. This shaking often has to be repeated 10 to 15 times to get the mercury toward the bulb end. It should be shaken down to about 95 degrees Fahrenheit (F). How low you shake it is not critical unless the animal's temperature is well below normal (hypothermic). If this is the problem, shake it all the way to the bottom and see

if it comes back up at all. It is helpful to lubricate the thermometer with petroleum jelly or a similar product before inserting it into the dog's rectum.

It is often helpful to have someone hold the dog's head while you take his temperature. If you are right handed, it is easiest to hold the thermometer in the right hand. Lift the dog's tail, if he has one, or steady his rump with your left hand. Gently insert the thermometer until it is about halfway into the rectum, depending on the size of the dog. It should be inserted at least two inches for all but the smallest dogs. If you don't have a cord on the thermometer, continue to hold it in place. If you do have a cord on the thermometer, clip it to the hair. Either way, leave it in place three to five minutes to get an accurate reading. Stay with the dog during this time to make sure he does not sit on the thermometer and make himself uncomfortable, or worse, break it off, leaving part inside. Unattended dogs may also pull it out, dropping it onto the floor and breaking it.

Reverse the procedure to remove the thermometer, unclipping it from the hair and grasping it by the end. Hold the tail with the left hand and gently pull it straight out. Wipe it with a tissue or paper towel. Read it. After reading, you can wash it with lukewarm water and a bit of soap. Do not use hot water, as it may break the thermometer. Clean the thermometer with alcohol or other disinfectant before you put it away for storage. You can store it in a vial of alcohol, or you can store it dry.

Normal temperature for the dog is 101 to 102 degrees (F), with an average of 101.5 degrees F (38.3 degrees Celsius (C)

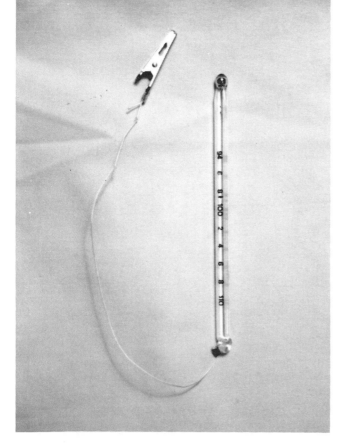

Thermometer with clip.

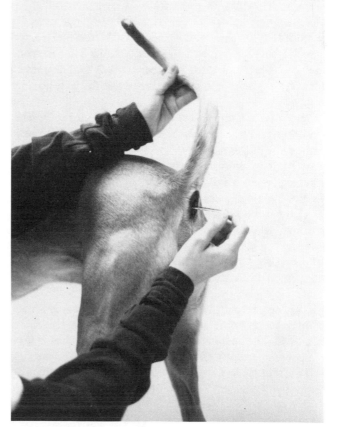

Taking the dog's temperature.

to 38.9 degrees C, average 38.6 degrees). Small dogs will run closer to 102 degrees F (38.9 degrees C).

Normal temperatures may run slightly higher in hot, humid weather, or if the animal has been in direct sunlight or left in a hot vehicle. Under these conditions, temperatures of 102 degrees F (38.9 degrees C) are not uncommon. The temperature is often elevated if the animal has just been exercised or is excited. Normal temperatures are usually a degree or so higher in the afternoon than they are in the morning. When you are checking the animal's temperature several days in a row, try to do it at approximately the same time of day. This will give a more accurate indication of changes from day to day.

Exposure to cold weather or winds or drinking large amounts of cold water may lower the animal's temperature briefly. A temperature which remains at 99 degrees F (37.2 degrees C) or less may indicate that the dog has been severely chilled and is suffering from hypothermia. Or it may indicate that he is going into shock or collapse, through internal bleeding or other causes.

The dog's body temperature is usually slightly higher one or two hours after a meal. Animals who are in unfamiliar surroundings or handled by strange people may also show an elevated temperature.

Fever is the term used when an animal's temperature is above normal. An elevated temperature (fever) will be seen from an infectious illness and from sunstroke (heat exhaustion).

It is well worth the effort to take your dog's temperature morning and evening daily for a week or so when you know the animal is healthy and in its usual environment. This gives you a base reading to use later to determine whether the animal's temperature is normal. A dog who is ill will generally be more than one degree above his normal (baseline) temperature for that time of day. Don't worry until a dog's temperature goes over 102.5 to 103 degrees F (39.2-39.4 degrees C) if the day is hot or the animal is excited and there are no signs of illness.

Do not be in a hurry to reduce a moderate fever. Fever is one of the body's active defensive mechanisms. The rise in temperature makes the body a less hospitable environment for many bacteria and viruses, helping the body to kill off the attacking organisms. When the temperature goes to about 103 degrees F (39.4 degrees C) or persists more than two to three days (or to the point where the animal has stopped eating and is becoming weak), then something should be done about reducing it. Of course, you should have been treating whatever is causing the fever all along, but the fever itself is not the problem in most cases—the real difficulty is the disease causing it.

There may be outward signs that the dog is running a fever. He may be trembling and sweaty. His skin may feel cooler than usual. The coat may seem to "stand up," and he may be humpbacked and miserable looking. Animals who are running a fever often have little or no appetite. They may be thirsty and depressed. Take the dog's temperature and record it for your veterinarian.

If the dog is shivering, or it is cold or windy outside, he should be brought into shelter and warmed up if at all possi-

ble. If you have to keep him outdoors, you can improvise a covering from a burlap bag, scrap of blanket or old quilt. He should have straw or deep shavings for bedding so that he will be warm and not lose heat to the ground or floor if he wishes to lie down.

Again, it is important to remember that fever is not the problem—it's part of the healing mechanism. Your dog's survival may depend on your quickly finding out WHY he has the fever and dealing with that underlying cause.

PULSE

The pulse which you can feel in an artery is an intermittent pressure wave caused by the heart forcing blood through the artery. The arteries alternate between expansion and contraction, and it is this pulse that we palpate (feel) and count. Counting the pulse rate is really counting the number of times the heart beats in one minute.

One of the easiest places to take a dog's pulse is inside his hind leg, on the femoral artery. You can lay the dog down to find the proper area (see photo). After you have done this, you can just reach inside the dog's hind leg while he is standing and take the pulse with your fingertips. Another method is to just put your hand around the lower part of the dog's chest. Move it around until you can feel the strongest beat of the heart. Or you can place the flat of your hand against the dog's chest, right behind the elbow. With the latter two techniques,

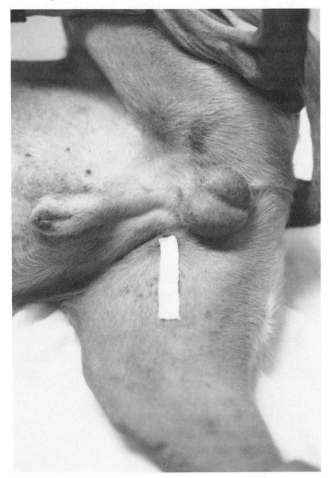

Tape marks area where the femoral pulse can be felt.

you will be counting the actual heartbeats, not the pulses, but the results are the same.

A stethoscope can be used to determine the dog's heart rate if you have one. Some people check the heart rate by pushing their ear against the chest wall behind the animal's elbow. Try this method if you do not have a stethoscope and cannot feel the pulse in one of the arteries. The heartbeat may be difficult to hear or feel on an obese dog.

Signs of heart or circulatory disease include pooling of fluid in the legs and belly (called edema). The dog may have a cough, may faint, or seem weak when he is exercised and may not have any energy.

THE STETHOSCOPE

A stethoscope is an instrument well worth having to make it easier to hear the sounds of internal organs. Inexpensive stethoscopes are available, and you don't need a top-of-the-line model. One key to being able to hear anything with a stethoscope is to find one that fits your ears. Try before you buy! If it doesn't fit in one direction, take it out of your ears, turn it 180 degrees, then try again. Some stethoscopes fit markedly better one way than the other. The earpieces should snugly fit your ears without pressure or pain. They should not be so loose that they rattle around. Some stethoscopes offer two different sides, one flat and the other bell- or cone-shaped. For most users, a stethoscope with only a flat side is sufficient.

After you have found an instrument that fits, the next step is to practice with it. The head of the stethoscope must be pushed firmly into the animal's side. Learn what the squeaking of the animal's hair sounds like against the head of the stethoscope and against its tubing. Then learn how hard you have to push to make firm contact with the animal's chest wall to avoid that noise and get the best sound.

Listen to a spot on the chest wall behind the left elbow for eight to ten seconds. Now, move two or three inches back, up or down. Compare what you hear with the sounds at the previous location. Are they more distinct or more muffled? Louder or softer? Cover a large area behind the elbow to determine where you can best hear the dog's heart. Examine the left side first. Then go to the animal's right side and repeat the procedure. On which side were the sounds clearer? If you'd like to hear lung sounds, go over the animal's whole chest in the same manner.

When using the stethoscope, the dog should be standing quietly. He should not be allowed to eat. Rattling choke chains, tags and other noises should be kept to a minimum. When you are getting used to a stethoscope, have people in the room remain quiet. After you have learned to listen with the stethoscope, you will become accustomed to ignoring outside sounds, but it helps not to have them around in the beginning.

Using a stethoscope is a skill where practice makes perfect. What at first is an unintelligible bunch of thumps will sort itself out into a distinct pattern of sounds. The loudest one will be a loud "lub," followed by a slightly softer "dub." This pattern is then repeated. Sharp ears may pick up two softer sounds in addition to the major two. These are normal, but

more difficult to hear in many dogs. Count only the "lubs," or you will get a pulse rate twice as high as it really is. Note the number of "lubs" per minute.

Dogs occasionally have what is called a sinus arhythmia. This gives an irregular heartbeat. If you are listening with a stethoscope, it will sound as if the animal's heart skips an occasional beat. This is normal, as long as the animal does not show fainting or other signs of heart problems, and as long as the heartbeat becomes normal when the animal is exercised. If you have trouble making sense of the heart sounds, ask your veterinarian on your next visit to listen with you and help you to understand them.

NORMAL HEART RATE

An adult dog's normal, resting heartbeat varies between 70 and 160 beats per minute, depending on the animal's size. Adult dogs of toy breeds may have a heart rate around 180 beats per minute. A young puppy may have a slightly higher heart rate, around 200 to 220 beats per minute. The pulse is usually slightly faster in the evening than in the morning. The heart rate may be raised by hot weather, exercise, excitement or alarm. It may be slower than normal with severe exhaustion, old age or excessive cold. Smaller dogs often tend to have faster heart rates, while larger ones have slower heart rates. Take the time to determine your dog's normal resting heart rate to establish the baseline.

RESPIRATION RATE

Respiration rate refers to the number of inhalations (or exhalations) per minute—the number of times the dog breathes in (or out). Do not count both in and out, or you will have a rate double what it really is. This is usually easy to count in the dog. Just stand back and observe the ribs moving in (or out). Do this from a distance, with the animal standing comfortably, without excitement. If you have a stethoscope, place it over the trachea, on the underside of the dog's neck, about halfway between the jaw and the chest. You can hear the air moving in and out. Again, count it as it moves in or out, but not both.

The normal respiratory rate for the dog is around 16 to 22 breaths per minute. As with temperature and pulse, respiration is usually faster in puppies. It increases with work, hot weather, overfilling of the stomach and pregnancy. Also, a fat animal will have a respiratory rate well above what is considered normal. Respiratory rate, like the pulse rate, is related to body size, exercise and temperament. It is often elevated when the animal is examined by strangers, as at a dog show or veterinary clinic.

GUT SOUNDS

Another area of examination is open to those with a stethoscope, that of intestinal sounds. These are the tinklings and bubblings made by gas as it percolates around and through the liquid and solid contents of the digestive tract. By listening to both sides of your dog's abdominal area for several minutes each, you can get an idea of what is normal. This can also be done by putting your ear on his flank. These sounds can be significantly increased when the dog is allergic to something in his food, has eaten something that he shouldn't have eaten, or is about to have diarrhea. What you are listening for is merely whether the sounds are more or less active than is normal for your animal. As with any of the other tests, you have to know the normal before you can detect the abnormal.

BLOOD

Blood is a fluid tissue consisting of a liquid, called plasma, and numerous cells. It is sometimes considered to be a connective tissue because of its cleansing and communicating functions from one part of the body to another.

Red blood cells are small round discs containing hemoglobin. This chemical can combine with either oxygen or carbon dioxide, whichever is in greater concentraton. Because of this characteristic, the cells take up carbon dioxide in the tissues where it is in greatest supply, and move it to the lungs. There more oxygen is available, so the cells dump the carbon dioxide (where it can be exhaled) and pick up a fresh supply of oxygen to carry back to the tissues.

White blood cells are one of the body's first defenses against infection by viruses and bacteria. The white blood cell component of blood also includes the platelets, which are involved with blood clotting.

Plasma is the term used for the fluid component of unclotted blood. It carries nutrients from one part of the body to another. For instance, it carries fats, amino acids (from the breakdown of proteins in food), and carbodydrates, taking these to cells throughout the body. There, the plasma picks up waste products, dropping them off in the kidneys and liver for removal from the body. Plasma also delivers hormones produced by the glands within the body to other sites where they are needed.

Serum is the fluid portion of the blood which is left after the blood has clotted. Antibodies which prevent disease and infections remain in the serum.

Blood helps to control body temperature by moving heat from deeper tissues to the surface where it can be dissipated.

It also helps to maintain water balance and a constant pH (acid-base balance) in body tissues.

Approximately 8% of an animal's body weight is blood.

Blood transfusions may be given to dogs who are in severe shock or have suffered from significant blood loss. Dogs do not have antigens against other blood groups as do humans, if they have never had a transfusion. If your dog needs a transfusion, let your veterinarian know if he has had one previously.

Blood pressure in dogs cannot be measured with a human blood pressure cuff—it simply does not work. Blood pressure measurement in the dog takes special instruments and techniques. It is rarely done except in university hospitals when special monitoring is needed, or in extremely large hospitals during lengthy, unusual surgery.

ANEMIA

A smaller than normal supply of red blood cells is called anemia. Dogs may have anemia from a number of causes. Bleeding, either internal or external, is the most common cause. Parasites may suck enough blood to make a dog anemic. These may be external, such as lice, or internal, such as various worms. Or the dog may simply not be producing a normal amount of red blood cells. Autoimmune diseases, in which the dog is allergic to parts of his own system, may cause him to be anemic.

Dogs who are anemic will have blood with reduced oxygen-carrying capacity. They may have less energy and ability to do work than normal, and may have pale mucous membranes.

If the animal is indeed anemic, it is important to find out why. Is there a deficiency of B vitamins or iron which are needed to produce red blood cells? Is the animal affected with internal parasites (worms) which are draining blood from him? Or is his bone marrow not producing enough red blood cells? Is a disease process involved? Anemia is seen with some kidney problems and with bone marrow depression. Has he recently suffered an injury causing severe blood loss? It is often necessary for your veterinarian to run a number of laboratory tests to determine the exact cause of anemia. Your clue that something may be wrong will be your dog's pale mucous membranes.

Chapter 5

VACCINATIONS AND INFECTIOUS DISEASES

Infection refers to the invasion of body tissues by various organisms. An example of an infection is an abscess, in which bacteria cause pus to form. An infectious disease is an illness caused by these organisms. They may be bacteria, viruses, yeasts or various parasites. A contagious disease is one that can spread easily from one animal to another, or from an animal to a human, depending on the organism involved. For example, an abscess is an infection, tetanus is an infectious disease, and canine distemper is both an infectious disease and a contagious one, as it can be passed easily from one dog to another.

You are probably familiar with viruses. They are tiny organisms which invade the cells of the body, causing disease. A good example of a human viral disease is the common cold. Bacteria also cause diseases in humans; tuberculosis is one example. Yeasts can also invade the body, causing disease. Some of these which affect dogs are discussed in the section on respiratory disease. Rickettsiae are tiny parasites which live within the white blood cells. Various species of them occur in dogs, cattle, sheep, goats and many other animals, as well as humans. They cause a variety of different diseases. Malaria is an example of this type of disease which affects humans.

Vaccines can be produced to protect against some of these organisms. Vaccines are fairly easy to make against most bacteria, and are produced if they cause severe enough problems. Vaccines can also be made against some viruses. The vaccine against smallpox in humans has resulted in total elimination of this disease in the world. Other viral diseases are currently impossible to vaccinate against. An example of

this is the common cold in humans. The virus is quite changeable, and does not produce a good immunity when made into a vaccine, at least with technology that exists at this time.

VACCINATION SCHEDULES

Specific vaccination schedules are difficult to recommend, as there are many variables involved. However, there are some guidelines to help you determine which to use and when to vaccinate your dog. If you are taking your dog to a veterinarian for the immunizations, you will of course be consulting with him and following his recommendations.

The bitch, especially when her vaccinations are current and her immune system is working normally, will pass immunity to her puppies, both through the uterus and in her milk. The colostrum (the first milk she produces after the puppies are born) is rich in antibodies against many diseases. They serve to protect the puppy until he is able to produce his own antibodies. However, the presence of antibodies from his mother (called passive immunity) in his blood will keep him from producing his own antibodies when vaccinated (this is called active immunity). The antibodies from his mother must be allowed to decay before his own body will produce an adequate immunity. How long this takes depends on how high his mother's immunity level is. It can be measured by having your veterinarian run a laboratory test called a nomogram. Nomograms are available for distemper and parvovirus only, and will tell at what age the puppy will be able to make his own antibodies.

Without this laboratory test information, knowledge of the area and its disease problems, evaluation of the possible risks and a bit of luck determine when and how often to vaccinate.

Ideally, one would start vaccinating puppies as young as 3-4 weeks and vaccinate them every two weeks with a vaccine containing at least distemper and parvovirus. Coronavirus vaccination can be given at the same time. This would be continued until the puppy is 16 weeks of age. While it is more expensive than a program with less injections, it gives the best probability for developing immunity, and is especially worthwhile with dogs of high economic or sentimental value. Admittedly, this is sort of a "shotgun" approach. But since you won't know when the antibodies from his mother are no longer there, the idea is to have vaccine present when they do go away. At least one of the shots will give active immunity— you just won't know which one.

A four-shot program would give an injection of the same type of vaccine at 6, 9, 12 and 16 weeks. A less expensive— and less protective—three-injection program would give shots at 8, 12 and 16 weeks. These programs have the advantage of being more economical than giving injections every two weeks for approximately three months, but sacrifice a degree of protection.

An alternative program is to give measles vaccine at four weeks of age. Distemper and parvovirus vaccines are then given at 8 or 9, 12 and 16 weeks of age.

If it is legal in your state and you have a reliable source of quality, major-brand vaccine and you wish to do so, you can give these injections yourself. This can save you some money. Rabies vaccinations must be given by a veterinarian in order to be considered legal in most states. This can be cheap insurance in the event your dog bites someone. In a few states, the vaccine is available and it is legal for the dog owner to give his own rabies vaccinations. It is important for all dogs to be vaccinated against rabies, but especially so for packs of hounds or hunting dogs who may be exposed to rabid wildlife in their travels.

Rabies vaccinations can be given as young as 3 months of age, then again at one year of age in a rabies problem area. From then on, the dog should have boosters every one, two, or three years, depending on the vaccine which has been used. Any dog who has never had a rabies vaccination, regardless of age, should have two injections initially, two or three weeks apart, before being placed on the revaccination schedule. Local and state laws often dictate these times and frequencies. Ask your veterinarian. He will know what the law is regarding rabies vaccination.

Depending on the disease in question, your veterinarian may prefer a different program than the ones outlined above. He knows what the current disease situation is and what the risk factors are for your area. Trust his judgment and use the program that he recommends. Let's discuss more about infectious diseases:

DISTEMPER

Distemper is a highly contagious viral disease of dogs and other canines, as well as ferrets, minks, skunks and raccoons. The distemper virus is closely related to measles virus. Canine distemper, by the way, is NOT related to the diseases called distemper in cats, horses or other animals, and is NOT contagious to these animals. Canine distemper is found throughout the world.

The heartbreaking part of distemper is that it may go through several phases, in different parts of the body. These may last as little as a week, but more often a it is a month or more before you know whether the dog will live or die. Meanwhile, the dog is severely ill, requiring extensive (and expensive) care. And the end result may still be a dead dog.

Distemper is spread through the air, by one dog coughing or sneezing on another, or via an object which is contaminated by a dog with distemper and then touched by another dog. You can bring distemper home on your shoes by unknowingly walking where an infected dog has walked. Infected dogs may shed the virus for months.

Distemper is characterized by an early temperature rise which has led some veterinarians to call it "102-1/2 disease." After a few days, the temperature drops to normal before it rises again, lasting for a week or more the second time around. In these early stages, there are no other particular signs of illness. You dog will just not be "up to par."

The first obvious signs of distemper are usually seen in the respiratory tract. The nose may be crusted with a thick, yellowish-gray discharge. Similar discharge will be seen in the corners of the eyes, and they may be matted nearly shut. The puppy will be listless and depressed. He will usually refuse to eat, and may develop diarrhea.

A form of distemper called "hardpad" shows severe drying, hardening and cracking of the pads of the feet. The end of the nose may also be extremely dry and cracked. This form, while very characteristic, has become rare in recent years. Dogs with hardpad usually also show signs of nervous system involvement.

The diarrhea may go on for a week or more, with the dog losing weight and becoming progressively more ill. The diarrhea may then stop, and the dog will appear to be getting better.

From here, the dog may continue to get well until he is recovered. Or, he may go into nervous system involvement. One form appears as twitching in one muscle or group of muscles. This may be all that happens, and the dog may recover, but have a twitch or nervous tic for the rest of his life. The twitch may appear either when he is awake or only in his sleep. Other dogs may have a head tilt or abnormal function of one or more limbs. A second form and an unfavorable sign is the development of a paralysis which begins in the hind end and progresses forward. Generally, a dog with this type of paralysis will not survive. A third form of nervous problem may occur—convulsions. These start with chewing motions of the jaw, accompanied by salivation. These are often called "champing fits." The combination of chewing motions and saliva often result in a frothy foam around the dog's mouth. This is not rabies. These seizures become more frequent and more severe until the dog falls on his side and paddles, running in place. Involuntary urination and defecation may occur.

From the time signs begin until the dog is either stabilized and recovering, or dies from the disease, may be as little as a week. Other cases may last three weeks to a month. This causes prolonged suffering for the dog, and expense, trouble and emotional turmoil for the owner until it is evident that the dog will either live or die.

There is presently no medication which can directly affect the distemper virus. Treatment is aimed at controlling secondary bacterial infections which may occur along with the distemper virus. For this, antibiotics are usually given. Good nutrition and supportive care may help to pull the dog through the illness. Vitamins are usually also prescribed, as well as supplemental fluids to assure that the dog does not become dehydrated. Drugs to help reduce the temperature may also be used.

No matter what treatment is used, a large percentage of dogs which come down with distemper die. Those who do not die usually show some degree of damage to the brain or nervous system which will persist for the rest of the animal's life.

Nursing is extremely important in treating a case of distemper. The dog should be kept warm and comfortable. Cleanse the eyes and nose with a paper towel or rag dampened with warm water. If the dog's nose is dry and crusted, application of petroleum jelly will make him feel better. When diarrhea occurs, it is treated symptomatically. The dog should be wiped, or washed as necessary to keep his hind end and hair clean. Long-haired dogs will be easier to keep clean if the hair on the hind legs and underside of the tail is cut short. The dog should be coaxed to eat whatever you can get him to eat. Plenty of water and broth will help to prevent dehydration. This is one disease in which your nursing may be the ONLY treatment determining whether your dog lives or dies. One caution, however. Keep in mind that even the very best of care may not save the animal. The canine distemper virus is a formidable foe.

Fortunately, prevention is quite successful, and distemper vaccination has greatly reduced the number of cases seen in recent years. Vaccinating your puppy will help to assure that he will not come down with the disease. Yearly boosters will keep his immunity strong.

Vaccines are made with either killed virus, or attenuated (modified-live) virus. The modified-live virus vaccines provide a more rapid onset of immunity, and the immunity is more durable.

Whatever vaccination schedule is used, it is important to have the last injection at or after 16 weeks of age, to be sure that the puppy is able to develop an adequate immunity. The distemper vaccination is normally combined with hepatitis, leptospirosis and other immunizations.

While the puppy is in the course of immunization, he should NOT be exposed to other dogs. If at all possible, do not take him out and around the streets, as he may walk where a sick dog has walked, and in that way be exposed to one or more contagious (and possibly fatal) diseases. Keep him at home. And keep other dogs from nosing him through a fence. If necessary, build a temporary, smaller run within your yard. If you take him out for exercise, do so only in a wooded or vacant area where other dogs are unlikely to have passed. After his complete series of immunizations, about 17 or 18 weeks of age, it is safe to take him out into the world.

It is important to give an annual revaccination to all dogs to insure that their immunity stays high. Even a dog 10 or 12 years old should still be vaccinated yearly. There is some evidence that older dogs may be particularly susceptible to distemper. Immunity from their "puppy" shots will have worn off long before this age.

MEASLES VACCINATION

Measles vaccine uses the virus of human measles to give puppies a temporary protection against distemper. The reason this vaccine works is because some portions of the virus are the same as those of the distemper virus, and it's less likely the puppy's mother passed measles immunity on to him. This vaccine can be given any time from about four weeks of age to about 9 or 10 weeks. It is most commonly given at six weeks of age, and develops protective immunity in less than a week. This will cover the period of time between the decline of the immunity the mother has passed on to the puppy and the time when he is able to produce his own immunity. The vaccine is not recommended for use in puppies older than 9 to 10 weeks

(Swango, 1989). It is a very effective vaccine, although it is still not wise to knowingly expose your puppy to a case of distemper. The puppy CAN come down with distemper after vaccination with measles vaccine, but it will usually not be fatal, and the risk of permanent damage is low.

Measles vaccine is NOT a substitute for distemper vaccine. It is only to be used in young puppies before they can produce an immunity against distemper. Measles vaccine should NOT be used in adult dogs or pregnant females. If used in the older female, this could prevent the vaccine from being effective in her puppies. It is also unnecessary, as distemper vaccine is effective in older puppies and adult dogs.

Measles vaccine MUST be given intramuscularly. Subcutaneous administration provides no protection against distemper. As a matter of fact, if you are EVER in doubt which way to go with a vaccine, give it in the muscle rather than any other way.

HEPATITIS

Infectious Canine Hepatitis (ICH) also occurs in other canines—wolves, foxes, coyotes, and skunks and bears throughout the world. The virus is very durable and may survive outside the animal's body for up to several months. This is not the same hepatitis which occurs in humans. Hepatitis is more common in young puppies and in elderly dogs.

The disease varies from a slight fever and eye discharge to a fatal illness. Very young puppies are more likely to die from hepatitis than are older dogs. The incubation period may vary from 4 to 9 days. The first sign is an elevated temperature, 104 degrees F (40 degrees C) or higher. As with distemper, the temperature may rise, stay high for 1-6 days, drop, and then rise again. The heart rate may be very rapid in response to the high fever.

The dog may be severely depressed and have little interest in eating, but be more thirsty than usual. The eyes may be reddened and runny. The nose may run as well. Some dogs will show signs of abdominal pain. The membranes of the mouth may be reddened, or may show pinpoint hemorrhages. Vomiting may occur. Edema may be seen under the skin of the head, neck and trunk. If injury occurs, the blood may not clot normally. This may be the most obvious (or sometimes the only) sign of ICH. Respiratory and nervous symptoms are not usually seen. Your veterinarian may need to run special laboratory tests to confirm that your dog has hepatitis.

As with distemper, there is no drug which will attack the virus of ICH. Nursing and supportive therapy are all that help. Daily blood transfusions may be given to seriously ill dogs. Also, large amounts of intravenous (IV) fluids will help the dog to survive. Transfusions and IV fluids must be administered by your veterinarian. He may wish to have you bring the dog in daily, or he might prefer to hospitalize the dog throughout the course of treatment. Antibiotics may also be given to help protect the dog from secondary bacterial infection.

Dogs who recover will eat well but gain weight slowly. A week to 10 days after infection, about a quarter of the recovered dogs will develop a bluish-white clouding (opacity) in the corneas of both eyes. This will usually go away with time. The only sign in mild cases of ICH may be this corneal opacity. Some dogs will show pain with this eye condition. They should be kept out of bright light. Atropine eye ointment may be given to help reduce the pain. Ophthalmic ointments containing corticosteroids are generally not used to treat the corneal opacity resulting from ICH. (Merck, 1986, p. 339).

Hepatitis is transmitted through feces, urine, or saliva from infected animals. Dogs who have recovered from the disease may shed virus in the urine for more than 6 months.

As with distemper, ICH may be prevented by immunization. Commonly used distemper vaccines include the hepatitis virus, so that a separate injection is not needed. The bitch who is vaccinated for ICH will provide immunity to her puppies through her milk, as with distemper. Most puppies, when vaccinated at 9 to 12 weeks of age, will develop an immunity to ICH. Sometimes, the vaccine may produce the same bluish coloration in the cornea which is seen with the disease. This is generally temporary, and will go away with time. Annual revaccination is recommended.

LEPTOSPIROSIS

Leptospirosis is a water-borne disease which occurs in dogs, man, cattle and many other animals. Over 175 different, distinct forms of this bacterium are known. A half-dozen different ones have been found in dogs in the United States. They can survive in surface waters for long periods of time. After an acute infection, the bacteria are shed in the urine in large numbers—for months or even years. In addition to dogs who have survived the disease, brown rats are also a source of infection.

Dogs of all ages can be infected. Males are much more commonly infected than are females, probably because they roam, poke their noses into areas urinated on by other dogs, and are more likely (because of their roaming) to contact infected waters. Cattle are also infected with some of the same varieties of *Leptospirae* which affect dogs, especially in the western states. Dogs may contract the disease from drinking where an infected cow has urinated upstream. The incubation period is 5-15 days.

Severe cases will have a sudden onset, with lack of appetite, weakness and vomiting. The temperature is around 103-105 degrees F (39.5-40.5 degrees C). The eyes may be slightly reddened. It can be difficult to diagnose the disease at this point. The temperature will drop sharply within several days, with the dog becoming more depressed and very thirsty. His breathing may become labored.

The first sign in some dogs may be icterus, a yellow coloration of the membranes of the eyes and mouth. The membranes of the mouth may also show irregular areas which look like burns or scrapes. These later dry and fall off in patches. The saliva may be blood-tinged, and the dog may have trouble swallowing. The dog may refuse to get up from a sitting position. He may show signs of pain when you palpate the lower back, or the abdomen just behind the ribs. Be gentle—jabbing at these areas can really hurt.

As the disease progresses, dogs are often severely depressed, and may have muscular tremors. The temperature drops gradually, as low as 97 degrees F (36 degrees C). The dog may vomit blood and have a bloody diarrhea. The dog may urinate frequently. The eyes may be sunken, and the blood vessels on the eyeballs may be filled and bright red.

Leptospirosis is not often fatal. Less than 10% of affected dogs die. In fatal cases, death usually occurs in 5 to 10 days. Some species of *Leptospirae* cause a chronic, progressive disease in which death may occur long after the dog has at least partially recovered from his original illness. This is because the bacteria have damaged the kidneys enough that they cannot adequately support the dog any longer.

Dogs with leptospirosis should be treated by or on the advice of your veterinarian. Tetracycline or streptomycin are two antibiotics frequently used. Fluid treatments and vitamin therapy will be used for dogs who have become dehydrated. Severe cases may require peritoneal dialysis. This is a procedure in which the veterinarian flushes fluids into the dog's abdominal cavity to remove toxic products which are not being removed by the damaged kidneys. This procedure is expensive, time-consuming and uncomfortable to the dog. It may, however, buy enough time for the dog's body to fight off the infection and resume functioning. In many cases it is worth a try. Personal hygiene is important for you and everyone else coming into contact with the dog. The disease can be transmitted to humans.

Prevention: If you are in an area with a leptospirosis epidemic, keep your dog confined to your own yard. During an epidemic, dogs should have booster vaccinations twice a year. This is also good insurance for dogs on the show circuit or in stud service. At other times, keeping your dog on a leash can be cheap prevention. When leptospirosis is diagnosed in a kennel, all dogs should be vaccinated. Kennel sanitation with an outbreak is very important. Rodent control is also important.

KENNEL COUGH (TRACHEOBRONCHITIS)

Infectious tracheobronchitis is a contagious viral disease which affects the trachea (windpipe) and bronchi (large passages in the lungs) in dogs of all ages. It is called "kennel cough" because it spreads rapidly through large numbers of confined dogs in kennels or hospitals, or through dogs at a field trial or dog show. Up to 80% of the dogs who are exposed to kennel cough will come down with the disease if they are not vaccinated. In most dogs it is self-limiting and mild. It can develop into a fatal pneumonia in elderly dogs, young puppies, dogs in poor physical condition or dogs that have other diseases. If your dog has kennel cough when he is a puppy, his lungs may be permanently damaged, and he may never reach his full potential for growth and development. Kennel cough does NOT infect people.

Stress and cold, drafts or high humidity may make the dog more susceptible to kennel cough. Long periods of barking (as many dogs will do in a kennel) may also contribute to the development of kennel cough by irritating the throat and trachea. Kennel cough may be complicated by bacterial infections.

Tracheobronchitis has an incubation period of 5-10 days. The dog usually has a history of having been in a kennel, clinic, or to a dog show or some other event where large numbers of dogs are present. Don't hold the disease against the kennel or clinic. It is common wherever numbers of dogs are gathered together, much like colds and children. No amount of sanitation will prevent it under those conditions. If your dog has been to a kennel and starts coughing shortly after he gets home, this is probably what is wrong.

The most prominent sign is a harsh, dry, rattling cough. For some reason, dog owners seem to become more aware of the cough late at night. Is the cough worse then, or are things just quiet enough to notice it? After he coughs, the dog may gag and act as if he is trying to vomit. If you press gently on the trachea or the base of the larynx, the dog will give a dry, harsh cough immediately. The dog may also have tonsillitis along with the tracheobronchitis, and may gag or vomit mucus from his throat.

Many dogs are bright and alert and seem to feel good except for the cough. Others may have little appetite and may appear depressed. The body temperature is normal at the beginning, but may rise as bacteria invade the dog's lungs.

The most severe signs are seen within the first 5 to 7 days, although the disease may go on for two to three weeks. If it lasts longer than this, pneumonia may be present, and the dog should definitely be seen by a veterinarian. If pneumonia develops, the dog may have a fever. Pus may run from his nose. He will be depressed, and refuse to eat.

Rest is an important part of the treatment, and the dog should be kept from exercise until he has stopped coughing to avoid further irritation to the respiratory tract. Remove the dog's collar, and if you need to restrain him, use a harness to avoid irritating his throat. Pressure from the collar may start the dog coughing. The dog should be kept from contact with other dogs to keep him from spreading the disease.

Cough syrups used for humans may be used, in a dosage appropriate to the size of the dog. Those with codeine are good, as are ones containing an antihistamine. In some cases, your veterinarian will let your dog cough for a week or so to help remove mucus produced in the lungs. Basically, if the dog is coughing up material, he should probably be allowed to cough in order to get it out of his lungs. When the cough becomes dry and non-productive, it should be controlled. If the cough reflex is stopped too early, mucus may accumulate in the lungs and cause pneumonia. On the other hand, every time the dog coughs, this prevents healing of the lining of the respiratory tract, which causes still more coughing. There's a fine line between continued irritation and the risk of pneumonia.

A cold water vaporizer may be used in the room where the dog spends most of his time. This will raise the humidity and help to soothe his respiratory tract. Encourage the dog to drink as much water as possible. This will help to thin the mucus so that it can be coughed up more easily. Keep the air temperature as even as possible. Keep the dog indoors if you can, and avoid chilling him. Do not give him a bath if you can avoid it. If you have to do so, be sure to dry the dog completely. Exercise and vigorous play should be avoided until the dog has stopped coughing. Only walk the dog long enough for him to urinate and defecate.

Antibiotics are sometimes given. Many veterinarians feel that they help to shorten the course of the disease. Without treatment, kennel cough can last from a couple of weeks to a month or more. Some veterinarians will take a culture to see which bacteria are causing most of the problem, and then treat the infection with an antibiotic specific for that particular infection. They may also use an antibiotic mixture containing a small amount of a corticosteroid. This will help the dog to feel better, after which he will begin eating. The steriod also helps to reduce the irritation which is causing the coughing. Steroids should not be used in dogs who have kidney disease. If the cough becomes worse or persists, or the dog has vomiting or diarrhea, take him back to your veterinarian for re-examination. Good nutrition, good hygiene, good nursing and "tincture of time" all contribute to recovery. Complete recovery may take as much as six weeks!

Vaccines are available against kennel cough, and may contain CAV1 or CAV2 viruses, parainfluenza or Bordetella. Immunization is a good idea if your dog goes to the kennel frequently, or to dog shows. The first series of kennel cough immunization is two injections two to four weeks apart. These can be given at the same time as the puppy is vaccinated against distemper. Annual revaccination is needed to keep the immunity current. If you have a dog on the show circuit or in field trials, vaccinating twice a year may be cheap insurance. Intranasal products are sometimes available. These usually require only one dose, with boosters every six months. Vaccination against distemper also seems to have some cross-protection against kennel cough, so keep that immunization current. Tracheobronchitis is a difficult disease to vaccinate against. However, you may not need to protect your dog if you keep him strictly at home, in your house or yard, and without "nose through the fence" contact with other dogs.

PARVOVIRUS

Also called "parvo," canine parvoviral infection is an infection of the digestive tract. It appeared as a serious problem in the summer of 1978 and is now found throughout the world. Some experts feel that it is a mutant form of feline distemper. However, the virus no longer infects cats. Coyotes, foxes and other canines are susceptible. Puppies seem to be more susceptible than adult dogs.

The virus is spread through contact with (and ingestion of) fecal material from an infected animal. Dogs which are infected will shed the virus in their feces for two weeks or more, and it may remain viable for years in the soil. The fact that you live in a remote location does NOT mean that your dog is safe from parvo. You may carry it home from town on your shoes, or it may be brought into your yard by a fox or coyote or a stray dog passing through the neighborhood.

Parvovirus causes a severe, degenerative infection throughout the digestive tract. Dehydration and electrolyte imbalance occur as severe diarrhea progresses. The dog may die as a result of endotoxic shock from dying bacteria in the intestinal tract releasing potent toxins. Or bacterial infection in the damaged intestine may be the cause of death. The incubation period varies from 3 to 12 days.

Diarrhea is perhaps the most prominent sign of parvo. A severe, watery, foul-smelling diarrhea may be streaked with blood, or be totally bloody. It will continue until the dog either recovers or dies. The diarrhea may cause a severe dehydration, which can occur soon after onset. The dog is depressed and will not eat. Vomiting may occur. Some dogs may show a fever early in the disease, but not all do.

Dogs may die suddenly of "shock" as little as two days after the disease begins. Lingering illness is rare. Dogs either recover or die quickly. In young puppies (4-8 weeks of age), the virus may cause damage to the heart, and the puppy may die within 12 hours, with no outward signs of the disease. Dogs with parvo should be kept in strict isolation to prevent spreading the disease to others.

Veterinary care is often the only chance to save a dog with parvo. Your veterinarian will give intravenous fluids to help replace those lost by diarrhea. This may be needed for 2-4 days, until the diarrhea lessens and the dog is stabilized. Antibiotics may be given.

Vaccination gives good protection against parvovirus infection. As with distemper, however, antibodies from the mother may prevent early immunization from giving protection (despite some companies' advertising to the contrary). So a period of susceptibility is difficult to avoid. The safest approach is to vaccinate the puppy every 2-3 weeks from the time he is weaned (or even two weeks before weaning) until he is 16-18 weeks of age. Slightly less than ideal, the immunizations can be given at the same time as the distemper vaccinations, based on the schedule used by your veterinarian. Keep the puppy STRICTLY ISOLATED FROM OTHER DOGS AND AT HOME until he is about 18 weeks of age. Do not let other dogs come to "visit" him, and do not take him out and around until after that age. You and others who will be around the puppy should also stay away from places where you might soil your shoes with dog feces. Annual boosters will keep your dog's immunity strong.

Parvovirus is resistant to many disinfectants, alcohol and most detergents. It can withstand high temperatures and freezing. A chlorine solution is one of the few disinfectants which will kill parvovirus. To clean up an area where an infected dog has had diarrhea, mix a 1:30 solution of household bleach (1 ounce of bleach to 30 ounces of water). This is, of course, not for internal consumption, nor should it be used on the skin. If you have been exposed to dogs who have parvo, you can use this to clean your shoes before walking into your house or coming into contact with your own dog. It is also a good idea to change into clean clothes before handling your dog if you have been in a household, kennel or other place where a dog has had parvo.

CORONAVIRUS

Canine coronavirus infection causes a severe infection of the stomach and digestive tract (called gastroenteritis). This virus disease is highly contagious among dogs, coyotes and foxes of any age, and is thought to exist throughout the world.

Coronavirus infection is transmitted from one canine to another as the dog eats fecal material from another infected animal. This may be as simple as the dog licking his feet after he has walked where an infected dog has had a bowel movement. Infected dogs can shed virus in the feces for approximately two weeks.

Signs are very similar to those of parvovirus. In fact, it is often difficult for you (or for your veterinarian) to tell the difference between the two without extensive laboratory tests. In a significant number of cases, both parvovirus and coronavirus will infect the dog at the same time, resulting in a more severe disease and a prolonged recovery, if the dog survives at all.

Diarrhea, vomiting, lack of appetite and depression are often seen with coronavirus infection. The disease may start very suddenly. The diarrhea may be very liquid, and may contain blood, as well as having a foul odor. The dog may become severely dehydrated due to fluid loss. Some dogs will show a fever, while others will have a normal temperature.

As with parvovirus, there is no specific treatment for coronavirus. Nursing care and supportive treatment are generally the same as treating a parvovirus infection.

If your dog has been immunized against parvovirus and comes down with a severe diarrheal disease, chances are good that it is due to a coronavirus infection. This disease may go explosively through a kennel, with many dogs becoming ill at the same time.

A vaccine is available to protect against coronavirus, and works well to prevent infection. This should also be a part of your dog's routine immunization program. Coronavirus vaccine can be given along with distemper vaccine. The first dose can be given around 9 weeks of age, a second at 12 weeks and a third dose at 16 weeks of age. At least one brand of vaccine combines coronavirus vaccine with distemper, hepatitis, parvovirus, and several other diseases for a rather complete "puppy shot." This can be given at the intervals recommended for the puppy's initial series of distemper vaccinations. As with most other canine vaccines, a single booster dose of coronavirus vaccine should be given annually.

RABIES

Rabies is a viral disease, found in warm-blooded animals throughout most of the world; there are sporadic outbreaks in populations of wild animals. In the northeastern United States it is most commonly spread through foxes, while the southeastern United States also sees it in raccoons and other animals. West of the Mississippi, skunks are a common reservoir. Bats may be carriers in certain areas. Rabies is perhaps more common in the summer, when both dogs and the wild animals that may carry the disease to them are roaming more freely. However, it can be seen at any time of the year.

Rabies affects the central nervous system, especially the brain, but the virus can be isolated from all tissues of affected animals. When the disease reaches its contagious point, the virus is present in the salivary glands. From there it passes into the saliva. It is most commonly transmitted from one animal to another by a bite or scratch contaminated with this infective saliva. Infection from one animal to another (or to a human!) may occur several days to weeks or months before signs of the disease become obvious.

The greatest danger with dogs contracting rabies is that they can then spread it to you and your family—through a bite, or by licking a cut or wound on your skin. They can also bite domestic animals, such as horses or cattle, who then become infected and present a hazard to humans.

The incubation period in dogs may be 15 days to as much as three or more months. In other animals, it may be as much as a year. Some animals, such as skunks and raccoons, may carry the disease, bite another animal, thus passing it on, and NEVER come down with the disease themselves. This is why it is not a good idea to keep skunks for pets. Other wild animals, such as foxes, may also be unsafe in a rabies area.

Rabies in dogs may go through three phases. A change in behavior is the first sign. This may be confused with digestive disorders, or any of a number of other diseases. The dog may stop eating and drinking and wish to be alone. More frequent urination may be seen, and males may show erection and sexual desire. After about 1-3 days in this stage, the disease moves on to either the "furious" or the "dumb" form. The dog either becomes vicious or starts into paralysis.

"Furious rabies" is the term used for dogs in the excitative phase. This is the "mad dog" of old. The animal becomes irrational, and generally will be aggressive and vicious. The pupils of the eyes are dilated, giving the dog an expression of exaggerated alertness and anxiety. The dog may attack any source of noise or motion. There are no signs of paralysis at this point in the disease.

Dogs with furious rabies may roam widely, biting anything that moves and eating peculiar objects such as sticks and stones. Veterinarians in rabies areas tell of dogs with the disease who bend and bite through the bars of their cages, breaking their teeth, with their jaws bleeding. The animals do not seem to feel any pain. Puppies with rabies may be abnormally playful and want to be with humans, but will bite as they play, quickly becoming vicious. The majority of cats who are affected will show signs of furious rabies.

Wild animals often show similar signs of rabies. Skunks will walk through a ranch yard, biting tires on tractors and cars. Foxes may bite porcupines, and a fox with porcupine quills should be treated as having rabies. DO NOT attempt to help him! Wild animals often also lose their fear of humans. This may lead them to approach your house or campsite or you! Consider that ANY wild animal that acts abnormally friendly MAY have rabies, and avoid contact with it. Rodents, at least in the United States, are not known to be commonly affected with rabies, so animals such as squirrels are not considered to be a problem.

If you kill an animal suspected of having rabies, DO NOT shoot it through the head, as this will destroy tissues needed for the rabies examination. Take the head to your veterinarian to be sent to the laboratory, being careful not to get any blood on your skin. Or, better yet, take the whole animal and let the veterinerian deal with the head.

The furious form of rabies may progress in the animal's last days, to the dumb, paralytic form. Or dumb rabies may occur from the start. These animals have paralysis of the muscles of the jaw and throat. They are unable to swallow their saliva, so they drool profusely, dripping long, stringy saliva. The dog may attempt to drink water. This will increase the spasms which are occurring in the muscles which control swallowing. Because of this discomfort, the animal may be afraid to drink water. Even the sight of water may cause these spasms. This reaction gave birth to the old name for rabies, hydrophobia ("fear of water"). The lower jaw may droop.

Dogs with dumb rabies usually do not attempt to bite, and they are not vicious. Unfortunately, the owner often attempts to check the dog's mouth for a foreign body, and is thus exposed to the disease. More than one veterinarian has been trapped in this way. A dog with dumb rabies may be totally oblivious to what is going on around him. He may sit in the middle of a busy street or highway, unaware that he needs to move to a safer place. Dogs with this form of rabies become paralyzed, followed by coma and death within a few hours. If you are in a known rabies area and your dog shows these signs, DO NOT examine him yourself. Take him to your veterinarian, and if necessary, leave him there for a few days of observation. If there is a chance that it's rabies, it is better to have him where he will not expose you and your family and friends. If it turns out not to be rabies, you are only out a few days board at the hospital.

Treatment: There is NO treatment for animals infected with rabies. "Any domestic animal that is bitten or scratched by a bat or wild, carnivorous mammal which is not available for testing should be regarded as having been exposed to a rabid animal." (Jenkins, 1989).

An unvaccinated dog or cat which is bitten by a rabid animal should be humanely killed immediately. If you are unwilling to do this, the animal must be placed in strict quarantine for at least six months. This means screened or wire fencing so that other dogs and cats cannot have contact with the animal. Provision should be made for feeding and watering it without need for entering the enclosure, and no one should handle or play with the animal. The dog or cat should be vaccinated immediately after the bite, and again after five months of quarantine.

If a dog or cat is exposed and has been vaccinated with a one-year vaccine, it must have been vaccinated within the previous year to be considered protected. When a three-year vaccine has been used, the vaccination must be within three years. Animals vaccinated in this manner should be given a booster immediately and observed for three months.

All species of livestock are susceptible to rabies. Cattle are among the most susceptible. If you know that one of your domestic animals has been bitten by a rabid animal, the best idea is to slaughter it immediately. If the animal is slaughtered within a week of being bitten, the meat can be eaten, provided you discard a liberal area around the bite (Jenkins, 1989). If you do not wish to slaughter the animal, it should be carefully quarantined for six months. Meat or other tissues, or milk from a known rabid animal should NOT be used for either animal or human consumption.

Rabies can be prevented by vaccination. This is cheap insurance not only for your dog, but, more importantly, for you and your family.

If you give your own rabies vaccinations, NEVER use a vaccine made for dogs in ANY other animal, as it may GIVE the disease, thus creating a hazard to you and your family. Dog-wolf or dog-coyote crosses are NOT genetically the same as dogs, and it is generally recommended that they NOT be vaccinated against rabies with vaccines meant for dogs, because of the danger of causing the disease. Unless the package flyer says otherwise, rabies vaccine is given deep into the heavy muscles of the thigh, in one location.

If you live in a rabies problem area, it is also a good idea to vaccinate your horses, cats, and valuable breeding cattle and sheep. Again, it is important to use only vaccine that is labeled as being approved for these species.

Help your dog to avoid the necessity for quarantine by avoiding situations that will lead to dog bites. Even the best-behaved dog will bite if he fears for his life. Dogs establish territories both inside and outside their homes. Strangers who invade this area may be candidates for attack. This is especially true of children who move suddenly and rapidly, in a manner which the dog may interpret as threatening. Minimizing your dog's exposure to strangers will help to avoid bites. It only takes a minute to put the dog out in the yard or into another room when company arrives. In addition, this will prevent him from becoming friendly with numbers of strangers, making him a better watchdog. If people are going to be spending some time with you, take a bit of time to introduce the dog to everyone who will be staying there. If the guests have brought a dog with them, be aware that one dog may become jealous when the other is petted, and bite either the other dog, a nearby person or both.

Avoid wild animals that act ill or are injured, especially in rabies areas. Be very wary of any nocturnal animals (such as a skunk, normally not seen during the day), that is out in the daytime. Minimize your dog's contact with wild animals by keeping him in your yard rather than allowing him to run loose. Keep him on a leash or under close control when you are out hiking or camping.

Rabid bats have been reported from every state except Hawaii. Because only an extremely small percentage of bats are affected, wholesale destruction is not justified. Colonies of bats eat literally tons of insects which are otherwise destructive to plants and crops. Only bats in colonies proven by laboratory tests to have rabies should be destroyed. It is, however, a good idea to keep bats out of houses, barns and other places that we and our animals inhabit. This can be done by screening over or sealing up holes where they enter.

RABIES AND THE DOG BITE

Any time you are bitten by a dog (or any other animal), cleanse the wound using a disinfectant such as povidone-iodine (Betadine®), scrubbing for a minimum of five to ten minutes. Consult the dog's owner, if known, to determine its current rabies vaccination status. In some areas, the dog MUST be taken to a kennel for a mandatory 10-day quarantine. If a dog who has bitten a human—even your own dog—dies within that 10 days, it is a good idea to have the brain examined to be certain it does not have rabies. If the dog has not been vaccinated, have the brain checked, even if the dog has an accident, such as being hit by a car. This is especially important in an area where rabies is common. Meanwhile, consult your physician to see if any further treatment is necessary. Tetanus immunization or antibiotic treatment for infection may be needed, depending on the bite. Under some circumstances, he may advise that you take a series of anti-rabies injections.

If you are bitten by a wild animal, the animal is not confined because the incubation periods are extremely variable. The animal should be killed and submitted for examination, again without damage to the head. Keep it refrigerated but not frozen until you are able to get it to your veterinarian. Testing for rabies may not be needed with rodents because of the extremely low incidence of rabies, but check with your veterinarian or physician to be sure. If the wild animal escapes after biting someone, rabies immunization is almost certain to be recommended for the bite victim. Why? The animal is presumed to be rabid unless it can be proved otherwise.

If you are in a high-risk area for rabies (such as parts of the southwestern United States, and parts of the southeast), and have reason to be exposed to wild or possibly rabid domestic animals, pre-exposure vaccine IS available for humans (Imovax®: Merieux Institute, Inc., P.O. Box 523980, Miami, Fl., 33152-3980). Three small doses are given within a month, to give you an immunity which will help to protect against rabies. Then, if you are bitten by a rabid animal, you only take two doses instead of an entire series. The series which you have already taken will allow your body to produce a good immunity with only a couple of injections after a bite. Do not feel that your series will completely protect you against the disease if you are bitten. You will still need the important booster injections. Consult your physician immediately if you are bitten.

Pre-exposure rabies immunization may be a good idea if you live in an isolated area, or if you are a veterinary assistant, a spelunker or archaeologist who frequents caves which are inhabited by bats, or if there is some other reason that you might be exposed to rabies. There is a small risk of reaction to the vaccine, so chances of exposure must be weighed against risk of taking the vaccine. Discuss this with your physician if you think you are a candidate for the vaccine.

TETANUS

Tetanus is rarely seen in dogs. It can occur when the causative bacteria contaminate a puncture wound. The incubation period is as little as five days. The length of incubation depends on the distance of the wound from the spinal cord, how many bacteria or spores have gotten into the wound, and how open or closed the wound is. Puncture wounds that are not open to the air favor rapid growth of the organism.

With tetanus, the dog's eyes are pulled back into his head. This causes the third eyelid to push out over the eyeball. The muscles of the jaw are rigid. The ears are pulled back and toward the center of the head. The muscles of the face stiffen, and the corners of the mouth are pulled back. The legs are paralyzed in rigid extension fore and aft. The signs look much like those of strychnine poisoning. History of a wound or possible exposure to strychnine may help to tell them apart.

Long-term hospitalization may be needed. The dog will be given sedatives to relieve the spasms and muscle contractions. This helps to relax the chest muscles and allows the dog to breathe. If the dog can be kept breathing and is given good nursing care, he will probably come out of the disease. Antibiotics will be given to control the bacteria. Drugs may be needed to raise the heart rate up to normal. The dog has to be turned from one side to the other every two to four hours. His body temperture will have to be maintained against its tendency to drop with this disease. Drugs are used to control muscle spasms.

Treatment is aimed at destroying the tetanus organisms, and relieving signs until the toxin is cleared from the dog's system. It may take as much as two weeks of treatment before you know whether the dog is going to live or die. Tetanus is rare enough that there is no need to vaccinate for it. Just be aware that it exists. Tetanus is one good reason for prompt antibiotic treatment of puncture wounds, whether from dog bites or other causes.

SALMON POISONING DISEASE

Salmon poisoning is a fluke-transmitted rickettsial disease. It affects both domestic dogs and wild canines. The dog becomes infected by eating a salmon or trout which is infected by an immature stage of a particular fluke (a type of flatworm). The fluke infection does not usually cause any problem for the dog, but the fluke is a carrier for the rickettsiae. The dog will pass infected fluke eggs in his feces, perpetuating the spread of both the flukes and the rickettsiae. A tiny, immature stage of the fluke then infects snails, which are eaten by the trout, and the cycle keeps going.

Salmon poisoning is only found in the northwestern United States. Fish infected with this disease are found on the Pacific Coast, from the coast of Alaska to San Francisco, but it is most common from Puget Sound to northern California. Salmon poisoning also occurs along inland rivers while the fish are migrating.

Signs of the disease occur suddenly five to nine days after the dog eats an infected fish. The signs usually persist 7-10 days, with death occurring in as many as 90% of the affected dogs, especially if the disease goes untreated. During the first day or two of the illness, the temperature may reach 106 degrees F (41 degrees C). It will stay the same or go down slightly during the next few days. The dog is weak, depressed and totally stops eating. Before the dog dies, the temperature will drop below normal. Around the fourth to fifth day, non-stop vomiting usually occurs. By the fifth to seventh day, diarrhea begins. It is often severe and bloody. Extreme weight loss and dehydration occur. The dog may have a crusted, runny nose, and the disease may look much like distemper. If the eyes are also crusted, distemper is perhaps the more likely diagnosis. Laboratory tests may be needed to tell which

disease the dog has. Whether it is salmon poisoning or distemper, the dog will need strong supportive treatment.

Salmon poisoning is treated with antibiotics. Among those which have been used are: penicillin, chlortetracycline, chloramphenicol and oxytetracycline. These drugs are best given intravenously or intramuscularly at first, depending on the drug. After the dog is stabilized and has stopped vomiting, the drug can be given orally. Treatment should be continued for two to three weeks. Dogs that are seriously ill may need intravenous fluids to stabilize their condition. If the dog has a bloody diarrhea, transfusions may be needed to replace the lost blood until the dog can produce enough of his own to replace what he lost.

Salmon poisoning can be prevented by keeping your dog from eating uncooked steelhead, trout, salmon and related fresh water fish. Feed only fish that has been thoroughly cooked, or that has been frozen for several days. Infected dogs should be isolated. Equipment used on them should be sterilized before it is used on other dogs to avoid direct transmission of the rickettsiae from dog to dog.

ELOKOMIN FLUKE FEVER

This rickettsial disease may be seen by itself, or as a complication to salmon poisoning. Its incubation period is slightly longer than that of salmon poisoning, around 9 to 12 days. It does not have the bloody diarrhea or severe dehydration seen with salmon poisoning. Less than 10% of the dogs with this disease die, but they may be very thin for many weeks after they recover. Some dogs will show staggering and signs of brain problems. Treatment and prevention are similar to those for salmon poisoning.

CANINE ERLICHIOSIS

This disease is caused by a rickettsial organism present in the dog's white blood cells. It occurs throughout the world and in parts of the U.S, especially in the southern states, and is found in both wild and domestic canines. It is carried by the brown dog tick (*Rhipicephalus sanguineus*), which may pass the organism to another dog as much as five months after it has fed on an infected dog. The organism can also be transmitted via infected blood, using the same needle to vaccinate more than one dog or via a blood transfusion. Injuries in a dog fight can transmit the organism from one dog to another.

The disease may occur as either an acute or chronic infection, depending on the degree of immunity which the dog has and the strain of rickettsia involved. Acute cases are usually seen in the summer and fall, when the brown dog ticks are most active.

Signs are often mild and may come and go. They include an intermittent fever, lack of appetite, and lack of stamina. The dog's fever does not respond to antibiotics. He may have drainage from the eyes and nose, swelling of the lymph nodes, and edema (fluid accumulation) in the scrotum and legs. The dog may show signs of nervous system involvement, as well as abnormalities in breathing. After the disease goes through this phase, it can enter a chronic phase. In many dogs, this may remain a mild disease that comes and goes for years.

Dogs rarely die in the acute phase, and may recover fully without treatment. Or the infection may progress to the chronic stage. During this phase, the bone marrow "overgrows," and white blood cells fill various organs of the body, such as the spleen, liver and kidneys. Signs vary, but the dog may show pneumonia, staggering, depression, paralysis and hypersensitivity. He may "waste away." The dog may have nosebleeds, or blood in the urine. The feces may be dark and tarry because blood is present. Small or large hemorrhages may be seen under the skin and mucous membranes all over the body.

German Shepherds, especially, seem to have a more severe chronic form of the disease. This may be related to stress, or to suppression of the immune system. Signs of the severe form are depression, lack of appetite and weight loss. The dog may have pale mucous membranes because of anemia, along with hemorrages. He may have a fever, and various organ systems may fail. Bone marrow depression contributes to the animal's lack of resistance. No matter what treatment is used, many of these animals will die.

This disease can only be diagnosed by blood tests done by your veterinarian. If only a few organisms are present in the blood, diagnosis may be very difficult, requiring several blood samples and other laboratory tests.

Erlichiosis is often treated with the antibiotic tetracycline. Acute cases are usually treated for a minimum of two weeks, while chronic cases may be treated for one to two months. Other medications, including a drug called doxycycline, are used in cases that do not respond to tetracycline. Dogs that are going to get well from the disease usually respond quickly and dramatically. Within two days of beginning treatment, the dog's appetite will return, and his temperature goes back to normal. Continue the treatment for the full course or the disease may come back. Dogs who are severely ill may need blood transfusions or fluid therapy to maintain their blood volume until the medication has a chance to take effect.

Oral tetracycline has been used for prevention, and has been given for one to two years in this manner. However, it has some possible side effects. Tick control, both by dipping the dog and spraying the premises to control ticks, is probably preferable as a way to prevent the disease. Kennels where the disease is a continuing problem may need to treat all dogs with tetracycline until the disease can be brought under control. Check with your veterinarian for the latest recommendations if you live in an area where this parasite is a problem.

HEPATOZOONOSIS

Canine hepatozoonosis is caused by the protozoan parasite, *Hepatozoon canis*. It is limited to southern Louisiana and the Texas Gulf Coast at the present time. It is spread when the dog eats an infected *Rhipicephalus sanguineus* tick (brown dog tick).

Signs of hepatozoonosis include weight loss, poor appetite, staggering or other abnormal gait, fever which does not respond to antibiotic treatment, diarrhea which may be bloody, and discharges from the nose and eyes. The dog may get better between periods of being quite ill.

Your veterinarian will diagnose this disease by finding a low blood sugar level in the dog. He may also find the parasite present in blood cells or in a muscle biopsy sample. There is currently no treatment which is consistently effective for the disease. Control of the ticks will help to prevent spread of the disease. Dogs in endemic areas should be routinely dipped to prevent spread of the disease.

BABESIOSIS

Canine babesiosis as a protozoal disease, much like hepatozoonosis. In the past, this disease was called piroplasmosis. Babesiosis occurs in dogs throughout the world. In the United States, it is seen primarily in the southern states. Like erlichiosis and hepatozoonosis, it is transmitted by ticks. It can also be spread from one dog to another via contaminated blood transfusions, or by using the same needle to vaccinate more than one dog. On occasion, it has been seen in puppies as young as three weeks old. The incubation period from time of infection until signs are first seen may range from 10 days to 4 weeks.

Young puppies who harbor large populations of the parasite suffer a peracute (very sudden) form of the disease. Signs include depression, weakness, lack of appetite and pale mucous membranes. They may be very briefly ill, go into shock and die. A heavy tick infestation is usually noted, or has been present on the puppy recently.

Acute babesiosis usually brings signs of anemia—pale mucous membranes, lack of energy and poor appetite. The dog may vomit. Lymph nodes throughout the body may be enlarged. The dog may be depressed, and have a fever—104 to 106.7 degrees F (40 to 41.5 degrees C). The dog may also have hemoglobin (from the red blood cells) in the urine, giving it a red-wine color. If an infected dog is worked or stressed, this may bring on clinical signs that were not otherwise apparent.

Dogs with chronic babesiosis may show a fever that comes and goes, weight loss and a poor appetite. Before they die, they may show yellowing of the mucous membranes (icterus or jaundice), and signs of kidney and liver failure. Dark urine and ticks may be seen, as above.

Your veterinarian will diagnose this disease by finding the parasites in a blood smear from the dog. Or he may use a laboratory test to detect antibodies produced by the dog's body in response to the organism.

Drugs are used which are specific for this particular parasite. Because babesiosis may occur in dogs that are also infected with ehrlichiosis, it is sometimes a good idea to use drugs which are toxic to both parasites. Severely ill dogs may need intravenous fluids and/or blood transfusions to keep them alive until the drugs can work. Dogs that recover from the disease can be carriers for quite some time. The disease may recur if the dog is stressed or his immune system is not working normally.

As with other tick-borne diseases, routine dipping should be combined with control of ticks on premises to prevent infection with babesia.

ROCKY MOUNTAIN SPOTTED FEVER

Rocky Mountain spotted fever is caused by the same rickettsial organism which causes the disease in humans. Most cases in dogs have been reported in the eastern United States, with occasional cases seen in other areas. This is one more tick-transmitted disease. For some reason, Siberian Huskies seem to have a more severe form of the disease than do some other breeds of dogs. The disease is seen from spring through early fall. In most dogs, the illness lasts two weeks or less.

Many different signs may be observed. These include fever, lack of appetite and depression. The sclera (white part) of the eyeball may be reddened. The dog's lymph nodes may be enlarged, and there may be discharges from the eyes and nose. The dog may cough or have trouble breathing. He may vomit and have diarrhea, and may show joint or muscular pain. The dog may have nosebleeds, blood in the feces (which may be dark and tarry), hemorrhages visible on the mucous membranes and blood in the urine. The dog may show signs of brain damage, including staggering and convulsions. As with the other blood parasites, blood tests may be needed to confirm the diagnosis. Tetracycline may be used, similar to treating erlichiosis. In some cases, other antibiotics may be given instead. Supportive treatment may be needed for a dog that is in shock or having organ failure. Dogs that recover from the disease are immune to it for six months to a year. The majority of dogs who are treated for spotted fever will recover successfully, especially if they are treated early in the course of the disease. No vaccine is available for dogs. It does seem that a number of dogs have a mild infection while they are young, and become naturally immune to the disease.

Rocky Mountain spotted fever is perhaps the most common tick-borne infection in humans in the United States, although Lyme disease is becoming more prevalent. The disease is not transmitted from dogs to humans, but both may catch it from infected ticks picked up on the same walk in the woods. You can also get it from contact with fluids from the tick as you pick the pests off your dog. Tick feces accidentally rubbed into the eyes or into a cut or scratch in the skin can also lead to human infection.

To prevent Rocky Mountain spotted fever, keep your dog out of tick-infested areas, or where large numbers of mice, ground squirrels and other rodents are found. These also include areas where deer are prone to travel. When you have returned from a tick-infested area, carefully examine your dog and remove all ticks that you find. Now go in the house and do the same for yourself. It is best to pull the ticks gently loose with tweezers or forceps. If you do not have one of these tools handy, protect your fingers with a tissue or paper towel. Do not crush or squeeze the ticks with your fingers, as this may get the infectious organisms onto your hands.

Wash your hands very carefully with soap and water or a disinfectant after picking ticks off your dog (or yourself). Do not flush the ticks down the toilet so as to spread the organisms to other areas. Perhaps the best method of disposal is to drown them in a strong disinfectant that will kill the parasites as well as the ticks. Or burn them up completely. If your dog is infected with spotted fever, be careful not to get his blood on your hands. Wash your hands well after working with him until he has gone through his complete course of treatment and has been pronounced cured.

If you live in a wooded area where ticks are an everyday problem, careful tick control is a good idea. The dog's kennel or bed area should be treated periodically with an insecticide. Schedule routine tick-dips and periodic grooming for all your dogs to make sure they are free of ticks. This is especially important if your dogs come into the house. Otherwise, they will just act to bring ticks indoors to you. (For a very thorough discussion of Rocky Mountain spotted fever, see Greene, 1987).

LYME DISEASE

Lyme disease is named after the town of Old Lyme, Connecticut. In 1975, it was discovered that a number of people in the town had a disease which seemed to be rheumatoid arthritis. Lyme disease travels widely throughout the human body, and causes many different symptoms, often beginning with a small rash, and signs of disease which may appear like a severe flu: fever, chills, headache and backache. The next stage may involve rheumatoid arthritis and/or nervous system problems. Lyme disease has been diagnosed in many parts of the world since the early 1900's.

The disease is caused by a bacterium, *Borrelia burgdorferi*. It is thought to be transmitted through white-footed mice, white-tailed deer, opossums and raccoons. It is picked up from these reservoirs by several species of *Ixodes* ticks, from which it is transmitted to humans. It also seems to be carried by some dogs, who can then transmit it to humans through the bite of those same ticks. (For a further discussion of Lyme disease in humans, see Reader's Digest, April, 1989, p. 88).

Signs of arthritis involving the large joints HAVE been seen in dogs. The arthritis may come and go, and may turn into a chronic form. The joints are usually not swollen, and the lameness may seem to shift from one joint to another. It may be accompanied by a fever, lack of energy, lack of appetite, and swollen lymph nodes. It should be considered if you live in area where Lyme disease occurs and your dog comes down with arthritis for which there is no good reason. It is important that this disease be correctly diagnosed to keep your dog from passing it to you, so take your dog to the veterinarian if you think Lyme disease might be the problem. It is easily treated with specific antibiotics when it is correctly diagnosed. In some cases, if the pet is felt to be a nonsymptomatic carrier, he may be treated with antibiotics. Discuss this with your veterinarian if someone in your family is infected.

The greatest importance of this disease is that your dog may transmit it to you, if only by accident, by carrying ticks which later bite you. It may be carried by tick nymphs which are only about 1/16 inch (1-2 mm.) long, and are difficult to see on the dog (or on yourself). If you live in an area where Lyme disease is known to occur, tick control on your dog is EXTREMELY important. It is thought that the tick needs to feed about a day before the disease can be transmitted in its saliva. Use tick repellent on yourself and your dog when you are going into tick areas. Check both yourself and your pet thoroughly when you have been in brush, grass or woods where ticks may be picked up. Be extremely careful during tick season, which is usually spring to summer. If you find any ticks, remove them as soon as possible. If at all possible, they should be removed intact. Mouthparts which are left in the skin may cause irritation and possibly infection. Your dog should be dipped frequently, or sprayed with a spray which kills ticks. This helps to kill ticks which are too immature to detect, or are hidden from your examination. There is no vaccine available against Lyme disease at this time, either for dogs or for humans.

BUBONIC PLAGUE

Bubonic plague has affected man far back into history. It was the "black plague" that devastated western Europe in the Middle Ages. Associated primarily with rodents, it was spread to humans by fleas from rats during that time. The disease is found in parts of the western United States, from the high plains to the Pacific Ocean. Thirteen states are involved, including Hawaii. The disease is more common in the desert southwest, and about half the reported cases of plague are from New Mexico. Arizona and California also have areas of plague activity.

Cases are now occasionally associated with dogs and cats. These animals pick up fleas from infected rodents, such as prairie dogs or ground squirrels, and pass the fleas on to the humans around them. Over 200 species of rodents have been shown to harbor the fleas which carry plague. In another scenario, the pets bring home infected rodents. In some cases, the dog (or cat) itself may become infected, and able to pass the bacteria on to the humans around it. Cats are more susceptible to plague than are dogs, developing a peracute and highly contagious pulmonary form of the disease.

The dog may become ill with a fever that may be as high as 105 degrees F (40.5 degrees C). If the disease lasts long enough, the lymph nodes, especially under the jaw and neck, will form abscesses which break and drain. The dog may recover and become normal without treatment, during the course of a week or so. Meanwhile, he can pass the disease to you or members of your family. The fluid from abscesses is especially infectious.Most cases of plague in animals (or

humans) are treatable with our current antibiotics. But, to do this, it MUST be diagnosed early in the course of the disease. If you live in New York City, it's a good idea to tell your doctor that you were just camping in New Mexico, or wherever, if you should happen to become ill. Otherwise, he might not suspect plague as a disease problem. Several people have died over the past few years because the physician had no reason to consider plague as a part of his diagnosis.

If you live or camp in an area where plague is found, keep your dog away from rodents as much as possible. Keeping trash and garbage cleaned up around your house and yard will make the area less attractive for rats and other rodents. Handle very carefully any dead rodents that you take away from the dog. It's not a bad idea to spray the rodent with insecticide—'most any one will do. Then pull a couple of plastic bags over your hand and up around your arm, one inside the other. Grasp the rodent through the bags, and then turn the bags down around the rodent, making a convenient bundle for disposal. Or, you could pick the rodent up with a shovel or pitchfork. Any way you do it, don't let fleas from the rodent get on you. Keep up flea control on your dog, with flea spray or flea powder if he has been in a rodent area. Do not camp where there are quantities of prairie dog or other rodent holes. If you see flies around a rodent hole, this often means that there is a dead rodent inside, and the fleas will be looking for a new home and a warm meal. Stay away from such holes, and keep your pets out of the area. If you find fleas on yourself, get rid of them immediately.

TUBERCULOSIS

Tuberculosis is, on rare occasion, found in dogs. It may be seen when family members are diagnosed as having the disease. A few cases have been reported in Basset Hounds. In this breed, it is thought to be linked with an immune deficiency which weakens the dog and makes him susceptible to the disease. Dogs with tuberculosis often show coughing, retching and difficulty in breathing. If someone in your family, or who has close contact with your dog, is found to have tuberculosis, it is a good idea to have the dog examined to make sure he has not caught the disease. Otherwise, he could possibly give it back to the humans around him.

Chapter 6

THE CANINE GOURMET

FEED COMPONENTS

All foodstuffs, whether they go into us or into our pets, are made of similar components. Protein provides the building blocks for muscle growth, and the basic ingredients for cellular maintenance. The nutritional value of protein depends on the amino acids which make up the proteins, and their digestibility. A greater quantity of protein is needed if the protein is of low quality. For dog food made from mixed plant and animal sources, a reasonable estimate of protein requirements in the food is: 15% to 18% for maintenance, 25% for breeding and growth, and 30% for hard work or severe stress. Meat, most meat by-products, eggs and dairy products provide high-value protein. These proteins are digested efficiently. Plant proteins have a smaller overall value because some are lacking in one or the other of the essential amino acids. But when balanced carefully with proteins from animal sources, they make a valuable contribution to canine nutrition.

Excess protein, if fed for a long period of time, can injure the kidneys, especially in older dogs whose kidneys are already damaged and not working well. A protein deficiency can impair growth, reproduction, health, physical performance and resistance to infectious diseases.

Carbohydrates come from starches and sugars. These compounds provide the energy which keeps the body functioning. They allow dogs to cope with the temperature of the environment around them. Grains which provide carbohydrates are the basis of most commercial dog foods.

Fiber comes from the cell walls of plants. They are largely indigestible, and add bulk to the dog's diet. Bulk helps keep the digestive tract moving and prevents constipation. Canids (dogs, coyotes, wolves, etc) roaming in the wild get plenty of exercise and do not overeat on a daily basis. They don't need much fiber in their diets. However, fiber is important in keeping domesticated dogs "regular," since they don't always get enough exercise.

As with other nutrients, the fact that a little fiber is good does not mean that a lot is better. Excess fiber may depress the efficient digestion of protein, fat, carbohydrates and some minerals. It may also cause bulky, loose stools. There is no current information that large amounts of fiber help a dog lose weight, except by causing him to digest his food poorly and run it through his digestive tract more rapidly than normal.

Fats and fatty acids are very concentrated forms of food energy. Fats are important for a shining coat and a supple skin. They also help to prevent dry skin. Too little fat can cause poor growth and poor reproduction. An excess of calories, whether from fats or carbohydrates, is merely turned into fat in the animal's body. This may be harmful to the animal's health and is certainly a waste of money. About five percent (on a dry-matter basis) of the diet should be fat. Dogs which are working hard, showing or breeding may need extra quantities of fat—as much as 13 to 35 percent of dry matter. Too much fat, especially if introduced suddenly into the diet, may cause diarrhea. Also, feeding the dog excessive fat may cause him to eat less total food, resulting in deficiencies of some nutrients.

Vitamins are needed in very small quantities. The body cannot make most of them, so they must be supplied by the dog's food. Vitamins are divided into two groups depending on whether they are soluble in water or fat. Water-soluble vitamins include all the B-vitamins and vitamin C (ascorbic acid). These are not well-stored in the body, and must be constantly replenished because they are rapidly excreted.

Fat-soluble vitamins (A, D, E, and K) are well-stored in the body and a continuous supply is not necessary. Any excess amount of the fat-soluble vitamins accumulates in the body and may even be toxic because of slow elimination. If you give your dog human vitamins, you may be giving him an excess of vitamins A and D. Both of these accumulate in the liver, and at high enough levels can cause toxicity.

Cooking and some types of processing may destroy certain vitamins. Most of these problems have been eliminated by dog food manufacturers. Extra amounts of vitamins are added during production to compensate for losses in processing and storage. Major dog food manufacturers continuously monitor their foods to make sure that vitamin content remains adequate, but not excessive.

Minerals are inorganic compounds found in the earth. Calcium and phosphorus are important for bone growth and maintenance. Balancing their quantities with that of vitamin D is important. An excess of one of the minerals or of the vitamin can lead to a deficiency of the other(s). It is easy to throw these important minerals out of balance with random supplementation.

Some dog foods contain as much as 120% of the calcium needed for growth. This can throw the phosphorus ratio out of balance. Calcium excess can also cause a deficiency of zinc. If this is not compensated by added zinc in the food, the result may be crusting and scaly skin lesions in puppies. The puppies may also be smaller than normal, and show delayed healing, skeletal abnormalities and poor immune response. Testicular degeneration may occur in an older dog with calcium and zinc imbalance. This problem has been seen in some generic dog foods which have too much calcium.

Calcium deficiency for long periods of time can cause a disease called nutritional hyperparathyroidism or osteoporosis. The bones may become thin and brittle, and may break spontaneously. The dog may also have problems with bone growth. Phosphorus excess can cause the same sort of imbalance, and in small dogs can lead to broken bones from something as minor as jumping off a sofa or step. Excessive phosphorus can come from feeding an all-meat diet, or having excessive quantities of meat in an otherwise balanced diet. Excess phosphorus can speed the progress of kidney disease and should be somewhat restricted for older animals. Minerals need to be carefully balanced in the dog's diet.

Excess sodium can cause heart disease, kidney disease and high blood pressure. Unfortunately, some dog and cat foods may contain as much as 20 times the amount of sodium necessary for good health. As with human diets, the amount of sodium should be regulated throughout the dog's lifetime.

Trace minerals, like vitamins, are needed in very small quantities. They are used to manufacture enzymes, hormones and vitamins. Trace elements necessary for dogs include iron, iodine, cobalt, zinc, manganese, molybdenum, chromium, and fluorine. Some of these elements are toxic in excess quantities, so random supplementation is not recommended. Excess magnesium, for instance, may cause the formation of bladder or kidney stones.

Water, while not a "nutrient" as such, is nevertheless extremely important to good food utilization and good health. Dogs should have a constant supply of reasonably pure water available at all times. Water is especially needed by dogs being fed dry dog food. Without it, severe digestive problems may result. Dogs which are both indoors and out should have water in both places so they can always get to it. Large amounts of water should not be given to a dog who is hot from being worked. Cool him down, giving a sip or two of water at a time between periods of walking him. The dog should be cooled completely before he is fed.

A balanced diet contains sufficient amounts of each of the nutrients, in their proper proportions. The amount of food needed for each animal depends on its individual metabolism, and on the stresses put on the animal. A dog whose only work is lying by the fireplace needs less perfect feeding than the dog which is working all day herding cattle in the mountains. Demands such as growth, breeding or other stress also require that the nutrition be more perfect.

The dog's diet should be balanced and complete, and contain adequate amounts of all the necessary nutrients. Excess nutrients can contribute to medical problems, especially in dogs who already have heart or kidney problems. Nutritional supplements are not needed when the dog is fed a well-balanced diet, and should not be used except on the advice of a veterinarian for management of a specific disease condition. A poor diet will not be improved (and will not be balanced) by adding a vitamin or mineral supplement. It is much better to switch to a diet containing the proper, balanced nutrients for the dog.

DO DOGS EAT MEAT?

Do dogs really eat meat? One recent dog book advocates feeding dogs a "natural" diet, namely, only raw meat mixed with a few raw green vegetables. In the wild, dog-family members do not eat "meat" in the sense that we think of a well-marbled piece of steak. When they are able to kill small animals, they eat them whole. They eat the intestines and their contents, which are not "raw" but are partially digested, nutrient-filled vegetable matter. They eat the bones (a good source of calcium and other minerals), hair (providing a bit of roughage or fiber in the diet), organ meats rich in vitamins, and, finally, the muscle mass that we think of as "meat."

Let's examine a larger animal such as a deer which has either been killed or found dead by coyotes or wolves. They will first rip open the belly and eat the intestines (again, filled with nutrients). They savor the organs: kidneys, liver, lungs and heart. They will eat the tongue (because it's both tasty and easy to get at). And, last and least, they will eat the loin and round and other cuts that we humans treasure. No, in the wild, canines do not eat "meat." They eat ANIMALS.

A good dog food should contain a certain amount of meat to provide high-quality, easily available protein. However, the fact that it also contains grains should not be a detriment. Some years ago, a nationally known brewery produced a dog food made mostly from grains, brewery byproducts and malt. Meat products were in the food, but were a minor part of it. The dog food produced fantastic, gleaming coats on healthy dogs. Unfortunately, it was discontinued because it never achieved adequate sales to the humans who had to buy it for the dogs. Seems it didn't have enough "meat" to suit the humans.

Soybeans may cause considerable gas or diarrhea when fed to some dogs, especially if added to the diet suddenly. Soybeans are not a good food ingredient for some dogs, particularly in large quantity. Raw or uncooked soybeans can be a real problem. However, small amounts of soybeans are added for their high protein value to commercial dog foods and are well tolerated by most dogs. In this use, they do not generally cause problems. This is because they are thoroughly cooked during the processing when dog food is made. Dogs of the Shar-Pei breed do not tolerate soybeans.

Someone may tell you that pork snouts and beef lungs are used to make dog foods. In some cases, this is probably true. But, the dogs like it just as well as they would a T-bone steak, and with careful balancing by the dog food manufacturer, a food is produced that is actually BETTER for your dog than feeding him the steak! Besides, it leaves the steak for you to eat!

TYPES OF DOG FOOD

A suitable dog food is one which provides all the dog's nutrient needs for good health and a long life. Stick to the same dog food. Dogs do not become bored when fed the same food day after day. On the contrary, it will provide a steady flow of balanced nutrients and helps to avoid digestive upsets. When you find one that your dog will eat without diarrhea or constipation and without becoming too fat or too thin, stick with it. The desire for variety in foods seems to be a learned trait in dogs. Your dog will happily eat the same food day after day if you don't teach him otherwise.

It should also be mentioned that feeding one's pets has more than nutritional significance. Feeding your dog can be a social experience for both pet and master.

PREPARED DOG FOODS

Prepared dog foods are manufactured and ready to feed to your dog. Manufacturers of good quality dog foods employ highly trained staff nutritionists. They utilize the latest nutritional research to provide your dog with a balanced and healthy diet. They also maintain kennels where dogs are raised through several generations to make sure they grow, reproduce and age gracefully on the same diet they offer you for your dog.

Moisture content in dog foods varies considerably from dry foods to canned foods. Dry foods generally have to have 10% or less moisture in order to prevent mold growth. Dry foods may take in moisture in damp climates, and mold if not stored in tightly closed containers. Canned dog foods will range between 70% and 78% moisture. Some of the water comes from the meats and other materials used to make the food and some is added to rehydrate dried ingredients. Moisture content has no bearing on the overall nutritional quality of dog food.

Dog foods come in a number of forms: dry meal, baked biscuits, soft-moist, canned and frozen. In the final analysis, the dog food you choose depends on convenience, cost, and what you, your veterinarian and your dog agree on. Your choices are:

1) Dry dog foods. Most of the energy in dry dog food is carbohydrate provided by starches from grains and grain byproducts. For optimum utilization, these grains must be cooked. In making dry dog foods, grains and cereal byproducts are mixed with plant protein sources (such as soybean meal), and animal proteins from eggs, milk, meat, and and meat byproducts. Vitamins and minerals are added, and the entire mix is run through cookers. Palatability is somewhat less than that of canned foods, but still adequate.

Dry dog foods are divided into meal and baked products. Meal products are the most popular dog foods today. Either type has all the necessary ingredients to provide a complete, balanced diet.

Dry foods have the advantage of being, for the most part, the least expensive of foods. You don't pay for water, nor do you have to lug processed water home from the store. Grain products are less expensive than meats, which also makes dry foods more economical.

Dry dog foods keep well and are convenient to store. In hot climates, the temperatures may allow insect eggs which are present to hatch, and fill your kitchen with grain weevils. In hot areas, dry pet foods MUST be either stored outside the house, or in tightly closed metal or plastic containers. Dry dog foods lend themselves well to self-feeding because they don't spoil readily.

Dry dog foods may be fed dry. Some dogs seem to truly enjoy the crunch of the dry food. If your brand is available in different sizes, try them to see which your dog prefers. Many dogs have definite preferences for either large or small crumbles. Most dogs which are fed only dry food soon after weaning will continue to prefer dry food throughout life. If the food is fed dry, the dog should have water available at all times.

Dry foods may also be moistened with water or fat-free broth to a light, crumbly consistency. If you add liquid, try just dampening it. Most dogs do not like, and will not eat, food of a mushy or soupy consistency (except puppies learning to eat). This is only a good idea if you are hand-feeding the dog. Spoilage may occur if the dog is being fed free-choice, causing illness when molds or bacteria grow in the dish. Dry dog food can also be moistened when you wish to have the dog eat slightly more than his normal quantity of dog food. Moistening the food may increase its palatability enough that the dog will eat 10% to 20% more than usual. Do not moisten any more food than the dog will eat within a few hours, especially in warm weather.

A few dry dog foods do not have adequate fat content for good nutrition. The low fat keeps the food from getting rancid in storage. These foods may result in a dog with a dry, harsh coat. In order to get a soft, shining coat (often called "bloom"), you can supplement with cooking oil or fat. Corn oil and pork fat contain fatty acids for the dog's coat. Begin with a teaspoon of corn oil, chicken fat or bacon grease per day on the dog's food. Work up to about a tablespoon per 30 lb. of dog per day. If the dog gets diarrhea, you are giving too much. Make sure that any fat or oil that you are feeding is fresh, not rancid.

Rarely, a dog will react unfavorably to the starch and fiber present in dry dog foods, resulting in the dog passing gas and excessive, sloppy stools, and sometimes causing chronic diarrhea. These dogs may do better when fed foods containing less starch and fiber, such as high-quality meat-based canned foods. However, allergies to some food ingredients may produce similar symptoms. Before you switch automatically to canned foods, first give the dog a week or two trial with another brand or two of quality dry food. Also be sure that the dog doesn't have any illness which could be causing the symptoms.

Dry foods are normally between 70% and 85% digestible. The remainder, naturally, is passed as feces. If you have a Poodle, the quantity passed is somewhat unimportant. If you have a Great Dane or Newfoundland, the amount of waste can be truly monumental, and disposal can be a problem. Some foods are much higher in bulk than others. Diets high in fat also result in the dog passing smaller amounts of feces. If your dog is passing excessive amounts of normal feces and has no disease problems, try other dry foods until you find one that results in less bulk. Low bulk foods also improve stamina because the dog is not carrying a large amount of food in the bowel in order to obtain the energy he needs.

2) Soft-moist dog foods. These are burger-style products, or soft crumbles which are packed in foil or similar pouches or packets. Like the dry foods, these are combinations of meat products and cereals. Soft-moist products are nutritionally complete, and they can be fed throughout the dog's life without additional supplementation. They do not need refrigeration and can be kept on the kitchen shelf. Soft-moist foods contain between 15% and 50% water. They also contain either a sugar or propylene glycol to inhibit bacterial growth. As with any food, the dog should have water available to him at all times. Soft-moist dog foods cost two or three times as much as dry foods on an energy or per calorie basis.

Convenience is a main advantage of soft-moist dog foods, as they are a good compromise between dry and canned foods. They are handy for people who would like to feed canned food, but do not want to open cans or have leftover dog food in the refrigerator.

3) Canned dog foods. These vary widely in quality and type:

A) Complete canned foods. These are nutritionally complete blends of meat, grains, vitamins and minerals formulated to provide a balanced diet. They can be fed as the dog's entire diet if you wish to do so. A safe and easy way to improve the palatability of dry dog food is to mix it with a high-quality canned food. If both foods are balanced and complete, there will not be any nutritional deficiencies, nor will there be problems created by excess nutrients. These products mix together more easily if the dry food is moistened slightly first.

B) All-meat canned foods. Made mostly of meat and poultry and their byproducts, all-meat canned foods vary greatly in protein quality, as well as water content. They are NOT complete diets. While they may be tasty to your dog, the continual and exclusive feeding of one of these products may lead to severe mineral deficiencies and even to fractures caused by an imbalance of nutrients for healthy bones. If fed at all, they should be used only as rare treats. They can be useful to encourage an ill dog to eat (if approved by your veterinarian) because they are so tasty.

C) Meat products with vitamins and minerals added. These canned foods are generally balanced in terms of vitamins and minerals, but they lack fiber and are not as healthful as a nutritionally complete food when fed for long periods of time.

The main energy source in canned foods is fat, with protein supplying as much as 40% of the rest of the calories.

With any of the canned foods, you are paying a premium for the small, individual specialized package (the can). You are also paying the company to package 74% to 80% water with the product. You have to carry this water home and find space to store it, in addition to going through the mess and bother of serving the food. Dog food manufacturers go to great lengths to manipulate canned foods to smell and look like "people food" (and some of the canned foods do smell pretty good), as well as appealing to our emotions in their advertising.

The disadvantages are perhaps counterbalanced by the greater palatability of canned food. Because of their high-quality protein, canned foods are also highly digestible.

Some small dogs are finicky eaters and will do better when fed canned food. However, this situation may have more to do with the dog having done a good job training his owner than to his specific nutritional needs.

4) Baked products. A few baked foods are balanced, nutritionally complete foods, packaged as kibbles. These can be fed as the dog's total diet, and have properties similar to dry foods. Most baked dog foods, however, are produced as biscuits, and fed as training aids or snacks. Remember that dog biscuits contain calories, too. Overusing them can devastate a careful diet plan.

5) Fresh or frozen meat. Plain meat is NOT the best diet for dogs. Remember, dogs in the wild eat animals, not meat. Feeding nothing but meat to a dog is like feeding a child nothing but ice cream. They may like it, but they will not remain healthy for long.

The author's personal preference is to feed a dry food, since it is the least expensive way of getting a quality product. Also, a dry food gives more chewing and more satisfaction to the dog that doesn't need much food for maintenance (an "easy keeper"). It makes him feel like he's getting more than just a smear in the pan for a meal.

Whichever type of food you buy, make sure that it states "nutritionally complete," "complete and balanced," or similar wording on the package or can. A statement saying that the product "meets National Research Council (NRC) Requirements" is also a guarantee of nutritional adequacy, as is "tested by procedures established by the Association of American Feed Control Officials" (AAFCO). These statements mean that the dog food contains all necessary nutrients, in adequate and balanced amounts, to maintain the dog throughout its life. A dog food which has passed feeding tests means not only that it meets certain analysis and standards, but that dogs can actually live and reproduce on it, going from one generation to another. The food is proven to work! Read the label to make sure you are buying adequate nutrition for your dog, and are getting what you think you are paying for. Remember, much of dog food marketing is aimed at making the food sound and look good to YOU, not your dog.

PRESCRIPTION FOOD OR NOT?

Prepared dog foods come in three broad categories: the common brands (let's call these "over-the-counter" brands), prescription foods and specialty foods. The basic differences between them is that the over-the-counter ones are for dogs with no needs other than a maintenance diet, while the other two are specifically designed with particular purposes in mind.

1) Over-the-counter dog foods are the ones that you see every day at the grocery store, at the pet shop and at the feed store. They are produced by companies from one end of the country to the other, ranging from small, local milling companies to major national corporations. You see dogs galloping toward them on T.V. and are faced with ads in many magazines. Foods produced by small mills may be very good, or may be totally lacking in major nutrients. If lacking one or more nutrients, they may occasionally cause nutritional deficiencies in dogs. Those produced by national corporations are backed by skilled nutritionists and a wealth of research. This is also true of the:

2) Prescription or therapeutic diets. These are available through veterinarians or specialty sources. They are formulated to meet special needs, such as a low-sodium diet for a dog with heart disease, or they might be lower in certain minerals to aid animals with kidney stones. Dog foods are also available for dogs with allergies to certain ingredients in common dog foods. Prescription dog foods are VERY effective when used for the conditions for which they are prescribed. They should be fed without any supplementation except as prescribed by your veterinarian, so don't give table scraps or treats unless he approves them. As with any other dog food, make sure that the prescription diet you are feeding is "nutritionally complete." This type of food is generally not needed by the normal, healthy dog. They tend to be expensive when compared to other foods. However, for a dog with a heart or kidney problem, or some other problem which can be helped by a special diet, the increase in health and longevity can be well worth the added expense.

3) Specialty diets. These foods are similar to prescription diets in that they are formulated to deal with specific situations. Unlike the prescription diets, specialty diets are not generally used in the treatment of diseases. You will find specialty diets for puppies, for dogs subjected to stressful situations and for the elderly dog, among others.

For the average, healthy, non-working, non-stressed, minimally exercised dog living in comfortable surroundings, a food intended for "maintenance" is quite adequate. These dog foods contain more fiber and carbohydrate and less fat and protein than foods formulated to meet special needs. My preference is to buy a dry dog food made by a major national manufacturer with a mid-range price. I've found that this approach is an excellent compromise, giving adequate nutrition at a reasonable cost.

An extremely cheap food may not have been made using quality ingredients, or the cost may have been held down by skimping on needed amounts of vitamin or mineral additives. Quality control may not have been quite up to par, and some batches may be lacking essential nutrients. Also, cheap foods might occasionally contain EXCESS quantities of some ingredients. Since it is much more expensive to take out, for example, excess Vitamin A than to leave it in, the resulting food may have more than the "minimum guaranteed analysis" stated on the label. It may even have a dangerous excess which could cause problems with other nutrients and their balance within the body. Too much of some things is as bad or worse than too little! Too much may actually lead to health problems that end up more expensive to treat than the original savings in food price. On the other hand, if you buy the most expensive food, you may be paying extra for advertising and fancy packaging, above and beyond the price of adequate nutrition.

PRESCRIPTION FOODS

Precision formulated prescription dog foods are available for specific ailments. Some of these are:

1) Urinary tract diets. These contain very limited amounts of protein and phosphorus. They are also low in salt. They can be used for dogs with renal failure, for dogs with kidney or bladder stones, for liver disease, and for copper storage disease. Still another prescription food is available for dogs with a tendency to form bladder or kidney stones from a mineral called struvite. When fed for a period of time (from 2 to 28 weeks), it is highly successful in dissolving these stones.

2) Intestinal Diets. A bland, highly digestible, low-residue diet is available for dogs who have had digestive tract problems. It can be used for a dog that has eaten something which has irritated his digestive tract, or that is recovering from a disease involving the intestinal tract. This food is also useful for dogs with colitis. Intestinal diets have low levels of fiber and fat, and is made from ingredients that are nonirritating. These foods have highly digestible, high-quality protein. They are usually fed in small amounts 3-6 times a day for a week to 10 days until the dog's digestive tract has healed. For a dog with a chronically sensitive digestive tract, the food may be given for a longer period of time.

3) Heart diets. Heart patients have available a diet with a number of differences compared to the ordinary maintenance diet. The major difference is a very low sodium content. This helps to decrease the amount of fluid which is retained in the body, thus reducing the workload on the heart. Heart diets have an increased amount of potassium to compensate for the potassium loss caused by diuretic drugs commonly used to treat heart disease. They have a slightly lower quantity of high-quality protein. They may also have slightly fewer calories to help the dog lose a bit of weight, again helping reduce the work load on his damaged heart. These foods may also have a slightly higher quantity of B vitamin.

4) Allergy diets. A diet is available for dogs with food allergies. Allergies to foods which the dog has eaten may occasionally show up as diarrhea, or gas and discomfort. More commonly, however, they will show up as skin reactions similar to those seen with inhaled substances (see Atopy). Allergy diets are made from ingredients which are not usually eaten by dogs; hence, it is unlikely the dog will be allergic to them. Often based on mutton and rice, allergy diets can be used on a long-term basis. Or, they can be used for several weeks to stabilize the dog's system as a diagnostic means to identify the food or foods to which the dog is allergic. To use an allergy diet as a diagnostic tool, feed it ALONE—no treats or people food at all! Give the dog distilled water to drink during this test. Feed the diet for several weeks until the signs of allergy are gone. Different foods can then be added back into the dog's diet, for five days each, until the offending one is found.

All in all, this is a rather amazing collection of foods designed to meet special needs. They are available through your veterinarian, and can literally add years to your dog's life, especially if he has kidney or heart disease. Your veterinarian can recommend a diet which is specific for your dog's ailment. What is right for a heart diet may not be right for another problem, and may even make the condition worse. So, your dog should have a complete examination before putting him on one of these diets. Don't give him one just because you think he has a problem.

Most dogs will readily eat prescription dog foods. However, if the food is not accepted after a day or two, you can try a few tricks: 1) mix warm water with the food and let it sit five to ten minutes before you give it to the dog. 2) warm it up and give it to the dog. He will probably be eating it readily after a few feedings. 3) mix it with the regular food, gradually changing the proportions over a 7-10 day period until you are giving only the new food.

SPECIALTY FOODS

Most dog foods are made for the average, mature to middle-aged dog. Considered maintenance diets, they are made for adult dogs who live in a comfortable, relatively stress-free environment with moderate exercise. They offer complete nutrition for the least cost. But, if your dog needs them, specialty foods are available.

Some dry and canned foods described above come in formulations made for special needs. Some of these are available at the grocery store, while others are available as prescription foods. Among these are:

1) Puppy Foods. These were among the first "convenience" dog foods to appear on the market, and are available in all the major types: canned, dry, and soft-moist. Young puppies that are growing rapidly require about twice the energy and nutrients of adult dogs of the same weight. Their needs can be met by feeding approximately twice the amount of regular dog food. However, it may be kinder to the puppy's digestive system to give a food which is higher in fat and protein. Puppy foods usually have higher quality ingredients than general purpose foods, and, as a result, are easier to digest. Puppy foods are convenient, but you can get the same effect by mixing a good general purpose dry food with a canned meat food.

Puppy foods should NOT be supplemented with random amounts of calcium, phosphorus, bone meal, or other mineral substances. If supplements are needed, your veterinarian will prescribe specific kinds and amounts. If the puppy is large and growing rapidly, his increased intake of food will give him a sufficient quantity of a balanced diet with puppy food alone. Unbalancing his diet by unwarranted supplementation may cause abnormalities in bone and joint growth. If these continue long enough, they may NOT be repairable, and the dog may never be normal.

2) Geriatric Diets. Old dogs accumulate a number of major and minor ailments. In general, they are less active than younger dogs and need fewer calories. Their efficiency of protein utilization declines. The daily intake of energy BUT NOT OF PROTEIN should decrease with advancing age (ALPO, 1984).

Contrary to the above reasoning, commercial geriatric dog foods often have a very low protein content. The restricted protein is meant to reduce the "workload" on the kidneys. However, it can also reduce renal (kidney) blood flow, and make filtration less efficient. Low-protein diets should not be fed to dogs who do not have chronic kidney failure (ALPO,1984). If your dog needs a low protein diet, it is important that the protein which IS present be of high quality for efficient digestion and a high rate of absorption of its amino acids.

Many geriatric foods have larger amounts of fiber to help prevent constipation and keep the intestinal tract moving. They may also have a reduced amount of salt or none at all. Increased amounts of vitamins may be present to make up for less efficient absorption, and perhaps, to counteract some of the aging processes. Some geriatric foods have the minerals specially balanced to meet the needs of the older dog. The aged dog seems to retain phosphorus and calcium as well as, or better than, the young dog. A higher intake of unsaturated fatty acids and zinc helps to keep the hair, coat and skin healthy on an aging dog. Because the dog cannot taste or smell as well as he did when he was younger, it is important that the food be palatable.

3) Reducing Diets. As with humans, a dog who is overweight can be put on a diet. Special dog foods with low nutritional density are available. These dog foods are also, deliberately, less palatable and less digestible. If a dog is put on a diet by cutting back on the amount of regular food, he will probably be hungry most of the time. He may be happier with a larger quantity of a low-calorie dog food. These allow the dog to feel full and still lose weight (see Overweight, below). These foods allow the owner to feed the usual amount without feeling guilty about enforced food restrictions.

4) Stress Diets. Maximum performance, whether in showing, hunting, working cattle, racing, or breeding, is a form of stress. Stress causes an increased utilization of protein and energy. Foods are available for stress or for special performance diets. They are similar to puppy food in that they are high in nutritional density and provide more metabolizable energy in the form of protein. These diets are sometimes used for dogs who are convalescing from surgery or fractures, from skin or skeletal disease, or from anemia or hookworm infestation. They can also be used for dogs who are starved or emaciated to help build them back up to normal.

NATURAL DOG FOODS

Some dog foods are advertised as "all natural." It is very much open to interpretation as to what is "natural" and what is not. One man's filler is another man's fiber. While these foods may meet the required "analysis," I question whether or not they have received adequate quality control to avoid excesses of some ingredients, such as vitamins, which may cause health problems when fed for long periods. Many of the companies producing these foods have not done ANY feeding tests, much less carried the tests through the number of generations necessary to demonstrate the value of the food. The "natural" labeling may be more a marketing gimmick to separate you from your dollars than sound nutrition for your pet. Besides, he has no idea whether it is "natural" or not.

Before you buy one of these foods, do enough research to find out if it really is best for your dog.

MAKING YOUR OWN?

To make your own dog food or not to...that is the question. By using a commerical dog food, you are taking advantage of the company's nutritional expertise. Also, the balance of protein and calories in good quality commercial dog food is regulated to the dog's needs. Homemade food can be used if you wish to take the time to make it. You can get recipes for homemade dog foods (for a regular dog food, as well as many specialized diets) from Hill's Pet Products, Inc., P.O. Box 148, Topeka, Kansas, 66601. Hills, by the way, is one of the nation's largest manufacturers of prescription and specialized diets for dogs and cats, and has been in the forefront of research on pets' specialized dietary needs for a number of years.

TABLE SCRAPS

Feeding table scraps should be done only if you do not have access to, or cannot afford, commercial dog food. Table scraps tend to be low in protein. They are also usually high in fat and calories, contributing to obesity.

Small dogs are especially prone to digestive upsets due to excess fat or spicy "pot lickings." Unless the dog has been raised from the beginning eating scraps and has a cast iron stomach, this sort of food may cause severe digestive problems. Curing them may cost much more than you have saved by feeding scraps.

MILK

Throughout nature, milk is a food for young animals, not for older ones, and dogs are no exception. Milk causes diarrhea in many adult dogs. It should usually not be given to them to drink, or used to moisten their food. If you have been giving milk to a dog and for some reason, quit for a while, but want to reintroduce it to the animal's diet, be sure to do so gradually to see if the animal will still tolerate it. Increase the amount given over 5 to 6 days. If you have given milk to the dog throughout its life, and he tolerates it well, by all means continue to do so. It can make the food more palatable, and provide fat and protein.

Also, cow's milk is a food for calves, not puppies. It can be used in an emergency, but should be replaced as soon as possible with a milk replacer specifically made for puppies, such as Borden's Esbilac®. You will save more puppies, more easily, and have fewer health problems.

EGGS

Eggs are perhaps the best, most convenient, high-quality protein supplement to use if you feel you'd really like to give the dog something extra. They also contain large amounts of quality fats. In the past, dog owners have been told to cook eggs before feeding them because the whites contain a protein which ties up one of the B vitamins, biotin. This is only true if the whites are fed alone in large quantities. When the white and yolk are fed together, the yolk contains enough biotin to compensate for the white. Biotin is synthesized by bacteria in the large intestine. If the gut is sterilized (as when the dog has been treated with oral antibiotics), raw egg whites should not be fed. Cooking is not necessary with clean eggs; simply crack them and break them over the dry dog food, about 1 egg per half pound of diet. Do not give the dog eggshells because dog foods contain plenty of calcium (ALPO, 1984).

However, if you are feeding an adequate amount of a high-quality, well-balanced dog food, the dog will already have enough of the amino acids contained in eggs, and you will probably not notice any difference from feeding them. As with any table scrap or supplement, eggs should, in any case, not make up more than 10% of the dog's diet.

BEER AND OTHER LIQUOR

Dogs, like humans, can acquire a taste for liquor. Some people get a kick out of seeing their dog drink beer. Also like humans, dogs can get drunk. This really can't be good for the animal.

Liquor given to (or accidentally drunk by) a puppy or small dog can be fatal. One New Year's Eve, we answered a call from a frantic client whose Samoyed puppy had finished a tall, strong drink that the owner had set on the floor while he went back to the kitchen to get the chips and dip. The puppy was nearly comatose, and required large doses of stimulants and artificial respiration for half the night before his survival was assured. We later calculated that the amount of alcohol he had consumed was equivalent to his 180-lb. owner drinking nearly a dozen strong mixed drinks—an amount which if consumed at one time might have meant danger for his owner!

TREATS

Dog biscuits, or small, fat-free meat scraps are good treats, when used IN MODERATION. Use them as training aids, or just to let your dog know that you appreciate him. Dog snack or treat foods are not complete foods, and should never be more than 10 to 15% of a dog's diet, at most. Dog biscuits are NOT low in calories—three large ones may contain 120 to 200 calories! Giving the dog cookies, ice cream, and similar foods brings us to...

JUNK FOOD

Dogs will eat almost any food which humans eat, especially if they see us eating it! They take the behavioral cue that this is O.K. because their "pack leader" is doing it. And, they truly enjoy much of the same junk food that gives us problems. While excess sugar does not seem to cause tooth decay in dogs, it can and does lead to obesity when fed in excess. Foods such as meat scraps which are high in fat may also cause obesity, as can gravies and sauces.

Feeding junk food can also lead the dog to beg and try to persuade you that he much prefers your food to his. If you give in and feed him human foods, you may displace good nutrition with empty calories. A small corner off a slice of bread given to a Chihuahua is, pound for pound, much like the average adult human eating half the loaf! You can see how little capacity would be left for good nutrition. In addition, feeding between-meal tidbits can also turn your dog into a constant food beggar who is a nuisance.

Your dog may choose not to eat a meal from time to time. This is much as he would have done in nature, where he would not eat every day. If you give him tidbits to try to tempt him to eat, you are surely training him to be a picky eater. If he does not eat a meal within twenty to 30 mintues (and you are not feeding him free-choice), pick up the food, and do not give him any until his next regular meal.

To have a healthy dog, avoid feeding junk food. Stick to a well-balanced, nutritious dog food. Or, if you wish to keep your veterinarian wealthy, feed LOTS of junk food...

BONES

Bones are GREAT for helping a dog to clean his teeth. Bone size, however, must be carefully matched to the size of the dog. The bone from a round steak is perfect for a Pomeranian. For a St. Bernard, it is a HAZARD. It can be swallowed whole and become a foreign body in the stomach (because the dog does not chew it before it goes down). If he does chew it, he'll probably only break it into sharp fragments, which may cause problems further down the intestinal tract. Or, it can catch between the dog's teeth, causing a violent reaction, with severe pain, pawing the mouth, and frothing at the mouth.

Bones such as those from pork chops, T-bones, and chickens or other poultry are easily chewed to pieces by a large dog (and that means almost anything, perhaps, above 30 lb). These fragments often go through the digestive tract until they reach the colon and rectum. In sufficient quantity, they set up nearly like concrete, often needing enemas (administered by a veterinarian) to get them out. In some cases, manual removal by a veterinarian or even surgery is needed to get them out. This problem is no job for the owner, as the dog often has to be sedated—the procedure can be quite painful. Don't feed ANY bone which the dog can chew into pieces.

Large knuckle bones are ideal for the large dog, again provided he doesn't chew off major fragments. Eating small fragments and gnawing the cartilage is O.K. Adjust the size of the bone to the size of the dog. A Pomeranian will be frustrated by a two-pound bone. Give him something more relative to his size (but still no poultry bones).

SUPPLEMENTS

If you are feeding a nutritionally complete commercial dog food, the manufacturer will have added all the vitamins and minerals needed by the normal dog. Additional vitamins and minerals are not necessary, but if used in recommended amounts, will not increase the overall amount to harmful levels. Do not, however, think that if a little is good, a whole lot is better. If you give more than the recommended amount, the total quantity of the dog's intake may result in an excess of vitamins, or a serious imbalance, and cause illness. This may be dangerous, or in the worst case, fatal to your dog. Your veterinarian will prescribe a specific supplement if he sees a need for it. Otherwise, supplementation is an unnecessary expense and bother.

WATER

A constant supply of clean water is essential for all dogs, and especially for those who are fed dry food. About 75% of the dog's body weight is water. Your dog must be able to drink when he wishes to maintain this percentage. The availability of water is a matter of life or death in hot weather. A dog may quickly die in a place like Phoenix in the summer if he is without water for even part of a day. Dogs under these conditions will appreciate water supplied in a bucket (for the larger dog, of course) which is cleaned daily. Or, you can use a lick-type waterer which attached to an outside faucet so that the dog can drink fresh water whenever he wants. Lick-type waterers should be checked often (daily in the summer) to be sure that they are functioning normally. A dog who is working hard, such as a hunting or field-trial dog, should be offered small amounts of water throughout the day.

Outdoor dogs in cold climates in the winter will appreciate a dish of lukewarm water at least twice a day. A heated bucket is convenient if you have a number of outdoor dogs. It will keep water (instead of ice) in front of them all day long. Dogs who are not given water in the winter will have to use calories of body energy to thaw the snow they eat in order to get water. If the dog cannot eat enough snow to supply sufficient water, he can develop digestive problems. Or, the dog may become thin if he does not have adequate food to provide the calories to thaw the snow. These problems are easily prevented by supplying clean, ice-free water to your dog.

It is not necessary to warm a dog's food, although an outdoor dog might appreciate a dash of warm water over his dry food in the winter.

WHEN TO FEED

Hand-feeding is perhaps the most common feeding system. The dog is fed a measured amount once or twice a day. Most foods, especially soft-moist or canned ones, taste good enough that dogs will overeat and become obese if given too much. Give the dog a measured amount adjusted to maintain the size, shape, and weight of dog that pleases you. By the time the dog is a year old, feeding once a day is generally satisfactory, unless working hard.

Feeding Free-Choice. Given their choice, dogs do NOT pick the nutrients that they need. Much like a child given a choice between ice cream and spinach, a dog will choose the ice cream. Offering a cafeteria of choices will result in the dog choosing the one with the best flavor, not the best nutrition. Sticking to one prepared dog food with all the necessary nutrients in it will give the dog all he needs.

"Free-choice" means putting out enough food that the dog can eat a little whenever he wants. It only works well with dry foods because they don't spoil.

Many "maintenance" dog foods can be offered to the dog on a free-choice basis. This can be an economical way to feed.

Free-choice feeding can also reduce labor which is important for kennels or breeders with large numbers of dogs. Even if you have only one or two dogs, free-choice may still be convenient. It can also help eliminate barking at mealtimes, which can otherwise disturb other dogs in the kennel, not to mention the neighbors. Frequent trips to the feeder may help reduce boredom. Timid dogs who do poorly in a competitive kennel situation when hand-fed once or twice a day may do well when fed free-choice. Puppies may be less likely to eat their own and their littermates' feces.

If fed in outdoor areas or runs, the food should be kept in a protective feeder to avoid rain and subsequent spoilage. When feeding any dry food, FRESH WATER MUST BE AVAILABLE AT ALL TIMES.

It has been suggested, but never proven scientifically, that feeding free-choice may help to prevent overeating and gastrointestinal distress in large hunting or working dogs. This may be helpful for inactive dogs, but those who will be working hard should have their food removed the evening before a day in the hunting field. After the event, the dog should be cooled down carefully, watered with small sips until he is no longer thirsty, and then given a small feeding before being put back with the free-choice feeder. The small feeding takes the edge off the dog's hunger and he is less likely to overeat.

There are some disadvantages to free-choice feeding. Puppies who are given a feeder may waste food by playing with it until the novelty wears off. One puppy may go to eat, and others may follow and eat even if they are not hungry.

The food used for free-choice feeding should have a low enough palatability to prevent overeating. Some of the maintenance foods which are higher in protein are too palatable, and the dog may overeat and become obese. If the dog overeats, try other foods until you find one that has a happy balance between flavor and nutrition so that the dog eats enough to stay in shape, but not so much that he becomes fat. If the dog still eats everything in sight, he may be a glutton. You'll have to hand-feed him. Some Dachshunds are like this.

Puppy foods, foods which are very dense in calories, and foods with 27% or more protein are generally too palatable, and will cause obesity in adult dogs when fed free-choice. These same foods may cause both obesity and skeletal problems in puppies. Some veterinarians recommend that free-choice feeding not be used until dogs have reached 80% to 90% of their adult size. This is perhaps not a problem if the dog food is chosen with these factors in mind.

Puppies who are kept outdoors or in kennels and are not going to be immediately housebroken will appreciate a free-choice container of dry puppy food in addition to feedings two or three times a day. If you are going to housebreak the puppy, he MUST be hand-fed. Puppies have a reflex which makes them want to have a bowel movement 15 to 60 minutes after they eat. If a puppy eats all day, he will tend to defecate whenever he wants (see Housebreaking).

Intermittent feeding. For the dog who is truly an "easy keeper," you might consider feeding him two days out of every three. At first, this might sound cruel. But think about it: in the wild, the canine may only eat once every two or three days, when he finds food or kills prey. Your dog might appreciate having a slightly larger ration two days out of three, rather than having a token amount every day.

Feeding when on vacation. If you take your dog to a kennel while you are gone, check with the kennel personnel to see if they would like you to bring his food with him. If the dog is on a special diet (such as reducing diet, or kidney diet), it may be important that he continues on the diet while in the kennel. Some kennels feed specially developed mixtures of foods which almost all dogs will accept. One kennel in Wyoming, for many years, mixed a high-quality, complete dog food with enough ground horsemeat to flavor it, and then cooked the mixture. Dogs loved it! When they were boarding nearly two hundred dogs on a holiday weekend, keeping track of individual diets was nearly impossible. Dogs who needed special diets were put into a specific area and fed separately. Most kennels prefer that you do not bring dog toys or treats, since they are easily lost, even in the most conscientious of kennels. You will be upset, as will the kennel personnel.

If you have a neighbor feeding the dog while you are gone, it is easy to give them the dog's food, or have it ready for them when they come each day to care for the dog. Some people measure each day's dry food into a plastic sandwich bag. The person doing the feeding merely places the measured amount into the feeding bowl and refills the water dish.

If you are only going to be gone for one or two days and your dog is on free-choice feeding, it is a simple matter to fill the feeder and leave him with a bucket or other non-tippable container of water. Have a neighbor check on him to be sure that he is not tangled or ill.

Feed dispensers are made which will meter out a measured quantity of feed, at the interval you select. You can set it to deliver the dog's regular feeding, once or twice a day. This may be useful for the dog who cannot be left with "all" the food that he wants. It is still a good idea to have someone check in to make sure the feeder is working properly so the dog does not go without dinner if the power goes off.

Working after meals. Don't work a dog or exercise him vigorously right after a meal. Give him at least an hour for his dinner to settle. Then, walk him a bit before you take him running or hunting.

Wolfing his feed. Some dogs gulp their food so rapidly that they vomit right after eating. Sometimes this is due to the dog becoming too hungry before he is fed. These dogs often benefit from twice-daily feedings. If the dog has been without feed for a couple of days for some reason, give him about half of his normal amount of feed at first. Then, in a couple of hours, give him the rest of the meal.

WHERE TO FEED

Pick a location to feed your dog which is out of the main traffic pattern in your house. It's hard for him to pay attention to his meal when he is in the middle of a hallway or the kitchen. Feed in the same place every time.

A dog dish with a wide, flat bottom will not tip and make a mess on the floor. It should have a smooth, easy to clean surface, inside and out. Keep the dish clean.

Dogs with long, floppy ears (like Cocker Spaniels) will appreciate a special long, narrow, raised dish which allows the ears to flop to each side. Or, the ears can be pinned together over the head. Clip the hair, not the meaty part, together with a wooden spring clothespin, if the dog does not object. If the dog soils the hair on his ears while eating, wipe the food off with a damp cloth after the meal. This keeps the dog smelling sweet and avoids skin infections.

HOW MUCH TO FEED

Use the recommendations on the dog food sack or can ONLY as a GUIDE for your particular dog. It is a starting point and no more. The dog's needs will differ depending on his individual metabolism, temperament, exercise, and the temperature where he lives. If the dog is new to you, begin with the recommended amount. Feed it daily for three weeks. THEN, decide whether the dog is fatter or thinner than you wish, and whether he has changed since you started. Adjust the amount being fed accordingly. Since the manufacturer is in business to sell dog food, the recommendations will usually be on the high side. Dog foods differ in bulk so that feeding a certain number of cups will result in widely varying calorie content from one brand to another.

Especially for a dog who is long-haired, it is important to FEEL the dog's condition every couple of weeks if you are not weighing him regularly. Many dogs, such as Norwegian Elkhounds, will look fat while they are extremely thin, because their build and hair coat appear so bulky. Stand behind the dog. Put your thumbs side by side, on the backbone, with fingers spread over the ribs. Ideally, you should be able to feel a thin layer of fat. If the ribs are visible, or the backbone protrudes noticeably, the dog is too thin, and should be evaluated for health or feeding problems. If there is so much fat that the edges of the ribs are totally covered and the chest feels smooth and only slightly wavy, the dog is probably too fat. Outdoor dogs should be checked often during the winter when there are heavier caloric demands on their bodies, to make sure that they do not become thin beneath their "winter woolies."

When trying out a new food or new quantity of food to see that it will do what you want, try it for three to four weeks. Either weigh the dog "before" and "after," or check him with your hands as mentioned above.

SPECIAL NEEDS

BREEDING AND PREGNANCY

The bitch may need to have her food increased slightly two to three weeks before breeding. A bitch who is on a lower-protein, maintenance-type dry dog food may benefit from the addition of moderate amounts of a nutritionally complete canned dog food. The portion of meat-based canned food can be increased during the pregnancy until it reaches three parts of dry food to one part of canned, by volume, for large and medium dogs can be brought to this level by the last ten days of gestation. For a smaller dog, a 1:1 mixture of canned to dry, by volume, may be a better mixture. Or, for a pregnant female

of any size, you can put her on a higher-protein content dry food than she has been fed previously. The increased protein will insure that protein levels will be adequate to cope with estrus, gestation, and lactation.

During the fourth and fifth weeks of pregnancy some bitches experience a period of mild to moderate loss of appetite. The cause is not well understood. It may be due to physical discomfort because of the increasing mass in her abdomen, or may be due to hormonal changes. You can help to keep up her daily intake by dividing her daily amount of food into two or three meals.

The bitch will not need much increase in food quantity for the first five to six weeks of gestation. Indeed, much of an increase early in gestation may lead to an unhealthy gain in weight. Also, early gestation is a delicate period for the fetus. Oversupplementation with vitamins A and D during this period has been linked to fetal abnormalities in some species, including humans. Because this might also be the case in dogs, be especially careful not to oversupplement early in pregnancy. (Actually, extra supplements are hardly ever necessary.)

Around five weeks of pregnancy, a gradual increase in feed quantity can begin. Approximately 10% more than maintenance level would be the most any female would require at that point. Around six to seven weeks, the amount fed may be raised to about 20% over maintenance. This will give adequate nutritional reserves to support the growing puppies, and prepare the bitch to produce an adequate quantity of milk.

The bitch should not be allowed to gain too much weight during pregnancy. Excess fat will make it difficult for her to whelp (give birth) without complications. It may also make her less fit to withstand a Caesarean section, or any other surgery which may be needed. An allowable weight gain can be determined by estimating how many puppies she is likely to have (determined by her past litters, or an average for her breed), and multiplying this number by the expected birth weight of each puppy. Then, add 10% of the bitch's initial weight to account for fluids and membranes which accompany the puppies. You can find the expected birth weight of a puppy by asking your veterinarian, or consulting with a long-time professional breeder of the particular breed of dog.

The normal gestation period for the dog is between 56 and 70 days, with an average of 63 days. Appetite may be used to help determine when the bitch is ready to whelp. Most bitches quit eating during whelping. This decrease in appetite may occur 12 to 24 hours before she is ready to have the puppies. Be sure to remove any uneaten food so that it will not spoil, and do not try to force her to eat. If the bitch goes more than 48 hours without eating, she should be examined by your veterinarian.

LACTATION

Nursing puppies, especially with a large litter, can put severe demands on the bitch's body. The puppies grow rapidly. In six to eight weeks, they will be approximately six times larger in size and weight than they were at birth. Until they are able to eat solid food, they are almost totally dependent on their mother's milk for their nutritional needs. To help her produce milk as efficiently as possible, her food must be high in digestibililty and nutritonal content. It must be palatable so she will consume enough for her needs. The nursing puppies will put a tremendous demand on her body, and the bitch may eat three to four times her normal quantity of food.

This is one period of her life where a high-quality, tasty dog food is very important. It is not, however, a good time to change dog foods. For that reason, either before breeding or early during gestation, the bitch should be put on the food that you want to use for the lactation period. She may not be able to consume enough dry food alone, so canned or soft-moist food may be added to her dry food. If she needs extra food during lactation, it is easy to increase the amount of the canned or semi-moist food, and she will already be used to it. Adding canned or soft-moist food is the easy way to give an increased amount of a well-balanced diet for the pregnant or lactating mother.

Immediately after whelping, increase the amount of food by one-half the non-pregnant maintenance diet. Divide the total daily ration into two or three meals. A week after the puppies are born, increase the amount to approximately twice the bitch's normal maintenance quantity. When the puppies are two to three weeks old, the bitch may eat (and need!) as much as three times her regular amount of food. Adjust the amount that you feed according to the litter size. A Labrador Retriever with a dozen puppies will need to eat all that she can to support these rapidly-growing puppies. A miniature Poodle with a single puppy will only need a small increase in her feed.

Be careful not to overwhelm the bitch's digestive system. If she has diarrhea or shows other signs of digestive problems, decrease the quantity (but not the quality) of the food. The intake of protein and fat should be maintained at fairly high levels. Feed less dry food and more canned or semi-moist food.

As the puppies begin eating solid food and decrease nursing, the bitch will automatically eat less. Gradually decrease the amount of food you are giving until she is back on a normal amount of her regular maintenance food by about the time the puppies are weaned.

PUPPY FEEDING

Puppies, especially of large breeds, grow rapidly and put a tremendous demand on their mother. The sooner you can get them to eating even a bit of supplemental food, the more you can help her carry their burden. Most puppies will eat some food on their own by 21 days of age. If the bitch is not well, or is severely drained by the puppies, begin feeding them around 16 days of age. Use high-quality canned or dry food, mixed with a bit of water or milk replacer to make a thin gruel. Put it in a low pan, with half-inch high sides. Saucers tend to tip when the puppies wade in, and are not very successful. Expect a mess, so feed on a cleanable surface, or outside on the lawn. Take each puppy in turn and dip his mouth into the gruel. You can also rub a bit of the mixture into the puppy's mouth. Some of the puppies will learn faster than others, but all should be eating by the end of their third week of age.

Keep the mixture out of reach of the female. Mix and feed small, fresh batches three or four times a day. Wash the container between feedings so that there will not be any spoiled or contaminated food left to harm the puppies. As they get older, decrease the amount of liquid until they are eating the canned food unmixed with water by the time they are weaned.

Most puppies are weaned around six to eight weeks of age. Shortly after weaning them, you can begin to introduce them to a dry puppy food. At first, dilute it with water, or broth, to make a stiff gruel. As the puppy gets larger, gradually decrease the amount of liquid until the puppy is happily crunching the dry food. Puppies can be fed either a mixture of dry and canned food (mixed half and half), or switched completely to a dry food.

Puppies need about two times the amount of energy and nutrients, compared to a mature dog, from weaning until they are half their expected mature weight. This is why puppies, especially of larger breeds, may not thrive or grow normally if fed a dry, maintenance diet meant for mature, sedentary dogs. Their food should be palatable and high in nutritional quality. It is best to feed them three to four times a day to help them take in enough food for their needs.

Puppies will vary greatly in the amount of food that they will need, or even eat. Adjust the amount of feed to the appetite of the puppy, but keep him from becoming fat. Puppies should be plump, but not overweight, please. Overfeeding may result in obesity. In large breeds, too-rapid growth may result in growth disorders such as osteochondritis dissecans (a disease of cartilage and bone). Excessive weight can also put too much stress on undeveloped bones and joints.

Avoid abrupt changes in diet which may cause digestive upsets such as diarrhea. Keep the diet fairly steady, making any necessary changes gradually.

Judge the proper amount to feed by the look and feel of the puppy. The puppy should look trim, with only a slight layer of fat over the ribs. If the ribs cannot be felt with gentle pressure on the rib cage, the puppy is too fat. If you can see the ribs easily as the puppy moves, the puppy is too thin. Adjust his diet to keep him in proper condition. Change the feed quantity weekly if needed. As with any food, change brands gradually over a week or so.

If you are feeding measured meals rather than free choice, puppies that are just weaned (about six weeks of age) do best if fed four meals a day, 4 or 5 hours apart. From 3 to 6 months of age, three meals a day are enough. But, be sure to increase the quantity at each meal to make up for having fewer of them, keeping the total daily intake unchanged. After six months of age, two meals a day are sufficient for most puppies, again, keeping the total daily amount the same. At 12 months of age, puppies of small and medium-sized breeds can be switched to once a day feeding. Puppies of large breeds and giant breeds may still be growing at 12 months of age and will gain better if kept on twice a day feeding. (For orphan puppies, see Orphan Puppies).

THE WORKING DOG

The dog used for hard work, whether herding cattle or sheep, pulling a sled, hunting, or in field trials, will need extra nutrient calories to fuel his muscles. Work also produces stress, which further increases the nutrient needs. A diet for hard work should be highly digestible and low in bulk so that the dog can eat enough to meet his needs. As much as 50% to 60% of the energy should be derived from fat, especially if the animal is working in cold weather. Another 30% to 40% can come from protein, and 10% to 25% from carbohydrate (ALPO, 1984).

Carbohydrate loading is commonly used by human runners and other endurance athletes. High levels of carbohydrates are eaten before extreme exercise in order to increase the storage of glycogen in the liver. This helps to provide a high muscle glycogen level which delays fatigue. In dogs and horses, the presence of excess glycogen in the muscles causes rapid muscle breakdown leading to the deterioration of the membranes around the muscle fibers. Myoglobin is released into the blood and must be removed by the kidneys. The urine turns tan or red. This disease is called exertional rhabdomyolyis ("muscle breakdown.") It is common in horses who are fed large quantities of grain while being worked, and then are fed the same amounts on "off" days. The condition is seen when the horse is put back to work. It does not occur in human runners (which is why carbohydrate loading works for us.) This problem is seen often enough in dogs that carbohydrate loading should NOT be used (Kronfeld, 1981.)

An alternate strategy of preparation for endurance-type exercise in the dog is fat adaptation. If dogs are fed a fatty diet for a prolonged period of time, they become adapted to using fatty acids from the blood instead of muscle glycogen or blood glucose. The strategy of feeding a high-fat diet results in improved stamina.

Food deprivation is NOT recommended for dogs which must work hard day after day. The hard-working dog should be fed, continuously, a high-fat diet. This diet should be introduced gradually to allow the digestive system time to adapt to the higher quantity of fat. Otherwise, poor digestion of the fat can lead to diarrhea. Reduce the quantity fed of a diet which is higher in fat, or obesity may occur. As with any feeding regimen, the diet should be balanced with the amount of exercise to maintain the dog at the desired weight and activity level.

Diets with 40% protein or more have been used successfully for sled dogs. These diets have high digestibility and low fiber content. They seem to reduce the incidence of rectal bleeding in these dogs, as well as improving performance by reducing intestinal fill. The dog has a smaller amount of food to lug around in his gut.

The quantity of red blood cells has been found to increase both with training or racing, as well as with increased dietary protein intake. This increase was found to occur during a three month racing season with dogs fed 32% to 39% protein, but not in dogs fed only 28% protein diets (Am. J. Clin. Nutr., 1977).

Dogs who are hard at work, such as retrievers or working cattle dogs, will benefit by a good feeding the night before they are to work. For most dogs, this means all they can eat. A light feeding in the morning of the work day will also help to keep the dog's energy high. This feeding should be given an hour or so before work begins. One or two "snack" breaks are also a good idea for the working dog.

Some working dogs may suffer from hypoglycemia. This is especially seen in some breeds of hunting dogs. The dog may become faint, or "fade" after several hours of work. These dogs will need several small meals during the day to maintain adequate levels of blood sugar and to keep the nutrients flowing to their muscles.

STRESS

Stress may result from illness, injuries, travel, breeding or showing, or physical demands such as racing or hunting. It can also result from training, especially when the dog does not understand what you want him to do. Many times, stress can be minimized by putting the dog into new situations gradually. For example, take the dog for short and medium-length auto rides before hauling him across the country. Train him gradually, breaking the learning into bite-sized lessons, keeping them short so that the dog is not fatigued. Keep in mind that good physical condition must be gained gradually—get the dog's body in shape for his retriever training at the same time you train his mind. Feeding dogs what will be or are under stress is much like feeding working dogs.

The dog who is ill may require a special diet. A dog with kidney disease, for instance, may benefit from a dog food designed to relieve the burden on the kidneys and provide the proper mineral balance for proper kidney function. The dog with a heart problem can use a food designed to compensate for his weakened condition.

A dog who is recovering from surgery should have a well-balanced, low-bulk, easily digested, highly nutritional diet. In some cases, your veterinarian may want you to continue with the dog's normal diet. If it is a high quality food, this may be a good idea, because the post-surgical period is not a good time to change the dog's diet. However, if the dog's normal diet is poor, or only marginal, changing to a better quality food may be a lesser evil than asking the dog to heal in the face of inadequate nutrition. Consult with your veterinarian if you have any questions about diet.

The dog who has had surgery on his digestive tract may be placed on a special food for intestinal problems. The diet will be low in bulk, highly digestible, and bland. It is not too palatable, and the dog may only eat a little of it. In some cases, your veterinarian may want to limit the amount of food the dog eats, and a bland food will help to do that. In other cases, it may be advisable to add a bit of grease-free broth or meat juices for flavoring to encourage the dog to eat. Again, consult with your veterinarian if you have any questions. If your veterinarian prescribes a bland diet, don't be tempted to unbalance it by feeding other food or treats. Some conditions calling for a bland diet are life-threatening with any other food.

THE OVERWEIGHT DOG

How do you determine if your dog is overweight? Many times it is obvious—the rolls of fat bulging between the last rib and the hip bone, the ribs that can't be felt with your fingers, and the general look of the animal. It's also suspicious if his abdomen is sagging, or if the stomach protrudes to the sides when viewed from above. If in doubt, consult with your veterinarian. He will tell you how much overweight your dog is, and give you a realistic goal for weight loss and condition. Several studies have determined that as many as 30-40% of American dogs are obese.

How do you determine your dog's weight? Small dogs, such as Chihuahuas can be weighed on a baby scale, if you have one handy. Larger dogs may stand on a bathroom scale by themselves. If your dog will not do so, pick him up, stand on the scale and weigh yourself and the dog together. Then, set the dog down and weigh just yourself. The difference is the weight of the dog. Some veterinary clinics have large platform scales. Most dogs will stand on these large scales long enough to be weighed.

Obesity is a serious health problem in dogs. It can significantly shorten your dog's lifespan and make him miserable while he is alive. Dogs who are overweight have more physical ailments than those of normal weight. Because fat holds anesthetic agents, an overweight dog has significantly reduced chances of surviving surgery, especially emergency surgery due to an injury. Excess weight strains the heart and puts extra stress on ligaments and tendons. Locomotion problems increase. These include herniated disks, ruptured ligaments, and arthritis. Dogs who are severely overweight can even have their legs collapse to where they must be euthanized because they cannot stand. Fat deposits may cause the skin to bulge into rolls which then rub against each other and produce skin irritations. The resulting skin diseases can be difficult to cure.

The overweight bitch, if she can even get pregnant, is more likely to have a complicated whelping. If she has to have a Caesarean section, she is less likely to survive than an animal of normal weight. Layers of fat make it difficult for your veterinarian to give your dog an adequate examination. Wounds heal more slowly in overweight dogs, and they have less resistance to viral and bacterial infections. Dogs who are overweight are also less resistant to the effects of heat. Some dogs may also be irritable because they are miserable. Dogs who are overweight show a 75% increase in cardiovascular problems, including congestive heart failure and high blood pressure. Chances of the overweight dog having cancer increase by 50%. The dog can also have digestive problems, including constipation, diabetes, and gas. The bad effects of being overweight begin when the dog is only ten to fifteen percent over his normal weight.

Some dogs are more prone to put on weight because of their conformation and heredity than others. Long-bodied, low-slung breeds like Basset Hounds gain weight easily unless the owner is careful. Big-boned breeds or individuals may conceal extra pounds and need to be evaluated more often than the "lean and mean" breeds. Have you ever seen an overweight Greyhound?

The only legitimate excuses for weight gain are as a side effect of medication, or because of a physical disorder causing the animal to put on fat. Both of them are very rare, however, compared to the "too much food" dogs.

Obesity is easier to prevent than to cure. Don't let it get started. As with humans, obesity comes from too much food, food with excess calorie content, or inadequate exercise. The first step in taking weight off the dog is to stop feeding "people food." Food which is fattening for us is fattening for your dog. Also, the size difference between us and our dogs must be taken into account. Allowing a small poodle to lick an ice cream dish is like one of us eating an entire bowlful. The foods which make us fat are even worse for our dogs because of their smaller size. Cut out all table foods and "treats." Stick to the diet without exceptions. It is kinder to control the food than to let your pet suffer from the medical problems that the obesity can cause. And ignore the whining and soulful looks. Do you really want to "kill your dog with kindness?" I hope that by now you are convinced that a fat dog is neither healthy nor happy. If you are paying attention to what your dog eats, he should never become obese. However, if you look at your dog and decide that he needs to go on a diet, here's what to do.

When first putting your dog on a diet, it may be helpful to put him outdoors or in another part of the house when you are eating meals or snacks. This keeps him away from the tempting odors and sounds of food preparation and consumption. He also can't beg if he's not present—and most obese dogs are skilled beggars. Do not feed an obese dog with other pets. It may be easier for the dog if you feed him before you or your other pets eat. Make sure he has plenty of fresh water.

Frequent small feedings, especially in the beginning, may make the new regimen easier for your dog to tolerate. With time, his stomach will shrink and be will become used to smaller meals and less food. Give your dog plenty of attention and emotional support to help compensate for the lack of groceries. Make sure that children don't tease the dog with food and make the diet more difficult. Hand-feeding may help when you are starting the dog on the new diet. Free-choice feeding usually cannot be used with the obese dog—he just helps himself! It may also be helpful to warm up food that you have stored in the refrigerator.

It is vital that you have the cooperation of ALL family members. It does no good to limit the amount of food if the four-year old is giving Fido cookies, or grandma is letting him lick the gravy pan. It is best not to give the dog anything but the diet food, but if you simply must give him a treat, give VERY SMALL quantities of carrots, green beans, other raw vegetables, or wheat bran cakes (with NO butter, oil, or salt added). These will add roughage, vitamins, and minerals, but almost no calories. Overall, it's better to just get the obese pet out of the begging habit—it's better for his long-term health!

Increased exercise will also help to reduce your dog's weight. It uses up calories as well as speeding up his metabolism. Start gradually. Taking an out-of-condition dog and making him walk a couple of miles is as miserable for him as it might be for you. Start with a few blocks and work up gradually. Stop and rest if the dog shows signs of distress such as excess panting or gasping. If you have any questions about starting your dog on an exercise program, or continuing one that you have started, be sure to consult your veterinarian.

Feeding a "diet" dog food can also be helpful. Some of the diet foods may have up to 40% less calories than regular grocery store brands of dog food. Special prescription reducing diets are available, and similar products are produced by some of the major dog food manufacturers and sold in grocery stores. While low in calories, these foods still supply all the protein, vitamin, and mineral requirements of adult dogs. "Diet" dog foods have fewer calories per amount of food so that the dog can feel full and satisfied yet lose weight—a lot like eating lettuce instead of ice cream. Don't expect quick reducing, but you should see steady, slow progress. These specialty foods work especially well when coupled with exercise. Don't feed more of the food just because it's a diet food, or you'll be right back where you started.

Dogs in the wild get plenty of exercise, having to either hunt down and kill or scavenge everything that they eat. Overeating is not a problem. And, the dog who might overeat in the wild is automatically regulated because he will be too sluggish to catch anything to eat until he goes without food for a few days. Now, under domestication, dogs often overeat if they have the chance. In many cases, we teach them to overeat by giving the dog attention and affection when feeding them. They soon learn that eating wins approval. Eat more, get more approval, and on and on. And, this often means snacks, not his regular meals. If we can avoid having the major part of our relationship with our dog centered on food, he will be less prone to overeat attempting to please us.

In extreme cases of obesity, it may be necessary to have your pet hospitalized until he has lost enough weight that he can go on a home-reducing program. Hospitalization can also be a last resort when a home program is not working.

Don't give up on the diet program. As with humans, the weight reduction may be slow. An overweight dog may only lose a couple of pounds per month, and it may take several months to reach your goal. Eventually, you will notice that your dog is feeling younger and more full of life. He will be enjoying the remaining years of his life, and you will be enjoying him!

Intermittent feeding can be used as a lifetime regimen with dogs who tend to be overweight. It involves feeding the dog two days out of three, and is suitable for dogs who are not working hard. It is also kinder to dogs on this feeding schedule if they are outdoors and not around food on the days they don't get to eat. A regular dog food can be used, and can be fed in nearly normal amounts. This program works well with dogs such as Blue Heelers who are "easy keepers". Remember to feed the dog on days that he will be working, preferably the evening before he goes to work.

THE UNDERWEIGHT DOG

Is the dog normal for his breed? A Greyhound normally will be leaner than a Norwegian Elkhound. And, by the way, is the Elkhound really thin? Feel through the hair on that Elkhound to see whether his ribs are covered with fat, or whether you can put your fingers into the spaces between them.

Begin by making sure that the dog is healthy. Take a stool sample to your veterinarian and have it checked for worms. If they are present, have the dog wormed. Then, see whether he gains weight in two to three weeks. If not, or if he shows signs of any physical illness, take him in to be examined by your veterinarian. If no worms are present and there is no obvious reason for the weight loss or thinness, have the dog examined by your veterinarian to find out what the problem is.

To put weight on the dog by feeding, you can simply increase the amount of food you are feeding providing the dog will eat it. If the dog food is not palatable to the individual dog, try another brand. Some cheap dog foods provide good nutrition, but have a poor flavor. Some dogs will not eat enough of them to maintain good condition.

Extreme thinness is one of the few instances where, if lack of calories is the only problem, one might recommend feeding "people food." Start with a tablespoon or so of bacon grease on the dog's food, and work up to two or three tablespoons per day, depending on the size of the dog. If diarrhea occurs, reduce the amount of grease. Corn oil can also be used. A bonus with this program will be a good, shiny hair coat. Fatty table scraps can also be given, again as long as they do not cause diarrhea. Bread, gravy, and other calorie-rich foods will usually put weight on the dog. Be sure to discontinue feeding "junk" when the dog is up to normal weight.

THE FINICKY EATER

Training (or lack of it) has much to do with the making of a finicky eater. If you insist that your puppy eats the good, nutritious food which he is given, and avoid feeding junk food, you will probably never have a problem with a finicky eater. As with many other problems, it is more easily prevented than treated. Getting the finicky eater to eat the food you want him to may be difficult. The dog will moan, groan, whine, beg, cajole, wheedle, complain, and in general try to make you feel guilty. Steel your heart and do what is good for the dog.

Cure the picky eater by putting out the food you wish him to eat at his regular mealtime. If he does not eat it within 15 minutes, take it away. Wait until his next regular mealtime and again put out the dog food you want him to eat. If you're feeding canned or moistened food, don't let it spoil between mealtimes. Repeat the process. Remember, THE DOG CHOOSES NOT TO EAT. You are not guilty of starving him. He will eat before he will starve himself. Do not fuss over him and the food, and do not give him ANY between-meal snacks. Really resistant cases may go two to three days without eating. Hold firm, he'll eat when he discovers he has no choice.

Sometimes it helps to put a bit of the new food on a plate and pretend that you are eating it, if the dog is accustomed to being fed from the table. Changing to a new food may be a matter of life and death if your dog develops heart or kidney disorders or other health problems which require an exclusive special diet.

Chapter 7

THE DIGESTIVE SYSTEM

TEETH

It is possible to tell the dog's approximate age by his teeth, up to about seven months of age. The puppy's first two pairs of incisors (front teeth) come in between four and five weeks of age. The third pair come in between five and six weeks of age. The first two pairs of permanent incisors erupt between two and five months of age. The third pair of permanent incisors comes in between four and five months of age. The temporary incisors are more thin and needle-like than are the permanent ones. The dog's permanent canine teeth come in between five and six months of age. As with the incisors, the permanent canines are thicker and broader at the base than are the puppy teeth.

A puppy will cut his permanent (adult) teeth around four to five months of age. This usually happens without any problem. Normally the "baby" teeth are pushed out of the way by the incoming permanent teeth, and fall out unnoticed. Keeping a good supply of tough chew toys and large bones for the dog to chew will help him shed his baby teeth normally. Occasionally, a baby tooth will refuse to fall out. This is especially noticeable when the dog has two canine teeth sitting side-by-side. If the baby tooth stays, the rest of the teeth may be permanently misaligned. Don't attempt to take the extra teeth out yourself. Have your veterinarian remove them (see Retained Puppy Teeth.)

TEETH CLEANING

A healthy mouth should have clean, white teeth with a coral pink gum tissue tightly and evenly surrounding them. The breath should have an acceptable odor. Early signs of problems include yellowing of the teeth and bad breath. There may be reddening of the gum tissue, especially where it adjoins the teeth, with a loosening and softening of the gum tissue there. As the gum disease progresses, the separation of the gum tissue from the tooth becomes irreversible. It is an indication of shrinking bone mass in the jaw, and a loss of ligament support of the tooth. In the later stages of periodontal ("tooth-surrounding") disease, the teeth are very yellowed, and may be loose. The breath is very bad, with a fetid or "rotten" odor. The gum tissue is red and swollen, with areas of ulceration. There is a softening of gum tissue, and it may separate from the neck of the tooth. At this point, teeth may be very loosened, or may fall out completely. The gums may be extremely sore, and the dog may refuse to eat.

Dogs rarely get cavities, but they do develop tartar accumulations which can lead to periodontal disease. This is a lot worse than cavities, because it can lead to kidney disease, heart infections, and other disease problems. Periodontal disease causes perhaps 95% of bad breath in dogs. Even some cases of vomiting and diarrhea may be due to periodontal disease. Painful teeth may cause the dog to be upset when his head or face are handled, and he may be irritable and grouchy.

Routine dental care is usually not necessary for the younger dog. Dogs five or more years old should have their teeth checked frequently. It is a good idea to examine the dog's mouth yourself once a month. Check for an accumulation of plaque or tartar around the gum area. Plaque will show up as a yellowish, grayish, or greenish scum or growth on the teeth around the gum line. Plaque can be scraped off with your fingernail or a soft object such as a wooden toothpick. If the tartar stays on the teeth for a long period of time, it will accumulate both bacteria and minerals, which harden it into tartar. Tartar, a hard, rocklike substance, is NOT easily removed with a fingernail or toothpick. Tartar shows the same range of ugly, unhealthy colors. Both can be accompanied by a foul, unpleasant odor.

Either plaque or tartar can cause an infection along the gum line. Neglected, the infection will work its way along the tooth, under the gum line. Given enough time, it will undermine the entire root of the tooth. At that point, the bacteria contained within the infected mass can be picked up by the bloodstream and carried throughout the body, causing infection in the kidneys, heart valves, and elsewhere. In fact, periodontal disease is one of the leading causes of kidney disease in older dogs. Routine dental maintenance is a cheap investment in continuing good health for your dog in his old age.

Keep an eye on your dog's teeth to make sure they stay healthy throughout his lifetime. Give him plenty of bones and hard chew toys so that he can remove plaque and tartar by gnawing and chewing on them. Dogs who have misaligned teeth often have trouble keeping their teeth clean and may need more frequent professional care by your veterinarian.

Why does periodontal disease occur? Where the gum meets the tooth, a narrow groove is formed. This groove is easily filled with soft food material. This material, when mixed with saliva and bacteria normally found in the mouth, builds up within the channel and sticks to the surface of the tooth. This is called plaque. When plaque is first formed, it is soft and only slightly stuck to the teeth. It can easily be removed by brushing the dog's teeth, or by the dog chewing hard foods or bones.

Plaque is the perfect place for bacteria to grow and prosper. As they multiply, the food material forming the plaque begins to rot. This putrefied food, along with the dead bacteria and their waste products, causes huge quantities of white blood cells to invade the gums around the tooth. This causes the gums to become inflamed. Then, minerals seep from the inflamed gums into the plaque, settling out to form a material called calculus. Plaque and calculus together are sometimes called dental tartar. If the buildup of calculus is allowed to continue, the material accumulates along with the dead white blood cells, forming a pocket of pus around the root of the tooth. This pocket begins to separate the gum from the tooth, forming a larger channel between the gum and the tooth. Still more food material gets packed into the space, and the process proceeds. This debris eventually becomes so toxic that it kills the tissues surrounding the diseased tooth. The thin bony walls that hold the tooth in place begin to erode, loosening the tooth.

If not treated, periodontal disease becomes progressively worse. The erosion process will eventually involve the whole bony socket holding the tooth. When it is no longer adequately attached, the tooth falls out. At this point, the hole is large enough that the dog can clean it out with his tongue. The food, debris, and pus disappear, the inflammation subsides, and the hole fills in with scar tissue, and the dog has one less tooth. However, chances of this involving only one tooth are small. Chances are very good that the entire mouth and all of

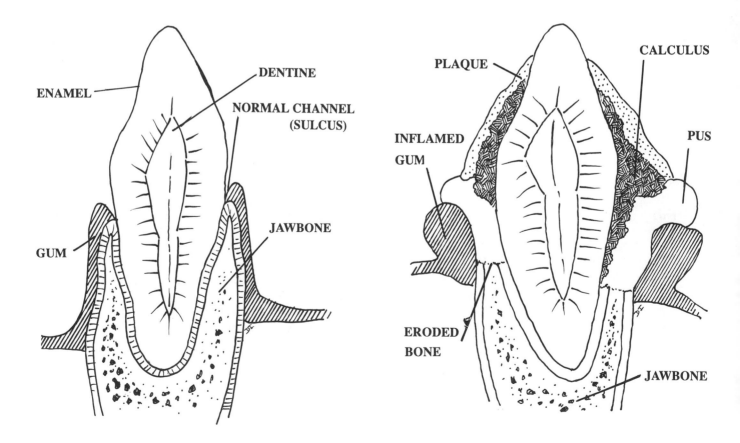

Normal tooth anatomy.   Gums recede as periodontal disease becomes worse.

the teeth are undergoing the same process together. If this is the case, it's only a matter of time before all the teeth fall out.

Many factors may contribute to dental disease in the dog. Among them are feeding canned or semi-moist dog foods. Advancing age seems to contribute to the development of tartar. Dogs who eat their own stools (coprophagy) seem to have more of a problem with tartar, as do dogs who chew and bite at their coats and eat large amounts of hair. Basically, any condition that contributes to dirty teeth is a potential cause of periodontal disease.

When you begin to notice tartar or plaque accumulation, it is time to take action. Soft tartar can be easily removed by gently brushing the dog's teeth. This can be done with a very soft toothbrush, or a piece of damp cloth or gauze wrapped around the end of your finger. Toothbrushes are made for dogs, with a convenient size and angle. They are very soft (even softer than a child's toothbrush) to assure that the dog is not irritated by the brushing and will tolerate the process.

It is a good idea to use a dentifrice made especially for dogs. Some of them are even beef-flavored! Most of these products do not need to be rinsed out of the mouth, which is very convenient. There are also some powdered products that can be squirted into the dog's mouth to help reduce the quantity of tartar and bacteria present. Human toothpaste is not good to use on dogs because it contains ingredients which cause foaming in the mouth, and which can cause stomach problems if they are swallowed. It's hard to teach a dog to spit! Baking soda and salt have been recommended for brushing dog's teeth. However, both have a high level of sodium and may cause problems with some dogs, especially those with heart disease.

It is best to brush the dog's teeth daily, especially with older dogs. Begin to teach him about brushing by handling his mouth for several minutes each day. After several days, hold the mouth gently closed with one hand. Lift the lip on one side of the mouth and brush the outside surfaces of the teeth. A circular motion is most effective, although a back-and-forth motion can be used. Brush a few more teeth each time, until your dog cooperates willingly with the procedure.

To clean the inside surfaces of the teeth, place your hand over the muzzle from the top. Gently squeeze and push the lips from one side between the back teeth. This will help to keep the mouth open. At the same time, pull the head back gently but firmly so that the mouth will remain open. Now you can brush the inside surface of the teeth on the opposite side. Repeat the process for the other side. When you and the pet have become accustomed to the procedure, it should only take one or two minutes. If you have a small dog who is not cooperating, you can wrap him completely in a towel or blanket, with just his head sticking out.

Brushing his teeth should be a pleasant routine for the dog. It is good to pick a time when you are both relaxed, such as after the evening meal. Give the dog plenty of praise and attention for allowing you to brush his teeth, and occasionally give him a small treat.

Oral cleansing solutions are available for use in the dog's mouth if you are not inclined to brush his teeth. One, for instance, contains chlorhexidine (Nolvadent Oral Cleansing Solution™, Fort Dodge.) This is a powerful disinfectant which helps to kill plaque-forming bacteria. Using it is simple—you just place the spout inside the dog's mouth and squeeze a small amount between the teeth and the side of the mouth. Then you just massage the cheeks over the teeth to spread the product over the surface of the teeth. The product also helps to eliminate bad breath, much like the mouthwash that we use. You can use this product as a dentifrice when brushing your dog's teeth if you wish. Oral cleansing is NOT a substitute for regular visits to your veterinarian.

A rubber chew device is available which has grooves in it to clean the teeth. This "dental exerciser" has grooves which are filled with a toothpaste especially for dogs. It has not been on the market long enough to know whether it is going to be totally effective, but may be worth a try. Hard nylon (Nylabone®) chew toys are also helpful for removing tartar. However, not all dogs will chew them. Try your dog and see if he will use the toy. Dogs who are on soft diets are in especial need of dental cleansing. The chewing action provided by chew toys and bones provides both cleansing action for the teeth and exercise for the small ligamentous fibers which help to hold the teeth in place.

Some biscuit-type products are recommended for keeping the dog's teeth clean. While hard biscuits certainly help and are better than no oral hygiene at all, they are not a cure-all, and are NOT a substitute for bones or other hard objects for chewing. Regular brushing of your dog's teeth is the best, all around form of dental hygiene for him.

If the tartar has become hardened, its removal is a job for your veterinarian. Normally this is done under general anesthesia. This allows your veterinarian to get down under the gum line and remove plaque which has accumulated deep under the gums. Removal of the deep plaque and tartar is crucial to continued good dental health. If your dog is very old, your veterinarian will probably use a gas anesthetic so that there is minimal risk and the dog will wake up quickly.

Some groomers offer tooth cleaning as a part of their service. However, they are not allowed to administer anesthetic or sedatives. For this reason, the cleaning they perform is cosmetic only, and does not adequately clean down into the groove between the tooth and gums. It should NOT be considered adequate dental hygiene for your valued pet. Have his teeth thoroughly cleaned by your veterinarian.

If infection has already invaded under the gum line, it may have undermined the roots of the teeth and loosened one or more of them. If this has occurred, removal is necessary. Please DO NOT ask your veterinarian to try to "save" the teeth at this point. Chances are good that infection has invaded much of the surrounding tissue, and perhaps even the bone in the area. Removing the tooth is the best insurance against future kidney and heart problems.

Several teeth may be removed in one session. This is not generally a problem to the dog, and is easier on him than anesthetizing him twice. In severe cases, half a dozen to a dozen teeth may be pulled. Again, don't worry about it. If they're that bad, they needed to come out. And, if they're that bad, they probably were easily pulled, almost falling out. A dog CAN eat without any teeth at all. He will lap the food into his mouth with his tongue. He then lifts his mouth upward (much like a chicken drinking) and swallows it. If you think about it, dogs rarely chew their food, anyway. Most veterinarians try to preserve the canine teeth (eyeteeth) if possible, as these teeth help to hold the tongue in the mouth and define the shape of the jaw. However, if preservation is not possible, it is better to remove even these teeth than to leave them as a source of infection.

TOOTHACHE

Your dog will not tell you that he has a toothache! You might perhaps notice that he is not chewing his food as much as he used to. He may be mouthing it and wallowing it around with his tongue and lips. Or, he may paw at the affected side, or rub it along the floor or ground. He may drool, and may have a foul odor from his mouth. These can also be signs that he has a foreign object caught in his teeth.

CAVITIES (CARIES)

Cavities are occasionally seen in dogs, and can occur on any surface of the tooth. If a cavity has been present for a while, gum tissue may have grown into the defect. It is worth having the cavity filled if your veterinarian does this kind of dental work, or if he can refer you to someone who does do it and you can afford to have the work done. Filling the cavity will prevent erosion into the pulp in the center of the tooth which will weaken the tooth and cause further decay. Or, the tooth can simply be removed.

RETAINED PUPPY TEETH

Some dogs may not shed their deciduous ("puppy") teeth when the permanent (adult) teeth are ready to erupt. If this occurs, the dog may have two canine teeth, side by side. This can cause poor alignment of the lower permanent canines, making them strike the roof of the mouth and causing ulcers. For this reason, many veterinarians prefer to remove the offending puppy tooth as soon as it is apparent that it is not coming out by itself. The dog must be anesthetized for this procedure, but it is relatively simple, and can prevent a lot of problems in the future. In some cases, it may be necessary to put braces on the lower canines to spread them sideways until they clear the roof of the mouth.

The upper or lower incisors (front teeth) may be retained. This may cause an uneven bite. It can sometimes be corrected by having your veterinarian remove these extra teeth as soon as possible. In some cases, braces may be applied for a short period of time to give the dog a more normal bite and better cosmetic appearance.

CAPS AND OTHER DENTISTRY

The canine teeth help to shape the dog's mouth, and keep the tongue in place between the lower pair. They are also an integral part of the armament of a guard or attack dog. Broken or chipped teeth can be repaired. In some cases, the teeth can be capped. Police departments sometimes use stainless steel caps on their working dogs—they are very impressive when the dog curls his lip at a burglar! Or, porcelain caps can be used, similar to those used on humans' teeth. Small holes are drilled in the portion of tooth which remains. Dental bonding pins, usually made of bronze, are inserted into the holes. These pins are drilled tightly downward into the tooth stub, with a portion of the pin left protruding. The top of the tooth is then rebuilt or attached, depending on the material used.

ROOT CANALS (ENDODONTICS) AND CROWNS

You may find that your dog's teeth are broken, discolored, or severely worn. This is especially true if you have taught your dog to, or allow him to, chase or play with rocks. This damage is commonly seen on the front teeth and the canines. The back teeth are rarely damaged in this way.

If the tooth is fractured deeply enough into the gum area, its roots will become exposed. The soft tissue inside the pulp cavity becomes infected and swells. The resulting pressure inside the hard tooth kills the blood vessels and nerve, leaving the tooth dead and discolored (usually gray, pink, or bluish.) The decaying pulp eventually forms an abscess in the root of the tooth. The abscess will leak bacteria and toxins into the body, causing heart and kidney problems much like gum disease. Meanwhile, the dog has a toothache and is miserable, and probably grumpy. He may eat poorly, if at all.

If the abscess occurs over the fourth premolar in the upper jaw, it may erode through the thin wall of bone that separates the tooth from the sinus, filling the maxillary sinus with pus. The dog's eye may swell partly shut, and a lumpy swelling or draining lesion filled with pus can be seen just below the eye.

Most owners, however, do not notice the abscesses which occur over the roots of the other teeth. If the upper canines are involved, the root abscess will break out into the nasal cavity, and is not detected. The other teeth are set more solidly into bone and rarely drain to the outside, effectively hiding the infections and abscesses. If you notice any of these signs, or discolored teeth, have your dog checked. If you do not wish to have root canal surgery performed, or cannot find a veterinarian to do it, or cannot afford it, simply have the tooth extracted.

If the tooth has worn away slowly and evenly, it may not have an infection in the root, and may not need a root canal operation, even if it is worn down to the level of the gums. If the center of the tooth tip is smooth and yellowish-brown, it probably has enough covering of dentin to not be painful to the dog. If the center of the tooth's tip is black or red, the pulp cavity is probably exposed, and it may be causing the dog pain.

A crown can be placed over the remains of the broken tooth to restore function. Caps are usually not put on incisors. Dogs are very hard on their teeth, and may break off caps. The more tooth length available after fracturing, the better the chance is that a crown will stay in place. After the surgery, make sure the dog does not chew rocks, or excessively hard objects. You will probably need to brush his teeth for the rest of his life to compensate for his inability to chew bones and keep his teeth clean by himself.

ORTHODONTICS (BRACES)

Yes, braces ARE available for dogs. Many dogs, especially those of short-faced breeds such as Pugs and Pekingese, suffer from teeth that do not have any normal relationship to each other. Longer-faced dogs such as Dobermans and Collies (just as examples, not singling them out as having any particular dental problems) may also have teeth that do not mesh. While many malocclusions are hereditary, a large number of them are acquired. These problems can come from something as simple as playing tug of war with a puppy, or a puppy who falls and hits his mouth while he is still small.

Braces are used to straighten the teeth, and bring them into a more normal alignment. Braces are also used to reposition front teeth that are not straight, or ones that protrude outward, improving the dog's appearance. Cosmetics are the main reason for canine orthodontics. Let's face it, dogs who are eating dog food don't exactly need their teeth for cutting or tearing flesh from carcasses. Even in the wild, dogs don't use their teeth for grinding up the meat once they have removed it from bones. Also, dogs don't worry about their teeth not being straight. So, in many cases, orthodontics benefit the owner rather than the dog. Orthodontic work should not, for ethical reasons, be used to correct misplaced teeth in dogs who are to be used for showing or breeding, as this would mask a serious hereditary problem. Better to just eliminate the dog from the breeding program and place it as a pet. Breeding these animals will eventually lead to a deterioration of the breed as a whole.

Timing is important in canine orthodontics, as it is in humans. In most cases, orthodontics should be put off until the facial bones are completely formed and have stopped growing. In most cases, complicated procedures cannot be done until the dog is one to two years of age. For most dogs, braces which are firmly fixed to the teeth and periodically adjusted by the veterinarian or dentist doing the work, are more successful than those that you have to apply and care for yourself. Small movements of teeth may take as little as two to eight weeks. If the tooth must be moved a long distance, the time period will be much longer. In some cases, when the teeth reach their new location, they will have to be stabilized by being bridged or otherwise supported by other teeth.

The dog who is wearing braces must be kept from chewing on bones or other hard objects. In order to avoid infection, bad breath, and gum infection, oral hygiene is important. Don't bother to get braces on your dog if you aren't willing to care for them. If you want orthodontic work done, ask if your veterinarian does it. If not, he may be willing to consult with a dentist who will assist him with it. Or, ask him for a referral to another veterinarian who does orthodontic work. It is a new enough technique in veterinary medicine that not all veterinarians do the work.

FOREIGN BODIES BETWEEN TEETH

Dogs occasionally get objects wedged between their teeth. Some examples are bones (especially those of poultry or brittle pork bones,) pieces of wood, corn cobs, or portions of toys. Most often, the object becomes caught between the upper teeth, wedged from side to side across the roof of the mouth.

A dog with something caught between his teeth may be quite irritated. He may salivate and paw at his mouth, and resist having his head handled. If the object has been present for some time, the dog may drool reddish or brownish saliva, coating his muzzle and front legs with it. An extremely foul odor may be present.

Before you examine the dog's mouth, think of rabies. Especially if you live in an area where it is common, consider taking the dog to your veterinarian if you haven't recently fed him any bones which were likely to cause problems.

To examine the dog, have someone hold him tightly. If he is resisting, have a strong helper hold him by the base of both ears. It may be necessary to have someone else hold his front legs so that he cannot paw you with them. If necessary, you can use a loop of gauze or 1/4 inch rope or cord to pull the lower jaw downward, opening the mouth so you can see clearly into it. If an object is visible, remove it, using a pair of forceps or clean needlenosed pliers. If the object has been there long enough to cause infection, the area may have a membrane of pus and debris built up over it. This should be gently removed with forceps or teased away from the surface with a cotton swab. All infected areas, as well as the place where the object was resting, can then be wiped with povidone-iodine solution. Use a cotton swab for a small area, or a pair of forceps holding a cotton ball for a larger area. The area should be swabbed once or twice a day until it is healed. Antibiotic treatment may be needed if the infection has involved a large area, or the dog is not feeling well.

TRENCH MOUTH

Trench mouth is caused by the overgrowth of bacteria and other organisms which normally inhabit the mouth. They cause problems after a predisposing factor, such as diabetes, damaged teeth, gum infection, autoimmune disease, hypothyroidism, kidney disease or other disease, has weakened the animal's resistance.

The gums may be reddened and swollen, and may be painful and bleed easily. If it progresses long enough, there may be ulcers throughout the mouth. The portion of the gums which holds the teeth in place may die, allowing the teeth to fall out. Periodontal disease is often present. In some cases, the saliva will be brownish and slimy, and may stain the face and front legs. The infection can also spread to the lungs, causing pneumonia.

Treatment of trench mouth begins by eliminating the original cause of the disease. Vitamin deficiencies, anemia, or diseases affecting the dog's general health must be treated. High doses of B-complex vitamins and vitamin C seem to help some dogs heal. Antibiotics are usually needed, often for several weeks. The type of antibiotic used will depend on the organism causing the problem, as well as whether a systemic disease is also involved. Yeast infections (often caused by *Candida* species) may require drugs such as nystatin. In addition to treating the original cause, the mouth will need to be cleaned out thoroughly and often. Mouthwash such as a weak potassium permanganate solution may be used. Have your pharmacist mix up a 1:4000 solution (Merck, 1973, p. 1520). Use it to flush the mouth or sponge the gums two or three times daily.

ULCERS IN THE MOUTH

Ulcers in the mouth may be associated with systemic diseases which reduce the animal's resistance. They can also be seen with kidney disease and diabetes as well as with foreign objects, and with damaged, fractured, irregular, or diseased teeth. Large accumulations of tartar may abrade the cheek or tongue and cause ulcers. The treatment of ulcers is the same as for foreign bodies between the teeth or for trench mouth. Deal with any underlying diseases and apply local treatment to the lesions in the mouth.

MOUTH BURNS

A dog may burn his mouth by biting an electric cord. This is particularly a problem with puppies. They will chew on almost anything. Or, the dog may eat or lick a caustic chemical in solid, powder, or liquid form. If the problem is chemical, you can rinse out the animal's mouth with lukewarm water. A small dog can be placed under a sink or bathtub faucet, while a garden hose works well for a larger animal. Rinse it for five to ten minutes. If you know that the chemical is acidic, neutralize it with baking soda. If it is alkaline, neutralize with vinegar or lemon juice. After rinsing and neutralizing, you probably should have your veterinarian look at the animal. It is possible that some of the chemical was swallowed and damaged the esophagus.

If the dog has not been observed to bite the cord or drink the chemical, your first signs may be a dog that does not eat or drink although he appears hungry or thirsty. Consider rabies (see below, and Rabies section.) You may see him salivating excessively, and he may not want you to handle his mouth or head. The mouth will show reddened membranes.

Keep the dog on a soft or liquid diet until he is healed. Flush the mouth with a solution of a teaspoon of salt per pint of lukewarm water. Or, you can use povidone-iodine solution. In most cases, using ointments on the affected surfaces (unless *Candida* yeast is involved) is of little or no use. Oral or injectible antibiotics may be needed for several days to help prevent the infection from going deeper—consult your veterinarian. Electrical and chemical burns in a dog's mouth can be hard to handle successfully.

ORAL TUMORS

Tumors are commonly seen in the mouth, especially in older dogs. Most of these tumors are malignant. "Malignant" means that they will grow rapidly and spread to other parts of the body. For the most part, those located in the rear of the mouth are more likely to be highly malignant than those in the front of the mouth. Since "benign" tumors are ones that are slow-growing, and don't tend to invade the tissues or spread to other

parts of the body) are uncommon, it is very important that any abnormal growth in your dog's mouth be examined as soon as possible, and probably removed at the earliest opportunity. All lumps should be considered malignant until proven otherwise. In some cases, radiation therapy is useful when combined with surgical removal of as much of the tumor as possible.

RABIES

Dogs with rabies may drip saliva, and may appear unable to swallow. These symptoms may cause you to think that the dog has something caught in his mouth. IF YOU HAVE ANY REASON TO BELIEVE YOUR DOG MAY HAVE RABIES, OR IF YOU LIVE IN AN AREA WHERE RABIES IS COMMON, DO NOT EXAMINE THE DOG'S MOUTH. TAKE HIM TO A VETERINARIAN IMMEDIATELY. Rabies is especially high on the list of possibilities if the mouth problems are accompanied by a change in the animal's voice or behavior or attitude. (For further information, see Rabies, in vaccinations chapter).

SALIVARY CYSTS

Salivary cysts (also called sialocele or mucocele) occur when saliva accumulates in the tissues around the salivary gland or duct. If it occurs under the jaw, it is sometimes called a ranula. This is the most common site.

These cysts occur when the salivary gland is plugged, either by infectious material, or when the duct is injured by being bitten by another dog, or hit, kicked, or otherwise damaged. The saliva can no longer exit through its normal channels, but is still being produced by the gland.

Saliva accumulates under the skin, making a soft, swollen mass, either under the jaw or on the side of the face behind the jawbone. The mass is cool (not hot, like an abscess.) It may be necessary for your veterinarian to clip a bit of hair from the area, disinfect it, and pop a needle (usually about 18 gauge, 1-inch) through the skin into the pocket. He will then attach a syringe and withdraw some of the fluid. If the swelling is a hematoma (blood-filled pocket,) blood (or serum, if it has been there for some time) will come into the syringe. If it is an abscess, the fluid may be pus, appearing whitish, greenish, yellowish, or tinged with blood, but will not be as bloody as the fluid from a hematoma. If it is a salivary cyst, the fluid will be mucus, and may be tinged with a small amount of blood. A tumor is slower-growing than any of these other problems, and would be firm, rather than fluid-filled.

Surgery is the only effective treatment. Your veterinarian will, in most cases, remove the contents of the cyst, and cauterize the lining so that it will not continue to produce fluid. He may have to re-establish a new duct if the old one is damaged. The surgery can be somewhat delicate, and is not always successful. In some dogs, it may be necessary to do a second surgery, and to make a permanent salivary duct which leads under the tongue, draining saliva there for the rest of the dog's life.

Some dogs may have an infection of the salivary gland similar to mumps. This swelling is usually firm or hard rather than fluctuant (fluid-filled.) It generally involves both sides of the jaw, just behind the vertical part of the jawbone. The salivary glands may remain hardened and slightly enlarged after the disease has passed. No treatment is needed.

FACIAL PARALYSIS

One side of the face may become paralyzed when the dog is hit by a vehicle or otherwise injured. Or, it may occur with inflammation of the inner ear, or problems within the brain. Facial paralysis can also be associated with tumors of the pituitary gland, or lack of thyroid hormone. Myasthenia gravis, similar to that in humans, can occasionally occur in dogs. Facial paralysis is uncommon in dogs.

A dog with facial paralysis will have a drooping ear on the paralyzed side. He will be unable to move the muscles that give him facial expression, so his nose may pull to the unaffected side. The eye on the damaged side may be opened wide, and he may not blink his eyelid if you gently touch the inner corner of the eye opening (toward the nose.) Keep the dog's eye moist if he is not blinking the lid, using any mild antibiotic eye ointment. Have him examined by your veterinarian. Food may pack inside the cheek on the affected side. You may have to experiment with suitable foods until you find one the dog can eat easily. These dogs will usually need careful feeding for the rest of their lives.

Depending on the cause and degree of damage, some dogs may recover slight function over a LONG period of time. Other dogs never recover, and may require eye drops or ointment to keep the eye moist. In some cases, the eyelids may be sutured closed so that the eye does not dry out.

ESOPHAGEAL STRICTURES

Constriction of the esophagus is generally due to the presence of scar tissue. The scarring may be because the dog has drunk or eaten a strong acid or alkali. It may occur after a foreign body, such as a bone or ball, has become lodged in the dog's esophagus. Or, it may occur when the dog is anesthetized and food mixed with acid flows backward into the esophagus. This is just one more good reason for a STRICT fast and an EMPTY stomach before your dog goes in for elective surgery. Because it takes some time for scar tissue to develop, strictures may occur weeks to months after the initial injury to the esophagus.

A dog with an esophageal stricture usually cannot eat solid food. He may vomit it, while keeping down liquids or gruels. Many of these dogs have ravenous appetites, yet lose weight because the food doesn't make it to the stomach. They do not usually show any signs of pain or discomfort.

Your veterinarian will diagnose this problem by giving the dog liquid barium to drink, followed by an X-ray of the esophagus while it is coated by the barium.

Two treatments are available. One is surgery, which is estimated to have less than a 50% success rate. The other is to anesthetize the dog and gradually stretch the area to a more normal size by threading dilators through it. This should only be attempted by a veterinarian who is trained in and familiar with the procedure. If your veterinarian is not, ask him for a referral to a university hospital or to a surgical specialist who is. Even in the most skilled hands, the procedure occasionally results in further injury and even more scarring.

FOREIGN BODIES IN STOMACH

A foreign body may be anything that the dog swallows other than food, water, or medication. He may eat metal, wood, rubber, cloth, etc. The dog may swallow a large bone as he chews on it. He may eat a wad of aluminum foil soaked with grease from a barbecue. Puppies may eat rubber balls, pieces of children's toys, or nylon stockings. A dog whose owner throws stones for him to retrieve may accidentally (or deliberately) swallow one of them. Dogs who have swallowed recently-made pennies may suffer from zinc poisoning (see Zinc Toxicity.)

Signs associated with the ingestion of foreign bodies are quite variable. Some objects may remain in the stomach for long periods of time without causing illness. Others will cause serious illness almost immediately. The dog may vomit occasionally, especially after he has eaten solid food. He may gradually lose weight. A large, rough object, such as a bone with sharp points, may irritate the stomach severely. It may tear the stomach lining, causing the dog to vomit blood. On rare occasions, the object may completely perforate the stomach wall, causing peritonitis.

Surprisingly, dogs are able to pass many odd items without damage. So, if you have seen your dog swallow something, do not try to get him to vomit. The anatomy of the stomach is such that it will probably not come back up. Wait and see if vomiting develops. Also, watch the stools for a few days to see whether the object passes. If the dog has swallowed string, cut off any that is still in his mouth or hanging out of it. Watch to see if the rest of it is passed.

A history of swallowing various objects, or of intermittent vomiting after meals, is suggestive of a foreign body in the stomach. Your veterinarian will probably diagnose the foreign body by taking an X-ray. The object may be visible on a plain film. Or, it may be necessary to give barium, which will coat the object and make it visible.

Some small objects can be removed from the stomach by passing an endoscope and pulling the object through it. Larger objects may require abdominal surgery for removal. If surgery is necessary, have it done soon, while the dog is still in good condition. Don't let him go downhill until he is unable to handle the surgery.

VOMITING

Vomiting is fairly common in dogs. Because of the structure of the stomach and esophagus, and the type of muscle of which they are made, dogs can vomit voluntarily and with little discomfort. Vomiting can occur from causes which have nothing to do with digestive tract illness. Dogs may vomit because they have become excited after eating (such as with vigorous play), have overeaten, or are worked soon after eating. They sometimes vomit if they become very thirsty, and then overdrink. They can also vomit to get rid of foods which they do not like. Sudden changes in diet may cause vomiting. Dogs will also vomit to get rid of garbage, or food which has spoiled from being in the dish too long. They may vomit from eating pieces of bone, or junk like aluminum foil and plastic. Dogs may also vomit because of motion sickness. So, occasional vomiting is not a cause for alarm, especially if you can see a reason for it. Frequent vomiting, on the other hand, should be cause for concern.

If your dog has vomited for one of the above reasons, keep him off food and water for a couple of hours. During this period, you can give him ice cubes to lick. Drugs such as Maalox®, Kaopectate®, and Pepto-Bismol® can be given to coat the stomach. (See below for dosages.) After a couple of hours, give water, about 1/3 cup at a time. He may WANT more than this, but if you overload him, it will just come back up again. And, repeated vomiting can irritate the stomach leading to yet more vomiting. Give water every 10 minutes or so until you have satisfied the dog's thirst and can put a dish of water down for him. Wait two to three hours (or until his next routine meal) before you give him any more food. Give 1/2 to 3/4 of his normal feeding, and then resume regular feedings at the next meal if he does not do any more vomiting.

Spitting up small amounts of whitish or greenish phlegm may mean that the stomach is empty at the time of vomiting, or that the dog has been eating grass. Vomiting or spitting up small amounts of phlegm may be due to an irritation in the stomach, or to an infection in the throat or tonsils. In any case, if it persists, have the dog checked by your veterinarian. Some dogs seem to eat grass like we would eat a vegetable, and do not vomit it. Don't worry about them.

Vomiting blood IS a cause for alarm. In this case, your dog should be examined as soon as possible. Vomiting which persists for any length of time is also a reason to have the dog examined, even if it is small in quantity. Vomiting when accompanied by depression, listlessness, and fever is often the sign of a systemic disease, and the dog should be checked the same day, if at all possible. Disease of the pancreas will cause vomiting, and so will kidney failure, liver disease, and infectious diseases such as hepatitis, distemper, or leptospirosis. Vomiting accompanied by weakness, depression, frequent (but unsuccessful) attempts to urinate, bloody stools, or severe abdominal pain are also indications for an immediate visit to your veterinarian.

Dogs who have swallowed a foreign object (a ball, toy, stone, etc.) will vomit, usually a short time after they have eaten. They may otherwise appear normal. Have the dog checked. X-rays may be needed to determine whether a foreign body in the stomach is the problem. Do not throw stones for your dog to chase or catch, and make sure that toys for your dog are too large to be swallowed. The dog should not be allowed to chew small pieces of children's toys, either.

Dosages of medications to help control vomiting and soothe the stomach are as follows: Pepto-Bismol® - 1/2 tsp. per 10 lb. (2.5 ml. per 4.5 Kg.), Kaopectate® - 2 tsp. per 10 lb. (10 ml. per 4.5 Kg.). Give either of these every four hours.

If you are using Maalox®, give 1/2 tsp. per 10 lb. (2.5 ml. per 4.5 Kg.) every eight hours. If your dog is on any other medication, consult your veterinarian before giving any treatment, for two reasons: 1) The medication itself may be causing the vomiting; 2) The vomiting may prevent absorption of the drug, and it may be necessary to change to an injectible form until the vomiting is under control.

TORSION OF THE STOMACH/GASTRIC DILATATION

Dogs who attempt to vomit and cannot bring up any material, and who at the same time have a swollen, painful abdomen may have a torsion of the stomach. This causes gastric dilatation (swelling) because, as the stomach twists, it closes off the opening where food enters the stomach. It can also close off the exit into the intestines. Gastric torsion occurs primarily in larger, deep-chested dogs such as German Shepherds, Great Danes, Irish Setters, St. Bernards, retrievers, etc. The cause is unknown. Apparently the stomach first becomes overfilled and distended with gas. Then, it turns around itself, closing off both the inlet and the outlet. The food which is trapped in the stomach ferments, and the stomach glands secrete digestive juices. More gas is produced, which causes the stomach to become enlarged like a balloon, and be extremely painful because there is no place for the gas to go. The dog cannot belch it up, or move it on through the intestine.

Dogs with torsion of the stomach will attempt to vomit, retching violently. They may salivate profusely, and may be restless and panting, and have vague abdominal pain. The abdomen behind the last rib may appear bloated and full. It will sound hollow if you thump it gently with a finger, like you were testing a watermelon. If this condition is not treated promptly, the dog may collapse and die. THIS IS AN EMERGENCY—GET THE DOG TO A VETERINARIAN AS SOON AS POSSIBLE. MINUTES COUNT. Handle the dog gently. Even asking it to walk a short distance may cause irreversible shock and death.

The veterinarian will try to pass a stomach tube to remove some of the gas and fluid. If this cannot be done, the dog may immediately be taken to surgery. A local anesthetic is given, and an opening in the abdomen made so that the pressure may be relieved through the wall of the stomach.

In some cases of torsion of the stomach (whether pressure is relieved via a stomach tube or through an incision), the decision may be made to anchor the stomach. This may be done by stapling or suturing it to the floor of the abdominal cavity or to the area of one of the ribs so that it is less likely to twist again. In most cases, this surgery will insure that the problem does not recur. Damage to the spleen may also have occurred, and it may have to be removed in part or completely. This is not a problem—dogs seem to do quite well without a spleen. If portions of the stomach wall have died because of pressure and loss of blood supply, they will have to be removed, too.

Surgery to repair the damage will need to be done immediately, in order to remove portions of the stomach, spleen, and intestine which have had their blood supply cut off and have died. The surgery is risky and involved because so many organs are affected. Strong supportive measures, such as large amounts of intravenous fluids, will be needed to keep the dog alive during and after surgery. Delay in performing surgery will certainly result in the death of the dog. The surgery is expensive because it is delicate, difficult, time-consuming, and it requires extensive life support. Make your decision immediately whether to have the dog treated or euthanize him. You have no time to delay—the dog won't recover without surgery.

Dogs who chronically overeat may be more likely to have a torsion. Prevention may include feeding the dog four or five times a day, a small amount each time. Do not return to once a day feeding, even after surgery, as this may increase the risk of recurrence. Do not allow strenuous exercise for an hour before the dog eats, and for at least an hour afterward. Make sure that water is available at all times so the dog does not become thirsty and then overdrink. Some people feel that a low-fat, bland diet may be helpful. Some also feel that excess calcium in the diet may predispose a dog to bloat by causing excess secretion of gastrin, a hormone made by the stomach lining (Walsh, 1975.) Feed a diet which has a controlled amount of calcium and avoid excesses of this nutrient from any source. Do not give the dog antacids or medicines which may contain calcium.

Other preventive measures are: try to avoid feeding foods which might cause gas formation in the stomach. Some dogs have trouble with gas when fed products containing large amounts of soybeans, while others have no problem. If you change foods, do so VERY gradually, over a period of one to two weeks. Avoid feeding all but the smallest amounts of table scraps or you may invite digestive upset. Some authorities feel that feeding wet food (canned food or moistened dry food) may be helpful in preventing torsion. No particular brand or type of food has been found to cause more problems than any other. Select one food and stay with it—do not change brands once you find one that works with your dog.

There is some evidence that the currently popular conformation may be a contributing factor to torsion of the stomach. For example, forty or so years ago German Shepherds had a level topline (from withers to rump,) and a "chest" and "waist" which were about the same diameter. Now, the breed standards are for the dog to be high at the withers and low at the rump, giving a deeply sloping topline from front to rear. Meanwhile, the chest has been changed to be extremely deep vertically, especially just behind the front legs, and the waist area has become very tucked up and small. Do these conformational changes contribute to the problem? No one is sure, but forty years ago veterinarians considered this a VERY rare problem.

This disease has also been called gastric dilatation volvulus (GDV), bloat, acute gastric dilatation, and gastric volvulus, in case your veterinarian uses one of these terms.

DIARRHEA

Diarrhea is a common problem in small animals. Most frequently, it is a temporary problem caused by dietary factors. For example, raw eggs can cause diarrhea in some dogs. And, if milk or rich gravies are added to the dog's food, or fed along with it, these may cause diarrhea. Removal of the offending food will usually stop the diarrhea. Excessive quantities of fats or oils in the diet may also cause diarrhea. If you are feeding fats or oil to deal with coat dryness or to provide extra calories for the working dog, be sure to add it to the diet gradually, increasing to the amount you wish to feed over a two-week period. If diarrhea occurs, reduce the quantity given, down to the point where the diarrhea stops.

A change in food can cause diarrhea, especially if the change is made suddenly. Eating garbage or spoiled food may cause diarrhea. Are you or your neighbors feeding your dog inappropriate foods? Some small dogs seem to have delicate digestive systems, and are easily upset by even minor changes in diet, resulting in vomiting and/or diarrhea. Table foods, especially if they are spicy, cause problems for some dogs. Other dogs will have diarrhea when given foods to which they are allergic.

A change of water or routine while traveling may cause diarrhea, as can fright or nervousness from being in unfamiliar surroundings. Some dogs may show diarrhea at times during bouts of vigorous exercise. This may be due to excitement or unexpected exercise and usually goes away after a few bowel movements.

Treatment with antibiotics may kill bacteria in the intestine, or change their kind and quantity. This may cause diarrhea. If your dog is on this type of medication and develops diarrhea, check with your veterinarian. He may be able to prescribe a different drug.

Some types of worms and other intestinal parasites can cause diarrhea. It may be a chronic, continuous diarrhea, or it may come and go between periods of normal stools. Diarrhea caused by internal parasites may be bloody, and should be checked by your veterinarian. Some of the parasites which cause diarrhea in dogs and cats are contagious to humans. For this reason, it is important to determine whether parasites are causing a dog's diarrhea, especially if it comes and goes, or does not clear up with home treatment.

Viruses and bacteria can cause diarrhea, and some of these are contagious from one dog to another. Diarrhea is one of the most prominent symptoms of both parvovirus and coronavirus infections. It can also be seen in the later stages of canine distemper, usually after the respiratory symptoms have been resolved. In some cases, it may accompany the respiratory symptoms. Chemical poisonings can cause diarrhea, but, fortunately, they are quite rare. Garbage eating is a much more common cause. Colitis (an inflammation of the large intestine) is also a relatively common cause of diarrhea.

Puppies and small dogs have very little in reserve to protect them against the weakness and dehydration that can accompany diarrhea. For that reason, their condition should be closely observed.

If the diarrhea is slight, and the dog has no other symptoms, keep him off food for the day. Give a medication such as Pepto-Bismol® or Kaopectate® in the same dosages used to control vomiting (see Vomiting). If the diarrhea persists, if it is bloody, or if the dog otherwise shows illness, have him examined by your veterinarian.

Medium and large-sized adult dogs with diarrhea should be taken off food for 24 hours. They can be given clear broth after five or six hours, but no solid food until the next day. Puppies have little reserve and should be given small amounts of food at regular intervals. Both puppies and adult dogs of any size must have water available at all times to help avoid dehydration.

After 24 hours, start the dog back on four to five small meals a day of his regular food, gradually working up to normal feeding quantities and times. Or, for a couple of days, you can use a food which is specially made for digestive tract problems. This type of food will contain only a small percentage of fiber. (If your dog has colitis, this type of diet is not indicated. A diet high in fiber may be needed, instead.) Carbohydrates in the diet should be easily digested. Also, the diet should provide a moderate amount of highly digestible protein. Avoid all table scraps, snacks, bones, and rawhide chews until the dog is well. These items may complicate the diarrhea and prolong healing.

Contact your veterinarian if the diarrhea lasts more than 48 hours, or if the dog shows signs of general systemic illness, such as vomiting, listlessness, depression, fever, etc.

Some dogs with severe dehydration will need intravenous fluids to stabilize their condition before the cause of the diarrhea can be diagnosed. Check the dog for dehydration by picking up a pinch of the skin over the ribs between your thumb and forefinger. Pull it upward about an inch, hold it there for a few seconds, and let it go. In the normal dog, it should spring back fairly quickly and stretch itself flat. In the dehydrated dog, the little ridge of skin will just stand there, or it may take five to ten seconds to flatten back to normal.

If the diarrhea goes on for a long period of time, your veterinarian may wish to take a biopsy of the intestine. A tiny section of tissue will be removed through a small surgical opening made in the abdominal wall. Only a stitch or two will be needed to close the opening. This procedure is done under sedation or general anesthetic.

CAMPYLOBACTERIOSIS

Until a few years ago, this disease was called vibriosis. It is a bacterial disease that causes diarrhea, especially in young puppies. The dog may have a poor appetite, and lack the energy to move around or play. Worms may be found on the fecal examination, and be considered the cause of the problem. After worming, the dog doesn't get well, and still has the diarrhea. Take him back to your veterinarian to be re-examined. It may be necessary for him to perform laboratory tests on a sample of the loose feces in order to find the bacteria which are present.

Campylobacteriosis is especially common in puppies from animal shelters or other areas where large numbers of dogs are gathered. The bacterium is normally found in the digestive tracts of many animals, where it causes little or no problem until it contaminates meat or milk. Pasteurization of milk and cooking of meat will kill the organism and prevent its spread.

This disease is usually treated with erythromycin or another suitable antibiotic.

One of the biggest problems with campylobacter infection is that it is also contagious to humans. If your dog has it, the best and safest course of action is to hospitalize him until the infection is well under control. If you can't do this, keep him confined to the smallest area possible, preferably one that is easy to clean. Thoroughly wash and disinfect all containers and materials that come into contact with the dog. Be sure to wash and disinfect your hands after you have handled the dog, or anything that comes into contact with him. Keep children from handling him (even petting!) until he is well.

In humans, the disease is more severe in young children, for the same reason it is more dangerous for puppies—lack of reserves. It causes vomiting, sharp stomach pains, and diarrhea, which may contain mucus (Williams, 1988).

PROTOZOAL DIARRHEA

Diarrhea caused by protozoan parasites such as *Coccidia* (called coccidiosis), *Trichomonas*, or *Giardia* is contagious from one dog to another. These organisms are normally present in the digestive tract in very small numbers. They multiply if the dog is stressed or sick, or his digestive tract is irritated by other problems such as worms or a viral infection. Diarrhea caused by these parasites cannot be treated by wormers, nor are they affected by antibiotics. Some home remedies may help temporarily, but the disease will inevitably return.

These diseases are spread from one dog to another by contact with feces from an infected dog. A healthy dog may lick his feet after having walked where a dog with the disease has defecated, and become infected. It can be spread by contact with contaminated water or food dishes left in pens where sick animals have been held. Protozoal diarrhea is a particular problem where numbers of young puppies are brought together, such as pet shops and kennels.

Dogs with protozoal diarrhea have a watery or "mushy" diarrhea, loss of appetite, and weight loss. Vomiting is sometimes seen. The disease is much more severe in weakened or young animals. It, in turn, can weaken the animal still further, making it susceptible to other diseases.

Your veterinarian will diagnose the disease by examining a stool sample under the microscope. In some dogs, several samples may be needed over a period of a few days, as it can be difficult to find the organisms on a single sample. The organisms tend to occur in waves and aren't present all the time. He will treat the dog with a drug which is specific for protozoan parasites.

Good nursing care will be needed to bring the pet through the disease, especially for a young puppy or very small dog. Keep the dog's cage or yard and his bedding dry, clean, and free of bowel movements because reinfection from his own feces can occur. Feed a high-quality, balanced diet, and make sure the dog eats! Encourage your dog to drink. Diarrhea can quickly cause dehydration. Replacement of the lost fluids helps prevent dehydration. Keep infected dogs away from healthy dogs. Isolate new dogs until you are sure they are free from infection. Isolate the affected pet to keep it from spreading the disease. If you have more than one dog, keep the sick one in a cage or kennel so that he cannot contaminate the yard, or another dog's food or water dishes. Disinfect runs and kennels with chlorine bleach (diluted 1:30 in water) or Lysol solution, diluted with water. Give vitamins as needed to help increase the dog's appetite and keep up his strength. Return the dog to your veterinarian for a recheck if he quits eating or drinking, becomes weaker, vomits more than occasionally, or if the diarrhea continues for more than two days without improvement after treatment has been started.

INTESTINAL OBSTRUCTION

Intestinal obstruction is occasionally seen in young puppies, and diarrhea may be one of the signs. In any dog with a diarrheal problem which does not clear up rapidly with home treatment, or is accompanied by other signs of illness, X-rays (possibly with barium,) laboratory blood and fecal examinations, and other tests may be needed to determine the cause of the problem. Do not let your dog play with string or yarn, as they may cause a fatal intestinal obstruction when swallowed.

CONSTIPATION

Constipation is a condition where the dog has infrequent stools, or strains to pass feces. The bowel movements which are passed may be small, hard, and dry. Do not worry if your dog does not have a bowel movement every day. Normal dogs, especially if not eating much and not getting much exercise, may only have bowel movements every two or three days.

Constipation is more often related to dietary problems than to any other cause. An irregular or imbalanced diet may cause constipation. An inadequate water supply is sure to cause it sooner or later, especially if you are feeding a dry food. Remember that the dog's body is 75% water. But, the water doesn't stay put. It keeps coming out the back end so you have to keep it going in the front end. If you are using an automatic or lick-type waterer, check it every couple of days to make sure that it is functioning normally. Check it once a day in hot climates, or the dog may be dead before he has a chance to develop constipation.

Feeding bones which the dog can crunch or chew up and swallow will often cause a stubborn constipation, or even an impaction necessitating surgical removal. For this reason, do NOT give your dog pork chop or rib bones, chicken or turkey bones, or any other bones which he can chew to pieces. Pieces of wood, foil, or plastic eaten by the dog may also cause constipation, as will hair or other foreign materials.

Older dogs often have trouble with constipation simply because their digestive system is less active. Older dogs receive less exercise as well. Changing to a diet with more bulk may be helpful. Giving the dog more exercise, within his physical ability, may be helpful, too. Two or three short walks each day may do more good than one long hike. Give the dog time to putter around and smell the smells which will help to encourage him to have a bowel movement. If you exercise him half an hour to an hour after you have fed him, this may also promote a bowel movement. Prostate disease, nervous disorders of the large intestine, tumors, and endocrine disorders or metabolic problems may also cause constipation in the older dog. Have him checked by your veterinarian if the problem persists.

A dog with hard feces impacted in the colon may strain, and pass little or no stool. He may be depressed, and may vomit or pass foul-smelling, blood-streaked stools.

Long-haired dogs may have fecal material caked onto the hair under their tails until they can no longer defecate at all. This is a horrible, foul-smelling mess, and the only way to fix it is to cut it off. Use clippers or scissors to cut off all the hair at the skin level until the entire mess is removed. Hair may have to be cut from the underside of the tail as well as the hind legs. Then, gently wash the whole area, using povidone-iodine solution. Afterward, a soothing cream may be applied. If sores are present, the dog may need injectible or oral antibiotics in addition to the local treatment of the area. Keep the hair in the area clipped to avoid having the problem in the future.

Mild cases of constipation may be treated by adding Metamucil® to the food. Give 2 teaspoons per 10 lb body weight up to a maximum of 6 teaspoons (10 ml per 4.5 Kg up to 30 ml maximum.) Metamucil® should NOT be used if your dog has kidney disease. Laxative products made for pets are also available. One of these is Laxatone® (Evsco.) It comes either in a squeeze tube like toothpaste, or in a pump dispenser. These products are flavored especially for pets, and most dogs take them readily.

DO NOT try to pour mineral oil down your dog's mouth. He cannot taste it, and instead of swallowing it, he might inhale it into his lungs. The resulting pneumonia could kill him. Another problem with mineral oil is that if given over a period of several days, it will tie up vitamins from the dog's body, and may eventually result in a vitamin deficiency. It is far safer to use another laxative.

Dogs who are straining to pass small quantities of blood-streaked feces may be given a pediatric Fleet® enema. Follow the package directions. Try this no more than twice. If it does not produce results and relief, consult your veterinarian. These enemas should not be used on puppies or small dogs unless recommended by your veterinarian. They should also not be used for dogs with kidney problems, or those who are taking diuretics for water retention.

A dog food containing a higher quantity of fiber will help to compensate for a less active digestive tract in the older dog, much as it does in humans. The bulk helps to stimulate the walls of the digestive tract, aiding the movement of food materials through the intestine. The fiber also helps to hold water in the intestine, softening the stool and making it easier for the dog to have a bowel movement. Don't feed your dog bones, snacks, or rawhide chews (if he eats them) if he is prone to constipation. Finally, the only thing your dog should ever eat, whether he is prone to constipation or not, is clean, wholesome, nutritious food and treats. Keep him away from and don't let him chew on, eat, or swallow anything else.

Splintering bones, rocks, string, yarn, garbage, foil, paper—the list of foreign materials is endless—can all, at one time or another, cause problems.

PANCREATITIS

The term pancreatitis refers to an inflammation of the pancreas. This organ, on the upper part of the small intestine, provides enzymes to the digestive tract. It also produces insulin to regulate the animal's blood sugar levels. Pancreatic insufficiency, in contrast to pancreatitis, is a deficiency of the products of this gland, whether digestive enzymes or insulin.

Acute pancreatitis can come on suddenly, and is very painful. The dog may show severe abdominal pain, and may have a fever. He will show depression and vomiting, and may have diarrhea. Signs of diabetes may also be seen because the inflamed pancreas is not producing enough insulin.

Pancreatitis can be VERY difficult to diagnose. Your veterinarian will use a combination of clinical signs and laboratory tests, often accompanied by a lucky guess, to make the diagnosis.

Some cases of acute pancreatitis improve within a day or two without treatment. The digestive organs get a rest because the dog will not eat. This period of inactivity gives the body a chance to repair the damage. However, some dogs won't eat or drink for many days. Eventually, if the problem is not diagnosed, the dog may have to be euthanized because he is starving to death and no cause is found to treat.

In cases of chronic pancreatitis, enough of the pancreas may have been destroyed that slowly, over time, the dog will have problems digesting food. He may have chronic diarrhea, and lose weight or stay very thin, even though he eats normal quantities of good food. He may have grayish, foamy stools. While the pancreas will never return to normal, the dog can have a normal life by supplementation with pancreatic enzymes to help him digest his food, and insulin to control diabetes (if it is present.)

Some dogs with pancreatitis may eat their own feces. When the problem is diagnosed and digestive enzymes are provided, this behavior usually stops. Dogs who are lacking in digestive enzymes may, in some cases, be helped by adding a teaspoon of meat tenderizer containing papain to each feeding. Your veterinarian can advise you, or, perhaps, prescribe a pharmaceutical preparation containing the necessary enzymes.

COLITIS

Colitis is a condition in which the large bowel (the colon) becomes inflamed and irritated. It may strike suddenly, or come on gradually, over a long period of time. If the problem develops rapidly, it may respond to less than a month of therapy, and heal well. If it has come on gradually, it may be more chronic, lasting for years, or even for the rest of the dog's life.

The inflammation of the colon causes the intestine to be less effective than normal at absorbing water back from the material in the digestive tract. Because of excess water being present, the main sign of colitis is diarrhea. The loose stool may be streaked with blood or mucus. The diarrhea may be continuous, or it may come and go. The dog may be depressed. He may have a fever, and show abdominal pain, weight loss, and his coat may be dull and dry.

Colitis may be caused by a number of different agents, including bacteria, viruses, parasites, tumors, food allergies, or the ingestion of a foreign body. Colitis should be suspected when your dog does not respond to standard treatment for diarrhea, and if the diarrhea persists for a period of time. Your veterinarian may need to run an entire battery of tests, including bacterial cultures, fecal exam for intestinal parasites, X-rays (possibly with barium to show irregularities and defects in the intestinal lining,) and colonoscopy (visually inspecting the colon with a lighted fiber optic tube inserted into the anus.) Biopsy of the colon and exploratory surgery to examine the abdominal organs may be needed. Additional tests may be needed throughout the course of the treatment to monitor the dog's progress.

The majority of cases of colitis, especially the chronic ones, cannot be cured. They can, however, in most cases, be managed well enough that the dog can live a nearly normal life.

Two approaches are commonly used to treat colitis. The first approach is to increase the amount of fiber in the animal's diet. Fiber can be, and often is, used to treat constipation. It can also be used to treat the diarrhea of colitis. The fiber stabilizes and lengthens the amount of time material takes to move through the intestine. This allows more water to be absorbed from the food material, and less to be lost in the stool.

The second approach is to feed a hypoallergenic diet, to avoid food allergies which may be at the root of the problem. With some dogs, it may be necessary to try both diets (high fiber diet and hypoallergenic diet) for a period of time, then use the one which works the best. A trial of two to six weeks may be needed on each diet in order to give it a fair evaluation. The diarrhea may become worse for several days before the dog's digestive tract stabilizes and adjusts to the new food. Be patient and give it some time. Whatever you are feeding, feed only the prescribed food. Do not feed ANY treats, bones, or anything else. Do not give ANY "people food" at all, or you may put the dog back to where you and he started, a miserable situation for the dog and an expensive proposition for you. Drugs may be used to help control the diarrhea and relieve the inflammation and pain. In some cases, antibiotics will be given to control related infections.

GALL BLADDER DISEASE

Gall bladder disease and gall stones are uncommon in dogs. Some dogs may have stones for many years without any signs or ill effects. Occasionally, gall stones may plug one of the bile ducts, causing liver disease. When signs are seen, they may include jaundice (yellow coloration of the mucous membranes) and vomiting. The dog may have a poor appetite, lose weight, and he may be dehydrated. The urine may be dark yellow to orange in color. Some dogs may have jaundice which comes and goes, with episodes of vomiting, over a period of years. The dog with an acute case of gall bladder trouble may show abdominal pain. In some cases, the stools may be clay colored because no bile is present to give them their normal color.

Gall bladder disease may initially be treated with antibiotics to control infection in the damaged area. Fluids may be needed to correct dehydration and electrolyte imbalances. As soon as the dog is medically stabilized, surgery may be performed to remove either the stones or the entire gallbladder, depending upon the problem. The dog may be kept on antibiotics for some time after surgery, again to control infection.

If gall stones have existed for a long time, and the bile ducts leading out of the liver have been blocked, liver damage may have occurred. The damage may be so extensive that the animal will never return to normal, even after surgery.

COPROPHAGIA

Dogs sometimes eat their own and other dogs' feces. When this behavior is seen in a dog that always seems to be hungry, is losing weight, and has an excessive appetite, the cause may be pancreatitis. The dog may eating his own wastes because they still contain many nutrients due to his inability to digest his food. Tests to determine whether this problem is present can be run by your veterinarian (see Pancreatitis.)

When coprophagia is seen in a dog of normal weight who is healthy, it is usually considered to be a vice. It may start because of boredom, especially in dogs confined to a kennel. The puppy may start to play with his feces because he is bored, and then begin to eat them. Coprophagia may occur when dogs are closely confined or overcrowded. It may begin from a bitch normally consuming her puppies' wastes to clean their bed area. And, one dog may learn this habit from watching another dog eat droppings.

In any case, after the habit has continued for a time, it usually becomes a firmly established vice. A medication is available to give in the dog's feed. It makes the feces unacceptable, so that the dog will not eat them. The problem is that when the medication is stopped, the dog usually resumes the vice. Most owners get tired of feeding the medication indefinitely, and give up, allowing the dog to do as it wishes. It has been suggested that putting a drop or two of anise oil or monosodium glutamate in his food may give the dog's stools a taste which the dog will find unpleasant.

The dog cannot eat feces that are not present. Keeping the kennel or housing area clean will eliminate the problem. You can schedule your dog's feeding times so that you can plan to clean up after him about a half-hour later. Plenty of exercise outside the kennel will help, as will a kennel large enough so the dog does not feel closely confined. Provide suitable toys and chew items such as large bones. Self-feeding (free choice) may help with some dogs who are left alone for long periods of time. If you choose self-feeding, make sure the dog does not overeat and become obese.

Dogs, especially farm dogs, often eat the feces of cattle or horses. These seem to be some sort of delicacy. They may take in eggs of parasites of these species, but the worms will not develop in the dog. This habit poses no threat to the dog. You, however, may object for esthetic reasons.

Dogs will often eat the contents of a cat's litter box. Cat food is extremely high in protein. Some of the protein is passed in the feces, making them attractive to the dog. Because some cat parasites can occasionally be infective to dogs, dogs should not have access to a cat's litter box.

ANAL GLANDS

Properly called anal sacs, two of these small glands lie beside and slightly below the anal opening, at about the 4 o'clock and 8 o'clock positions. They are about the size of a pea or larger when they are filled. Each sac has a small duct which opens into the anus. They are evolutionary relics in the dog. Their walls are lined with small glands which produce a fluid secretion that is musky and unpleasant smelling. The scent glands in a skunk are fully functioning anal sacs and certainly are not relics! In the dog, fluid is passed with each bowel movement. It probably serves to help the dog mark his territory. The dog may also squeeze these sacs out when frightened.

Many dogs, however, have glands which fail to empty properly. The duct becomes blocked, and the secretions accumulate. As the glands become full, they press on the adjacent structures, and the dog becomes uncomfortable. He may sit and scoot along the floor, dragging his hind end. This dragging causes some people to think the dog has "worms." This action is one of the most common signs of full, uncomfortable anal glands. Or, the dog may lick or bite at his hind end. He may strain and have pain when he has a bowel movement.

Anal gland problems are more common in smaller dogs, probably because the openings to the glands are smaller and less likely to empty by themselves. A too-soft diet may not give enough firmness to the feces for it to press on the glands as the dog defecates. Obese dogs may have poor muscle tone, including the muscles around the anal glands. A dog with a seborrhea who is producing excessive secretions all over his body may also have excessive anal sac secretions.

With any of these problems, the contents of the anal glands may remain in the gland rather than being emptied gradually, a little at a time, as is normal. The glands may then become inflamed or even infected, causing an abscess. This may break and drain to the outside, leaving an opening near the anus which is oozing an odorous, blood-tinged material. Or, the material may harden inside the gland, called "impaction". The abscess may be felt as a hard mass just under the skin on the side of the anus. One or both glands may be involved. With either an abscess or an impacted gland, the skin over the area may be discolored, and the dog may show severe pain.

Many dogs, especially smaller ones, need to have their anal glands squeezed out regularly to give the animal relief. This may be needed every six weeks to three or four months. The dog will usually show discomfort, chewing, and scooting when it is time to do it again. You can take the dog to your veterinarian to have it done.

Or, you can squeeze the anal glands out yourself in one of several ways. Some dogs get relief by having the whole anal area squeezed with a wad of paper towel across the entire area, from side to side. Or, you can put on a disposable glove, and lubricate your index finger with petroleum jelly or a similar product. Insert this finger about an inch into the anus, and squeeze the thumb and index finger together, first at the four o'clock position,and later at the 8 o'clock position. You will feel the anal gland as a nodule in the skin, from the size of a pea to a small marble. No matter how you do it, if the anal gland feels hard, like a small pebble, and you cannot squeeze any material out of it, it might be impacted and you'll need assistance from your veterinarian.

You can squeeze moderately hard. This is often necessary if some of the material has dried and clogged the duct leading from the gland. Be sure to keep your face out of the way, as it can squirt out quite forcefully. The brownish secretions will end up inside the glove and can be disposed of by turning it inside out as you pull it off your hand. Because the secretions are quite odorous, the whole operation is best done outdoors, wearing old clothes, just before you give your dog a bath. Wipe the dog's anal area gently with a dampened paper towel or cotton wad to clean it for him, when you are finished. The dog may be slightly uncomfortable for a day or so after you have emptied his anal glands. He may avoid having a bowel movement. It may be helpful to give him a bit of pet laxative, or a meal that is slightly laxative one feeding after the anal glands are expressed (see Constipation, above.)

If the glands are untreated, or if the openings are too small for them to be cleaned out well, an abscess may form. It may be so painful that the dog avoids having a bowel movement.

If unnoticed long enough, the abscess may break and drain to the outside, leaving a raw, painful sore. If caught in time, before it breaks and drains, your veterinarian may lance it to provide drainage. In either case, the dog will have an open sore that you will need to swab out for some days or weeks. It is not pleasant but it WILL heal with time.

Some dogs have continuing problems with anal gland drainage or even abscesses. In these cases, it may be necessary to surgically remove the glands. Your veterinarian will take them out. The surgical opening may be either left open or sutured shut. Healing may take a bit of time. You may need to swab these areas until they are healed. After the healing is complete, you (and your dog) will be glad not to have the problem any longer.

PERIANAL FISTULA

Perianal fistula occurs when draining tracts, called fistulas, develop in the area of the anus. The fistulas seem to be caused by the dog's tail spreading a film of feces across the hind end, contaminating the hair follicles and glands in the area. They become infected which results in non-healing tracts that continuously ooze pus and have a very foul odor. It is most common in German Shepherds, and is also seen in Retrievers and Setters. The condition is more common in dogs over 7 years of age than in younger animals. Dogs with fistulas may have other skin problems. They may also have contributing problems, such as low levels of thyroid hormone.

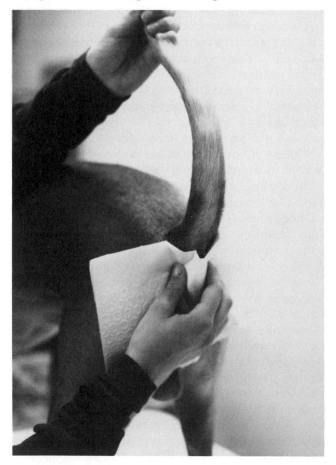

Expressing anal glands with paper towel.

Expressing anal glands, using gloved finger.

The draining tracts are filled with chronic inflammatory tissue. They often tunnel from the skin surface into the lining of the rectum and anus. Because of the involvement of deeper tissues, severe infection may result if the disease is not treated as soon as possible.

The dog may try to lick and bite the anal area and the surrounding skin. He may have a changed attitude, lowered appetite, straining, and diarrhea.

Antibiotics, steroids, and other medical treatments, by themselves, are not effective. Surgery will be required. Your veterinarian may wish, however, to put the dog on antibiotic treatment for a week to ten days prior to surgery. This helps to control infection in the area, making the surgery easier and safer (Greiner, 1981).

Surgery is needed to remove the draining, infected areas. Recent research suggests that tail amputation may, in most cases, resolve the problem with little further complication, once it has been cleared up (van Ee, 1987).

Complications after surgery may include constriction of the anus, inability to control defecation, and recurrence of the fistula. These are more likely to occur if the initial disease has been allowed to progress for some time without treatment. Fecal incontinence may occur in about one-fourth of dogs who are treated surgically. About half the dogs surgically treated in one study had total resolution of the problem (Budsberg, 1981).

PERINEAL HERNIA

This hernia occurs when a sac lined with peritoneum (the lining of the abdominal cavity) pushes out into a weakened area between the anus and its surrounding muscles. Perineal hernia is more common in male dogs between 6 and 8 years of age, especially those who have not been neutered. Hormonal influences, probably testosterone, seem to be involved. Dogs with prostate disease often have perineal hernia. Boston Terriers and Welsh Corgis are especially prone to this problem. Chronic straining due to continuing constipation or diarrhea may contribute to a perineal hernia.

Dogs with perineal hernia may show pain when they try to defecate, accompanied by much straining. The dog may pass gas, and have irregular bowel movements. The area beside the anus may appear swollen and bulging. A large percentage of cases occur to the right side of the anus. The mass is soft and spongy. If you press very gently on it, it will be considerably reduced in size. This is because you are pushing a portion of the rectum back to a more normal position within the dog's body. If the swelling is firm and painful, it may contain the urinary bladder or prostate. Perineal hernias require emergency care if they interfere with the dog's ability to urinate.

Surgery is the only reliable treatment for perineal hernia. It is a good idea to neuter the dog at the same time. Even with both of these operations, many hernias will recur. Also, healing after the surgery sometimes is complicated by infections, fistula formation (see Perianal Fistula, above,) rectal prolapse, and complications involving nerves supplying the tail and anal area.

RECTAL PROLAPSE

Rectal prolapse occurs when continued straining pushes one or more layers of the rectal lining out of the anal opening, where they are visible. The straining is usually due to either intestinal problems such as diarrhea, or to a urinary problem.

Young puppies are especially susceptible to rectal prolapse. It can occur because the puppy has worms which cause a loss of protein from the blood. This is added to vitamin loss, continuing diarrhea, and non-stop straining to defecate. Rectal prolapse can occur with any severe diarrhea for these reasons. Other causes are tumors of the colon or rectum, bladder or kidney stones, bladder infection, and diseases of the prostate gland. A bitch who is straining excessively to have puppies may push the rectal lining out. Dogs with perineal hernia may also have rectal prolapse, as can Boston Terriers, who have a hereditary weakness of the peritoneum and muscles of the anal area.

Rectal prolapse is diagnosed when you see a reddish, wrinkled mass of tissue sticking out from where there should normally be an anal opening. It may be small and rounded, or it may be large and long, resembling a sausage. The large protrusion may be more than just a simple prolapse. It may be one piece of intestine which has telescoped inside another piece. If it has been out for some time, it may be dried, crusty, and blackened.

An anal prolapse may not be a simple thing to repair. It is best to take the dog to your veterinarian for examination, diagnosis, and treatment. Treatment usually includes surgery. If the portion of intestine sticking out has died, it may be necessary to amputate it. Understand in advance that this repair may be quite expensive. If it's in a young puppy, are you willing to spend the money? After the prolapse is replaced, it may be necessary to feed a special diet, or keep the animal on a stool softener until he has healed. If the original cause was diarrhea or a urinary problem, that, of course, must be treated or the prolapse will recur.

If you do not have access to a veterinarian, you can attempt to replace the prolapse yourself. This may or may not work, but if you have no other help and want to try to save the dog's life, it's worth a try. If the prolapse has dried, moisten it very gently with lukewarm water. Add enough povidone-iodine to the water so that it is the color of weak tea. If the prolapse is severely swollen, pack sugar onto it, patting it gently, all the way around. This will help soften it and draw out some of the fluid which is making it swollen. Alternate the sugar and water treatment for half an hour. After it has softened, locate the opening in the middle. Begin to gently tuck the edges into the middle, like you were rolling a sock. Continue until all of it is back in the dog. Insert a finger into the rectum and gently push the lining forward, flattening and straightening it as much as possible. The dog will need antibiotic treatment for a week or so. If the prolapse has been caused by diarrhea, this must be treated. The dog must be kept on a soft diet for one to two weeks until the prolapse is healed. Keep a close eye on the dog for those two weeks. It is not unusual for the prolapse to recur.

PERITONITIS

Peritonitis is not strictly a disease of the digestive tract. It is an inflammation or infection of the peritoneum, the membrane which lines the abdomen. Peritonitis may be due to trauma such as a penetrating abdominal wound, whether from a tree branch, a bullet, an arrow, or some other object. It may be due to rupture of some part of the digestive tract allowing intestinal contents to drain into the abdominal cavity. Or, it may be a more localized infection due to rupture of an abscessed lymph node.

Signs of early peritonitis may be as vague and nonspecific as lack of appetite, vomiting, and fever. Or, a case which is rapidly becoming critical may show severe signs within a few hours. These may include a high fever and fluid in the abdomen. The dog will show a lot of pain, standing with a humped back, being reluctant to move, or not wanting anyone to touch his abdomen. If your dog is acting like this, get care for him immediately. You have a possible emergency on your hands. A similar human condition is acute appendicitis. He may rapidly go into shock. Laboratory tests may give conflicting answers, suggesting several different diagnoses. In some cases, it may be necessary for your veterinarian to tap the abdomen with a needle to see what kind of fluid is present.

This may enable him to make a positive diagnosis. In some cases, it may be necessary to do exploratory surgery to confirm it. Don't hesitate if surgery is recommended. It may be your dog's only chance!

Without prompt and intensive treatment, the dog with severe peritonitis nearly always dies. With treatment, the chances are much better. In most cases, it will be necessary for your veterinarian to give large amounts of intravenous fluids to counteract the shock and replace the fluid which was lost into the abdominal cavity. Oxygen therapy may be needed to counteract the respiratory depression that occurs. Electrolyte imbalances will have to be corrected. Antibiotic therapy will be needed. Corticosteroids will be needed to treat the shock. It may take several days to a week or more of hospitalization before you will know if the dog will live or die. Be prepared for the veterinarian's bill—a full-blown case of peritonitis is expensive to treat.

Acute pancreatitis may follow a case of peritonitis. This is because the digestive juices and enzymes which spilled from the damaged intestine have partially digested and damaged the pancreas. The dog may end up either being deficient in pancreatic enzymes, or become diabetic. Even with these possible problems, many of the dogs who have peritonitis can be saved, and will have long, useful lives after recovery. Prompt and aggressive treatment is the key.

Chapter 8

REPRODUCTION

TO BREED OR NOT TO BREED

Is there a market for the puppies you would produce? By market we are speaking not only of being able to sell the offspring, but to find homes for those you plan to give away. Please remember that there are always more dogs available than there are homes for them. Currently, 16 to 18 million dogs and cats pass through the nation's animal shelters each year. About 13 million of these animals are eventually put to sleep (euthanized) because homes are not available. This includes young, healthy animals as well as older, unhealthy animals that no one wants. If the number doesn't shock you, think seriously of heaps and tons of dead dogs in a crematorium or city dump. This fate may await the puppies that you produce. Now, do you REALLY want to breed your bitch?

Is your dog a purebred or a mutt? If a mixed breed or "Heinz 57," there may be no way to find homes for the puppies. And, you might end up having to take them to the pound, or place them in less than desirable homes. Remember, if you place the puppy with someone and in a month or so he is not so cute and ends up in the pound, it is effectively the same as if you had taken him there yourself. Is that what you really want? Little puppies are cute, but sometimes people don't want them when they are older.

If your dog is a purebred, registered animal, is there a good chance that you can sell the puppies? Do you know other people who have had the same breed of dog and are successfully selling puppies? Just because you saw a breed for sale in the classified ads for "$800 each" does not mean that this is what the breeder actually got for them, or that he actually sold all he produced. Do your homework. Call and see how many puppies the breeder has. Call back in a couple of weeks to see if he has any left. Ask what is the least he will take for a puppy. If they are 14 or 16 weeks old, you can be sure that they are NOT selling like hotcakes!

If you have a purebred, do you have one with a desirable bloodline? In some breeds it doesn't matter, but often in Retrievers, Setters and other working dogs there are lines which become popular, and sell for much more than dogs of comparable quality from less-popular or well-known heritage.

There is an old wives' tale which says that the female will be a better (or more settled, calmer, etc.) dog if she is allowed to have a litter of puppies before she is spayed. Most veterinarians do NOT feel that this is true. All that does is produce more unwanted puppies to be put to sleep. If you want to have her spayed, it will be far more convenient to have it done before the first heat. Her maturity and final form will in no way be affected by your decision. This also saves you the bother of putting her into a kennel, or keeping her indoors and having all the males cluster around your house, fighting for a chance to get at her.

Some people want to breed their dog so that their children can see her having puppies, and witness the "miracle of birth." Animals have some ability to control the time at which they have their offspring. The chance of your children seeing puppies born is perhaps 1 in 10. They are much more likely to arrive in the middle of the night or when the kids are at school than when there are spectators. This is NOT a good reason to breed a dog. Go to your library and borrow a video for the kids to watch if you want them to see the birthing process.

There are definite reasons for the high selling prices of some breeds . For example, a friend decided to get an English Bulldog bitch to raise puppies and help put himself through school and paid a considerable amount of money to buy one. Well, this breed often has reproductive problems, beginning with hormonal upsets that keep them from coming into heat. After a LOT of expensive hormonal evaluations and therapy, the dog finally came into heat. He took her to the male. After repeated artificial inseminations (most Bulldogs cannot breed normally) and several heat periods, she finally became pregnant. Because the puppies' heads are very large and the female's birth canal very small, the litter had to be delivered by Caesarean section. The results: one puppy. It was traded for the stud fee. When my friend graduated four years later, that one puppy was all that had been produced. Considering the hormonal treatments, artificial insemination and Caesarean section, the net loss was considerable. Find out if there are problems like this in the breed that you hope will make you rich.

In general, there are two types of dog breeders who seem to make money: those to whom the dog is a pet and hobby, and any monetary gain is incidental and welcome; or serious breeders with professional, long-term kennels. Breeders who make money usually breed either for show or field trial or other working-type dogs. They stay in it through thick and thin, through high prices and low, and they make, in most cases, a small living which compensates them for their devotion to their particular breed or type of dog. Very few people have gotten wealthy from dog breeding.

What about breeding your male? There is no physiological need for him to reproduce. While the male dog seems to take pleasure from the coital process, it is by no means a necessity for his well-being. If dogs are not deliberately being chosen and kept for breeding purposes, most of them make better pets if neutered. They are less prone to run away from home looking for a female, and get hit by a car, poisoned, attacked by another dog or even shot. Some males are nearly impossible to contain as long as they are driven by their raging hormones, and will climb fences or dig holes to escape when they smell a female in heat nearby.

Whether male or female, the dog to be bred should be a reasonably good example of its breed so that it will produce quality offspring. It would be rather counterproductive to breed a 25-lb. mature Doberman or a 35-lb. mature Sheltie. Either of these would be far outside the normal range for its breed. The dog should be free of hereditary defects. If he or she is a member of a breed prone to hip dysplasia, radiographs should be taken to show that the individual is not affected by the trait. Orthopedic Foundation for Animals (OFA) certification can be obtained to verify this soundness.

The male dog, by the way, reaches puberty several weeks later than a female of the same litter. Sexual maturity usually occurs soon after he reaches his adult weight. In smaller dogs, adult weight may be reached by six to eight months of age, while it may take a year or more in larger dogs. The age for onset of puberty is determined by the size and weight of the dog, as well as his breed and heredity.

BREEDING SOUNDNESS EXAM, FEMALE

There are two ways to approach breeding the female. The first is to put her with the male and see if you get puppies a couple of months later. This is cheap, easy and usually works best only when you don't want puppies. The second way is to have the female examined before she is bred.

Many veterinarians begin with a complete health history. This will include the bitch's immunizations and previous illnesses. If the dog is receiving any drugs that may harm the puppies or affect her pregnancy, she may be taken off them. Her ability to reproduce may need to be re-evaluated. Be sure to let your veterinarian know if the bitch has been on any medications previously. Some drugs, especially corticosteroids or hormones, may affect her current ability to reproduce. Tell him how old she was when she first came into heat, how often she comes into heat, and any breeding behavior that you have observed. Let him know whether she has had puppies before, and how many were in the litters. He also will need to know if she was bred naturally or by artificial insemination.

Have your veterinarian go over the dog's nutritional program to make sure that it is adequate for breeding. He will also advise you on how she should be fed during pregnancy. The bitch should be in good condition—neither too fat nor too thin, and have good muscle tone.

If you are going to get OFA certification, X-rays should be taken so that they can be sent in for evaluation. This should not be done when the bitch is in heat . A blood sample should be checked to see that the bitch does not have canine brucellosis (discussed below). It is also a good idea to check for heartworms and other blood parasites. If the bitch is over seven years old, it may be a good idea to run a CBC (complete blood count), urinalysis and blood chemical profile to make sure she does not have any disease which might affect her health or that of her puppies.

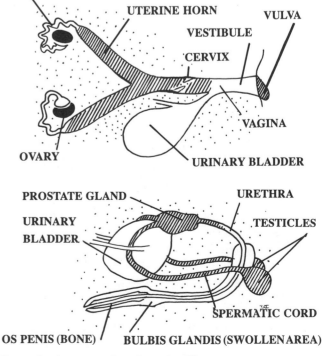

Reproductive tracts, female and male.

Booster vaccinations should be scheduled a bit more than 30 days before breeding, so that the vaccine will not interfere with early growth of the embryos. Otherwise, it may cause early abortion, resorption of the embryos or abnormal development of the puppies. The boosters will ensure that her colostrum (the first milk that she produces) is full of antibodies which will protect the puppies against disease until they are old enough for their immune systems to produce their own antibodies. When you take her to the veterinarian, take along a fresh fecal sample to be checked for worms. Any worming that is needed can be done well before breeding. A female who is infected with ascarids may pass them on to her puppies while they are in the uterus. External parasites such as fleas should also be removed. Any dental care or any other surgery which requires anesthesia (other than that of an emergency nature) should also be done about six weeks before breeding.

BREEDING SOUNDNESS EXAMINATION, MALE

The male should also be examined for breeding soundness. This would include a physical examination by your veterinarian to show that he is in good health, normal, free of worms and blood parasites, and in fit shape to breed. It should also include a semen examination to show that the dog is fertile and can reasonably be expected to impregnate a normal female. Both testicles should be in the scrotum, and the penis should be checked to make sure that it is normal and will extend fully from the prepuce (sheath). Many male dogs have a surface infection (called balanoposthitis) on the shaft of the penis. This is why most male dogs lick themselves around the prepuce. Mild cases are not a problem. Severe cases should be treated with a topical antibiotic prescribed by your veterinarian a few days before mating. The male should also have a blood test to make sure he does not have canine brucellosis.

BRUCELLOSIS

Brucellosis is a disease of the reproductive tract which can cause both females and males to become sterile. It is a bacterial disease, and is spread by contact with vaginal secretions of a female who is infected with the disease and has aborted.

Brucellosis infection occurs in dogs after the bacteria penetrate the membranes of the vagina, mouth or eye. The disease is transmitted as a venereal disease only when an infected bitch is in heat. The disease may also be spread after abortion or whelping, by nasal or oral contact with aborted puppies or their membranes, or contact with drainage from the vagina. An infected bitch may infect her puppies while they are still in the uterus, or through her milk after they are born.

Dogs with brucellosis are not usually seriously ill, and may show no symptoms at all. On a rare occasion, a dog may develop a fever or have swollen lymph nodes throughout the body. Some may have a poor haircoat, less tolerance to exercise and generally less vigor. A history of infertility may be the most prominent sign. Both males and females may be carriers of the disease, spreading it without showing symptoms themselves.

A bitch infected with brucellosis may abort puppies between days 45 and 59 of her pregnancy. She may have a greenish-gray or brownish discharge that persists for as long as six weeks. Or she may carry the litter to term and have both live and dead puppies. The puppies that live may have swollen lymph nodes, fever and convulsions. These puppies are a major source of infection for future generations of dogs. Nearly all infected females may have healthy litters after the first infected litter. Bitches who are infected with brucellosis will have normal heat cycles and interest in breeding.

Brucellosis bacteria can live in the testicles and prostate gland of the male, where they cause infection and infertility. Male dogs can spread the bacteria in both their semen and urine. Infected males who are not treated may shed bacteria for several years. Males may sometimes show lesions on the skin of the scrotum because they lick and bite at the area (because of pain of infection of the epididymis). Or the scrotum may become enlarged because of fluid accumulation. Some males may show pain when ejaculating. Dogs who have been infected for a long period of time may have small, soft testicles.

Rare cases of brucellosis may show spinal pain because the bacteria have established themselves in small blood vessels in the disks between the vertebrae. These dogs will usually stagger and be uncoordinated. Other dogs may show anterior uveitis, an eye problem with signs of pain, spasm of the eyelids, reddening of the blood vessels of the conjunctiva and reluctance to be in bright light. Others may show kidney problems or damage to the nervous system.

Canine brucellosis is slightly contagious to humans, and a few cases have been reported. The symptoms are much like influenza: chills, fever, headache, backache, weakness, enlarged lymph nodes, joint aches and weight loss. Humans may recover spontaneously or after treatment with antibiotics, especially tetracycline. Diagnosis is difficult in humans because serum tests are hard to interpret, and the bacteria are difficult to culture. Most cases are seen in owners who have handled bitches that aborted. If there is any reason to suspect brucellosis, membranes and dead puppies should be handled only while wearing rubber gloves, and you should disinfect your hands carefully afterward, using providone-iodine or a similar product.

Many veterinarians can perform a rapid brucellosis screening test in their offices. Negative results to this test are quite accurate. However, this test does give some false positive readings. If your dog tests positive, further tests are necessary to confirm the presence of brucellosis. This can be done by a serum test or by culturing lymph, blood, bone marrow, prostate fluid or vaginal discharge. If the dog is being treated with antibiotics, the drugs must be stopped for a week or so before a culture can be done accurately. Most veterinarians do not do these tests in their own labs, but send them out to a specialty lab, as the bacteria are difficult to isolate and grow. Do not allow your dog to be euthanized without one of these tests positively confirming that he or she has the disease.

The stud dog should have been tested within the past 3-6 months, especially if you are in an area where brucellosis is known to be a problem in dogs. All females bred to him then and afterward should test negative. Your own bitch should have a negative serum test within a month of breeding. Dogs (male and female) used for breeding, or considered of value as pets, should NOT be allowed to breed indiscriminately with strays. Stray dogs are considered to be a major reservoir for canine brucellosis.

Infected dogs can be treated, but because of the risk of the disease to humans, this may not be advisable. Discuss this with your veterinarian if your dog is positive on serum test or culture. Even when treated, the disease may leave a male dog sterile. If the male is to be kept, it may be advisable to neuter him to prevent his passing the disease to other dogs, even on accidental matings. Infected females may later produce healthy litters, but remain a source of infection for males. For that reason, spaying is recommended for the infected bitch. If the veterinarian who is doing the spay is not the one who diagnosed the disease, be sure to tell him that she is infected so that he can take precautions against becoming infected himself.

Antibiotic treatment may or may not be successful. It is often VERY expensive, depending on the antibiotics used. Brucellosis organisms are resistant to most of the common (and cheap!) antibiotics. Dogs who recover on their own from brucellosis are thought to have good resistance against reinfection. This recovery may take as long as three years, during which time the dog is shedding the bacteria, which are hazardous to other dogs as well as humans. Dogs who are treated with antibiotics, however, are susceptible to reinfection. For this reason, they should be kept from contact with other dogs, and should not be bred within at least three months after antibiotic treatment. Attempts to develop a vaccine for canine brucellosis have not been successful to date.

If you are buying a dog from a environment for breeding purposes, it is a good idea to have him or her tested for brucellosis, or to buy the animal with a guarantee that he or she does not have brucellosis. Two negative blood tests, at least one month apart, should be obtained before the animal is considered free of the disease. Within the kennel environment, good sanitation will help to prevent spread of the disease. Dogs who are infected should be handled with rubber gloves. They should never be bred, not even by artificial insemination.

BREEDING THE BITCH

How old should the bitch be before she is bred? The female dog will first come into heat somewhere between six and 18 months of age. In general, small dogs such as Poodles will be closer to six months, while large dogs such as Newfoundlands will be much closer to 18 months. The female may be fertile at her first heat cycle, and may successfully accept the male, become pregnant and produce puppies.

The bitch should be physically mature before she is bred. Small dogs may be bred on the second heat, or around one year of age, whichever comes later. Larger dogs, such as Saint Bernards, may need to be as much as two years old before they are sufficiently mature to be bred. The first time a bitch comes into heat, it may be a "split" or false heat. The dog may bleed for two to five days, and then seem to go out of heat, followed by a true heat two to four weeks later.

The age of the female also has a bearing on puppy survival. Research has shown that bitches who were over two years of age weaned more healthy puppies than those who were younger when they gave birth. Aged females also have less reproductive success. As many as half of all bitches over five years of age may fail to conceive and produce puppies normally.

Is the female too old to have puppies? What is too old? a Poodle of 14 will be a younger animal, physically, than an eight-year-old Great Dane. It depends on the longevity of the breed as to what is old. If she is in good physical and mental condition and gets around normally, there should be no reason why the older female should not be bred. She will need careful attention to her feeding, care and exercise. It is especially important that she not become overweight. In general, older bitches are more prone to having a prolonged course of labor.

FINDING THE MALE

It is important to locate the male to which you want to breed your female before the onset of her heat period. That will give you time to consider which one you like, his bloodlines, and his conformation and traits, before you have to take your female to him. You can also make the necessary financial arrangements in advance. If the male is registered, you will want to make sure that his registration papers are in order so that the breeding will be valid and recognized by the appropriate kennel club. If you plan to ship the female to the male, make arrangements, as far as possible in advance of the crucial part of her estrus cycle.

THE BASICS OF HEAT CYCLES

The time from the beginning of one heat cycle or period to the beginning of the next one varies from 4 to 14 months. The length of the heat cycle varies from one dog to another, but is fairly consistent with any one dog. Heat cycles are divided into proestrus, estrus ("heat"), metestrus and anestrus.

Proestrus is the portion of the cycle where the female is "coming into" heat. This lasts 2 to 15 days, with an average of about 9 days. During this time, the female may drop spots of brownish or bloody fluid from the vulva. The first sign may be spots on the carpet or flooring; they are normal. The vulva will begin to swell.

During proestrus, the bitch may act nervous and "not be herself," and she may want to be outside more than normal. Some dogs who are normally "homebodies" may be inclined to run away. Males begin to be interested in the female, but she is not yet interested in them. She will usually be grouchy and snap at a male during this phase of the cycle. The bitch may stand with her front end to the ground and her hind end raised toward the male, teasing him. When he approaches, she will run away. If you are going to breed her to your own male, it is often best to separate them at this time. Otherwise, when the female is into full heat and wants to be bred, the male is so "gun-shy" from having been snapped at that he will not breed her.

Bitches who have a very short proestrus may only be in this portion of the cycle a couple of days. Then they are ready to receive the male, and to conceive. These may be missed if you are using the "average" number of days for breeding. If this seems to have happened to your bitch, she should be taken to your veterinarian for a vaginal swab the next time she shows any signs of coming into heat. Your veterinarian can check daily swabs to determine where she is in her cycle and when she should be bred. It is very difficult to look at only one specimen and see which stage she is in. It is much more informative for your veterinarian to watch the cell types change from day to day as the dog progresses through her heat cycle.

Estrus is the part of the heat cycle in which the female is fertile and will accept the male. This period will last from 3 to 21 days, with an average of about one week. The vaginal discharge during this part of the cycle is clear or straw-colored in most females. In others, however, it may remain bloody throughout the heat cycle. The female will present herself to the male as she did previously, often with her front end down on the ground and hind end raised in the air. The tail is often kinked to one side. This time she will stand, allowing the male to mount and service her. The vulva may twitch up and down. This motion is called "winking."

If the bitch can only be serviced a few times by the male, it is best to do so on days 9 and 11, counted from the beginning of protestrus (when you saw the brown spots and the vulva started swelling). If you have the time and the male is convenient, or she has been shipped to a male, start on day 9 and breed every other day until she will no longer accept the male. If you have not noticed the onset of her heat cycle, breed her every two to four days from the time she will take the male until she is no longer interested in him. An occasional female may accept the male for more than three weeks. This extension of estrus is considered to be abnormal, and you may want to have her checked by your veterinarian.

If you are taking the bitch to a male and she is not accustomed to travel, or she has to be shipped, this should be done during the proestrus period. Otherwise, bitches who are shipped while in estrus often go out of it soon after arriving at their destination, probably due to stress. In any case, the female should be taken to the male.

A site should be chosen for breeding that is not normally used for training the male. Otherwise, he may have negative associations with a training area and may not perform satisfactorily for breeding. The footing should be good so that the male will not slip—grass, soft dirt or gravel are often used. Some breeds which do not easily breed naturally (such as the English Bulldog) may need a rack to raise them to the level of the female's rear end. This type of device should be comfortable for the dogs to use (with help from humans, of course).

The female should be brought to the breeding area first, and then the male should be introduced to her. Reliable supervision should be present at all times so that if the dogs fight, they can be separated. Some selection does occur in dogs, and not all pairs which are put together will mate naturally. If the dogs fight, or do not mate, what do you do next? If the male is willing and the female is not, she may not be quite far enough into estrus to want to accept him. You can either wait two days and try again, or take her to the veterinarian to have a vaginal smear taken. This will give you an idea of the approximate stage of her cycle, and will help you to decide whether to sedate and/or hold her to allow the male to mount, or to wait and try again. Vaginal smears also allow the female to be bred on the days on which she is most likely to conceive. This may be necessary with a heavily-used male who cannot be allowed to service the female more than a couple of times. Every-other-day use of the male will not cause a drop in semen quality. Daily use will cause a drop in sperm count after 5-7 days (Merck, 1986, p. 1086).

An experienced male will mount from the rear, holding the female with his front legs around her "waist" area so that she cannot sit down. After a few pelvic thrusts, the penis enters the vagina, ejaculation occurs and the thrusting stops. The male dog has a small, elongated bone in the penis, called the os penis. This helps to keep his penis straight as he mounts the female.

The shaft of the penis has an area, the bulbis glandis, which becomes enlarged upon erection. Meanwhile, the female's vaginal muscles clamp down on the male's penis behind the bulbis glandis. This results in what is called a "tie." The male and female may stay hooked together for up to half an hour after he has ejaculated. The male usually swings one leg over the female so that they are facing opposite directions while still hooked together. "Tying" is not necessary for pregnancy, as most of the semen is passed in the first few thrusts. Tying is natural, and the dogs should be left together until they come apart naturally. Attempts to force them or pull them apart may injure one or both of them. If it's your female and you didn't want her bred, the damage is already done and it doesn't do any good to be angry at the male. If this has occurred outside the yard, you may wish to stand by to protect the pair, as other dogs may occasionally attack one or the other while they are incapacitated.

Once the female has been bred to the male you have selected, keep her away from all other males. It is possible for the bitch to have a litter sired by more than one male, and you may get undesirable puppies if another male gets to her while she is still in heat.

Metestrus (also called diestrus) is the two-month period after the end of estrus. It is considered to begin when the female no longer allows a male to mount or mate with her following a heat period. When the female goes out of heat, the discharge from the vagina will change to a whitish color. This discharge will last for about a week. During the remainder of the two-month period, her vulva will return to normal size, and there will be no discharge. Diestrus ends with whelping if the bitch is pregnant. A false pregnancy can occur near the end of metestrus if the bitch has a hormonal imbalance. Normally, metestrus will blend into anestrus, without any distinction.

Anestrus lasts two to ten months. In this final phase of the cycle, the ovaries rest from egg production.

If the bitch fails to conceive after she has been bred, both the male and female should be evaluated for infertility. If the male sired other litters of puppies during the time he bred this female, it is not necessary to check him, as he has already proven himself fertile. Otherwise, a semen sample can be checked to make sure the male has adequate numbers of sperm cells present in his semen.

ARTIFICIAL INSEMINATION

Artificial insemination (AI) may be used when there are physical reasons that the two dogs cannot get together. For instance, Basset Hounds often have a penis which hangs extremely low. Combined with their length and their being extremely front-heavy, this may make it impossible for them to mate naturally. Other oddly built breeds, such as the English Bulldog, have similar breeding difficulties. Artificial insemination is also useful where either males or females have a lameness or other physical defect which makes it impossible for them to breed naturally.

AI is also used to impregnate a female when she cannot be transported to the male. The semen is collected from the male and shipped to the female. It can be sent by overnight delivery service for use the next day. Properly diluted, the semen can be refrigerated several days and still work well. Undiluted, dog semen does not store well. Pregnancy success rates are higher with fresh, cooled diluted semen than they are with frozen semen. However, frozen canine semen has been successfully stored for over five years, despite the loss in potency.

AI can be used to breed more than one bitch from the same ejaculation. The semen may be either fresh and chilled, or frozen. AI can also be used when the female is vicious to the male, or if he is young, timid, or afraid of the female.

Check with your breed organization or studbook to make sure that semen shipment or AI are allowed by them, or you may end up with unregistered and unsaleable puppies, or at least puppies worth MUCH less than you had hoped.

Artificial insemination can be performed by most small-animal veterinarians if they have both the male and female on their premises. In some cases, it is advisable to take both the male and female to the clinic or kennel just as she is coming into heat, and leave them there throughout the cycle so that they can be accustomed to the surroundings in which the work will be performed. Also, most small-animal veterinarians can handle frozen semen to impregnate the bitch. Be sure to make arrangments ahead of time so he can schedule your bitch when she is expected to be in fertile heat and at the time you expect the semen to arrive.

How is AI done? The veterinarian will collect semen from the male by massaging him to ejaculation. The semen will then be frozen or chilled if it is going to be shipped. If the semen is going to be used fresh, it will be placed into a syringe. A special tube with a rounded tip is inserted into the female's vagina, and the the semen is injected. This operation should be performed at two-day intervals just as

natural breedings would be. Having the bitch reside at the clinic during the process also allows the veterinarian to run a series of vaginal smears to determine the optimal time for breeding.

MISMATING

A mismating is when the female is bred to the wrong male, or is bred when she was not supposed to be bred at all. First, let's clear up an important misconception in this area. The male to whom the female is bred for one litter has NO influence on future litters. In other words, the bitch is not "contaminated," as many people would lead you to believe. If your purebred rare dog is bred to a common mutt, this litter (if you allow her to have it) will be crossbred puppies. But there will be NO influence at all on future litters. In most cases, it is safer to just go ahead and allow her to have the puppies than to abort her and try again. Aborting the litter may injure the bitch, reducing her ability to conceive and whelp in the future.

Injections of hormones may be given by your veterinarian to produce an abortion in a female if you do not care about her future reproductive abilities. One type should be given as soon as possible (within a day or so) after the mismating has occurred. Another (Dexamethasone) may be given as late as 45 days into the pregnancy. The problem with these injections is that they cause a high incidence of pyometra ("pus in the uterus," uterine infection). This condition generally necessitates spaying the bitch to save her life. The injections may also cause bone marrow suppression, a sometimes fatal condition. It is just as easy (and safer!) to allow her to become pregnant and have her spayed as soon as she is out of estrus if she is a pet and not a breeding animal. While you are waiting for her to go out of heat, it is necessary to keep her, if at all possible, from being bred again if you do not want her to be pregnant. The more times she is bred, the higher the probability is that the matings will result in a pregnancy.

The same recommendations hold true when you want the bitch to have puppies, but not this time. If she is bred by accident, it is usually better to let her go through the pregnancy and have the puppies. If you do not want the puppies, most veterinarians will euthanize them for you as soon as they are born. If the puppies never have a chance to nurse, the bitch will not start a milk flow, will not bond to them, and will have minimal side effects from the pregnancy. Then you can go ahead and mate her at her next heat if you want—to the male of YOUR choice. Pregnancy has less likelihood of permanent damage to her reproductive system than an abortion does.

Vaginal douches after mating are of little or no use in preventing pregnancy in the dog, and their use may cause injury or infection in the female. This technique should not be attempted.

If you wish to use your dog for future breeding, it is far easier to keep her from getting pregnant in the first place by careful confinement than it is to try to fix the problem later. And, just because your female wouldn't think of climbing out of your yard doesn't mean that an enterprising and athletic male won't climb in. They can and do! Otherwise, it's easier to have her spayed and not worry about the problem any more.

ABORTION

In the section on mismating, we have discussed deliberate abortions in order to end an unwanted pregnancy. This section deals with the spontaneous or unwanted abortion. Abortion may end a wanted pregnancy, or work to keep the female from becoming pregnant. This may be due to bacterial disease. One of the most common is infection with *Brucella canis* (see Brucellosis, above). Any bitch who does not become pregnant when bred by a known fertile male should be checked for brucellosis. Bacterial infections of the uterus (metritis, endometritis) may cause similar problems. The only way to diagnose them is for your veterinarian to check a culture from the vagina or uterus, or, in some cases, to take a biopsy sample from the uterus. In this examination, a small piece of tissue is taken from the lining of the uterus, and examined for normal cellular structure and/or the presence of bacteria. Bacterial uterine infections may necessitate treatment with antibiotics for a prolonged period of time (3-4 weeks). These are usually given either orally or by injection, as douches will not reach the area of infection in the bitch's uterus. Also, residue from an antibiotic douche may remain in the uterus, causing death of sperm cells if the dog is mated within a week or so after this treatment.

If you don't wish to breed the bitch again, ovariohysterectomy (spaying) is the easy cure. Your veterinarian will perform the surgery after the bitch's infection has cleared up as much as possible and she is healthy enough to withstand the surgery. If you DO wish to breed her again, bacterial cultures, blood tests, urinalysis and possibly a thyroid hormone evaluation may be needed before you attempt to breed again.

INFERTILITY

A herpes virus can cause a vaginitis in dogs which may result in infertility or abortion. It can be diagnosed by the presence of lesions which look like small fluid-filled vesicles which progress to pustules and ulcers. (They look much like chicken pox.) There is no treatment for this problem. This is not the same herpes virus that infects humans.

Hormonal imbalances or deficiencies may cause infertility or abortion. One of the more common causes is hypothyroidism, in which the thyroid gland is not producing enough hormones for normal ovarian function. The bitch may not come into heat at all, or may have abnormal, irregular cycles due to hypothyroidism. Males who are hypothyroid have little or no interest in breeding. And they may have such low sperm counts that they do not impregnate females, even if they are interested. Your veterinarian can run tests to see if your dog is hypothyroid. The problem can at least be partially corrected with hormone therapy.

Cysts or tumors on the ovaries may also cause the bitch not to come into heat at all. In most cases, the only sure diagnosis is an exploratory laparotomy—surgery in which your veterinarian opens the abdominal cavity and "takes a look" at the ovaries. If only one ovary is affected, it may be removed. The other ovary may still be functional. In some cases, hormones from one ovary will suppress function of the other one to the point that it never returns to normal. If the dog is very valuable as a breeding animal, it may be worth removing the abnormal ovary (especially if the problem is a cyst) and seeing what happens. If you do not need the dog for breeding, a complete ovariohysterectomy will end the problem permanently.

Some cysts or tumors may produce an excess of hormones, which keep the female in heat continuously. Hormone injections may be used in an attempt to resolve the cyst. If injections do not work, surgery may done to collapse the cyst(s) within the abdomen, or to remove the abnormal ovary if only one is involved. If a tumor is causing the bitch to stay in heat, the affected ovary should, of course, be removed.

Malnutrition or extreme parasitism may cause abortion, but these problems are usually so severe that they are easily seen.

Males who have tumors in the testicles are generally infertile. If only one testicle is involved and is removed, the other may regain reproductive function. However, in many cases, hormones from the affected side have destroyed the function of the other testicle. Don't get your hopes up that you will have a fertile male after surgery is done.

Extremely high environmental temperatures may cause either temporary or permanent low sperm count in the male. Breeding males should be kept cool in the summer if you wish to maintain their reproductive ability at a good level.

In some males, part of a membrane from the embryonal development of the penis may be attached to the sheath. This will keep the male from getting his penis out of the sheath, and will prevent him from breeding. Your veterinarian can do a simple surgical correction to repair the problem. In some dogs, the end of the sheath is too small, and will either not allow the penis to come out when the male has an erection, or will not allow it to go back in after he has bred the female. In either case, a simple surgical procedure will correct the problem.

Perhaps 50% to 90% of failures of the bitch to become pregnant are due to the owner not paying close attention to her. She may be cycling silently with little in the way of outward signs until she is fully in heat. Or she may be going through the phases of her heat cycle much more rapidly than "average," and is out of heat before she is taken to the male. These problems can be lessened by careful observation and recordkeeping from one heat cycle to another.

A bitch with an irregular cycle should be taken to the veterinarian for a vaginal smear as soon as you even SUSPECT that she is coming into heat. A smear should be taken every day or every other day throughout her cycle to allow your veterinarian to evaluate the cell types which are present and the changes that occur in them. In this way, he can give you a good idea of when she should be bred. One single smear is usually of little value. What is important is not which cells are present on a given day, but the changes in cell types occuring from one day to the next.

Because the normal bitch only cycles one to three times a year, and the bitch with reproductive problems may cycle even less often, it will take several months or longer for a proper reproductive evaluation to be conducted. An entire heat cycle should be used to observe her, checking vaginal swabs, hormone levels, vaginal or uterine cultures, and performing other tests as necessary. You could find yourself with a considerable commitment in terms of time and money to determine why the bitch has not become pregnant.

PREGNANCY DETERMINATION

Most normal, healthy female dogs become pregnant when bred to a normal, healthy male. Most of the time, nature works as intended (or as the owner didn't intend!). The bitch will have an increased appetite, and may begin to gain weight. Around the twenty-first day of pregnancy, if the dog is not overweight, your veterinarian may be able to palpate the tiny puppies as a string of lumps in the uterus, assuming that the patient cooperates and will relax. Around the thirty-fifth day of pregnancy, the lumps in the uterus are no longer individually distinct.

A few veterinary practices have ultrasound machines, which can make a determination of pregnancy around day 21 to 35. If ultrasound is not available, the next possibility is at around 45-48 days. X-rays then may be taken to check for fetal skeletons. If you are pretty sure the dog is pregnant, positive veterinary diagnosis may not be necessary. This diagnosis, however, is important where a large male has bred a small female. If puppies are definitely present, whelping problems can be anticipated, and arrangements made for a possible Caesarean section. This situation is more of a problem when a small female has only one or two puppies. They may each become so large that they will not come out through the birth canal. If she has a larger number of puppies, chances are good that they will individually be small enough that she can give birth to them normally. At any rate, it is better to know ahead of time and anticipate the problem than to have to deal with an emergency. Exposure to X-rays at this stage of the pregnancy will NOT cause problems for the puppies, as they are too far along in their development to be affected by the low dosages used. There are currently no chemical or biological tests which can be used to determine canine pregnancy.

Weight gain will occur in the pregnant bitch. This may vary normally from about 20% of her body weight up to as much as 55%. Weight gain can also occur, however, with a false pregnancy, so the fact that the dog is getting heavier does not guarantee that she is pregnant. Most of the weight gain occurs in the second half of pregnancy, when the puppies are rapidly growing larger.

CARE OF THE PREGNANT BITCH

The gestation period in dogs may range from 56 to 70 days, with an average around 63 days. In other words, be prepared from the 56th day on, counted from the first day the female accepts the male. If the bitch has been bred several times, she may not whelp until 71 or 72 days after the first mating. This means that the first mating was not the one which made her pregnant. The length of gestation varies greatly from one dog to another. However, as with heat cycles, a bitch will usually carry her puppies very close to the same number of days from one litter to another. Around fifty days of pregnancy, the breasts will begin to enlarge in many females. This does not occur in all of them—some do not show breast enlargement until after the puppies are born.

Adequate (but not excess) nutrition is necessary for the bitch. Malnutrition may cause her to have puppies that are too small to survive after they are born. Also, a malnourished mother may not care for the puppies properly, and may not provide adequate milk for them after they are born (see Canine Gourmet chapter). During pregnancy, she will need a larger quantity of food to give more calories. The daily ration should be divided into three or four smaller feedings, as there will be less room left in the digestive tract for food as the puppies take up more of the abdomen.

Normal exercise, especially during the first half of pregnancy, will help to keep the bitch from becoming overweight. It also will keep her in good muscle tone to help make her delivery easier. On the other hand, don't allow the dog to run free without supervision. Later in the pregnancy, she will restrict her own activity as she becomes less comfortable with exercising, but don't let her get fat and lazy. Keep her from any strenuous exercise for the last three days before her anticipated delivery date.

Drugs given during pregnancy may be hazardous to the fetuses, and should not be given except on the advice of your veterinarian. If you have to take her to a veterinarian for an injury or illness, be sure to tell him that she may be pregnant. In some cases, it may be necessary to treat the bitch and risk the puppies in order to save her life. The antibiotic tetracycline may cause liver failure in pregnant bitches. Some drugs may require higher concentrations in the pregnant bitch, while half as much only of others may be needed. Some antibiotics, aspirin and many wormers cannot be given to the pregnant dog. Diethylcarbamazine (DEC), a heartworm medication, seems to be safe to give during pregnancy. It is best, if possible, to have all worming and other necessary treatments done before the bitch is bred, as a part of getting her ready for breeding and pregnancy.

WHELPING

Fifty-six days have passed since you have first bred your bitch to the male. You are expecting puppies around 63 days, but it doesn't hurt to be prepared a bit early. Now, what do you do?

It's good to have a whelping box for the bitch to use while giving birth. It should be long enough that the mother can stretch out at full length. It should be low enough that she can step comfortably in and out, yet high enough to keep the puppies from crawling out. A cardboard box can work nicely for a small female, and can easily be discarded if it becomes soiled. The bottom can be lined with layers of newspaper. These can then be covered with clean towels, rags, mattress pads or carpet. Be sure that whatever you use goes completely to the edge of the box so that the puppies cannot crawl underneath the padding and smother. There should not be any loose strings or holes in which the puppies could become tangled. Hay and sawdust are too dusty to be good bedding. Farm dogs can be whelped on straw, if it is VERY clean and dust-free. Whatever you use, the area should be clean, dry, free of drafts and attractive to the bitch. The prettiest box in the world isn't much good if she won't stay in it.

If you can keep the whelping box at a temperature of about 80 degrees (26.7 degrees C.), more puppies will live. Chilling is one of the commonest causes of death of newborn puppies. They cannot regulate their own temperature for as much as two weeks after they are born. A 250-watt bulb can be suspended above half the box, or the box can be placed near a radiator or electric heater. A heating pad can be used under about half the box IF your female is not prone to chew cords or the pad itself. If you are doing this, it should be put in place several days before the puppies are due. A thermometer should be placed in the box, and checked frequently to see that the proper temperature is being maintained. If it is too hot, the bitch will not be inclined to use the box. If it is too cold, you are not doing any good. Remove the thermometer after you have the temperature adjusted to around 80 degrees. The box should be introduced to the female about two weeks before she is due. The bitch is more likely to use the box if the box is placed near where she normally sleeps, or near you (in your bedroom, perhaps?).

If the bitch has long hair on her belly, like a Schnauzer or Collie, clip her quite close with a pair of clippers (or have your groomer do this) about a week before she is due. Otherwise, sometimes puppies will begin sucking on a lock of hair because they can't tell it from the nipples. It's not very nutritious. If she has long hair under her tail and around her vulva, this should be clipped at the same time. The female can more easily be kept clean and fresh with the long hair gone from this area. Clipping the mother's belly also allows the puppies to have direct contact with her skin, which provides them more warmth than if her skin is insulated by the hair. It may make females with heavy hair more aware of the cold, and they may be more likely to snuggle with their puppies.

Within two or three days of the time she is due, wash the bitch's belly and vaginal area with a good pet shampoo and lukewarm water. Then, rinse it a half-dozen times to make sure that ALL soap is off the skin and hair. The soap on her skin may be ingested by the puppies as they nurse and make them ill. Dry her off with a towel and keep her in a warm place until she is completely dry.

Delivery of a litter may occur quite rapidly, within three or four hours after the bitch goes into hard labor. Or delivery could take as long as 18 to 24 hours. The bitch may be able to delay whelping for up to 24 hours if she is upset or stressed—which is why she may not whelp when the kids are all standing around watching.

No drugs are available at the current time to safely induce delivery at a time that is convenient to us. So we have to take potluck and watch to see when she is going to have puppies.

How do you know that whelping is near? Two or three days before the event, the bitch may become restless and nervous. She may pace and whine, and lose her appetite. She may urinate and defecate frequently because of the decreasing space within her abdomen. Nesting behavior is usually seen within 12 to 24 hours before the puppies are born. The bitch may paw and turn around at her nest box (or your bed or an open drawer or the corner of the carpet). The muscles of the pelvis and abdomen will relax and look loose or sagging. At this point, the bitch may go into the first stage of labor, when contractions of the uterus begin. Right before puppies are born, she may repeatedly scratch at the carpet or ground. A dark greenish discharge from the vulva may occur several hours before the birth of the first pup, as well as throughout the whelping process. This is normal. It is stale blood breakdown products being released as the membranes separate from the uterus.

The bitch may show droplets of milk oozing from the nipples. This may occur a week or two before she whelps. Or it may occur a few hours before she has the puppies. Some bitches do not show any mammary development until the puppies arrive and attempt to nurse. This depends a lot on the bitch, and is perhaps more common with ones having their first litter.

Take the bitch's temperature twice a day. Write it down so that you know what is normal for her and can see when it starts changing. Her temperature will drop to between 98 and 100 degrees F (36.7-37.8 degrees C) within 24 hours of the time that she is going to whelp. This is VERY important, as it is the single most consistent sign that the bitch is going to whelp. Keep track of her temperature from about the 56th day on. If her temperature falls to this level and she has not whelped within 24 hours, have her examined by your veterinarian. Her uterus may simply not be going into contractions as it normally should, or something else could be going wrong.

The bitch may experience labor pains from time to time within a day or two before whelping. As long as these are occurring one or two at a time and she is not settling down, they are just "practice runs." When the bitch lies down and is having rhythmic contractions, labor has begun in earnest, and she will voluntarily push with her abdominal muscles, during the contractions. From the time that this occurs it should not be more than two hours until you have the first puppy.

It may take as much as two to three hours between the first and second puppies if the contractions are weak, or as little as 30 minutes if they are strong. Intervals between the rest of the puppies should be shorter. During intervals between puppies, the female will continue to strain if there are more puppies to come. If it is longer than about three hours between puppies, the bitch may be having problems or be getting tired. Consult your veterinarian for advice. Also, if she strains hard and constantly for more than an hour without producing a puppy, she should be examined as soon as possible. An emergency situation may have developed.

Delivery of the entire litter is usually completed within 6 hours. However, in some cases it may be spread over 24 hours without problems. A litter may range from a single puppy to nearly two dozen. Toy breeds tend to have litters of between one and four puppies. Larger breeds have larger litters. Most breeds average between four and eight puppies. It is thought that runts are not merely the smallest puppies, but may even be a separate group of puppies for some reason. It is not known whether this grouping is due to some genetic factor, to unequal competition for nutrients while in the uterus, to having a different father if the breeding was unsupervised, or to other factors.

When whelping starts, it is a good idea to have the bitch in the whelping box. She won't want to be moved until all the puppies are born. Children should either be VERY quiet or out of the room. Noise should be kept to a minimum, and the lights should be turned down. Keep enough light so that you can see what is happening, but not so much that it is harsh, glaring or distracting for the mother. No strangers should be around a whelping bitch if it can be avoided. This may upset the bitch so much that she will not pay attention to giving birth and taking care of the puppies. If the female is distracted or frightened, labor may be prolonged, and she may have less milk than she would otherwise. She may be paying so much attention to the people around her that she accidentally rolls over one or more of the puppies and smothers them. Some bitches may even become aggressive to the people around them if they are not left alone for whelping. The whelping bitch is not a circus performer—be quiet and unobtrusive.

Everything which touches the mother or the puppies should be either sterile or as clean as possible. Be sure to wash your hands before touching her. Scrub well with soap and plenty of water. Brush under your fingernails with a fingernail brush to get any dirt that is caught there. Dry your hands with a clean cloth or paper towel. If you have a disinfectant available, rinse your hands with it. Povidone-iodine mixed with water until it looks like weak tea works quite well.

When the puppies appear, they may come feet first or head first. It doesn't matter which—they are usually rather sausage shaped, and either way is normal. When the puppy begins to emerge from the birth canal, you can GENTLY help. If you do help, keep your movements slow and quiet so you don't disturb the bitch from her work. Grasp the puppy with a clean rag or paper towel. Pull only on the puppy's legs and not on the head, if at all possible. Work with the mother. Pull when the mother pushes, and relax when she does. If the puppy is head first, you can tear open the membranes covering its face as soon as you can see it. It should not take more than three or four pushes to remove the puppy from the mother. Some puppies may not be covered with the sac. This is normal. The mother may pass one puppy, and then a couple of sacs within 5 or 10 minutes, and then another puppy or two. This is also normal.

If the bitch is having the puppies, and you just want to watch, that's OK. If she does not remove a membrane from the puppy's head after a few seconds, gently remove it yourself, or the puppy may suffocate. She will usually lick the puppy vigorously to stimulate its breathing. She will chew at the umbilical cord to separate it from the membranes. At times, this action may be vigorous enough to tear the puppy's abdomen open, exposing the intestines. Or, it may cause an umbilical hernia. These accidents are rare, but be watching carefully and be prepared to intercede if the mother seems to be a little rough with her puppies. Let the mother lick the puppy and chew the umbilical cord apart (unless she is too rough about it).

If you are helping with the delivery, remove all the membranes from the puppy's body. Tie off the umbilical cord about an inch from the puppy's body, using string which you have soaked in alcohol. Now dip the end of the umbilical cord into tincture of iodine. Using scissors that have been dipped in alcohol, cut the cord on the side AWAY from the puppy, leaving the string on the part attached to him. Dip the end of the cord into the iodine again. Do these steps rather quickly in order to go onto the next procedure:

Wrap a single layer of cloth or paper towel around the end of your finger. Use this to clean out the puppy's mouth, removing mucus and fluid. Take the puppy and cradle it between your two hands, head downhill. Swing the puppy GENTLY in a long, wide arc, using the whole length of your arms. If you use too much force, you may lose your grip and throw the puppy to the floor. You are helping mucus to flow out of his lungs. If you do this too vigorously, you may rupture the diaphragm or cause other internal damage. Having the puppy supported by your full hand will keep the head from swinging from side to side, which may cause injury. Sway the puppy from one side to another six to eight times. Repeat the mouthwiping. If the puppy is still not breathing, blow GENTLY into the puppy's nose until the chest expands. Too much force will rupture his lungs. Squeeze it VERY GENTLY to help it exhale, and repeat the artificial respiration. Efforts to get a puppy breathing may continue up to 20-30 minutes if you really want to save him.

Now take the puppy in your hands and rub it vigorously but gently with a paper towel or a rag. This will remove mucus from its hair and help to stimulate breathing. By this time, the puppy should be gasping nicely. If it does not, repeat the gentle swinging. If you are taking the puppies away from the mother, they can be placed in a box held at 90 degrees F (32.2 degrees C). Otherwise, the puppy can be placed at the mother's breast for nourishment and warmth. Allow him to find the nipple by himself if at all possible. The struggles and crying help to strengthen the puppy and get his lungs open and working properly.

If you come to the box and find that the mother has had a puppy, has not cared for it, and it is chilled, take it to the sink and run lukewarm water (NOT HOT!) gently over it, holding it with the head straight down. Now, dry and rub it as above.

If all is going well, you should have a puppy which is warm, partly dry and breathing with a normal rhythm. If the bitch is having another puppy, pass this one to a family member and help her with the next. As soon as the bitch is through having puppies (if they are coming close together), you can put all the little ones up to her to nurse. If she is going a long time between puppies, they should be given to her to nurse as soon as they are dried off and breathing normally. The sooner they get good nutrition into them, the better start they will have on life.

The bitch may reach around and take the placenta (membranes or afterbirth), either picking it up after it is passed, or actually pulling it out of her body. She may then eat it. This is normal—let her do it if she wants to. The placenta seems to be laxative, and may also help to start the flow of milk. The cleaning process seems to help the bitch bond to the puppies. In some cases, the bitch may start by cleaning vigorously and end by eating one or more puppies. This cannibalism is especially common with first-time mothers who are anxious and nervous. It may simply be that she doesn't know the difference between the afterbirth and a puppy. It may be necessary to have her tranquilized, and to remove the puppies in order to save them.

When the bitch is through having puppies, she will stop straining and relax. She will start licking them and paying attention to them. At this point, you can wash her off with a warm, damp rag if she is soiled. Do not make a big production out of this, or take her away from her puppies. Just get the big pieces and leave the rest for her to clean up herself, or you to deal with in a day or two. Put clean bedding in the litter box if it is soiled with birth fluids. Make sure that everything is warm and cozy, and then LEAVE HER ALONE. She needs time and quiet to bond to the puppies. If you pay too much attention to her, she may think that she is supposed to be with you, and leave her puppies at this critical time, which may be fatal to them. She is a mother now, with a mother's responsibilities. Don't distract her, or make her choose between you and the puppies.

The puppies' umbilical cords will separate nearer to the body than you have cut them off initially. This is a natural separation point, and is normal. Keep dipping the end of the umbilical cord in tincture of iodine (or povidone-iodine or merthiolate) until the hanging piece has fallen off. Do this 2 to 3 times a day. The remnant of the cord will usually fall off in 2-3 days.

Occasionally, one hears stories that someone "took their dog to the veterinarian to be whelped (or have a Caesarean section) and the veterinarian kept ___ of the puppies and sold them." This is nonsense. Most veterinarians are extremely ethical, and would not think of doing this. If you have ever fed an orphan puppy—getting up every couple of hours for the first week or so to feed him, coddle him and keep him warm and wiped—you know that no one in his right mind would do this for a dog to which they had no emotional attachment. Besides, what value would the dog have without registration papers? Sheer nonsense!

Breeders who whelp large numbers of bitches and produce valuable puppies may wish to invest in a heated incubator with oxygen capabilities. One is available from Thermocare Inc., P.O. Drawer YY, Incline Village, Nevada, 89450.

WHELPING PROBLEMS

Call your veterinarian immediately if you have a puppy stuck in the birth canal and you cannot pull it out within several minutes. He may be able to give you helpful suggestions over the phone. Or he may want you to bring her in right away. A stuck puppy IS an emergency.

If more than two hours pass between puppies, or if the bitch quits straining and you suspect that there are more puppies, have her examined as soon as possible by your veterinarian. Likewise, if she is still straining, but appears to be doing so only weakly, have her checked. If she is still very enlarged, or she is a dog who normally has a large litter, or you have had her X-rayed, and the required number of puppies have not come out, get her to a veterinarian as soon as possible. A Caesarean section may be required to deliver the remainder of the puppies.

Occasionally the mother "wears out" during delivery. This can occur if she is old or in poor condition, or if many people, or people whom she doesn't know, are present. It may also occur if she has been straining for a long time. The uterine and abdominal contractions become weaker and weaker and she may stop squeezing the puppies out. If you suspect that this is happening, take her to your veterinarian immediately. Take along the puppies she has already had, so that you can care for them if you have to wait for her for a while.

Injections of oxytocin may be given to stimulate the tired uterus to begin pushing again. Your veterinarian will use about five to 20 units of oxytocin, given approximately every thirty minutes for two or three treatments. This drug usually produces less effect at each subsequent injection. It may be necessary to give one injection for delivery of each puppy, until the uterus can no longer be stimulated to contract. A side advantage of oxytocin injections is that the bitch is stimulated to produce a good, strong flow of milk. Even with oxytocin, delivery may be slow, with as much as a couple of hours between puppies. The use of oxytocin to stimulate the delivery is best done at your veterinarian's office where help is available if problems occur. In the worst-case scenario, all but the last one or two puppies are passed before the mother's uterus becomes totally tired, and a Caesarean section has to be done to get the rest. When one of these cases is finished, you may wonder why you didn't have the surgery done at the beginning. Still though, it is often better if the puppy is born naturally, so it's worth trying.

Other factors may affect the bitch so that she has a difficult birth. One of these is a previously fractured pelvis which narrows the birth canal. If your dog has had a fracture which has not healed well, it is worth having her spayed so that she will not become pregnant, unless you really want puppies and are willing to consider a Caesarean section.

Difficult births may also be due to problems with the puppies. One or more puppies may be deformed, or extremely large. Dead puppies may hamper the birth process. Bitches with narrow pelvises who are having puppies with large heads (English Bulldogs, for example), have a high incidence of abnormal deliveries. For many of these individuals, the only way they can have puppies is by Caesarean section.

Sometimes a puppy gets stuck crosswise at the fork of the uterus. The uterus has two horns and is "Y" shaped. Now, imagine a puppy lying crosswise across where the two horns come together. Not only can he not get out but none of the others can, either. Sometimes when a small dog has only one or two puppies, all the nutrition goes into growing HUGE puppies, and they will not come out of the mother. This is especially true if she has been bred to a much larger male. All of these situations may require a Caesarean section to save the bitch and/or her unborn puppies.

CAESAREAN SECTION

If you are planning on a Caesarean section, you will be taking her to the veterinarian when her temperature drops, and if the calculated days of gestation suggest that she is very close to giving birth.

In performing this surgery, an incision is made down the midline of the abdomen, and the puppies are removed from the uterus. Depending on the anesthetic used and how well the surgery progresses, you may or may not be able to take the bitch home right after the surgery. She should be able to nurse the puppies soon after the surgery is completed. Stitches will need to come out in 10-14 days. If you are planning to have the dog spayed anyway, ask your veterinarian about it before he starts surgery. If conditions are favorable, he may be able to do it at the same time. Also let him know if you do not want the puppies. That way, his staff will not be tied up in an attempt to save puppies that you do not want. If you do not want them, the puppies will be quickly and painlessly euthanized shortly after they are removed from the uterus.

Before the veterinarian does the Caesarean section, you should make a decision as to whether the bitch or her puppies are more important to you. Tell the veterinarian so that if there are complications and he is able to save either the bitch or the puppies but not both, he knows what your choice is and can act accordingly.

THE NORMAL NEWBORN

If any of the puppies are dirty, wipe them gently with a clean, damp washcloth. When the puppies are all cleaned, check each one over to see if there are any defects or injuries from the birth process. The skin should be complete, with no bruises or tears. The coat should be shiny and clean. The umbilical cord should be dry and clean, and there should be no sign of an umbilical hernia. If a hernia is present, it will look like a bulging area or small knob where the cord attaches to the puppy. The membranes of the mouth should be pink. Check to make sure the puppy does not have a cleft palate (split in the roof of the mouth).

Newborn puppies should be rounded and plump. They will usually breathe between 15 and 35 times per minute. The heart rate is over 200 beats per minute until they are a couple of weeks old. The rectal temperature is usually around 96 to 97 degrees F (35.6-36.1 degrees C). The rectal temperature will gradually increase to 100 degrees F (37.8 degrees C) by one week of age. If you have a chilled puppy that is less than a week of age, he should not be warmed any higher than 97 to 100 degrees F (36.5 to 37.8 degrees C).

A normal newborn puppy should be able to crawl and turn himself right-side up. He should be able to nurse shortly after birth. Some newborn puppies may not nurse well the first day after they are born. However, by the second day they should have the hang of it and nurse eagerly. The puppy will mostly sleep and nurse for the first week.

CARE AFTER WHELPING

The bitch should pass one set of membranes per puppy. Keep count to see that she has done so. Retained membranes may lead to uterine infection. However, if you haven't been watching her all the time, she may have passed and eaten some of the membranes. In that case, don't worry right away. Just keep an eye on her after whelping for odorous drainage, or passing of fragments of membranes from the vagina.

The day after the bitch has whelped, take her to your veterinarian. He will palpate the abdomen to see that all puppies have been born. He may give her an injection of a hormone, oxytocin. Oxytocin helps to shrink the uterus (which also expels fluids and any membranes that are left inside). It stimulates milk production. If you see anything abnormal about the puppies, have them examined by your veterinarian at this time. Put them in a SMALL box (just big enough for them all to sleep in a single layer), and cover them with a towel or piece of cloth. Be sure that you are not smothering them, but that you keep them snug and warm. If you need to take one puppy to be examined, take them all.

If you are having tails docked (clipped), or dewclaws removed, you will have this done at three days of age. Some owners or veterinarians prefer to wait until 4 to 10 days of age, but many people feel that the puppy is less sensitive to pain at the younger age. If there are no abnormalities, wait until the declawing day to take the puppies to the veterinarian, rather than risk chilling them and disrupting their routine twice at this very tender age.

It is a good idea to take the bitch's temperature twice a day for ten days to two weeks after whelping. If it goes over 103.5 degrees F (39.7 degrees C), she may have an infection of the uterus (metritis) or of the mammary glands (mastitis). Have her checked by your veterinarian as soon as possible. It is also a good idea to squeeze a couple of drops from each of the mammary glands once a day. Colostrum, the milk produced for the first two or three days, is slightly thick and may be straw-colored or yellowish. After about the third day, normal milk should be bluish-white. It should not be off-colored, bloody, sticky or odorous. If any of these occur, have her checked. Meanwhile, take the puppies off her and put them on milk replacer until your veterinarian has examined the bitch. Milk from a bitch with mastitis can make the puppies very ill.

You can offer food to the bitch soon after she has finished whelping. If she has eaten the placentas, she may not be hungry yet. She may also have a black, watery diarrhea for 24 to 36 hours after whelping if she eats the placentas. This diarrhea is normal and is not a problem unless it continues for an extended length of time.

Keep a close eye on the bitch's vulva for a couple of weeks after whelping. A small amount of drainage may be seen for up to six weeks after whelping. Odd colors are OK—it may be greenish, blackish, or reddish but should NOT show fresh blood. The draining material should not have a foul odor, nor should there be very much of it. If fresh blood, a foul odor and/or a large amount of drainage are present, consult your veterinarian right away, as the bitch may have a a uterine infection.

For the first three days, other than the visit to the veterinarian, leave the new mother alone with her puppies as much as possible. Do NOT let children handle the puppies. Keep a close eye on the puppies for signs of illness. Remember, "A Quiet Puppy is a Happy Puppy." Quiet puppies are well fed, warm, comfortable and healthy. It is normal for them to whimper for a few minutes when they wake up, or when their mother gets in and out of the box. But there should not be any prolonged or loud, continuous crying. This crying may occur if a puppy gets caught in the bedding and cannot get to his mother. Or it can occur if he is not feeling well, or is cold or hungry. If ALL the puppies are crying much of the time, it is probable that the mother does not have enough milk (or any at all), or she has an infection in the breasts (mastitis) so that the milk there is not good. If the problem is only with one puppy, take him to your veterinarian to be checked. If all of them seem to have a problem, take the mother as well as the puppies to the veterinarian.

Puppies are so small and have so little reserves that diseases can easily be fatal to them. Take them to your veterinarian at the first sign of a problem if you want to save them. If you are not interested in saving every last puppy at any price (which may be the most realistic course if they are mixed breed and you are not certain about finding homes for them), you may be able to get by, making your best guess as to the problem, and treating it as best you can with home treatment and nursing. Be careful, however. Some problems in puppies may reflect a serious problem in their mother. You may want to consult with your veterinarian.

For the first few days, most bitches want to be with their puppies almost all the time, and will usually only get out of the box when they need to urinate, defecate or eat. Some will stay so close to their puppies that they become constipated, or have urine retention. The bitch should be taken outside for a short walk several times a day so that she will urinate and have a bowel movement.

Some bitches may be very protective of the puppies and may not like you to handle them. Limit the number of visitors and strangers around the puppies for the first three days. After that, it is good to have your entire family handle the puppies on a regular basis so they will be socialized to humans at an early age. Socialization to the world of dogs is also important. It is good to find "doggy" companionship for puppies who have been orphaned, so that they will be comfortable in the dog world when they are grown. This is especially important if they will be used as breeding stock. Otherwise, they may be so bonded to humans that they will not breed normally.

The puppies will soil their nesting box. On the third day, when their mother is outside taking care of her needs, change the bedding. Once a day, wash her breasts and belly with a washcloth and clear, warm water. DO NOT USE SOAP OR DISINFECTANT PRODUCTS.

The milk that the bitch produces for the first 24 hours is called colostrum. It is thicker and more yellowish than the milk produced later in lactation, and contains antibodies against diseases such as distemper. In humans, much of the baby's early immunity is transferred from the mother through the placenta, before the baby is born. This is not the case in dogs, and the colostrum is essential to protecting the puppy until his body is capable of producing antibodies against disease when he is vaccinated.

The bitch's appearance and milk production are the best way to know if you are feeding her enough (see Canine Gourmet chapter). Dogs with extremely large litters who are producing large quantities of milk (imagine a Labrador Retriever with 12 or 14 puppies) may need extra vitamins and calcium. Consult your veterinarian for products and dosages. It is very important that the female have clean water available at ALL times. Without it, she cannot produce an adequate quantity of milk.

If you have a small, sensitive scale (how about a postage scale?), weigh the puppies soon after birth. If you weigh them again in 10-14 days, you should find that they have just about doubled their birth weight if they are growing normally.

Puppies' eyes will open around 10-14 days of age, and from that point you will notice rapid mental and physical growth. When the eyes first open, the iris is usually bluish-gray. It will change to the normal adult color around 4 to 6 weeks of age. Before this time, the puppies' vision is poor, and their ability to see is still developing. The ear canals open around 13-17 days of age, a few days after the eyes open.

Newborn puppies cannot stand. They move by making "swimming" motions with their legs and sliding along on their bellies. Puppies may have occasional muscle twitches. This is normal. They will begin walking when they are about 14-16 days of age. They are very curious and interested in the world around them, and become lost quite easily. For this reason, it is good to keep them confined in a whelping box, box stall or other simple environment where they won't become trapped behind or under objects. Puppies need the bitch's licking to stimulate their urination and defecation for about 2-1/2 weeks. They will be able to shiver by about one week of age.

As the puppies grow larger, the mother will spend less time with them, and will have less patience with them. Their sharp toenails may scratch her breasts, and their teeth are sharp when they nurse. You can trim the puppies' nails, which will help for a time, but this is nature's way of being sure their mother weans them.

You can begin feeding the puppies around 16-18 days of age, and the entire litter should be eating a puppy-food gruel by 21 days of age. You can put the food in a shallow pan or small cookie sheet. It is normal for the puppies to walk through the food, sit in it, fall over in it, even romp in it for a few days until they figure out what it is and get the hang of eating. If you are feeding a dry puppy chow, it should be soaked in water until thoroughly moistened before feeding. This may help to prevent the puppies from becoming bloated after feeding. Cat or kitten food is not properly balanced for puppies and should not be fed to them.

COMPLICATIONS AFTER WHELPING

Retained puppies, as well as retained membranes, will be discovered on your day-after-whelping visit to your veterinarian. At any time, if the bitch is not feeling well, she should be examined as soon as possible.

Eclampsia (also called puerperal tetany) may be seen in small, excitable or nervous breeds of dogs. The most obvious sign of eclampsia is an excitation and twitching. The first signs may include whining, pacing, panting, nervousness and restlessness. The bitch may walk with a stiff gait.

It is most common in Poodles, Chihuahuas and small Terriers, usually those weighing less than 45 lb (20 kg). On rare occasions it will occur in larger dogs. It is generally seen within one to three weeks after whelping, although it is occasionally seen during late pregnancy. For the most part, it develops at the peak of lactation, when maximum demands are being placed on the bitch's body for calcium and other minerals. The cause is not known, other than that it seems to be involved with hormone metabolism. The bitch's parathyroid gland does not allow her to utilize enough calcium to keep up with the body's needs during gestation or lactation.

If you notice these early signs, call your veterinarian. He may want to see the dog and may also begin treatment before the situation is life threatening. Within 8-12 hours (or less), the signs may progress into stumbling, falling, trembling, twitching and convulsions The increased muscular activity can elevate the body temperature, to as much as 107 degrees (41.6 degrees C.). THIS IS A LIFE-THREATENING EMERGENCY. The bitch should be taken to a veterinarian as soon as possible, even if it is the middle of the night. He will give an intravenous injection of a calcium and electrolyte solution, very slowly, until she is stabilized. This will often relieve the symptoms within as little as 15 minutes. The drug must be given very slowly to avoid cardiac arrest.

The puppies should be removed immediately from a bitch with eclampsia. Keep them away from her for 12 to 24 hours to reduce the calcium drain on her body. During this time, they can be fed a milk replacer. If they are old enough (say, anything more than 16 days), they can be weaned. If they are younger than this, they should be returned to her after the 24-hour period. Do not keep them away from the bitch longer than 24 hours before returning them to her. The milk in her breasts will no longer be fresh, and may cause illness in the puppies. If the eclampsia returns when the puppies are again nursing, you will have to raise them as orphans.

A bitch who has had eclampsia with one litter will be prone to have it again. It may, in some cases, be prevented by feeding a high-quality, balanced diet with a 1:1 ratio of calcium to phosphorus, or slightly higher on the calcium. A slight excess of calcium is acceptable. Large excesses may cause other mineral imbalances and should be avoided. There is NO evidence that large amounts of calcium will prevent eclampsia, and it may interfere with normal gestation. Giving excess calcium before whelping may cause, rather than prevent, eclampsia. The diet fed during pregnancy should continue after whelping. Help the mother out by beginning supplemental feeding of her puppies as soon as possible. Vitamin D, carefully balanced with the calcium level, may also help prevent further problems with elcampsia. Calcium carbonate may be given during the peak of milk production to bitches who have had eclampsia previously. Calcium carbonate, 500 mg per 11 lb body weight (500 mg per 5 kg) per day has been recommended. One Tums® tablet = 500 mg. calcium (Smith, F., 1986). If the dog is experiencing an acute attack of eclampsia, this is NOT a substitute for veterinary treatment. It is used only after she has been stabilized by intravenous calcium/electrolyte therapy.

Hypoglycemia (low blood sugar) is occasionally seen in bitches before they whelp. The dog may appear weak, show convulsions and go into a coma. Your veterinarian will test her blood sugar to confirm this problem. He will treat it with an intravenous glucose solution. The problem seems to cure itself after the puppies are delivered.

Occasionally, the new mother may fail to produce any milk. It is not unusual for the bitch to show little or no development of the breasts before she whelps, particularly with her first litter. However, within hours after the puppies' birth she should be producing milk. The breasts should show enlargement, and you should be able to squeeze out droplets of milk from each nipple by pinching it gently together between your fingers and massaging outward from her body. If she has just whelped, the milk should be white or a bit yellowish. You should be able to get some out of each nipple—check them all.

If the puppies are not getting any milk, or if they are not getting enough of it, you will notice that all of them whine and cry much of the time. They will settle into a restless sleep for brief periods, only to wake and cry again. They are hungry. Have the bitch checked immediately. Your veterinarian will give her an injection of oxytocin. If this works, you're in business, provided there is no infection in the breasts. If it doesn't work, you get to feed the puppies by hand (see Orphan Puppies). This situation may also happen after the first day or so—the bitch may stop producing milk.

Mastitis is the term given to an infection of the breasts (mammary glands). It may result from bacteria invading through the nipples, especially if sanitation is poor. Infection may also occur because the gland has been injured, or because bacteria have been brought there via the blood, from an infection elsewhere in the body. If mastitis develops, the puppies act like they are hungry: restless and crying. In mild cases, the breasts (one or more of them) may be swollen, reddened, bluish or purple, hot (or in some cases, much colder than the others) and painful. The affected gland (or glands) may feel hard or have lumpy areas in them. Normal mammary glands should be soft and pliable. You may not be able to squeeze out any milk at all. If you can, its color may be grayish, reddish or off-colored instead of the normal whitish to slightly bluish color. It may contain clumps, clots, or stringy pieces, and may be sticky.

In severe cases of mastitis, the bitch may be droopy, have an elevated temperature, drink more water than normal and generally look ill. She may ignore her puppies. This is more serious—take her to your veterinarian, quickly! Watch the puppies closely to see that some of them do not become ill from ingesting the spoiled milk.

Whether the mastitis is mild or severe, the bitch will need treatment with antibiotics for a week to ten days. You will need to milk out the infected gland(s). Warm packs will help to resolve the infection and relieve her pain. If only one or two glands are affected, you may be able to cover the nipples with Band-aids® and let the puppies nurse from the rest of them. After several days of antibiotic treatment, the puppies can be allowed to nurse all the glands as usual. If the infection has progressed to gangrene or localized into abscesses, the puppies cannot be allowed to nurse and you will have to raise them as orphans.

The mammary glands sometimes become swollen and hard with milk. This condition may be hard to tell from mastitis. You should have your veterinarian look at the dog. The swelling may be so painful that the bitch will not allow the puppies to nurse. Covering her breasts with towels soaked in warm (not too hot) water will help to relieve the swelling and pain, as well as stimulating circulation in the area. Gently milk out the glands, and help the puppies to nurse. Reduce the bitch's feed to lower her milk production. If overproduction and swelling are continuing problems, get the puppies onto solid food as soon as possible (any time after about 16 days of age), and wean them when they start eating well. If the breasts become engorged with milk during weaning, use the warm compresses, but do NOT milk her out or massage her breasts, as this will stimulate continued milk production. You want production to stop.

Occasionally, a bitch may seem to have no milk at all. If you squeeze on the nipples, nothing comes out. This can happen if the bitch is on a poor diet, especially one with low-quality protein. This may occur when a Caesarean section is done before the bitch's temperature has dropped. Keep track of her temperature to make sure that she does not have an infection such as metritis. Encourage the puppies to suck, as the suckling action may help her to produce milk. In some cases, oxytocin may be given, as above, to bring about milk letdown. There is no drug that will stimulate milk production if the bitch is not making any at all. Make sure the bitch has adequate food (and is eating enough of it) and drinking enough water for milk production.

Metritis is an infection of the uterus. It may occur when the bitch does not pass all the afterbirth (membranes) at the time the puppies are born. It can also occur if she has retained one or more dead puppies in the uterus. A few cases have been seen after apparently normal births with nothing having been retained. Most cases develop within one to three days after whelping. The bitch may have a foul-smelling fluid draining from the vulva. She may have a fever, be depressed, stop eating, stop producing milk and drink more water than usual. She may have little or no interest in her puppies. Get her to a veterinarian as soon as possible.

Blood tests and X-rays may be needed for your veterinarian to confirm the presence of metritis. If you do not want future litters, the simplest solution is to have an ovariohysterectomy (spay) performed immediately. If you wish to keep the bitch for future litters, the veterinarian may treat her with antibiotics placed in the uterus, antibiotic injections or oral antibiotics, perhaps for three to four weeks. He may give the hormone oxytocin, or other hormone injections, to try to eject the infected material from the uterus. There is a risk with hormone treatment in that the uterine wall, which has been weakened by the infection, may rupture, causing a fatal peritonitis. Or infection may spread throughout her system, again with fatal results. If the dog lives through the treatment, the uterine lining may be damaged enough that she will never carry another litter to term.

For some bitches, the safest course of treatment for metritis is a spay, performed as soon as possible. Be aware that doing surgery on an infected uterus carries much more risk than a "routine" spay for a healthy animal. In some cases, the bitch may not live through the surgery, or will die soon afterward. Chances are this is NOT the veterinarian's fault—she was just too badly infected to survive.

The mother may ignore one or more of the puppies. If she is ignoring all of them, have your veterinarian check her immediately. She may have an illness or infection. No infection, no illness? Then, look for social causes. Is she so much a member of your family that she is not "acting like a dog?" You may pay for having excessively spoiled her by getting to play mother to her litter! It may help to move the puppies into an area of the house where you are. For instance, if you are fixing dinner, move the box into the kitchen. Pay attention to her when she is in it, and ignore her when she is not in it. This will help to reinforce the idea that you want her to stay there with the puppies. You may also have to spend some time sitting by the box and petting her and telling her that this is where you want her to be. Then, when you go to bed, take her and her puppies to the bedroom.

You may not be guilty of having excessively socialized the bitch to you. She may have been removed from her own litter at a very early age, or she may have been raised by hand. Either way, she would not have gotten an "example" of mothering skills from HER mother. Or she may simply lack the skills for genetic reasons. Some bloodlines in all species (including humans!) are not good mothers. This condition is inherited, at least in horses. You may have either to help her raise the puppies or raise them yourself as if they were orphans. Think long and hard about whether you want to raise another litter out of this female or one of her offspring and, perhaps, perpetuate the problem.

NEWBORN PUPPY PROBLEMS

A litter of puppies will pile together if they are cold. A single puppy may be so cold that the bitch has pushed it out of the way. This puppy is probably either sick or has a defect. Have it checked by your veterinarian if you want to save it. If the puppies are widely separated from each other, they may be too hot. Also, puppies that are panting and have reddened gums may be too hot. A rough, dry haircoat on a puppy is either a sign of illness, or of the mother neglecting it. A puppy which has decreased muscle tone and looks "flat" is probably seriously ill, and saving it may not be possible. Have it checked by your veterinarian as soon as possible. Bluish color and labored breathing are also problem signs, possibly of a congenital heart defect.

Hypothermia is a common cause of death in newborn puppies. Until the puppy is several weeks old, his system is not capable of regulating his body temperature. If he is not getting (or eating) enough food, is in a cold environment or is neglected by his mother, he may become cold. At this point, his mother may decide that she doesn't want him. This is a natural reaction on her part. However, it may be fatal for the puppy when he is pushed away from the only convenient source of both warmth and food. Puppies cry constantly when they first become chilled. Later, they will stop crying, and stop moving. The bitch may push the cold puppy out of the nest as if it had died.

Feeling the puppy is not an adequate test of its temperature. A puppy which feels warm may still be cold enough to be dying. If the puppy's rectal temperature drops below 93-94 degrees F (33.9-34.4 degrees C), he may not be able to nurse effectively. Chilled puppies cry pitifully and weakly. If not rewarmed, they may die within a few hours.

Take its temperature, and if necessary, warm it until the rectal thermometer registers between 97 and 99 degrees F (36.1 to 37.2 degrees C), and NO higher.

Gently warm the puppy by wrapping him in a towel and placing him on a hot water bottle filled with lukewarm water. Electric blankets or heating pads may get the puppy too warm and should not be used. Do not warm the puppy so fast or so hot that the skin is burned, or that you overheat and get his body temperature too high. Be careful not to warm the puppy too rapidly. Too-rapid heating raises the oxygen needs in the outer tissues, while the heart and breathing rates are still too slow to adequately oxygenate them. You are just trying to bring him back up to normal, not parboil him. Rewarming may take one to three hours, depending on how badly the puppy is chilled.

In many cases, when you have warmed the puppy, the bitch will take it back again. If it does not warm up within an hour or two, it is unlikely to do so, and will probably die. Hypothermia may also cause hypoglycemia, by slowing the action of the digestive enzymes. A sugar-water solution (two parts sugar to one part water), diluted honey, or corn syrup can be used to treat this problem. This allows the necessary sugars to be absorbed directly from the stomach without needing any digestion. Use a medicine dropper to place a few drops at a time in the puppy's mouth. If he swallows, you've probably got it made. After the puppy is warm and has been fed, he can be allowed to nurse normally.

Cleft palate is a defect which is sometimes seen in newborn puppies. Much of the time it is hereditary. A few of the breeds in which it is seen include Chihuahua, English Bulldog, Boston Terrier, German Shepherd and Toy Poodle. A few cases of cleft palate are thought to be caused by factors affecting the mother during pregnancy while the puppy was developing, such as nutritional deficiencies, drug or chemical exposure, or stress. If the puppy has a harelip (split upper lip), check the roof of his mouth to see whether or not it is cleft, as the two problems are often found together. If no harelip is present, the first sign of cleft palate may be milk dripping from the puppy's nostrils as he tries to nurse. Pneumonia is common because the puppy will inhale milk while trying to drink.

Puppies with cleft palate who are not treated usually die either of pneumonia or of starvation because they cannot produce enough vacuum in their mouths to suck milk out of the nipple. In general, correcting cleft palate is difficult surgery because the patient is so small. Most veterinarians like to have the puppy about three months old before attempting corrective surgery. At this age, the puppy has a better chance of surviving the anesthesia. Meanwhile, you will have to try to keep the puppy alive for that long, which usually means feeding it by hand with a stomach tube.

Cleft palate and harelip occur because the puppy did not quite grow together on the midline as he was being formed in the uterus. If the defects are large enough, the kindest course of action is to euthanize the puppy. Puppies which are successfully treated should not be used as breeding stock because of the high probability of passing on the defect. Frankly, since the puppy, as an adult, could only be a pet, the bother and expense of dealing with cleft palate hardly seem worth it.

Umbilical hernia is another hereditary defect which is fairly common in dogs. You may first notice it as a small bulge where the umbilical cord was attached to the puppy. Feel the swelling. If it is hot, it may be an abscess—have the puppy checked as there may be infection in the stump of the umbilical cord. If the swelling is of normal temperature, it is very likely an umbilical hernia. If it is small, it will probably go away with time. What happens is that the puppy grows, but the hernia stays its original size. So, a "half-inch" hernia, which is large in a puppy, is negligible in an adult dog.

The biggest problem with an umbilical hernia is that a piece of intestine may crawl out through the defect (a hole) in the abdominal wall and become strangulated. It is pinched off by the edge of the defect, and blood flow is no longer possible. The piece of intestine may die, endangering the life of the puppy if prompt treatment is not given. If the umbilical hernia is large, feel it gently a couple of times a day, gently pushing its contents back into the abdominal cavity. If you are suddenly unable to push them back in, take the puppy to your veterinarian right away.

Umbilical hernias can easily be corrected surgically. Most veterinarians prefer to wait until the puppy is at least three months old so that it is better able to tolerate anesthesia. If the hernia is not giving the puppy any touble, you may even wish to wait until you spay or neuter it, around six months of age. Many times the hernia repair can be done as part of the other surgery, under the same anesthetic. It's a lot less expensive than having it repaired separately. If contents of the abdomen are not pushing into the pouch, there is no harm in waiting.

Lack of anus (atresia ani) is the condition where the newborn puppy does not have an anal opening. This condition may be noticed as you check the sex of the puppy. The skin below the tail may bulge slightly where the opening should be. In some cases, the only problem is that the skin itself has not opened. Your veterinarian can quickly remedy this by puncturing the skin and making the opening that should have been there. In other puppies, part of the digestive tract may be missing, and these puppies should be humanely euthanized.

Canine herpesvirus can cause respiratory disease in adult dogs. Puppies born to infected bitches contract the disease while in the uterus or while passing through the birth canal. They can also become infected by contact with an infected dog after they are born. In newborns, the disease causes severe (permanent) damage to the kidneys. Signs in tiny puppies include crying, sudden illness and pain.

Keeping the puppy's temperature above 101 degrees F (38.3 degrees C) may be helpful in treating canine herpesvirus. Maintain the litter of puppies at this temperature for three hours. You can use a carefully regulated heating pad, or a heated incubator if you have one. While they are being treated, give water with a dropper or nursing bottle three or four times per hour to keep them from becoming dehydrated.

For the rest of the day, keep the litter at 95 degrees F (35 degrees C). Do not raise their temperature over 103 degrees F (39.4 degrees C).

Treatment of herpesvirus infections is generally not very successful. In most cases, you can expect to lose at least part of the litter. In general, puppies who have reached the stage where they are constantly crying have already suffered hemorrhages throughout their bodies. If they survive this crisis, many will suffer from chronic kidney disease during their first year of life. For this reason, many owners treat only the puppies that are not yet crying. By the way, this is NOT the virus that causes fever blisters and similar problems in humans, but is in the same family of viruses.

Diarrhea can be a problem in newborn puppies, especially if they are orphans who are being hand-fed. Good sanitation will help to prevent it. Overfeeding may also cause it—avoid giving them too much formula, or giving a few large meals instead of more frequent smaller ones. As with human babies, dehydration can quickly kill the puppies because of their lack of bodily reserves. Cow's milk formulas can cause diarrhea when used for prolonged periods to feed some puppies. Switch to a canine milk replacer as soon as possible.

If the puppy which has diarrhea is valuable, take it to your veterinarian as soon as possible. If you wish to try home treatment, first look into the feeding problems mentioned above: sanitation, overfeeding, cow's milk. Then give the puppy one-half to one teaspoon (2-5 ml) of Kaopectate® or a similar product. Give this with an eyedropper, keeping the puppy's head level. For a larger puppy, just dribble it into his mouth with a spoon, again keeping his head level. Repeat this every two to three hours. Keep the puppy hydrated by giving him canine milk replacer as normal, or at least giving him water from a bottle if he will take it.

Trauma is a common cause of puppy death. The bitch may roll over and crush the puppy, or she may deliberately eat one. Some females may accidentally bite the puppy hard enough to puncture his body, or squeeze him hard enough to cause an umbilical hernia while carrying the puppy around. These things are most often seen with bitches that are frightened or nervous. Limiting the number of visitors (and strangers) around the mother for the first few days after the puppies are born will help to prevent these situations. Providing a stable, stress-free environment may keep the rest of the litter from being killed or "worn out" from too much motherly attention. If the bitch shows this kind of behavior for more than one litter, she should not be kept in the breeding program. This type of behavior can be inherited, and you may be breeding it into your dogs by keeping her. Tranquilizing the bitch may be helpful, but providing a quiet, stable environment from the beginning may be more helpful.

CAUSES OF PUPPY DEATHS

Under average kennel conditions, as many as 1 in 4 of the puppies that are born will die before they reach three weeks of age. Under good kennel conditions, losses may be as low as 1 in 10. Under home conditions, losses may be more or less, depending on both care and luck.

Malnutrition in the bitch, both during pregnancy and afterward, is a major cause of puppy loss. This may because she is not given (or does not eat) enough food, or because the bitch is unable to absorb certain necessary nutrients. It may be because her food is of low digestibility, her diet is unbalanced or needed ingredients are lacking.

The puppy may suffer malnutrition because he is too weak to nurse, or does not nurse effectively. He may simply not drink enough milk to maintain himself or to grow. He may be oversupplemented so that his diet is imbalanced, or he may be unable to digest milk. Puppies which do not nurse well may quickly become hypoglycemic and die. The supplementation of these puppies with milk replacer with a small amount of corn syrup added may give them enough energy that they can recover and nurse on their own. Some puppies which die soon after birth are simply not developed enough to make it out in the world.

It is important for the newborn puppy to take a good, strong first gasp. This helps to open up and inflate his lungs. If he has not gotten them fully expanded and opened up, this will have to occur gradually over the next three days. During this time, the puppy may be weak, and it may be in doubt whether he will make it. Don't despair—many of them make it.

Some large puppies will have the umbilical cord pinched off by pressure as they pass through the birth canal. Or, the placenta may separate too soon, and the lack of oxygen from these situations may make the puppy try to breathe while he is still immersed in birth fluids. He may inhale some of these fluids, leading to his being born with lungs filled with fluid rather than empty and waiting to be filled with air. Removing as much fluid from the puppy's mouth and throat right after he is born is helpful. So is gentle swinging with his head held downward. Placing him in an incubator which has a gentle flow of oxygen added to its atmosphere can be helpful. Unhumidified oxygen should not be used for more than about four hours, or you risk drying out the linings of his lungs and causing even more problems. The atmosphere in the incubator should be enriched with oxygen, NOT 100% pure oxygen! A puppy who has fluid in his lungs may also be gently taped to a board. The board is then propped at a 45 degree angle, with the head downhill, in an incubator. The puppy will begin to cry, and this crying will help to open up the lung passages. The head-down position will help to drain fluid out of the lungs. Do not leave him on the board for more than half an hour to an hour.

As with chilled puppies, puppies who are not breathing adequately will not nurse well. For the puppy to be vigorous, it is necessary that his lungs expand normally and that he breathes stongly.

Puppies which die within one to three days after birth, with signs of weakness and rapid decline, should be examined for signs of hemorrhage. You may see blood clots on the lips or tongue. All puppies are born with only a marginally effective clotting mechanism. This may be due to a vitamin K deficiency. For these puppies, treatment with vitamin K may significantly increase their survival. In some cases, hemorrhages may occur because a puppy was rewarmed too rapidly or subjected to temperatures above 103 degrees (39.4 degrees C). In some cases, it may be necessary to combine history, examination of the puppies and laboratory tests to find the reason for the hemorrhages.

In some cases of hemorrhage, the bitch may bite the umbilical cord off too close to the puppy's body, or pull too hard on the stump. The blood vessels pull back into the puppy's abdomen, and he bleeds to death internally. These puppies will have blood or blood clots in the abdomen.

Puppies which are four days to two weeks old and are crying and bloated should be examined to see if their rectums are red and swollen. This may be a sign of "toxic milk" syndrome. Their mother looks healthy and normal. This distinguishes the problem from acute metritis, where the bitch will be sick. The puppies should be removed from their mother and placed where the temperature is 85-92 degrees F (29.4-33.3 degrees C). Feed them a 1:20 mixture of corn syrup in lukewarm water until they are no longer bloated. When the bloat is gone, you can feed them a normal milk replacer product for the remainder of the day. Meanwhile, take the bitch to your veterinarian for examination. What has happened is that her uterus (or part of it) did not drain out completely after the puppies were born, or there is an early infection in it. Your veterinarian will treat the bitch with a combination of antibiotics to control the infection and drugs to drain the uterus. In many cases, the puppies can be returned to their mother within one to two days.

Puppy septicemia may occur anytime from shortly after birth to six or seven weeks of age. Many of the cases occur within one to two days after birth. The very young puppies become hypoglycemic, chilled and dehydrated—signs much like many of the other puppy diseases. Many will die within 10-12 hours after the illness begins. Older puppies breathe rapidly, have swollen abdomens, cry from time to time and die within 12-18 hours. At first, only one puppy may be affected. Soon others become ill, until most or all of the litter is sick. Few, if any, of the puppies in the litter will survive the first week.

Many bacteria are involved in puppy septicemia. In some cases, the exact species which is causing the problem can be determined only by laboratory cultures. Septicemia is especially a problem in kennel situations. Puppies who do not get enough colostrum shortly after birth are more susceptible than those who nurse adequately from the very beginning.

This section has presented only a short listing of the more common problems which can befall newborn puppies. If you have puppies that are ill or are not doing well, and want to do everything possible to save them, gather them up and take them to your veterinarian for diagnosis and treatment. Even then, don't be too disappointed if a few of them don't survive. A seriously ill puppy is a challenge for your veterinarian to diagnose and treat under the best of circumstances.

ORPHAN PUPPIES

It may be necessary for you to act as mother to newborn puppies if part of the litter is born, and the mother must go to the veterinary clinic for a Caesarean section or other treat-

ment. This is generally temporary, and you can turn their care over to their mother as soon as you get her back. It's another story when the mother dies at whelping time, or when she is not producing milk, or when, as sometimes happens, she rejects the litter. Long-term supplemental feeding may be needed for a very large litter. Then, you're looking at a committment of a LOT of time and effort for 3-4 weeks. Are you willing to put in the effort? If not, have the veterinarian euthanize the puppies right now, and save yourself time, trouble and heartache.

Borden's Esbilac® is one common canine milk replacer which is readily available. It is specifically formulated to have fat, sugar and protein content similar to that of bitch's milk. In addition, it is highly digestible, and puppies seem to do well on it. Other companies have similar products available. Esbilac®, for instance, is mixed one part powder to two parts cold water. The container of powder should be kept in the refrigerator after opening. After mixing, Esbilac® is fed at 2 tablespoons (30 ml) per 4 ounces (125 grams) of body weight per day. Divide this amount into equal portions for each feeding. Large puppies may be fed 1/3 of the total amount every eight hours. Smaller or weak puppies may need to be fed every 3-4 hours, around the clock. Feed them through the night for the first several days until they are doing well. Then you can let them sleep through the night if they will and just feed them during the hours you are up and around. Feed milk replacer at room temperature or very slightly warmed. As with baby formula, you can put one or two drops of the puppy formula on the inside of your wrist to judge its temperature.

Cow's milk is considerably different than that of dog's milk. It has less protein, sugars and minerals than puppies need. Cow's milk often will give them diarrhea or cause serious digestive upset. In an emergency, you can mix together one cup of homogenized milk with one-half teaspoon of corn syrup and two egg yolks. Mix this in your blender, or stir it until thoroughly mixed. Consider this mixture as a TEMPORARY measure only, until you are able to get a suitable canine milk replacer.

In an emergency, you can feed puppies with a medicine dropper. If you don't have one handy, steal one from a bottle of nose drops or children's vitamins. Just be sure to wash and rinse it well before use. An eyedropper is also useful for puppies that are extremely small or weak. For emergency use, you can try a doll-sized baby bottle. Most doll nipples, however, do not work very well for feeding puppies. Pet stores or veterinarians have special pet nursers with nipples which fit the puppy's mouth and are of the right shape and softness so that the puppy can nurse easily. It is a good idea to obtain nipples, bottles, formula and other supplies before the bitch whelps—just in case.

Wash all utensils thoroughly after each use with hot, soapy water. Rinse well to remove ALL soap. Formula can be mixed every two or three days and kept in the refrigerator. Shake well before you measure the amount needed for feeding. Cleanliness is not only next to godliness, it will help prevent serious illness in your puppies.

Be sure when feeding the puppy that you hold him nearly level, and squeeze one drop at a time when using a medicine dropper. If you fill him too fast, or hold his head up, you may force liquid into his lungs and he will get pneumonia and die. If milk comes out of the puppy's nose while nursing, you are feeding him too fast (or he may have a cleft palate). When using the nipple and bottle, put the nipple in his mouth, and pull it up and away slightly. This helps the puppy to raise his head and will encourage vigorous sucking.

Warm the formula to around 100 degrees F (37.8 degrees C.). The puppy, especially at first, may not open his mouth and nurse automatically. In that case, place him on his stomach and open his mouth with your finger. Put the nipple on top of his tongue. The puppy should start nursing. If he does not, squeeze the bottle to let out a drop or two of milk so that he can get the taste of it. If he still won't nurse, feed him a drop or two at a time until he gets enough. When you are finished, the puppy's belly should be nicely rounded but not tight or bloated looking. Burp the puppy much as you would a human baby, placing him on your shoulder and patting his back. As with a human baby, use a towel on your shoulder!

When you increase the amount of formula that you are giving, the puppy may have excessive diarrhea. If this occurs, return to the previous lower level of feeding for several feedings before trying to increase it again. Diarrhea may upset the bacterial balance in the puppy's system. Supplementing the formula with an oral product containing normal digestive bacteria may be helpful. One product is Bene Bac® (Pet-Ag, Inc., Elgin, Il., 60120). If diarrhea persists, or the puppy becomes weakened or is otherwise ill, consult your veterinarian.

Feeding is only part of your job. Puppies have very poor intestinal circulation when they are first born. The mother makes up for this by licking them. Do YOU have to lick them? No, not really. After you have fed them, take a washcloth dampened with warm water and wipe their skin. Work from head to tail, down first one side and then the other, then down the back and down the belly. This also helps to clean the milk mess off the puppy's face and the other mess off the other end. Now take a dry rag and stroke a few more times to help dry the puppy. A reasonable amount of gentle petting will also help things along—you can let your children stroke the puppies for a few minutes four or five times a day (after you have done the washcloth scrubbing). Normal bowel movements will be yellowish and have some shape to them.

Prepare an appropriate-sized incubator box for the orphan(s). It is important to provide good ventilation, but keep drafts away from the puppies. For very small, delicate puppies, you can use a clear plastic cover with holes in it, or even clear plastic wrap, safely secured to the box so that it will not fall and suffocate the puppies. Poke some air holes in the plastic wrap.

The puppies must be kept warm to compensate for the absence of their mother. Their box should be heated to between 85 and 90 degrees F (29.4 to 32.2 degrees C) for the first week, 80 degrees F (26.6 degrees C) for the second week, 75 degrees F (23.9 degrees C) for the third and fourth weeks, and around 70 degrees F (21 degrees C) for the fifth and sixth weeks. Smaller puppies generally need higher temperatures

than do larger ones, but not much higher. Set the box halfway on a heating pad.

If the box is very thick, you can put the heating pad inside at one end, wrapped securely in a towel so that the puppies cannot burrow under it. Begin by turning it to low, and check the temperature in the box every hour for five to six hours until you are sure the temperature has stabilized. Use a thermometer, at puppy level. The bedding at the end with the heating pad should be around the desired temperature. If not, turn it up, give it the same time to stabilize, and check it again.

Having heat at only one end of the box will allow the puppies to crawl to the other end if they are feeling too warm. Whatever heat source you use, make sure it will not burn the puppies, or cause a fire hazard in your house. A bit of humidity will make the puppies more comfortable. A humidifier in the room, or a pan of water near the box, will be helpful. Placing an old-fashioned, wind-up alarm clock with a good loud tick in the box may help to keep the puppies calm and quiet.

WEANING

Weaning is the process of getting the puppies to stop nursing their mother or your bottle, and eating solid food. You can begin supplemental feeding as early as 16 days of age. This is especially important if their mother has had eclampsia, is old or in poor condition, or is nursing a very large litter. Not all puppies will eat at this young age, but it's worth a try. Each day more and more of them will eat until the whole litter is eagerly awaiting your arrival with food. This will take a significant load off their mother (or you!). If your bitch doesn't have any of the above problems, it is often easier to wait until the puppies are 18-21 days of age. They will be a little more ready to eat because they are more developed.

The puppies' first food can be either a commercial milk replacer such as Esbilac®, or puppy chow mixed into a thin gruel. Mix the puppy chow either with water or Esbilac®. Do not use cow's milk, as it may cause diarrhea in some puppies. Or you can use a product meant to bridge the gap between mother's milk and solid food. One such product is Puppy Weaning Formula® (Pet-Ag, Inc., Elgin, Il., 60120). It can be used from about four to eight weeks of age, after which the puppies can be fed puppy food mixed with water or milk replacer.

Whichever food you are using, place the mixture in a shallow pan (not more than about a half inch deep). Do this where you want to feed the puppies in the future. If possible, feeding outdoors will help keep the puppies from making a mess all over the house. Mix just a small amount of food each time, and discard what the puppies do not eat within about 20 minutes. Allowing the mixed food to sit part of the day can allow it to spoil, causing digestive upset in the puppies.

There are two ways to introduce the puppies to the food. One is to dip your finger into the food and let each puppy suck on it. You can then lead their heads down toward the mixture. Or dip their faces gently into the food. The object of the game is not to drown them in it, but to get a bit onto their mouths. As they lick it off, they will get the idea about lapping and eating. Don't worry if the pups walk into the container. That's normal for the first day or so. About the time you are convinced that the little dummies will NEVER learn to eat, they will suddenly all get the hang of it and slurp like crazy! Keep fresh water available, in a container that the puppies can reach, while you are introducing food. If the puppies' first food is a gruel of milk replacer, convert to puppy chow soon after they have learned to eat.

After around five weeks of age, the puppies' sharp teeth will usually cause their mother enough discomfort that she will be glad to have your help in weaning them. She may nip at them as they irritate her breasts, and this also helps the weaning process. At this point, you can keep the mother away from the puppies (or vice versa) for several hours every day. At six weeks of age, just keep them together at night.

Reduce the mother's amount of food at this time to slow her milk production so that she will not be too uncomfortable. If her mammary glands become very swollen and miserable, take a damp, warm towel and apply it to her breasts for a few minutes. This should help to relieve the discomfort. If she is not much more comfortable in a couple of days, have her checked by your veterinarian. DO NOT allow the puppies back with her, or squeeze milk out of the glands for her. The pressure of the retained milk helps to shut off the flow. As long as you or the puppies keep removing it, she will keep producing it, prolonging her discomfort. The puppies should not be allowed back with their mother until she has completely stopped producing milk and her breasts have receded to nearly their normal size and shape.

After all the puppies are eating the puppy chow gruel, you can gradually make it thicker until it is just a thick mush, and finally you can begin feeding it dry.

Young puppies need to eat more frequently than do older dogs. The puppy's stomach is small and cannot handle much food at a time. Several small meals will be more comfortable and efficient for him. Space them as regularly as you can for easy digestion (and well-spaced elimination, which makes for easier housebreaking). From six weeks to about three months of age, the puppy will do best on four meals a day, spaced four to five hours apart, during the hours that you are awake. From 3 to 6 months, three meals a day are enough. From six months to a year of age, two meals a day are sufficient. You can continue to feed two meals a day to dogs of large breeds (such as Saint Bernard and Newfoundland) until a year-and-a-half to two-years of age to help them attain their maximum growth. From this point on, you can either continue with two meals a day, or feed once a day—depending on the dog and what is most convenient for you, if you are not feeding free choice. If you wish to feed the dog free choice, you can do so any time after he is completely housebroken.

Puppies should, if at all possible, go to their new homes between 6-1/2 and 7 weeks of age. If they are taken away from their mother before that age, they are often inadequately socialized to the canine world. This can result in reproductive and behavioral problems later in life. Males often will attempt to mount humans, making a nuisance of themselves on people's legs. They may refuse to breed a female, instead turning to the humans to whom they are socialized. Females may leave their puppies or refuse to care for them, or show other signs of poor mothering. When puppies are left with their mother much beyond 7 weeks of age, they may become TOO socialized to the dog world, and may not bond well to humans.

Incidentally, dogs who have been in kennels all their lives generally make LOUSY pets, as they have not had adequate contact with humans at the young, critical age. They are often extremely shy. They are hard to train because they have not come to think of humans as part of their "pack." Some people feel that these dogs were "beaten," but that is generally not true. Their cowering and distrust are merely because of lack of social contact with people.

SPAYING

Why spay? Spaying prevents pregnancy and the birth of unwanted puppies. It avoids the need to kennel or restrain the bitch during her heat period. There is no attraction of males who tear up your shrubbery, urinate on everything, get into fights, climb your fence and generally make a nuisance of themselves. It keeps the female from roaming because she is in heat and is looking for a mate. It avoids reproductive-related problems such as tumors, pyometra and false pregnancy.

When to spay? In general, most veterinarians do not like to spay dogs before they are five to six months old. The more mature the dog is before she is spayed, the better she is able to withstand the anesthesia. Spaying at this age will catch most females before they come into their first heat (estrus) period. There is no need to let the female have a heat period before she is spayed. You can avoid the problems associated with estrus by spaying her before it occurs. There is evidence that the hormone, estrogen, which is secreted by the ovaries when she comes into heat, may sensitize the breast tissue to later tumor deveoplment. About 50% of mammary tumors are malignant and life-threatening. Early spaying may help to prevent these tumors from occurring.

It is also not necessary to let the female have a litter before she is spayed. There is no evidence that it changes her disposition, or makes her "calmer" or "more settled." Spaying does not slow or change her physical or mental development, nor does it alter her personality. It does not change the dog's activity level (except to remove the fact that she might normally have gone roaming, looking for a male, when she was in heat). Dogs who get fat after they are spayed do so because they have too little exercise and too many groceries, NOT because they were spayed. Spaying does not make the dog any less a guard dog than she would be without the surgery. Leaving her reproductively intact just produces puppies for whom homes must be found, or who go to their deaths because no homes are available. Ask any animal shelter operator how they feel about unspayed pet dogs if you are still unconvinced.

What about spaying the older dog? A dog who is not in heat or pregnant can be spayed at any time. Dogs who are in heat can be spayed, but there is slightly more risk, because the hormones cause the blood to clot more slowly, and there is more blood to deal with during spaying. Dogs can be easily spayed during the first month of pregnancy. When the dog is in heat or pregnant, veterinarians often charge a bit more because the dogs bleed more easily and the surgery takes more time and is more difficult. If the dog has just had a litter, wait until milk production has completely stopped, but before she gets pregnant again. A good time for the operation is usually between two and four weeks after the puppies are weaned. If you have a bitch that you have been breeding and no longer wish to breed, it is strongly urged that you consider spaying her to prevent the same problems which can occur in all unspayed females.

What is a "spay?" The word "spaying" brings visions of a simple piece of surgery. The technical name, "ovariohysterectomy," gives a better view of the operation. It is removal of the entire reproductive tract—uterus, Fallopian tubes, ovaries, and part of the ligaments that hold these organs. A spay is major abdominal surgery, but is routine to veterinarians because they do a large number of them.

PREPARATION FOR SURGERY

The dog should be in good condition, preferably not overweight, and preferably not in heat or pregnant. Call several days in advance to make an appointment for her surgery. Most veterinarians schedule a limited number of spays per day, and will not accept any more than that in order to have time for any emergency cases which must receive care. A few veterinarians like to have the dog brought to the clinic the night before surgery is to be performed. Most of them, however, like to have her come in the morning of surgery.

The dog should be kept off food and water before surgery. Do not give any food after her evening meal, and no water after midnight. That means closing the toilet so she can't sneak a drink, too. DO NOT try to be "nice" to the dog and feed or water her after these times. This is one time you could kill her with kindness! If she has anything in her stomach, she may vomit when she is given the anesthetic, or even after the surgery is completed. If she inhales this material, it will probably cause pneumonia and death. The food material and the bacteria on it cannot be removed from the lungs. Incidentally, this surgical preparation holds true for all surgery on dogs—young or old, male or female.

THE OPERATION

A general anesthetic is used, which means that the dog is completely anesthetized and is unconscious during surgery. She does not feel any pain, and does not know what is happening. Often a combination of drugs are used. The veterinarian may begin by administering a tranquilizer or narcotic sedative. This will help the dog to relax and will relieve any anxiety that she might feel by being in strange surroundings and around people whom she does not know.

Following sedation, the veterinarian will administer a short-acting anesthetic. This will take her to unconsciousness, and allow him to open her mouth and place a tube in her trachea. This tube will then be attached to an anesthetic machine which will deliver a mixture of an anesthetic gas and oxygen. The mixture can be precisely regulated to keep the dog in a surgical level of anesthesia. Many veterinarians use an intravenous anesthetic agent instead of gas. Recovery may be slower, and the level of anesthesia cannot be as easily controlled. However, intravenous anesthesia is an acceptable way to get the job done.

After the dog is anesthetized, she will be placed on a surgery table, with her belly upward, and gently tied in place. She is still connected to the gas anesthetic machine at this point. The veterinarian will make an incision in her belly and remove her uterus, ovaries, Fallopian tubes, and some of the associated ligaments and blood vessels. The stumps of the blood vessels are carefully tied off to prevent internal bleeding. For a normal dog who is not overweight, the incision may be as little as an inch long. This incision is then sutured.

When the surgery is over, the machine is disconnected and the tube is removed. Within a short time, her breathing will clear the remaining anestheic from her body, allowing her to wake up quickly and safely. The dog is put into a recovery area. She will still be groggy for a period of time, which is called the "recovery period."

Especially at some low-cost spay clinics, the dog may be sent home while still groggy. This may last for the rest of the day and part of the night. Put the dog in a darkened, warm place, and leave her alone! Check her every half hour or so to make sure that she is OK. If you have the dog out and around your family, she will try to walk and to follow you, and will be very upset that she cannot. If you leave her alone in a quiet place, she will sleep off the anesthetic normally. It is normal for the dog to "go up and down," alternating between periods of being more and less conscious. But she should gradually progress toward being MORE conscious. DO NOT give her any water until she is able to walk without staggering and acts like she knows where she is. Then only give her a couple of sips every half hour. Do not give her any food until the next day.

AFTERCARE

The dog should be restrained from excessive activity for two to three weeks after she is spayed. She should not hop up into a car or pickup, or onto the sofa or bed, as the stretching involved may tear open the incision.

Keep an eye on the incision. If reddening or swelling occur, or if pus oozes from the area, get in touch with your veterinarian within a day. The dog should feel well and eat and drink normally. Short walks are OK, but running is not a good idea for a couple of weeks after surgery. Swimming or bathing the dog are NOT OK, until the incision is completely healed. Water could seep into the incision and cause infection.

The stitches may be hidden, with no removal required. If stitches are visible, they should generally be removed in 10 to 14 days. You can remove them yourself with a pair of fingernail scissors. Clip about 1/16 inch (1 mm) to one side of the knot. Take your fingernails or a pair of tweezers, and pull out the stitch. Or you can take the dog back to your veterinarian for removal. The price of removal is normally included in the price of the spay. Many veterinarians like to remove the stitches themselves because it gives them a chance to see the dog to make sure everything is OK.

If the dog is fat, pregnant or is difficult to spay, she may have a long incision. This may also be the case if the dog has already been spayed. Sometimes it is very hard to tell that a dog has already been spayed without going inside and looking, surgically. Don't laugh—this can easily happen if you take in a stray or get a dog from a shelter. It will take a longer incision to deterimine that the dog has already been spayed. A long incision should not have any more trouble healing than a short one. As we say in the veterinary world, "incisions heal from side to side, not from end to end." However, with a longer incision, it will be even more important to limit her activity. If the dog has a thin or weak abdominal wall, or is overweight, she may come home with a wide bandage around her belly. This may also be the case if the dog has suffered excessive bleeding (which is usually due to her hormonal status rather than to any fault of the veterinarian). Carefully follow your veterinarian's recommendations for aftercare in this case.

The most serious problem which can occur after a spay is for the incision in the abdominal wall to completely come open (this is called wound dehiscence). This usually occurs either from excessive activity or due to infection of the surgical site. If the wound opens, intestines may drop out through the hole. THIS IS AN EMERGENCY. Your immediate care may make the difference between life and death for your dog. Soak a towel or strip of bedsheet with lukewarm water. Wrap it around the dog's belly. The idea is to keep the intestines moist and as free from dirt as possible. Get the dog to your veterinarian as soon as possible. If you cannot contact your veterinarian, take her to the nearest other clinic or emergency clinic. This is a VERY rare consequence after surgery, but it is good to know how to take care of it if it occurs. Remember, not having it happen is the reason for limiting the bitch's activity after she has been spayed.

If the bitch was in heat when she was spayed, or had just come out of heat, it is very important to keep her confined for a week or two after the surgery. Otherwise, the hormones still in her body may make her attractive to males. One of them may attempt to breed her, and can cause severe internal damage.

SPAYING THE VERY YOUNG DOG

Some humane societies and veterinarians are experimenting with spaying puppies and kittens as young as 8 weeks. They find this avoids the situation where animals are adopted and never brought back or never taken to a veterinarian for spaying or neutering. In most cases, the animals are carefully screened for anemia caused by parasites, as well as other illnesses such as diarrhea, dehydration and hypoglycemia. Early spaying be useful in this situation, where a particular end is desired. However, for my own animal, I would wait until 5-1/2 to 6 months of age, depending on the size and development of the animal.

ALTERNATIVES TO SPAYING

The easiest alternative is simply to keep the dog confined when she is in heat—the abstinence method of birth control.

You can put her in a kennel. With some dogs, this may necessitate her being there for an entire month. Kenneling is expensive, and you are without your pet. If you keep a large female inside the house, the blood spotting early in the heat cycle may seriously stain a light-colored carpet. If you keep her in your yard, she may stay in OK, but a male may climb or dig under the fence and breed her. A small dog may be kept in the house and only taken out on a leash. This may not be too inconvenient, although you may have to tolerate a gang of amorous males keeping you company.

Small harnesses are sold which hold a sanitary napkin. These keep spots off the carpet, but do NOT keep a male from breeding the female. Similarly, "poodle panties" do not prevent pregnancy.

Injections of male hormones are given to female Greyhounds to keep them out of heat while they are being raced. Some of these females will come back to normal fertility with appropriate treatment. Others will stay infertile and will never produce puppies (Moses, 1988).

If you think you would like to breed your dog at a later date, but do not want to do so right away, consult with your veterinarian. There are two drugs available, Ovaban® and Cheque®. These pills can be given to keep the dog out of heat. They must usually be started BEFORE the dog comes into heat. So check with your veterinarian about these drugs before you need them. These drugs do have a small percentage of reactions, which may include pyometra (an infection which causes the uterus to fill with pus). If this occurs, the dog may have to be spayed anyway.

A very few veterinarians offer a tubal ligation as a method of birth control. Their theory is that it allows the ovaries to function, retains the uterus within the dog's body and keeps her partly "intact." It still allows her to come into heat and be serviced by a male, although puppies will not result. This surgery, in the opinion of most veterinarians, has all the disadvantages of having an intact female (coming into heat, males hanging around and breeding her, a uterus which can still become infected, ovaries which can have tumors, mammary tumors, and the general fuss of caring for a bitch in heat), and none of the advantages (removal of the organs so that diseases do not occur).

NEUTERING

The term "neutering" applies to removal of the reproductive organs of both male and female dogs. It is most commonly associated with the removal of the testicles and epididymis of the male (castration). This surgery renders the male unable to reproduce, and has many advantages if you do not specifically want to keep the male intact for breeding. It reduces roaming, especially if performed before dog becomes sexually mature and establishes a territory. While roaming, the male has a greater chance of getting hit by a car, getting into a fight with another male, becoming lost, or contracting a contagious disease from another dog. Neutering reduces his tendency to urinate to mark his territory, especially in the house. A dog that is already sexually mature before being neutered may continue to exhibit mating behavior, may still roam, fight and mark his territory. Castrated dogs also are less likely to develop prostate infections or cancer in their old age. In general, the neutered male is simply a more pleasant, more acceptable pet. In some areas, the neutered male and spayed female have the advantage of much cheaper licensing fees.

When should the male be neutered? Much like spaying in the female, it is preferable so have the surgery done before the dog is sexually mature—around 6 to 8 months of age. At this point, you may notice him lifting his leg to urinate, and may begin to roam and fight. However, neutering can be done at any time beyond that age, providing the dog is in good health.

Preparation for the surgery is the same as for spaying: no food or water the evening before surgery. The surgery itself involves putting the dog under general anesthesia, as for spaying. The incision is not usually made directly over the scrotum, as there is a tendency to form a seroma when this is done. It is made on the midline ahead of the scrotum. The testicles and epididymis are removed, and the incision is generally sutured closed. The stitches may be entirely buried so that removal is not necessary. Or they may be exposed, in which case they should be removed in 10-14 days. Some veterinarians use stainless steel sutures so that they prick the dog's tongue when he tries to lick, preventing premature removal by the dog.

If the dog licks excessively after he is neutered, he may end up tearing the incision open. Give your veterinarian a call if he is doing a lot of licking. The veterinarian may prescribe a bad-tasting medication to put on the area. A deterrent such as Variton® Creme may be used to keep him from worrying at the surgical site. Or, your veterinarian may wish to put a collar or bucket on the dog to keep him from reaching and irritating the incision.

These instructions apply to castration of the normal male dog, one who has both testicles in his scrotum. If the dog is a cryptorchid, the surgery is much more complicated, as well as more expensive. In such cases, the surgery is about the same as a spay in the female.

CRYPTORCHIDISM

The normal puppy's testicles develop inside the abdomen while he is in the fetal stage. They descend into the scrotum at birth or within 10 days after birth. If they are going to descend into the scrotum, they will ALWAYS do so before six months of age. If one or both testicles do not descend into the scrotum, the dog is said to be a cryptorchid (meaning "hidden testicle"). About 10 percent of dogs have this problem. It is hereditary, and dogs with this defect should not be bred. For this reason, surgery done to pull the testicle(s) into the scrotum is considered by most veterinarians to be unethical. There is no medical treatment which will make the testicle(s) descend into the scrotum. Cryptorchids are disqualified from AKC shows.

Neutering a cryptorchid is more like spaying a female than neutering a normal male, and a dog with one descended and one retained testicle will probably have two incisions when he is neutered—one where a standard castration would be performed, and one more nearly like a spay incision. Expect to considerably pay more for this surgery than for a routine castration.

An undescended testicle will still produce male hormones, and is many times more likely to develop a tumor than a normal testicle. For this reason, a cryptorchid dog should always be neutered to prevent the development of an internal tumor when he is older. Neutering also removes any chance of passing on this genetic defect.

REPRODUCTIVE PROBLEMS

FEMALE

False pregnancy (also called pseudopregnancy or pseudocyesis) is occasionally seen in dogs. The bitch may have all the signs of a real pregnancy, including weight gain, nesting behavior, milk production and even labor pains, but no puppies are born. If all this activity has led you to assume she is pregnant (logical assumption!), the first step is a visit to your veterinarian. He will examine her, and may even wish to take X-rays to confirm or deny the presence of puppies. False pregnancy is why you see newspaper pictures of dogs adopting litters of kittens, squirrels and other beasties. They may attempt to mother a toy, a slipper, a piece of clothing, or even piles of shredded newspaper or cloth. Some dogs may try to nurse themselves. This particular activity can be prevented by a collar or side stick.

In the wild, false pregnancy is thought to serve a very real purpose, as it allows nonpregnant females to assist in feeding another female's litter of pups. Or the nonpregnant female is able to adopt a litter whose mother has been killed or is ill, thus helping to insure survival of the pack and its offspring.

False pregnancy may be curtailed by the use of hormones, but at the risk of upsetting her system and causing later problems. Tranquilizers may be helpful for the female with a severe behavioral upset. Some bitches in false pregnancy are found to be hypothyroid. This may be worth testing for if you wish to keep the female for breeding stock. If she is perfectly healthy, it may be easier to just let her mother the kittens or squirrels (providing their mother approves, or they are in need of a mother!). False pregnancy is almost certain to recur at the bitch's next heat cycle. Spaying is the best and most certain cure.

Infertility may be due to many different causes. Hormonal imbalances may prevent the bitch from coming into heat, or may keep her from carrying a pregnancy to term if she is bred. Conformational abnormalities of the reproductive tract (malformed uterus, etc.) may prevent impregnation. Some of the malformations are not possible to correct, but many can be bypassed by artificial insemination. Bacterial, fungal or viral diseases of the reproductive tract may keep the dog from becoming pregnant. Laboratory tests may be necessary for your veterinarian to determine whether any disease processes are present and what treatment is needed. Laboratory determinations of hormone levels may also be needed. In extreme cases, if nothing else is found and you really want to breed the dog, it may be necessary to do an exploratory laporatomy—that is, to go into the abdomen surgically and "take a look," firsthand. Any dog with a reproductive problem should be examined by a veterinarian.

Some females may have dispositional problems when breeding is attempted. Either they may attack the male, intimidating him, or they may show no interest at all, making breeding difficult. Careful restraint may be tried, with the bitch's owner holding her while the male's owner directs and controls his dog. The female should be muzzled so that she cannot bite either the handlers or the male. Artificial insemination is the easiest way around this problem. But do you really want to perpetuate the problem by raising litters from this bitch (no pun intended!)?

Vaginitis is an inflammation of the vagina. It may occur in any bitch—whether spayed or intact, young or old. It is most commonly due to bacterial infection. Sometimes this is associated with a conformational defect in the vaginal area. The most common sign is drainage from the vulva. The drainage may be bloody, clear or pus-like. This odor may attract males, even with a spayed bitch. The bitch may lick continuously at her vulva. Have her checked by your veterinarian. It may be necessary for him to have a blood sample checked at the laboratory to tell this disease from pyometra, if the dog is unspayed. In general, the dog with vaginitis is otherwise normal and feels well, while the dog with pyometra may show other signs of illness.

Treatment for vaginitis usually includes antibiotics via injection, orally or both. Antibiotic or very dilute povidone-iodine douches may be used twice daily for as long as four weeks. Young bitches who have not come into their first heat often do not need any treatment—the problem will disappear when they do come into heat, unless something else is wrong.

Vulvitis is an inflammation of the vulva. Symptoms may be similar to those of vaginitis, only with less drainage. The vulva may be swollen, and the dog may lick it. As with vaginitis, antibiotics will be needed at the infected area. Treatment is similar to vaginitis.

Vaginal hyperplasia is an overgrowth of the lining of the vagina. It begins on the floor of the vagina, and becomes larger during proestrus and estrus. It will reduce in size as the bitch goes out of heat. It is usually seen during the first few heat cycles. Enough growth may occur that a lump of tissue protrudes from the vagina. In older dogs, this may look similar to a tumor. For this reason, it is important to have the dog examined by your veterinarian. He may wish to take a sample of the tissue for examination by a lab in order to tell if it is a tumor or just hyperplasia. Vaginal hyperplasia is usually not treated if it is not causing problems. However, you may have to put an ointment on it to keep it from drying out, and the area should be kept clean. An Elizabethan collar may be needed to keep the bitch from chewing the area. The bitch may be bred by artificial insemination, and the mass usually goes down by the time she is ready to whelp. If the mass becomes very large or causes problems with urination, it may be necessary to surgically remove some or all of it. The problem will generally recur with each heat cycle. Spaying will not make the mass go away any sooner than if the dog is not spayed, but it will prevent it from happening again with each heat cycle.

PYOMETRA

Pyometra is an infection in which the uterus becomes filled with pus, due to a bacterial infection of the lining. Estrogen injections, sometimes given for "mismating," may contribute to the occurrence of pyometra, as can some drugs used to produce abortion or to prevent pregnancy. A hormone imbalance within the bitch's body may also initiate a case of pyometra. Pyometra is most commonly seen in middle-aged dogs, around 7 to 10 years of age. When hormones are used to produce abortiton, the disease can be seen in bitches less than a year of age.

Signs of pyometra will vary, depending on whether the cervix is open or closed. If it is open, a bloody, pus-like discharge may be seen dripping from the vulva. It may stain the hind legs and cake the hair, and often is associated with a foul odor. Pyometra often occurs 4 to 8 weeks after the bitch goes out of heat. In addition, the dog may be depressed, vomit and quit eating. She may drink more water than normal, and also urinate more frequently. If the uterus is closed, depression, vomiting and lack of appetite may be the only signs—drainage will not be seen. If not PROMPTLY treated, pyometra can quickly result in shock, dehydration, coma and death. THIS IS AN EMERGENCY, even if it's the middle of the night. If drainage is present, it is not quite so urgent, but it is still serious.

Pyometra is sometimes difficult to diagnose, and your veterinarian may need to run blood tests, and possibly take an X-ray to confirm the diagnosis. Spaying the dog immediately is the best treatment, even though the risk from anesthesia is high. If you wish to salvage her for breeding AND she is not too ill, a more conservative treatment using hormones and antibiotics may be tried. In some cases, prostaglandins have been used to drain pus out of the uterus and attempt to save the dog's reproductive capability (Brown, 1985). However, overall, spaying seems to save more animals than do more "conservative" treatments. This is because the large quantity of bacteria present in the uterus is spreading infection throughout the body. It's like having a balloon filled with pus inside the abdominal cavity. The blood supply to the uterus is less than adequate, making it difficult to transport antibiotics into the infected area.

Spaying a dog with pyometra is a delicate piece of surgery. The uterine wall is thin and tears easily. The dog is already ill and has less physical reserves than a dog being spayed under normal conditons. She will also have less tolerance to anesthetic than she would otherwise have. For these reasons, there is significantly more risk than in a normal spay (but less risk than if she is NOT spayed). Also it's more expensive surgery because of the complications. Intensive care, including large quantities of intravenous fluids, may be necessary to save the animal's life. After surgery is performed, the bitch will be kept on antibiotics for about 7 to 10 days to get rid of the rest of the bacteria in her body. If you and your veterinarian try conservative treatment and are successful, it is highly probable that the problem will recur at later heat cycles. The dog should be bred at each heat cycle until you no longer wish to breed her. She should then be spayed.

Pregnancy sometimes prevents the conditions from developing in the uterus which lead to pyometra.

Mammary tumors are occasionally seen in dogs. They are much more common in unspayed dogs, although they are occasionally found in spayed females; they are extremely rare in male dogs. Spaying the bitch before she has had her first heat period dramatically reduces her risk of mammary tumors. About 50% to 60% of unspayed dogs develop breast tumors by age 10 (Shirk, 1988). The two hind mammary glands have tumors much more frequently than the three front pairs. Tumors may occur in just one gland, or in several. These tumors have a roughly 50-50 chance of being malignant.

The safest course is to assume that all mammary tumors are malignant. As with similar tumors in humans, it does not pay to wait. Have the dog examined by your veterinarian. Most veterinarians prefer to remove the lumps within a reasonable length of time (say, a week or two, at your and his convenience). The affected mammary gland(s) will be removed. If the growth is extensive, lymph nodes in the area may also be taken out. Chemotherapy and radiation treatments of these tumors are still in the experimental stage. It is usually not worth risking your dog's life to save her mammary glands. If you still want her to have puppies, they can either survive on the glands that are left, or be raised as orphans by hand.

Long haired dogs who are older than four or five years should have the breast area palpated at least once a month. Feel for abnormal lumps or swellings, hardened areas, or areas of unusual softness. Lumpy, puckered, abnormally shaped glands are easily seen in shorthaired dogs. A breast exam should be part of your routine care of the dog, especially for the bitch.

MALE

Infertility in male dogs occurs in the ones we most want to breed (naturally!). In the wild, or in city dogs who are running loose, infertile dogs do not reproduce themselves and are eliminated from the genetic pool. In contrast, we select purebred dogs for how they look, perform, etc., rather than how fertile they are. And we go to great lengths to help those who are less fertile to reproduce because we like their "breed characteristics."

Infertility may be due to conformational or developmental problems, hormonal abnormalities, or infectious causes (such as brucellosis).

Finding the cause of infertility begins with a complete physical examination, including a medical and breeding history. Laboratory testing for brucellosis is important. Your veterinarian will check a sample of the dog's semen to find out if it is normal. Some males may be rendered temporarily sterile by the administration of drugs. Be sure to tell your veterinarian if you have given the dog any medication within the last six months or so.

Phimosis is the condition where the dog cannot extend his penis from the sheath. The dog may have been born with an abnormally small opening in the sheath. Or the opening of the prepuce (sheath) may be constricted by shrinking of scar tissue after an injury, or due to a tumor or fluid accumulation (edema) in the area. If the opening is constricted enough, the dog will have trouble urinating, the prepuce may swell and pus may drip from it. Usually it is not obvious, and no signs are noticed until the dog attempts to mount and breed a female.

Treatment for phimosis depends on how severe the constriction is, and how you intend to use the dog. If he is urinating normally and you do not intend to use him for breeding, treatment is probably not needed, although castration is a good idea. If the constriction interferes with urination, or the dog is to be used for breeding, the opening of the prepuce must be enlarged surgically. Your veterinarian can do this quite easily.

Paraphimosis occurs when the dog has an erection and gets the penis out of the sheath, but is unable to get it back in. In most cases, this is due to long hairs around the opening of the prepuce pulling back into the sheath along the shaft of the penis, and binding it in the extended position. If this continues long enough, the dog will be unable to urinate and will have urinary tract and bladder problems. The blood supply to the penis will be shut off, and gangrene may occur.

Treatment for paraphimosis begins with re-establishing drainage of the veins from the penis. Hair which is holding the penis out should be gently clipped and removed. The penis is then soaked in a strong cold sugar solution. Use 1-2 ounces of sugar in 10 ounces of water (30-60 grams in 300 ml). The penis can then be lubricated with a water-soluble lubricant such as K-Y Jelly® (Johnson & Johnson, New Brunswick, N. J., 08903), and gently slipped back into the prepuce. If you can't get the swelling down enough to replace the penis, keep it packed in cloths soaked in the cool sugar solution. You may have to do this for an hour or two. The sugar solution actually pulls fluid from the swollen tissues.

When the penis has been returned to the sheath, it must be pulled out daily to prevent adhesions from forming. Otherwise, the lining of the sheath may grow to the surface of the penis, and it may never function normally again. It is often helpful to grasp the end of the penis with a clean soft cloth or piece of paper towel to help pull it out. At the same time, an ointment or cream with a combination of an antibiotic and a corticosteroid should be applied, and the area should be massaged (see balanoposthitis, below). Mastitis medications made for cattle are often used here, too. The extension, treatment and massage should be continued for ten days to two weeks.

If the dog is not urinating normally, it may be necessary for your veterinarian to put a catheter in place. It will be left until the effects of the paraphimosis are healed. Signs of gangrene include a foul odor from the area, and a blackish or bluish discoloration of the tissue. The tissue may be cold to the touch. If any of these signs occur, be sure to have your veterinarian examine the dog. In severe cases, it may be necessary to amputate the penis and/or the prepuce. It may still be possible to collect semen from the dog and breed by artificial insemination if he is a valuable stud dog.

Tumors are sometimes seen in the testicles of male dogs. Perhaps the most common is the Sertoli cell tumor, which is found in testicle(s) which are retained in the abdomen in cryptorchid males. About fifty percent of all retained testicles will be affected. While this tumor is usually slow-growing, if not removed in time it may spread through the dog's system, eventually causing his death. This is why it is strongly recommended that all retained testicles be removed while the dog is young. Other tumors, such as seminomas and interstitial cell tumors, are occasionally seen.

Signs of testicular tumors may include swelling of one or both testicles, misshapen testicles, and puckering of the skin on the scrotum. There may be signs of hormonal imbalance. The dog may have hair loss (usually symmetrical from one side to the other). This hair loss often begins over the collar area, tail-head area and loins. He may have seborrhea, or the skin may be blackened. Feminization may occur. Signs of feminization include swelling of the mammary glands, lack of interest in females, prostate problems, and a hanging, floppy prepuce (sheath). Other males may be attracted to the dog.

Neutering is a simple and effective cure for most testicular tumors, especially if done early, before they spread to other parts of the body. If the dog is so old or in such ill health that it is too risky to anesthetize him, testosterone treatment may be of some help. This is only effective if the dog is not showing feminization or overgrowth of the perianal glands.

Balanoposthitis is the name given to an infection of the sheath and shaft of the penis. It occurs because the area is warm and damp, making an ideal site for bacterial growth. Mild cases are present in MOST male dogs, and are the reason why they spend considerable time licking themselves. No treatment is needed. Dogs with severe infections show swelling of the sheath and pain, and may have a considerable amount of pus dripping from the opening of the sheath. If severe enough, the dog may show fever and other general signs of illness. This condition DOES need to be treated.

Less severe cases of balanoposthitis may be treated by extending the penis and cleaning both the shaft of the penis and the lining of the sheath with a mild disinfectant such as povidone-iodine. An antibiotic ointment can then be squeezed into the sheath daily for 7-10 days. Mastitis ointments made for cattle are often used. The tip of the tube is inserted into the end of the sheath, and the fingers are used to pinch the skin shut around the tube. A teaspoon or so of the ointment is then squeezed into the prepuce. Withdraw the tube tip while still holding the prepuce closed. Then massage the ointment along the shaft of the penis a half-dozen times. Severe cases may need injections or oral antibiotics for the same period of time in addition to the local treatment. Whatever treatment is used, chances are very good the infection will recur with time, and may need re-treatment.

Inappropriate mounting behavior is often seen because the male puppy was taken away from his mother at an early age, and was never adequately socialized to the dog world. Instead, he has become "attached" to humans, and thinks that your legs, or those of members of your family or friends, should be objects of his attentions. The dog will grab around the leg with both his front legs, and make thrusting motions, often with an erection. This can be both annoying and embarrassing—it is seldom funny. Disciplinary measures can be helpful in curbing this behavior—period! You, as "leader" of his pack, have to make it clear that he is not allowed to "breed" anyone else. This can be done with a newspaper, your boot or a 2 x 4, depending on the size of the offending dog. Meanwhile, shout at him in your most evil and dominant tone, in whatever words you use for discipline, that this behavior will not be tolerated. A few sessions should establish your dominance and teach him the rules of your pack. Neutering may help in some cases. Just kidding about the 2 x 4, but sometimes it is tempting to grab one when you are dealing with one of these young, undisciplined testosterone factories.

Transmissible venereal tumor is passed from one dog to another at breeding time. It can affect either males or females. In males, the tumor looks like cauliflower-shaped masses, or granules of varying size and shape. These are reddish or cream-colored, and may have ulcerated or dead areas on them. In females, one or more similar masses may bulge from the vagina. Tumor growth is usually first noticed about a week after mating.

If not treated, about two-thirds of transmissible venereal tumors will go away by themselves within two months, as the dog's body develops immunity against the foreign cells. Of the remaining one-third, most will grow deep into the local tissues. Only a small percentage of the tumors will spread (metastasize) throughout the body, to sites which include the skin, lymph nodes in the area, testicle, and other organs. Surgical treatment works well. Radiation treatment works quickly and consistently. Chemotherapy works well, especially if the disease has spread throughout the body.

For diseases of the prostate gland, see Chapter on Urinary Tract.

Chapter 9

THE IMPORTANCE OF NURSING

THE IMPORTANCE OF NURSING

> "...grant me the serenity
> To accept the things I cannot change,
> Courage to change the things I can,
> And wisdom to know the difference."

These words by Rheinhold Niebuhr seem particularly applicable to the field of veterinary medicine. There are those problems we CAN change, such as suturing a wound, splinting a broken leg, giving the proper antibiotics to help kill infection-causing bacteria or helping your dog to give birth to her puppies.

The rub comes with problems that we cannot directly relieve—those that leave the veterinarian and dog-owner both feeling helpless. If you are cursing your veterinarian's inablility to change the course of a case of distemper (which is caused by a virus) in your beloved dog, stop and consider how little human medicine can do for the common cold! Or, for that matter, AIDS. Medicine has not developed to the point where we can even influence, and certainly cannot cure, most

viral diseases. Problems such as distemper and parvovirus infections can be prevented by immunizing your dog against them, but there is little that can be done if you don't immunize him and he catches the disease. A dog with one of these problems leaves us feeling helpless. While cures may indeed be found for some of these diseases within our lifetimes, there is, at present, only nursing care available to help the animal that has the disease.

It is with diseases such as distemper that you can influence the outcome of the disease through careful and diligent nursing care. Veterinary medicine cannot heal these diseases directly—we can only give the animal the best conditions possible, hoping that his immune system and bodily defenses are strong enough to overcome the problem. The day-to-day nursing care and help that you supply can, quite literally, often make the difference between life and death. Even when dealing with diseases where a veterinarian can do something, good nursing care will often help the dog heal faster and more completely. Let's discuss some specifics about nursing the sick dog:

1) Shelter. The dog who is seriously ill must have moderate temperatures. If he lives indoors with you, this is generally not a problem. Move his bed to a warm, draft-free corner, out of the main traffic pattern but close enough that he can see what is going on the house while he is resting. If he sleeps quietly at night, you might want to put a lightweight blanket over him. Or put a coat on him if you have one handy. An old jacket or sweatshirt will fit a large dog and give him some warmth and comfort.

If the dog normally lives outdoors and is sick in the winter, bringing him inside may save his life. If he has diarrhea or a similar problem and you cannot bring him inside, do the best you can for him outdoors. Make him a small, warm corner in a shed or garage, boxing it off with a couple of pieces of scrap plywood. Or stop by an appliance store and get a box from a television set or a dryer to make a temporary doghouse. You can heat it with an infrared lamp, the kind used to keep calves warm. But be careful that it is well secured and cannot be knocked over, or it may cause a fire. Also make sure that it does not overheat the dog. A deep bed of clean, dust-free straw will provide comfort and insulation. You could also use burlap bags, old blankets or carpet. In an emergency, a horse trailer or other draft-free trailer can make a shelter, or you can put the dog in a car or pickup cab to keep the wind, rain or snow off him for the night—if he's not vomiting or doesn't have diarrhea!

If it is summer and is hot outside, it is still a good idea to have the dog indoors so that he will not get too hot. And he will not have to fight flies, gnats, mosquitoes, and other insects. When it's summer in the southwestern United States and 110 degrees F (44.4 C), the dog doesn't need heat stroke added to his problems!

If your home isn't air conditioned and your area is experiencing a hot spell, a fan will help move air and make the dog more comfortable. If the dog is outdoors and you can't move him (such as having a very large dog collapse and you're a small person at home by yourself), any shade that you can provide may save his life. A tarp thrown across a couple of sawhorses placed on either side will give a bit of shade. Or park a vehicle beside the dog for shade until you can get help to move him. If you either can't move him or get shade for him, cover his face with a rag or towel to help keep his eyes and mouth shaded. Sponge him with cool (not cold!) water several times a day to help keep his temperature down to normal until you can get help to move him.

2) Nutrition. Your dog should have good, high quality food that is easy to digest. It should have adequate nutritional content to provide for healing damaged or diseased tissues. The animal who is ill probably will not eat as much as normal, making it doubly important that the food provide as many nutrients as possible in a small quantity. On the other hand, avoid sudden changes to over-rich food that can add digestive problems on top of the existing illness. Use your judgment or ask your veterinarian any questions regarding feeding your sick dog.

3) Water. Water is very important—VITAL—to maintaining the fluid balance within the body in order to aid healing. Your doctor often advises, "Take two aspirin and drink lots of fluids." Especially with virus diseases, it is important that the body not become dehydrated. Dehydration can cause serious complications for an already-sick dog. The water should be fresh and clean and changed frequently. Try to keep it cool, but not cold, in summer. If the dog will not drink, he may lick ice cubes—it's worth a try. A light chicken or beef broth might entice him to drink liquid. Keep the salt content low unless your veterinarian advises otherwise.

In winter, if the dog is outdoors, offer him warm water several times a day. Or use a bucket with a heater in it. Make sure that the dog is not getting an electric shock from the heater, and watch to see that he is indeed drinking and not just splashing it on the ground.

4) Freedom from insects. If your dog is indoors, this should not be a problem. Can you imagine lying in bed with a cold and having flies buzzing all over your body? Your sick dog surely can't enjoy it either. If he's outdoors, you can spray the area lightly with an insecticide that is safe for use around dogs. Cover him with some fly netting or put him in a screened area.

Insect repellent can be used ON the dog. When using a new insect repellent, try a small spot on the dog's neck and let it sit for 12 hours or so. Do something else to protect him during this time. Testing this small patch will let you know if he is allergic to the product before you marinate him in it. If the patch doesn't show any reaction, you can use it on the rest of the dog according to directions. Some of the stick-type insect repellents used for horses can be used around the dog's eyes or nose. Again, test a small patch first. Poisoned baits may help to reduce fly numbers in the area—make sure they are set safely outside the dog's reach.

5) Grooming. Don't overdo it, but a sick dog should be brushed to help remove dirt, stimulate circulation in the skin,

and just generally help the animal feel better. Sponging drainage from the eyes and nose with a dampened paper towel, or wiping it away with a tissue, will make him feel better and reduce the number of insects that are attracted to his face. Wipe mucus from just inside his nostrils with a cotton swab and then coat them with petroleum jelly to keep them from drying and cracking. The dog's sense of smell is very important to his appetite, and cleaning his nose will help him to be more interested in eating, which, in turn, will help to keep his strength up.

It will be very helpful If the dog is able to go outdoors to have a bowel movement and/or to urinate. When he comes back in, make sure that he is clean so that he does not soil his bed. Wipe him clean if necessary. He should not be allowed to lie down with damp hair, as this may cause an infection on the skin. If the dog is unable to go outdoors, you will have to take care of him. Put plastic or rubber matting down on the floor then put down layers of carpet or other disposable material. Last, put down towels, blankets or rags which are either washable or disposable. Mattress pads work well. The bedding should be soft so that the dog will not develop sores from lying on it. The items can be washed or thrown away when soiled. The dog should be turned from one side to the other a half-dozen times a day to keep him from getting pressure sores ("bedsores") from lying on one side all the time.

You can make a diaper by pulling a soft piece of cloth or towel up between the dog's hind legs and around the tail. It doesn't need to be pinned in place, especially if the dog is lying down. When it becomes soiled, wipe the dog gently with a cloth moistened in warm water. Dry him with a soft towel or rag, and dust the area with a light coating of talcum powder. This process will help to prevent skin irritation and reduce odors. On a long-haired dog, it is helpful to clip all the hair off the hind end and underside of the tail so that it can be more easily kept clean. Be careful not to irritate the skin with the clippers. You will have enough trouble keeping the skin healthy without creating more problems.

6) Exercise or rest? The decision to exercise or rest your dog depends on the illness and your veterinarian's instructions. If you don't understand or agree, ask the veterinarian why he is recommending the rest or exercise. Also, be sure you understand how much, when, and what kind of exercise to give the dog.

7) Medication. Pills or injections should be given as close to the prescribed times as possible. The veterinarian may tell you to give a pill every 12 hours because the drug only stays in the blood for 14 hours. If you go much beyond this time interval, the animal may be without adequate levels of antibiotics in his body, giving bacteria a chance to start growing again and maybe get ahead. Bandages should be changed or wounds cleaned according to your veterinarian's instructions.

If you have any questions about treatment or progress, don't hesitate to call your veterinarian. Most veterinarians would rather get an extra call or two than to have an owner treat the animal in a way that would be harmful or delay healing. Regular medication or bandage changes will result in faster healing than treatment in "fits and starts." Do what you are supposed to do, and do it when you are supposed to do it, and you will save time and save money on medications, bandaging materials and extra veterinary visits.

8) Miscellaneous. Some dogs do best with a companion around, while others should not be fussed over and pushed around by their normal companion. Separation may be the only way for the animal to get some rest and relaxation. And, speaking of rest—don't worry your dog to death by hovering over him. Take care of him so that he is comfortable, but don't fuss with him all day long. That's why hospitals have visiting hours—so that sick people can get some rest!

Strangers may be upsetting to a sick dog—think of that before you have all your friends over. This may be a good time to go over to see them for a change, and leave Fido at home to get some sleep. It's definitely NOT a good time for the kids to have a slumber party at YOUR house! When you are home, your dog may appreciate it if you just sit by him from time to time, perhaps just touching him with your hand or foot as you read the newspaper or watch T.V. Knowing that you care can make a real difference in your dog's recovery.

Last, but definitely not least, hang in there. Many problems can be cured if we just keep after them long enough to give the animal a chance to heal himself.

9) Medications in general. The medication meant for your pet has been specifically chosen by your veterinarian for your pet's needs. Unless directed otherwise, give ALL the medication until it is gone. Or consult with your veterinarian and get his advice that it is OK to stop giving it. Perhaps the most common cause of a dog not getting completely over a disease, or having it come back again, is that the owner does not give all the pills as directed because the dog was "getting better". Stopping too soon allows the bacteria to come back, as they may not have been completely controlled at that point. If you think that your dog is having a reaction or side effect to the medication, please let your veterinarian know right away.

Be sure that you understand how to give the medication. Your veterinarian will be glad either to write out instructions, or give you a demonstration of what he wants done. Or ask his receptionist or technician if you feel more comfortable dealing with him or her. But—ask SOMEBODY if you aren't sure how to do it.

Give all medications with as little fuss as possible. Keep an eye on your pet for signs of excitement, such as panting and weakness. If you have any question about it, stop your attempt and consult your veterinarian before continuing. Better to miss one dose than to fight the dog and kill him or cause a relapse.

Now that we've discussed some important points about nursing, let's cover some treatment methods which you may be using.

ORAL MEDICATIONS

LIQUID MEDICATIONS

Liquid medications are sometimes given to dogs. Often, your veterinarian will prescribe a human pediatric liquid medication, especially if it is an antibiotic or other drug which is not easily available in veterinary dosage or form. Human anti-diarrheal drugs are often given to dogs in liquid form. They are convenient, safe, and most of us have them handy. Human cough syrups can also be used, especially the pediatric formulations.

Liquids should be measured as closely as possible. You can use a measuring spoon, the kind from your kitchen. You can ask your veterinarian for a syringe, or get one at the feed store if they can legally be sold in your state. Use it without the needle, of course. You can also buy a small measure at the drugstore which has a calibrated cylinder and a spoon-like top. You just pour the liquid in it up to the amount needed, and use it to pour the medication into the dog's lip. Or you can use a plastic pill vial obtained from your druggist. You might ask him to calibrate it with a line at the proper level.

Approximate measures are: 20 drops = 1 ml (cc), 1 teaspoon = 5 ml, 1 Tablespoon = 15 ml, and 1 cup = 250 ml = 8 oz.

The easiest way to give liquids to a dog is by putting the liquid in the pouch of his cheek, outside of his teeth. Hold his head with one hand (have someone else hold the rest of the dog if necessary). Pull out the flap of the cheek, and place the liquid in it. Do not put in more than a teaspoon or so at a time. You can hold the dog's head SLIGHTLY above level, but NO more than that. If you hold it too high, you risk having him inhale some of the medication. With some drugs, inhaling them could be fatal. Wait until he swallows before you put more into the pouch.

Maybe he won't swallow. What do you do then? You can stroke his throat gently, in a downward direction, from the base of his tongue part way down the neck. Or you can put a small drop of the medication on his nose. When he licks it off, he will end up swallowing the rest of it. When his tongue pokes out through his teeth, you will know that he has swallowed. You can also tell that he has swallowed by watching his throat bob as the medication goes down.

Continue until you have given the whole dosage of medication. Wipe the dog's face with a dampened washcloth or paper towel. If medication is left on the face, it may cause the hair to come out. At the very least, it may become smelly and spoiled, and will cause discomfort to both you and the dog.

Coat supplements and some worming medications can be given by mixing them with the dog's food. Try a bit of the medication with just a little food in the bowl, however, before you give the dog the rest of his "spiked" dinner. Otherwise he may smell the different odor, and leave the medicated portion of his meal in the bowl. Important medications such as antibiotics should not be given with food because they might not be eaten. It is often easier to give the dog his medicine before you give him his dinner. In this way, his dinner becomes a reward for taking the medicine. Some oral medications are irritating to an empty stomach; feeding right afterward may help. Ask your veterinarian about feeding along with, before or after giving the medication.

PILLS AND TABLETS

Pills and tablets are handy, and many common medications come in a variety of dosage sizes which are made to accommodate dogs from Chihuahuas to Saint Bernards. Your veterinarian may also prescribe human drugs, as this allows him to give some of the modern antibiotics which may not yet be available in veterinary form, as well as drugs which are so rarely used for animals that they are not produced for the veterinary market.

You give pills to a dog by placing one hand over the top of the muzzle. Press the cheek into the space behind the canine teeth, and gently but firmly open the dog's mouth, pressing inward and upward. Pull the upper jaw upward and backward, toward the dog's back. Do not pull it too far back, or the dog will fight you. However, pulling it a little way back will make it easier to hold. Do not count on keeping his mouth open by wrapping his cheek over his teeth with your fingers. The dog may bite through both the cheek and your hand. It is also very helpful if you are clearly dominant over your dog, so that when you speak sharply to him if he struggles he will stop immediately.

Next, using your other hand, pull the lower jaw down, and place the pill as far back on the tongue as possible, in the middle of it. Close the dog's mouth, and hold it gently shut. Hold it shut until he has swallowed. It will help some dogs to swallow to stroke the throat as if it were a liquid medication. Pinching his nostrils shut as you close the mouth will cause many dogs to swallow.

You can also use a "pill gun" which holds the pill, allowing you to place it far back into the dog's throat. You can then squeeze the plunger (much like a syringe), which pushes the pill out onto

Drop the pill onto the back of the dog's tongue, pushing it down with your finger.

the dog's tongue. Be careful! You can injure the throat area if you go too far back into the throat with the instrument.

Sometimes you can feed the dog his pills, using any food which is "legal" for his diet to disguise the pills. Putting the pill in a piece of cheese, hot dog or meat works well with some dogs. But don't use a hot dog or other salty meat for a dog on a salt-restricted diet. Some dogs will learn to take the pill if you give them a (legal!) treat afterward. You may try a couple of the treats, such as hot dog slices, without pills, followed by the one with the pill. If you are going to be giving the dog pills for a long period of time, it is well worth your while to train him to take them readily, and make it easy on BOTH of you. Some dogs will also take the pill if you coat it with butter and then offer it. Margarine works with some dogs and doesn't work with others. You can use sugar pills, harmless vitamins, or small round dog treats as trial pills to see which, if any, of these methods will work for your dog.

Capsules are occasionally used for dogs. They may also be used for special medications which are measured and placed into capsules in order to give something too bitter or distasteful for the dog to take as a powder or a liquid. If you are giving a capsule, you may have trouble with it sticking to the dog's tongue, with him spitting it out later. This can be avoided by lubricating it with a bit of salad oil before you pop it onto the dog's tongue. This will make it slide down without sticking.

Whatever method you use, watch the dog carefully for several minutes after you have given him the pill or capsule, to be sure that he has indeed swallowed it. If he spits it out, try again until you get it down him. If you have tried everything and still can't get him to take the pill or capsule, ask your veterinarian for help. He may be able to think of something you haven't tried. Or he may be able to convert to a liquid or injectible form of the drug. He may have you bring the dog into the clinic for daily treatment. It's cheaper to train your dog.

OTHER ORAL MEDICATIONS

Paste medications are sometimes used. These commonly include vitamins, laxatives and high-calorie supplements. They come in tubes much like toothpaste, and the dosage is usually measured in inches of material squeezed out of the tube. The paste can be easily squeezed onto the dog's tongue, and he will usually swallow. Many of these products are made with liver extracts and other good flavoring agents, and most dogs accept them eagerly. Nutri-cal® (Evsco Pharmaceuticals) is an example of a nutritional supplement which comes either in a tube or in a pump-type dispenser.

Powdered supplements or medications are occasionally used. Sometimes they can be mixed with gravy, jelly or peanut butter ("sticks to the roof of your mouth..."). Or, they can be put into empty gelatin capsules and given that way.

EYE MEDICATIONS

To put any medication on the eyeball, it is often easiest to have the dog in a sitting position, with his head extended upward. A small dog should be placed on a table or counter, as this gives you better control of him and a better working angle for putting medication in the eye.

After you have put the drops or ointment in the dog's eye, distract his attention for a minute or two to keep him from rubbing his eye and injuring it or removing some of the medication. This can be done by playing with him, taking him for a walk or feeding him.

Eye medications occasionally cause sudden allergic reactions or irritation, resulting in an itching, weeping, reddened eye. These are individual reactions to the particular medication being used, and are more annoying than serious. However, if a reaction occurs, discontinue treatment immediately and consult your veterinarian as soon as possible. He may wish to change your dog to a different medication, or the same medication in a different base. These medications, as is true of all drugs, should be kept out of the reach of children. Wash your hands after treating your dog's eye. This can keep you from getting an infection if he has one, as well as keep you from getting any of the medication into your eyes or mouth by accident.

EYE DROPS

Eye drops are a common form of medication. They are used to carry antibiotics, corticosteroids, atropine and other drugs onto the surface or into the interior of the eye (as with glaucoma).

Putting drops into your dog's eyes is easy. Hold his head slightly above level. Rest your hand which is holding the dropper or dropper bottle on the bridge of his nose. Then drip the drop onto the surface of his eyeball. Or you can drop it onto the sclera (white area) just inside the skin at the inner corner of his eye. To avoid contamination of the dropper vial, do not touch the tip to the eye. Just get it close and allow the drop to fall.

Most eye drop medications must be put in rather frequently, as the dog's blinking washes them off the surface of the eye and flushes them away with his tears. Many eye drop medications need to be put in the eye four or five times a day, or even more often. Let your veterinarian know if you cannot follow this sort of schedule. The product may be available in an ointment. Ointments remain on the eye much longer than eyedrops.

With some eye medications, more often is better. However, with drugs such as atropine, an excess may cause irregularities in the heartbeat. Make sure that you know whether the dosage is critical, or if "more really is better." Artificial tears and some other drugs can be used almost as frequently as you feel like using them.

EYE OINTMENTS

In some cases, eye ointments are used because they have a longer duration of action than eye drops. The greasy film helps to hold the medication in place and keep it from being washed away by the dog's blinking. They are used in other cases because the oiliness provides good lubrication for the corneal surface. Eye ointments are used to carry the same drugs as drops: corticosteroids, antibiotics, etc.

Eye ointments are even easier to use than drops. Again, you will hold the head with one hand and steady the other (holding the tube of ointment) against the dog's forehead or muzzle. The dog will normally close his eye when you get near it with the end of the tube. Pull the lower lid down, and squeeze a small amount of ointment into the pouch that is formed, using a steady, gentle pressure. Try not to touch the tip to the eye, in order to avoid contaminating it. In most cases, you will want to squeeze out about 1/2 inch (1.3 cm). When you are through, pull the tube gently away from the eye and stop squeezing. Some of the time you will leave a small tag of ointment on the eyelashes. Use a tissue to wipe it gently out of the way as your dog closes his eye again.

Some eye ointments are very stiff when cold. Warm the tube in your hand or in warm water before using it.

If you are using chloramphenicol ointment, be careful. Chloramphenicol is a good antibiotic, and seems to be safe for your dog. It can in rare cases, however, cause some blood problems in humans. Wash your hands well, with soap, to remove any traces, after using it.

If your dog's eye is injured and you use an ointment with a corticosteroid in it, you may cause the loss of the eye. If in doubt, use an ointment containing only an antibiotic (the names of corticosteroids often end in "-sone"). Either your pharmacist or your veterinarian can quickly tell you if the ointment contains a corticosteroid. If the dog's cornea has been cut or torn (such as having run into a branch on a bush or tree limb), DO NOT put ANY ointment in it if you can get the dog

Squeeze ointment into inner corner of the dog's eye.

to a veterinarian within an hour or so. An oily ointment may prevent the successful suturing of the laceration.

OTHER EYE TREATMENTS

Powders are occasionally recommended for use in dogs' eyes, but usually not by veterinarians. Powders are occasionally used in animals such as cattle. It is generally not a good idea to use them in dogs' eyes. They may be a bit coarse and irritating, leading to violent attempts by the dog to scratch his eye, creating even more damage.

In some cases, such as with a prolapsed eye, it may be necessary to suture the dog's eyelids shut. This is an extremely safe and secure treatment, especially with dogs like Pekingese, whose heads are hard to bandage without choking them. They're a lot like bandaging a bowling ball with eyes and a mouth. The sutured eyelid will act as a bandage, allowing the eye to heal. The stitches are usually removed within one to two weeks, depending on the problem, and, usually with no ill effects. In some instances, you will be asked to put eye ointment into the corner of the eye, under the sutured lids, to help healing. This is a simple and very effective process. Ask your veterinarian to show you the first time, if you are uncertain how to go about putting the ointment in the eye.

EAR MEDICATIONS

Ear drops and washes are commonly used on dogs. Ear drops work well to spread a medication evenly over the surface of the ear. Washes contain products to dissolve wax in the ear, helping to liquefy and remove it. To put either drops or washes into the dog's ear, hold his head steady (or have someone else hold it if he is really trying to move around). Lift the ear flap with one hand and drop in the medication with the other, using the number of drops, or measurement on the dropper, which has been prescribed. Drop it into the largest, darkest opening that you can see. Let go of the ear flap and massage the ear canal below this opening with your thumb and forefinger, rubbing firmly. This helps to spread the liquid around the ear surface, and to work it into the nooks and crannies. It also helps to work debris loose so that the dog can shake it out. Last but not least, it "scratches" the dog's ear for him, and often makes him feel more comfortable. When you have done all this, get out of the way, as many dogs will shake their heads vigorously. This is natural. The dog will not shake out enough of the medicine to cause any problems. However, because of this shaking, ear treatment is best done out of doors, and NOT while wearing good clothing!

Ear ointments are used much like drops. The recommended amount (say, 1/2 inch) is squeezed into the ear and it is massaged. Ointment may be hard to get out of the tube if it is cold. Warm it in your hand or in warm water before you use it and it will be much easier to squeeze from the tube.

Powders are occasionally sold in pet supply outlets or feed stores for use in ears. The dog with an ear problem usually already has material caked against the ear drum and on the lining of the ear canal. He does not need anything more gumming up the area. Powders do nothing toward cleaning this material out of the ear. Powders go in easily, they don't come out. For these reasons, they are NOT good to use in dogs' ears.

COLD

Cold therapy is often a valuable treatment for injuries, such as bruises, sprains, muscular strains and similar problems which have JUST occurred. Cold helps relieve pain. Cold therapy is also good for dogs that have just been burned.

Cold helps to reduce the inflammation which is occurring in the FRESHLY injured tissues. It can help reduce swelling, probably by slowing circulation in the injured area and reducing the amount of fluid which leaves the blood and lymph vessels and pools in the damaged tissues. It can also help stop bleeding by constricting capillaries in the area. The less blood that escapes from the blood vessels and into the tissues, the less there is to be removed in the healing process. Think back to the times when you have had a severe, large, purple bruise—and remember how long it took for it to heal! If you can avoid some of this blood being present in the first place, the wound will heal more quickly and easily. For all these reasons, prompt application of ice or cold water may significantly reduce healing time by partially reducing the damage from the injury.

Cold is most valuable when used during the first 24 to 48 hours after the injury has occurred. After this time, it is of little or no value. By slowing circulation, it may even hinder recovery.

Ice may be used to chill an injured area if it is available. Ice cubes can be placed in an ice bag or plastic sack, and then wrapped in a towel or rag. This may be held over the injury by a loosely applied elastic bandage. This procedure works best if you can hold the dog, or sit beside him so that he remains still while it is being applied. The refreezable, artificial-ice bags are convenient, and often stay frozen longer than ice made with water. They can be molded around a box of frozen vegetables or package of meat and then frozen so that they approximate the curve of the dog's leg. If you use ice or cooling material, be sure to wrap it in a towel or some other barrier to avoid freezing the skin.

Cold water may be run directly onto the area with a garden hose. Or you can pop the dog into the bathtub or shower. Tiny dogs may fit nicely under the kitchen faucet. Don't keep the dog in the cold water for a long period of time, or you may drive him into hypothermia.

If you are using cold water on a dog who has been burned, do not use it for an excessive length of time as it may contribute to the shock that the dog is experiencing. In general, if the animal is in shock, large amounts of cold water or ice should not be used. Treatment with cold water should also not be used if infection is present.

When water is put on an open wound (this includes third degree burns where open tissues are present), the dog's tissues tend to absorb it. This may carry infection into the cut, and swell the tissues, slowing the healing process. For this reason, cold running water should not be used on open wounds—use an ice bag instead. Again, be careful using ice so you don't freeze the skin, as that will severely retard healing. The injured dog doesn't need frostbite in addition to a cut!

Cold should not be used for more than twenty to thirty minutes at a time, as it may then cause the blood vessels to open up and increase circulation to the area—just the opposite of what you want. Using cold in addition to a compression bandage will help to prevent this problem. Place the cold material over the bandage.

Heat and cold may be used alternately in some problems after 24 to 48 hours have passed. This treatment is often used on sprains and similar injuries. Temperature therapy can be a tricky business, although it is a valuable adjunct to treatment. If you aren't sure how to go about it, ask your veterinarian for advice.

HEAT

Heat may be used to warm a chilled dog, such as a very ill outdoor dog in a cold climate, a puppy born in a snowbank, a puppy who has wandered into the rain and is suffering from exposure, or a puppy suffering from hypothermia from any cause. You can fill plastic gallon jugs or similar containers with warm water, and use them as hot water bottles to help warm the dog. If you put very hot water in the bottles, wrap them with a thick cloth or a towel to avoid burning the dog's skin. A chilled dog may be warmed in a tub of lukewarm (NOT HOT) water. He should then be carefully dried. A good way to do this is first to wipe him with towels or other cloths and finish the job with a hair dryer. The puppy can be returned to his mother after he is warmed and dry.

Infrared lamps can be used to heat puppies in a garage or in a horse stall. Make sure they have plenty of bedding. Be very careful with these lights, as they can burn the dogs if they are too close. They also present considerable fire danger if they get near bedding or other flammable materials. The bitch may knock the bulb down and break it, and then injure herself and the puppies. With a bit of ingenuity you may be able to find a substitute method for providing heat which is at least as effective and much safer. Hard plastic kennel heaters are available which can keep the mother and puppies nicely warm—and safe, too. (One source of kennel heaters is R.C. Steele, 15 Turner Drive, Spencerport, N.Y., 14559).

Heat is often used on injuries after 24 to 48 hours have passed. At this point, heat helps to stimulate circulation in the area. The increased blood circulation in the area aids the body in removing toxic products and makes healing more rapid by bringing in fresh oxygen for the cells. Heat also helps the body's circulation to remove blood and other fluids from the area. This in turn reduces the swelling, allowing the cells to become more nearly normal.

Heat should not be used if infection is present in an area— or even suspected! Heat can cause the infection to spread. It can also cause problems because of increased absorption of infection-related toxins into the body. Increased circulation in the area may lead to severe edema and swelling, which may further complicate the infected injury. If heat is used on a fresh injury, it may make the problem worse than it would have been without it. For this reason, DO NOT use heat on a fresh injury, nor any time within 24 to 48 hours after the injury.

Hot water can be applied with moist cloths, as when a bitch has edema in her udder. Make sure the cloths are not so hot that they scald the animal or the problem may get rapidly worse instead of better. Second degree burns are severe problems all by themselves. Begin with lukewarm water and gradually make it hotter as the animal becomes accustomed to it. If the cloths are too hot for you to handle with comfort, they are too hot to put on the dog.

The dog may be put into the bathtub and given a heat treatment. Begin with lukewarm water, and gradually heat it up as the dog becomes used to it. Again, if it is uncomfortable to you, it will be uncomfortable to the dog. This type of therapy is used, for instance, for Dachshunds and other dogs with disk disease. In some cases, your Jacuzzi or whirlpool may be helpful. Consult with your veterinarian if you think it may work, and be sure your filter can cope with the hair that will fall into the tub. Grooming the dog before the bath will help to reduce the amount of hair shed into the water.

Deep heat and diathermy have been used to produce heat below the surface tissues. These should be used only under the direction of your veterinarian, as severe damage to bones and other underlying tissues can occur with improper usage. Like Jacuzzis and whirlpools, they are sometimes used on dogs who are paralyzed because of disk problems. Like other forms of heat, deep heat techniques should not be used for at least 24 to 48 hours after an injury has occurred; likewise, they should be NOT used when ANY infection is present.

Infrared light has occasionally been recommended as a way of producing heat in tissues. It is not a good idea because of the very great danger of skin burns. Like a sunburn, these burns may not show up until some time after the treatment which caused them.

SOAKING SOLUTIONS

Epsom salts (magnesium sulfate) are sometimes used to help draw swelling and fluid out of an injured area. This material can be used to soak a large dog who has strained himself hunting or working. One or two cups of epsom salts are used per gallon of water. You can use hot or cold water, depending on how fresh the injury is. Commercial soaking solutions are available. They are mainly based on epsom salts, with menthol and other aromatic substances added. The aromatic substances are generally oily and become stuck in the dog's hair and make a mess. Plain magnesium sulfate is probably better, and also cheaper. Epsom salts are usually available from a drug store. You might even end up using it on yourself, for soaking aching muscles, sprains or similar injuries! Before you use a soak of epsom salts on either your dog or yourself, carefully check for cuts, scrapes or other breaks in the skin. Do not soak an area that has anything but intact skin.

MASSAGE

Massage is often used in addition to heat treatments to help heal sprains and similar problems. Massage often helps to lessen swelling and reduce pain. Many people like to use liniments, "braces" and other products, rubbing them into the skin over the injury. In general, these don't help much, and make a real mess in dogs' hair. They may produce some reddening and irritation in the skin over the injury, but don't do anything for the underlying tissues. Improvement is often due not to the product, but to the massaging action of applying it. For best effect, massage should be repeated three or four times a day. Massage often helps to keep scar tissue from forming adhesions between the skin and the underlying tissues.

REST

Rest is often used to help keep leg problems, such as osteochondritis dissecans, from getting worse. It also helps with disk problems and pelvic fractures. Some leg injuries will be made much worse if the dog continues to move around and use the leg: more fluid and blood may leak from the injured area, causing more swelling and pain, and lengthening the time necessary for healing.

Make sure you know what your veterinarian wants in the way of rest for your dog. He may want the dog totally confined to a small space. My favorite area for total confinement is a playpen. It keeps the dog from exercising, while allowing him to see and be a part of what is going on in the household. Perhaps the best location for the dog is one that is out of the main traffic pattern, but close enough that his "humans" are visible. Your veterinarian may want the dog to have a small amount of exercise, or he may want the exercise limited to going outside a couple of times a day to urinate and defecate. Be sure that you know what the veterinarian has in mind, and follow his instructions. Don't feel sorry for your dog because he was "cooped up all day," and take him out for an hour's walk in the evening. You could set his progress back considerably—or even cause permanent damage. It will also be helpful if you move a chair near him, so that you can just be by him, perhaps while you are watching television or reading the paper. After all, he is still a member of the family, and not in isolation.

EXERCISE

Exercise is frequently used to help your dog lose weight. It can also be used to build up the dog's muscles and tendons after prolonged confinement. In either case, it is VERY important to start gradually. With a very fat dog, once around the block may be all that he can do as a beginning. Give him lots of encouragement, and don't carry him if you can avoid it. It is better for him to get halfway down the block and back by himself than to get accustomed to being carried. You can't do the exercise for him! Match your pace to his, at least while he's getting in better shape.

Be careful about turning your dog out to play with another one if he is recuperating from surgery or injury. He may forget that he has a problem, and reinjure the area or tear something loose if they start to play vigorously. It's better to keep him by himself and exercise him gradually. Otherwise an hour's exuberance might undo months of treatment and rest.

Swimming is excellent exercise for building up dogs who have had leg injuries or leg surgery. It helps the animal to build up both lung and cardiovascular capacity without jarring his legs. Swimming can strengthen the dog so that when he begins walking or running longer distances, he will not reinjure his previous problem. Swimming is sometimes used as therapy for dogs with disk problems.

ACUPUNCTURE

Acupuncture has been touted as a cure-all for anything and everything that ails. It has also been debunked as being total quackery. Like many disputes, the truth probably lies somewhere in between. No one knows for sure HOW it works. However, there are definitely times when it DOES work. It can often help relieve pain, as from arthritis. If you've tried everything else, and an acupuncturist who is familiar with dogs is available, why not give it a try? This author will be the first to encourage any treatement which works.

Acupressure (kiatsu or shiatsu) is often helpful, especially with bruises and fresh bleeding under the skin. You can press your thumb firmly into the area, and hold it there for six to eight seconds. Release the pressure SLOWLY, gradually removing your thumb from the area. This action will press the blood and stale fluids out of the area, allowing fresh lymphatic fluids to seep into the area. If you can do this three or four times a day, it can make a difference in how fast the bruise will heal.

ELECTRICAL STIMULATION

This technique has had much the same history of controversy as acupuncture. It is likely that the best use of the technique is for pain relief. It has been widely used for pain therapy in humans following muscular injury. In some cases, it may be used in conjunction with acupuncture.

INHALANT TREATMENTS

A humidifier may help your dog breathe more comfortably if he has distemper or kennel cough. In some cases, a vaporizer may be used to raise the humidity of the air around him and make him more comfortable. Check with your veterinarian about whether you should use one that puts out cold moisture or steam.

Your veterinarian may treat certain diseases and lung conditions by putting your dog in a cage with a nebulizer. A nebulizer creates a small fog of medicated droplets so that the medication can be inhaled directly and deeply into the lungs. Nebulization is not usually a treatment that you would be using at home.

ENEMAS

Constipation can largely be prevented by watching what your dog eats, and making sure that he gets plenty of exercise. In some cases, however, such as a pelvic fracture with loss of efficient bowel function, it may be necessary for you to give your dog an enema. You can use ONE pediatric Fleet Enema®, in accordance with your veterinarian's instructions. Lubricate the tip of the enema tube with petroleum jelly or other lubricant, and insert it gently into the dog's rectum. This procedure is best done out in your yard, or someplace else where you can easily clean up afterward, or can walk away from the mess. If the enema does not work within an hour or so, make an appointment with your veterinarian to have the dog examined. Fleet Enemas® should not be used on very small dogs or young puppies, or for dogs with kidney disease.

INJECTIONS

"Injection" is the general name given to the process of putting a vaccine or medication into the animal's body with a syringe and needle. Injections placed under the skin are known as subcutaneous (S/C or Sub-Q for short) injections. Injections made into the upper layers of the skin are called intradermal injections. Intradermal injections are not usually given by the dog owner, but are used by the veterinarian for skin testing, as for allergies. Injections into the muscle are called, logically enough, intramuscular injections. Specialized injections may be made into the joints; this route is called intra-articular. Others are intra-abdominal, intrathoracic, intravenous, etc., depending on where in the body the material is being deposited by the injection.

There are advantages to giving your own injections. Depending on the availability of quality vaccine, you may be able to save substantial amounts of money, especially if you have several dogs. It can be much more convenient to bring vaccine home, instead of taking dogs to a clinic, especially if you have a kennel or pack of them—or just one large, boisterous dog (and a small car!). You may be more likely to keep vaccinations current if you can vaccinate the dog at your convenience, which will give your dog better protection.

Make sure that you get vaccine from a reliable source. It must be refrigerated throughout the distribution chain. If it sets in the back of the feed store for a week until they get around to unpacking it, it will not be any good, even if it is then refrigerated. You will be falsely relying on it for protection. When you go to town to get vaccine, take a cooler and a couple of ice packs to keep it chilled. Refrigerate it when you get home, and keep it refrigerated until use. Vaccine which has passed its expiration date may no longer give good protection and should be discarded.

Do not use syringes which have been cleaned with any chemical disinfectants or alcohol. These products do not kill some contaminants, which may later cause disease in the dog. And they do not kill all the blood-borne parasites which can be transmitted from one dog to another. On the other hand, they CAN kill modified-live vaccines, rendering them useless. Use only new, sterile, disposable needles and syringes. You can use the same syringe for more than one dog if you have not drawn blood into it. Use a new needle for each dog.

Before we go into the common types of injections and how to give them, let's discuss a few problems and liabilities involved in your giving injections to your own animals.

There is some risk of reaction any time you give injections to your dog. The risk is very small, but you should take it into consideration before deciding to give your own injections. If you are not comfortable living with this small risk, spend the money and take the dog to your veterinarian for his immunizations. Be sure that you know how to begin to treat an anaphylactic reaction if it should occur (see below).

If you are giving an injection to your own animal, you are obviously assuming the risk of doing so. By giving your own vaccinations and antibiotic injections, you may save considerable time and money as compared to having your veterinarian give them. You can give the injections when they are scheduled, without waiting for anyone but yourself. If your animal requires a prolonged course of antibiotic injections and you live a long way from nowhere, your veterinarian may PREFER that you give these "shots" yourself. In fact, it may be the only way to get the drug into the dog.

NOTE: If the dog is insured, the policy may REQUIRE that any immunizations or injections be given by a veterinarian, and the policy may be voided if you treat the animal yourself—be sure to check with your insurance agent or read the fine print in the policy (and the big print, too) before giving the animal ANY medication.

You will be taking the responsibility for any reactions that may occur. Reactions are of two types: local and systemic. Systemic reactions are the most serious and life-threatening. Fortunately, they are also extremely rare. One systemic reaction which may occur is anaphylactic shock. Read on...

ANAPHYLACTIC SHOCK

Anaphylactic shock is the name given to the most serious systemic reaction that may follow an injection. It occurs most commonly after injections of vaccines, antibiotics or products for desensitization from allergies. Normally, it does not occur the first time the animal is given a drug (although in exceptional cases it will occur the first time). More frequently, it follows the second or subsequent exposures to the product. Anaphylactic shock is basically a very acute, powerful allergic reaction; the body usually requires previous exposure to the substance to become allergic to it. Anaphylactic shock can occur after the dog is stung by a large number of bees, fire ants or yellow jacket wasps. It can occasionally occur because of allergy to something the animal has eaten. Food allergy anaphylactic shock is even rarer than anaphylactic shock in general.

What happens in anaphylactic shock? This problem usually occurs within a few minutes to four or five hours after the offending material has been injected. Signs of anaphylactic shock include pale, cool mucous membranes, increased heart rate, and difficulty in breathing. The dog may have sudden, acute, explosive diarrhea and vomiting, both of which may be bloody. He may have hives, or may have generalized swelling as his skin fills with fluid. Collapse and death can follow, usually due to complete failure of the dog's circulatory system.

If the problem is not treated promptly, the dog can quickly DIE. If the animal survives long enough for you to call a veterinarian, or to get him to a clinic, he will probably make it anyway. It will be important for the veterinarian to know that you gave an injection within the preceding few minutes or hours. Be sure to tell him what you have given.

Treatment for anaphylactic shock must be immediate and sure. Epinephrine (also called adrenalin) is the drug which is used. An approximate dosage is .005 ml per lb (.01 ml per kg) of a 1:1000 solution. Check the vial which you have to make sure of the dosage and method of administration BEFORE you need it. Chances are good you will never have to use it. But, if you do, there will be NO TIME to stand around reading the label. Give the epinephrine intravenously if you can hit the jugular vein. Otherwise, give it intramuscularly or subcutaneously, depending on the instructions on the bottle. If the reaction was due to an injection, an amount of epinephrine equal to that already given should be injected locally around the site of the vacine or drug first injection, to help slow absorption of the first material. A small spot of white hair regrowth may occur at the site of local epinephrine placement. So don't give it in a visible area on a dark-colored show dog.

A bottle of epinephrine and suitable syringe and needle (say, a 3-cc syringe and 20-gauge, 1-inch needle) should be handy and ready WHENEVER you give an injection. It need not be on your person, but it should never be more than a few yards away in your medicine kit. It is often convenient to tape a sterile syringe (still in its plastic case) and needle (same) to the vial of epinephrine so they are always convenient—and so you are never tempted to use them when you are short of supplies. Don't cover the label. You will want to re-read it before you give the first shot to your dog.

If epinephrine is not available, prompt administration of an antihistamine solution according to the directions on the label may save the animal's life. Epinephrine is usually preferred if you have it (and there is no excuse not to have it). It is available from veterinary supply companies. In a small town, you can get it from your veterinarian or perhaps from a pharmacy with your veterinarian's prescription.

Occasionally, hives (also called urticaria) may be seen as a milder systemic reaction following an injection. Your veterinarian should be consulted if they are numerous or if they do not go down within 12 to 24 hours.

LOCAL REACTIONS

Reactions may occur at the injection site itself. These local reactions do not usually show up right away, but may be seen from a few hours to as much as a week later. Swelling is the main sign, and it can range from a mere bump an inch or so in diameter to a large blob. Pain may accompany the swelling. There are several causes of local reactions:

An allergic reaction can occur at the injection site. It will usually occur within a few hours after the injection is given, and will go down in several days (with or without treatment).

The swelling may be due to an infection. Infections can happen when bacteria are carried into the tissues by the needle when the injection is given. Or it may be due to bacteria being brought by the bloodstream to tissues which were damaged or weakened by the injection. Abscesses tend to form in the

swelling, and feel hotter to the touch than the surrounding area. After several days, the abscess may come to a point, getting a soft area—usually in the middle—at the highest part of the swelling. The presence of the point indicates that it is time to drain the abscess.

An abscess may affect the animal's general well-being, causing him to go off feed and appear generally "droopy." An abscess on the neck may cause the animal to turn stiffly. Because of the chance that the animal may be sore after an injection (even if he does not develop an abscess), it is not a good idea to vaccinate an animal right before a show or field trial.

The possibility of an abscess makes it important to utilize injection sites that will drain well if an abscess occurs. This is why intramuscular injections are often made in the lower part of the hind leg.

The animal may get a hematoma at the injection site. This is a blood clot which occurs because you have punctured a small (or large) blood vessel in the process of giving the injection. Because it occurs either under the skin or deeper in the muscle, it is impossible to prevent a hematoma from occasionally happening. But, by utilizing good injection techniques and giving injections in the proper sites, the possibility of getting a hematoma can be minimized. It would be a good idea to ask your veterinarian to coach you in both injection site selection and proper technique. If he refuses, and you are determined to give injections to your dog(s), find one who will coach you.

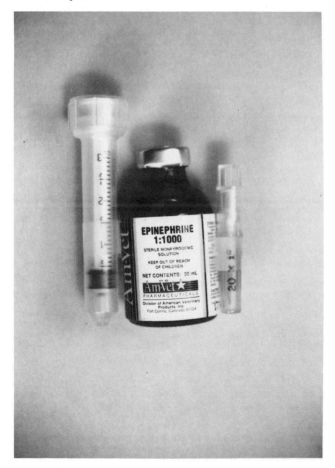

Epinephrine with sterile needle and syringe.

As sometimes happens after a human "flu" shot, the vaccine itself can make the dog feel ill for a day or two. Don't worry if your dog is droopy for up to two days after an injection, as long as he does not show any signs of illness.

LEGAL COMPLICATIONS

In some cities and states, vaccine is available through the feed store, drugstore or through your veterinarian, so that you can purchase and give it yourself. In other areas, it is illegal to even so much as possess a syringe or needle. Make sure that "doing-it-yourself" is legal where you live.

If you are treating your own animal, you are accepting the risk of anything that might happen. The dog is your property, and generally—short of cruelty—you can do about anything you want to with him. It becomes another matter entirely if you are treating a dog belonging to a friend or neighbor. Several things happen if a reaction occurs, whether it is an anaphylactic reaction that causes the animal's death, or "merely" an abscess or other "minor" complication. The first thing that happens is that you feel horrible and will probably lose a friend. The second thing is even worse. There is a good possblity that the animal's owner may sue you for the loss of his animal—his property—and stand a good chance of winning.

Finally, YOU may be changed with practicing veterinary medicine without a license, which is a serious crime in some states—enough to get a stiff fine or even a jail sentence. It usually doesn't matter whether the other person is paying you. What does seem to matter is that you were illegally practicing medicine on someone else's animal.

How do you avoid this problem? Easy. Don't work on other people's animals. Period. If someone wants you to help him and you know how to give injections, that's fine. Show him how to give the injections himself (and make darned sure you're right or that could be another possible liability) or, even better, suggest he ask his veterinarian to show him how or tell him to get a copy of "The Dog Repair Book."

Some veterinarians are reluctant to teach their clients how to give injections because of the problems which may occur. However, if you offer to pay them for the time it takes to teach you, it will be money well spent, and will often change the resistance to cooperation. This is because many veterinarians get so tired of being milked for free information by clients, who then misunderstand or misuse it, that we get a little gunshy about freely dispensing it. If, however, you can make your veterinarian understand that you are aware of the dangers, and that, despite the risk, you would like to learn to give injections properly, he may change his mind.

Now that we have discussed some of the advantages and dangers of giving your own injections to your dog, let's talk about the hows and whys of technique.

ROUTE OF INJECTION

It is very important that injectible drugs be given in the manner prescribed on the label. A drug which is meant for intravenous injection but given in the muscle may cause the animal severe pain. It can cause a large chunk of muscle to die. If a drug meant for intramuscular use is injected into the animal's vein, carriers and other agents in the medication may cause a severe reaction and/or death. If there is ANY doubt as to which way a vaccine should be given, give it IN THE MUSCLE. Better yet, read the label or the package insert and do only what it says. The dog you save may be your own.

PROCEDURE FOR GIVING INJECTIONS

What do you need in order to give an injection? You need the vaccine or medication which is to be injected. See whether it is labeled for intramuscular or subcutaneous use. You need alcohol or other disinfectant for the skin. You can apply it with a cotton ball or just spray or flood it onto the skin. If the dog has long hair, you should part it and inject into the "valley" that you have formed. If the animal is very dirty (muddy or bloody), it is good to comb the dirt from the skin before beginning the injection. In warm weather, the area can be washed or hosed off first. This is unnecessary when the animal is reasonably clean; alcohol will clean the skin sufficiently.

Syringe sizes should closely match the injection that is being given. Too large a syringe is awkward with a small amount of liquid. Syringes are sized in cubic centimeters, also called cc's. A cubic centimeter is the same, for practical purposes, as a milliliter (ml). If someone gives you a dosage in milliliters and your syringe is calibrated in cubic centimeters, they are the same thing. A 3-cc syringe is adequate for most vaccines, as well as dosages of antibiotics and other drugs for smaller dogs. A 12-cc syringe is adequate for most antibiotics and other drugs for larger dogs, and is probably the largest size that you will need for most "small" animals. In most cases, you will not inject more than four or five ml in any one site, especially intramuscularly. This is because larger amounts cause considerable pressure and pain, and probably slow absorption as compared to dividing the same dosage into smaller amounts and giving it in a couple of places.

Syringes come with two different types of tips. Luer-lock syringes have a threaded end which you have to screw onto the needle. Luer-slip ends, which merely slide into the end of the needle with a snug fit, are also available. While you may prefer the Luer-slip ends for horses, either one is suitable for dogs. If you have both dogs and horses, and treat both, you may wish to keep only syringes with Luer-slip ends on hand, as they are handy for both species. Syringes have the business end either centered or offset to one side. For most injections, it doesn't matter which you use.

The size of the needle depends on the material you are injecting. Most vaccines, for instance, are placed under the skin. They are generally given in small doses and are usually liquid enough that they flow easily through a needle. For these reasons, a small needle can be used, causing the animal less discomfort. My preference is a 20-gauge needle, 1 inch long, for both intramuscular and subcutaneous injections. These needles will also handle penicillin and similar small-quantity antibiotics which are given to dogs. If you are giving vaccine to a VERY small dog (say, under six pounds), you may wish to use a smaller, 22-gauge or 23-gauge, 1-inch needle.

Removing metal cap from bottle.

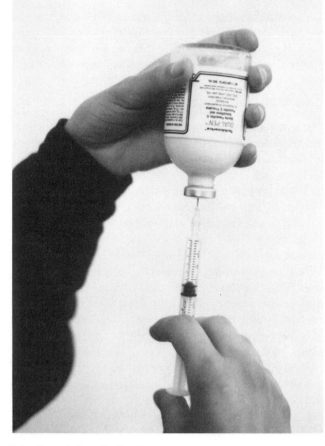

Injecting air into the bottle.

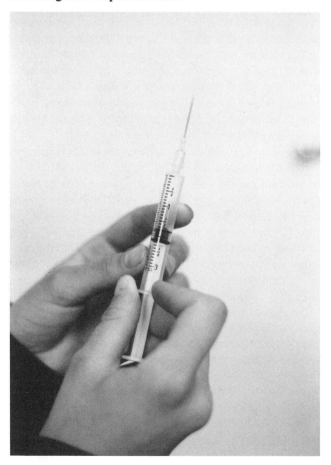

Drawing air into the syringe.

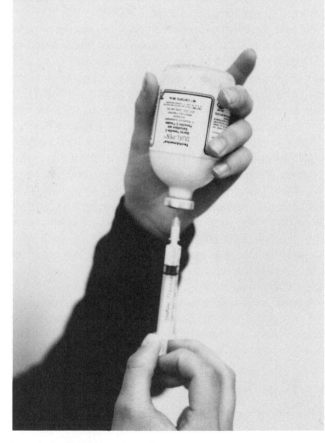

Drawing medication out of the bottle.

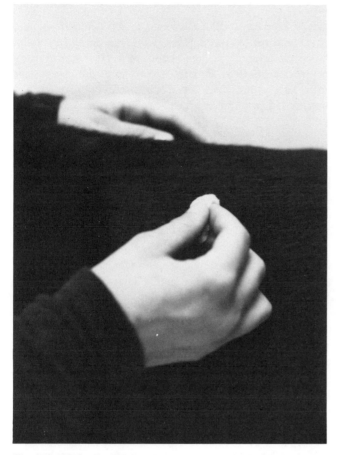

Cleansing injection site.

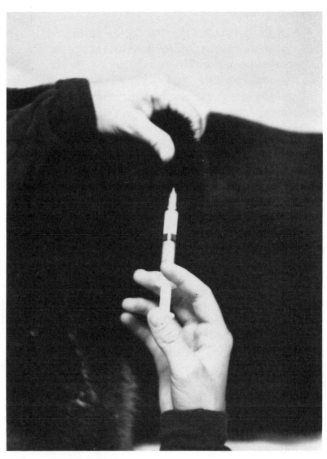

Injecting medication.

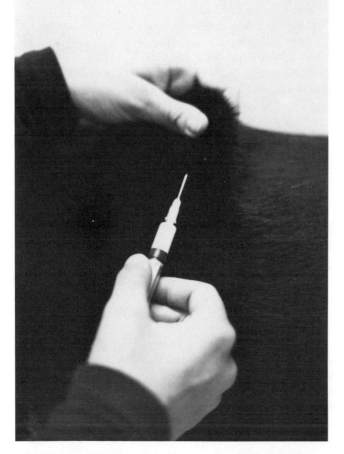

Subcutaneous injection: inserting needle at base of skin.

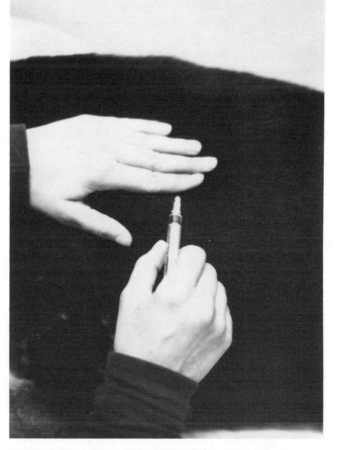

Holding skin firmly down while pulling out needle.

Needles and syringes may be purchased individually in sterile plastic containers. Some veterinarians prefer needles and syringes made by Monoject (Monoject Division, Sherwood Medical Industries, St. Louis, MO., 63103). Others are made which are less expensive, but some brands are not consistently sharp and are more subject to breakage.

There is no excuse today for using anything but new, sharp, disposable needles and new, disposable syringes for dogs. The old-fashioned needles could be sharpened, but it seems no one ever bothered to do so. Using a dull needle on a dog can cause him considerable pain. Pretty soon, you have a wrestling match each time you give an injection.

No method of cold sterilization (such as soaking in alcohol) will kill some virus diseases, or all the parasites which may be transmitted through the blood from one dog to another. Boiling the needles and syringes also does not always kill these organisms. The ONLY sterilization method which kills viruses and parasites is sterilization with live steam under pressure. Your veterinarian uses a contraption called an autoclave to prepare instruments for surgery with live, pressurized steam. Most dog owners do not give enough injections to bother with such sophisticated methods. Besides, disposable syringes and needles are very inexpensive. So don't try to save a few cents and maybe lose a dog because you are using a needle which is not sterile. Use a separate, new, sterile needle and syringe for each dog.

If you are treating the same dog day after day with a medication, such as penicillin, you can put the syringe, with needle still attached (after you have used it) in the refrigerator along with the penicillin bottle. This will keep the penicillin in the syringe from spoiling. Then, take the syringe out when it is time for injection, put a fresh needle on it and give the injection. You can use the same syringe for three or four days in this manner if you have NOT drawn any blood into it in the process of injection. If you do draw blood, start with a new syringe for the next injection.

Now it's time to fill the syringe with the medication or vaccine. Let's assume that you are starting with a new bottle of the product, such as penicillin/streptomycin. Take the tip of a fingernail or sharp knife and remove the small, protective flap of metal covering the center of the bottle cap. It will usually have one or more raised edges which make it easy to remove. Place the needle on the syringe, remove the protective sheath, and draw air into the syringe, in an amount equal to the amount of drug you are going to remove from the bottle. for example, 2 cc of drug will need about 2 cc of air to replace it in the bottle. This need not be an exact measurement. Shake the bottle well. Wipe the center of the rubber cap with a cotton ball moistened in alcohol. Rubbing alcohol from the drugstore is fine for both this and for wiping the dog's skin.

Hold the bottle of medicine upside down and insert the needle (attached to the syringe with air in it) into the center of the rubber cap. Inject the air from the syringe into the bottle. This equalizes the pressure and prevents a vacuum from forming in the bottle, allowing you to remove the medicine more easily. Draw out the amount of drug which you need. If there is a bubble of air in the top of the syringe or hub of the needle, merely inject it back into the bottle and draw out enough product to fill the syringe to the required amount. Measure to the top of the black plunger in the syringe (with the needle upward), not the bottom of it. Now you're ready to give the injection. Proceed according to the instructions given later in this book for subcutaneous or intramuscular injections, depending on which one the drug label tells you to use.

Perhaps the single biggest cause of problems while giving injections is the owner's attitude. If you are upset or anxious about having to give your dog a shot, you are probably going to communicate it to the animal. He will then become upset and will squirm and protest. One thing that helps is to have your assistant (the one who is holding the dog's muzzle with one hand) rub the dog's ear FAIRLY HARD while talking to him. It sometimes also helps to have the helper blow in the dog's nostrils. But he should keep his face safely out of reach of a nip. These actions take the dog's mind off what you are doing.

If it bothers you too badly to give an injection, it's probably best to have your veterinarian to do the dirty work. But if you are determined to do it, get your own mind under control before you approach the dog. Take a deep breath, slowly let it out, and RELAX! You're just giving your dog a shot to help him, not facing a firing squad! Now that you are calm, cool and collected, approach the dog.

Pick the site where you are going to place the needle. Cleanse a spot two or three inches in diameter with disinfectant. Having a large area disinfected allows you some leeway. If you don't hit the exact spot you have in mind, you can still hit within the cleansed area.

Be sure to safely dispose of your needles and syringes so that they cannot be used by children or addicts. They are tools, not toys. When you are finished using it, you can disable a needle by bending it over before you throw it away. Bend it against a hard surface while holding the syringe. DON'T use your finger to bend it. Put the syringe on a firm surface and step on it with a hard shoe heel, cracking it so that it cannot be reused. Watch that you do not put the needle in the trash and reach in and scratch or stick yourself on it. If you drop it in a soup can or old milk carton, it won't be a hazard for the sanitation engineer who picks up your trash.

SUBCUTANEOUS INJECTIONS

The most commonly used site for injecting vaccines into dogs is the loose tissue right under the skin. "Subcutaneous" means "under the skin," hence the name of this injection. This is also a convenient site to give large quantities of fluids, and is sometimes used for dogs with severe diarrhea or parvovirus infection.

Safe restraint of the dog is important. If the dog is not carefully held, he may turn and bite you when you give the injection. Have someone hold the dog for you at a convenient height. A small dog can be placed on a counter, a table or a bench, while a large dog can be held on a convenient spot on the floor. If you think the dog may become nervous and urinate, make sure he is on an easily cleaned floor or out in the yard.

A dog with a pointed nose, like a Collie, can be held with the left hand under his jaw, holding the muzzle slightly above level, and the right arm around the dog's shoulder. This assumes that the helper is standing on the dog's left side. Reverse the position of the hands if the helper is to the dog's right side. If the dog is antisocial or nasty, he can be held with both hands just below his ears, taking a good grab of both ears and the skin below them (from behind). If the dog is REALLY nasty, your helper can straddle him and sit on him while gripping his ears and skin to control his head. Just make absolutely SURE your helper has a firm grip and is strong enough to hold the dog. If not, don't try to vaccinate the dog, or wait until you get STRONG help.

Now, here's how to give the injection. For subcutaneous injections, let's assume that you are right-handed (reverse the directions if you are left-handed). You are on the dog's right side, with his head to your right. Two convenient sites are over the shoulder, and over the ribs just behind the shoulder blade and a couple of inches below the backbone. Pick up a fold of skin with your left hand, between thumb and forefinger. With the syringe in your right hand, insert the needle just through the skin. Don't thrust the needle as if it were a dart. Firmly push it through the skin as if you were sewing heavy canvas. A new, sharp needle will encounter almost no resistance. The needle stays attached to the syringe, rather than separated as is often done when injecting a horse. Be extra careful not to stick the needle clear through the fold of skin and into your thumb or finger! It is better to insert the needle below your finger at the base of the fold rather than directly into the fold itself.

When the needle is under the skin, pull back gently on the plunger to make sure you are not in a blood vessel. If you get blood back into the hub of the syringe, you have hit a blood vessel. Withdraw the needle and insert it at another nearby spot. If no blood appears in the syringe, go ahead and gently inject the contents of the syringe. It should flow in smoothly. If it does not, you may have the needle within the skin (intradermally) rather than under it. If this happens, withdraw the needle and reinsert it, holding it at a slightly more vertical angle in relation to the skin. In most dogs, you will be going about 1/8 to 1/4 inch deep for a subcutaneous injection.

Your veterinarian may give fluids subcutaneously. He might put several hundred milliliters (one or two pints) of fluid under the dog's skin to treat an illness. Several days after fluid has been given in this manner, you may notice large amounts of fluid hanging in pouches of skin under the dog's belly. Gravity has pulled the fluid down into the area because it has not yet been absorbed. This is fairly common on dogs because the skin over their chests is quite loose, and it is easy for the fluid to migrate from the area up high where it was originally placed. If the pockets of fluid are cool and soft, there is no problem. If they become hot and more firm, consult

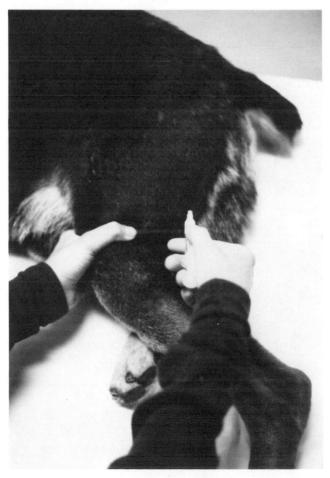

Intramuscular injection. Be sure to pull back on plunger before injecting here, too.

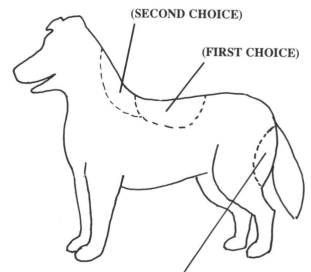

SUBCUTANEOUS INJECTIONS

(SECOND CHOICE)

(FIRST CHOICE)

INTRAMUSCULAR INJECTIONS

Injection sites, in order of preference.

your veterinarian immediately about possibly draining them, and the dog's possible need for antibiotic treatment, as an abscess may be forming from an infection.

INTRAMUSCULAR INJECTIONS

Some vaccines can be given to dogs ONLY by the intramuscular route. Rabies vaccine and measles vaccine are the most important of these. Remember, if you are EVER in doubt about the way to give a vaccine, put it in the muscle rather than under the skin (subcutaneously).

There are several reasons for using the intramuscular route. A large dog has large muscles which provide plenty of space for injecting materials. Many antibiotics are specially formulated to be injected intramuscularly. The muscles have a good blood supply, giving a rapid absorption of medication into the blood, which will then spread it throughout the body. For many people, intramuscular injections are more difficult to give than are subcutaneous ones. For many dogs, intramuscular injections may be somewhat more painful than subcutaneous injections. This is especially true of tiny dogs. Tiny dogs have little muscle mass and have more of a tendency to tense their muscles.

When should medication be given intramuscularly? Vaccines should be given intramuscularly when so directed by the labeling or package flyer (insert). This is especially important with rabies vaccine. If you have a choice of giving a rabies vaccine either subcutaneously or intramuscularly, put it in the muscle, as this seems to give a longer acting, more durable immunity. If the vaccine says it SHOULD be given intramuscularly, be sure to do so, as in some cases the vaccine may actually CAUSE rabies if given subcutaneously.

Just because you have been giving a drug in a certain manner, don't forget to read the label occasionally for good measure. Manufacturers sometimes change formulas (and recommendations for administration) in midstream. Do NOT automatically assume that since you gave the medication subcutaneously a year ago, that a new bottle is necessarily still the same. Read the label to make sure. Any medication that your veterinarian prescribes to give in the muscle should be given according to his directions and dosage.

Where do you give intramuscular injections? Sites for injection into the muscles should be chosen with an eye to avoiding bones, main blood vessels and areas where the absorption of the material would be poor. The site should cause the animal as little discomfort as possible. It should be in an area which will allow good drainage if the worst possible side effect, an abscess, should follow the injection. While abscesses are a rare complication, if you give every injection in a site which would not cause problems if one developed, you are protected.

The only common site for intramuscular injection in the dog is the large muscle on the back side of the hind leg. In small or toy dogs, this is the ONLY major muscle in their bodies! Also, it has good drainage if anything should go wrong and an abscess develop. In most dogs, the shoulder muscles are not large enough, and they are too near critical bones and nerves to use them as sites for intramuscular injections.

The dog should be restrained by someone helping you, as described for subcutaneous injections. Disinfect the skin and proceed. If you are right-handed, hold the needle and syringe in your right hand. Hold the dog's hind leg with your left hand, stabilizing the muscle as you insert the needle into it with your other hand. You will push the needle gently but firmly through the skin, with the needle attached to the syringe. In a small dog, you will place the needle halfway through the large muscle on the back of the leg, or about 1/2 inch (1.3 cm) deep. On a large dog, you can insert the 1-inch needle to its full depth.

Pull gently outward on the syringe plunger to see if you get any blood. At first, it is helpful to hold the syringe with one hand and pull on the plunger with the other. As you become more experienced, you can pull out on the plunger while steadying the syringe barrel with the same hand. This procedure is done to make sure that you are in the muscle and NOT a blood vessel. If you do get blood, don't panic. Pull the needle out and place it an inch or so away from the first site. It is not a good idea to just push the needle deeper or to pull it out to a shallower position along the same track. Reactions or infections are more commonly seen when drugs are placed in an area where bleeding has occurred, especially if vaccines or oily solutions are used. Pull the plunger back at the second site and check again for blood. There will be a little in the hub of the needle from the last puncture, but that is not a problem. No more blood should rush into the syringe. If you do not get blood the second time, go ahead and inject. It does not hurt

Owner restrains guard dog for an injection.

to inject the small amount of blood which is in the syringe. It's just going back into the same animal.

You can inject the medication as fast as you can comfortably push on the plunger. It is probably no more painful than doing it very slowly. The longer you take, the more chance there is that the animal may move his leg and pull the needle out, forcing you to start over and stick him again.

Some people find it easiest to hold the hub of the needle with one hand and inject with the other. This helps keep the needle and syringe coordinated together. Occasionally, if you do not do this, the needle will pop off the syringe and medicine will spray all over you.

When you are finished, don't be in a hurry to get free. Place the fingers of one hand against the skin at the base of the needle and hold it toward the dog as you withdraw the needle and syringe. Holding the skin in this fashion helps avoid pulling it away from the underlying tissues as you remove the needle. If not done in this way, air will sometimes be sucked into the tissues. Remove the needle smoothly. Don't jerk it out. After you have removed the needle, don't forget to handle the dog. Praise and pet him and tell him that he was good. Any goodwill you can create will make it that much easier the next time you have to give a shot, whether it is tomorrow or next year. Try to leave the dog with a good feeling about the whole procedure. It doesn't hurt to give the dog a treat, provided it's a "legal" treat and it won't mess up his diet.

If you cannot get it done any other way, you can put a collar and leash on the dog and tie the leash to a fence or post. You can then hold a hind leg, pulling on it until the dog is snugly stretched. This way, you can give the injection by yourself. If you have any doubt about being able to give it by yourself, wait until you have adequate assistance. The leash and post approach will not endear you to the dog—treat afterwards or not!

If you have to give injections for several days in a row, alternate sides from day to day. Give it in the right hind leg one day, and the left one the next. Also try to alternate between sites on the same leg. You might give it higher up on the right leg the first day, and perhaps a half-inch or inch lower on the third day.

When you are repeating injections of a drug like penicillin into a muscular area, you will sometimes hit a pocket of the drug which you have given previously. When you pull out the plunger on the syringe, you get penicillin instead of blood or nothing. No problem—just pull the needle out and move it to another site. This happens because the body has not absorbed all the previous dosage. Just be aware that it occasionally happens.

INTRAVENOUS INJECTIONS

Some drugs are given by the intravenous route. They may be given this way so that they will take effect within a short time, rather than having to wait several hours for the material to be absorbed. Anesthetics are commonly administered this way. Certain antibiotics may be given intravenously in severe infections so that they can begin working immediately. Other medications are given intravenously because they are very acid, very alkaline or otherwise severely irritating to tissues. It is possible to give these products intravenously because the bloodstream dilutes them as soon as they are injected. The same products, when injected into the muscles or under the skin, will damage or kill the tissue and may cause large areas to slough. Several anesthetic agents are very irritating to tissues. If the person administering one of them misses the vein, or if the animal moves and pulls the needle out of the vein, some of the drug will be deposited in the surrounding tissues. A few days later, the color of the skin may begin to change and it may die and slough, leaving a nasty weeping sore. Intravenous injections with some drugs must be given very slowly to avoid reactions or having the animal collapse.

Because of the possibility of severe complications during and after intravenous injections, the technique will not be described in this book. If it is necessary to treat your animal with intravenous injections for a prolonged period of time, your veterinarian will either treat the animal or hospitalize it. It is definitely not a "read and do" procedure. You are not likely to find a veterinarian willing to teach you the technique—too many things can go wrong that can endanger your dog.

INTRADERMAL INJECTIONS

Intradermal injections are made into the upper layer of the skin. Your veterinarian will use this route for testing for allergies. He will inject small amounts of allergen extracts into the skin of the dog's belly. Intradermal injections make a small lump under the skin. This is normal, and will go away within a week. If the dog has a reaction, one or more of these blebs may be swollen, spread out or reddened. As long as they don't get any worse after about eight hours, this is OK. If they become reddened and hot, or greatly swollen, an abscess may be developing and you should have the dog examined by your veterinarian. The intradermal route is not normally used for products to be given by the owner, as it is tricky and used more for diagnosis than treatment.

INTRA-ARTICULAR INJECTIONS

Intra-articular injections are those made into the joints. Several serious complications can follow injections into the joints. Infection may occur if sterile surgical technique is not used. The point of the needle may penetrate the joint cartilage, damaging it and starting an arthritis. Bleeding may occur because a small blood vessel in the joint capsule has been punctured. The blood which leaks into the joint may cause severe problems, including arthritis, at a later date. For these reasons, joint injections should be left to your veterinarian. Again, this is not a "read and do" procedure.

Chapter 10

EMERGENCY CARE

RESTRAINT AND SAFETY

Before you can treat the dog, you must restrain him safely so that neither you nor he will be hurt in the process. No matter how much you trust him, he will be in pain, and may bite you because of it. He will act by instinct, not because he wants to hurt you. You must protect yourself.

When you pick up a puppy, support him securely and comfortably. Tiny puppies may be picked up by cradling one adult hand (or two child-hands) around them. As they grow, two hands are needed to make sure puppies will not fall, and to keep them comfortable and feeling secure.

An adult dog should have security if you pick him up. Small dogs may be picked up with one hand under the chest, and then snuggled to your body. Slightly larger dogs can have one hand placed in front of the chest and the other behind the rump. Very large dogs are best left foursquare on the ground unless it is necessary to move one if he is injured.

Small dogs who are injured can easily be picked up with a blanket folded into quarters. Press it firmly over the dog, being especially careful to cover his head until you have picked him up. Keep the blanket between you and him until you have him in a safe place and can evaluate whether or not he is hurt. You can pin his head with the blanket and examine his legs and the rest of him before you open it up and further

An emergency muzzle: Using gauze or rope, tie overhand knot and pull snug on top of dog's muzzle.

look him over. An injured dog is in pain. He is frightened, and he is very likely to bite.

A larger dog (any one larger than can be restrained with a blanket) who is injured should have his mouth muzzled before you do anything else. Use a piece of gauze if you have it handy. You will need a piece about six feet long. Double it. Tie an overhand knot in it, making a loop six or eight inches across. Drop this loop over the dog's nose, with the knot on top of his muzzle, and pull it snug. Pull the ends under the jaw and tie another overhand knot. Pull that snug also. Now tie the ends snugly behind the dog's ears, and you are finished. If gauze is not handy, a piece of thin rope or a long piece of cloth will work well. Then you can figure out how to carry him.

You can restrain a large dog safely on his side (lying down) until he is examined. Do this by kneeling at his back, holding his topmost front leg with one hand and the upper hind leg with the other. Meanwhile, lean your forearm (the one that is holding the front leg) across his neck.

A stick four to six feet long with a sliding loop on the end can be used to restrain a dog who is vicious, or whose intentions are unknown. The same type of stick should be used to handle an attack dog who must be controlled in the absence of his regular handler. Or you can make a sliding loop and rope the dog. If necessary, one person with one of these loops can be on each side, stretching the dog between them. If you think you might need to know how to use these techniques, see if the animal control agency in your area uses them, and ask for a demonstration.

A large dog can be moved on a stretcher, a board or a folded blanket carried by a couple of people. Any strong piece of cloth, such as a tent, can be used as a stretcher in an emergency. You can tie a knot in each corner and push a strong branch or pole through the knots—one on each side. To do this, however, takes two people, so that the surface can be kept tight. If the dog seems to have back or head injuries, move him on a piece of plywood or other hard surface to avoid complicating any injuries to the spinal cord. A small dog can be cradled in your arms (while someone else drives!). Like the large dog with head or back injuries, keep the back from moving as much as possible.

Carry a larger dog who has an injured front leg with his hind legs lower than the front ones. This will help to slightly lower the blood pressure and lessen the bleeding in the front leg(s).

If you are alone and need to carry a large dog, stoop down with your back to him. You can lift him up, putting him on your shoulders with his feet in front. Be sure that he is MUZZLED if he is conscious. Otherwise, in his confusion and pain, he may bite you in the face.

CARDIOPULMONARY RESUSCITATION (CPR)

CPR may be needed if your dog has drowned or was just hit by a car. In a few cases of injury or accident, prompt attention may make the difference between life and death. Unfortunately, most dogs whose hearts stop cannot be resus-

Tie second overhand knot underneath, pulling snug.

Tie bow or square knot behind dog's ears to complete muzzle.

citated. It is always worth a try. If, after twenty minutes, there has been no sign of recovery, there probably never will be, and it's OK to stop. If the dog has bitten an electrical cord, or otherwise tried to electrocute himself, prompt CPR may get him going again and save his life. Of those who are resuscitated, many will have enough damage to their tissues that they will later die. But it is still worth a try.

The gravity of the problem must be recognized right away, and treatment begun immediately. The dog may be unconscious and unresponsive. If you touch his eyelid, he may not blink. He probably will not be breathing, or, if he is, he will be gasping deeply and irregularly. He may not have a heartbeat. His membranes can be blue or grayish, pale white, or even normal in color.

Remember the letters ABC when doing CPR. They stand for:

> Airway
> Breathing
> Circulation.

As a rule of thumb, use 60 to 120 compressions per minute and 8 to 12 breaths per minute.

AIRWAY. Make sure the dog has an open airway. If there is any question, gently pull his lower jaw upward and backward, so that his head is above the level of his back. The dog should be lying on his side. Grasp his tongue and pull it outward. In some cases, this will stimulate the dog to breathe. If it does not, it still helps to open the airway.

BREATHING. If you have an oxygen tank and face mask available, you can use this, with a gentle flow of oxygen (up to 30 to 50 psi (pounds per square inch)) for a large dog, if you have a gauge on it). Oxygen from a welding tank can be used if medical oxygen is not available. If no oxygen is available, you can breathe for the dog, using your cupped hands around his nose, or using your mouth on his muzzle. Hold his mouth shut while you are doing this. For a small dog, you will only use part of each of your breaths. Watch the chest, and do not expand it more than it would if the dog were breathing for himself. Otherwise, you could force too much air into his lungs, and rupture them. Use 8 to 12 breaths per minute. After each breath, take your mouth away, and allow the dog's body to exhale by itself.

CIRCULATION. External compression is used to stimulate the heart and circulate blood throughout the body. If you have someone to help you, have him hold his hand on the femoral artery (see Pulse). Use whatever technique gives the strongest pulse. For a small dog, you can put your strongest hand around the bottom of the chest, and squeeze your thumb and fingers together. Stabilize the dog with your other hand behind his back. The dog can be lying on either side. The important thing is that you BEGIN CPR IMMEDIATELY. For a larger dog, such as a Newfoundland, you can put two hands over the heart and push with them together. You will be pushing toward the floor or ground on the other side of the

Lean lightly on the dog's neck to restrain him.

Mouth-to-nose resuscitation.

dog's chest. Or you can put the dog on his back and use your hands over the sternum (breastbone) to push. Use whatever technique seems to produce the best pulse quality. At its best, external cardiac massage will only produce 20% to 40% of normal blood pressure—but even that is better than 0%.

Research at the Duke University Hospital has shown that if you can get 120 to 150 beats per minute going, with a strong pulse quality, many dogs regain consciousness. The most successful techniques seem to use a brief duration of compression, done with moderate force, at a high rate of speed. If you have two people, one should do the cardiac compression while the other breathes for the dog in between periods of cardiac compression and monitors the pulse quality.

Adjust the force of your resuscitation efforts to the size of the dog. Too-hard pushing can tear the liver, with the animal bleeding to death because of this damage. Or it can break ribs, which puncture the lung or heart and cause death. You can push strongly, but not TOO strongly. Regardless of which method of artificial respiration is used, after you have inflated the lungs for each breath, remove ALL pressure completely. Allow the lungs to empty by themselves before you add the next breath. If you don't, the body cannot get rid of the carbon dioxide that has accumulated between breaths. The basic pattern is breathe—compress heart 5 times—breathe—until the dog recovers or you quit.

If you have epinephrine, a small quantity can be given—intravenously if possible. Otherwise give it subcutaneously or in the muscle. Use about 2/10 of a ml of a 1:1000 concentra-

External cardiac massage, just behind dog's elbow.

tion. The dog may die anyway, but it is worth a try if you cannot get to a veterinarian right away.

Whatever you do, get the dog to a veterinarian as soon as possible, even if you get him breathing and his heart going again. If he has had enough damage to stop his heart or breathing, he will need serious supportive care if he is going to live. And the veterinarian will have to deal with the problem which caused the stoppage in the first place.

BREATHING DIFFICULTIES

Early signs of respiratory distress include stretching the head upward toward the back and an anxious expression. The dog may breathe with his mouth open, pulling the corners of the mouth backward as he inhales. His heart rate will be increased. He might hold his elbows outward, and have little or no interest in what is going on around him. Later, if the condition worsens, the dog will gasp and strain for air. These signs occur with an obstruction in the airway. They are seen with short-faced dogs (such as English Bulldogs, Pugs, etc.) who have a long soft palate in a short facial structure. The soft palate flops over the airway in the back of the throat and literally chokes them. Similar signs are also seen with advanced cases of pneumonia. If the cause is pneumonia, the difficult breathing will be accompanied by fever and general signs of illness.

If a foreign object is lodged in the throat or trachea, hold the dog by his hind legs. A large dog may take two people to hold. If you cannot get him completely off the ground, at least hold his hind legs up in the air. Shake him vigorously. You can slap him on the sides of the rib cage, alternating blows on one side and then the other. Also try applying pressure up into his abdomen (similar to the Heimlich Maneuver for humans). If these actions are not successful within two or three minutes, get him quickly to the nearest veterinarian. He can do a tracheotomy (cut a hole in the trachea on the underside of the dog's neck), if necessary, to bypass the blockage.

If you are absolutely certain that a foreign object is causing the dog's distress, you are unable to get it out, and you are a long way from a veterinarian, you can try a desperate first-aid measure. DO NOT do this if you can get the dog to a veterinarian quickly. Lay the dog on his back, with one person holding the front legs and head and another holding the hind legs. Locate the trachea where it lies near the skin surface. This is about halfway between where the head joins the neck and the neck joins the chest. You can feel the trachea as a firm, bumpy object, much like a long, bumpy garden hose. Disinfect an area about 2 x 4 inches with alcohol or other disinfectant. Stabilize the trachea with the fingers of one hand. Feel for a space between two of the rings. With the other hand, pop a large, new, sterile hypodermic needle through the space between the rings. Use a 16- or 18-gauge needle, 1 inch long. Go straight in, perpendicular to the skin. You will need to end up with the needle in the lumen (open cavity) of the trachea. If you use a longer needle, be sure not to push it in too far and go completely through the airway. When you are in the right place, you will hear air whistling in and out of the needle. This little amount of air should give the dog a bit of relief, and may buy you enough time to get him to your veterinarian. Leave the needle in place while you transport the dog. Have one or two people hold the dog and the needle so that it does not come out. This technique would not be of any help with the problems mentioned below.

Small dogs, especially if they are overweight and middle-aged or older, may suffer from a collapsed trachea. This collapse occurs because the rings which make up the trachea are not complete circles of cartilage. Instead, they are half-circles with the top part covered by a membrane. The fatter the dog gets, the more the fat presses downward and into the trachea until the dog finally cannot breathe adequately. Some dogs with tracheal collapse may have a cough that sounds much like a goose honking. Others will have a dry, hacking cough. The dog will have frequent episodes of coughing or respiratory distress. Give oxygen if you have it handy. Get the dog to your veterinarian. Surgery may be needed to cure the defect.

Pleural effusion is an accumulation of fluid in the chest cavity. The fluid is present outside the lungs, between them and the chest wall. The fluid may be blood from being hit by a car or from a penetrating wound. Or it may be lymph from a ruptured lymphatic vessel. It can be pus from an infection, or exudate from a tumor. Whatever the fluid, if enough of it is present it will cause breathing difficulties because it takes up space into which the lungs would normally expand as the dog breathes. It will be necessary for your veterinarian to drain as much of the fluid as possible, as quickly as possible. The cause for it must be found and corrected. If the cause is an infection or a tumor, the prognosis is poor at best.

RESPIRATORY ARREST

Respiratory arrest is just that—the dog stops breathing. It must be corrected IMMEDIATELY. If it goes on more than three to five minutes, the dog will have heart failure and will die. As a rule of thumb, more than four minutes without air will cause irreversible brain damage. Newborn puppies, however, can tolerate up to about ten minutes without harm. Efforts at resuscitation should continue more than 20 minutes if oxygen has been given, or if the animal is colder than normal (the dog has been in cold water or exposed to cold temperatures). Either of these conditions will tend to prolong the time before the brain damage occurs.

Respiratory arrest can occur from diseases such as chronic heart disease, blood clots in the lung following treatment of heartworm disease, and chronic lung disease of any kind. It may result from depression of the centers within the brain which control breathing, caused by brain injuries, lack of oxygen to the brain, infection or increased pressure within the cranial cavity. Overdosages of depressant drugs can cause the dog to stop breathing. These drugs include tranquilizers, narcotics or barbiturates. Paralysis of the respiratory muscles is sometimes the problem, as from poisoning by organophosphate insecticides or fractures of the spinal cord.

Signs of respiratory arrest include slow, irregular labored breathing. The chest will stop moving and the dog's membranes will turn blue.

Treatment is similar to the treatment for shock: make sure the dog has an open airway and begin artificial respiration.

Use mouth-to-nose respiration if necessary. Give oxygen if it is available. Remove the cause of the problem if you can determine what it is and correct it. Get the dog to a veterinarian IMMEDIATELY. In most cases, you won't be able to find the cause, and if you do, you won't be able to correct it. DO NOT waste a lot of time trying.

OXYGEN USE

Precautions: Before you use oxygen, be sure you understand and use appropriate safety measures. A steel tank pressurized to 2,000 or 3,000 psi is dangerous. Also, oxygen facilitates burning. No combustibles or open flame should be anywhere near the oxygen.

Any oxygen tank used to treat an animal (or human) MUST have a regulator attached before the main tank valve is opened. Otherwise, the pressure can be so strong that the tank may travel like a rocket. Open the valve gradually and gently. Be sure the tank is solidly held so that it will not fall over or roll around. The hose coming off an oxygen tank can be used to give oxygen to the animal by running it into the corner of a plastic bag. Place the open end of the plastic bag over the dog's head. Leave it loosely open so that the exhaled carbon dioxide can escape. You are not to replace the air the dog is breathing with pure oxygen—you are only to enrich it with the pure oxygen.

Oxygen must be kept away from cigarettes and other smoking materials, open flames (what about the pilot light on your cook stove or water heater?) and electrical connections. It is explosive in combination with grease or oil, and should be kept away from them or a serious fire or explosion can result. If you are not absolutely sure about the safety of using oxygen, don't use it. It won't help you, your home or your dog if you destroy your home in the process.

It is a good idea to give oxygen whenever the dog is not breathing normally. It can be given to a weak newborn puppy. It is helpful with respiratory distress, such as that from heat stroke. It is useful in helping dogs who are in shock.

Pure (100%) oxygen without any air should NOT be given to animals. It can cause permanent eye damage in puppies less than three weeks old if present in excess concentration for more than a short period of time. Pure oxygen also decreases blood flow through the lungs, drying up the mucus which helps to protect the lungs against infection. There is no treatment for oxygen toxicity—and too much oxygen is toxic.

CONVULSIONS

A convulsion or seizure is sometimes due to epilepsy. If this is the case, it will be over in a few minutes; the dog will wake dazed and tired. The convulsions or seizures may be due to a poisoning by lead, strychnine, organophosphate or another toxic substance. Convulsions also result from low blood calcium (eclampsia) in a small bitch from just before to shortly after whelping. In a young puppy, they can be caused by a large quantity of certain worms. They may be due to an injury to the head or a brain tumor. Finally, they can result from an infection with bacteria or viruses, especially if the brain is infected. With almost all of these non-epileptic causes, seizures often continue until treated or until the dog dies.

What do you do for a dog who has a seizure? Stay calm. Move any sharp objects out of his way. Keep your hands out of his mouth. You can't help him, and you can easily get bitten. Dogs do not swallow their tongues. Prevent the dog from falling off a porch or down stairs. If the convulsions do not stop within five minutes, get him to a veterinarian as soon as possible. Unfortunately, if a severe poisoning is the cause, the dog may die on the way if the trip is longer than just a few minutes.

FRACTURES AND OTHER LIMB INJURIES

Dogs receive fractured bones from a number of causes. Perhaps the most common cause is being hit or run over by an automobile. Fractures also occur from falls, being kicked by a horse, bite wounds (such as a large dog attacking a small one), gunshot wounds, and blows from blunt instruments (such as a small dog and a boot!). Natural disasters such as windstorms and hurricanes may cause fractures, as can nutritional deficiencies or imbalances, and tumors of the bone.

Life-threatening fractures include those of the skull which damage the brain, rib fractures that prevent proper breathing or inflict damage on the lung, fractures of the jawbone and larynx that obstruct breathing, and injuries of the vertebral column that threaten the spinal cord. IF YOUR DOG HAS ONE OF THESE, GET TREATMENT FOR HIM IMMEDIATELY. Other fractures (limbs or pelvis, for example) may cause severe pain, but with proper treatment most will heal and your dog will regain normal function.

Fractures may be closed or open (where the bone has pierced the skin from the inside to the outside). Fractures where the skin has been pierced from the outside, with an object penetrating the bone, are also considered "open." This type of open fracture may occur with a gunshot wound, for example.

Sprains and other injuries to the ligaments and muscles are often hard to tell from broken bones. The injured area will be swollen and tender, much like a fracture. If you can get the dog to a veterinarian, have him examined. If you cannot get veterinary care fairly quickly, apply ice and give the dog a night's rest to see how he feels. Sprains and other soft-tissue injuries generally heal well with time and rest.

Joint luxations and subluxations are commonly known as dislocations. Dislocations often occur when the joint is hit by an external force (again, as by a car), or the dog lands awkwardly on a leg. The weight of his body may tear the ligaments loose, allowing the joint to pop out of place or hang loosely. Dislocations are common in the toe, jaw, knee and hip joint. The dog may hold the injured joint or limb at an abnormal angle. Do not attempt to replace the dislocation. Put an ice pack on it and take the dog to your veterinarian. In most cases, anesthesia will be needed to allow replacement with as little pain as possible. The sooner the joint is reset, the better the chance for normal and complete healing. Anesthesia also has the advantage of relaxing the dog's muscles, preventing

further damage as the joint is maneuvered back into place. If left more than a day or so without resetting, it may be impossible to replace without surgery.

Avulsions are injuries occurring when part of a limb is torn partway loose, usually by a hard blow during an accident. The same kind of injury can occur when a tail is caught in a door or otherwise injured.

How do you tell if your dog has a broken bone? He will often be suddenly lame, carrying a leg completely off the ground or putting weight on it only reluctantly. If the dog has a neck or back injury, he may be uncoordinated, or even totally unable to rise or walk. A dog with a broken leg will probably show abnormal movement, such as part of a leg moving sideways. A reduced range of motion of one leg might be the only sign. The dog may show pain and swelling. When the leg is examined, a grating sensation can sometimes be felt. Damage to the skin and muscle may be seen, with bleeding, bruising and torn skin.

If the dog is lying down, or has just been hit, your first priority is to ensure that the dog has an open airway. Deal with any life-threatening injuries first. Minor bleeding can be ignored until the dog's primary needs are met. Remember ABC: Airway, Breathing, Circulation.

Whether you saw your dog hit by the car, or if he comes home limping, your first move MUST be to muzzle him. He will be in pain and could accidentally bite you. If there is bone sticking out through the skin, or obvious angulation of the limb, there is no need to check the dog further. Just gather him up and take him to your veterinarian. Leave him muzzled, as you will probably hurt him while moving him, no matter how careful you try to be, and he might accidentally bite you.

Skeletal fractures, other than those few mentioned above, are obvious, painful and dramatic, but rarely life-threatening. Do NOT give any painkillers or sedatives. These drugs can depress the dog's blood pressure and put him into shock. And they also tend to mask signs of head injury or nerve damage. They complicate recovery from heart and lung involvement in the emergency. Do not give your dog ANYTHING to eat. If he is thirsty, give him a sip or two of water—just enough to moisten his mouth, until you and/or your veterinarian determine the extent of his injuries. You could let him lick a couple of ice cubes, which will let him dampen his mouth without swallowing much liquid, which might later interfere with surgery.

If no broken bone is obvious, you can begin to examine the dog further. Again, make sure that he is muzzled. If possible, have someone hold the dog's head. Feel over his head and neck, looking for lumps, bumps or rough edges. Feel gently down each leg, one at a time, looking for swelling, grating or lumps. Move each joint in turn through its normal range of motion. If it causes him pain, do not force it to move. If you find a possible broken bone, leave him muzzled, gather him up and take him to a veterinarian. If you do not find anything that appears broken, remove the muzzle, and ask the dog to move a little. Watch how he moves across the room or yard. Is he favoring one leg? Dragging a toe, or not properly moving a leg through its normal arc, could mean that there is nerve damage or that there is a fracture that is not apparent.

Use direct pressure to stop any bleeding. For instance, if blood is spurting from an artery, put a sterile gauze compress over it. If you don't have sterile gauze handy, use a clean handkerchief or a paper towel. Sanitary napkins are also good, especially for large open wounds. If the wound is deep, put the sterile gauze or clean material directly on the wound surface. If the material does not come up to the level of the surrounding skin, fill in the space with anything that you have handy. Crumpled paper, or a rolled-up sock or rag, can be placed on top of the first layer. Then wrap a bandage around the whole thing. The filler will help to put pressure on the bleeding area deep in the cut. The bandage should be snug but not too tight. In most cases, this is much better than using a tourniquet. And you will not have to worry so much about cutting off the circulation below the bandage.

DO NOT put cotton batting or cotton balls on a wound. The cotton fibers will get caught with the clotting blood and will be nearly impossible to remove later, and their presence will delay healing.

DO NOT worry about splinting or setting a fracture if you can get the dog to a veterinarian within a reasonable length of time. This is true even if you have to drive three or four hours to a suitable clinic. If you are 40 miles back into the mountains on horseback and a horse steps on your dog, you will have to splint the leg.

Veterinary care for the injured dog will usually start by an evaluation of the patient to inventory his injuries. The veterinarian will then treat the dog for shock, and administer antibiotics to prevent infection. He may suture open cuts. If there are fractures, many veterinarians do not treat them until the next day. Do not feel that he is neglecting your dog. A night in a cage (with four boring walls to help him rest quietly) will make your dog a better candidate for a successful outcome of surgery in the morning. It will allow his body to stabilize and give the medications a chance to take effect. Then the veterinarian can safely cast, splint or pin the leg. The delay also gives the swelling a chance to go down; if a cast is applied it will fit better and do a better job of holding the leg.

If the dog has suffered a dislocation, your veterinarian may need to suture ligaments and tendons back together, depending on what has been torn. A dislocated hip will be put back into place and be either pinned or bandaged to hold it in place, depending on the direction it has dislocated and the direction of force needed to hold it while it heals. Consult with your veterinarian to find out what will be required and what it will cost. If the dog's tail has been torn apart (an avulsion), the torn end will usually be amputated. The tail does not have a very good blood supply, and is extremely hard to splint successfully.

Pelvic fractures are common in dogs, most generally caused by being hit by a car. There are two ways of handling these injuries. Your veterinarian can use multiple bone pins to put all of Humpty Dumpty's pieces back together. This surgery can cost $800-$1,000 or more. As an alternative, you can confine the dog to a small space—about the size of a child's playpen for a small to medium-sized dog, and only slightly larger for a dog such as a Labrador Retriever. Pad it with fairly firm material such as carpet scraps or a small mattress, cut to fit the area. Firm material will enable the dog to turn around without getting tangled in his bedding.

Confinement will be necessary for about four weeks minimum, and perhaps as much as six weeks. You can pick the dog up and take him outside two to three times a day. Support his hind end as he urinates and defecates. The rest of the time should be spent in the confined area. Some dogs will be more comfortable and at ease if they are in the kitchen or living room, in sight of much of the family's normal activity. Give the dog plenty of quiet attention. Do not let children induce him to romp or become excited. The key to success is for the dog to use his rear legs as little as possible. The dog may heal with some limping and may no longer win races, but this course of action is worth considering if you do not have the money for expensive corrections. This assumes, of course, that the dog does not have any complications affecting the urinary system or bowel. You can tell whether this is the case by watching to see that he is urinating and defecating normally. You will need to feed him less than his normal amount of food. If he cannot defecate easily, feed a high-fiber diet or use a laxative. Enemas may be needed from time to time. Because the bone pieces from a pelvic fracture tend to reduce the size of the pelvic canal, a female should not be allowed to become pregnant, unless you are prepared to pay for a Caesarean section.

What do you do if you live in the middle of nowhere and your dog has been hit by a car or similarly injured? You cannot get to a veterinarian, or do not have the money to do so. Give first aid for any open cuts. Check the dog for concussion. Now put him in a warm, QUIET place. You can use a playpen if you have one, or a box which is just slightly larger than the dog. If you have a crate for him, that will be fine. Just shut him in. Otherwise, he will try to follow you around as he normally does, and may severely aggravate his problems. Let him rest quietly overnight. Most veterinarians do this with many of their accident patients after checking them over. Give him half an aspirin or a whole one, depending on the dog's size. Go away and leave him alone. In the morning, you will be able to evaluate the dog's condition and the problems that are still troubling him. You can splint a leg as best you can, or apply other treatment. Please note that this treatment is to be used ONLY when you CANNOT do anything else—you could easily return in the morning to a dead dog if his injuries were severe. Yet, if you could do nothing else...

CUTS

Skin cuts can occur when a dog is hit by a car or ripped by fighting with another dog. Farm and hunting dogs often get tears from charging through barbed-wire fences.

Cut arteries may bleed severely, and if not stopped may be life-threatening. The end of the nose and the nasal cartilages are richly supplied with blood vessels and bleed profusely. Cuts on the tongue, ear flaps, tail, feet, penis and mammary glands may bleed excessively from arteries. Pressure must be used to control arterial bleeding, and the dog should be taken to a veterinarian as soon as possible. Dogs who have eaten warfarin (rodent poisons such as D-Con®), or who have hemophilia or other clotting disorders, can bleed excessively from even minor cuts. If the bleeding is severe, or has continued for some time, the dog may have to be treated for shock. An ice pack may be used to help slow bleeding, but do not leave it on for longer than about 15-20 minutes.

Blood which is coming from an artery is bright red and will flow irregularly, sometimes spurting in time with the heartbeat. Blood from a vein is darker in color and flows evenly.

DO NOT use "clotting" powders which are made for cattle or other livestock in your dog's wounds. They can cause severe burning and pain. And it will be nearly impossible to suture the wound and have it heal if one of these products has been used. The only clotting products which are useful for dogs are silver nitrate sticks, epinephrine or styptic pencil. These can be used when you are clipping toenails, and get one a bit short so that it bleeds. None of these products are useful for open wounds. A pressure bandage is the only good way to control open-wound bleeding, whether arterial or venous.

Your veterinarian will repair the laceration in somewhat the following manner: If the cut is large, he will completely anesthetize the dog; if it is small and the dog is calm, he may either sedate the dog or just have a capable assistant hold him. He will probably muzzle the dog, although you probably would have muzzled the dog when you first took a look at the injury. He will then wash it with providone-iodine solution (mixed to about the color of weak tea), or a similar MILD disinfectant. He will soak gauze sponges with this solution and lay them in the wound to keep it clean while he clips the hair from around the edges of the wound. He will clip the dampened hair back from the edges at least 1/2 inch (1.3 mm) all the way around. This keeps the hair from getting into the wound, and from irritating it as it heals. It will also keep the area cleaner.

He will anesthetize the skin edges by injecting small amounts of a local anesthetic such as xylocaine around the periphery of the wound, using a syringe and a very fine needle (about 25 ga. 5/8 inch long). The anesthetic will be injected about half an inch under the skin edge (away from the hole), in spots about a half-inch apart, in order to deaden the skin all the way around the wound. Following the use of the anesthetic, he will finish cleansing the wound, removing any hair, grass, dirt or other foreign material. He will cut out any hanging shreds of arteries, tendons or shredded muscle. He will then trim around the edge if the cut is more than a couple of hours old, or has a ragged edge, removing as little tissue as possible. In some cases, he will only take off about 1/16 of an inch (1 mm)—the least amount that he can trim off. If the wound surface is dried, it may be trimmed, again taking off the very thinnest layer possible. Trimming the wound in this fashion will give a fresh, clean surface which will heal well. Some veterinarians like to flood the wound with a penicillin or penicillin-streptomycin product at this point, using 1 to 5 ml, depending on the size of the wound.

The veterinarian will use a surgical needle with a very sharp point to suture the skin. It is shaped like a half-circle. He pushes it through the skin with a pair of needle holders. This is a pair of forceps with a special gripping edge to hold the needle securely. He will use a pair of "tissue forceps" with his other hand. These are like a large pair of tweezers with a toothed edge. He will put the needle through the skin, first on one side and then the other, coming through about 1/8 to 1/4 inch (3-6 mm) back from the skin edge, depending on the location of the cut and thickness of the dog's skin. After he has passed the needle and suture through both sides of the wound, he will tie a square knot to complete a simple stitch. The stitches are just barely pulled snug. The skin will swell, and if they are put in too tightly they will cut through the skin and pull out.

Many veterinarians like to begin suturing in the middle of a wound so that they come out with the same amount of skin at both ends, with no wrinkles or puckers. The suture is often a nylon product similar to nylon fishing line, although a fine stainless steel suture is sometimes used. After the suturing job is finished, the veterinarian may apply a powdered nitrofurazone product (such as Topazone® powder) along the stitch line. This helps to dry any discharges which drain from the wound area, as well as kill any bacteria in the immediate area. A very fine once-over with the powder is all that is needed. It doesn't do any good to have the material caked thickly on the stitch line, and may even cause harm by keeping the stitches moist under the crust.

Some veterinarians now use skin staples (the same kind used in human hospitals) instead of sutures. Whether staples or sutures are used, they will usually be removed in about ten days.

Keep an eye on the stitch line. It should continue to be clean and free from pus, blood or drainage. If the sutured wound becomes filled with pus because of infection, or filled with serum or other fluid, it will need to be drained. Return the dog to your veterinarian. He will open the incision by removing one or two stitches at the lowest point of the pocket. He will then push the blunt end of a pair of forceps into the pocket to open it up so that it will drain out through the hole. You will then need to swab the pocket out twice daily, using a product such as povidone-iodine and long cotton swabs (you can get them at the drugstore). This will take the pressure off the suture line and allow the rest of the wound to continue to heal. Do not be afraid to press gently with the swabs—you will not damage any tissues which have already healed. You are just cleaning out dead and infected material that is coming off the damaged tissue surfaces. Do not let the drain hole seal over all at once, or the pocket will just fill up with pus again. It should get smaller day by day, as it heals from the inside out. Each day you should notice that the depth to which you reach with the swab gets more and more shallow. The condition and its treatment are very much like an abscess.

SHOCK

Shock refers to a condition where the dog's blood pressure is lowered, causing inadequate blood flow through the tissues. Shock can result from severe blood loss, whether from a bleeding cut or from a ruptured spleen, liver or internal blood vessel. Acute heart failure results in shock. Shock may occur from fluid loss from diarrhea, severe vomiting or the plasma loss that occurs with burns involving large amounts of skin. Shock also results with massive crushing injuries, such as when the dog is hit by a car, leading to severe internal bleeding. Shock may occur when injury to the heart or heart disease results in lessened blood output so that blood pressure throughout the body drops. Severe stress, whether psychological or physical, may cause shock. Infections with some kinds of bacteria cause shock. The bacteria produce toxins which affect the blood vessels, causing blood to "pool" in the internal organs, with a deadly drop in blood pressure. Lack of hormones from the adrenal gland may leave the dog's system unable to maintain normal circulation and blood pressure. Anaphylactic shock occurs when drugs or toxic substances trigger a severe allergic reaction within the body.

Whatever the initial cause of the shock, the events that follow are much the same. Some event decreases cardiac output, lowering the blood pressure. The adrenal gland and sympathetic nervous system cause arteries and capillaries in the skin and limbs to shut down. The spleen contracts and blood is shunted away from the skin and intestines. The kidneys retain sodium and water. The whole process leads to complete circulatory collapse, ending with heart failure.

SIGNS OF SHOCK. Signs include a rapid heartbeat and weak pulse. The dog will be breathing rapidly and shallowly, or he may be panting. He will have a poor capillary refill. To check capillary refill, push your finger firmly into a pinkish portion of the dog's gums. When you release your finger, the color should return within 1-2 seconds. If it takes longer than two seconds to return, the dog's circulatory system is not doing well. The dog's temperature may be below normal, and he will probably be weak, depressed and restless. His eyes could have a "glassy" stare. The gums will become pale. If the shock continues to progress, he will go into a coma, and his pupils will become dilated.

TREATMENT OF SHOCK. Support the dog's respiration. Make sure that his airway is open. Open his mouth and check it to make sure he can breathe. Be careful—you can still get bitten if he is unconscious. If he is unconscious, pull outward on the end of his tongue, and tilt his head backward to open the back of his throat. If you have oxygen available, use it if you can do so safely. If there is visible bleeding, control it as soon as possible, preferably by direct pressure or bandaging. Keep the dog's head slightly lower than the rest of his body to increase blood flow to the brain (the same idea as raising the feet and legs of a human in shock).

If the weather is cool, keep the dog covered with a coat or blanket until you move him. In hot weather, get him into shade. Keep the dog quiet, and avoid any noise that may make him attempt to move. Do not move him any more than you have to. Do not give painkillers or sedatives. Delirium or restlessness may be more due to lack of oxygen to the brain than from pain. Painkillers can mask severe symptoms, and depressant drugs will further compound the shock.

If there is no visible bleeding, but you think the dog is bleeding internally into his abdomen, wrap a long piece of cloth tightly around the dog's abdomen as a binder. A strip of bedsheet works well. His membranes may be pale grayish in color, and he will be either weak or prostrate.

At this point, your dog needs more help than you can give. Get him to the nearest veterinarian as soon as possible. It will be necessary, in most cases, to give intravenous fluids, and possibly a blood transfusion, as well as intensive drug therapy to save the animal. Emergency surgery could also be required. Keep the oxygen on him while you are driving him there if you can. BE SURE NOT TO ALLOW ANYONE TO SMOKE AROUND THE OXYGEN.

CONCUSSION

The dog's brain can be damaged by being hit by a vehicle, blows from a blunt object, falls from heights, bite wounds and other traumatic encounters with his environment.

If you did not see the dog get injured, you may notice a skull fracture—one area of the skull may be caved in. The scalp may be torn, and the dog may have a nosebleed. He may not be aware of who you are or where he is. The pupil of one eye may be enlarged, while the other is smaller than normal. The difference in size of the pupils is the most definite sign of concussion. The dog may be uncoordinated, staggering or falling. In cases of severe damage, the dog may be unconscious. The dog may be making involuntary noises. He might circle or tilt his head to one side.

Treat for shock. If the dog becomes nearly normal within a few minutes, you can observe him closely for 24 hours. Take him to a veterinarian immediately if he does not return to normal within one to two hours, if he is obviously severely injured or if his condition becomes worse. If you are taking him to the veterinarian, keep his head slightly elevated to help reduce any bleeding which may be occurring in the cranial cavity, even though he might be in shock.

PUNCTURE WOUNDS OF THE CHEST

DO NOT MUZZLE THE DOG WHO HAS A PENETRATING CHEST WOUND. It may interfere with his breathing. Make sure the dog has a clear airway. Remove blood, mucus or vomited material. Handle him carefully so that you do not get bitten.

The presence of air within the chest cavity is called pneumothorax. A pneumothorax is somewhat comparable to a sucking chest wound in a human. The difference is that in a dog, BOTH lungs are likely to collapse, while in a human, there is a good chance of one lung remaining partially functional. Pneumothorax in the dog is an emergency and must be cared for promptly.

Pneumothorax may occur because of the rupture of some of the air sacs of the lungs. The ruptured sacs leak air into the chest cavity from the inside. Or it may occur with an open chest wound. This can happen when an object penetrates the chest cavity from the outside. These wounds are generally obvious. Penetration may occur in small dogs who are bitten by very large dogs. If the penetrating object is still in place and is small, DO NOT REMOVE IT. This would apply, for instance, to a small tree branch which had pierced the dog's chest. Just bandage it in place, while keeping it from penetrating any deeper. As long as it is there, it acts as a cork, plugging the hole. Get the dog to your veterinarian as soon as possible.

A large or immovable object (one you can't take along with the dog) will have to be removed before you can haul the dog. It is important to bandage the dog securely, sealing the hole to prevent air from entering the chest cavity. Use a piece of plastic (a plastic bag will do in an emergency) to seal the hole. This helps keep the lung from collapsing. Put as many gauze sponges over this as are needed to cover the hole or bleeding area. Then put a large pad over them, to apply direct pressure on the area. You can use a small folded towel or piece of clothing or rag. Finally, bandage around the whole chest. Bandage snugly so that the materials will not fall off, but not so snugly that the dog cannot breathe. Give oxygen if you have it safely available. Get the dog to a veterinarian as soon as possible.

PENETRATING WOUNDS OF THE ABDOMEN

Treat as for chest wounds with respect to removing or leaving the penetrating object and bandaging. If the intestines have been pulled out or are dangling out of the wound, take a deep breath and get control of yourself—it's not pretty. Have someone hold the dog so that he cannot walk and drag the intestines in the dirt or step on them. Dampen a long, clean rag with lukewarm water and wrap it around the dog's abdomen and up over his back, around and around to support the intestines in a sort of hammock. Do not attempt to replace them in the abdomen. Let the veterinarian do that so he can inspect them for damage and clean them. These wounds look gross but, surprisingly, many dogs survive the injury. Get the dog to a veterinarian as soon as possible.

PUNCTURE WOUNDS

The most common cause of puncture wounds is the dog bite. These wounds are small at the skin surface, deep, and become infected quite easily. Clip the hair away from the wound opening. If there is some doubt as to where the punctures are, it is better to clip away too much hair than too little. Cleanse the area with povidone-iodine wash. If the puncture wounds are large enough, swab down into each one with a cotton swab. If the bites are extensive, or if your dog becomes infected easily, it would be worth taking him to your veterinarian for an antibiotic injection. This will help to prevent the possibility of tetanus, even though it is remote. Antibiotics will help to prevent an abscess from forming.

HEAT STROKE

The most significant sign of heat stroke is an elevated body temperature. The dog may have a rectal temperature of 105 to 110 degrees F (40.6-43.3 degrees C). Life-threatening complications may quickly follow. These include edema (fluid accumulation) within the brain, acid-base imbalances, and coagulation of the blood within the blood vessels.

Heat stroke usually occurs when the air temperature is high. It may occur as low as 90 degrees F (32.2 degrees C). Most commonly, it occurs at temperatures between 100 and 115 degrees F (37.7 and 46.1 degrees C). Most dogs who are unconfined will not stay in conditions which will raise their body temperature to the point of heat stroke. For this reason, it is usually seen in dogs that are confined, especially in places with poor ventilation or in the sun. A good example is a vehicle on a hot day, especially if the windows are rolled up. A dog in a transport crate is an even better candidate for heat stroke. It can also happen to a dog that is chained so that he is unable to move to an area that would be more comfortable for him. If the dog has been in a fight or is otherwise excited so that his temperature is raised, he is especially vulnerable.

High humidity can contribute to heat stroke. The dog is not able to evaporate as much moisture as usual through the membranes of his nose and mouth, even though he is panting as hard as he can. Young puppies and very old dogs have less heat tolerance and are more prone to heat stroke. Dogs of short-faced breeds are also less tolerant to heat. Lack of water can also contribute to heat stoke. Fat dogs have more trouble with the heat than do thin dogs.

One family took their dog on a 30-mile trip with the car windows open. They had walked the dog in shade at each stop. However, while in the car, the dog had been sitting in the sun on this hot afternoon. Despite adequate ventilation, the dog's core temperature became hot enough to cause heat stroke and the dog died. Be sure to provide shade, even if you are driving along with the windows open.

The first sign of impending heat stroke is hard and fast panting. The heart rate is above normal. The dog's mucous membranes are bright red. If you were to take his temperature, you would find that it is above normal. As the condition progresses, the dog goes into a stupor. The legs and feet are hot to the touch. The bright red membranes of the mouth become pale. The dog may now have a watery diarrhea, which he cannot control. If it becomes bloody, or if hemorrhages are present on the mucous membranes, clotting may be occurring within the blood vessels. Coma and respiratory collapse occur unless the dog is treated.

Take the dog to the nearest veterinarian if you are near a clinic. If you cannot get to a veterinarian, proceed as follows:

Treatment begins by lowering the dog's body temperature. Get the dog out of the sun or enclosed area, into shade or an air-conditioned building. You can immerse his legs and trunk in a tub of cold or iced water. Take his rectal temperature at least every ten minutes. Stop cooling him when his body temperature reaches 103 degrees F (39.4 degrees F). His temperature will continue to drop, and it is easy to get him too cold and make him hypothermic. After you stop bathing him, keep taking his temperature every 10 minutes to make sure that he does not return to an elevated temperature. Ice water enemas have been recommended as a method of treating heat stroke. The disadvantage is that they interfere with the only way you have of monitoring the dog's progress and making sure that you do not have him too cold: the rectal temperature. Evaporative cooling methods which work to cool humans do not work well on dogs because of their hair coats.

As soon as you have the dog cooled and his temperature has stabilized below 103 degrees F (39.4 degrees C), get him to a veterinarian for follow-up treatment. He may give corticosteroids, mannitol or other drugs to help reduce the edema in the brain. If the blood is starting to clot in the blood vessels, he may administer intravenous fluids to dilute the blood and stabilize the dog's circulatory system. Antibiotics may be given to help prevent infection due to the dog's weakened condition.

The best treatment for heat stroke is prevention. If it's hot for you, it's probably miserable for your dog, who cannot sweat and cannot remove his coat and throw it on the seat beside him. If there's the least doubt, leave him at home, where he will be alive when you get back, rather than taking him with you and returning to the car from shopping, to find him dying or dead.

DROWNING

Most dogs can swim fairly well, if introduced to it gradually. Dogs may drown when they have never learned to swim, and are suddenly thrown, or fall into the water, such as diving out of a boat in the middle of a lake. They may drown when they try to swim across a lake or large river and become exhausted. A tragedy that can occur is a dog getting into a steep-sided swimming pool, pond or irrigation canal, and finding that he cannot get out. First, if rescue is necessary, make sure that you, or the person who goes after the dog, can swim well. Do not compound one tragedy with a second. You can drop a rope around the dog's neck and tow him to dry ground to avoid having him try to climb on top of you. Drowning dogs act like drowning people.

When you have the dog back on dry ground, hold him up by the hind legs, with his head hanging clear of the ground. A large dog may require two or more persons to do this. Hold him for 10 to 20 seconds, while slapping him on alternate sides of the chest wall. You should slap gently on a small dog, and harder on a large dog such as a German Shepherd. Begin CPR on the dog. If you still hear gurgling noises, stop every couple of minutes to hold him up again to drain water out of his lungs. It is also helpful to have him lying with his head downward if possible while doing the CPR. As long as you can feel a heartbeat, there is hope. Keep him warm. When he regains consciousness, take him to a veterinarian for examination if he has been unconscious for more than a couple of minutes, or has swallowed much water, or if he otherwise looks ill.

In some cases of cold-water drowning, your veterinarian may wish to put the dog into a barbiturate-induced coma to reduce metabolism within the brain, reducing damage to brain cells. This may give the dog his best chance of recovery.

POISONINGS

When we say "poisoned," the first thing that comes to mind is some vicious person deliberately trying to kill the dog. Luckily, these cases are quite rare. More often, the dog poisons himself accidentally by getting into insecticides, herbicides, or chewing on a poisonous plant because he is bored and it is convenient. Dogs are sometimes poisoned when a tick or flea dip is mixed incorrectly and is too strong. If you suspect that your dog has been poisoned, bring along the container when you take him to the veterinarian. This will help the veterinarian determine what the problem is, and what needs to be done about it.

Dogs are three to four times more likely to be poisoned than cats. They are less finicky about what they eat. They are more likely to chew and worry at items that a cat would disdain as inedible. They are more likely to roam and be exposed to dangers.

In general, a dog should be encouraged to vomit if he has ingested a poison. The exceptions are acids, alkalis and petroleum or other aromatic chemicals. With these items, give cream, milk or water to dilute the substance. Do not bother trying to get the dog to vomit if you are close to a veterinary clinic. Get your dog to the clinic and let the veterinarian take care of it. He has injectible drugs which will make the dog vomit almost immediately. Activated charcoal may be given with any poisoning or suspected poisoning. It may cause constipation if not followed later by a laxative. Keep this in mind after the initial crisis is past (Buck, 1986). Do not give any drug to a comatose or unconscious animal.

Pesticides are chemicals used to kill insects and other pests in and around the house and garden, as well as on your pet. Their use is based on the principle that they are more poisonous to the pest than to you or your dog. Most of these are safe WHEN USED in recommended dosages and at appropriate intervals. However, they can all be deadly when used in excessive amounts, or accidentally misused.

Organophosphate and carbamate poisonings will be discussed together because they are quite similar. These poisonings can occur from home and garden insecticides and related products. The dog can obtain a toxic dose if he eats them or walks on freshly treated foliage. Organophosphates may cause toxicity when the dog is dipped in an overly strong solution of flea or tick dip. Reactions to flea collars and dog wormers containing these products may also occur. Pets can be poisoned when these compounds are incorrectly mixed, or when the animal is treated at the same time with the same chemical for both internal and external parasites. Poisoning may occur if these chemicals are inhaled by the pet. Very small amounts, even the quantity left in an "empty" container, can cause death. Store these materials out of the reach of your dog (and children!), and dispose of the empty containers promptly and properly.

Common organophosphates include dichlorvos, DDVP, vapona, malathion, fenthion, parathion, trichlorfon, chlorpyrifos, prolate (Phosmet), Ruelene (commonly used for cattle grubs) and diazinon, to name but a few. Malathion is one of the safest of these compounds, while parathion is one of the most toxic. Names of organophosphates often contain "phosphoro." Carbamate insecticides cause the same symptoms. Some of the carbamates are carbaryl (Sevin), aldicarb, some formulations of Golden Malrin (Zoecon) and propoxur (Baygon). Over 100 of these products are currently manufactured under many different names. Carbamates are also the main ingredient in some ant traps, such as Raid Ant Trap (S.C. Johnson & Son) and Black Flag Ant Trap (Boyle-Midway). Dogs chew them open and are poisoned. Be sure to place these traps where dogs can't get them (Hornfeldt, 1987).

Signs of organophosphate poisoning may occur within as little as five minutes after the dog has been exposed to the product. Most reactions occur within 12 hours after exposure. The dog may have a garlic odor on its breath or coat. The pupils of the eyes are constricted—this is one of the most consistent signs. The dog may be restless and confused. He will salivate, and have tears running from his eyes. Fluid is pouring into his lungs. As he breathes, this will come out the nose and mouth as frothy bubbles. He will gasp and strain to breathe, and may turn blue because the fluid keeps his lungs from exchanging air. His breathing difficulties can be due to irregular muscular contractions as well as fluid production in the lungs. The muscles of the face and tongue begin to twitch, followed by twitching of all the muscles in small, short convulsions. The dog might show muscular temors, incoordination, stiffness, cramps and vomiting. He may urinate and defecate (this may be a watery diarrhea). He may show muscular weakness along with the twitching, which can progress to convulsions and paralysis. If severe enough, the dog will go into a coma, followed by death. Death may occur within a few minutes, or the dog may live several days before dying.

ORGANOPHOSPHATE POISONING IS AN EMERGENCY. Get the dog to a veterinarian as soon as possible. He will treat the animal with drugs to specifically counteract the toxicity. Give oxygen if it is safely available. Artificial respiration may save the dog if he goes into respiratory failure and you have someone to administer it while you are heading for the veterinary hospital. Even with prompt treatment, some dogs cannot be saved. If the dog comes through the initial crisis, he has a good chance of returning to normal.

If there is no way you can get the dog to a veterinarian, do the best that you can. Remove the dog's flea collar. If an insecticide or dip has caused the problem, give the dog a bath, using soap and water. Wear rubber gloves so that there are not two victims! Give activated charcoal if you have it on hand and can give it rapidly (see strychnine, below). Do not give charcoal or anything else if the dog is in convulsions, or is having so much trouble breathing that he cannot swallow adequately. Oxygen is also helpful. If you can keep the dog alive, eventually his body will eliminate the toxin. On the other hand, a sufficiently large dose will kill him before you have a chance to help him.

Prevention of this type of poisoning includes keeping pets away from containers of insecticide. Be sure to safely dispose of empty containers. Carefully wash all sprayers, buckets and other objects which have come into contact with the product. Distribute the spray or dip carefully and evenly so that there are no pools from which the dog can drink. Confine all pets until treated yard areas have dried completely. Do not store insecticides in unlabeled containers (if possible, do not store them at all).

DO NOT mix insecticide unless you have written instructions for that specific product, whether on the label or in a separate folder. One of my clients lost a dog when a friend gave her a bottle of insecticide and said to mix it one part insecticide to 10 parts water (1:10). The label did not give instructions, and the flyer accompanying the bottle had been lost. After the tick dip was applied, the dog went into or-

ganophosphate poisoning and died. A later check with the feed store revealed that the recommended dilution was equivalent to a 1:128 solution!

NOTE: Many flea and tick dips which are perfectly safe for your dog may be fatal to your cat. DO NOT use the same product for both unless the directions say it is safe for cats. Cats ingest the material as they groom. What is safe on the outside of the cat may not be safe on the inside!

Organochlorine insecticides include products such as aldrin, dieldrin, heptachlor, endrin, chlordane and lindane. The use of these products is severely limited because they persist in the environment and some are known to cause cancer, but stocks are still sitting around in garages and barns. Toxicity can occur when a pet eats contaminated food, or the compound is carelessly used and the dog gets into it. Mothballs contain a related substance which causes similar signs when eaten. (I never said dogs have a high IQ!)

Signs of organochlorine poisoning include twitchiness, restlessness, vomiting, salivation, depression and incoordination. These signs may be followed by blindness, convulsions, coma and death. Get the dog to a veterinarian as soon as possible. If the convulsions can be controlled, the dog will probably survive.

Toxaphene is an organochlorine insecticide that is often used as a cattle dip. A dog may fall into the vat while cattle are being dipped, or drink some of the material which has dripped off the cattle, or run out of a truck where the cattle have been sprayed. Dogs are best kept away from cattle dipping or spraying operations. If the dog falls into a vat, he should be washed off immediately, first with clear water, and then shampooed and rinsed throughly. Wear rubber gloves as you are doing this so that YOU do not get poisoned by this material. The concentration used for cattle can be toxic to humans. If the dog has drunk some of the dip, treat as described above for organophosphate poisoning, including, if possible, a quick trip to a veterinarian.

Pyrethrins are natural insecticides derived from several species of *Chrysanthemum*. They are commonly used in flea control products. Pyrethrins are fairly safe to use around dogs, as mammals metabolize them quite well. Man-made pyrethrin-type compounds are somewhat more toxic. The man-made materials include products such as allethrin, tetramethrin and fenvalerate. In some products, the pyrethrins are combined with other insecticides which make them much more toxic. Be sure to read the label so you will know what you are using.

Signs of pyrethrin poisoning include vomiting, salivation, lack of appetite and difficult breathing. The dog may be hyperactive, staggering and have seizures. Or he could be somewhat depressed. First aid is the same as for strychnine. Get the dog to a veterinarian as soon as possible.

Rotenone is derived from the roots of a plant. It is fairly safe when used according to directions. Large quantities can cause toxic reactions in dogs. Depression and vomiting are the signs most commonly seen. There is no specific antidote for this poisoning. Bathe the dog thoroughly with detergent to remove as much of the product as possible from his coat. Wear rubber gloves while giving the bath. Give activated charcoal. If the dog goes into convulsions, your veterinarian can administer drugs to control them.

Naphthalene is used in some types of mothballs. A poisoned dog may show lack of appetite, depression, vomiting, twitching, diarrhea and dilated pupils of the eyes. Induce vomiting, give charcoal to limit the absorption from the digestive tract, and get the dog to a veterinarian as soon as possible.

Household chemicals such as lye and bleach may get on the dog's skin if he is not kept out of the way while you are cleaning. Concentrated solutions of any of these products may be quite caustic if they get on the dog's skin. Flush with plenty of lukewarm water. Then wash the dog thoroughly with soap and water, rinsing well. If the dog has drunk one of these products, you can give olive oil or egg white, but DO NOT try to make the dog vomit. Get him to a veterinarian as soon as possible.

Acids may be spilled on the dog's skin. Battery acid, swimming pool chemicals and certain cleaning agents are all strong acids. The dog will be in severe pain when suffering from an acid burn. Flush the area with large quantities of cool water. Apply a paste made of baking soda (sodium bicarbonate). If the dog has drunk the acid, treat as described above for household chemicals.

Ivermectin is a safe antiparasitic drug when used according to label directions. One of the most common products is Heartgard-30® (Merck), which is used to control heartworms. Toxicity may occur when a product formulated for cattle or horses is used in dogs. Imagine, for instance, the difficulty in accurately dosing a 40-lb. dog with a paste wormer made and measured for a 1,200-lb. horse! It is all too easy to accidentally overdose the dog. Collies are especially susceptible to ivermectin toxicity, and are easily poisoned by overdoses which would be tolerated by other breeds of dogs.

Signs of ivermectin toxicity include salivation and vomiting. The dog may stagger, tremble and become disoriented. This may progress to weakness, with the dog unable to stand, followed by stupor and coma. Get the dog to your veterinarian as soon as possible. Treatment of ivermectin toxicity may be successful, but may take one to two weeks of intensive, expensive treatment for the dog to fully recover. The message? If you are worming a dog, use a dog wormer.

Metaldehyde is the toxic component of baits used for snails and slugs. These baits are often placed where dogs can get them, and are palatable enough that some dogs will eat them. A dog who has eaten snail bait may vomit, salivate and become uncoordinated. Increased heart and respiratory rates, muscular twitching and convulsions are common. Some dogs appear to be blind. About half the dogs who eat snail bait die. Give olive oil and/or activated charcoal and get the dog to a veterinarian as soon as possible. The best prevention is to keep the dog away from areas where snail bait is being used. It is also a good safety measure to use a meal formulation rather than pellets. Pelleted snail baits are more easily picked up by the dog.

Warfarin and **coumarin** are toxic components of some common rodent poisons. The dog may be poisoned by eating the bait, or by eating carcasses of rodents poisoned by these compounds. These poisons work by inhibiting one of the K vitamins necessary for the blood to clot normally. This results in spontaneous bleeding. The dog may have hemorrhages of various sizes visible in the membranes of his mouth or eyes. Large hematomas can form under the skin if he bumps himself or is otherwise injured. His blood may not clot if he is bitten or cut. In some dogs, a poor appetite, droopiness or difficulty in breathing might be the only signs noticed.

Anticoagulant toxicity from older formulations of these compounds is most often seen with exposure to small amounts of these compounds over a period of three to 10 days. One large dose may not be a problem. A dog may eat a whole box of this type of poison ONCE and survive, but a teaspoon every day for a week could easily kill him. Take the dog to your veterinarian. He will give Vitamin K, and chances are the dog will be fine.

Newer anticoagulant products, such as brodifacoum and diphacinone, cause similar symptoms. However, just one dose may be sufficient to cause symptoms in dogs. Prolonged Vitamin K therapy is necessary if a large amount of either of the newer products has been eaten.

Vitamin D3 (cholecalciferol) is the active ingredient in some of the newer rodenticides. It is NOT safe when eaten by dogs in anything but the smallest amounts. Signs of toxicity include vomiting (which may include blood) and a severe bloody diarrhea. The dog's body temperature may drop as low as 96 degrees F (35.6 degrees C). Coma and death soon follow. Signs may appear one to two days after the dog has eaten the material, and become progressively worse.

Induce vomiting with syrup of ipecac as soon as possible after you know that the dog has eaten a vitamin D3 rodenticide. Get the dog to a veterinarian. If you wait one or two days until signs appear, it may be too late to save the dog— irreversible damage likely has taken place. In some cases, large amounts of intravenous fluids, as well as other drugs, may be needed to try to keep the animal alive. As with most poisonings, it's a lot easier to prevent than to cure (Gunther, 1988).

Thallium is another substance used for rodent and predator control. A dog with acute thallium poisoning shows a lack of appetite, vomiting (sometimes with blood) and possibly bloody diarrhea. Chronic poisoning will result in hair loss, and thickening and ulceration of the skin. Laboratory tests will confirm the presence of this toxin. Early diagnosis and treatment often have good results.

Sodium fluoroacetate (1080) has been used to control both rodents and predators. An extremely potent and long-lasting toxin, its use has been strictly limited in the past few years, but stocks still exist and may sometimes be misused, either accidentally or deliberately. Dogs may be poisoned by either eating material containing the compound, or by eating animals that have been killed by it. Within one-half to two hours after eating it, the dog will become restless and irritable. He may then wander aimlessly, barking, urinating and defecating, while running around. Violent convulsions often occur. The dog may appear to get better, and then go back into seizures. Dogs poisoned by 1080 usually die within 2 to 12 hours after signs begin. There is no known treatment for this toxicity, and most affected dogs will die. If you suspect this poisoning, get the dog to a veterinarian as soon as possible. Intensive supportive therapy might make a difference.

Strychnine poisoning. Strychnine is used as a rodent, predator and skunk poison, as well as being given maliciously on occasion. Dogs can also be affected when they eat poisoned rodents or birds.

A dog who is poisoned by strychnine will become nervous and excited, and may salivate. As the poisoning progresses, the dog will go into convulsions, becoming stiff like a sawhorse. His head will be pulled toward his back as his neck muscles contract. His front legs will be pulled forward, and the back legs will be pulled backward, like a sawhorse. The dog will gasp and choke as the muscles of the larynx constrict. He may turn blue as the larynx closes, shutting off his breathing. He will froth slightly at the mouth as he gasps for air, and his lips will be pulled back, exposing his teeth. Spasmic convulsions will rack his body, coming in waves. Any stimulation such as a loud noise will start a new wave of convulsions.

There is NO effective home treatment for strychnine poisoning. If untreated, the convulsions become more severe, and the dog dies of asphyxiation—a very unpleasant death. Give activated charcoal, but only if you can do so VERY quickly, before signs appear. Do not attempt to give it if the dog cannot swallow or is already into convulsions. Get the dog to a veterinarian as soon as possible. Take him to the nearest one, even if he's not your regular veterinarian. He will anesthetize the dog to stop the convulsions, and treat the dog to remove the toxic material from the stomach and digestive tract. If the dog survives the first 24 hours, his chances of making it are good. The dog may have to remain under anesthesia for many hours while his body slowly removes the strychnine.

Sticky traps are used to catch both insects and rodents. A dog may stumble into one and become stuck to it. Use butter (margarine does not work as well) or a mechanic's hand-cleaning product to dissolve the adhesive material. Then wash the dog in liquid dish detergent. Rinse very well. These things are more messy than toxic, but it is best not to have the material on the dog.

Antifreeze (ethylene glycol) is quite attractive to pets, both dogs and cats, because of its sweet taste. Antifreeze poisoning occurs commonly in the winter, spring and fall, when people are draining radiators. Ethylene glycol poisoning can also occur when dogs drink color film-processing chemicals. High blood levels occur within one to three hours after the dog has drunk the liquid. A high percentage of dogs die if not treated soon after drinking ethylene glycol.

Signs of antifreeze poisoning include vomiting, abdominal pain, diarrhea, depression, incoordination and staggering. The dog may have difficulty breathing, rapid heart rate, lowered body temperature, muscle twitching, convulsions, blood in the urine and kidney failure. Eventually, the dog becomes very drowsy, enters a coma and dies. Get the dog to a veterinarian as soon as possible. He may have to treat the dog intravenously for two to three days, and with luck may be able to save him. The sooner treatment begins, the better are the chances of survival. Don't wait to see if the dog develops symptoms if you know that he has drunk antifreeze. By that time it is almost always too late.

Ethanol (ethyl alcohol or **drinking alcohol).** Dogs may become intoxicated on alcoholic beverages, much as do humans, and the signs are similar. Depression and stupor are the most common signs. Staggering and incoordination may be seen. The dog might retch or vomit, and have trouble breathing. Alcohol intoxication may be fatal in a puppy or small dog. The central nervous systems of puppies may be more susceptible to alcohol. Or maybe a puppy's liver is less able to metabolize it than is that of an adult dog. Whatever the reason, pupppies are very susceptible to the effects of alcohol. If you are starting treatment within two hours of the time the dog has drunk the alcohol and the dog is not severely depressed or comatose, induce vomiting. Give activated charcoal. Get the dog to a veterinarian as soon as possible for treatment.

Dishwashing detergent is useful for removing some tars and toxins from a dog's coat. However, it should not be used on very young puppies, puppies of small breeds, or very small, thin-skinned dogs. Some of these products contain enough ethyl alcohol to be absorbed and cause toxicity. The dog should be rinsed thoroughly.

Fertilizers may be eaten by dogs. Some of these may contain herbicides or other chemicals which make them more toxic. Give milk, cream or water to dilute the fertilizer. Get the dog to your veterinarian for treatment. Be sure to take an empty bag or label so that specific treatment can be given.

Carbon monoxide is a colorless, odorless, non-irritating gas. It is generated by furnaces, stoves and vehicle exhaust, especially if operated in a confined area without adequate ventilation. Carbon monoxide poisoning can occur when a dog is carried in the trunk of an automobile. The dog may be depressed, have an elevated temperature, and his muscles may twitch. His mucous membranes can be either muddy color or cherry-red. Give artificial respiration if necessary, and administer oxygen if safely available. It may be necessary to hospitalize the dog for a couple of days of treatment.

Chocolate can be toxic to dogs in excessive quantities. It contains theobromine, a stimulant similar to caffeine. Theobromine can cause an irregular heartbeat. Some of the most prominent signs are related to central nervous system stimulation. The dog may be restless, excited and nervous. He may have panting, vomiting, diarrhea, depression and frequent urination. The mucous membranes might be bluish. As the poisoning progresses, muscular tremors, seizures, coma and even sudden death may be seen. Most fatalities occur 6-24 hours after the chocolate is eaten (Hornfeldt, 1987).

Signs of chocolate poisoning begin four or five hours after the chocolate is eaten. It has been determined that a four-ounce chocolate bar may be lethal to a five-pound dog, and 16 ounces could kill a 20-lb. dog. Some dogs may also have trouble digesting the milk sugar in the chocolate, resulting in a case of diarrhea. Don't let your dog overdose on chocolate chips! Caffeine can cause similar signs with an overdose.

There is no specific treatment for chocolate poisoning. If you know that the dog has eaten the chocolate, it is helpful to get him to vomit, even if it is several hours later. Do not induce vomiting if convulsions are occurring. Give activated charcoal if you have it available. Get the dog to your veterinarian.

Pennies minted after 1982 may cause toxicity if swallowed by your dog. They are made of 96% zinc, and eating just one of them could be fatal. Nuts and bolts may also contain large enough quantities of zinc to poison a dog. These objects usually don't pass through the digestive tract. Instead, they just sit in the stomach and are dissolved by the stomach acid. The zinc compound from reaction with the acid destroys red cells in the dog's blood.

Symptoms of "penny poisoning" include jaundice (yellow coloration of the mucus membranes and conjunctivae—also called icterus), vomiting and difficulty breathing. If your dog has these symptoms, or you have seen him swallowing pennies, have him examined by your veterinarian immediately. He may wish to X-ray the dog to determine whether pennies are present. Surgery may be necessary to remove the coins, but recovery should be complete. Keep all pennies out of the reach of dogs to avoid zinc toxicity, as well as foreign-body reactions in your dog's stomach (Knapp, 1989).

Lead poisoning can occur in dogs who chew on surfaces painted with lead-containing paints. About half the dogs suffering from lead poisoning get it from eating paint. Putty, linoleum, fishing weights, shotgun pellets, grease, batteries, drapery weights and solder can also cause lead poisoning if the dog eats them. Signs may occur three days to two weeks after the dog eats the substance containing lead. The dog may show signs of abdominal pain, and will often cry when his abdomen is handled. He may have vomiting, diarrhea and lack of appetite. If the nervous system is affected, he will show hysteria, nervousness and barking The dog may stagger, tremble and have convulsions. Blindness and deafness can occur.

Lead poisoning is most often seen in dogs who are less than one year of age, living in an inner-city area where buildings are old, or in a house that has been recently remodeled. Like some insecticides, lead-based paint is pretty much off the market, but some is still around. If you are remodeling, ask your contractor to avoid lead-based paint. Teething and curiosity may lead a puppy to chew items that an adult dog would not touch. Glazed ceramic food bowls, particularly from Mexico, may not have been fired well enough to bind the lead pigments in the glaze. The lead can slowly leach out into the food or water and be a source of chronic lead exposure.

Treatment for lead poisoning involves administration of chelating drugs to help remove the lead from the dog's system. This could take one to two weeks of hospitalization, and can be quite expensive. Surgery may be needed if the dog has eaten a large solid item like a wheel weight. If you have a dog affected by lead poisoning, and have young children, consult your physician about the possibility that they were exposed to the same materials. Many large cities have clinics which test children for lead poisoning free of charge.

Arsenic poisoning. Arsenic is found in some herbicides and insecticides. The dog may be poisoned by walking in a recently treated area and then licking his feet. It is also found in many ant poisons, such as Terro Ant Killer (Sanoret Chemical). Arsenic is a component of some rodent poisons, such as Vacor (Rohm & Haas). It may also be present in wind-borne smoke or dust from some smelters.

The most common sign of arsenic poisoning is vomiting. The vomited material will often have a garlic-like odor. The dog may be restless and weak. He may show considerable abdominal pain, along with diarrhea which will sometimes be bloody. The membranes can be bluish. In a severe case, shock, collapse, coma and death are likely to occur. Get the dog to a veterinarian as soon as possible. Several days of intensive treatment may be necessary before you know whether the dog is going to live or die.

Cocaine may poison a dog, whether it is given deliberately or he gets into it accidentally. Signs of cocaine toxicity are those of stimulation of the central nervous system. The dog may salivate profusely, twitch or shake, vomit, have an increased heart rate, and can go into convulsions. The effects of cocaine on the heart can be life threatening. In addition, a fatal respiratory depression is possible with a large enough dose. Get the dog to a veterinarian as soon as possible. And be sure to tell him what the dog has eaten. The signs of cocaine intoxication are not specific, and he might not otherwise figure it out in time to save the dog. There is no specific treatment for cocaine toxicity. All the veterinarian can do is treat the symptoms that are occurring at the time. If you cannot get the dog to a veterinarian, and it has not been more than a couple of hours since he has eaten the cocaine, induce vomiting to remove as much of the material from his stomach as possible. Give oxygen if it is safely available.

Marijuana cigarettes or marijuana-containing foods are rarely fatal to dogs, but will cause obvious signs of sickness. These may include depression, drowsiness, lowered body temperature, incoordination, salivation, vomiting and a slowed heart rate. The pupils of the eyes may be widely dilated. A mild case may be treated by keeping the dog warm and in a quiet, darkened area until he recovers. If the heart rate is severely slowed, veterinary treatment may be necessary.

Plant poisonings are sometimes seen in dogs. They are more common in winter when both the dog and the plants are kept indoors. Some decorative Christmas plants are very toxic. Puppies are especially susceptible to poisoning by plants as they chew on anything and everything around them. Older dogs, especially if they are the only pet, may become bored when left alone for long periods of time, and may chew on plants if they are available.

Some offending **house plants** are: Diffenbachia (dumb cane), ivies, azaleas, philodendron and schefflera. Plants such as poinsettias and mistletoe may cause irritation and blistering of the membranes of the mouth and stomach. The dog may show lack of appetite, vomiting and paralysis of the tongue. Mistletoe may cause a slowed pulse. Get the dog to your veterinarian so that he can monitor the dog's pulse and administer specific antidotes if necessary.

Diagnosis is often difficult if the dog was not observed eating the plant. If the dog has vomited, look for plant material in the vomitus. Look for chewed edges or missing leaves on your plants. The dog should be encouraged to vomit.

Most plant poisonings can be successfully treated by your veterinarian, as he will, in most cases, just treat whatever symptoms occur. The best prevention is to keep house plants where the dog cannot reach them, or in a room in which the dog is not allowed. It also helps to make sure the dog gets plenty of attention, exercise and a balanced diet.

A number of common **outdoor plants** are also toxic to dogs. Among these are croton, Lily of the Valley, oleander, privet, rhubarb, lupine, monkshood, autumn crocus, bleeding heart, castor bean, daffodil, hyacinth, black locust, marigold, nightshade, mountain laurel, bittersweet, morning glory and horse chestnut.

It might be a good idea to keep your puppy confined to a run or a pen until he becomes mature enough not to chew on all your plants. For a dog who only gets into one flower bed, it is often helpful to set out a number of mouse traps. Just "set and forget" them—unbaited, of course. They will discipline the dog for getting into the area, and, best of all, they even work when you are not around.

Outdoors, **yew trees** may cause signs of shaking, weakness and collapse, and trouble breathing if the dog eats their leaves. The heartbeat may become fast and irregular, and coma, convulsions and death can result if the dog is not treated. Try to get the dog to vomit, and get him to your veterinarian so that he can wash the dog's stomach out thoroughly, and administer drugs for the heart problem if needed.

Oleander and **Lily of the Valley** can cause poisoning with symptoms of dizziness, depression, and a rapid, weak heartbeat. If untreated, the dog may stop breathing, and his heart may stop. Treatment is to induce vomiting and seek veterinary help.

Nettle poisoning can occur in dogs. One report tells of hounds in Arkansas who became poisoned while hunting (Edwards, 1983). The dog may show nausea, retching, clawing at his face and nose, and vomiting, which can be severe. Muscle twitching, staggering, weakness, and partial paralysis of the rear legs can also occur. The dog may bleed from the nostrils and have trouble breathing. Dogs inhale chemical-filled hairs as they run through the nettle plants and get them in their eyes and on their tongues and skin. Nettle poisoning looks much like organophosphate poisoning, but without the extreme stimulation. Bathe the dog, wearing rubber gloves. Antihistamines are helpful. Other supportive treatment may be needed.

Dogs are susceptible to most of the same **mushrooms** that poison humans. *Amanita* is perhaps the most toxic genus. If you know (or suspect) your dog has eaten one or more poisonous mushrooms, encourage him to vomit. Take him to a veterinarian for further treatment if other signs appear.

Blooms of blue-green **algae** occur on ponds and lakes in the upper Midwest and southern Canada during dry, hot, summer weather. Pets become poisoned by the endotoxin that these algae produce when they drink water from the pond. Signs of algae poisoning include vomiting, muscular twitching and staggering, followed by paralysis and convulsions. Death may occur within an hour or two after the dog drinks the water. Encourage vomiting. Give activated charcoal if you have it and if there are no convulsions. Get the dog to a veterinarian as soon as possible.

Aflatoxin is the name given to a toxin produced by the growth of *Aspergillus flavus* or *Penicillium* molds on feed. They are often found on corn, peanuts or cottonseed that has molded, whether in the field or in storage. Acute toxicity requires continuous exposure for 20-30 days, at a minimum of one part per million in the diet (Morgan, 1985). Signs include weakness, lack of appetite and depression. The dog can have diarrhea, which may be bloody. His blood may clot poorly, and he might show jaundice due to liver damage. Collapse and death may occur within a week to 10 days after signs begin. The symptoms are treated as they occur. See your veterinarian if you think this toxicity is affecting your dog. To avoid aflatoxin poisoning, do not give feed, whether grain or dog food, which has molded. Aflatoxin can be produced even in foods which do not look moldy. If your dog seems to have become ill from food, your veterinarian may have it tested by a laboratory.

Poison ivy does not seem to bother dogs. The main problem is that the dog can carry the toxin to YOU on his hair, after he picked it up by running through or rolling in the plant. You may be affected if the dog rubs against your bare legs, or you may get it on your hands when you pet him. If you know that your dog has been in contact with poison ivy, put on rubber gloves and give him a good, thorough bath with dog shampoo and plenty of water.

Garbage poisoning may occur when a dog eat eats spoiled food, especially ham, chicken and milk products. Some staph bacteria on these foods produce an enterotoxin which causes nausea, abdominal pain, diarrhea and collapse, usually within four to five hours after the dog has eaten the material. The good news is that it is rarely fatal. The bad news is that other strains of staph bacteria may be present which produce a lethal toxin. This results in uncoordination, difficulty in breathing and violent convulsions. Signs can appear anywhere from five minutes to 24 hours after the material has been consumed. It may be fatal, regardless of treatment. Since you don't have any way of knowing what your dog is likely to encounter, don't let your dog roam to eat garbage, or get into your own trash can.

Botulism is uncommon in dogs, but may occasionally be seen. The dog will become paralyzed, followed by coma and death. If recognized early enough, an antitoxin may be given, and the dog might be saved. Dogs are somewhat resistant to botulism. All of these poisonings are best treated by your veterinarian. Prevention includes keeping the dog out of your garbage and the neighbor's garbage, and keeping other people from feeding him meat or bones which may be spoiled.

Dogs may ingest a number of **pills** and **drugs**, whether by accident or by being given them deliberately. The possibilities range from accidental dosages of prescription drugs, whether heart medications or antibiotics, to deliberate dosages of illegal drugs. A partial list would include tranquilizers, amphetamines, narcotics, cocaine, heroin, etc. An overdose with some of these drugs can be fatal, because most dogs are smaller than we are, easily resulting in an overdose situation. When the dog and his family move into a new house, and the dog finds medications which have rolled into a corner, or he finds pills which have been left after a party, he could get a critical overdose. If the dog gets into medication, take the pill bottle, or some of the medication or substance you have found, to your veterinarian immediately. Some drugs, such as antibiotics, will cause little or no harm, while a large dose of heart medication may severely upset a toy dog.

Treatment for an unknown drug poisoning is largely symptomatic. Observe the dog carefully, and consult your veterinarian if the signs are anything other than mild and transient. By the way, a dog can eat a month's supply of birth control pills without any harm.

Nonsteroidal anti-inflammatory drugs, such as ibuprofen (found in Motrin®, Advil®, Nuprin®, etc.) can cause poisoning in dogs, especially when eaten in large quantities. Naproxen (Naprosyn®) may cause similar signs. With any of these drugs, the dog may be staggering and incoordinated, and depressed or in a stupor. Vomiting can occur, as well as diarrhea (which may be bloody or blackish). Bleeding into the stomach will sometimes occur, and may be life-threatening. If the drug has been deliberately given for several days, the dog may have enough internal bleeding that he is also anemic and pale. Kidney failure can occur. The prognosis for survival is good if the kidney failure can be reversed. In some cases, it may not be possible to completely reverse it. If you are sure your dog has consumed one of these products, encourage vomiting. Give activated charcoal and get the dog to your veterinarian for further treatment.

TREATMENT OF POISONINGS IN GENERAL

If you know or suspect that your dog has ingested a toxic substance, what can you do? You can begin by calling your veterinarian and getting his recommendations. If he is close, take the dog to him as soon as possible. If you can't get him or another veterinarian and there is no emergency veterinary clinic close by, call the nearest poison control center and ask for their recommendations for the particular substance you think (or know) that your dog has ingested. This is important because vomiting should be induced with some substances, and is totally wrong for others.

In general, vomiting should be induced if the dog is seen eating or drinking most poisonous substances. If you know that he has swallowed petroleum products such as kerosene or gasoline, or a caustic (acid or alkaline) substance, or DO NOT induce vomiting. If the dog has drunk an acidic solution, DO NOT give him sodium bicarbonate (baking soda)! The gas-forming reaction can rupture his stomach. Give him milk or cream to dilute the substance, and get him to a veterinarian as soon as possible. Also, DO NOT try to get the dog to vomit if he is unconscious, has any signs of nervous system problems, or is showing tremors or convulsions.

You can get the dog to vomit by giving syrup of ipecac at one teaspoon per 5 lb body weight, to a maximum of three teaspoons (one to two ml/kg body weight to 15 ml maximum). Do not give more than one tablespoon (15 ml) to even the largest dog. The dose may be repeated in 20 minutes if the dog does not vomit with the first dose. Do not give more than two doses of it. Syrup of ipecac does not work on all dogs. It can usually be purchased at a drugstore. If you do not have syrup of ipecac, you can put a couple of teaspoons of salt on

the back of his tongue. A third method you can try is to give him a half-and-half mixture of 3% hydrogen peroxide and water. Pour it into his lip pouch. Table salt and hydrogen peroxide do not always work. Syrup of ipecac is better if you have it available. After he has vomited, offer milk or cream again and get him to the veterinarian as soon as possible.

Activated charcoal is one substance which can be safely administered after any toxin. It can be helpful with substances as diverse as organophosphate insecticides, accidental drug overdosages and herbicides. Activated charcoal is also helpful with garbage poisoning. It is safe, and can be kept on hand to use if needed. SuperChar®-Vet (Gulf-Bio-Systems, Inc., 5310 Harvest Hill Road, Dallas, Texas, 75230) is one brand which is available. It comes as a liquid which can be given in an emergency. It should be given to your pet in the bathtub or outdoors, as it can stain. Burned or charred toast is mentioned in some books as an emergency antidote. It does NOT work. Keeping a bottle of activated charcoal mixture on hand is cheap insurance.

TOAD POISONING

Toad poisoning occurs when dogs eat toads of the species *Bufo marinus*. It may be fatal. Because the poison is found in the skin and salivary glands of these toads, it can also occur if the dog only handles the toad in his mouth. Poisoning can occur with other toads of the genus *Bufo*, but is not usually fatal. These toads are found in the more tropical parts of Texas and Florida, as well as in Hawaii, and along the Colorado River in California and Arizona. Dogs often find the toads at night under yard or street lights. The toads' skin contains a drug which affects the heart much like digitalis. The dog will begin by salivating profusely. He may paw at his mouth, shake his head and make faces. His membranes may become blue (cyanotic) due to the ineffective heart action. He may have convulsions and collapse, and his heart may stop. If you have the toad, kill it and take it with you for possible identification. Take a moment to wash out the dog's mouth with water, as thoroughly as you can. Get the dog to a veterinary hospital as soon as possible for specific treatment. Handle the toad without getting any material from his skin on you. It is toxic to humans also.

SNAKEBITE

A dog may be bitten by a poisonous snake when he blunders into one of them, or if he deliberately attacks a snake. He may be merely curious and want to see what the snake is. When he reaches out his nose to check it, he gets too close and the snake strikes. Snake bites in North America which are poisonous to dogs are most often from pit vipers. These snakes include copperheads, the cottonmouth or water moccasin, and some 32 species of rattlesnakes. Pit vipers have a slit-shaped pupil of the eye, much like a cat, in contrast to the round pupil of the non-poisonous snakes. These snakes have two modified salivary glands which produce venom. The venom glands are attached to a sizeable pair of fangs, which serve to inject the venom during a bite.

Coral snakes are also poisonous, but for the most part they are small and limited to small geographic areas, which reduces animals' exposure to them. In northern parts of the country, snakebites are most common in summer (the snakes are hibernating during the colder months), but in the south and southwest, snakebites can occur any month of the year.

Several factors determine the severity of a poisonous snakebite. The weight, age and general health of the dog will determine its reaction to the venom. Some species of snakes are more poisonous than others. For instance, in the western United States, the bite of the Mojave rattlesnake is generally more severe than that of the Western Diamondback. Bites on the dog's head may be quickly fatal, while those on the extremities may give more time for treatment. A glancing bite which injects little or no venom may not be a problem, while a head-on bite which strikes deeply into the dog's tissues may be quickly fatal even if you get veterinary help soon. The smaller the dog, the more likely the bite is to be fatal, other factors being equal.

Snake venoms are composed of proteins which include enzymes that dissolve proteins in the victim, destroying capillaries and tissue at the area of the bite. They contain neurotoxins, which damage the nerves and may cause paralysis, including the respiratory system. Other components of venom cause hemolysis (dissolving) of the red blood cells, and damage to the heart and circulatory system. Coagulation times may be increased, with the blood not clotting normally. In addition, the large amount of dead tissue at the bite wound offers an ideal place for bacterial growth. Infection and gangrene may occur. And if the dog lives through the initial crisis, large areas of tissue may slough, leaving large, ugly ulcers that are slow to heal.

You may see the snake bite the dog, which makes the problem easy to diagnose. Otherwise, you must look for signs that a bite has occurred. Bites occur most frequently on the forelegs, shoulders, head and neck. If necessary, clip the hair away from the area. This may help to tell a snakebite from the bite of a wasp or spider. One or two fang wounds may be seen. The wounds appear as small punctures. If the snake has struck the dog more than once, several fang marks may be seen. The dog may show extreme pain at the site of the bite wound, swelling, and discoloration of the area. These symptoms are not seen with bites from nonpoisonous snakes. The dog may show excessive thirst and other signs of shock.

If the venom has gone directly into a blood vessel, the dog may immediately become unconscious, with or without convulsions. The size of the swelling and amount of signs depend on the amount and toxicity of the venom which was injected. The dog will probably have no appetite, and may be listless for several days after a snakebite. A large injection of venom is nearly always followed by a large tissue slough. In some cases, full-blown signs may not develop until several hours after the bite has occurred. If you KNOW that the dog has been bitten, it is usually worth having him hospitalized by your veterinarian for 24 hours' observation.

It's worthwhile to know the snakes in your area, and to be able to identify those that are venomous. This will keep you from treating a dog who has been bitten by a harmless bull snake, or from not treating a dog bitten by a rattlesnake. The treatment may cause damage, so it is important that it not be applied, except as a lifesaving measure. If possible, kill the snake for identification, but do not endanger yourself or get bitten doing it.

FIRST AID FOR SNAKEBITE

Immobilize the dog as much as possible until he can be treated, whether by you or by a veterinarian. Unnecessary physical activity will increase absorption of the venom. Do not use excessive heat or cold on the bite area. Do not give tranquilizers, as they may add to the effects of the snake venom to give an even more severe reaction. Painkillers should not be given, at least until the animal is examined by a veterinarian, as they may mask important signs.

IF AT ALL POSSIBLE, THE BEST FIRST AID AND TREATMENT FOR SNAKEBITE IS TO GET THE DOG TO A VETERINARIAN AS SOON AS POSSIBLE. He has the specialized drugs that may make the difference between life and death for the dog. He may have or be able to quickly obtain antivenin which can be given. The best first aid for snakebite, whether for your dog or yourself, is your car keys and a cool head!

THE FOLLOWING MEASURES ARE ONLY TO BE USED IF YOU ARE MORE THAN ONE TO TWO HOURS FROM A VETERINARIAN. YOU MAY CAUSE DAMAGE BY USING THEM. IF YOU CANNOT GET TO A VETERINARIAN, THEY ARE WORTH A TRY.

If you cannot get the dog to a veterinarian right away, begin by isolating the venom. If the bite is on a leg, put a flat tourniquet between the bite and the heart. It should be tight enough to slow the venous and lymphatic flow in the surface tissues. It should NOT be so tight that blood flow to the leg stops. You should be able to insert a finger under the tourniquet easily. When properly applied, it may be left in place up to two hours. It should NOT be loosened at intervals because this could allow the venom to be circulated from the bite area. If you can get to the veterinarian within a reasonable length of time (an hour or two), DO NOT use a tourniquet. In many cases, more damage has been done by a tourniquet than by the snakebite. If used incorrectly, it may result in gangrene and/or loss of the leg!

If you are not within one to two hours of a veterinarian, it is worthwhile to try to remove as much venom as possible. Make an incision in a straight line through both fang marks, extending to the gray-blue tissue (fascia) covering the muscle. Be careful not to cut through vital structures such as major blood vessels, tendons and nerves. Do not use X-shaped incisions, because the tips of these areas will die and are very prone to infection. Apply suction with a snakebite suction cup for at least 30 minutes to remove as much venom as possible. It is not a good idea to suck the venom with your mouth, because it may enter your body through any cuts or open areas in the mouth. If you are in ANY doubt about this step, don't. Get the dog to a clinic as soon as possible.

An antivenin is available for the toxins of North American pit vipers. One brand is Antivenin Polyvalent (Fort Dodge

Laboratories, Fort Dodge, Iowa, 50501). If you live in a snakebite area, and have dogs which you value for their economic or sentimental value, you may wish to keep some of this on hand. Its main drawback is that it is VERY expensive, and as much as 5 vials (50 ml) may be needed for a small dog (the smaller the dog, the larger the dose). Ideally, the product works best when injected intravenously. If you cannot do this, intramuscular injection is better than not giving it at all. Or if you are close to a veterinarian, take the antivenin to him and have him inject it. Additional doses may be needed every two hours if symptoms such as pain and swelling remain or recur. The earlier the antivenin is given, the more effective it is.

Your veterinarian may give the dog antihistamines to help delay or suppress any allergic reactions which might occur, either from the snakebite or from the antivenin. Antihistamines also help to calm the animal and reduce his activity. One drug which is commonly used is Benadryl® (Parke-Davis). A small dog may be given 12.5 mg once a day, while a dog over 50 lb (23 kg) may get up to 25 mg once a day. He may also give antibiotics to help prevent or reduce infection in the dead tissues. Intravenous fluids may be needed, as well as blood transfusions. The wound should be cleaned as well as possible. It may be useful to place a loose bandage over the wound to keep the dog from worrying it. The dog should be placed in a cage or small run to limit his activity, and in most cases will be hospitalized for AT LEAST 24 hours.

CORAL SNAKEBITE

Bites by coral snakes are uncommon because these snakes are shy and move around mostly at night. Also, most of them are fairly small so that it is not easy for them to get their mouths around a dog's limb. The fangs are in the rear of the mouth, so the snake must bite and hang on in order to inject venom into the wound. The bites tend to have very small punctures. There is generally little or no local reaction at the bite, which makes them even harder to find.

Clinical signs may not develop until 2 to 12 hours after the bite has occurred. However, when signs begin, they rapidly become serious. Treatment may not be successful if it is begun after signs occur—a real Catch-22, since you may not know the dog was bitten until signs begin. Death is primarily due to respiratory paralysis. If the breathing apparatus is not completely paralyzed, pneumonia can occur after the dog has recovered from the bite, and he may still die.

If you suspect that your dog has been bitten by a coral snake, he should be treated before any clinical signs occur. The product commonly used is Antivenin (*Micrurus fulvius*, equine origin,) (Wyeth). The dog should be immediately taken to a facility which has a respirator, as well as equipment for intensive care, in case his breathing stops. All dogs who are bitten by coral snakes should be hospitalized for 48 hours, and carefully monitored. It may take several weeks for the dog to recover completely.

The above mentioned antivenin does not neutralize the venom of the Sonoran coral snake (*Micruroides euryxan-*

thus). These snakes are found in southern Arizona and northern Mexico. Treatment is largely supportive. Again, respiratory support may be needed.

GILA MONSTER BITES

Gila Monsters (and the related Mexican beaded lizards) are the only lizards in the world which have developed a venom. They tend to bite and hang on, probably more out of fear of being dropped or flung away than out of viciousness. These lizards do not have fangs like the poisonous snakes. They have grooved teeth, from which secretions of their modified salivary glands are directed into the bite wound. In many cases, you may have to pry the gila monster off the dog. Use a couple of sticks to separate the jaws and watch that it doesn't bite you in the process. Gila monsters can swap ends with lightning rapidity.

If enough venom has seeped into the bite wound to cause problems, the dog will usually show severe pain at the bite site within just a few minutes. The dog may have a severe drop in blood pressure. In a small dog, this drop may be life-threatening. The dog may salivate, have tears running from his eyes, and urinate and defecate frequently.

Give a dosage of aspirin appropriate to the size of the dog to help reduce the pain. Get the dog to your veterinarian for treatment. The lowered blood pressure may make it necessary for him to give intravenous fluids to keep the dog alive. No antivenin is available. Antihistamines do not seem to help. If the dog survives the blood pressure drop, he will probably come through the crisis OK.

Please don't kill the gila monster. They are sluggish, basically non-aggressive, and only bite when prodded or annoyed. And there aren't many of them left. You are lucky to be able to see one!

INSECT STINGS

These include stings by bees, hornets, wasps and ants. Multiple stings are common because the insects are found in colonies with large numbers of individuals. A dog who has been stung once may be allergic to the venom on a later sting, resulting in a severe, life-threatening anaphylactic reaction. The dog may also have severe local swelling and pain with the stings. This usually becomes more tolerable within an hour or so after the stings have occurred. If the dog is stung severely around the neck or face, he may have enough swelling that he cannot breathe. This is, of course, a real emergency. Anaphylactic shock may occur. Get the dog to a veterinarian as soon as possible so that he may give appropriate treatment.

If the dog has only one or a few stings, and minimal reaction to them (other than pain and annoyance), you can give him Benadryl® (see snakebite, above, for dosage information). Observe him carefully for signs of breathing difficulty, severe swelling or shock. A paste made of a bit of meat tenderizer and water can be put on the stings and may help to remove some of the pain. Be careful not to get it into the dog's eyes. The dog's face may be swollen and comical for a day or two, but one or two stings are usually more annoying than life threatening (except in an allergic individual).

TICK PARALYSIS

Occasional ticks secrete a toxin which keeps the nerves from normally transmitting impulses. Tick paralysis occurs when one of these ticks attaches itself to the dog (or child, sheep or calf). The first sign is incoordination. An ascending paralysis occurs. First, the dog becomes incoordinated, and is then unable to move his hind legs. The paralysis moves upward, eventually involving the front legs. Within one to two days, the paralysis may involve the respiratory centers in the brain, resulting in death. The dog has a normal temperature, and looks normal other than being paralyzed.

Usually, only one tick is causing the problem. However, you have to remove ALL the ticks from the dog to get that one. You can pick the ticks off, being careful that you get them all. Check especially carefully around the neck and head. Look into the ears and remove any ticks that you find there. Or you can use in insecticidal spray or dip. This is a better idea than manual removal, since manually removing them invariably leaves some mouth parts imbedded in the skin, which often results in infection. Also, a dip will get all the ticks, including the one carrying the problem.

After the offending tick is removed, the dog will improve dramatically. He is often noticeably better within a couple of hours, and completely well within two days. Continued attention to tick control will prevent recurrence of the paralysis.

BURNS

Burns, in general, are most severe when they involve very young or very old dogs, and when they involve the head or joints and result in the formation of scar tissue.

A superficial burn only affects the outer layer of the skin. These are often called first degree burns. The skin may be reddened, and may later peel (much as a sunburn does on our skin). These burns may be hard to find if the dog's hair is not burned, or his skin is dark colored. First degree burns may be quite painful, but they need little care and heal rapidly.

Partial thickness (second degree) burns go completely through the outer layer of the skin into the middle layer. The site may be reddened and swollen, and may ooze a yellowish plasma. Blistering may be seen, especially if the burn is from flame or scalding liquid. The site is painful, but less so than with a superficial burn. These burns heal with little or no scarring IF they do not become infected. Healing usually takes about two weeks to a month.

Full thickness (third degree) burns go clear through the epidermis and dermis. These layers are coagulated and deadened. Portions of the skin may be charred. They may be severely swollen. Dry gangrene can occur, with the entire damaged skin layer peeling off, exposing underlying tissues. Because the nerve endings have all been burned, the area is insensitive. The hair is either gone, or pulls out easily. Infection and severe scarring are common. These are severe burns, and should be examined by a veterinarian.

Shock may occur if more than 15% of the skin surface is burned. If more than 50% of the body is involved, consideration should be given to euthanizing the dog promptly, without treatment, for humane reasons. You know how much a small burn from touching an oven or barbecue hurts. Imagine how extremely painful that would be over half the animal's body— and the nerve endings rejuvenate fairly quickly. Euthanasia is the kindest course of action.

FIRST AID: If burn has just occurred, apply ice compresses or cold water for 20 to 45 minutes. Treatment with cold water is useful within two hours following the burn. Cold water helps to reduce the extent of the burn, and decreases its depth by dissipating heat. It also relieves the pain. Be careful not to chill the dog excessively, thus making the shock worse, or to cause frostbite on the skin by leaving ice on it too long.

If the burn is more than just a tiny one, there is a good chance for infection. Cover the burn with a clean, dampened cloth or gauze. Do NOT use cotton, because the loose fibers get caught in the surface of the wound and are very difficult and painful to remove. Do not put ointments, grease or butter on the wound! They don't help, and they make treatment much more difficult. Get the dog to your veterinarian or emergency clinic as soon as possible.

Treatment for severe burns may necessitate intensive treatment by your veterinarian. Treatment may include administration of fluids to replace those lost through the damaged skin surface, and antibiotics to help prevent infection in the damaged skin. Corticosteroids may be given to help reduce inflammation and swelling, especially in the lungs. Lung damage occurs both from inhalation of hot gases, and from toxic products and particles in the smoke. Drugs may be given to reduce pain. Infection is the most common cause of death in dogs who survive the initial burn.

Hot water and other liquids can cause burns when they are accidentally dropped onto the dog, or he walks into them. With hot water burns, soak the dog in cold water or apply ice as described above—the quicker, the better.

Chemical burns may be caused accidentally or deliberately by battery acid and many other chemicals stored around the household. If the burn is caused by an acid, it should be neutralized by a mild alkali, such as baking soda, dissolved in a glass of water. If the burn is caused by an alkali, it can be flooded with vinegar or lemon juice. Anything but a small chemical burn should be examined by a veterinarian as soon as possible. If you do not have any of these neutralizing agents handy, or do not know the cause of the burn, rinse the dog in cool water for at least five minutes. Get him to a veterinarian as soon as possible.

Burns due to solvents and petroleum products should be handled with care. Avoid volatilizing the product if at all possible, because the fumes may cause pneumonia (in both you and the dog!). Wash the dog with a strong detergent, either Ivory® dishwashing liquid or a similar product. Be sure to rinse it all off.

Burns due to flames are most often seen with a house or apartment fire. They are also seen when a dog is deliberately doused with gasoline and set on fire. The odor of gasoline or other petroleum product on the dog is the first clue that such an act of extreme cruelty has occurred.

Burns caused by hot tars or grease are difficult to treat. Carefully remove as much as you can by blotting it off with paper towels or clean rags. Cut away the hair very gently, if necessary, to get the material away from the skin, so that you can see just HOW MUCH damage has been done. If you have an ointment containing polyoxyethylene sorbitan, coat the remaining hair and the skin with it. Neosporin® ointment, and some other antibiotic ointments, contain this solvent. If there is just a small spot of tar, you can rub the ointment in, put a bandage over it, and leave it for six to eight hours to soften the tar. If you do not have one of these drugs, rub salad oil, lard or shortening gently into the hair and skin. Then wash the dog as above. This treatment should be done at home only with small or minor burns. Major ones should be taken to a clinic where the dog can be sedated and supported with intravenous fluids as he is cleansed.

Burns from direct heat primarily occur in association with food and cooking. They may occur when a dog licks a hot barbecue grill. The dog may be burned as he hungrily gulps dry dog food to which excessively hot water has been added. In this case, his esophagus and stomach may suffer burn injury, in addition to the damage to the mouth and tongue. Scalding injuries can occur from hot grease or food which is spilled on the dog as he begs near the stove or lies in the middle of the kitchen floor. Just another reason to have a well-trained pet who will stay out from underfoot and not beg!

Friction burns may occur when a dog has a rope or cord dragged rapidly around a leg or over his skin. They also happen when a dog is tied and falls out of a vehicle or trailer and is dragged on the road. They frequently occur when a dog is hit by a car and skids along the pavement. Similar injuries may occur to the foot pads after vigorous exercise on a hard, rough surface such as asphalt pavement. Excessive shearing forces created by sudden stopping and turning may lead to separation and detchment of the entire pad surface. In some cases, it may be necessary to use skin grafts to replace the area damaged by friction burns.

Remove as many of the sticks and stones, and as much of the dirt as is possible. Wrap the injured, abraded area in a sheet or towel dampened with cold water. Take the dog to your veterinarian as soon as possible.

Begin by treating any burn OTHER than the tar or grease burns with cold water as described above. Remove hair from the area and clean it very gently. A small burn can be gently washed with povidone-iodine solution. Small burns may be treated by applying an ointment. You can use aloe vera cream, gentamycin cream, chlorhexidine (Nolvasan®) solution or silver sulfadiazine cream (Silvadene Creme). Povidone-iodine cream can also be used. Nitrofurazone cream is also a good product to apply to small burns. However, some bacteria are resistant to it. If you are using nitrofurazone and no improvement is seen, change to one of the other drugs. Petroleum-based (greasy) ointments should not be used on a fresh burn.

Small burns should not usually be bandaged. If the dog wants to lick the area, he should be restrained from doing so, either by an Elizabethan collar or a side stick, whichever is appropriate. It is very important to keep the burned area clean to avoid infection, so the dog should be kept from rolling in dirt or otherwise getting it dirty. If you are treating a burn and it shows pus, discoloration or signs of infection, have it checked by your veterinarian. Some dogs may need to be sedated for a few days, or given painkillers to reduce the pain. If a burn is this bad, you should see your veterinarian.

ELECTRICAL BURNS

Puppies, especially, may chew electrical wires. This may result in severe burns to the membranes of the mouth, in addition to possibly stopping his breathing and/or heart. If the puppy is still near the wire when you find him, either knock the wire out of the socket with a wooden stick or with the leg of a wooden chair. Then you can take care of the puppy. If it has just occurred, start CPR immediately. In some cases, you can restart a heart that has been stopped by the electrical shock and revive the dog. If the dog has a heartbeat, but is not breathing, begin artificial respiration. Take him to your veterinarian as soon as possible. The resulting burns in the mouth should also be checked by your veterinarian, as there is a good chance for infection.

SUNBURN

Sunburn is not common in dogs. It may occur when a dog is sheared extemely closely and then allowed out in hot, midday sun before a week to ten days have passed for hair regrowth. Dogs with white areas on the end of the nose may have severe problems with sunburn (see Collie Nose).

SMOKE INHALATION

A dog who has inhaled smoke may also have burns on his face, lips and mouth, as well as singed whiskers and hair. He may become unconscious. He may be hoarse, and may have cherry-red membranes in his mouth, either from extreme heat or from inhaling carbon monoxide.

For smoke inhalation, give oxygen if it is safely available. Continue administering it for 30 to 45 minutes . This will help to remove much of the carbon monoxide that the dog has inhaled. If you think your dog has taken in much smoke, take him to a veterinarian as soon as possible. If you're not sure and are willing to wait and see, observe the dog carefully for 24 hours. Lung edema may occur that long after smoke is inhaled, with the dog making gurgling noises as he breathes, and appearing depressed and weak. If this happens, get the dog to a veterinarian as soon as possible. Other signs of severe lung damage include aggressiveness or irritability, stumbling or incoordination, drowsiness, collapse and convulsions.

The lungs can be damaged enough that pneumonia follows. If this happens, the dog will show depression, fever, lack of appetite, and may have trouble breathing. This can occur as much as a week or so after exposure to smoke. Again, take the dog to your veterinarian, as he may need intensive treatment.

LIGHTNING STRIKE

Dogs are on rare occasion struck by lightning. The dog may be walking with the owner on a high ridge, or may be standing next to a fence which is hit by lightning. The dog who survives may be dazed and staggering or unable to stand. If the dog was wet, he may have burns on his body. The soles of the feet may be burned. First aid consists of letting the dog rest and treating the burns. It may be necessary to clip some of the hair off in order to determine the extent of skin burns. If the feet are burned, it will be necessary to bandage them for protection.

FROSTBITE AND HYPOTHERMIA

Hypothermia occurs when the core temperature of the body drops significantly below normal. It may occur accidentally from exposure to cold weather when the animal cannot get to shelter because he is unconscious, injured, caught in a trap, left outside by the owner or unaccustomed to a new, cold climate. It may occur when the animal has increased susceptibility to cold because he is elderly, ill or injured. It can also occur when the dog is accidentally or deliberately locked in a freezer, refrigerator or food locker. A wet dog exposed to cold (or wind) can easily become hypothermic. Think twice before you just toss your wet retriever into the back of the pickup and drive off down the road.

As hypothermia progresses, the body core temperature falls and metabolic processes slow. The skin and extremities are very susceptible to frostbite and freezing. Blood vessels in the skin contract in order to shunt blood to the internal organs. The heart rate and cardiac output decrease. The pulse becomes weak. Urine output from the kidneys falls. Breathing becomes shallow and slow, and the dog may shiver. The dog may become mentally slow, and the pupils may be dilated. Any frozen skin or limb becomes bluish or pale, and may have little or no feeling. Terminally, ventricular fibrillation occurs and the heart stops.

Mild hypothermia occurs at a body temperature of 86-90 degrees F (30-32 degrees C). This may be endured for 24-36 hours. Moderate hypothermia occurs at a body temperature of 72-77 degrees F (22-25 degrees C). A dog may survive between 4 and 24 hours with this temperature. Severe hypothermia occurs at a body temperature of 60 degrees F (15 degrees C). The maximum survival time at this body temperature is 5-6 hours. It may be as little as 1-2 hours if the dog is ill or diseased (Morgan,1985).

Treatment begins by returning the core temperature to normal. Shock must be treated, including giving oxygen. The frozen tissue must be thawed slowly enough that it does not suffer damage. Bring the dog indoors and wrap him in blankets. This is sufficient treatment for a mild case of hypothermia. More severely chilled dogs should be placed on hot water bottles (not TOO hot!), in a tub of warm (not HOT) water, or on an electric heating pad. When a dog with moderate to severe hypothermia is rewarmed, there is a chance of an "after-drop" in the core temperature. First the skin warms up, then the core begins to warm. Take his temperature every fifteen minutes for three to four hours, to make sure that it does not drop again.

Frostbite (cold injury) occurs when body tissue actually freezes. Frostbite can occur from exposure to cold or windy conditions, or contact with cold liquids, glass or metal. A sled dog who licks the axe which has been used to cut meat is the classical example of this problem. Flood the area with lukewarm water to release him. Freezing from contact with dry ice or liquid nitrogen can also cause frostbite.

Dogs are especially prone to freeze the footpads and scrotum, usually from long-term contact with deep snow or cold surfaces. The scrotum will show reddening and scaliness. Small areas may even slough. These can be treated with any mild healing ointment. Reduce or remove contact with the cold surface to allow it to fully heal. Long-eared dogs occasionally freeze the ends of the ears.

Deeper tissues may be frozen if an animal is injured and unable to return home, or is caught in a trap where he cannot move around to keep warm. The damage can be quite severe. However, prompt medical treatment may save large areas of tissue, and may make the difference between life and death for the dog. If your dog has deeply frozen tissue, DO NOT attempt to thaw it. Keep the frozen areas insulated so that they stay frozen. Protect the frozen tissue so it is not injured in transit. Get the dog to a veterinarian as soon as possible. Tissue damage is increased if the frozen tissue is thawed and refrozen again.

If you absolutely cannot get the dog to a veterinarian, do the best that you can, and realize that the dog may die no matter what you do. This treatment should NOT be attempted if there is any chance that you can get the dog to a hospital within 6 to 8 hours. Thaw the frozen tissue rapidly. Use warm, not hot, water—100 to 112 degrees F (37.7 to 44.4 degrees C). Do this only if you know that you can keep the tissues from refreezing again. Otherwise, leave them frozen until you are able to permanently thaw them. If some areas have been thawed previously, they should not be rapidly rewarmed.

The thawed part will become reddened and swollen. Blisters may occur on the skin. The dog will often attempt to scratch or chew them. It may be necessary to put an Elizabethan collar on him to keep him from doing so. Most veterinarians feel that it is better to leave the lesions open than to cover them with dressings, bandages or damp ointments.

Dogs with severe cases of frostbite should have systemic antibiotics to help prevent infection. It may take two to three weeks before it is clear which tissue is healthy and will live, and which is dead and will need to be removed or amputated. If at all possible, preserve the pads of feet which have been frostbitten. A dog who has suffered from frostbite should have a high-calorie, high-protein diet, in addition to a vitamin supplement. This is especially true if the dog has been suffering from malnutrition, or has been in a trap so that he has not had any food for a period of time.

Frostbite is rare in dogs that are healthy and well fed. It is of the utmost importance that dogs who are kept outdoors in cold climates have enough food to produce sufficient heat to keep their body temperatures normal. Extra fat can be added to the diet if needed to provide enough calories. Be careful to increase the amount of fat in the diet gradually to avoid causing diarrhea. That would both lose the benefit of the fat and lower the dog's resistance. Both frostbite and hypothermia are fairly uncommon in long-haired dogs because of their protective coats. Dogs in general instinctively seek shelter from extreme cold.

ALLERGIC REACTIONS

Allergic reactions may occur with insect bites, such as the stings of wasps and bees. Exposure to other allergens may occasionally produce itching eyes, with tears often running down the dog's face. He may be sneezing and have difficulty breathing. His face may be lumpy and swollen. In a severe case, the dog can collapse and become unconscious. With a severe reaction, get the dog to your veterinarian as soon as possible. With a mild reaction, you can either wait to see what happens—most of them will go away within two to 24 hours—you can give an antihistamine (such as Benadryl®) for a mild reaction. For dogs that weigh 25 lb., give 12.5 mg. once a day; dogs over 50 pounds should have 25 mg. once a day. Do not use these drugs on puppies or pregnant dogs without your veterinarian's approval.

CHOKING

Choking can result when the dog swallows a bone, toy or piece of food which is too large. This occasionally happens when two dogs are trying to eat together. One may wolf his food as fast as possible so that the other does not get it. If there are large pieces of meat or bone, a fragment may lodge in the back of the mouth. The dog will usually make retching motions and paw violently at the side of his face. The problem comes on suddenly, with no previous signs of abnormality. One person can often relieve a small dog which has choked. If the dog is a large one, do not attempt it by yourself. Get help. Push the lower jaw open and tilt the head back. USING EXTREME CAUTION, try to remove the object with your fingers. If this does not work, kneel behind the dog, and try a Heimlich maneuver as you would in a human. Wrap your arms around his body just behind the ribs. Squeeze hard a few times, pressing upward and inward. If the object does not come out, take the dog to your veterinarian as soon as possible.

Do NOT attempt to relieve "choking" in a dog which has been acting peculiarly. If you look into the dog's mouth and do not find a problem, and he still acts like he is choking, have him examined by a veterinarian. These, in rare cases, may be signs of rabies. Don't take a chance with your life and those of family members.

MISCELLANEOUS EMERGENCIES

Most eye injuries are emergencies. Check the chapter on Eyes for specific recommendatons.

Torsion of the stomach is a severe emergency. Take the dog to your veterinarian or emergency clinic immediately (see Torsion of the Stomach).

SKUNKED

If you live out in the country or on a farm or ranch, your dog may be curious enough that he will check out a skunk. The skunk normally wins and the dog comes home smelling terrible. Some dogs try it once and learn from the experience. Most, however, just keep on getting skunked, once or twice a year. Begin care by washing the dog's eyes thoroughly with lukewarm water. Then apply a mild antibiotic eye ointment or a couple of drops of olive oil. This will help to relieve any stinging in the eyes.

You can get some of the odor out of the dog's coat by giving him in a bath in tomato juice. Follow this by a bath in shampoo and water. You can also try a rinse of household ammonia, diluted 1:10 or 1:20 in water. Be sure not to get this solution in the dog's eyes. These methods may not get rid of all the smell, but they will make it more tolerable. You can try diluted lemon juice instead of the tomato juice. A product called Skunk-Off® will also help to get rid of the odor. You may be able to get it from your veterinarian or at the local pet shop or feed store. Believe it or not, the odor WILL wear off in time—if the dog does not contact another skunk!

FISH HOOKS

Dogs occasionally get caught by fish hooks. This is especially true if the dog tries to get a cheese ball off a hook, or is standing in the way of a child's wild cast. The dog will usually have the hook through his lip or in his tongue. Or, he may step on a hook and catch it in his paw. If you are close to town, take the dog to a veterinarian and let him clip it out. If not, you'll need to take care of it yourself. If it is only in a little way, you may be able to pull it out the way it went in (backwards). If it is deeper, you will need to grit your teeth and push the barbed point on through the skin or tongue. If it looks like it will go through one of the large blood vessels on the underside of the tongue, DON'T try to take it out yourself—get him to a veterinarian. Those vessels bleed profusely.

After you have pushed the barbed end through the cheek (or wherever), clip the eye end off with a pair of pliers. Now you can pull the hook on through, continuing in the direction it went in. Dab the area with an antiseptic if you have some handy. Keep an eye on it for the next week or so to be sure there is no infection at the site. If infection does occur, take him to your veterinarian for antibiotic treatment.

PORCUPINE QUILLS

Porcupine quills are a hazard for the farm or hunting dog, or for the city dog who is visiting in the country. The dog will come home with a face full of quills. He may also have them in his chest and front legs. Occasionally a dog will roll over with a porcupine and have them all over his body. If at all possible, take him to your veterinarian for care. The veterinarian will anesthetize the dog so that he will not feel pain while the quills are being removed. If the dog has quills inside his mouth, they may even be bad enough to pin his tongue to his lower jaw. These will have to be removed under anesthetic. Don't bother to remove the rest of them if the dog is going to have to be anesthetized anyway.

If the dog is just sitting around and not bumping into anything, the quills do not hurt. Trust me on that—I sat on one once, and it didn't hurt unless I slid in and out of my pickup truck. A serious case of quills may take a veterinarian AND his technician, both picking as fast as they can, more than half an hour to get them all. You can't do it nearly this fast with a dog that is awake, so why bother? It doesn't hurt to leave the quills in until the next day if you can't get to the veterinarian until then. Just don't tempt the dog by trying to feed him if he is unable to eat because of the quills.

So your dog only has a few quills, and none of them are near the eye, or inside the nose or mouth? You can take them out yourself if you have to. In this case, it will be easier if you take them out as soon as possible. If you have two people, one can hold the dog while the other pulls the quills. Be careful not to get bitten in the process. A muzzle is a good idea if it won't get in the way. You can pull the quills out with a pair or pliers or forceps. I have not found that cutting the tips off makes them any easier to pull out. Just go ahead and pull them out. It also seems to be easier to pull them straight out rather than twisting them. If the tip of a quill has gone completely through the cheek, you can either pull it through from the inside, or clip the tip off and pull the rest of the quill from the outside.

Quills SHOULD be removed. They have a backward-facing barb, and will continue to work forward until they are taken out. If not removed, they may evenutally work into the brain or other vital organ. Even if you or your veterinarian have done the best possible job of removal, quills or pieces of quill may work to the surface of the skin later. When they appear, your veterinarian can make a tiny incision and remove the piece of quill. You can feel these as small, hardened lumps under the skin or mucous membrane. Have them removed at your earliest opportunity. They are not an emergency, but should be removed within the next couple of days. If the bump containing the quill breaks, use a pair of small forceps or tweezers, and make sure the piece of quill has come out. Swab out the hole with povidone-iodine, just as you would an abscess.

BANDAGES AND SPLINTS

You can put a bandage on your dog to keep a wound from bleeding seriously until you can get him to a veterinarian. It is a good first aid practice. If you live in a remote area, this may be your only treatment. If at all possible, after you have given first aid, take the dog to your veterinarian for further care.

Bandages are often essential to help stop bleeding. They can also be used to keep a wound clean and free from dirt and other contamination. They can keep the dog from chewing and licking at the area. In some cases, they may support weakened tissues so that healing can occur more rapidly and efficiently. A bandage can help to control the edema and swelling that

Bandaging materials: spoon splint, roll gauze, elastic and regular tape, Vetrap® and cotton.

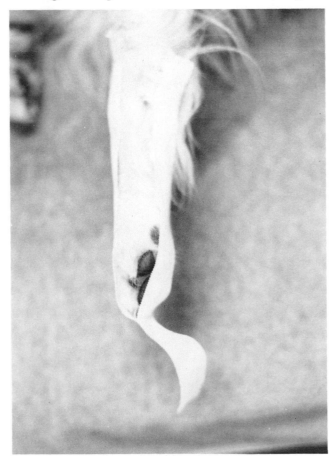

Tape on top and bottom of leg. Top piece is longer than lower one, so that some adhesive is left exposed.

occurs after the circulation to the leg is damaged by a wound. A splint can immobilize a fractured leg, allowing it to heal.

It is useful to keep simple bandaging materials on hand in case your dog is injured. And who knows, they might come in handy for you or someone in your family. Gauze sponges are useful; 2 x 2 and 3 x 3 inch (5 x 5 and 7.5 x 7.5 cm) are convenient sizes. Non-stick pads are handy for putting directly on open or bleeding wounds. Telfa Pads® (Curity/Colgate Palmolive) are one example of these. A plain, porous adhesive tape should be on hand—one-inch (2.5 cm) width is useful. Waterproof tapes should not usually be used, as the dog may sweat severely under them and become badly infected. It is also useful to have an elastic bandaging material. Elastikon® (Johnson & Johnson) tape is one example—two-inch width (5 cm) is handy. If you are using elastic tape, it is helpful to pull eight to 10 inches off the roll before you lay it onto the bandage, so that it is not put on under much pressure as you pull it from the roll. Otherwise, it is easy to get it too tight. Vetrap® (3-M), which is often used on horses, can also be used on dogs. Plain roll gauze is sometimes useful; two-inch width is convenient. Roll cotton is useful for some types of bandages. You can buy it at your drugstore. Cotton is available in one-pound (1/2 kg) rolls. Remember not to place cotton directly on an open wound or on a burn.

If your veterinarian has bandaged or splinted the leg, and the bandage comes off, take the dog back immediately. Don't wait until the next day, but get it checked promptly. A slipping bandage or a loose cast can cause severe damage in only a few hours.

BANDAGING A LEG

A bandage is used to stop bleeding and protect a wound on a leg. If you have to bandage a wound on a leg, go ahead and wrap all the way down to the end, including the foot. This will keep the dog's foot from swelling below the bandage. Some blood may soak through the bandage. Do not worry about that, as long as it is not actively dripping through. However, if it is dripping, wrap several more layers of gauze or tape over it, tightening it very slightly.

If you are not going to have a cut sutured, you can wash it with povidone-iodine solution before bandaging it. Moisten the hair around the edges of the wound with the solution. Lay a gauze sponge in the cut to keep hair out as you clip it. Clip the hair back from around the edges, about a half-inch on all sides. Now remove the hair-covered sponge and pick out any hairs which may have fallen into the wound. Pat the wound out gently with a sponge moistened in the povidone-iodine solution. When you have the wound clean, pack it with nitrofurazone ointment. (This treatment is not necessary if you are taking the dog to your veterinarian to be sutured.)

Put a non-stick gauze pad over the wound itself, to keep it clean and to avoid damage to its surface. Wrap the entire leg with roll gauze. Begin two to three inches above the injured

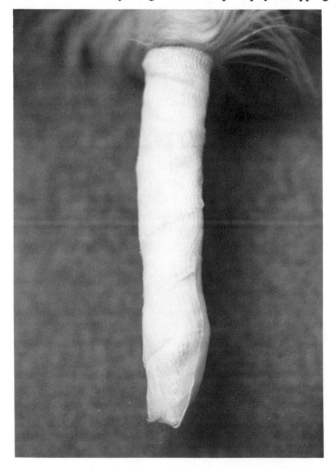

Wrap over leg with gauze, at least two layers. Now, stick tape to the gauze on the back of the leg.

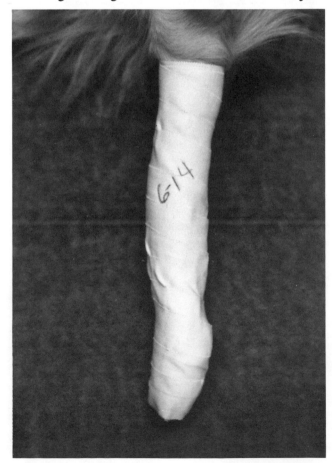

Put tape overall. Date it so you know when it was applied.

area and wrap completely down around the toes, pulling the gauze snug but not tight. When you get to the bottom (just beyond the toes), give the roll a half twist. The twist will help to get you turned around and headed back up the leg. Now wrap back up the leg to where you started. Using a roll of one-inch adhesive tape, begin wrapping tape about two inches ABOVE where the gauze ends. Starting above the gauze will help to keep the bandage from falling off. Don't be afraid to wrap tape onto hair. It helps to keep the bandage in place, and avoids many problems. Wrap tape down over the gauze to the bottom of the foot. Tear the tape off the roll and pat the end down flat. Whether you are wrapping with gauze or tape, be sure to wrap in a spiral pattern rather than in circular rings. Otherwise, the rings may act as tourniquets and cut off circulation in the leg. Overlap each layer between one-third to one-half on the previous one.

Tear a half-dozen strips of tape six to 10 inches long, depending on the dog's size. Place the middle of each strip over the bottom of the toes, and smooth the ends upward on each side of the leg. Do one from front to back, one from side to side, and the others at angles between. This will give a "bumper" or a "boot," which will protect the toes and help to keep the bandage from wearing through.

Finally, begin taping again from the bottom just above the toe area, and wrap 'round and 'round as you did before, going up the leg. Stop where you first started the first wraps of tape above the gauze, and your bandage is complete.

Most bandages should be changed every three to five days. Change it sooner if the dog gets it wet or soiled, or if he licks or chews enough to get it wet. A small amount of licking and chewing is to be expected. However, if the dog simply won't leave it alone, remove it and check for a problem. When you change the bandage, cut down the side opposite the injury. Split the bandage apart midway down the leg, where the tape runs over the gauze and it is easy to start separating it. Then, you can pull each half away from the other until you can pull the bandage free. It may be helpful to cut the hair loose at the top. But cut the hair from the tape rather than from the leg. Otherwise you will soon have a leg with no hair. You need the hair to protect the skin of the leg, and to keep the bandage from falling off.

SPLINTING A FOOT

The dog who has broken a toe or a bone in the lower foot can be immobilized by a spoon splint, or lightweight wood or plastic shaped to the same shape. This type of splint is useful for emergency protection, and can be used when you are in the back country until you get to a veterinarian. Do not use it if you can get the dog to a veterinarian within six to eight hours.

The best splint for a foot injury is a metasplint or spoon splint, called that because it is shaped like a spoon. It allows room for the dog's pads, and avoids the pressure that may

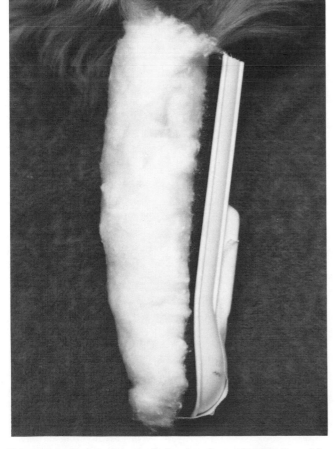

Put tape on foot as for simple leg bandage. Pad the leg with cotton. Place in splint.

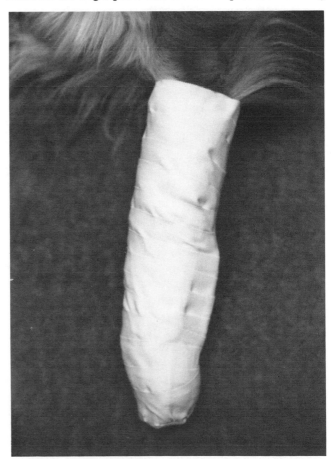

Tape over splint and leg together.

occur with a flat piece of wood or plastic. Pad the splint carefully with cotton batting, torn so that it is one continuous, flat sheet. The batting can extend a half-inch or so beyond the edges of the splint, so that the sharp edges do not gouge the dog's leg.

Put a cotton ball or small puff of cotton between each pair of toes, to keep them apart and to keep moisture from causing sores between them. Don't forget the dewclaw. Put a piece of tape down the bottom side of the dog's leg, sticking it well to the hair. This piece of tape should extend about four inches beyond the dog's toes. Do the same with a piece on top of the dog's leg. The top piece should extend about a foot beyond the dog's toes. Stick the end of the bottom piece to the top piece. Putting the two pieces together like this will leave a sticky area on the top piece hanging free. This sticky area is of the utmost importance in keeping the splint from sliding off the dog's leg. Now dust the dog's hair, as high as you are going to put the bandage, with boric acid powder or talcum powder. Fluff it well into the hair, especially between the toes.

Wrap the dog's leg with gauze, applied gently. (DO NOT pull it too tightly!) Two or three layers of gauze are about right. Put one or two thin layers of cotton around the dog's leg. Lay the dog's foot in the splint. Next, pull the tape down and stick the sticky area to the bottom (back) of the splint. Tape over the entire splint, foot and leg, exactly as described above for bandaging the foot. Use porous adhesive tape rather than the waterproof kind. Write the date you applied it on the bandage.

For a broken toe, about three weeks in the splint are sufficient. For other broken bones in the foot, four to five weeks may be better. In general, younger animals need to be splinted for less time than do mature ones.

Any splint or bandage must be kept clean and dry. Keep the dog indoors. If you have to put him outside in the morning while there is still dew on the grass, put a plastic bag over the splint. Secure the bag with tape or a rubber band. Let the dog out just long enough to urinate and defecate, bring him back inside and remove the bag. Also use a bag if it is raining, or if there is snow outside. Do not bathe the dog until he is completely healed. If the dog goes swimming or otherwise gets wet, the bandage must be changed as soon as possible to avoid infection developing underneath it.

If the dog chews on the bandage, you can get a bitter apple spray. This stops some dogs but not all of them. Other dogs respond well to a very light coating of petroleum jelly, liberally sprinkled with cayenne pepper. Variton Creme® (Schering) is also useful to keep a dog from chewing a bandage. Just put a very light coating of it on the areas that the dog can reach. A product called Ro-Pel is available (Burlington Bio-Medical, Farmingdale, N.Y.). It is extremely bitter, and is useful to keep a dog from chewing his bandage.

However, chewing may be a sign that the bandage is too tight, or that there is infection underneath. If it has been several days since you have changed the bandage, it may be worth changing it and looking for the problem. If you didn't find any problem, and the new bandage is O.K., then put on the bad-tasting stuff.

SPLINTING THE FRONT LEG

For a front leg, a straight piece of wood, split lengthwise to make a splint, will work well. Make it slightly narrower than the width of the leg. You can put it either on the inside or the outside of the leg. If there is a cut or wound, put the splint on the opposite side. Pad the splint well with cotton or even rags, leaves or the soft inner bark of a tree if you have nothing else. Be sure to MUZZLE the dog first.

Pull the leg gently to the point where it is nearly straight. Wrap the leg well with cotton batting. If you do not have that, use cloth or blanket material, making it about 1/2 inch thick. This wrapping should be barely snug, NOT tight, and as smoothly wrapped as possible. Lay the leg on the splint, and wrap snugly over both splint and wrapped leg, using gauze if you have it. Wrap a layer or two of adhesive tape over this. If at all possible, use a porous tape, or a product such as Vetrap®. If worst comes to worst, you can use duct tape or any other tape that you have handy. Now that you have the leg immobilized, you can take the dog out on a stretcher or on horseback without further damage.

SPLINTING THE HIND LEG

To make a splint for the hind leg, you can use 1/4-inch plywood. Lay the dog on his side, with the good leg DOWN. Put the plywood on the floor under the leg, and trace around it (it hurts less, and you can move it where you want). Cut about 1/2 inch (12 mm) inside the lines you have drawn, all the way around. You want the splint to be smaller than the leg so that the leg will not slide around on it. It should, however, be about 1/2 inch longer than the leg so that the toes do not touch the ground. Pad the splint with cotton. Wrap the leg in thin sheets of roll cotton (about half the thickness of the sheet—it usually splits easily), 'round and 'round until you have a padding about a half inch thick. Put the leg in the best position you can. Put the splint on the outside of the leg. Tape it snugly to the splint with porous adhesive tape, as described above. The leg will shrink with lack of use, and the splint may become loosened. It may be necessary to replace it. If you have had the splint on for three weeks or so, it is a good idea to unwrap the leg and apply fresh bandage material.

For a hind leg, use a limb or branch that is as nearly hind-leg shaped as possible. As a rule of thumb for any broken bone, you want to immobilize AT LEAST the joint ABOVE and the joint BELOW the break.

ROBERT JONES BANDAGE

The Robert Jones bandage is a thick, bulky bandage made with roll cotton. It can be used to stabilize fractures or dislocations which occur at or below the stifle and elbow joints. It puts enough pressure on the area to help prevent soft-tissue swelling, helping to control pain. It is also useful as first aid for fractures. And it may be handier than a solid splint if you do not have any wood or plastic material handy. Since it is bulky and porous, it can absorb considerable quantities of moisture if the dog gets into dew or water. It will take between 1/2 and 2 lb (1/2-1 kg) of roll cotton to make the bandage. Unroll a 1-lb roll of cotton. As you reroll, tear it up the middle, leaving right and left halves. The 6-inch-wide cotton strips are much easier to handle than the 12-inch roll.

If there is a cut or wound, it should be cleansed with povidone-iodine, and covered with nitrofurazone ointment and a non-absorbent dressing. Put tape on the top and bottom of the leg (see Splinting the Foot). Lightly bandage over the wound with gauze and tape. Make sure the bandaging is not too tightly applied.

Begin wrapping with one of the cotton strips at the foot and wrap upward. Leave the dog's two longest toes exposed. If the nails are not colored, and you notice that they are turning purple, the bandage is too tight. If the toes are cold, or if the dog chews his toes, the bandage may be too tight or there may be an infection underneath. Wrap the cotton up the leg, pulling it evenly snug. Wrap it as far upward as you can, either into the armpit or the groin. Wrap a layer of gauze over this, again working from toes to top. Pull the gauze snug. For this type of bandage, gauze four to six inches wide (10-15 cm) works better than narrower sizes. Stop the gauze about one inch (2.5 cm) short of the top of the cotton. This will leave a comfortable cushion of cotton at the top. It will keep the gauze from sliding over the top of the bandage and cutting into the dog's skin. Now you can stick the first two pieces of tape that you applied to the back side of the gauze. This will help keep the bandage from sliding. Put a layer of tape over the entire bandage, again wrapping from bottom to top. You can use

either porous adhesive tape, or an elastic product such as Vetrap® (3-M) or Elastikon® (Johnson & Johnson).

The bandage is easily removed by slitting the outer tape with a sharp blade. You can then pull the layers of cotton apart, or unroll them. If you are putting on a fresh bandage, leave the first two pieces of tape in place. Just cut it off at the toes, and put new pieces of tape over the top of it to make new stirrups to hold the new bandage in place. This will avoid the irritation of removing the tape and then having to put new tape on the irritated skin.

Any bandage may rub at the groin or armpit area. It may be necesary to cut a notch in the bandage material to leave room for the dog to move his leg. It also may be useful to dust the dog's skin at the top of the bandage (in the armpit or groin) once or twice a day with baking soda, talcum powder, or medicated powder.

In an emergency, a Robert-Jones bandage can be made from layers of blanket, towel or sleeping-bag material. Several layers of material can be laid all over the leg until it reaches about 2 inches (5 cm) thick. Then, it can be wrapped overall with gauze and whatever kind of tape you have handy. Pull the tape fairly snug. This type of bandage will give the dog nearly as much protection as would a solid splint.

BANDAGING THE HEAD AND NECK

It may be necessary to bandage the dog's head if he has a hematoma on one or both ears. It is important not to make a

Robert Jones bandage (soft cast or splint).

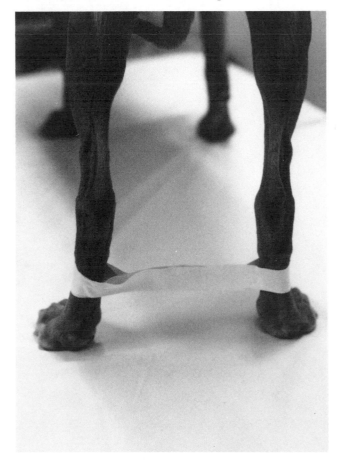

Hobbles can be used on hind or front legs.

head bandage too tight. The lower half of the bandage forms a collar as it encircles the throat. You should be able to slip two fingers under each side of it. If you get the bandage too tight, the dog can have trouble breathing or swallowing. You can slit whichever edge of the collar is tight. Just cut one or more slits until you have relieved the discomfort. Then you can lay tape over the cut area to reinforce it. This procedure will keep you from having to redo the entire bandage.

If a head bandage slips, it will usually slide to the rear. If this happens, the dog may have trouble breathing. Remove the bandage immediately to relieve his discomfort and try again. The dog may scratch at the bandage with his hind legs, trying to remove it. If this happens, it may be necesary to put hobbles on him. You can hobble either the hind legs or the front ones, whichever the dog is using to worry at the bandage.

HOBBLES

Hobbles can be easily made for either the front or hind legs—whichever are trying to remove the bandage. Use one-inch-wide porous tape. Tape around one rear leg, sticking the tape to itself. Leave about six inches of slack—the normal width between the dog's legs. Tape around the other rear leg, returning to stick to the tape that is already between the dog's

rear legs. Go from one rear leg to the other three or four times. This will keep the dog from scratching or pawing.

BANDAGING THE CHEST

It may be necessary to bandage the chest if the dog has a penetrating wound, or has damage to the skin in the chest area. The main thing is to avoid getting the bandage too tight. Otherwise, the dog may not be able to breathe adequately. As with a head or neck bandage, you should easily be able to slip two fingers under either edge of it. If you are using elastic tape, be sure to pull it off the roll and lay it on WITHOUT tension. If the dog has trouble breathing, take the bandage off immediately. Chest bandages slip quite easily. To anchor it, the bandage should be stuck to the hair for 1-1 1/2 inches (5-8 cm) at both the front and rear. Again, hobbles may be needed to keep the dog from scratching at it.

BANDAGING THE ABDOMEN

Bandages on the abdomen should be secured to the hair much the same as those on the chest. The abdomen should not be bandaged too tightly, although it may have a slightly more snug bandage than the chest. If put on a male, the bandage should not go over his prepuce, or he may not be able to

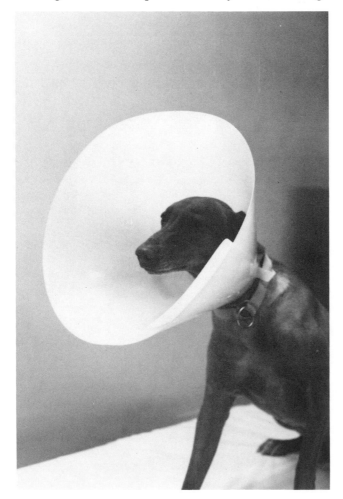

Elizabethan collar.

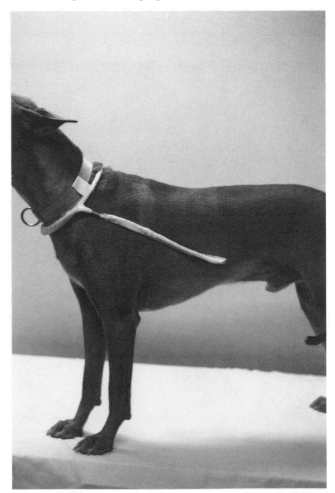

Side stick. This one should be about four inches longer—to the hollow of the dog's flank.

urinate. It should be notched out in front of the prepuce, if necessary, to avoid urine contamination.

ELIZABETHAN COLLAR

An Elizabethan collar is used to keep a dog from chewing at a bandage or splint. Or it may be used to keep a dog from licking at an open wound or skin infection. Ready-made Elizabethan collars are available in several sizes, depending on the size of the dog. The collar must be large enough to go around the dog's neck and meet on the other side, and must extend outward far enough to keep him from reaching around the edge of it and chewing or licking. After the collar is put on the dog's neck and snapped or laced together, it should be tied to the dog's collar with pieces of gauze or scraps of nylon cord. This will keep the dog from rubbing or pawing it off over his head.

If you don't have a collar handy, your dog can be a "bucket head." A bucket works just as well as an Elizabethan collar. Buy a soft plastic bucket or wastebasket. Get one that is three or four inches deeper than the distance from where the back of the dog's neck meets his shoulders to the end of his nose. Remove the handle. Cut a hole in the bottom of the bucket.

Don't make the hole too large. You want to have to PUSH to get it over the widest part of the dog's head. This will leave it plenty loose for the dog's neck. Cut a small hole and try it, then cut and try until you just barely can get it on over the dog's head. When you have the hole the right size, punch two holes through the bottom on each side. These will be used for gauze or cord to tie the bucket to the dog's collar. The base of the bucket will be at the dog's collar, and the open end will be toward his nose. The dog is generally able to eat and drink by putting his head down over his dishes. He will bump around and into everything. Ignore the dog's initial discomfort. He will soon learn to navigate quite well with the bucket. And buckets will work well on some dogs who can get around the Elizabethan collar.

A side stick works well on some dogs. It can easily be made from lightweight aluminum rod, bent to shape and covered with adhesive tape. Bend the aluminum rod around a can or flowerpot slightly larger than the dog's neck. You will be making a circle in the middle of the rod, to start. This will make one complete turn around the mold, and halfway around again. You will end up with the two straight ends facing you. The side stick can be stabilized with a loose wrapping of tape around the dog's chest to keep it from going upward or down.

Chapter 11

SKIN CARE AND DISEASES

The dog's ability to grow a good hair coat is largely dependent on inherited factors, aided by good nutrition. The use of special shampoos or medications has little effect on the hair coat of a normal dog. They are, however, valuable in eliminating parasites or diseases.

Most dogs who are kept outdoors seem to have two major periods of shedding, followed by the growth of new hair. These periods occur in the spring and fall, and are probably related to changes in day length. A major shedding occurs in the spring, with the hair becoming more coarse and less dense. A lesser shedding occurs in the fall, with the coat becoming softer and more dense as the undercoat thickens to insulate against cold of the coming winter. Dogs who are kept indoors and exposed to many hours of artificial light tend to shed all year round. The stress of pregnancy may lead to heavy shedding, as can whelping and nursing.

GROOMING AND SKIN CARE

To some people, "grooming" means ears with ribbons and painted nails. But think about how your dog lives. If he's a country dog, his day probably includes a trip through the burs, a swim in the pond and a roll in the horse manure behind the barn. If he lives in the city, his day may include cheat grass from a vacant lot caught in his toes and a few ticks hitchhiking from around the neighborhood. Your taking just a few minutes a day will help to keep him clean and comfortable, and will keep you ahead of skin diseases and parasite problems. Grooming is a valuable investment in cleanliness and health.

Daily grooming will help to remove normally shed hair from the coat. It also helps avoid some of the scratching, biting and chewing that a dog may do if this hair is not removed. The dog's attempts to remove the hair (biting, scratching and chewing) can start an infection or skin irritation. Regular grooming moves flakes of dead skin ("dandruff" or "scurf") away from the skin so they can fall off. It distributes skin oils throughout the hair coat so that it will be soft and shiny. Long-haired dogs need brushing to remove surplus undercoat and keep the hair from matting and tangling. Grooming allows you to observe the dog's skin for injuries, ticks, lice, fleas and other problems.

It is easy to get your dog accustomed to being groomed when he is a small puppy. It may be harder to train him to accept grooming when he is older. If you put him on a bench or table, he will know that this is business rather than play. It will also make it easier for you to work on him. Or use a corner of your porch or patio, or a special corner of the yard. You can even keep the grooming tools there so they are always handy. Reassure the dog and be gentle with him, and he will soon enjoy the attention of being groomed.

Simple equipment is all that is needed for home grooming. A short-bristled, slightly stiff brush is good for a short-haired dog. A long-haired dog will need a comb with blunt, widely-spaced teeth, and a brush with long bristles. A wire doggy brush is good for grooming the kinky hair of Terriers. Scissors with blunt ends are good for cutting mats off a long-haired dog. Nail clippers made especially for dogs will allow you to clip his nails yourself.

Comb carefully through the dog's hair to work out snarls and remove loose hair. If it is matted, begin by working from the outside of the mat, straightening the hair bit by bit. If this does not work, surgery is in order. Work a comb under the mat, between it and the skin. Then, cut it away with your scissors, cutting between the comb and the mat. Always point your scissors AWAY from the dog's body. They develop a quick dislike for being groomed if they are cut or constantly poked with the end of the scissors.

Follow the combing with a vigorous brushing. Brush in the direction that you want the coat to lie. The brush helps to distribute oil from the skin onto the hair to make the coat shiny and sleek.

If your dog is long haired or wire-haired and is shedding heavily, try to get as much dead hair as possible out by vigorous combing. Follow again with a brushing. Wire-haired breeds need to be gone over with a stripping comb, or plucked periodically. Either have a professional groomer do this job, or get someone familiar with the operation to show you how it is done.

Dogs with short, smooth coats can generally be kept clean with a daily once-over with a stiff, short-bristled brush. This is best done after a walk or run—the exercise helps to loosen the hair by stimulating circulation. Don't forget grooming because the dog looks so sleek. The hair deposited by a black Doberman on a beige carpet will leave you crying.

Check the dog's mouth occasionally to see if he has any dental problems or tartar which may cause disease. Chipped or broken teeth may cause pain and dispositional problems. Have them checked the next time you take the dog to your veterinarian.

Check the dog's feet occasionally to be sure that there are no stickers or grass awns (pointed grass seeds) between the toes. Dogs with hair in their feet, such as Cocker Spaniels and Pekingese, should have the hair clipped from between their toes frequently. This helps to keep them from gathering stickers, and makes it easy to detect the abscesses which frequently occur when these dogs run outdoors.

NAIL TRIMMING

Check your dog's toenails at least once a month. If he gets plenty of exercise, he probably keeps them worn down (except for the dewclaws). If he plays mostly on grass or soft ground or spends much of his time indoors, or if he is old or less active, the nails will probably grow faster than they are worn off. If allowed to grow too long, they can cause his feet to spread or splay and will make it difficult for him to walk. Or the nails may curl around and penetrate the pads of his feet. Either problem may result in pain, lameness or possibly arthritis.

Use nail clippers which are meant for animals. Two basic types are available. One type looks like scissors with short ends which hook toward each other like a parrot's beak. The other type has a guillotine-type blade. The nail fits into the hole and is neatly cut off. The latter type is my favorite, but use whichever one works the best for you and fits your hands best, because they both work equally well on the nails. After a long period of use, the trimmers will become dull and the blades will tend to crush the nail instead of cutting it. This can be very painful for the dog, and it may cause irreversible damage to the nail. When the clippers stop cutting cleanly, buy a new pair. Toenail clippers meant for humans work quite well for nipping the ends off puppies' toenails.

It's often easiest to have someone help you for the first trim or two. If they hold the dog, you can put all of your attention into trimming the nails.

You are just cutting off the transparent tips of the nail, beyond where the blood (seen as a dark center) ends. This area is easy to see on dogs with white nails. It is impossible to see on dogs with dark or black nails. For dark nails, you will be guided by the angle of the nail—where the curve near the foot changes to the curve at the end (see illustration). In general, cut off less than half the length from the end of the nail to the quick. You can also start by cutting off a little bit at a time and working back toward the dog's foot. Just try not to exceed that halfway point.

It is a good idea to have your veterinarian demonstrate nail trimming before you attempt it the first time. Ask him for a

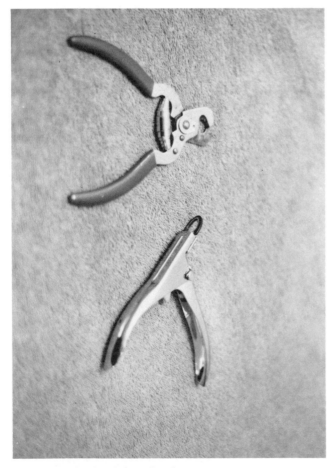

Two types of nail clippers for dogs.

Do not trim nail any shorter than where angle changes.

demonstration when you have the dog in for a vaccination or checkup. After that, it's easy for you to do at home. Nail clipping can be done with the dog sitting on a bench or table, or with him lying on his side or back. It doesn't matter—use whatever works out best for the two of you.

If the dog has never had his nails trimmed, or if they have not been trimmed for a long time, the quick (the tender, blood-filled center) will have grown out toward the end of the nail. If you trim it back to a normal length, it will be very painful to the dog. He may come to associate nail trimming with pain, and be reluctant to have it done again. The nails may also bleed severely. Handle these by only trimming them back one-fourth to one-third of the length. Give the dog five to seven days, and then trim the nails again. This will give the quick time to draw back toward the dog's foot. Take off a small portion again. Do this three or four times over a month's time, and you will have the nails back to a normal length.

Don't forget to trim the dewclaw. This is the vestigal toe (or in some breeds, several toes) located on the inside of the leg just above the paw. They may be present on the front legs, hind legs or both. If your dog has dewclaws, they will need trimming even worse than the rest of his nails. They do not receive ANY wear. If not trimmed, they can grow around in a circle and back into the skin at the base, or into the side of the leg, causing infection and pain.

If your dog has long hair, you may have to feel into his "feathers" to tell whether he has dewclaws. Many puppies have these removed at three days of age. This is a good idea, even with "mutt" puppies, as a dewclaw that isn't there will never need to be clipped, and it will not snag in brush or weeds, causing painful tearing. If your dog continually snags his dewclaws, they can be removed at any time. If done at the same time as neutering, spaying or other surgery, the cost is very minimal.

If you do trim a nail too deeply, your dog will let you know it. He will probably yelp and attempt to pull his foot away from you. A drop of blood may appear on the end of the nail. Hold the foot firmly, while telling the dog to hold still. Dab the blood away with a tissue or paper towel. Then touch the area with a silver nitrate stick or styptic pencil to stop the blood flow. Now, you know for SURE (finding out the hard way) where the quick is in each nail. Cut the rest of them a bit farther away from the dog's foot. And don't worry too much about it—it happens to the best of us! Silver nitrate (and blood!) may stain a light-colored carpet, so the operation is best conducted out of doors.

Some dogs do not like to have their feet held, even if they have never had a nail clipped too close. This seems to be a personal preference. You just need to establish that you are the leader of the pack and are dominant over your dog. Hold one or the other of his feet from time to time when you are not working on them. Do not let go of the foot until the dog relaxes and lets you have it. Then praise him and let him have it back. A few sessions like this when you are watching T.V. or sitting in the living room will go a long way toward letting you trim the dog's nails without fuss or protest. Hold the foot a bit gently, rather than in a death grip or tug-of-war with the dog.

BATHING

If you brush or comb your dog daily or even three or four times a week (and he doesn't visit a skunk or roll in a not-so-fresh fresh carcass), he should rarely need a bath. Let's face it—in the wild, dogs don't get a whole lot of baths, especially with skin-drying shampoos! Too many baths cause far more problems than too few. Dogs with dry, itchy skin and scaling coats often just need a few less baths. If your dog has dry, scaly skin, try bathing him less often and see if it clears up. Baths should be an occasional extra in the grooming process for most normal dogs, rather than a substitute for frequent brushing and combing.

When does the dog need a bath? When he becomes so dirty that you can't stand him, has a bad odor, or both. Or when he needs a dip or bath to remove parasites from his coat. Also, the dog will need a bath when he has gotten into a foreign substance such as road tar.

An ideal soap or shampoo should lather well, rinse out easily without leaving a residue in the coat, and remove debris and dirt without removing too much of the natural oils. It should not irritate the skin or eyes. Irritation from the shampoo may result from depletion of natural skin oils, excessive softening of the skin surface, or from the mechanical effect of the foam. Some dogs may be sensitive to ingredients of the soap or shampoo. Some shampoos contain soaps that form an insoluble curd in hard water ("bathtub ring") which remains on your dog's coat. This residue will leave the hair dull and tacky-feeling. A final rinse with water to which a little vinegar or lemon juice has been added will help to remove the residue or film on the hair. Or try a different shampoo. It is especially important to rinse the dog well to completely remove any soap or shampoo that you are using.

Most shampoos contain detergents. These do not leave a film in hard water, but they tend to remove more of the natural oils from the dog's skin and coat. Many detergent-based shampoos have oils such as lanolin added to help replace the oils lost in the shampooing. These oils lubricate the hair, leaving it shinier and easier to comb.

Use a shampoo made specifically for dogs. Human shampoos are much too drying for dogs, and may also contain ingredients which irritate the dog's skin. A human shampoo may leave the dog itching and scratching, and may start skin problems. Even "baby" shampoos are not good for use on dogs. They are much the same as the rest of our shampoos, only the pH is balanced so they don't burn when they get in the eyes. This still doesn't make them right for the dog's skin. And don't use your dog shampoo on your cat unless the label says that's OK.

Hair conditioners similar to those sold for people are available for dogs. They add shine and body to the hair. They also help to reduce static electricity, which can make a dog's coat snarl and "flyaway." The conditioner may be slightly acid to help remove any hard water film that remains on the hair. Protein conditioners leave a film of protein over the dog's hair, giving it more body and shine. Fatty or oily conditioners put a fine film of oil on the hair, making it shiny and easy to comb. They will cause the coat to lie flat, and should not be used if you want the coat to fluff.

Get everything ready before you begin. Have towels to dry the dog, a hair dryer if needed, and all your shampoos and other conditioners. When you bathe the dog, prepare to get wet and/or dirty. Put on grubby pants and an old sweatshirt and get ready for the mess. Brush all dirt and mats out of the dog's coat before starting the bath.

It is very important to protect the dog's eyes before bathing him. Put a dab of petroleum jelly, a couple of drops of mineral oil, or a 1/4" strip of eye ointment (obtained from your veterinarian) in the eyes just before you begin. Blink each eye open and shut a couple of times to spread the film over the eye.

If the dog's ears are dirty, clean them before you give him his bath. Wrap a cloth or piece of paper towel around the end of your finger, and gently remove only the material that comes out easily. NEVER use cotton swabs to probe down into the dog's ear canals. This only packs dirt down onto the eardrum (and contributes to job security for your veterinarian!).

What about hair in the ear canals? Dogs such as poodles often have fine hair growing far into the ear canal. The hair traps dirt, grass awns and foreign objects, and it helps to keep the ear canal moist and hot, which is an ideal environment for bacterial infection.

To pluck or not to pluck—that is the question. This is a matter of personal preference. Some veterinarians feel that hair should not be removed from the ear canal. My preference is to go ahead and pull out as much as you can get. Begin by plucking it with your fingers, taking a small amount at a time. When you have gotten all that you can in this manner, you can finish by using a pair of forceps to pull out the rest of the hair, as far down the canal as you can see, WITHOUT gouging the dog or pinching him with the forceps. DON'T FORCE the instrument into the ear canal. If you go too deeply, you may push the forceps through the eardrum. Do this before the bath, and before you fill his ears with cotton.

Tuck two to four cotton balls down into each ear. Count them so you know how many you need to get back. Don't force them down into the canal—just put them in as far as they go easily with gentle pressure. You are not plugging the ears tightly shut. You are using the cotton balls just to keep water from going down into the ear canals during the bath. If the ends of the ears need cleaning, wash them gently with shampoo and pat them dry with a towel.

Toy dogs and puppies are easily bathed in the sink, and the spray attachment is great for rinsing them off. Just be sure not to spray it forcefully into the dog's eyes or ears. Larger dogs can be bathed in the tub, shower or outside in the yard.

Use warm water for the bath, sudsing the shampoo gently through the dog's hair. Use the least amount of shampoo which will do the job. This will make rinsing much easier. Rinse VERY thoroughly, because soapy residue can irritate the skin. Oil rinses and conditioners are available for dogs who have dry skin or dandruff problems. These products also give the coat a nice sheen.

Wash and rinse all of the dog except the head. Leave his head until last, because he'll want to shake when you wash it. Wash his head last, trying to keep the shampoo out of his ears and eyes. Rinse well. If you have a shower with solid doors,

this is the ideal time to get out of the way, shut the doors and allow the dog to shake until he feels comfortable. Now you can take the dog out and dry him.

Get the dog as close to dry as possible by rubbing him with towels. If it's a nice day, he can finish drying outside, but keep him on a leash until he is dry or he will roll in the grass or dirt. If it is cold outside, dry him with a hair dryer set on the warm setting (NOT hot). This is great for dogs like Collies with heavy undercoats that seem to take forever to dry. Keep the dog inside and out of drafts until he is completely dry. DON'T FORGET TO REMOVE THE COTTON BALLS FROM HIS EARS!

Old dogs and dogs under six months of age need special care in bathing. They can become chilled easily, leading to illness. Keep the dog warm and protected for at least 3-4 hours after the bath. It is worth taking extra time to dry him thoroughly. Dry, powder shampoos are available and can be used if you are concerned about getting your dog wet. However, they can be drying to the coat because they absorb a lot of the natural oils.

CLIPPING

Some breeds of dogs need regular grooming to keep them looking neat and clean and smelling good. Poodles are perhaps the first to come to mind, but many Terriers need similar grooming. If you have a mixed-breed dog who comes from a background of long-haired parents, he may need regular clipping to keep him looking fresh. How do you decide if the dog needs clipping? If he has hair which continues to grow, gathering unshed undercoat hairs, burs and other debris as it becomes longer, he is probably a candidate for regular clipping. If he is unkempt, ill-smelling and unpleasant to have around, he will need clipping and bathing. How often he will need clipping depends on how fast the particular dog's hair grows. It may be once a month, or every two or three months.

You can do the grooming yourself, if you are willing to learn how to clip the dog. You can save considerable money by doing so. Check out a book on grooming at your local library. Expect to spend about seventy dollars on a good, sharp set of clippers. Small dogs will be trimmed with a regular-sized set of clippers. Large dogs, such as an Old English Sheepdog, will need larger, coarser clippers. If you are clipping for show, you may need both kinds of clippers.

Expect to spend some time experimenting. The first clip job may be a bit rough, the next one better, and soon you will be doing a thoroughly professional job. Expect also to spend the better part of a day to clip a medium- to large-sized dog—between the clip, the bath, and the drying and fluff. If you feel awkward doing the job, remember that the difference between a bad haircut and a good haircut is two weeks.

If you have a long-haired dog and do not like to groom him, however, you will want to find a professional groomer. This should be someone who gets along well with the dog, and does a job which is pleasing to you. This does not necessarily mean a show clip, but what YOU want done to the dog. At one time I was working at a veterinary clinic which did grooming, and a woman brought in a show-quality, snow-white Pekingese. She requested a poodle clip. This was very unusual, so I questioned her further. Yes, "like a puppy clip—short all over with a pompon on the end of the tail." I did as she asked, and waited rather anxiously for her evaluation of the result. She was thrilled. "I hope Dr. X is gone again next summer when Fido needs clipping—you did a beautiful job," she said. So find someone who does what you want, not what they want.

The groomer should have a clean facility so that your dog does not come home with parasites as a bonus. Clippers and combs should be kept clean and disinfected so that the dog does not get ringworm or other contagious diseases. If you like, the groomer can also clip the dog's nails and pluck the hair from his ears. A good groomer should also be on the alert for problems such as skin disease, tumors or ear infections, and should tell you about them so that you can take the dog to your veterinarian for examination and treatment.

A seasonal, yearly trim should be routine care for most long-haired dogs. Even a dog living in our very northern states can suffer miserably during the summer. They become hot and sweaty under their haircoat. This is especially a problem with dogs with fine undercoats, such as Collies, St. Bernards and the sled dogs in general. If they are not routinely combed and brushed, the undercoat accumulates. The hair collects burs and grass awns, which do not fall out. In addition, the dandruff from the skin cannot sift out through the hair. It remains next to the warm, moist skin. Soon the dog develops a "hot spot." This is an area of infection on the skin, down under the hair. A spot may start as a slightly reddened area. It can then progress until it is weeping, pus-covered, angry red lesion several inches across. Meanwhile, given the same environment elsewhere on the dog, other hot spots are probably occurring (see Hot Spots).

In my opinion, ALL long-haired dogs that are not being groomed on a daily basis, and who do not need show coats, should be sheared once a year. Do this when the weather turns hot—around the end of May or first of June up North, sooner in the southern states. You can take him to a groomer to have him sheared. Or you can shear him yourself, using a large clipper with a wide, coarse blade. Cut WITH the lay of the hair, not against it, and you will get a close, even clip that still leaves enough hair that the dog will not be sunburned. If this is the first time you have ever clipped a dog and it is a little ragged, try not to laugh at the dog and keep the kids from laughing at him. Surprisingly, he will be sensitive to how he looks. And remember, the difference between a good haircut and a bad one is about 14 days. It WILL grow out! By the time winter comes, the dog will be back with a full, fresh, new coat, ready to face the cold.

Don't tell me that the dog needs his coat for insulation from the summer heat. I'll believe that when I see you in your arctic down jacket in the middle of the street in the middle of a hot sunny day in July! If you notice, dogs which originally came from hot climates have either short hair (Basenji, Greyhound) or a long, sparse coat (Saluki). Those from colder climates usually have thick, full coats with a large quantity of soft, insulating undercoat (Norwegian Elkhound, St. Bernard, all the sled dog breeds such as the Husky, etc.).

Clipper rash or clipper burn is the name given to reddened, scraped-looking, irritated patches in areas where the dog has been clipped. It may be due to a groomer who uses dull blades, or does not keep them cleaned out so that they glide smoothly through the dog's coat. It may be due to letting the clippers get so hot that they irritate the dog's skin. Or it may be that your dog is unruly and wiggles around a lot. In any case, talk it over with your groomer. The cause may be something he can change if the clipper burn is called to his attention. Give him another try the next time you need the dog groomed. If it happens again, try another groomer to see if the problem is the groomer or the dog.

If the rash is causing the dog much irritation, he may lick and chew at it, irritating it further and maybe even starting an infection. It may be necessary to take him to your veterinarian to get an injection of an antibiotic and/or a drug to help reduce the itching for a few days. In some cases, topical medication may be needed, too.

FEEDING FOR A HEALTHY COAT

An adequate, well-balanced diet will help your dog to have a healthy coat. Most high-quality, complete dog foods have all the nutrients necessary for good skin and hair health. Added fat may be needed if you are feeding dry dog food. Extra fat is not usually necessary if you are feeding a canned dog food. In some cases of skin disease, such as seborrhea, added fat may make the skin problem worse. Some dry foods contain adequate fat, but the fat is not adequately protected by antioxidants and becomes rancid in storage. If you add fat to the diet and do not see a definite improvement within one to two months, it may not be worth continuing the supplementation. If you add it and DO see a difference, then you know it was needed and it will be worthwhile to continue the supplementation.

HOT SPOTS

"Hot spots" is the name given to an acute, moist dermatitis. This disease is most often seen in dogs with dense, heavy haircoats. The things that can start a hot spot are many and varied. It may occur just because the dog has a lot of old, dead hair and skin scales held near his skin. It may begin because of allergies. Or it may start because of injury to the skin as the dog licks, chews or scratches at impacted anal sacs or infected ears. It may be caused by irritation from external parasites such as ticks, fleas or lice, or from ANY minor skin irritation.

The lesions can develop within only a few hours. They are red, moist and extremely painful. If not treated immediately, they often spread rapidly, and can quickly become infected. *Staphylococcus* bacteria ("Staph") often invade the area, although other bacteria can be found in the lesion. Some people feel that a high level of protein in the diet contributes to the development of hot spots. There is no evidence that this is true.

Some hot spots will first be noticed as a patch of missing hair. They begin by oozing serum. Then they become crusted over with exudate, they may be covered with matted hair.

Many hot spots will have a yellowish center surrounded by a reddened ring of irritation. If you feel the areas, they often feel "hot," compared to the surrounding skin.

The first line of treatment for hot spots is to clip ALL affected areas. If a fancy coat is not needed, it doesn't hurt to shear the entire dog, as above. If the dog is in severe pain or the spots are very extensive, it may be necessary to take him to the veterinarian so that he can be completely anesthetized for the shearing.

After the hair has been removed from the area, the spots can be VERY gently cleansed with povidone-iodine solution, or with a mild antiseptic soap. If there are a lot of hot spots, or they are very large or severely infected, take the dog in for a veterinary examination. It may be necessary to give the dog injectible antibiotics for several days, in addition to topical treatment, to clear them up. In some dogs, injectible corticosteroids may be needed for up to a week or so to break the itch-scratch cycle.

Ointments should not usually be used on hot spots because they prevent air from reaching the moist, weeping lesions. However, lotions containing a combination of antibiotics and corticosteroids are often used. As the lesions heal, softening preparations may be used if the skin is dry and crusty. These may include preparations such as nitrofurazone ointment, or even a product such as carbolated petroleum jelly. If the lesions are still weeping and moist, an astringent drug may be used to help dry them up. It may be necessary to put an Elizabethan collar or bucket on the dog's head to keep him from chewing at the spots until they are healed. The original cause of the hot spots—whether anal glands, ear problems or parasites—should also be treated to keep the dog from getting them again. Help to prevent them next year by shearing the dog early! If you don't shear the dog, be fanatic about combing and brushing him on a regular schedule.

SEBORRHEA

There are only a limited number of ways that the skin can react to insult or injury. For that reason, many illnesses or disease problems cause the same set of symptoms. Many groups of symptoms, for example "seborrhea," should not be thought of as a specific disease but as a description of the current condition of the skin. Seborrhea comes in two forms. "Seborrhea sicca" is a dry, dull haircoat with a lot of dandruff. The greasy form of seborrhea is called "seborrhea oleosa," and is an oily haircoat with yellow flakes and a rancid, unpleasant odor.

Seborrhea is a general term describing symptoms ranging from slight dandruff to greasy, crusted, scaling, hairless areas. The skin is a living organ which continuously produces new cells and sheds the old ones from its surface. If too many new cells are produced, or too few old ones shed, the old ones will accumulate. In normal, healthy skin, the proper amount of fat is present to keep the skin supple and the surface from drying. Fats also keep the coat shiny and sleek. If an excess of fats is produced by the skin cells, the surplus may accumulate along with the old, shed cells, forming a greasy, foul-smelling mass. This is also an ideal place for bacteria to grow, adding to the odor. Waste products from the bacteria are irritating to the skin.

Seborrhea may occur secondary to hormonal upsets such as hypothyroidism. It may cycle on and off in bitches who have irregular or prolonged heat cycles, or a history of false pregnancy. It is seen in male dogs with Sertoli cell tumors (which commonly develop in testicles which are retained in the abdomen). Male dogs who are producing excess quantities of female hormones may also show seborrhea. Dogs with excessive corticosteroid production (or who have been given excessive quantities of corticosteroid medications) may show seborrhea.

Nutritional factors such as a fat-deficient diet are a common cause of seborrhea. Homemade diets and poor-quality dried foods, epecially if they have been stored more than six months, are often low in fat and can cause seborrhea. It can also be seen with prolonged feeding of some generic dog foods. The first signs are a dry coat with dandruff. Later in the course of seborrhea, the skin and hair feel greasy. Pancreatitis may cause it by hindering fat digestion and absorption. Vitamin A deficiencies, zinc deficiencies, and feeding excess calcium to puppies may also cause seborrhea. Interestingly, Vitamin A excess can cause similar signs. Your veterinarian will want to question you about the dog's dietary history in order to find the causative factor. A laboratory analysis of the food may, ultimately, be the only way to know for sure what, if any, dietary factor is involved.

Parasites which live on or in the skin can cause seborrhea. Flea bite dermatitis is one of the most common causes of seborrhea. Scabies and demodectic mange can cause it. *Cheyletiella* mite infestations and lice may cause severe dandruff-type scaling. Some autoimmune diseases may cause seborrhea.

Seborrhea is seen as a specific disease in some breeds. Among these are Cocker Spaniels, Springer Spaniels, Basset Hounds, West Highland White Terriers, German Shepherds, Poodles, Dachshunds and Labrador Retrievers (Campbell, 1985). Certain bloodlines show a higher incidence of the disease, suggesting the involvement of hereditary factors. Signs appear early in life and become progressively worse. Males and females are equally affected. Hereditary cases are tough to control, probably because the skin does not react "normally."

It must by now be obvious that there are a LOT of causes of either a dry, dandruffy coat, or a fatty, greasy one. In many cases, diagnosis will be a job for your veterinarian. But first rule out the obvious causes. Do you have the dog on a well-balanced, quality food WITHOUT any random supplementation? Comb through his coat with the proverbial "fine-toothed comb" to see if you can pick up any fleas or flea dirt. Fleas are slightly larger than a pinhead, and will jump rapidly. Lice, on the other hand, are about 1/8 inch long, dirty gray in color and cigar-shaped. Flea dirt is small, rounded specks of reddish-black material (actually, your dog's dried blood that has had a trip through the flea's digestive tract). If the dog is in a false pregnancy, spaying may prevent the recurrence of both that and the seborrhea. If none of these are present, it's time to see your veterinarian and get a positive diagnosis. Shampoos, baths and pasting various medications on the dog's skin are all useless if the underlying disease problem is not identified and treated.

When you have identified and have begun to correct the underlying disease problem, THEN you can begin treating the skin itself. Dogs with the oily form of the disease will need to be "degreased." Selenium-based shampoos are valuable for this, as are those with benzoyl peroxide or salicylic acid. To get the best effect, the shampoo should be left on for 10-15 minutes. In the beginning, bathe the dog as often as necessary to remove the scales or control the odor. This may be as often as every 3 to 4 days. Dogs with the dry form of the disease can be bathed with hypoallergenic, mild shampoos. Afterward, the oils can be replaced by using a capful of a product containing essential fatty acids mixed into a pint of warm water. Put this in a spray bottle and mist it over the dog's coat daily. If the dog is long-haired, it may be useful to shear him until you have the seborrhea under control.

BLACKHEADS

The development of blackheads (comedones) on the skin of the back is common in Schnauzers, but may occasionally be seen in other dogs. These are crusty, pointed pimples which stick up above the surface of the skin. They usually do not cause itching or pain unless they become infected. If infected, they can cause an intense, miserable itching. The dog may need antibiotic injections, as well as possible corticosteroid treatment. A simple case of blackheads can be treated a couple of times a week with the same shampoos as for oily seborrhea (see above). A benzoyl peroxide ointment may be applied daily to help loosen the blackheads. Look for one among the acne medications in your drugstore. Because that's really what this is—a case of acne! You can also rub the dog's back with denatured ethyl alcohol twice a week to help prevent further blackhead formation. Stop using alcohol if the dog's skin becomes dry and itching.

PYODERMA

Pyoderma is a pus-producing bacterial infection of the skin. *Staphylococcus intermedius* or *Staphylococcus aureus* ("Staph") are the most commonly involved bacteria. Some cases of pyoderma are basically self-limiting. Others may be resistant to treatment and can ultimately threaten the dog's life. Staph skin infections do not seem to be transmitted from dogs to humans.

Pyoderma may occur in skin folds, such as the facial folds of an English Bulldog, Pug, Boston Terrier, Pekingese, Boxer or Shar-Pei. In young puppies, demodectic mange may also be present, complicating the disease.

Pyoderma may occur in the lip folds of dogs such as Cocker and Springer Spaniels. These infections may start from an accumulation of food and saliva in the folds. Once started, it may then be complicated by excessive salivation or tartar on the teeth.

Fold pyoderma may occur around the vulva in bitches who are fat or have very wrinkled skin in that area. It is also common in fat young bitches who have an immature, recessed vulva. Irritation from urine soaking into the folds or continual dampness from urinary incontinence may compound the problem. The bitch may show pain on urination. She may lick the area of the vulva (or as close as she can reach if she's fat) continuously. Pyoderma can also occur around the tail folds in dogs with corkscrew tails, such as Pugs, Boston Terriers and English Bulldogs.

The permanent cure for these skin fold pyodermas is surgical removal of the extra skin. If you don't wish to have surgery done, the problem can be managed medically with an antibiotic-steroid cream or lotion. This may need to be applied for the rest of the animal's life. Clipping the hair out of the fold will help to reduce the irritation and keep it cleaner. The area can also be treated with Domeboro® solution (Miles Pharmaceuticals, West, CT, 06516). This product is available at most pharmacies. This medication helps to dry and soothe the irritated skin.

Pyoderma may be seen as an acne on the chin or muzzle of short-haired dogs such as Great Danes and Dobermans. Most of these cases are seen in young dogs, three to 12 months of age. Many dogs outgrow the problem when they become sexually mature. Antibiotic-steroid creams or lotions are the primary treatment. If the lesions are severe, the dog may need antibiotic treatment for one to two months.

Pyoderma may be seen on the top of the end of the nose in long-nosed dogs. In most cases, it seems to result because the dog has been rooting in dirt, or pushing into it with his nose. The dog develops a deep, painful sore on the bridge of the nose. This may spread to other parts of the face. The hair follicles may be so badly damaged that even when the disease is cured, the nose remains scarred and hairless (see Collie Nose for a condition which may look similar).

German Shepherd pyoderma is a deep (many layers of the skin are infected) pyoderma common in middle-aged Shepherds who are otherwise healthy. In this breed, the lesions usually start over the hips and outer portions of the thighs. Early in the disease, they are well hidden by the coat, and may be quite mild. Later, they are very painful. If the dog has fleas at the same time, the pyoderma may be misdiagnosed as flea-bite dermatitis. If the dog is treated with systemic corticosteroids, he may temporarily improve, only to become much worse later. German Shepherd pyoderma tends to recur even after appropriate treatment and apparent cure. The dog is healthy except for the severe skin problem. Defects in the dog's immune system may be the underlying cause of at least some of the cases.

Puppies may have a puppy pyoderma. This is not contagious. It is usually associated with debilitating factors such as other disease conditions, poor diet, parasitism or unsanitary living conditions. Pus-filled pimples occur, primarily on the thinly-haired skin of the belly. They rupture, covering the skin with honey-colored crusts.

Another form of pyoderma occurs when Staph bacteria infect the hair follicles, producing a pimple at the base of the hair. This ruptures, leaving a yellowish crust. Areas of seborrhea may be mixed in with the pimply areas. In short-coated breeds, the small bumps may lift the hairs, giving a ruffled, bumpy appearance to the coat. This may be diagnosed as a case of hives or other skin allergic reaction, which it is not. Most cases involving the hair follicles are associated with parasites such as *Demodex*, fleas or food allergies. Pyoderma can also be seen with Cushing's disease, hypothyroidism or seborrhea.

Dogs with pyoderma will usually need treatment with appropriate antibiotics for at least three weeks to a month. It is very important that you keep the dog on the entire course of treatment if he is to be cured, especially with German Shepherd pyoderma. Corticosteroids may give temporary relief because they reduce irritation and itching. They should, however, be avoided with pyoderma because of the tendency to make it recur, or to become worse than it would have been otherwise. If there is an underlying cause, such as food allergy, inhalant allergy or hypothyroidism, it should be found and corrected so that the problem does not recur. Pyoderma also occurs with infestations of skin parasites such as fleas, scabies or demodectic mange. Getting rid of the parasites will allow the pyoderma to heal.

HORMONAL SKIN DISEASE

Imbalances in almost any of the body's hormones are reflected by skin problems. These may occur as loss of hair which is bilaterally symmetrical (the same on both sides of the dog). A lack of thyroid hormone, a lack of adrenal hormone, an excess of adrenal hormone, or lack of estrogen are among the imbalances which cause skin signs. (See Endocrine Chapter for a further discussion of these problems).

ACANTHOSIS NIGRICANS

Acanthosis nigricans is the name given to a skin disease which is particularly common in Dachshunds. The skin becomes blackened and thickened, especially over areas where friction occurs, such as the elbows, hocks and belly. The cause is not known, but some of the affected dogs have lower than normal thyroid activity, and this may contribute to the problem. Other hormonal imbalances may cause darkening of the skin, including, on occasion, diabetes mellitus. In some cases, it may be due to demodectic or sarcoptic mange.

As with other hormone-related problems, the darkened spots are symmetrical from one side of the dog to the other. They are often seen first in the armpits and groin area. The skin is swollen, the hair becomes thinner, and a grayish-blue, brown or black coloration appears. Early in the disease, there is little or no itching. As the disease progresses, the darkened spots may extend to both the inner and outer surfaces of the legs, the sides and belly, ear flaps and under the tail. The skin becomes progressively thickened, deeply folded and blackened. Seborrhea may be present, with an accumulation of greasy material, scales and crusts. At this point, itching may occur, and the dog may damage the skin by scratching.

Acanthosis is usually a chronic disease. Some cases can be controlled by appropriate hormone therapy, but a total, permanent cure is rare. Appropriate tests (or trial therapy) should be used to determine if a hormone deficiency is present. Antiseborrheic treatment will help to reduce the pain and itching. If the dog is overweight, reduction to a normal weight may help considerably.

RINGWORM

Ringworm is caused by a number of species of fungi which infect the hair follicles, causing the hairs to fall out. Ringworm is often first seen around the dog's head and ears, especially in thin-skinned young puppies. The patches are usually rounded and scaly. Inside the spot, the hairs may be broken and short, or they may have completely fallen out, leaving a hairless spot. Pimples and bumps may surround the edge of the spot. Severe cases of ringworm may cause hairless, crusted, reddened, scaly spots over much of the body.

Most species of ringworm are easily transmitted to both humans and cats. If you or your children have spots at the same time as your dog or cat, it may be ringworm. One species of ringworm (the most common one) is strongly fluorescent. If you have a Wood's lamp or other black (ultraviolet) light, shine it on the lesions in a darkened room. If there are tiny, brightly sparkling fluorescent areas, it's probably ringworm. There are also several kinds of ringworm fungi that do not fluoresce, so the fact that an animal does not "glow in the dark" does not rule out ringworm. Sarcoptic mange is also contagious to humans, but the spots are usually scaly and irregularly shaped. Sarcoptic mange may itch intensely in both dogs and humans from the mites burrowing through the skin.

Products containing iodine are highly successful in treating ringworm. These are used directly on the skin lesions. Povidone-iodine products work well. Shampoos which contain iodine also work well (such as Weladol Shampoo ®, Pitman-Moore). Chlorhexidine products are also effective (Nolvasan® solution, shampoo or ointment, Fort Dodge Laboratories). Tolnaftate cream does not seem to be effective in small animals, although your physician may prescribe it for you.

Griseofulvin is a drug which is used for systemic treatment of ringworm in animals. You can get it from your veterinarian. CAUTION: it can cause defects in unborn puppies, and should absolutely NOT be used in pregnant animals. Occasionally, dogs will have digestive upsets from griseofulvin. It can be useful, however, when trying to clear up ringworm infections in a number of animals in situations where it is easier to give pills or liquid medication than to treat individual skin spots. It enters the skin and hair, so that new hairs growing out are resistant to attack by the fungus.

If the dog who has ringworm also has an infection in the skin (shown by pimples and crusts forming), it may be necessary for him to have antibiotics for a period of time. Consult your veterinarian.

When dealing with ringworm, it's best to treat the whole herd at one time—dogs, cats and humans. Careful sanitation is important. Wash the animal's bedding thoroughly in a 1:30 solution of chlorine bleach. Or you can provide disposable bedding and change it once a week until the outbreak is cleared up. Wash all grooming tools with the same solution. Keep children from handling pets as much as possible to avoid passing the fungal infection back and forth (yes, it goes both ways). Wash your hands carefully after handling the dog.

ABSCESSES AND OTHER SWELLINGS

Your dog has a large bump on his shoulder. Or maybe on the side of his ribs. How do you decide what it is? Begin by feeling it carefully. If it is solid and hard, it may be a tumor, especially if the dog is old. But if it appeared suddenly, it may be a blood clot, a serum pocket or an abscess. How do you tell them apart? You can take the dog to your veterinarian to have him examined, and this is truly the best approach.

If the swelling is on the midline of the belly or in the groin area, it very possibly is a hernia. If you press gently on it, it may feel doughy. If you are able to squeeze (gently!) the contents back into the abdomen through the hole in its wall, it is surely a hernia. Take the dog to your veterinarian for treatment. DO NOT, under any circumstances, stick a needle into one of these. You could cause a fatal peritonitis (infection of the abdominal lining). The hernia may contain a loop of intestine just under the skin.

If you can't get the dog to a veterinarian and you're sure the swelling is not a hernia, you will have to examine the swelling. Clip all hair off of and an inch or so around the swelling in all directions. Use a pair of clippers with a fine blade, or a pair of scissors. Now you can feel it more carefully. An abscess may be noticeably hot compared to the surrounding area. It may have a spot at the highest area where the skin feels thin (the "point"). Or it may be discolored, bluish or reddened, and it may feel fluid-filled.

Carefully wash the bump with soap and water. Dry it with a paper towel. Now rinse it with povidone-iodine. With someone carefully restraining the dog on his side, pop a sterile 16-gauge or 18-gauge needle carefully into the lump. You want to go JUST through the skin. Now attach a syringe to the needle—a 3-cc one is fine. Pull outward and see what comes out.

If you get blood, the swelling is a hematoma. Leave it alone. With time, it will go down and scar tissue will form. It may contract and leave a wrinkled scar. In some cases it may become infected, and later become an abscess which will need to be treated. If the dog develops more hematomas, he may have hemophilia or another disease. Consult your veterinarian.

If you get thin yellowish or straw-colored fluid, the lesion is a seroma. This may have formed as a serum pocket after the animal was kicked or otherwise injured. It will go down after a long period of time.

The fluid may be thickened and yellowish, greenish or reddish. This is pus. It means that the lump is an abscess. It will need to be drained. Wear plastic or rubber gloves and be careful not to splash or squirt the pus onto yourself or your helper. Put the dog on a thick pad of newspapers so you can throw away all the infected material. This can be done by making an incision at the lowest point of the abscess. Make a single vertical cut about 1/2-inch long, so that pus will drain out the lower end. Drain the pus out onto paper towels or rags that you can throw away. Now swab the hole out with

povidone-iodine. Use a pair of forceps with a tiny piece of cotton on it, soaked in iodine. Or you can use cotton swabs. Clean the hole out thoroughly.

You will need to clean out the abscess daily with povidone-iodine until it is healed. This is to allow it to heal from the inside out. Each day the hole will get slightly smaller. Do not allow the outer hole to close until the inside is completely healed. Otherwise, the pocket will only fill again with pus. If it suddenly seals shut, just pick off the material that is sealing it and keep on swabbin'. The dog may need treatment with antibiotics for five to 10 days, depending on the extent of the abscess.

If you cannot draw any fluid from the lump, it could be a tumor. Have the dog examined by your veterinarian. Skin tumors sometimes spread throughout the body. He will probably want to take X-rays of the dog's chest and abdomen to see if there has been any spreading. He'll also, probably, suggest surgery to remove the tumors.

COLLIE NOSE

Collie nose is a severe case of sunburn which occurs on top of the bridge of the nose, usually toward the outer end. While it may occur in any dog, it is most common in Collies, Australian Shepherds, Shetland Sheepdogs and animals of related breeding. It may also be seen in Welsh Corgis, white German Shepherds and Weimaraners. Heredity seems to play an important role in this disease. It is more common in areas where the sun is bright and intense, such as Colorado, Wyoming, Florida, California and Hawaii. It is uncommon in coastal areas where it is cloudy much of the time. It is more common in summer when the sun is most intense and days are longest.

The affected area becomes reddened. In some dogs, it seems to begin in an area that is white or without pigment. In others, it seems that normally colored areas lose their color after they are affected. The area may become ulcerated and eroded, leaving an area sunken well below the level of the surrounding skin. During seasons when the sun is less intense, the damaged areas heal with a thin, weak skin. This skin does not have any of the hair or glands of the normal skin it has replaced. It may bleed quite easily if brushed or injured. The dog may be quite sensitive about having his head handled. If the dog has similar lesions on the ears, or at the corners of the eyes or mouth, the problem is not considered to be Collie nose.

The treatment depends upon how badly the nose is damaged, and how much trouble it causes the dog. You can begin by keeping the dog inside during the day. It will take a minimum of two weeks to see any improvement. If you have to take him outside to relieve himself, keep that time as short as possible. The dog can be hospitalized at your veterinarian's clinic if you do not have a place to keep him.

A sunscreen can be used on the damaged area. Get one with as high an SPF (sun protection factor) as possible. Use a product which contains PABA (paraminobenzoic acid). Presun® (Westwood Pharmaceuticals) is an example of one of these products. A black, indelible marking pen can be used to blacken the pale skin and provide temporary relief.

Ointments containing corticosteroids in combination with antibiotics, such as Panalog® (Solvay), may be useful if the dog does not wipe the medication off his nose. This combination of drugs will give relief from the inflammation, as well as providing antibiotics to help control infection in the damaged skin. Systemic corticosteroids are often used to relieve inflammation if the damage is of long duration. It will not, however, prevent further sunburn, so keep the dog indoors.

Tattooing often gives the dog permanent relief. It must be done when the lesions are healed as well as possible. They should be completely covered by skin, even if it is the thin and weak kind, if at all possible. There should not be any redness in the area, nor should there be any serum oozing from the lesions. It may be necessary to confine the dog, darken the area with a marking pen, and treat him with corticosteroids for several weeks before the tattooing can be done.

Your veterinarian will completely anesthetize the animal for tattooing. Many veterinarians use an electric tattooing device to put black ink into the area. The dog may be given antihistamines and/or corticosteroids for a week to 10 days after tattooing to relieve swelling. A combination of serum and ink may ooze from the tattooed area after treatment. Cool, wet cloths may be used to gently blot the area a couple of times daily. This seems to give most dogs considerable relief. The skin of the nose on most dogs turns grayish or blackish in color a week or two after tattooing.

Treatment is much more successful if done before deep erosions invade the cartilage or the bony areas of the nose. Most dogs do very well after they are tattooed. If the dog was not completely healed when he was tattooed, some areas may not take the ink well. In that case, the darkened area will remain in good shape, and the areas which are still unpigmented will need to be retattooed after they and the tattooed area have healed.

SPOROTRICHOSIS

Sporotricosis is caused by a fungus which is found in decaying leaves and bark throughout the world. At body temperatures, the organism exists in a yeast form.

Sporotrichosis is commonly seen with infected puncture wounds. Hunting dogs often have the disease because they get stuck with thorns and branches as they go through brush. Cat's claws are often contaminated with the fungus. A cat scratch can develop into the disease.

Humans, by the way, are infected in much the same manner—from puncture wounds and getting clawed by cats. Humans can also get the disease by contact with pus from treating a dog or cat who has an abscess due to this organism. For this reason, it is best to wear rubber gloves or disposable plastic gloves when treating an abscess, whether it is on your dog or your cat. When you are through, carefully remove the gloves. Wash your forearms and hands with a povidone-iodine scrub or solution.

Dogs with sporotrichosis may have numerous, nodular lesions on the skin, especially on the head and trunk. Some of these may be ulcerated and draining, or they may be covered with crusts. In some cases, the lesions may extend down the legs. This disease should be suspected when the dog is treated with antibiotics and shows little or no healing. Your veterinarian may diagnose sporotrichosis by staining a sample from one of the draining lesions or abscesses and finding the yeast organisms. In many cases, he may wish to send a sample to a laboratory for culture to confirm the diagnosis. In some dogs, sporotrichosis is hard to diagnose, and a second set of samples may have to be submitted.

The dog may be treated with potassium iodide, which is given with his food. Or a special anti-fungal drug may be given. The organism is quite hardy and resistant, requiring three to four months of treatment before he is cured. Treatment may be continued for a month or more after the dog appears cured. Do not stop treatment too soon, or the disease may come back. Corticosteroids should not be given while the dog is being treated, or the disease may not be completely eliminated and may flare up when treatment is stopped (Kirk, 1989, p. 633-634).

LICK GRANULOMA

Lick granuloma is the name given to a lesion resulting from self-mutilation. It is also called pruritic nodule, neurodermatitis and acral lick dermatitis (ALD). This condition occurs when the dog begins licking one portion of his body, generally his foot or lower leg, and does not stop until severe damage is done. Most commonly only one side is affected, although occasionally the dog will chew both legs. It is usually seen in older dogs (5-12 years of age), and in large breeds, especially German Shepherd, Labrador Retriever, Doberman Pinscher, Boxer, Great Dane, and Golden Retriever (Scott, 1984). Twice as many males may be affected as females (Mandelker, 1989). Boredom is thought to be a major cause of lick granuloma. The classic case seems to develop in a dog which is left alone for long periods of time.

In some cases, it is felt that there may be an initiating cause—such as a cut or abrasion, infection or abscess, musculoskeletal pain, or foreign objects such as grass awns involving the area—and the dog may be licking because his foot hurts for one of those reasons. However, most veterinarians feel that the problem has an emotional cause, such as boredom or lack of exercise. Changed social factors in the dog's home environment may start the chewing, such as a new puppy, a death in the family, or the dog being left alone all day with nothing to do.

The dog licks and chews, usually at the side or top of his paw or the area just above it. In some cases he may chew the stifle or hip, or top of the hind paw. Occasionally the dog will chew more than one area. First it will just be damp. Then the hair will be removed and the skin becomes reddened. If the problem continues, the dog may chew down through the skin, and then into the tendons. Finally, in extreme cases, the dog may gnaw clear to the bone. The problem may go on for years, if no successful treatment can be found.

Begin by examining the dog's foot carefully. Be sure that there is not any foreign substance or object on or in the skin—no grass awns, pine pitch or anything similar. If you find something like this, take care of it promptly. However, in most cases, you will not see any reason for the licking, even with careful examination. If your dog is one of the breeds listed, or is an especially nervous individual, you can suspect that the problem is lick granuloma. Incidentally, most dogs who chew at their feet either have a foreign object in them or are chewing because of allergies. These are dogs who start chewing and don't stop.

MANY treatments have been tried for lick granuloma. The bad news is that they are not very successful. Bandages and casts have been tried. Most dogs just chew them off and then continue chewing on the foot. Physical restraints such as muzzles and Elizabethan collars have been used. These may help temporarily—only as long as the dog will leave them in place. The dog will go back to chewing as soon as they are removed. Bitter substances have been applied to the wound, or to a bandage over it, also with little effect. These dogs have such a strong drive to chew that almost nothing will stop them. In effect, you may cure the initial problem, but the licking has become a habit, resulting in continuing self-mutilation.

Many drug therapies have been tried. These include corticosteroid drugs, either applied to the lesion or injected under it. Tranquilizers and sedative medications have been tried in attempts to keep the dog dopey enough that he will not chew. Injecting cobra venom under the lesions has been tried with some degree of success. It does not, however, appear to be currently on the market. Surgical removal of the chewed area, radiation therapy, cryotherapy (freezing) and acupuncture have also been tried.

In one report, a mixture of three ml. of Banamine® added to one eight-ml. bottle of Synotic® was used to treat a number of dogs (Scott, 1984), and showed considerable success. This was used without a bandage. Long-term therapy with antibiotics (two to three months) has helped in some cases. In some cases, megestrol acetate (Ovaban®) has been used to control the licking. Again, these treatments do not work in all dogs, but are worth a try.

If you can find an initial cause for the licking, that should be removed, quickly, before the habit of licking is established. Increasing the amount of exercise may be helpful for some dogs. For those who are bored being home all day, it may be useful to get them a companion, or take them to a place where they can have companionship during the day. The dog may be emotionally crippled or disturbed enough that it may not be possible to leave him alone ever again.

HIVES

Hives are raised, rounded, itching bumps in the skin. They are caused by an allergic reaction like the one that causes anaphylactic shock. Hives may come on quite suddenly. They may occur because of something the dog has eaten, or some chemical he has gotten into, such as a perfume or insect spray. They may be due to insect bites or stings. Or they may be because he has had an injection of a substance to which he is allergic.

A related problem, called angioedema, does not have separate bumps. Instead, the skin of the face and neck is swollen with fluid. It is most often seen in puppies. The lips may be half an inch thick, the muzzle may be swollen until it bulges, and the eyes may be nearly closed. The ears may be thickened and rubbery. Rarely, the tissues of the neck and throat may swell enough that the dog's life is threatened.

Take the dog to your veterinarian for treatment. Mild cases of hives or angioedema are easily treated with antihistamines. More severe cases may need an injection of a corticosteroid or epinephrine to stop their progress. If the dog has trouble breathing, give oxygen if possible and get him to a veterinarian immediately. This is an emergency. (For information on related problems, see Anaphylactic Shock).

CANINE ATOPY

Canine atopy is the name given to allergic skin disease which occurs in dogs due to substances which they have inhaled. It is the equivalent of humans' hay fever. Instead of sneezing, the dog itches. Allergies are especially common in Terriers, Poodles and Golden Retrievers, although they may occur in any dog—whether mutt or purebred, large or small, male or female.

Some dogs are affected by these allergies on a year-round basis. Others are affected only seasonally. The dog's skin itches. He may chew, lick and scratch. All of this worrying at his skin may produce infection. The feet are the area most commonly chewed. The saliva contains iron, so the dog's feet may look yellowish or brownish. The dog may scratch at his flanks, ears, armpits and groin. Some dogs rub their faces on the carpet, furniture or lawn, or paw at their faces with their feet. Bacteria may invade the scratched and irritated areas, causing infection. Signs often begin between four months and four years of age. As the dog continues to worry at his skin, infection and pyoderma may occur. The skin may become thickened and darkened with pigment.

Grasses are common causes of skin allergy when the dog inhales their pollen. Kentucky bluegrass is a prominent cause in many parts of the country, while dogs in warmer climates are miserable when the Bermuda grass is blooming. Trees and weeds produce pollen which cause skin irritation after the dog inhales them. In cooler climates, trees tend to pollinate in the spring, grasses during the summer and weeds in the fall. In more mild climates, plants may be pollinating nearly year-round, leading to a continuing problem. Molds and house dust cause year-round misery for some dogs. Others are affected by dander from various animals, including horses, cats and humans. Yes, your dog may be allergic to you!

The seasonal occurrence of skin problems may be the first sign that your dog's problem is allergic. At this point, your veterinarian may put the dog on corticosteroids to keep the itching under control. This medication may be needed for several months at a time, or even on a year-round basis for some dogs. Because of their side effects, you may not wish to keep the dog on corticosteroids for a prolonged period of time.

Desensitization may be used in dogs, much as it is in humans with hay fever. To desensitize the dog, one must first know exactly which substances are causing the problem. Your veterinarian will use one of two tests to determine this.

The first test for atopy is the skin (intradermal) test. Ideally, for this test, the dog must be kept off corticosteroids for one week for every month that he has been on them. If he has not been under treatment, then this step is not necessary. He should be kept off other drugs for seven to 10 days. He is then kept off food (a total fast, except for water) for 12 hours before the testing is done. If the dog has a severe skin problem, he should not be left in misery during this waiting period. Treatment with soothing baths, antibiotics to control skin infection, and, possibly, short-term oral corticosteroids do not interfere with skin testing.

The dog may be lightly sedated if necessary. His belly or chest is clipped, and tiny amounts of the testing materials (called antigens) are injected. Antigens are extracts of possible offending substances—foods which are commonly in dog foods, plants which are common in the area and substances which are found in the dog's home. Each extract is injected separately. For instance, elm tree extract and oak tree extract would be injected into different spots and marked (or mapped) so that the tester knows where each one was done.

The injections are placed between the layers of skin (intradermally). This makes small bumps which will remain for several days. The tests will be evaluated ("read") in 15 to 30 minutes after injection. Those which have swollen or reddened (or both) are considered to be positive. In unusual cases, reactions may be seen as much as 24 hours after the tests are done. If your veterinarian hasn't mentioned it, it may be worth checking your dog the day after his tests. Notify your veterinarian if any of the spots are swollen, reddened or otherwise abnormal. He may want to have you bring the dog back so that he can see which spots have reacted. It is important that the tests be evaluated by someone who does the testing frequently, and is familiar with reading them. These tests never discover all the dog's allergies, but should discover the ones which are giving him the most trouble. If those are then treated, improvement can be expected.

Skin testing has disadvantages. It must be performed and read by someone trained and experienced with the procedure. Also, the same antigen from different suppliers may give different results.

The other basic form of allergy tests is a "blood test." This is a test which measures substances in blood serum to determine the materials causing the allergies. One of these is called the ELISA test. Another is called the RAST test. The advantage is that the blood tests are easier to use and "read." However, many veterinarians feel that skin testing is more accurate than the blood tests, if the skin testing is done by a trained, experienced person.

Avoiding the substances to which the dog is allergic is the best means of preventing these skin allergies. Unfortunately, it is not always practical. If, for instance, he is allergic to Bermuda grass (which is common in southern dogs), romps on the lawn may have to be severely limited during the season in which it is pollinating. Keeping the lawn mowed short so that it does not pollinate will also be helpful. If the dog is allergic to weeds or trees which have only a short pollinating season in your area, avoidance may be the best control. It will save your pet the discomfort of desensitization treatment. If the dog is allergic to pollen, it may be helpful to keep him indoors much of the day. Air conditioners allow the windows to be closed, keeping pollen exposure to a minimum.

Molds are worse at night, unless the dog spends the day in a basement or outdoors. Molds may be as bad indoors as outdoors. You can do a crude test for molds in the house by putting slices of potato in saucers. Add just enough water to keep them moist. Place them in various areas of your house. You can later compare the slices with each other to see which area has the largest amount of molds (Ackerman, 1988). Old houses with damp, musty basements have plenty of mold, as do houses near marshes or lakes. Dogs are best kept out of most basements if at all possible. If you need to have the dog in the basement, paint the floor and walls with a mold-resistant paint. Humidifiers, vaporizers and air conditioners are all good places for molds to grow. They should be cleaned frequently, and kept in good working order. Dehumidifiers reduce the amount of molds and dust mites, and may be helpful. Electronic air cleaners sometimes work well. Vacuum and dust frequently, at least once a week. Put the dog outside for two to four hours after you vacuum so that he can avoid the dust which hangs in the air after vacuuming. Or vacuum right before you run errands and take him with you.

Your bedding, as well as the dog's, should be washed frequently. Avoid comforters and pillows filled with down or kapok, as the dog may be allergic to them. Wash synthetic pillows once a year to keep them dust-free. House plants grow large quantities of molds. Remove them if possible. If you wish to keep them, spread fish tank charcoal over the surface of the soil. Aquariums can be an important source of mold. Add algae killer to the water, and carefully disinfect all decorations when you clean the tank.

Control house dust as much as possible, especially in the room where the dog spends most of his time. Use a dog bed stuffed with synthetic materials. A room without carpeting will help to keep down dust that bothers the dog. Keep the dog well groomed, as well as any other pets that you own. Clean or change furnace ducts and filters often. Dust furniture and other surfaces with dampened paper towels or rags which can be thrown away after use. Perfumes, cleaning products with strong odors, and smoke from fireplaces or smoking may also bother the dog.

After the tests have been performed to determine the substances to which the dog is allergic, he can be placed on a course of treatment (desensitization). This treatment uses a mixture of antigens put together for your dog's specific needs. In most cases, not more than 10 antigens are put into the mixture. If the dog has a very large number of substances to which he reacts strongly, it may be necessary to have two different antigen mixtures made. They can then be administered alternately.

These "allergy shots" are given once or twice a week. The dog should be watched closely for one or two hours after each injection to make sure there are no reactions to it. If a reaction does occur, epinephrine may be used for treatment, at 0.2 ml – 0.5 ml of a 1:10,000 solution. This can be repeated every 20-30 minutes as needed. Give oxygen if you have it available. It is worth sitting at the veterinarian's office 10 to 20 minutes after each injection in case there is an immediate reaction.

Eight to 12 months of treatment may be needed before any relief is seen. If the problem is seasonal, you may see relief, only to have the allergies return at the next pollen season. Over a period of time, the dog's allergies may change, or he may acquire new ones. This is especially true of young dogs. It may be necessary to retest the dog and change his antigen mixture as needed.

Other dogs may never show benefit from the program, and for them it should be discontinued. Each animal is unique, and can only respond to treatment as allowed by his own immune system.

Food extracts, while used for testing, are usually not put into treatment mixtures. This is because desensitization to foods is not very effective. Keeping the dog off the offending foods works much better. There is a special dog food made for dogs who have food allergies. It is made of mutton and lamb, and is free of foods such as wheat and corn, to which most allergic dogs react. In many cases, the simplest and kindest course of action is simply to feed this diet for the rest of the dog's life.

If the dog is old, or you do not wish to have desensitization treatments for him, corticosteroid drugs may be given, either by injection or in the form of tablets. These may be sufficient to control the allergies for the remainder of the animal's life. Antibiotics may be given to control infection where the dog has damaged the skin. Antihistamines work well on only about one-third of the dogs on which they are used. When they do work, however, they work well, and can be used for long periods of time if needed. Dietary supplements containing omega-3 fatty acids (DHA, DPA and EPA) are helpful to some dogs, and may be used with or without immunotherapy. They do not seem to have any harmful side effects. Products such as vitamin C and aloe vera have been tried, but do not seem to work well. Medicated baths may also be helpful for some dogs. The benefit is short-lived, and frequent baths may be needed. Use a hypoallergenic or sulfur-based shampoo. Baths may give the dog some relief until a program of medication or testing and desensitization can be started. Oil rinses containing essential fatty acids, or sprays or lotions containing these acids, may give the dog temporary relief. These products can also help to reduce the amount of corticosteroids needed during the early phases of treatment. For some dogs, putting on a sweater or vest may be very helpful, if only by reducing the amount of damage he does to himself by scratching and chewing. It's worth a try.

HAIR LOSS (ALOPECIA)

Alopecia is a general name given to hair loss anywhere on the dog's body. Generally the skin will appear healthy, just bare. Hair loss may be due to physical causes. The dog may have gotten tar or glue into his hair, and pulled out the hair while trying to clean out the mats. A child may have taken a pair of scissors or knife and snipped out a patch of hair. Or the dog may have chewed out a patch of hair on his leg because of nervousness or irritation.

Hair loss may be due to hormonal excesses or deficiencies. Alopecia due to hormonal causes often occurs as a pattern of thin or missing hair which matches symmetrically from one side to the other. Hair loss is not a disease, but a symptom of an underlying cause which must be found and cured before the hair will return.

Chapter 12

EXTERNAL PARASITES

FLEAS

Fleas are hard-shelled, six-legged wingless insects. They are reddish, brown or black. While they are only about 1/32nd of an inch long (less than 1 mm), they may leap as much as eight inches high and 12 inches distant (20 cm/30 cm). These prodigious feats are due to their extremely strong legs. Fleas reproduce quickly. One mating pair, which may live as long as a year, can create 250,000 progeny in that year. Fleas do not do well in very cold areas such as the northern United States and parts of Canada. They do not thrive in hot, dry climates, or in high altitudes such as Colorado and Wyoming. However, everywhere else seems to be perfect, from the flea's viewpoint.

Fleas are perhaps THE most important external parasite which infests dogs. *Ctenocephalides felis* is the most common flea species in the United States. It infests both dogs and cats. If they're not handy, these fleas are not above nipping the nearest human! These fleas will die in one and a half to two months without a blood meal from a dog or cat. Human blood does not have the components needed for their reproduction. *Ctenocephalides canis* is sometimes found on dogs in the United States. The human flea, *Pulex irritans*, is often found on dogs, especially in Mississippi and Georgia. Fleas which otherwise infest poultry are also seen on dogs and cats in the southeastern United States. Different species of fleas infest wild animals, but these do not seem to affect domestic dogs and cats. Fleas can serve as intermediate hosts for some other parasites such as tapeworms, and for some infectious diseases such as plague. They can carry the tapeworm *Dipylidium caninum* to a small child (or the dog himself) who accidentally swallows a live or dead flea.

SEX AND THE SINGLE FLEA

Understanding the life cycle of the flea helps us understand how to get rid of them, both on the dog and on our premises. Adults of *Ctenocephalides felis* must have a meal of dog or cat blood in order to reproduce. The young adult flea must find one of these animals and get lunch before it can mate and lay eggs. Given a choice, the adult flea will spend its entire life on the dog or cat, unless it falls off or is removed by scratching. Tapeworms may be passed to the dog who accidentally eats a few fleas while grooming himself or chewing at his miserable, itching skin.

The female lays small whitish eggs, mostly on the dog or cat's hair. These eggs fall off into the animal's bedding, onto the carpet and lawn, and everywhere else the pet goes. A female flea may lay 20 to 30 eggs per day and several hundred during her lifetime, especially if she has frequent blood meals. The eggs incubate two days to two weeks before hatching.

The flea eggs hatch into tiny whitish maggot-like larvae. These larvae feed on any organic material which is handy, such as dandruff from the pet, dried blood, or feces from the adult fleas. These larvae burrow down into the lawn, carpet, or cracks in tile or flooring. They grow and molt twice, in a time span of one week to six months. This may occur in as little as two or three weeks inside your house, where they are not susceptible to sunlight, drying or freezing. Now the flea larva is in the third stage in which it spins a white cocoon. In a few days, a pupa is formed inside the cocoon. Favorable conditions for speedy completion of the life cycle include a high relative humidity (70%-85%), and a temperature of 65 to 85 degrees F (18.3 to 29.4 C). These are nearly year-round conditions in much of the southern and southeastern United States! Vibrations from a person or pet moving around in the vicinity of the pupa seem to stimulate it to emerge as a young adult.

Under ideal conditions, the flea's entire life cycle may be completed in two to three weeks. It may take as long as a year if the conditions are not as favorable. The instant the flea emerges from its cocoon, it begins looking for dinner... your dog, your cat, you... . From egg to death of the adult, the flea's entire lifetime may be around six months to a year. If its surroundings are suitably humid, the flea may live four months to a year without a meal. Fleas spend as much as 90% of their life cycle elsewhere than on host animals. Adult fleas are thought to prefer to stay on the host animal if at all possible. However, at any given time, only about one flea in a hundred will be an adult. The rest of the population will be in the egg, larval, or pupal stages. These immature stages MUST be eliminated if you are going to get control of the 1% that you can SEE!

FLEA ALLERGY

Flea allergy (flea bite dermatitis) is one of the most common causes of severe itching in the dog. This reaction develops after the dog has been bitten by fleas. His body develops antibodies against the flea saliva. Six to 10 weeks later, when he is bitten by a flea, he may itch intensely from the allergic reaction that has developed. Then he scratches intensely! Pretty soon, he has reddened sores from pawing and chewing at himself. He's miserable, and you're miserable because he's miserable. If the situation is allowed to continue, real damage to the dog's skin can take place.

Some of the most severe cases of flea bite dermatitis occur in dogs which have grown up in northern states and have been moved to flea-infested areas later in life. Many southern dogs who have been exposed to fleas all their lives have a minimal problem with flea allergy. Dogs who have continued exposure to fleas may have less problem with allergy than dogs who intermittently have fleas. Perhaps the dogs develop a resistance to the flea bites. For your dog's sake, it might be better for him to have a few fleas all the time rather than to be rid of all of them and then get them back again. For that reason, you should either make a full commitment to getting rid of fleas, or decide to let the dog live with a few fleas all the time. Off-and-on, half-hearted attempts to eliminate them will only set the stage for flea bite dermatitis.

Dogs who are not allergic to fleas may carry large numbers of them without noticeable problems. Those who are allergic to fleas develop small bumps, much as we get with a mosquito bite. These may go away without further problem. Flea bite dermatitis begins when the bumps develop into an itching, crusted pimple. These bumps are especially seen over the loins and back, inside of the thighs, flanks, belly and neck. If the dog is severely sensitive to the bites, lesions may occur all over the body. All this itching causes the dog to scratch severely. First the skin becomes reddened. Then the dog may scratch it with his toenails as he tries to relieve the itching. These scratches may become infected, oozing pus. Areas of broken hairs may be noticed where the dog has scratched continuously. An odorous seborrhea may accompany the other signs. If the dog continues to damage his skin for a long period of time, it may become thickened, wrinkled, and pigmented with brownish or blackish material. Staph dermatitis (pyoderma) may accompany the skin damage. If the allergy and its itching and infection cause the dog enough trouble, he may lose weight and become anemic.

Dogs commonly develop flea-bite allergies between three and seven years of age. Occasional cases are seen in puppies as young as six months, or in old dogs. In moderate climates, the dermatitis may be more common in the spring and fall.

Flea bite allergy (dermatitis) is a more severe problem in dogs who have other allergies, whether to food or to inhaled materials. Their strong reaction to the bites is related to their generally overstimulated immune systems. Diseases such as sarcoptic mange may also be present, complicating the allergic problem. Skin testing is sometimes used to confirm that the dog's problem is flea bite allergy. Skin testing for flea allergy is quite accurate.

Desensitization injections can be very helpful for some dogs with flea bite allergy. These injections will be needed for varying lengths of time. In some cases, they may be needed for the rest of the dog's life. (For further discussion of desensitization for allergies, see Atopy). Some dogs will need antibiotic treatment for the eczema or dermatitis which has occurred. Some will need corticosteroids to reduce the inflammation, irritation and itching. Doses of antihistamines may also be needed.

FLEE, FLEA

It is a good idea to consult your veterinarian for current techniques of flea control. He can recommend a combination of products for your dog (and cat), house and yard, which are compatible and effective. He can correlate factors which may influence your choice of products, such as whether or not you have small children or exotic pets. Each program must be tailored individually for the size of the indoor and outdoor areas which are involved, as well as the time of the year. The program will depend on whether you live in an area where there is freezing weather part of the year, or whether the climate is moderate year-round. Also, some insecticides work well in one part of the country, but are nearly useless in other parts because the pests have developed a resistance to them.

Because of the mobile, on-the-pet, off-the-pet nature of fleas, it does little good to treat your house and leave the yard untreated, or to bathe the dog and leave the car that he rides in untouched. It's much more effective simply to declare war on the little beasts, and dedicate one day every two weeks for a month or so to eradicating them if that is the way you've decided to go. Remember, off-and-on, half-hearted measures don't work. Then you can go to one day every two to three months for a maintenance program.

Reinfestation is the biggest reason for failure in flea control. Fleas come back into the house, carried by the dog, the cat and the people. Some people wonder why they should fight fleas in the summer when the dog will just go outside and get more of them. Why not wait until the weather gets cold and take care of it then? Because it won't work. While you are waiting for cold weather to arrive, fleas are becoming firmly entrenched in your house and yard and reproducing like crazy, guaranteeing that you are going to have a long, hard battle to eliminate them. Fleas can remain frozen for many months and thaw out, good as new. Each flea that you don't get this year is one more that starts the next year. Meanwhile, your pet has suffered several months of needless misery, especially if he is allergic to the flea bites. Most household flea problems start with just a few fleas infesting the pet, and multiply from there. The key strategy is to act before the few become many.

Prevention should begin before the flea season starts. This varies from one part of the country to another. The pet should be dipped as soon as fleas start. Spraying the premises and house should begin no more than 2 1/2 weeks after dipping the dog.

Sanitation is an important part of flea control, both indoors and out. It should be done before any insecticidal products are used. Vacuuming indoors helps to remove flea eggs and larvae from carpeting. Vacuum carpets and corners, under the sofa and chair cushions, inside closets, and between the mattresses and box springs. Spray an insecticide into the vacuum cleaner bag and discard it when you are finished. CAUTION: It is not safe to put moth balls in a closed vacuum cleaner bag while you are using it, as the fumes which are generated may be both toxic and explosive. Do not put a piece of insect strip or flea collar in the vacuum cleaner bag, as the vacuum cleaner motor may spread unsafely high levels of the product throughout the house.

Having your carpet steam cleaned is quite effective in removing and killing the eggs and developing stages of the fleas. Ask the cleaning company to use an insecticide in the cleaning solution. Or you can buy the appropriate product where you rent the steam cleaning machine if you plan to do it yourself. Mop the floor using normal household cleaners. Take special care to clean dirt and debris out of cracks and corners. This will keep flea eggs and the organic material on which the larvae feed from accumulating. Caulk holes and cracks in the walls and mopboards. This alone will eliminate a large number of fleas. They're in there, but they can't get out.

The dog's bed should be washed thoroughly, and dried at as hot a temperature as possible to kill fleas which have fallen off the animal. The same cleaning should be used for any throw rugs, sofa throws and pillows where the dog spends time. If he spends time on your bed, wash all that bedding, too. If you use disposable bedding for the dog, throw it away once a week during the initial phase of the flea war. Discard it in a sealed plastic bag, preferably after spraying it with an insecticide.

Outdoor cleanup is just as important before you treat the premises with insecticide. Mow the lawn. Rake up all dead leaves, weeds and thatch from the lawn and yard. Houses on pilings and house trailers on blocks will require special treatment and cleaning underneath in the crawl space to eliminate trash which harbors the fleas. Remove rotting lumber, and plan to treat your woodpile along with the rest of the yard. Haul the debris away so that the fleas go with it. Bermuda grass and similar lawns have runners along the surface which make good living places for fleas. Controlling fleas is harder in these lawns than in bluegrass and ryegrass lawns. Places where the dog sleeps outdoors need special treatment, both in cleaning and in treatment with insecticides. If the dog has dug holes in the yard or under his house, these should be treated for fleas.

For more information on cleaning up for pest control, in addition to a wealth of general advice on pet cleanup, see the book, "Pet Cleanup Made Easy" by Don Aslett (Writer's Digest Books, 1507 Dana Avenue, Cincinnati, Ohio, 45207). I highly recommend this book to any pet owner!

There are no flea control products which kill the flea eggs. For this reason, you have to treat, AND KEEP ON TREATING, until you have killed all the fleas which hatch from the eggs which are on your pet and premises. Then, your job is to keep the dog from becoming reinfected. This is why one intensive campaign, with careful cleaning, will make a good start toward the effective, safe elimination of fleas. Many flea control programs begin with treating pets, house and premises on day one, day 14, and again on day 30. After this careful beginning, you can treat every two to three months.

Which product should you use? Literally hundreds of them are available, in forms from shampoos to foggers to mists to dusts—and everything in between. There is no such thing as a perfect flea control product. As with any other pesticide, these chemicals must strike a delicate balance between toxicity to the pest and toxicity to us, our children and our animals. And we are constantly dealing with pesticide resistance in fleas, just as we see with other insects and with intestinal parasites.

A sample program for a household with young children, and with sensitive pets such as birds or cats, might be as follows. This program can be used with dogs who are being given systemic organophosphate insecticides such as fenthion or cythioate, PROVIDED you choose a house and yard insecticide different than organophosphate or carbamate.

Day 1. Thoroughly clean house as above. Spray all surfaces, crevices, and the bottom couple of feet up the drapes and walls with an insecticidal spray. Do NOT use one which contains carbamates or organophosphates. Follow this with foggers meant to kill adult fleas. Before spraying, remove birds, fish or other pets from the area. Take out all their food and water dishes. Be sure to cover or remove all the people food too. Air the house well before you (and the pets) return. Several hours after the fogging is completed, wash both food and water containers and fill them with fresh contents. Wash any people dishes and utensils that were exposed to the insecticide. The entire house must be done at one time. Otherwise, fleas just move from one room to another. For the dog house and garage, use products made for indoor use. If you have sprayed the house with a microencapsulated product, avoid vacuuming as long as possible to allow the microcapsules to work. The microcapsules release the active ingredient over a period of time.

Clean the yard. In the evening, cover it with a spray or dust, being careful to work the material into all corners and crevices, around plants, into bushes and under low trees. Be sure to treat the children's sandbox. Dusts or granular products can be applied with a fertilizer spreader. The next day, water it in thoroughly. Allow the area to dry completely before you return your pet (or children!) to it. When you treat the dog house, be sure to spray it inside and out—roof, ceiling, floor and walls. If the dog gets into a crawl space or under the porch, this area should also be treated.

Do not give the dog fenthion or cythioate on the same day you treat the premises or house. Treat your cat at the same time with a product which is appropriate for cats.

Day 14. Same as day one, including the cleaning.

Day 30 or 31. Repeat the whole process again for the third time.

From then on, clean and treat the house every two to three months just like day one. Every two weeks retreat the yard and premises, cleaning as necessary. Do this as long as the nighttime temperature is above 50 degrees F (10 degrees C).

You can treat your dog by dipping or shampooing him instead of giving him a systemic insecticide. Again, be sure not to use an organophosphate or carbamate insecticide on a dog at the same time you are using these products to treat the house or yard. Otherwise, your dog may receive an overdose. If you are using a pyrethrin-type product in the yard, this can be used on the dog at the same time without problems. Microencapsulated products last for varying periods of time; consult product directions for reapplication intervals.

Carbamates and organphosphates belong to a class of chemicals called cholinesterase inhibitors. If you are looking for a product without these, it may say, "does not contain cholinesterase inhibitor."

For dogs who are NOT on a carbamate or organophosphate insecticide, products such as malathion are good to use in the yard. Foggers containing methoprene use insect growth hormones to kill the larvae, and can be used in conjunction with any other insecticide. These products work well in the house.

You can call in an exterminator to treat the house and premises, while, at the same time, you take the dogs and cats to the veterinarian or groomer for a dipping or treatment. However, cleaning before the exterminator arrives is essential. One problem with exterminators is that they sometimes treat only the perimeter of the room, which does not get rid of the fleas. It is necessary to treat the carpeting, furniture, under the furniture, a foot or two up every wall, and the lower part of the draperies to reach all the areas where fleas commonly hide. Be sure to treat all rooms in your house, whether your pet frequents them or not. You have probably carried some fleas around on your body as you go back and forth, and you do not want to leave any safe haven for the pests. Discuss the job you want done with the exterminator to be sure he understands how thorough you want him to be. Also find out what insecticide he will be using so you can tell the veterinarian or groomer.

FLEA CONTROL PRODUCTS

This section is merely a once-over of flea control formulations which are available. New products are being developed every day, and old ones are being removed from the market.

Flea control products come in a wide variety of forms: shampoos, dips, dusts, powders, sprays (both water- and alcohol-based), mousses (foams), foggers, mixed, unmixed, and any other way a manufacturer thinks you may buy the product. You should have no problem finding the product(s) you need for your particular situation.

Shampoos are primarily used to clean the dog's skin and haircoat. Shampoo ingredients themselves will kill some of the fleas living on the dog. In addition, the shampoo may contain pyrethrin-type products to kill fleas present at the time he is bathed. These generally do not have any residual killing effect for flea control. For that reason, the shampoo won't kill any fleas picked up after the dog is bathed.

Shampooing may be followed by a dip or spray with residual killing action. If you plan treatment after bathing the dog, be sure to dry him with a towel so that the dip or spray that you use isn't diluted by water in the dog's coat. Some flea shampoos do contain an insecticide with residual action, such as carbamate insecticides. If you are using one of these shampoos, do not dip

or spray the dog, nor treat the premises at the same time with a carbamate or organophosphate-type product.

Dips are meant to have some residual activity against fleas. For that reason, they are not to be rinsed out of the dog's coat, but should be allowed to dry there. The dog should not be towel dried after the dip is applied. Allow him to dry naturally, or use a blow dryer. Confine the dog while he is drying so that he does not roll and rub the dip out of his hair. Most dips should not be used on puppies less than four months of age unless recommended by your veterinarian.

Dipping may be done in a vat of prepared insecticide. Many veterinary clinics and dog pounds in the south keep a vat mixed up and ready at all times. Or the "dip" compound may be sponged onto the dog. In addition to the residual effect, dips give good immediate kill of the fleas when the dog is well saturated with the product so that it makes contact with the fleas. Dips can soak into a thick or matted haircoat better than a spray. It is a good idea to wear rubber gloves while you are applying the dip.

Be sure to mix a dip according to directions. With insecticides of any kind, it's not true that if "a little bit is good, a lot is better." A "lot" may be fatal! Most dips cannot be stored for more than about a day after they are mixed and still retain their effectiveness. Mix each batch fresh, right before you are ready to use it. Be careful when discarding leftover dip so that you do not put it where an animal might drink it, or contaminate a water supply. Some of the insecticides in a dip will kill fish, so be careful that it doesn't run into a stream.

Dusts or powders were once the most common method of flea control on pets. They have been largely replaced by sprays. Dusts often have some repellent activity in addition to killing fleas. They are still convenient for use on the dog's bedding, and for parts of the yard where he often sleeps. Dusts are also among the safest of flea control products to use. One disadvantage is that they leave a visible coating on the dog, you, the floor, and anything else that gets in the way. Some dusts are useful for treating carpet and flooring, furniture and vacuum cleaner bags before they are discarded.

Flea powders are convenient to use when you are grooming the dog. They can be combed into the coat as you groom, pulling the hair backward and working the dust down toward the skin. Put the combings in a plastic bag and sprinkle them with flea powder before you throw them away. A flea powder containing 5% carbaryl can be mixed half-and-half with talcum powder. This gives a 2-1/2% product which is safe for use on puppies and kittens.

Powders do not work well on dogs with dense undercoats, such as Chows and Siberian Huskies. They also may not work well on dogs such as Dachshunds, which merely shake them off.

Sprays or mists give a quicker kill of adult fleas living on the dog than do dusts or powders. They are also easier to apply to the underside of the dog than are dusts. Many pump-type sprayers are well tolerated by even shy dogs. They have the disadvantage of giving your hand quite a workout if you are using them on a very large dog. These products are usually pre-mixed and ready to use straight from the sprayer. But read the directions to make sure.

You can lift the dog's coat with a comb as you are spraying, which will allow the spray to penetrate better. The dog should be well dampened but not soaked. Sprays can be used from time to time on your grooming tools to kill any fleas that might linger there.

Aerosol flea sprays are available for use on pets. Some can be used on either dogs or cats, if the animal will tolerate the noise and air blowing on him. These usually cost about twice as much as pump spray products. If you are concerned about the environment, try to find an aerosol that doesn't use a fluorocarbon as the propellant.

Sprays which are meant for animals can be used on the dog's bedding, or on your furniture or carpet. However, they are usually much more expensive than sprays meant for that purpose. And they often contain coat conditioners, repellents and other ingredients which don't do your carpet any good.

When applying spray to an animal, be sure not to get the spray into his eyes, nose or mouth. Puff a bit of the spray onto a cotton ball and wipe it around the dog's face. Make up a routine and use it each time that you spray so that you don't miss any spots. Be sure to spray between the toes and footpads where fleas can hide. As much as possible, try to keep the dog from licking himself after the spraying.

Many sprays are formulated for use outdoors in the kennel or yard. The concentrated form is often called an emulsifiable concentrate. These are usually applied with a garden-type sprayer after diluting them with water to the proper mix. Most of these products contain either carbamate or organophosphate insecticides, which give a reasonably good residual insecticidal action. Otherwise, you would have to spray every day. These products often have a strong and rather unpleasant odor. Do not use a yard or kennel spray on your dog. It may contain compounds as carriers which are harmful to the dog, the product itself may be harmful. A few products are available which can be used as either dips or premise sprays. If you use one of these, read the label carefully to avoid giving your dog an overdose. The concentrations may differ for the different uses.

Some ready-to-use sprays are diluted in water. These are generally cheaper than others, which are diluted in alcohol. Water-based sprays do not soak into a greasy coat, which is a problem if your dog has seborrhea. They are slow to dry on both animals and fabrics. On the other hand, they don't catch fire.

Alcohol-based sprays cost much more than those mixed with water. They catch fire easily, so the freshly treated dog, furniture, carpet and other items must be kept away from fire and flame. One advantage is that they dry quickly. Another is that the alcohol penetrates the flea's shell very easily, giving a much more rapid effect than do water-based sprays. In addition to the fire hazard, there are several disadvantages to alcohol-based products: The alcohol may dry out the dog's coat; it may be irritating to inflamed or injured skin. The alcohol may damage some plastics and wood finishes. It is very important that sprays with an alcohol base be applied in an area with good ventilation.

Sprayers which are used for diluting and applying indoor or outdoor insecticides should be washed well with soap and water after use. Otherwise, seals and hoses may be damaged by long-term exposure to the organic solvents.

Foams or mousses are now available for flea control. Some of these contain microencapsulated pyrethrins. The pyrethrin-type insecticide is enclosed in microscopic capsules to give a long-term release of the insecticide. Foams are good for use on nervous dogs. You spray the foam onto your hand and then rub it into the dog's coat. An example of a foam product is Sectrol Two-Way Flea Foam (Animal Care Products/3M).

Foggers or bombs are used indoors. While the label on the can may say it will treat several thousand square feet, in reality most of the fog falls within 15 or 20 feet of the container. The material does not go into the corners of rooms and through doors very well. For these reasons, it is usually more effective to use one smaller fogger for each room. Foggers also do not treat behind draperies and under furniture, including tables and chairs. If you have a serious pest problem, it is best to spray under furniture, behind drapes and behind things in the closets before fogging.

The insecticides contained in foggers are effective against fleas, as well as ticks and mites. They have the added advantage of getting rid of flies and moths. Most foggers contain an organophosphate insecticide with residual action. This residual action on the carpet often does a good job against the larval stages of fleas. Until you are sure that you have the flea problem under control, it is a good idea to spray and fog every room twice a month. Usually, if combined with good sanitation, this can be done for three treatments, and then the household can be put on an every-two-to-three-month schedule for fogging and spraying.

Systemic flea control products are used in the dog to control fleas, ticks, lice, and other sucking and biting pests. They kill the pest when it feeds on the dog's blood or body fluids. One of these products, Proban® (Haver) is given orally as a liquid or tablet. It contains an organophosphate insecticide which then spreads throughout the dog's body. It works quite effectively to kill adult fleas on the dog. It begins to work within two to three hours after treatment, with peak action about eight hours later. It seems to be safe, convenient and effective. It is used on a year-round basis in many parts of the southern United States.

Systemic insecticides should not be given to dogs that are sick, that have kidney or liver problems, that are recovering from surgery, or that are stressed. Depending on what your veterinarian recommends, Proban® is given every three days or twice a week. This seems to be often enough to break the fleas' life cycle. Proban® should not be used when any other carbamate or organophosphate insecticide will be applied to the house or yard. It is safe to use it along with pyrethrins, rotenone, and methoxychlor. If your dog needs to be anesthetized, be sure to tell the veterinarian that the dog has been on Proban® if he was not the one who prescribed the drug.

Systemic insecticides do not work well on dogs with flea allergies. The flea must bite the dog in order to be killed. Meanwhile, when it bites, it injects the saliva which causes the problem in the first place. The dog still gets a reaction because of the saliva, and he keeps right on itching. Non-systemic products which contain flea repellents in addition to flea-killing insecticides are good to use on allergic dogs. These help keep the fleas from climbing onto the dog at all. The lack of effectiveness of systemic insecticides for allergic dogs applies equally to the "drop-on" insecticide, fenthion.

Fenthion is also a systemic organophosphate insecticide. It is currently formulated for use by dropping a measured amount on a spot between the dog's shoulder blades. It is absorbed through the skin and spreads throughout the body much like Proban®, mentioned above. One formulation is Pro-Spot™ (Haver). Again, it kills the flea that bites the dog. This drug is not effective against ticks. Almost all of the drug is absorbed within eight hours after application. The dog can then swim or be bathed. The dose is repeated every two weeks. As with Proban®, be sure to tell your veterinarian that the dog is being treated with the product and when the last treatment was if he needs to be anesthetized for any reason. Fenthion should not be used on dogs less than 10 weeks of age. It should not be used at the same time as organophosphate or carbamate sprays are being used on the house or yard. It should be used with caution on dogs who live in households with young children or elderly people. The dog should not be touched for two hours after application. Organophosphates aren't just hazardous to fleas. They can harm people too.

Insect growth regulators are among the latest entries into the flea-control arsenal. One of these products is methoprene (Precor® Vet-Kem). This hormone keeps the flea pupae from changing into adults, and they eventually die without reproducing. It comes as a spray for use on dogs. It is rapidly degraded by ultraviolet light when sprayed on premises outdoors. However, it seems to be stable when sprayed on the dog. It is very safe. Methoprene is good to use in areas where babies will be crawling. Because it does not kill adult fleas, methoprene should be used on the dog along with a fast-acting product which will kill the pests. Methoprene is also available in foggers. These products give good long-term flea-killing action. Some foggers also contain a fast-acting insecticide to kill the adult fleas. Read the label carefully to see which one you are getting.

Flea collars are plastic strips impregnated with an insecticide which is released slowly. The collar has the disadvantage of being near the dog's head, while most of the fleas are on the dog's back, hind legs and tail. Flea collars only kill the small percentage of fleas which are near his head. They are convenient, but are only a small part of the flea control picture. They don't do much by themselves.

When you buy the flea collar, make sure it is fresh. Change it at the recommended intervals, whether three months or up to a year, to keep it effective. Make sure that there is at least an inch of space between the dog's neck and the collar. This space will allow the dog to pull his head out of the collar if he gets caught by it, and it prevents the insecticide from irritating his skin so much. A breakaway collar which will release and fall off if the dog gets caught is an excellent safety feature.

Flea collars work better on smaller dogs with short hair than they do on giant longhaired ones. Never use a flea collar on a puppy less than two months old. Do not put one on a sick pet, or a dog who does not have fleas. Flea collars are not very

helpful to dogs with flea allergies, as the flea is already on the dog and biting before the collar can kill him. Besides, the fleas living and biting near the dog's tail can do so in perfect safety, unthreatened by the collar.

Check the dog frequently to make sure there are no sores, reddened spots or areas of hair loss under the collar. Some dogs have severe allergic reactions to these collars. The reaction may be bad enough to require your veterinarian to treat it with antibiotics and other medications, especially if the problem goes for some time before you notice it. Some owners and veterinarians prefer to air out the collar for two or three days before it is put on the dog. Airing it helps to reduce the initial high concentration of chemical present in a fresh collar.

If the flea collar becomes wet, it can release much more insecticide than it is supposed to. Remove it immediately if the dog is out in the rain or has gone swimming. Put it back on after the collar and the dog have had half a day to a day to dry.

If you suspect that your dog will need surgery, take off the flea collar immediately. But BE SURE to tell your veterinarian that you have done so, as he will take this into account when administering anesthetic to the dog. Take it off four or five days before scheduled surgery such as a spay or neuter. Again, be sure to tell the veterinarian.

Flea traps can be used because fleas, like other insects, are attracted to light. You can make a flea trap by setting a lamp (safely secured so it will not tip) over a pan of water. Put a few drops of dishwashing detergent into the water to break the surface tension so the fleas will sink and drown. Or you can buy a trap which has a light and uses a sticky surface to catch the fleas. One example is the Pulvex Flea Trap (Zema Corporation, P.O. Box 12803, Research Triangle Park, N.C., 27709, or at your feed store or pet shop).

Traps can be used in one room until you no longer catch fleas, and then taken to another room. Be sure to rotate it back through each room within about 15-20 days to catch the new crop of pests as they hatch and mature.

A flea comb with very fine teeth (30 or more per inch) can be purchased at the drugstore or pet shop. This comb can be used to remove fleas from tiny puppies and kittens. Use it along with cleaning and spraying the house or premises to minimize the flea load until the young animals are old enough to tolerate being treated with insecticides.

Dog beds filled with cedar shavings are a nice touch. They are considered to repel fleas, but this has not been proven. They probably do a better job if a bit of flea powder is dusted onto the covering! A cedar bed may be less prone than others to absorb "doggy odor."

Avon's Skin-So-Soft bath oil seems to act as a flea repellent, reducing the number of fleas on the dog. Use 3 tablespoons (45 ml) per gallon of water as a final rinse when you bathe your dog. Or you can mix it with flea dip to give added protection.

Citrus extract (d-limonene) is derived from the peel of citrus fruits. Some of these products have caused toxic reactions in cats. If you wish to use them, Hill's VIP Products is one reliable brand which is available. They seem to be fairly effective at killing fleas, but they may not offer the residual insecticidal action that pyrethrin products do.

"Natural" flea-control products vary from somewhat workable to totally useless for anything except separating you from your money. Giving the dog sulfur or garlic does not seem to help control the flea problem. In addition, anemia is sometimes seen in dogs who are fed garlic pearls. Doses of thiamine (one of the B vitamins) has been proven to be ineffective against fleas (Halliwell, 1982).

In one study, brewer's yeast was given to dogs at the rate of 50 mg/lb/day (110 mg/kg/day). Dogs who were given the yeast had 55% fewer fleas compared to dogs not given it. It does not prevent fleas, but does seem to lessen the load a bit (Bradley, 1983).

Ultrasonic boxes for use in the house do not seem to be helpful, and may eventually cause damage to your ears. Fleas do not have ears. They are attracted to dogs by the dog's body heat, the vibrations as the dog moves by, the change in light level caused by the dog's presence, and the increase of carbon dioxide in the area from the dog's breath.

Diatomaceous earth, boric acid and silica gel are sometimes recommended for flea control. They act to kill the fleas by drying out their body fluids. Boric acid is found in 20 Mule Team Borax laundry detergent. Diatomaceous earth is used in swimming pool filters, and can be purchased from pool suppliers. These products have a very abrasive structure, and can rapidly cut through the fibers on your carpet and the upholstery on your furniture. They do seem to be fairly effective, however, at killing fleas.

GENERAL CONSIDERATIONS

One of the best flea control measures is to make your dog a strictly indoor dog, with trips outdoors only on a leash to a specific location. Take the dog out several times a day to urinate and defecate. This is especially easy with toy dogs. You will have a much better chance of flea control than with the free-running dog.

Watch where you walk your dog. It may be worth driving him to the woods or a park which is out of the way rather than to take him hiking down the streets where plenty of other dogs have left fleas and ticks for him to pick up. If you go to the woods in an area where Lyme disease is present, take appropriate precautions for you and your dog. Ask your local health department for details on your locale.

For young puppies, use an insecticide only on your veterinarian's advice. Then use as little spray as possible, using a cotton ball to apply it. Or use a flea comb as mentioned above. Do not use an insecticide on a pregnant bitch unless your veterinarian recommends it.

Whichever product you use, pets and children should be kept off the carpet and out of the yard until it has completely dried. It is not a good idea to use carbamate or organophosphate insecticides on carpeting where small children will crawl. Pyrethrin and methoprene products are considered to be much safer.

Whether you have sprayed, fogged or had an exterminator treat your house, many veterinarians feel that birds should not be returned to it until the odor of the product is gone. Wiping cage surfaces with a clean damp rag before putting the bird back in his cage will give an extra measure of protection. Reptiles and rodents should be removed from the house as are dogs and cats while the household is being treated.

If your dog shows any unusual signs shortly after he is sprayed or dipped, assume that the treatment has caused the reaction until it is proven otherwise. Bathe the dog immediately to remove the insecticide. Be sure to wear rubber gloves while doing so. Use a non-insecticidal pet shampoo if it is handy. If not, use human shampoo or dish detergent. Fix the problem first and worry about the dry, itching skin later. Meanwhile, have someone gather up the insecticide container and call your veterinarian or poison control center. Prepare to take the dog to the nearest veterinarian if necessary. (For further information on insecticides, see Emergency Chapter.)

Before using any insecticidal product on your carpet, furniture, drapes or walls, patch test a small, inconspicuous area. This way you can make sure it will not stain or otherwise harm the fabric or paint.

FLEAS AND YOUR CAT

What is a section of flea control on cats doing in a dog book? Fleas love cats. The free-roaming cat is one of the biggest factors in keeping your dog and your home well supplied with fleas. It does little good to confine your dog, treat him for fleas, treat the premises, treat your car, and let this little four-legged flea taxi run loose. He goes freely from one yard to another, where the tiny pests hop on for a ride home. Now, don't get me wrong. I LOVE cats! It's just that letting your cat(s) run loose can easily negate all your dog-flea control efforts when the cat(s) bring home every stray flea in the neighborhood.

The single easiest thing you can do to help reduce your flea population is to keep your cat indoors! It is not harmful to do so. Cats are small and rather convenient, and can be taught to accept confinement. Keeping the cat inside also makes his veterinary care cheaper, as he is less likely to fight and get abscesses, to catch leukemia and other cat diseases, and to get injured by cars or be in other accidents. Cats, by the way, can have flea allergy very much like dogs. So let's control fleas on the cat.

Be sure that whatever flea product you use is specifically labeled for use on cats, or is recommended by your veterinarian for use on them. Don't just take the word of a pet shop employee that it's OK for cats. Many products meant for dogs are toxic to cats. Chlorpyrifos and Blockade® (Hartz Mountain) have been found to be toxic to cats. DO NOT use these products on your cat (Whitley and Melman, 1987). Most organophosphate powders and dips are dangerous when used on cats. Chlorinated hydrocarbon (lindane) insecticides are not safe for use on cats. Remember that anything you apply to the outside of the cat will eventually end up inside the cat when he grooms himself.

Many cats do not care to be dipped or sprayed. Some of the new foam products seem to be well tolerated by even the grumpiest cats. One which is usable on either dogs or cats is Sectilin™ Flea & Tick Mousse (Bio-Ceutic). Flea powders can be used on shorthaired cats, but do not work well on longhaired cats. Again, check the label.

LICE

Lice are wingless insects. They are flattened from top to bottom, and are often brownish or dirty gray in color. Dogs have several kinds of lice. *Trichodectes canis* is the common biting louse on dogs. It can act as an intermediate host for the tapeworm *Dipylidium caninum*. These lice are very active and can cause considerable skin irritation. *Linognathus* is the only sucking louse which feeds on dogs.

Lice are host-specific. This means that a dog louse only lives on a dog. If he gets on you or another animal, he would crawl around, but would not feed or live there. A dog louse can only survive a few days if he is removed from the dog.

Lice spread from one dog to another by close contact. For that reason, they are often a much worse problem in the winter in northern states, when dogs huddle together for warmth. They are especially bad on long-haired, matted, outdoor dogs. Lice are one of the few pests seen on ranch dogs in Wyoming, Colorado and other cold states in the winter. Not all dogs on a given ranch are infested with lice, so the infestation may have to do with an individual being weakened or having a lack of resistance. A massive louse infestation may cause severe anemia. If not treated, it may be fatal. A dog with anemia will have mucous membranes that may be nearly white instead of pinkish. Lice may also be spread from one dog to another by using contaminated grooming equipment.

Lice may first be noticed on the neck and shoulder area, especially under the collar. The dog may itch and scratch, causing injury to the skin and hair loss. The dog may be restless and annoyed. You can diagnose a case of lice by holding a sheet of clean white paper under the dog. Scratch and rub clear down to the dog's skin, doing it quite vigorously. If lice are present, the tiny (about 1/16 inch, 1 mm) cigar-shaped insects will be seen to fall onto the paper. Lice move by crawling rather than hopping. On a dark dog, the louse eggs ("nits") may be seen as tiny white or yellowish specks glued to individual hairs.

Treatment of lice is much the same as for fleas. Many of the same products work well. Check the label to make sure. Or consult your veterinarian for specific recommendations. Be sure to treat (or dispose of) louse-infested bedding. Also disinfect all grooming tools.

TICKS

Ticks are arachnids rather than insects. That is, the adults have eight legs instead of six; tick larvae have only six legs. All ticks have four stages in their life cycles: egg, larva (seed ticks), nymph and adult. All stages of both sexes are parasites and feed on blood and lymphatic fluids. The adult male has a hard shell which does not expand after feeding. Adult females, nymphs and larvae swell to several times their

original size after a meal. Ticks may hibernate through the winter, becoming especially active in the spring when searching for a meal.

Hard-shelled ticks are the most common ones which affect dogs. The brown dog tick (kennel tick, *Rhipicephalus sanguineus*) is perhaps the most common. It is found in tropical and temperate regions of the world, especially in the southeastern United States, Central America, Africa and Europe. It affects dogs and wild carnivores, and, in some cases, may parasitize cats and humans.

Other hard-shelled ticks which may infest dogs in the United States include the Rocky Mountain spotted fever tick or wood tick (*Dermacentor venustus (andersoni)*), the American dog tick (*Dermacentor variabilis*), and the winter tick (*Dermacentor albapictus*). Ticks transport numerous diseases to animals and man, including babesiosis, Rocky Mountain spotted fever and tularemia.

The brown dog tick is a three-host tick. This means that it requires three hosts at different stages in its life cycle. These may be different species of animals, or three different animals of the same species. It may have a life cycle as short as eight weeks. After feeding and mating on the final host (the dog), the female drops off, and crawls horizontally until she meets a vertical object. She then crawls upward on this object, often a wall or fence, and lays several thousand eggs in a protected crack. In about three weeks, depending on the temperature, the eggs hatch. The larvae (seed ticks) find a new host as soon as possible. Under ideal conditions seed ticks can live for eight months or more without a meal. When they find a new host, they feed for three days to a week, drop to the ground and molt into nymphs in about a week. The nymph crawls up vegetation to await a new host, feeds for three days to two weeks, drops off and molts in about two weeks into an adult. Male ticks may remain attached for several weeks or months. The females feed for about a week. The ticks are dependent on blood for their existence.

Most brown dog ticks live for about two months. Under ideal conditions, they may live as long as a year without feeding. The life cycle and habits are similar for other ticks which infest dogs. Rocky Mountain spotted fever ticks may take two years or more to complete their life cycle.

Ticks may be found anywhere on the dog's body, but are most common in the ears, around the neck and between the toes. Tick bites may cause irritation and inflammation. In sufficient numbers, they can suck enough blood to cause anemia. Dogs with large numbers of ticks may lose weight, have no appetite and lack energy.

Most dogs don't notice a few ticks. As the number of the pests increases, the dog spends more and more time licking, biting, chewing and rubbing in an attempt to get rid of them. All this activity may cause irritation and raw spots, which then become infected. The skin may be swollen enough to engulf small ticks. Tick bites often heal slowly. Occasionally, individual female ticks may product a toxin which causes tick paralysis.

It is not a good idea to pick ticks off your dog. An anaphylactic reaction may occur if you crush a portion of the tick into the open sore where it was feeding. And you may get infectious organisms on your hands, which is a hazard to you. You can spray a tick-killing insecticide directly onto the tick. You are not likely, however, to notice small seed ticks nestled among the hairs. For that reason, it is a good idea to dip the whole dog. Dead ticks may not drop off for several days after treatment has occurred. Dip the dog every two weeks until you have the infestation under control. In some areas of the United States, the brown dog tick has a definite resistance to certain insecticides. If this is the case, consult your veterinarian for one that works.

To get rid of ticks on the premises, you can call an exterminator. Or you can do it yourself, using an insecticide recommended for ticks. The house and yard should be treated every two weeks throughout the summer. This treatment may be necessary year-round in warm climates where the brown dog tick is a continuing and serious problem. Be especially careful to apply the insecticide to vertical areas such as walls and fences, and to crevices and cracks. It's a good idea to keep tall weeds and grass cut back near the house. If you are fighting both ticks and fleas, work out a schedule of cleaning and treatment that uses an insecticide effective for both pests.

MANGE MITES

SARCOPTIC MANGE

Sarcoptic mange, also called scabies, is caused by the mange mite *Sarcoptes scabiei var. canis*. The mites are microscopic in size and cannot be seen with the naked eye. They live burrowed completely within the skin, mostly on dogs. Sarcoptic mange is highly contagious from one dog to another. Carrier dogs who do not show signs are sometimes seen. For that reason, only one or two dogs out of a group or kennel may have signs of the disease.

Sarcoptic mange can be transmitted occasionally to humans. The infection is usually mild and doesn't last long. It is worth considering if your dog has skin problems and members of your family are itching too. The itching may begin within 24 hours after exposure to the infected dog. You may notice severe itching with reddened areas. These are most common on the arms and torso, especially around the waist, where clothing fits tightly.

The sarcoptic mange mite goes through its entire life cycle from egg through larva, nymph and adult in 10-21 days. It spends its entire life on the host. Transmission from one dog to another (or to a human) is by direct contact. The mites mate on the surface of the skin and both males and females burrow through the epidermis. The female lays eggs in the tunnel she has made. They hatch in three to eight days, and the larvae migrate to the skin surface, where they molt twice to become adults. They reach the adult stage four to six days after they hatch from the eggs. Adult mange mites cannot survive much more than a day off the host because they dry out. For this reason, reinfection from the house or premises after treating the dog is not a problem.

Dogs who come into contact with sarcoptic mange may show signs anywhere between 10 days and two months later.

This depends on how closely and for how long the animal was exposed. A typical dog with scabies is a thin-skinned puppy which has just come from a pet shop or animal shelter where it has been exposed to numbers of other animals.

Sarcoptic mange mites seem to prefer areas of skin with little or no hair. They are found on the dog's belly, hocks and elbows. The chest and legs may also be affected. Perhaps the most common site is on the tips of dogs' floppy ears.

The most common sign of sarcoptic mange is intense itching. The dog may scratch while you are carrying him or leading him, or even trying to give him his dinner. The area affected by the mange may show hair loss. There may be reddish pimples, which become covered with thick yellow crusts. If the mange continues long enough, the combination of irritation and the dog's scratching may lead to thickening and wrinkling of the skin.

Your veterinarian will diagnose scabies by taking a skin scraping from the dog and examining it under the microscope. This is a very difficult disease to confirm, and repeated scrapings may be necessary. The mites burrow deeply into the skin, so don't worry if the veterinarian scrapes hard enough to draw a little blood. In some cases, it is not possible to recover mites in a skin scraping. In this case, your veterinarian may choose to treat the dog for mange anyway, based on his clinical observations and experience.

Because carriers who do not show any signs of scabies can exist, it is important to treat all dogs in a household when one is found to have sarcoptic mange. The dog's hair should be clipped. Then he should be bathed in an antiseborrheic shampoo. An example is SebaLyt® (DVM Products). This type of shampoo will help to remove the crusts so that medication can penetrate into the skin. It may be necessary to bathe and dip the dog(s) every five days for eight consecutive treatments in order to control the mites.

Whatever dip is used, it must be applied thoroughly to the entire dog. It is not enough to treat the spots which are showing signs. Be careful with the dip around the animal's eyes and ears. Lime-sulfur dip is a classical treatment for sarcoptic mange. This is applied in a 2%-4% solution, mixed with warm water. Be careful to make the proper dilution. If applied full strength, it may cause scalding (chemical irritation) of the dog's skin. The greatest disadvantage of lime-sulfur is that it smells like rotten eggs. Perhaps the odor would be better if you think of it as an expensive mineral spa! One such product is LymDyp® (DVM Products). Check with your veterinarian to see if you should be treating your cat, and which product should be used on him.

DEMODECTIC MANGE

Demodectic mange is caused by both the presence of and the dog's reaction to the mite *Demodex canis*. Almost all normal dogs have small numbers of these mites in their hair follicles and sweat glands. Normal humans even have small numbers of demodectic mites, usually on the skin of the face (we never know it). The life cycle of *Demodex canis* from egg to adult takes about 20 to 36 days, and the entire time is spent on the host animal.

Demodectic mange is transmitted from the mother to her puppies within the first three days after birth, while they are still nursing. In these puppies, hairless spots first appear on their muzzles. It seems to be especially common in thin-skinned dogs such as Chihuahuas. In some kennels, the disease has been eliminated by either taking the puppies by Caesarean section or removing them immediately from the mother and raising them as orphans. Getting rid of bitches who pass it to their puppies is also helpful. There seems to be some hereditary susceptibility to the disease. Some bitches may develop demodectic mange in association with heat periods or whelping. Then the disease clears up, only to return with the next reproductive cycle. In many cases, it is thought that the dog's immune system is not functioning to suppress the mites as it would normally. Demodectic mange is not considered to be contagious between healthy adult dogs.

Demodectic mange is most commonly seen in purebred dogs less than one year of age, but it can occur in any breed of dog. In dogs this age, a localized form of the disease occurs. The dog will have one or more small, rounded areas of hair loss. These may be reddened or darkened compared to the rest of the skin. They are most common on the head and neck, but may occur on the front legs too. The affected areas usually do not seem to itch. About one in 10 of these localized cases will progress to a generalized mange.

The more generalized form of demodectic mange is seen in dogs less than a year and a half old. The dog's skin may be reddened, swollen and thickened. There may be crusting, seborrhea (greasy skin) and considerable hair loss. The dog may show intense itching. The feet may be involved; if they are, the case may be nearly impossible to treat. If the damage and secondary infection goes deeply into the skin, the dog may show lack of appetite, have a fever and be severely weakened. Severe, generalized demodectic mange can kill the dog if not treated quickly and intensively. Because of inherited susceptibility, dogs with generalized demodectic mange should never be used for breeding. The American Academy of Veterinary Dermatology has passed a resolution that all dogs with generalized cases of demodectic mange should be neutered (Newsletter, 1981).

Your veterinarian will usually diagnose demodectic mange by finding the mites on a skin scraping. Skin biopsies may be necessary in Shar-Pei or other dogs whose skin has become so thickened that no mites can be found on scrapings.

Dogs with only localized lesions of demodectic mange do not usually have any problems with their immune systems. Nine out of 10 of these dogs will get better within one to two months, with or without treatment. A benzoyl perioxide gel, such as Pyoben Gel™ (Allerderm), may be rubbed into the lesions once a day. Be careful not to get the product into the dog's eyes.

Treating a generalized case of demodectic mange can take a long time, be very expensive, and is often disappointing. The disease is especially difficult to cure in the older dog. Some dogs may need treatment for the rest of their lives.

Before treating a case of generalized demodectic mange, your veterinarian may wish to run a series of laboratory tests to see if the dog has any other disease problems. Several topical drugs are used, all of which are available only on veterinary prescription. This is one instance where it's worth starting with your veterinarian. Pet-shop mange remedies often do not work, and using them will only delay your seeking help early enough to have even a 50-50 chance of treating the disease.

EAR MITES

Infestations of ear mites are caused by the mite *Otodectes canis*. This infestation is also called otodectic mange. These mites may infest dogs, cats and even humans. If the ears become severely inflamed and infected with bacteria, the mites may abandon the ears, infesting other parts of the dog's body. The mites spend all of their three-week life cycle on the host animal.

Common signs of ear mites include rubbing the ears, twitching them, scratching, head shaking and groaning as the dog attempts to put a foot in his ear.

The dog's ears are usually filled with a brownish or black waxy or granular mass. If you observe VERY carefully, you may see small white mites moving around on this material. The mites are about the size of a grain of salt. If you take a cotton swab and put a bit of this material on a white piece of paper under a bright light, the mites may be seen moving slowly across the paper.

The ears should be infused with a half-teaspoon or so of mineral oil (2-3 cc), heated to lukewarm. This can be gently massaged around to help loosen the waxy material. The oil will also kill some of the mites. In some cases, your veterinarian may wish to sedate the dog so that he can clean and wash the ears clear down to the eardrum. The dog will then be treated with a product containing an insecticide as well as antibiotics to help clear up the accompanying infection. This will usually be ear drops which will need to be put in every few days for several weeks. Ear mites are rather resistant and difficult to treat, so it is very important that you carefully follow the recommended treatment schedule. Other dogs in the household, as well as cats, should be checked for ear mites and treated at the same time. In some cases, you may be treating the whole "herd" for five or six months. It is easier to do them all at once than to treat one and then treat the others as they come down with the mites, passing them back and forth to each other.

Ear mites may live for months off the animal. For this reason, it is important that the house and any spots outdoors where the dog spends considerable time be treated with the same type of residual insecticide you would use for flea control.

FLIES

HOUSE FLIES

House flies, stable flies, mosquitoes and other flying insects may attack dogs who are kept outdoors. This is especially true if the dog has tear-staining which keeps his face wet, diarrhea, or a similar problem. Flies can make a dog truly miserable. The best solution is to use a fly or mosquito repellent. Ones made for humans can usually be used on dogs. Just be sure to keep it away from the animal's eyes and mouth while spraying it on him. Repellent creams are made for dogs which can be smeared directly on the face. Some repellents made for fleas will also work on flies. It may take a couple of tries to find the product which will make life more comfortable for your pet.

BLOW FLY MAGGOTS

Common blow flies normally lay their eggs in dead carcasses and rotting meat. If a dog is allowed to have rotting tissue or filth on him, these flies will lay their eggs on this material. This may occur when a long-haired dog gets a wire cut or is ripped open in a dog fight, and the owner does not notice the wound. Or it may happen when a long-haired dog has diarrhea or is not clean about his defecation, and feces become matted in the hair of the rear end.

The blow fly eggs may be seen as masses of white or yellowish eggs, which are laid in the filth or wound. Within about 12 hours, they hatch into maggots. The maggots grow to about 1/2 inch (13 mm) long. They burrow throughout the dead tissue, eating it as they go. If the filth has laid against the dog's skin long enough, areas of the skin may be devitalized enough to be attractive to the maggots. The maggots will then burrow under the skin, weaving in and out through holes. In the same manner, they will go deep into a wound, moving around wherever there is dead tissue.

Your first sign of a problem may be the living maggots crawling on the dog, or falling off as he walks. The first step in treatment is to clip all hair away from the wound or to clip off all hair containing any filth, even if it means shearing the whole dog. Now you can see how bad the problem is. Maggots can be removed from deep holes with tweezers or forceps. If the wound is more open, spray them with an insecticide (one safe for use on dogs) to kill them so that they do not reproduce and make more blowflies. Antibiotic treatment may be necessary to control the infection which occurs in the surrounding damaged tissue.

At one time, screwworms were a problem in the southern and southwestern United States. These are the same type of worm, but they eat live tissue, instead of dead, and can easily kill an animal. Dogs are susceptible as are any animal. If you live in an area where screwworms are a problem, it is important that you keep the hind end clipped on long-haired dogs so that a filth situation does not develop. The dog should be inspected frequently so that any tiny wound or tear can be treated before the flies lay their eggs in it.

CUTEREBRA INFESTATION

The rodent or rabbit bot-fly may infest dogs. Young puppies with thin, delicate skin are most commonly affected. The adult flies are usually not noticed. Female *Cuterebra* lay eggs in or near nests of rodents or rabbits. These hatch into infective larvae in response to body heat given off by an animal. A puppy may pick them up by nosing around a burrow. The tiny larvae, 1/16 inch (1 mm) long, usually enter the puppy through the skin of the mouth or nose, but may also go in through cuts in the skin. They will then migrate to various locations under the surface of the skin.

The larvae may grow to be as much as an inch long and 1/3 inch in diameter (25 mm long, 8 mm in diameter). They may be grayish, brownish or black. They often occur in late summer or early fall, and are commonly seen on the skin of the chest and neck. You will first notice a thick-walled abscess under the animal's skin. The grub may have made a breathing hole through the skin—this is very circular in shape, and has smooth edges. It does not look like a cut or injury. Pus may ooze out through the hole. You may be able to see the larva squirming under the skin.

Do NOT squeeze the sore, because rupture of the worm may result in anaphylactic shock. The breathing hole has to be surgically enlarged to permit removal of the bot (or bots). You can take your puppy to your veterinarian to have this done. If you can't get him to a veterinarian, have someone hold the puppy securely. Clip the hair from around the lump. Using a very sharp knife or razor blade, make a tiny slit, starting at the edge of the hole and working away from it, like the spoke of a wheel coming from the hub. A slit 1/8 to 1/4 inch long (3-6 mm) should be sufficient. The larva can then be VERY carefully squeezed or lifted out. Don't rupture the worm! The abscess can be swabbed out with povidone-iodine solution to remove any pus which is present. Continue treating as you would any abscess, until the hole has healed from the inside (see Abscesses in Skin Care and Disease Chapter).

Chapter 13

INTERNAL PARASITES (WORMS)

ASCARIDS

Ascarids are large, thick worms. They may be over 8 inches (20 cm) long and 1/8 inch (3 mm) thick. The adults live in the dog's small intestine, and occasionally in the stomach or large intestine. They live on intestinal contents and do not attach to the lining of the intestine as do many other worms.

Two species of ascarids are found in dogs. *Toxacara canis* is the most common roundworm found in dogs. These worms can cause serious disease in young puppies (and kittens). *Toxascaris leonina* is less common, and causes a less severe disease. Dogs are usually infested with one ascarid or the other but not both.

TOXACARA CANIS

Eggs of the ascarids are passed by the dog. At this point, they are not infective—they would not cause infection if eaten by another dog or other animal. They develop to the infective stage in a few days to several months, depending on environmental conditions. If the temperature and humidity are favorable, the eggs may remain infective to dogs or cats, as well as to humans, for a number of years. They can survive through the winter in soil or in feces. Their extended survival is important to remember in terms of transmission to humans, especially children.

The dog becomes infected by eating eggs which have reached the infective stage. The ingested eggs hatch in the small intestine in a couple of hours. If the animal is a puppy under three months of age, the larvae go through an intricate migration within the body. They go through the lining of the intestine, into lymphatic vessels, through the lymph nodes draining the intestines, and into the liver. From there, they travel via the hepatic vein out of the liver to the heart and into the lungs. They make this journey within three to six days after the eggs are eaten. In the lungs, the larvae stop and grow

to about 1/16 inch (1 mm). They then migrate up the respiratory tract into the trachea and on into the throat, where they are swallowed. They reach the stomach and pass into the large intestine. The entire journey takes 10 days to two weeks. At any given time the puppy may be infected with both the migrating larvae moving through his body (from eggs that he has just eaten), and adult worms in the digestive tract (from eggs that he ate a couple of weeks ago).

Many of the worms are either vomited or passed in the feces by the time the dog is six months old. If a lot of worms are present, the untimely exit—from the worm's point of view—may be due to mechanical irritation of the bowel. As the puppy gets older, the larvae seem less likely to migrate up the trachea to be swallowed. Instead, they migrate through the dog's tissues, and can be found in other parts of the body—including kidneys, liver, brain and lungs.

Some of the migrating larvae become surrounded by tissue capsules, especially in the kidney and skeletal muscles. These larvae may never leave these capsules—unless the dog is female and becomes pregnant. Pregnancy, for some unknown reason, reactivates the larvae. Then they, in addition to those from any eggs that she has just eaten, migrate via the placenta (fetal membranes) into the unborn puppy's liver. Not all larvae are awakened at any one pregnancy. Some remain in the body of the bitch to infect subsequent litters. The larvae stay within the puppy's liver until it is born. They then migrate to the lungs, go up the trachea and are swallowed, and reach in the intestine. They arrive there as soon as three weeks after the puppy is born. This is how a puppy raised under the most sanitary conditions can still have worms. He was born with them! If ascarid infestations are heavy enough, the puppies may be stillborn. Transmission of ascarids from the bitch to her puppies is an extremely common problem.

In some females, some of the larvae activated from tissue capsules, as well as ones which are newly hatched from eggs that she has eaten, migrate to the mammary glands. This migration occurs late in the pregnancy or within a few days after whelping. The puppies then suckle infective larvae directly from their mother in the milk. These larvae go into the intestine and quickly become adult ascarids. Overall, however, the infection of the puppies through the placenta is more important. An infected bitch may show negative stool samples before breeding and during pregnancy, but have positive stool samples after she has whelped.

And if those weren't enough ways for your dog to get ascarids, there are more to come! Ascarids are found in the tissues of many other creatures, ranging from earthworms, monkeys, birds, sheep, rodents and rabbits, to other animals, including humans. Rodents and rabbits are perhaps the most important ascarid hosts for city and farm dogs. The dog eats a mouse or rabbit which is carrying the ascarids. He scrounges a meal from the carcass of a dead farm animal or deer or other game animal. The ascarid larvae are encapaulated in the tissues of the other animal much as they are in the non-pregnant dog. When they are eaten, the dog's digestive juices release them from the capsules. These larvae migrate via the trachea, ending up in the intestine as if the dog were a young puppy that had ingested ascarid eggs.

Puppies may have such a severe infection with ascarids that they will die. Older dogs have more natural resistance against the worms, as well as greater reserves, and are usually not as badly affected.

Puppies may die of pneumonia within two to three days after they are born. This is due to large numbers of larvae migrating through the lungs. These larvae were acquired while in the mother's uterus. If the puppy survives this initial migration period, his next crisis may occur at two to three weeks of age. At this point, large numbers of worms have matured in the digestive tract and are robbing him of large quantities of nutrients. If the adult worms are up to eight inches long and the whole puppy is only four inches long, it doesn't take many worms to totally drain him! He's starving to death.

During this second crisis, the puppy may have a dull, dry haircoat and a severely swollen pot belly. He may have alternating spells of constipation and diarrhea. The diarrhea often contains mucus and/or worms. The puppy may be vomiting. The vomited material may also contain adult ascarids. He may have a cough and nasal discharge because of pneumonia from migrating larvae that have not yet reached the intestine. The puppy's breath may have a sweet odor, and he may show signs of abdominal pain. He may be anemic. In some cases, signs of nervous system disturbance may be noted. These signs may include restlessness and muscle twitching. In some puppies the disturbance may go as far as convulsions ("fits" caused by worms).

If enough ascarids are present in the puppy's intestine, they may completely block it. The blockage may cause the intestine to rupture, followed by peritonitis. Adult worms may occasionally cause a perforation of the intestine. Or they may block essential passages such as those leading from the gall bladder or pancreas into the intestine.

If a puppy anywhere from three weeks of age onward vomits or passes in the feces one or more large worms, it is reasonably safe to assume that they are ascarids. Take a fecal sample, along with the worm, to your veterinarian for confirmation. In most cases, it is best to let your veterinarian prescribe the proper medication after examination of the puppy or puppies, rather than buying something at the grocery store. When extremely strong wormers are used in puppies with signs of pneumonia, the large number of dying larvae in the lungs may cause further complications and possibly death.

Piperazine products are safe for use with ascarids in the intestinal tract of young puppies. Be sure to use the drug according to label dosages. The dosage varies with the form of piperazine which is used. These products have no effect against larvae encapsulated in muscles and other tissues of the bitch.

Meanwhile, the puppies will need good nursing care. They should have a clean, warm, dry place to stay. Make sure the bitch is on an adequate quantity of a good-quality dog food, and encourage the puppies to eat a good puppy chow as soon as possible to supplement the (contaminated) nutrition they are getting from their mother.

Fenbendazole can be used in newborn puppies at 45 mg/lb (100 mg/kg) to kill the migrating larvae. This is given for three days (Lloyd, 1983). The puppies must be weighed on a sensitive scale, and the dosage carefully calculated. A second treatment is needed two to three weeks later when worms are beginning to mature in the digestive tract.

CONTROL OF ASCARIDS

There are three important sources of infection with *Toxacara canis*. One is infective eggs in the environment, which have come from the feces of a dog with ascarids. The second is larvae in the tissues of the pregnant bitch. The third source is larvae in the tissues of animals that the dog might eat. Sanitation is of the utmost importance, especially in kennels where large numbers of dogs are kept.

Larvae transmitted from their mother via the uterus and her milk, and possibly eggs transmitted via her feces, are the most important sources of infection for the puppies. The bitch should have a fecal examination before she is bred, and be dewormed if necessary. Treatment during pregnancy will also be helpful in reducing or eliminating the transmission of ascarid larvae to the puppies.

Transmission of ascarids from the female to her puppies can also be stopped by raising bitches on wire so that all fecal material falls through, leaving no infected eggs to be accidentally eaten. The bitch is bred repeatedly until all the ascarid larvae have migrated out of her tissues. This usually takes about three pregnancies. From there on, assuming she doesn't become reinfected, she will produce ascarid-free puppies.

Fenbendazole can be given to the pregnant bitch to produce uninfected puppies. Consult your veterinarian for current availability and dosage. This drug must be given from about the 40th day of pregnancy until two weeks after the puppies are born. Starting treatment later in pregnancy than about the 40th day does not adequately protect against the migrating larvae. The dosage must be carefully calculated, because there is some evidence of nervous system damage to the unborn puppies if too much is given to the bitch.

All puppies in areas where ascarids are a problem should be wormed within two weeks after they are born. They can then be treated every two to three weeks until at least three months of age. The dosage of wormer must be carefully calculated so that it gradually increases as the puppy grows.

With careful deworming of the bitch during pregnancy, it is possible to have puppies born without ascarids. They are, however, susceptible to infection with them after birth. For that reason, careful sanitation is important. If possible, the nursing bitch should be kept on wire mesh so that all feces fall through. Or she can be walked daily to an area where the feces are immediately picked up and disposed of, preferably by burning if legal in your area, or placed in the garbage. The point is: Don't let the puppies get anywhere close to their mother's feces.

A careful, continuing program can avoid contamination of the environment on a long-term basis. All adult dogs on the premises should have routine fecal examinations for ascarids. Two to four times a year would be a good interval in an ascarid area. The dog should then be treated with appropriate wormers. Some of the "pet shop" products are not effective, and may give you a false sense of security. When you have your veterinarian do the fecal examination, he can keep you advised of currently effective wormers to help control the worms.

Sanitation is vital in preventing both infection of puppies and reinfection of adult dogs. The dog can become infected from eating feces or, in areas which are contaminated by feces, simply by picking up spilled dog food off the ground, ingesting ascarid eggs with the food. He can also become infected by eating rodents, carcasses, dirt or earthworms. Anything you can do to keep him from eating these items will be a giant step toward having him remain free of ascarids. Feces should be removed daily, whether from a kennel run or from the corner of your yard. Do not allow other dogs to visit your premises, or pick up their feces and disinfect the area carefully after they have defecated. Dogs who are kept in kennels with concrete runs that can be easily hosed clean, or runs with wire floors, will have the best sanitation. Gravel cannot be completely cleaned.

Ascarid eggs, unfortunately, are resistant to cold, drying, many common disinfectants and low-temperature composting.

TOXASCARIS LEONINA

This ascarid is much less common in dogs than *Toxacara canis*. This worm has eggs that are possibly even more resistant than those of *Toxacara*. These worms are smaller, ranging up to 4 inches (10 cm) long and 1/8 inch (2 mm) thick. These ascarids have a much simpler life style than *Toxacara*. The dog becomes infected by eating infective eggs, or hosts whose tissues contain larvae within their tissues. There is no migration through the trachea, or infection via the mother's uterus or milk.

Eggs are passed in the feces from a dog or other animal infected with *Toxascaris*. Within as little as three days they become infective, and can cause infestation when eaten by the same or another animal. The larvae attach to the walls of the small intestine. In an extremely heavy infestation, they may migrate through the abdominal organs, muscles or lungs. Once they arrive in those locations, they do not develop any further, nor do they migrate to anywhere else. Eggs will be present in the feces one and a half to two months after the dog eats infective eggs, thus completing the worm's life cycle. Adult worms are occasionally passed in the feces.

While *Toxacara* infection is most common in puppies, *Toxascaris* infection may be seen in dogs of any age. Dogs do not seem to develop any resistance against it as they get older. *Toxascaris* is found within the tissues of rabbits, mice and chickens, and may be passed to dogs who eat the tissues.

This ascarid causes few specific clinical signs. When found in a fecal sample, the treatment is similar to that of *Toxocara*. Sanitation is similarly important. *Toxascaris* eggs are extremely resistant to both high and low temperatures, and survive cold winters well. Because reinfection may occur, fecal examinations two to three times a year are a good idea in an area where this pest is found. Be sure to remove any adult worms that you find, because they are a great source of continuing infection.

ASCARIDS AND CHILDREN

Both *Toxocara* and *Toxascaris* may infect humans, especially children. These infections are called visceral larva migrans because the larvae migrate through the viscera (organs). While many infestations do not cause any problems, in some children the larvae may migrate into the eye(s), where they are an important cause of childhood blindness. Or they can migrate through other organs, causing liver damage, pneumonia or encephalitis (if they invade the brain).

This disease is NOT a reason to get rid of your dog or cat. It IS a good reason to clean up after him on a daily basis. Either walk your dog on a leash or teach him to defecate in one spot if you live in a part of the country where ascarids are a problem. You can further protect your family by having your veterinarian check a sample of the dog's feces two to three times a year, and deworm the dog if ascarid eggs are found. It is an excellent idea to limit your children's exposure to puppies and lactating bitches, especially if you don't know the dog's worming status. Keep your children from eating dog feces or dirt which may be contaminated by dogs. Keep a cover on the children's sandbox so that ascarids are not acquired from the feces of passing cats.

HOOKWORMS

Hookworms of several different species infest dogs in the United States. *Ancylostoma caninum* is the most common species. *Ancylostoma brasiliense* is seen in the southeast. *Uncinaria stenocephala* is seen throughout the northern United States and northward into the Canadian Arctic as well as the cooler portions of Europe, Australia and South America.

Hookworms are reddish-brown or white. They range from 1/4 to 3/4 inch (6 mm to 18 mm) long. You are not likely to see these in the feces. The only good way to diagnose a hookworm infestation is by a veterinarian's examination of a stool sample.

Most hookworm infestations are acquired when the dog eats the infective larvae. The larvae, however, are also capable of penetrating the skin. If the dog has not had hookworms before, most of the larvae which are eaten will develop to maturity within the small intestine. If the dog has had several infections with hookworms, he will often have some degree of immunity. In these dogs, the larvae will migrate through the tissues. They may stay in one place for quite some time, coiled up in a tiny capsule. In a pregnant bitch, the larvae are stimulated to leave the capsule, crossing the placenta into the developing puppy. When the puppies are born, the larvae in their bodies continue migrating until they reach the small intestine. Hookworms can also travel into the bitch's mammary glands to be passed in her milk, much like ascarids. The time from eating infective larvae to passing eggs in the feces from the resulting worms is about two and a half to three weeks. However, a puppy who has been infected in the uterus may pass eggs in his feces as soon as 12 days after birth.

Hookworms live on blood they suck from the lining of the intestine. An adult dog may carry a few hookworms without showing any signs. Puppies, on the other hand, may show signs of disease with relatively few worms. The puppies may not do well and may be weak. They may have pale mucous membranes, a sign of anemia. Some puppies may show signs of pneumonia. The puppy's feces may contain enough blood that they are dark, tarry, fluid and foul-smelling. Both anemia and dark, foul-smelling stools can come on quite suddenly as sufficient numbers of the larvae become mature worms and begin sucking blood from the intestine.

Overall, the anemia is perhaps the most prominent sign of hookworm disease, and the one most likely to kill the dog. Hookworms attach to the intestinal wall. They move to another feeding spot a half-dozen times a day, soon resulting in many small bleeding areas in the intestine. The bleeding, in addition to the blood the worm itself has taken, can cause severe blood loss.

By the time you notice that a puppy or dog has hookworm disease, he is in BIG trouble. Chances are good that he will need supportive treatment, which may include blood transfusions, to keep him alive until a wormer can take effect. Powerful wormers are required which can only be obtained through a veterinarian. Treating a dog who is sick with hookworms is not a do-it-yourself project. It is very important that a severely anemic dog be handled very gently and that stress be avoided, or he may go into shock and die.

If the dog has hookworms, but they are not causing severe anemic illness, some of the drugs used to eliminate them are toluene (Vermiplex) or dichlorvos. A single treatment works to remove them (until the next time the dog becomes infected). Two drugs were used years ago that are completely outmoded today. One is n-butyl chloride, which kills only about half the worms that are present. The other is tetrachloroethylene. It is about 90% effective, but may cause liver damage and should not be used in dogs that also have tapeworms. These two drugs are mentioned here because you might run across them and be tempted to use them. Don't. More effective, safer drugs are available.

It is almost impossible to prevent hookworm infection in areas where they are present, unless you almost completely confine the dog (or cat, as they can be infected, too) to your house or to its kennel. Dogs kept in concrete-floored kennels which are exposed to direct sunlight have perhaps the lowest chance of reinfection. As with other worms, careful sanitation and daily removal of all feces is necessary. Pets who roam freely will continue to pick up hookworms, and will need periodic treatment to remove them. Don't mess around with home remedies trying to treat hookworms. At best, they will remove only a few of them, allowing the dog to miserably coexist with those that are left. At worst, they may allow him to die for lack of treatment. Take advantage of the modern wormers which are available, and use them three or four times a year, or as otherwise prescribed by your veterinarian.

WHIPWORMS

Whipworms are white, 1-1/2 to 3 inches (40-75 cm) long. The short tail end is thickened, and the longer head end is thin, like the lash of a whip. They live in the caecum and colon, where they attach to the lining and suck blood, much like hookworms. *Trichuris vulpis* is the species which commonly occurs in dogs. It is found sporadically all over North America. Eggs from whipworms may survive in the environment as long as five years if conditions are favorable. However, they are very susceptible to drying and temperature extremes.

The life cycle of the whipworm is simple. The dog eats the infective larvae. They develop in the hind part of the small intestine. This takes about two and a half months. They then enter the large intestine, where they may live for over a year.

As with hookworms, a dog may carry a few whipworms without showing any signs. Dogs with large numbers of whipworms may develop a colitis, with alternating spells of diarrhea and normal stools. Mucus and blood may streak the feces. To make diagnosis difficult, these dogs may not show any worm eggs in their feces, depending on the current reproductive stage of the worms. Some veterinarians in whipworm areas prefer first to treat the dog as if he had whipworms before resorting to endoscopic examinations and other therapy for colitis. In puppies and younger dogs, the dog may show weight loss and anemia much like the conditions seen with hookworms. Treatment of whipworms is similar to that used for hookworms.

Whipworm eggs are occasionally found in human feces, and it is well to be aware of the possibility of human infection with this parasite. (See Ascarids, above, for environmental control measures). Flame throwers used to kill weeds can be used to sanitize concrete runs. If used carefully, this is a fast, cheap, safe method of disinfecting runs. Rearing and maintaining dogs on wire also works well. Avoid overcrowding in kennels. Exposing run areas to sunlight helps to dry out and kill the worm eggs. Exposure to sunlight is only effective after careful cleaning, however, as feces will protect the eggs quite well against drying.

STRONGYLOIDES

Strongyloides, the intestinal threadworms, are very small worms, 1/10 inch (2 mm) long. They are almost transparent in color, and they bury themselves in the lining of the small intestine. *Strongyloides stercoralis* is the species which is seen in dogs. It also may infest the small intestine of domestic and wild animals, as well as humans. The disease can be quite serious in humans. Keep this fact in mind if your dog has a case of strongyloides.

The worms which parasitize animals and humans are all females. They lay eggs which are fertile without any assistance from male worms. Each female may lay several thousand eggs per day—a lot for such tiny worms! The eggs hatch within the digestive tract, and tiny larvae are passed in the feces. It may take less than a day for the larvae to become infective. The tiny larvae can penetrate the dog's skin, producing reddening and itching in the area where they enter. Or they may penetrate the membranes of the mouth. Regardless of the point of entry, they then migrate through the circulatory system, into the lungs, up the trachea and then to the intestines. On the way through the lungs, they may produce pneumonia.

Strongyloides can cause severe disease in young puppies. It is more commonly seen in the summer when the weather is damp and hot. Signs are similar to those caused by hookworms. A continuing diarrhea, which does not get better with routine treatment, is perhaps the most common sign of strongyloides infection.

It is important to take the freshest fecal sample possible to your veterinarian for diagnosis of strongyloides. Otherwise, the few eggs that are present may hatch into larvae, which are extremely difficult to find in the fecal sample. Avoid overcrowding dogs in kennels or in your home. Keeping dogs in small cages or small runs concentrates the fecal contamination and can quickly lead to heavy infestations in the animals. Strongyloides is a frequent problem in young puppies in kennels. As with other internal parasites, sanitation is of extreme importance in preventing reinfection. With this parasite, it's important to keep it from spreading to you!

SPIROCERCA

Spirocerca lupi are worms which cause nodules in the esophagus in dogs. The adults of these worms are bright red, 1-1/4 to 3 inches (30 to 75 mm) long. Dogs acquire the infection by eating either an intermediate host, such as a dung beetle, or a transport host, such as a chicken. The larvae migrate through the wall of the aorta in the chest, spending about two months in this area before moving on to the esophagus.

Most dogs do not show any signs with spirocerca infection. If the lesions in the esophagus become very large, they may become cancerous. The dog may have trouble swallowing, and may vomit after trying to eat. The worms only pass eggs from time to time, so the chances of finding them in any single fecal examination are slim. In areas where spirocerca are present, dogs should not be allowed to eat chickens, and they should not be fed raw chicken scraps.

HEARTWORMS

Heartworm disease occurs in dogs (and, to a lesser extent, in cats) in many parts of the world, especially those areas with subtropical or tropical climates. Canine heartworm disease can also be called canine dirofilariasis, from the name of the worm, *Dirofilaria immitis*. It is widespread in North Africa, Europe and southern Asia, including China and Japan. As many as 60% of the dogs in Japan may be affected. Canine heartworm disease has long been recognized in the United States in the southeastern coastal areas. In that part of the country, as many as 90% of dogs who do not receive preventive treatment may be affected. However, during the past 20 or so years, the disease has spread to become a major problem along the entire east coast and throughout the Midwest,

especially Wisconsin, Michigan and Minnesota. Heartworm disease occurs in small numbers of humans. Controlling it in dogs may help to prevent its spread to humans.

Heartworm disease is less common west of the Mississippi River, but more and more cases are being reported. Inititally, it was felt that most of these cases were dogs who have lived in one of the problem areas and then moved to the West. Now, however, cases are being seen in native dogs. These cases are assumed to be carried by mosquitoes from non-native dogs. Because heartworms are transmitted by mosquitoes, the disease is more common along river valleys and other places where water is abundant. The good news is that heartworm disease is completly preventable.

Heartworm disease is carried from one dog to another by mosquitoes. The mosquito sucks larvae (called microfilariae) from an infected dog along with blood as it feeds. The microfilaria then incubate within the mosquito for 10 to 20 days. This incubation is an essential part of the parasite's life cycle. Fleas and other insects cannot carry heartworms from one dog to another. Only mosquitoes can host the incubating microfilariae.

From the time the mosquito injects the incubated microfilaria into the dog's body, the worms begin a long and complicated life cycle, requiring at least six months to complete.

The microfilaria are microscopic in size and circulate within even the tiniest blood vessels of the dog's body. In contrast, female adult heartworms may be over 10 inches (25 cm) long, while males are half to two-thirds that size.

During the incubation period within the mosquito, the larvae (microfilariae) change from first-stage larvae to third-stage, infective larvae, and migrate to the mosquito's mouthparts. As the mosquito feeds on another dog, a drop of hemolymph (mosquito blood) containing the infective larvae is deposited onto the dog's skin. The microfilariae (usually only a few per mosquito) penetrate the dog's skin and go into the subcutaneous tissues, where they molt. The dog is now technically infected, but will not yet show any clinical signs. Clinical signs are due to the adult worms being in the heart.

During the next two to four months, the larvae will molt twice, becoming fifth-stage larvae. These migrate to the right side of the heart, continuing to mature into adult worms. At this point, they are living inside the heart, within its right ventricle. Around six to seven months following infection, the worms (now mature) will produce first-stage microfilariae, which are ready to be picked up by new mosquitoes, thus completing the life cycle. The adult heartworms may live as long as six to seven years, and microfilarie can live up to three years. You can see how one infected dog can spread the infection via mosquitoes to many other dogs around his area. And he can do this for a long time before he becomes sick or even shows early signs of the disease. In fact, heartworms are often found on autopsy of dogs dead from other causes, but caused little or no harm to the dog.

Dogs who live outdoors and are exposed to mosquitoes in a heartworm area have a much greater risk of becoming infected than do indoor dogs. Dogs with long haircoats do not have any less risk of heartworm disease than do those with short hair.

Clinical signs of heartworm disease may develop as soon as six months following the bite of an infected mosquito. However, not all dogs with adult heartworms in the right side of the heart will show signs of the disease. The severity of the disease varies with the size of the dog's heart, the number of adult worms present, the length of time the infection has been going on, the age of the dog and his overall health.

The most common sign of heartworm disease is lack of stamina, or decreased tolerance to exercise. This sign is an especially significant warning if you live in a heartworm area, and the dog is not receiving preventive treatment. The second most common clinical sign is a cough which becomes gradually worse over a period of several weeks or months. If the disease is not treated at this point, the heart will eventually become enlarged. This is actually a form of congestive heart failure. Worms which are present in the pulmonary arteries (the arteries which go to the lungs) will increase blood pressure within the lungs and slow circulation of blood, due to their bodies forming partial plugs in the arteries. The worms also cause lesions within the blood vessels themselves. Eventually, the dog will have a severe cough most of the time. He will have no energy or stamina, and will tire quickly from very little exercise. He may have trouble breathing even when resting, and may occasionally faint.

If the disease goes on for a long time, the right side of the heart becomes thickened and less efficient as a pump. The dog will develop congestive heart failure, followed by signs of liver failure—including fluid accumulation within the abdomen. The kidneys may also be damaged by the poor blood circulation, so that the dog may drink more than normal and urinate more often. Normal blood clotting mechanisms may be altered, leading to irreversible bleeding disorders. These disorders may show up as bloody urine, coughing up blood, nosebleeds, and bleeding from bruises or when blood samples are drawn. If the dog has bleeding episodes, his chances for survival are poor.

Some dogs with heartworm disease may show no signs at all until they suddenly become weak and stop eating, have trouble breathing and collapse. Many of these dogs will die no matter how rapidly and intensively they are treated. This is called the caval syndrome. It occurs when large numbers of adult heartworms mature at the same time, blocking most of the blood circulation. The lack of circulation causes sudden kidney and liver failure.

Heartworm disease cannot be confirmed by clinical signs alone. Other diseases, especially in the older dog, can show the same signs. Laboratory testing is needed to show the presence of microfilariae in the blood. The test requires only a few drops of blood from your dog. In addition, X-rays of the chest will show the enlarged heart (and maybe enlargement of some of the blood vessels to the lungs). X-rays will give a good idea of how severe the disease is, and how much damage the heart has sustained. Many veterinarians prefer to do these X-rays before beginning treatment, as it gives them a better idea of how to proceed with treatment. If the heart is severely damaged, it may be necessary to stabilize the dog's condition before treatment to get rid of the worms can be started. In some cases, an electrocardiogram may be taken. It cannot diagnose heartworm infection, but can give good information about the status of the heart before treatment is started.

A bitch who has heartworm disease with very large numbers of larvae in her blood may give birth to puppies who also have microfilariae in their blood. These puppies do not generally have adult worms, and are usually not treated until they are four to five months of age. Dogs can have clinical signs of heartworm disease, but not have detectable microfilariae in the blood. This is known as occult heartworm disease, and may occur in 15% to 25% of all dogs infected with heartworms. New diagnostic test kits allow veterinarians to detect the disease in these dogs so that they can be treated. The test detects the presence of antibodies against adult heartworms.

HEARTWORM TREATMENT

Treatment of heartworm disease in the dog has two phases. First the adult heartworms must be killed. Then the microfilariae which are circulating in the bloodstream must be eliminated. Treatment may be long, difficult and expensive. However, if it is started early enough in the course of the disease, nearly 100% of dogs can be treated successfully. Complications that arise from treatment can be more easily managed early in the disease. Much of the damage to the pulmonary arteries can be reversed when the worms are removed, and the majority of dogs return to normal function with a normal life expectancy. Dogs with severe infection may require considerable special treatment, but if they survive the treatment, there is a good chance for them return to normal health.

Before treating the dog, your veterinarian may want to run laboratory tests to evaluate the dog's overall health and make sure he will tolerate the treatment. The veterinarian may run a complete blood count (CBC), urinalysis and blood chemical profile to check kidney and liver function, as well as other tests. If the dog is over five years of age, or has other disease (for example, kidney disease) associated with the heartworm infection, treatment may be needed before he can be given medication to kill and remove the adult worms. If the dog has any other medical problems, they too may need to be stabilized before the dog is treated for heartworms. This preliminary treatment may include one to two weeks of cage rest, diuretics to remove excess fluid, corticosteroid therapy, and aspirin to reduce blood clotting. These procedures greatly increase the dog's chance of survival.

The dog will have to be hospitalized while he is being treated to eliminate the adult heartworms. As many as four injections of a drug are given intravenously over a two-day period. The injections must be given very carefully so that none of the drug is deposited outside the blood vessel. Treating a case of heartworm disease is not a home project! Drug sensitivity reactions are the first complications that may occur, with either liver or kidney injury. Even after a single injection, the dog may show loss of appetite, vomiting, diarrhea, lack of energy and icterus (yellowing of the membranes, indicating liver damage). These signs may occur within a few hours, or as long as several days later. For this reason, your veterinarian will want the dog where he can administer supportive treatment if and when it is needed.

The second set of complications from treatment to eliminate adult heartworms may begin around six to seven days after treatment. As the adult worms are killed, they leave the heart and are pumped into the lungs, where they may clog the smaller blood vessels (an "embolism"). Blood circulation within the lungs may be severely impaired, and the dog may have trouble breathing. In severe cases, the dog may die. Aspirin may be given to help reduce blood clotting and lessen the effects of the embolism. Your veterinarian may prescribe forced rest for your dog for four to eight weeks. DO IT! Your dog's life may depend on it. The veterinarian may want the dog confined to a cage or small pen. Be sure the dog does not become excited. Limit the amount of company or contact from children that he gets, and try to keep him calm. Gradually begin to exercise him when your veterinarian recommends it.

Some dogs may need a second course of treatment four to six weeks after the first course. If the dog has had a reaction with the first course of treatment, there is very little chance of having problems on the second treatment, so go ahead and have it done. If you don't do it, you will probably lose the dog to the heartworms anyway.

Around four to six weeks after the last treatment for adult heartworms, your veterinarian will treat the dog to eliminate the microfilariae circulating in the dog's blood. One common treatment involves giving tablets daily for 10 days. Three to four weeks after this treatment ends, a blood sample is checked to see that there are no larvae still present. If any are found, the treatment is repeated. If the blood sample is "clean," the dog can be put on preventive medication. In some cases, ivermectin has been used to treat for microfilariae. Collies seem to have a high incidence of severe reactions following treatment with this drug, and it should not be used in that breed. Otherwise, it seems to be a fairly safe treatment. It should NOT be used as a home treatment. If there are adult worms present in the heart, the drug can kill them, and the dog may die suddenly.

Some years ago, surgery was done to remove heartworms from the heart and blood vessels. However, studies have shown that surgery does not significantly improve blood circulation to the lungs. Today, surgery is rarely done, except occasionally on dogs with the caval syndrome, where physical removal of the blockage may be the dog's only chance of living.

Many factors influence the outcome of treatment for heartworms. For this reason, it is difficult for your veterinarian to provide an accurate prognosis. Most dogs who are treated do quite well. Occasionally complications do occur, but they can usually be controlled. Some dogs die because they are treated, but this is, fortunately, quite rare. Early detection and treatment greatly increase the dog's chances of survival. Do not hesitate to have your dog treated, because it's his only chance to live to old age. If you do not have him treated, there is a good chance the disease will kill him, probably sooner rather than later.

HEARTWORM PREVENTION

Has all this convinced you that heartworm disease is easier to prevent than to treat? I'll guarantee you that prevention is certainly cheaper! Elimination of all mosquitoes is impossible, so preventive medication is the only realistic course of action.

Where heartworm disease is considered to be endemic (the southeastern coast, parts of the northeastern United States, the upper midwest and California), treatment with preventive drugs is recommended for the duration of the "mosquito season." The length of time that mosquitoes are active will vary, however, from one place to another, and even from one year to another. For that reason, many veterinarians are recommending treatment throughout the year in heartworm areas. What if you live in an area, such as Wyoming, where heartworms are not a problem and dogs are not routinely treated with preventive medication? As long as your dog stays there, he should have no problem with heartworms. But if you take him to an area where heartworms are a problem, such as the Gulf Coast or Jersey Shore, be sure to put him on a program of preventive medication. CAUTION: This is important even if you are just going there for a short vacation. One encounter with an infected mosquito is all it takes to give your dog heartworms.

Diethylcarbamazine citrate (DEC) is one drug which is used to prevent infection with heartworms. It is available in liquid form, pills and chewable tablets. DEC acts by keeping infective larvae from developing within the dog. It must be given daily, and is highly effective. Heartworm disease may occasionally be found in dogs who have been given DEC. These infections usually occur when the treatment was begun AFTER the dog had been exposed to infected mosquitoes. Or infection can occur if treatment is stopped before the end of the mosquito season. Also, a week or two of very warm weather during the winter may allow some mosquitoes to become active and transmit the infection. For this reason, year-round administration is the safest. Missing two or more days' dosage may allow the dog to become infected with heartworms. Daily administration of this drug is VERY important. Be fanatic about it. Your dog's life may depend on it.

DEC should NEVER knowingly be given to a dog with circulating larvae in the blood, or to a dog who is infested with adult heartworms. Some dogs may not show any ill effects. However, many dogs will show signs, ranging from weakness and disorientation to collapse and shock or death. For this reason, your dog should be examined by a veterinarian BEFORE preventive medication is begun, and a blood sample should be checked to see that there are no microfilariae in the blood. DEC is not recommended for dogs under two months of age.

Ivermectin is another drug which is used to prevent heartworm disease. This drug is sold under the name Heartgard-30® (MSD Agvet). Dosages come in packets according to the weight of the dog, and do not need refrigeration. Ivermectin has the advantage that it can be given once a month instead of daily. Treatment can begin on puppies as young as six weeks of age if you live in a heartworm area. As with DEC, it is IMPERATIVE that the dog be tested for heartworms before the drug is given. Ivermectin is NOT recommended for dogs infected with adult heartworms. It is not effective on adult heartworms in dosages which are safe for the dog. Using it would leave adult worms still producing microfilaria and continuing the disease.

Since only one or two tablets of ivermectin are given, it is of the utmost importance that the dog swallow them. Watch him for several minutes after you give the drug to make sure he has swallowed it. If there is any question about whether or not he has gotten the dose, another should be given. The initial dose of the season must be given within a month after the first exposure to mosquitoes. And the final dose of the season must be given within a month after the last exposure to mosquitoes. But with such a handy product, there is really no reason not to give it on a year-round basis in endemic areas.

If you are replacing DEC with ivermectin, the first dose of ivermectin must be given within a month after stopping the DEC treatment. Thirty days is the effective period for this drug. If at all possible, do not go over this period by more than a day or two without treating the dog, or you may risk allowing adult heartworms to develop from the larvae circulating in the blood. All dogs should be observed closely for eight hours after treatment, as most reactions to the drug (they are quite rare) occur within this time period. Treat the dog on a morning when you are going to be home or can have him with you all day. Signs of toxicity may include staggering, twitching, salivation, vomiting and disorientation (see Ivermectin Toxicity). Contact your veterinarian if these signs of toxicity, or any unusual signs, appear.

Whichever medication you are giving, be sure to increase the amount as the dog grows from a puppy. An amount sufficient for a 15 lb (7 kg) puppy will not give protection when he reaches 60 lb (27 kg).

Many veterinarians recommend twice-yearly blood tests for microfilaria for dogs who are on heartworm preventive medications. This schedule allows a check on the medication, to make sure that it is working in your dog. It also allows early treatment if the prevention fails for any reason, or if the dog was developing an infection before treatment was started, and it was not detected.

TAPEWORMS

Small numbers of tapeworms (also known as cestodes) rarely cause discomfort for dogs and are well tolerated. Severe infections can cause loss of appetite as well as intestinal problems. In rare cases, tapeworms can also infect humans. Some common tapeworms of dogs include *Taenia* species, *Echinococcus* and *Dipylidium caninum*.

Tapeworms can be transmitted to your dog through infected fleas or lice, as well as other insects such as crickets and cockroaches if your dog eats them. They can also infest your dog if he eats an infected rabbit or rodent, or infected game meat such as deer or antelope. The dog eats the infected insect or meat, taking in the larva of the tapeworm. Within two to four weeks, the tapeworm has completely developed. Its head end attaches to the lining of the intestine, with up to several hundred segments being linked together to form the entire tapeworm. The entire worm may be several yards (meters) long. The segments are meant for

independent living, and can move by themselves. Each may contain more than 200 eggs. The segments break off, a few at a time, and you may see them crawling on the dog or its bedding or feces.

You will notice that your dog has tapeworms if you see small whitish, gray or yellowish worm segments in the dog's feces or on the hair of his hind end. These resemble grains of rice. The dog may "scoot" across the ground or floor on his hind end as adult tapeworms break off and exit, irritating the anus. Have a stool sample checked by your veterinarian. However, some of these worms may not pass obvious eggs, and the main sign of their presence will be the rice-like particles on the hair.

Treatments for tapeworms are 90% to 100% effective. However, if the dog continues to eat insects or infected meat, he will become reinfected. Thus, for the scavenging farm dog, or the city dog who eats insects, periodic treatment may be needed. Most current tapeworm remedies kill the worms within the digestive tract. They are then digested, so you may not see any of them in the feces. One available drug, Scolaban®, is safe if the directions are carefully followed. It is of the utmost importance that the dog NOT be allowed to exercise for 24 hours after this drug is given.

It is also important to control fleas and lice on the dog. Control of parasites within the dog's living area (or your house, if he's an inside dog) is also important. Try to keep the dog from scavenging on carcasses. Do not feed uncooked meat or game scraps. If your dog has tapeworms, it is not a good idea to feed lawn clippings to your rabbits or other livestock, as this may pass tapeworms to them. The grass may be contaminated with the dog's feces.

PINWORMS

Pinworms are NOT a parasite of dogs and cats. And, children don't get pinworms from dogs or cats. This worm simply doesn't live in these animals. They are strictly passed between humans, usually because small children are careless about sanitation and don't wash their hands after using the bathroom or before eating.

A misinformed physician may want you to get rid of the dog or cat because the child has pinworms. Don't do it if the only problem is pinworms. Your dog or cat isn't to blame.

WORM NOTES

Scooting the hind end on the ground or licking the hind end are not generally a sign of worms, except occasionally tapeworms. More commonly they are signs of anal gland problems. A puppy who is chases his tail is also NOT a sign of worms. This probably starts out as a game. If it results in a lot of attention from the owner, it may become a habit.

Routine fecal examinations are a good idea. They should be done on young puppies, as young as two to three weeks of age if you live in an area where worms are a problem. For the adult dog, they should be done two to four times a year. For a fecal examination, take a fresh sample of feces to your veterinarian. Most veterinarians do these tests for a nominal charge.

My initial intention when writing this section was to tell you which wormers to use for which worms. In general, you still have to have the fecal sample checked so that the dog can be treated for the specific worms. Wormers are poisons. They are just designed to be more toxic to the worms than to the dog. Because of that toxicity, they should not be used routinely or lightly. However, since the most specific and most effective wormers are available only to and through veterinarians, this section will serve you better if I tell you about "worming" in general and let your veterinarian deal with your specific situation.

Many formulations of wormers are currently on the market, including injections, pills, chewable tablets and pastes. Some of these are safe enough that your veterinarian will sell them to you and let you administer them yourself. Be sure to weigh your dog before you go to the clinic so that he can give you the proper dosage. Other medications are so toxic that veterinarians will only administer them in the clinic.

And, let's face it. If there is an emergency in the middle of the night, your veterinarian is more likely to get out of bed and take care of your animal if he knows who you are. Give him a profit on the worming and he will be more willing to take care of you on your emergency needs at inconvenient times. There's nothing wrong with being a good and valued customer.

Some people will say when your puppy is ailing that "he just needs worming." Worm medicines are not so safe that they should be given indiscriminately, without good reason. And if the dog is suffering from an illness, the worm medication may weaken or injure him sufficiently that he will die. For that reason, it is very important that you take a fecal sample in for examination BEFORE you worm your puppy or dog.

A positive fecal sample does not necessarily mean that worms are the cause of the dog's diarrhea or illness. The worms may just be there along with another problem. And a negative fecal sample does not always mean that the dog does not have worms. The female worms may just not be producing eggs at the time you take the sample.

All parasites which inhabit the digestive tract shed some stage of their life cycle in the feces. This stage may be an egg, a larva or a segment. An appropriate incubation period is necessary before the stage in the feces becomes infective to another animal, whether of the same species or an intermediate host. The incubation period is generally a minimum of two to six days to as long as several months or more, depending on the environmental conditions. This time in the parasite's life is an easy and effective point at which to break the cycle of infection. There is no easier preventive measure than cleaning up the animal's feces and disposing of them properly. If done daily, this can significantly reduce the animal's risk of reinfection and can limit the spread of the parasite to other animals.

Chapter 14

EYE PROBLEMS

EYE EMERGENCIES

The brief list that follows describes emergencies involving the eye. It gives instructions for coping with these emergencies. In all cases, after you have given first aid, get the dog to a veterinarian as soon as possible.

As a general rule, if it isn't relatively easy to examine an injured eye, DON'T try to do so. If you fight the dog, or end up putting too much pressure on an injured eye, you may cause it to rupture. Rupture is especially a risk if the cornea or sclera is cut or weakened. Gently place cold compresses over the area. In most cases, if you need to bandage an injured eye, it is just as well to bandage both of them. Otherwise, the normal eye will keep trying to move and cause unwanted movement of the injured eye.

A dog may aggravate an eye injury by trying to rub it with his paw, or by rubbing his face on the ground or against furniture. A bandage will help to protect the eye. If the dog tries to paw the eye, "hobble" him by taping his front legs together with about six inches of space between them. Tape around one leg (not too tightly!), leave about six inches of tape, and go around the other leg. Now, tape around the center tape again, and back around the first leg.

Injuries which penetrate the globe of the eye, or cuts on the surface of the eyeball. Cover the eye with a gauze bandage or clean cloth, but be sure there is no pressure on the cornea itself. If the object penetrating the cornea is something like a splinter or thorn, DO NOT REMOVE IT. You might cause permanent and irreparable damage by trying to take it out. Restrain the dog by taping his front legs together so he cannot paw the eye. Have someone hold him while you get him to the veterinary hospital. Let the veterinarian remove the object.

Acute corneal ulcer or abrasion. This may be due to an injury or fight, or to the dog merely dragging a dewclaw across the surface of the eye as he rubs his face with a paw (a very good reason for removing dewclaws on all puppies). The dog may have run into a weed or piece of brush, or he may have been scratched by a cat. If you look at the cornea from the side, you may see a scalloped or dished-out spot, or a long, deep scratch. The dog will produce excessive tears, and will obviously be in pain. He may rub the eye with a paw, which will not help—especially if that's what caused the problem in the first place. There is no need to bandage the eye if you can get to a veterinarian within a short period of time. If it will be several hours before a veterinarian can treat the eye, bandage with a soft, clean cloth or gauze over the eye. Moisten it with water over the injured eye. Be sure not to bandage the dog so snugly that you choke him. Tape a cotton ball or gauze sponge over the dewclaw on the injured side to keep the dog from catching it in the bandage if he tries to paw the eye bandage.

Prolapse of the eyeball. This is where one or both eyes have popped partially or totally out of the eye socket. This occurs in breeds of dogs, such as Pekingese and Pugs, that have eye sockets which are extremely shallow. The globe is usually popped out of place by a sharp blow such as the dog being hit by a car or kicked by a horse. Many cases of prolapse, with prompt attention, can be saved as cosmetically acceptable eyes. A few will regain full vision, again with prompt treatment and luck. Cover the eye with a bandage of gauze or very soft cloth. Moisten the part right over the eye with a bit of water to keep the cornea from drying, since the dog cannot blink to spread tears over the cornea. Do not attempt to replace the eyeball. If you apply any pressure, it may cause further damage to the eyeball. Replacement can only be done with the dog completely anesthetized. Keep the animal quiet and get him to a veterinarian as soon as possible.

Descemetocoele. This is a condition in which a small piece of membrane from within the eye protrudes through a hole in the cornea (the clear covering of the eye). It will be seen as a small bulge on the cornea which obviously comes from within the globe itself. Bandage the eye and transport the dog to your veterinarian as soon as possible.

Acute glaucoma. This is a sudden increase in fluid pressure within the eyeball. If untreated, it can lead to a permanently damaged retina and blindness. With prompt treatment, chances for a cure are good. It is extremely painful; the dog may keep his eye closed, and may seem sensitive to light. Excessive tear production may occur. The eyeball may appear larger than normal, and the blood vessels in the sclera (white area) may be swollen and red. The cornea may be clouded or reddish. The pupil may remain dilated (wide open) even when a bright light is shined in the dog's eye. The dog may have trouble seeing. Many dogs show little or no pain with glaucoma, which may mislead you into thinking that it is not serious. Don't be fooled— it IS serious.

Uveitis. You may notice that the dog's eye is red or "cloudy." He may try to hold it closed, and may not want you to examine the area, because it is quite painful. Tears may run down the dog's face, and he may try to avoid bright light. The blood vessels of the sclera may be very enlarged and reddened (this is called "injected"). If you can open the eye, the pupil (opening) may be constricted. If this problem is not treated promptly, it can lead to glaucoma, cataracts and/or retinal detachment. Any of these may lead to permanent blindness.

Hyphema. This is a fancy name for blood in the globe of the eye. It may be due to an injury or blow, or to problems within the eye itself. It can be seen as a red cloudiness just inside the cornea, or a small area of red which has settled to the lowest point inside the cornea. It is important for your veterinarian to determine whether the hyphema is due to injury to the eye, or to a clotting disorder or similar problem. Laboratory tests may be needed to make this determination.

Eyelid Lacerations. These can bleed profusely. If not sutured, they can cause permanent scarring and deformity of the eyelid opening, and damage to the cornea from facial hair rubbing on it. Apply a bandage or clean cloth to put direct pressure on the bleeding area to control the bleeding. Cold compresses are also helpful to control the bleeding. If you use a cold compress, be careful not to freeze the eyelid and other tissues with ice.

Chemicals splashed into the eye. These should be flushed out immediately, using plenty of clean water. Use a garden hose, or pop the dog into the sink or shower. If necessary, get in with him to keep his eye open and facing the water. Flush gently for five to ten minutes. Then apply a gauze bandage or clean cloth to protect the eye until you can get the dog to a veterinarian.

Orbital abscess. This infection may be a single large sac of pus present in the bony orbit behind or beside the eyeball, putting pressure on it. Or it may be a diffuse infection called a cellulitis. It may be due to an object which has penetrated this area from the skin, mouth or conjunctival sac. Bites or other wounds may cause an orbital abscess. Infection may spread from an infected upper molar tooth or sinus. Signs usually come on rapidly. The eye may bulge outward or turn at an odd angle, and the sclera may be reddened. The dog may object if you try to open his mouth, and he may have a fever.

Sudden vision loss. The dog may suffer sudden vision loss from problems within the eye such as detached retina or retinal degeneration. Vision loss can occur because of inflammation of the optic nerve, or because hemorrhage may have occurred within both eyes because the dog has been hit by a car or otherwise injured. It may also occur with some poisonings and some brain tumors.

ALL OF THE PREVIOUS CONDITIONS ARE EMERGENCIES. THEY REQUIRE IMMEDIATE TREATMENT. PROMPT TREATMENT MAY MEAN

THE DIFFERENCE BETWEEN A SIGHTED ANIMAL AND A BLIND ONE.

GLAUCOMA

Glaucoma is an elevated fluid pressure within the eyeball. Fluid which is produced normally within the eyeball is not drained from the eye at a normal rate. The increased pressure can damage the optic nerve, cornea, lens and other structures within the eyeball. Early signs are hard to detect. The "white" of the eye may be reddened, and the blood vessels may appear enlarged. The dog may show that his eye hurts by rubbing the side of his face, avoiding bright light and having excess tears running from his eyes. He may not wish to have his eyes examined.

Unfortunately, glaucoma looks much like several other eye problems. If the eye with glaucoma is left untreated for as little as THREE days, vision may be lost because of irreversible damage to the retina and optic nerve. The course of the disease varies. It may stay mild for many months, or may change slowly or rapidly. Some animals can go from a mild case to a severe case within a few hours. Dogs who lose the sight in one eye may compensate so well with the other that the loss of sight is not noticed until it is far advanced.

If the case of glaucoma is advanced, the pupil of the eye will be widely dilated, and will not shrink if a bright light is shined into the eye. At this point, the cornea may become cloudy and whitened, and the eyeball may become enlarged. The eyelids

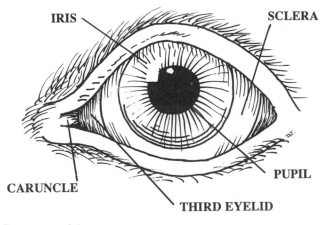

Structures of the eye.

may not close over the globe to protect the cornea as they usually do. Tears are not spread over the globe, and the cornea will dry out, becoming gray or blackish and scarred.

Some cases of glaucoma can be treated with medication. Drugs may be given to help increase the flow of fluid out of the eyeball. Other medications help to decrease fluid production. Either approach will reduce pressure within the eyeball. Some of these drugs can cause muscular weakness because of potassium loss through the urine. If this occurs, let your veterinarian know so that he can adjust or supplement the medication accordingly. Epinephrine is sometimes used to medicate dogs with glaucoma. It may turn pink and look like blood when put into the eye. It may irritate the membranes of the eye. This is not a problem—you can ignore it unless the irritation is severe. In some cases, mannitol solution may be given intravenously by your veterinarian. This helps to reduce pressure within the eyeball until further measures can be taken.

In many dogs with glaucoma, medication alone does not give long-term control. Or you may not be able to give medication often enough to keep the problem under control. In these cases, surgery may be necessary. If the glaucoma is caused by a displaced lens, it will have to be removed. Surgery may be done to reduce the production of fluid within the eyeball, or to allow the fluid to drain more rapidly and efficiently.

If the dog has an enlarged, blind eye, there are two types of surgery which may help. In some cases, a silicone implant can be placed into the globe, creating a cosmetic appearance. This only works if the cornea has not been damaged before this surgery takes place. If the cornea is damaged, total removal of the eye (called "enucleation") is the surgery of choice. There are seldom any problems with removal of an eye, and removal gives permanent relief from the continuing pain associated with glaucoma (see Blindness, below).

Glaucoma is an inherited disease in some breeds of dogs. Those most commonly affected are Basset Hounds, spaniels, Fox Terriers, Norwegian Elkhounds, sled dogs (Malamute, Siberian Husky and Samoyed), and miniature and toy poodles. It may not occur until later in life, after the dog has already reproduced. If he has a close family history of glaucoma, the dog should not used for breeding.

CORNEAL ULCERS

A corneal ulcer is a dished-out area on the clear area of the eyeball (the cornea). It may be caused by an injury—whether from a dogfight, barbed wire scrape, or because the dog has dragged a dewclaw across his eye as he scratches the area with his paw. Or it may be caused by a foreign body, such as a foxtail or grass awn, which has become lodged in one of the eyelids and is being dragged across the eyeball when the dog blinks. Seed hulls are also prone to lodge inside the eyelid, or cling to the eyeball like a suction cup. They too can cause ulcers.

Bathing a dog with soap or detergent and getting it into the dog's eye may damage the cornea. Be sure to rinse out all soap or shampoo, immediately and thoroughly.

Burns caused by strong alkali, such as lye, may cause a corneal ulcer. Strong acids, such as battery acid, may cause corneal burns. Mace may cause damage to the cornea if sprayed in the dog's eyes at close range. If any of these materials have been splashed or sprayed in the dog's eyes, flush his eyes for AT LEAST 15 to 20 minutes with water. Get him to your veterinarian as soon as possible.

Dogs with very prominent, bulging eyes—such as Pekingese, Lhasa Apso, Shih Tzu, Boston Terrier and Pugs—may have a special eye problem. Lagophthalmos is the inability to close the eyelids fully. The dog cannot blink them together, and they may remain slightly open even when the dog is sleeping. This allows an area in the center of the cornea to dry out, and can lead to a corneal ulcer. Surgical correction will allow the lids to close more normally, preventing the damage that would otherwise occur.

If you look across the surface of the dog's eye from the side, you will see a dished-out area, lower than the rest of the surface of the cornea. The dished-out area is the ulcer. A dog with an ulcer is usually in severe pain, and may blink his eye or even hold it shut. He may rub at his eye and show increased tear production, or even a bit of mucus or pus in the eye. He may be reluctant to have you handle his head, and may not want to be in bright light.

If you have determined that the dog has a corneal ulcer, take him to your veterinarian, if possible. Before you do so, put a cotton ball or small piece of gauze over the dewclaw on the side where the eye is injured. Tape this in place with two or three wraps of adhesive tape. These should be snug but not tight enough to stop circulation to the foot. This is to keep the dog from further injuring his eye if he should rub it with his paw.

If you cannot get the dog to a veterinarian, treat him as soon as possible with an eye ointment containing ONLY one or more antibiotics. The product should NOT contain a cortisone or corticosteroid-type drug, as they may cause the problem to become worse, with eventual loss of the eye. Eye drops, again containing ONLY an antibiotic, can be used if you do not have eye ointment. An ointment will last longer and is preferred over drops if it is available.

Put the ointment in the eye every half hour for four to six treatments, and then every two or three hours for the rest of the first day. From then on, treat the dog at least four times a day. It is important to treat the ulcer intensively with antibiotics to prevent bacterial infection (or to treat the infection if it has already occurred). Without antibiotic treatment, infection may occur, become rapidly worse, and result in perforation of the cornea and loss of vision in that eye. The ulcer should heal within three to five days. Treatment should be continued up to eight to 10 days to make sure that total healing has occurred. It is safer to treat for a couple of extra days than to stop too soon. If a foreign body has caused the problem, it must be removed when treatment is started. Leave the dewclaw bandaged until the eye is completely healed.

If the ulcer becomes larger, deeper or fails to heal, see your veterinarian at once. In some cases, a fungus may be involved, and the antibiotic will not do any good. Also, if the foreign body causing the ulcer is a thorn penetrating the surface of the eyeball, its removal is best left to your veterinarian, who will remove it after sedating the dog enough to make sure no further damage is done to the eyeball.

KERATOCONJUNCTIVITIS SICCA (KCS or DRY EYE)

Keratoconjunctivitis sicca is a condition in which the dog does not produce an adequate quantity of tears. A lack of tears may be due to damage to one of the nerves, usually due to a head injury. It may be from irritation from foreign bodies in the conjunctival sac (the area behind the eyelids, next to the eye), from eyelids which roll inward so that the skin rubs on the cornea, or from hair on hair-covered nasal folds irritating the eye. It may occur when the dog cannot completely close his eyelids over the cornea and the cornea dries out.

Inadequate tear production leaves the surface of the eyeball dry. As the dog blinks his eyelids together, the rubbing of this unlubricated tissue causes considerable pain. The dog may have a thick, pus-like material clinging to or oozing from the eye. If you look across the corneal surface from the side, it may look dull and dryish.

If KCS goes on for a long time, the irritation to the cornea may cause an ulcer to form, or blood vessels may grow out across the surface of the cornea in response to the irritation. These are followed by black pigmentation and scarring of the cornea. If the deposition of pigment in the cornea continues for a long period of time, the dog may become totally blind. For this reason, it is important to treat the disease before it progresses very far (see PK, below).

KCS can be treated by using various kinds of artificial tears, as recommended by your veterinarian. These serve to replace the tears which the dog's body is not producing. Antibiotics may be helpful in some cases.

In a few cases of KCS, an initiating cause can be found. One of these is lack of a normal amount of thyroid hormone. Another is the administration of certain sulfa drugs. Surgery to correct hair or eyelashes rubbing on the eyeball surface may provide relief. If any of these is the case, treating (or removing) the cause will often result in improvement.

If normal tear production does not resume within a reasonable length of time (say, six months or so), the parotid salivary duct can be transplanted so that it discharges into the conjunctival sac, allowing saliva to take the place of tears in lubricating the eyeball. This can often provide a dramatic cure.

PIGMENTARY KERATITIS (PANNUS)

Pigmentary keratitis (PK) is the response of the cornea to chronic irritation. It may begin with KCS, and anything causing KCS can lead to pigmentary keratitis. It is also associated with a syndrome called pannus, which is especially common in German Shepherds.

The continuous, chronic irritation causes blood vessels to grow out across the surface of the cornea. These blood vessels are a relatively normal response to the chronic irritation, and are trying to heal the cornea. The response becomes abnormal when the blood vessels persist for a period of time, and black pigment follows them out from the sclera (white part of the eye) onto the cornea. As pigment covers the cornea, the dog will gradually go blind, because light cannot enter the eye.

Treatment begins with curing the original cause if possible. Eyelid surgery may be necessary if the lids are not closing normally. Surgery may be needed to keep the nasal folds from rubbing hair across the cornea. Similar surgery may be needed if the eyelids are rolling inward and dragging hair across the eyeball.

Pannus in the German Shepherd seems to have a genetic association with the breed. A similar disease is seen in Border Collies and Greyhounds. The disease may involve autoimmunity and other factors. Pannus may involve both eyes, and is more common in dogs three to five years of age or older. The first sign that you will probably see is a black spot on the edge of the cornea, usually toward the outer corner of the eye.

While pannus can sometimes be temporarily arrested with drugs, the disease usually progresses until many of these dogs become permanently blind. In some cases, surgical thinning of the layers of tissue on the cornea makes the disease more susceptible to medical treatment. Pannus in some dogs may be controlled with medication, which must be given for the rest of their lives.

ENTROPION AND FACIAL FOLDS

Entropion is the condition where the eyelid folds or rolls under, bringing its hair into contact with the surface of the eyeball. It commonly affects only the lower eyelid, and both eyes may be involved. It is especially common in Chow Chows, Shar-Pei, English Bulldogs, Pekingese, and other dogs with wrinkled, shortened faces.

Some Shar-Pei, as well as other dogs, may have facial folds which are high enough to roll against the surface of the eyeball, bothering the dog as soon as his eyes open at two to three weeks of age. In some cases, temporary sutures may be placed in the folds to hold them away from the eye until the dog "grows into" his eyelids. He may or may not need further surgery as he grows older.

Entropion can be temporarily controlled by pasting the hair down with petroleum jelly or mustache wax. Surgery should be done to correct the problem permanently. Your veterinarian will remove a thin strip of skin from the lid, and suture the area back together. This "plastic surgery" will prevent the eyelid from rolling inward, and should permanently cure the problem.

ECTROPION

Ectropion is when the lower eyelid bulges outward like a little bag. This condition is common in Cocker Spaniels, Bloodhounds, Bassets and St. Bernards. The dog's sagging, drooping lower eyelid collects all sorts of dirt and debris, in addition to becoming reddened and irritated by exposure to sun and wind. Simple cases with occasional conjunctivitis can be treated by washing the conjunctival sac with sterile saline solution or artificial tears, followed by an antibiotic-corticosteroid ointment. Cases of ectropion which are making life miserable for the dog can be treated surgically by taking a piece out of the outer corner of the dog's eyelid. This procedure tightens the lower lid up against the eye and eliminates the bulge.

TRICHIASIS

Trichiasis is the condition in which eyelashes are pointing toward the surface of the eyeball, rather than away from it. It may be due to injury of the eyelid and scar contraction, or it may be a hereditary problem. It is common in Toy Poodles and Pomeranians. Your veterinarian may use electrolysis to remove the offending lashes if there are only a few of them. If a large number are involved, or a whole extra row of them are present, surgery may be needed. These techniques are relatively simple, and if done before permanent damage occurs to the cornea, can generally provide permanent relief from irritation.

PROLAPSE OF THE EYEBALL

Prolapse of the eyeball (also called proptosis of the globe) is when the eyeball is popped partially or completely out of the dog's eye socket. This condition is more common in dogs with shortened faces and prominent eyes, such as Pekingese and Lhasa Apso. In these breeds, a minimal blow is all that is needed to pop the eyeball out of place. It can occur in dogs of other breeds who are kicked, hit by a car, or otherwise injured by a sharp blow to the side of the head.

Cover the dog's eyeball with a dampened gauze sponge or piece of cloth. Transport him immediately to the nearest veterinary clinic. If the injury has just occured, your veterinarian will anesthetize the dog and attempt to replace the eye in the socket. It may or may not turn out to be a functional eyeball after healing occurs, depending on the damage to the optic nerve and blood vessels. In some cases, it will be necessary to remove the eye later. Restoration of sight occurs in enough cases that it is worth a try, however.

CATARACTS

Cataract is the general term which refers to the clouding of the capsule or fibers of the lens within the eye. Cataracts begin with a slight clouding of the lens, progress to diffuse white lines or rays within the lens, and eventually end with the whole lens being completely whitish. At this point, the dog will be totally blind. Light cannot penetrate the opaque lens.

Occasionally, a puppy may be born with cataracts. They can also occur in dogs who have diabetes mellitus and Cushing's disease. Some cataracts are due to objects which penetrate and damage the lens. These may include thorns, cat claws, shotgun pellets and similar objects. Most cases of cataracts in the dog are considered to be of hereditary origin.

Hereditary cataracts which develop later in life are found in some breeds, including Miniature Poodles, Boston Terriers, Cocker Spaniels and Afghan Hounds. A certain percentage (about one-third) of the hereditary cataracts will be reabsorbed spontaneously. For these animals, enough recovery may take place that the dog will have functional sight. These animals can be treated medically and watched for a period of time. If enough resorption does not occur so that the animal can see adequately, surgery is still advisable to remove the opaque lens.

Other than the few animals mentioned above, there is no medical treatment for cataracts. There is no medication that can remove cataracts once they develop, whether given systemically or put on or into the eye. Surgery is the only treatment for cataracts. The object of cataract surgery is to restore the animal to functional vision. Dogs adjust rather well to loss of sight, especially when kept in a familiar environment. Their vision is not badly impaired until the cataracts in both eyes are near maturity (becoming very opaque). For that reason, you, the owner, are the best judge of when surgery should be done. When the dog is constantly bumping into objects and cannot live a normal life, the time for surgery has arrived. Cataract surgery is best performed by a veterinary specialist, familiar with and skilled in the procedure.

Some dogs may have a damaged or diseased retina, which cannot be evaluated through the clouded lens. This is one reason why surgery for cataracts sometimes fails to restore the animal's sight.

SENILE SCLEROSIS

Senile or nuclear sclerosis is a normal, common, age-related change in the lens of the eye. The lens is deep within the dog's eye, not on the surface. You may see a wedge-shaped cloudiness in the lens. It may be whitish or bluish. It may have a ground-glass appearance. Senile sclerosis is seen in most older dogs. It rarely causes problems with vision.

CONJUNCTIVITIS

Conjunctivitis is an inflammation of the membranes which line the eye area—the conjunctivae. The conjunctiva lines the fold at the bottom and top of the eye, and folds back onto the inside of the eyelid.

Signs of conjunctivitis include pain, swelling of the conjunctiva and redness. In some cases, small reddened nodules may appear on the surface, similar to those occurring on our eyes when we rub them too much and irritate them, and then look at them in a mirror to see why they are uncomfortable. Discharge may be present. The discharge may just be extra tear production, strings of ropy mucus, or yellowish or grayish pus. It may dry in the corners of the eyes. It is important to determine whether the problem involves only the eyes, or is a symptom of a more serious problem, such as canine distemper.

Your veterinarian will begin to treat conjunctivitis by thoroughly examining the eye. He will make sure that there are no foreign bodies, such as grass awns, caught in the conjunctival sac. He may also check to make sure that the reddening and infection are not associated with a case of glaucoma or other severe eye problem.

Most cases of conjunctivitis are due to bacterial infection. A pus-like exudate is a prominent feature of these infections. An antibiotic ointment or drops are usually used to treat a simple case of conjunctivitis. Most drops should be put in the eyes five to six times a day, and ointments at least three to four times a day. It may be necessary to treat the eye(s) for a week to 10 days. Keep the dog's face and eye area wiped free of tears and exudate. You can wipe them off with a washcloth or paper towel dampened with lukewarm water. If it is fly season, apply an insect or fly repellent recommended for dogs. It may be necessary to keep the dog indoors or in a screened area to protect him from flies until his eyes are healed if he is normally an outdoor dog. If the conjunctiva tends to be dry, it may be necessary to use an artificial tear solution in addition to the antibiotic ointment or drops.

If the conjunctivitis becomes worse, if it does not heal completely within five to seven days (with steady improvement each day), or if the dog shows other signs of disease, take him to your veterinarian for examination. Continuing conjunctivitis may be a sign of a systemic illness. Or it may be due to an eye disease such as keratoconjunctivitis sicca (dry eyes, KCS). Or the dog may have eyelashes or hairs on the eyelid which are rubbing on the cornea and keeping it continuously irritated.

Follicular conjunctivitis is an inflammation of small follicles in the conjunctival sac. It looks like a number of small reddened, irritated granules. Your veterinarian may treat it by sedating the dog and scarifying or cauterizing the granules. It is then treated with an antibiotic-corticosteroid ointment. Follicular conjunctivitis may recur in 2-4 months. It is not a serious problem, which is fortunate because there is no permanent cure for it.

CONJUNCTIVITIS IN NEWBORNS

Bacterial conjunctivitis is especially common in newborns, both puppies and kittens. As soon as their eyes open, they may become stuck shut with a pus which soon hardens into crusts. Meanwhile, the infection continues behind the closed lids. If let go long enough, it will erode the cornea and the animal will be permanently blind. Treatment begins by opening the eyelids. Gently pick off any crusty material with the edge of your fingernail. Separate the eyelids, and remove any remaining pus or exudate with a cotton swab, trying to pull it away without touching the cornea with the swab. Rinse the eyes with a saline eyewash and pat them dry with a tissue. Treat them with an antibiotic eye ointment. The cleaning should be done twice a day and the ointment put in four to five times a day if at all possible. If treatment is started as soon as the problem is noticed, most puppies will have normal sight and no permanent damage. If neglected, blindness is a real possibility.

TRAUMATIC CONJUNCTIVITIS

Conjunctivitis may be caused by an injury to the dog's eye, whether by a cut or a puncture. The hunting dog may, for example, run his eye into a thorn and scratch the conjunctiva. After you have checked to see that there is no foreign material left in the eye, it can be gently irrigated with a lukewarm solution of one part povidone-iodine to nine parts water. It can then be treated with an antibiotic ointment until healed. Make sure there is NO damage to the cornea before treating an eye

in this manner. If the cut is more than 3/8 inch (1 cm.) long, the dog should be taken to your veterinarian for suturing.

CONJUNCTIVAL HEMORRHAGE

Bleeding within the conjunctiva may occur when the dog's eye is injured, whether being hit by a car, being kicked, or running into an object such as a tree. The resulting blood clot (hematoma) will reabsorb naturally within one to three weeks, depending on how much blood is in the area.

Bleeding within the conjunctiva is generally a sign of another problem. Hemorrhage under the conjunctiva may be associated with certain infectious agents, especially *Rickettsia*. Most bleeding resolves itself when the primary disease is treated.

If the dog shows hemorrhage into the conjunctiva and you do not have any knowledge or evidence of injury, this may be a sign of a clotting disorder within the dog's system. It may be due to a disease such as hemophilia, or an autoimmune disease. Have him checked by your veterinarian.

CONJUNCTIVAL ADHESIONS

Adhesions between the conjunctiva and the cornea may occur when the conjunctiva heals an ulcer on the cornea which has been caused by injury or infection. The two surfaces may become permanently grown together with fibrous tissue. These may result in the dog being unable to move his eyeball normally, or may keep his third eyelid from moving. If the conjunctiva grows to the cornea, a permanent whitish or blue spot, through which the dog cannot see, may result. These adhesions are commonly due to chemical damage or to physical injury (as from being hit by a car or scratched with a piece of brush as the dog runs through the woods).

Treating one of these adhesions is a job for your veterinarian. With the dog under anesthesia, he will surgically separate the attached areas, and make the surfaces as normal as possible. A large soft contact lens may be placed in the dog's eye for some time to keep the two surfaces from growing back together while they both heal. In some cases, however, surgery is not successful. The two surfaces may grow back together, or a permanently damaged spot may remain on the cornea.

EYEWORMS

In the western United States, a parasitic worm, *Thelazia californiensis*, can infect small animals. The worm lives in the conjunctival sac, next to the eye. The dog may not show any signs, or it may show signs of a mild conjunctivitis. Treatment consists of removing the worms, which may be 1-15 inches long (25-400 mm), and are quite thin. There may only be one worm in an eye, or there may be several. They can be taken out with forceps or tweezers, or picked out with your fingers. This must be done very carefully, so as not to damage the cornea or other portions of the eye. If you cannot get them easily, take the dog to your veterinarian. He will use a topical anesthetic on the surface of the eyeball to make it easier to remove the worms. The dog will need treatment with an antibiotic eye ointment for the accompanying conjunctivitis. Control of flies helps to prevent reinfection with the parasites.

Cuterebra larvae may grow in the conjunctival sac, or in the delicate tissues around the eye in young puppies. These are short, fat worms about a half-inch long. They have to be picked out. Surgical removal may be needed if the larva is within the skin. If there is any question about getting one of these worms out of his hole, take the puppy to your veterinarian for surgical removal of the larva. If you rupture it while attempting to remove it, a severe anaphylactic reaction may occur.

TEAR STAINING

Tear staining of the face is common in many breeds of dogs, especially the toy ones. This overflow may be caused by either increased tear production or decreased tear drainage through the tear duct into the nose. These problems are especially common (and noticeable) in toy and miniature Poodles, Lhasa Apso, Pekingese and other small dogs.

Tear production may be increased because of irritation or pain. In the small dogs, this is commonly due to eyelashes or hairs rubbing the eyeball. In some cases, stray eyelashes will be growing in the conjunctival sac, again rubbing on the eyeball. Or they may be along the upper eyelid. These problems are cured by electrolysis to remove the offending eyelash, or surgery to remove a number of them. Facial folds and eyelids which roll inward may rub onto the cornea, causing the same problem. In some breeds, especially the Lhasa Apso, extra hairs may grow from the caruncle. This is the small pinkish nodule in the inner corner of the eye. These hairs are easily removed surgically.

Decreased tear drainage may cause tear staining on the face. Tears normally drain into the nose through two tiny holes in the inner corner of the eye. Tears are squeezed into these holes as the dog blinks. The blinking also results in a pumping action.

In some dogs, these tiny holes may become plugged because of conjunctivitis or another infection causing pus which cannot flow through the holes. In many short-faced breeds, the drainage system is not totally normal in the first place, and may never drain well. This is also common in Miniature and Toy Poodles. Some of these dogs have a slight ectropion (sagging) of the lower eyelid, which squeezes tears across the face rather than into the drainage system. Surgical repair of the lower eyelid may be helpful.

Still other small dogs may have the opening into the tear drainage system completely missing. They were simply born without it. An opening may be surgically created by your veterinarian. In a few dogs, the entire drainage system is missing. This can't be repaired.

Scarring from infection, surgery or injury may damage the area of the openings into the tear ducts. Tumors in this area may also block the drainage system. Older dogs who have never had tear staining and suddenly acquire it should be checked for tumors.

Finding the cause and curing it as best as possible will give your dog the most comfort. Tear staining is ugly for the owner to look at. It often turns pinkish or rust-colored. If you cannot get the cause of the drainage problem repaired, cream bleaches are available which can make the drainage lighter in color and less prominent. The condition can be miserable for the dog as flies collect on the drainage. Cream fly repellents can be wiped on the dog's face to make him more comfortable. As with any other skin product, patch test a small spot first, elsewhere on the dog, and then be careful not to get the medication into the dog's eye.

DISORDERS OF THE THIRD EYELID

The third eyelid is the little flap of tissue in the inner corner of the eyelid. It has several functions: It helps to protect the cornea; when the dog blinks, it helps to restore the tear film across the eye; it contributes to tear secretion; and also has some immune functions. The third eyelid is stiffened by a small, T-shaped support cartilage.

Prolapse of the gland of the third eyelid occurs when this small gland becomes swollen and protrudes from the inner corner of the eye. This is often called "cherry eye." When this occurs, the dog may also have conjunctivitis. The cartilage may be bent as the gland bulges, turning the third eyelid inside out. The problem seems to be inherited, and is especially common in Cocker Spaniels, Beagles, English Bulldogs and St. Bernards. One or both eyes may be affected. Some years ago, the glands were routinely removed by surgery. It has been found, however, that the gland produces about one-third of the tears. Current treatment favors suturing the gland back into place, rather than risking developing a dry eye.

Occasionally, the cartilage of the third eyelid may roll outward on itself. This is most common in giant breeds of dogs, and may occur in one or both eyes. Surgery is done to carefully dissect the cartilage out of the third eyelid. This leaves the third eyelid in place to function reasonably normally. There is no other way of correcting the problem.

Tumors occasionally affect the third eyelid. These are usually seen as a smooth pinkish nodule sticking out of the inner corner of the eye. Some can be successfully removed by themselves, while others will require removal of the entire third eyelid. Treatment, if done early enough, is usually successful.

RETINAL DISEASES

The retina is the area at the rear of the eyeball where the nerves which allow normal vision are found. Retinal detachment may occur as the retina comes loose from the rear part of the globe of the eye. This may occur suddenly, leaving the dog totally blind. This sudden blindness often happens in Toy Poodles. Retinal detachment may occur after injury or surgery, or due to high blood pressure or kidney disease. The retina will not reattach by itself. Surgery to reattach the retina may be available, but the cost may be prohibitive.

Progressive retinal atrophy (PRA) affects a number of breeds of dogs as a hereditary problem. Among those affected are Toy and

Miniature Poodles, Springer Spaniels, Norwegian Elkhound, Irish Setter, Labrador Retriever and Golden Retriever.

Retinal diseases generally get worse until the dog is completely blind; there is no cure for them. The best idea is to prevent them by careful attention to bloodlines and avoiding breeding affected animals, or those related to affected animals.

WHITE SPOTS IN EYES

Dogs of several breeds who have a blue merle coat may have white spots in one or both eyes. Or the iris (colored part) of the eye may be completely white. This is called a wall eye, watch eye, china eye or glass eye. These white spots are occasionally seen in dogs with other coat colors, such as black and white Border Collies. Dogs with these spots seem to have normal vision. The spots are not a problem.

BLINDNESS

Blindness is not a serious problem in the pet dog. Many dogs go blind so gradually that the owner does not realize this has occurred until he moves to another house or changes the furniture around, and notices that the dog suddenly bumps into things. Even when blindness occurs suddenly, as from glaucoma, most dogs adjust quickly and are still good pets. Most animals, in fact, accept the handicap more readily than do their owners.

A blind dog should never be allowed outdoors alone unless he is in a securely fenced yard. Otherwise, he may blunder into the street and get hit by a car. Or he may be attacked by another dog, and have no idea of where to go or what to do. He will, however, enjoy a walk on a leash with you. Keep his food, water and bedding in the same location. The dog will "learn" his environment quite rapidly, and blind dogs are rarely a problem to their owners because of lack of vision.

If you have a dog who is blind and you move, you might consider putting the dog in a kennel during the time that you are moving. This will keep him from being confused by all the movement and change going on around him. When you are settled, and most furniture is in its permanent place, bring him into the new environment and let him explore it. I had a blind cat who moved through several "new" homes, finding each one a grand new adventure of smells to explore.

Chapter 15

EAR PROBLEMS

Healthy ears begin with preventive maintenance. Dogs who have hair growing down into the ear canal should have it removed when they are groomed, as part of their routine maintenance. If you take your dog to a groomer, make sure that he uses good sanitation, disinfecting all clippers, brushes, and cages, as well as his hands, between animals, so that bacteria and ear mites are not spread from one animal to another. If you have ear mites in another animal (whether dog, cat or rabbit) in your household, it is often a good idea to treat all the animals at the same time so that an infected animal will not spread the parasites to one that has just been treated and cleared up.

If you do your own grooming, use the same disinfectant as you expect a groomer to use between animals if you have one with an ear infection. You can disinfect grooming supplies with povidone-iodine solution between dogs, or you can use a product such as Roccal®. If you are working with several dogs, you can mix a pan or bucket of the solution, and keep grooming supplies in it between animals. The business end of clippers should be brushed with a disinfectant solution after unplugging them so that you do not get shocked. They should, of course, NOT be dipped into the disinfectant solution.

Routine maintenance should include cleaning the ears, beginning when the dog is still a puppy. Take a bit of baby oil on a gauze sponge or cotton ball. Wipe all of the ear surfaces that you can see. COTTON SWABS SHOULD NOT BE USED FOR ROUTINE EAR CLEANING (See Ear Infections, below). If the dog has a large accumulation of wax, mix together equal parts of vinegar and baby oil. Warm this mixture to body temperature. You can easily do this by running warm water over a dropperful of it until it is lukewarm. Then wipe the water off the outside of the dropper and put half a dropperful into each ear. Massage the base of both ears until you hear a "squishy" sound. Using a gauze sponge or piece of cotton, remove the wax which you have worked loose. The dog will shake his head when you let go

of him, removing still more of the material. For that reason, the operation is best done out of doors or in the garage, while you are wearing old clothes. The mixture of vinegar and oil mentioned above can be used in your dog's ears after he has been swimming. This will help to prevent infection and clean out any material in the ears.

If the wax keeps coming back rapidly, the dog needs to be checked for infection or ear mites.

EAR FLAP PROBLEMS

Flystrike is perhaps the most common problem affecting the skin of the ear. It is a seasonal problem in dogs which are confined outdoors in an area infested with flies. Adult stable flies bite the dog, suck blood, and produce a reddened area of sores. Blood and serum ooze from the fly bites, causing dry crusts. The dog is miserable. He may shake his head or scratch his ears, producing scrapes and bleeding. The lesions are usually confined to the tips of the ears, and are especially seen in dogs with upright ears. Sometimes they may be found elsewhere on the face. They especially occur with dogs who

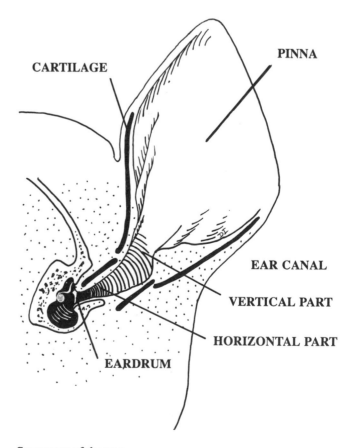

Structures of the ear.

are chained or kept outside where they cannot escape from the flies.

Healing a case of flystrike begins by getting rid of the flies, or protecting a dog from them. Keep the dog indoors during the day for a few days until you can get the itching under control. If the dog has to remain outdoors, use a fly or mosquito repellent on his entire body, especially concentrating on his head and ears. (Be careful not to get any in his eyes.) Or a paste can be made from flea powder and put on the area. Skin-So-Soft bath oil (Avon) can be used to help keep the flies away. An ointment or cream containing an antibiotic plus a corticosteroid (such as Panalog®) will help to control the infection and reduce the itching. It will also soften the crusts so that you can remove them in one or two days. If you scrape the hard crusts off, you just do more damage to the skin. Let them get soft before you try to remove them. If you can determine where the flies are coming from, spraying that area or removing garbage or other material will help to reduce the dog's discomfort. Plan on keeping insecticide on his face and ears throughout the summer. Housing should be provided so that the dog can get away from flies, or a screened area could be made for daytime use.

Scabies can produce intense itching on the ends of a dog's ears. This is especially seen in dogs such as Poodles with drooping ears. The dog will scratch his ears. The ends may be reddened, and some or all of the hair may be gone. Yellowish crusts may appear on the ends of the ears due to the seepage of serum from the injured skin. The dog may also have lesions on his elbows, legs and the lower part of his chest. Small hairless spots near the eyes may also be due to scabies.

Scabies is often difficult to diagnose in a skin scraping. For that reason, your veterinarian may treat the dog based on the signs that he is showing.

Frostbite may occur on the ears when a dog is left outdoors for a long time in extremely cold weather. The tips of both ears are usually frostbitten. The skin may be cold, pale and have no feeling if you pinch it gently. Once rewarmed, it becomes reddened and painful. To care for frostbitten ears, bring the dog into a warmer area and warm the ear tips with lukewarm water for half an hour. Petroleum jelly can be used to soften the ear tips and help protect the frozen areas. Check the tip of the tail and the scrotum, as these areas may also be affected. It is hard to get the dog to sit in a pan of warm water, so use warm, moist towels to warm a frostbitten scrotum. A dog who has had frostbite once will be much more susceptible to it in the future. The original event damages blood circulation to the affected skin. The dog should be kept out of the cold after frostbite has occurred.

A torn ear flap may occur when a dog is in a fight. Or it may happen when he catches his ear on a barbed wire fence or a piece of sharp metal. This may be a small nick in the edge of the ear, or it may be a major split which cuts the ear in half. For best healing, take the dog to your veterinarian as soon as possible so that the ear can be sutured. Be aware, however, that no matter how skillful the surgeon, the ear may not heal smoothly. Ears are thin sandwiches of skin with a bit of cartilage in the middle. Often, as they heal, the scar contracts. This leaves a wrinkled, "cauliflower" ear.

FOREIGN BODIES IN EAR

Foreign bodies in the ear are a common problem, especially in late summer and fall, when foxtails, cheat grass, and other plants are becoming ripe and drying. The awns or seed heads, as well as other parts of the plant, break off quite easily. The dog's ears often act like scoops to pick up one or more of these plant pieces on a day's walk. Foreign bodies are especially a problem in dogs with drooping ears. Dogs with upright ears are often able to shake such objects out. The ear flaps of dogs with drooping ears help to hold the objects in. The dog may pull the affected ear downward.

Hard, often sharp, foreign objects result in severe irritation, inflammation, and sometimes pressure necrosis (death) of the eardrum. They may also cause the dog to shake his head severely enough to cause a hematoma of the ear. In addition, he may paw at the side of his face enough to rub a spot raw, which may be hairless and bleeding. Get the dog to the veterinarian as soon as possible—the next morning is good enough. In all but the calmest dog, it will be necessary for the veterinarian to totally anesthetize the dog in order to remove the foreign body without puncturing the dog's eardrum. Plan on leaving the dog for the day or overnight. If there is much inflammation or infection in the ear canal, it may be necessary for you to administer ear drops or ointment until it is cleared up.

HEMATOMA OF THE EAR

A hematoma of the ear is an accumulation of blood within the flap of the ear. It is like a giant blood blister. It usually occurs in dogs with large ear flaps, such as Labrador Retrievers, Spaniels, etc. Foreign bodies, ear infections and mite infestations all cause a great deal of irritation, pain and itching deep within the ear. The dog tries to get relief by flapping his ears violently, or pawing at them with his feet. The mechanical damage separates the layers of the ear flap, and breaks small blood vessels. Blood pools in the area of separation. Bite wounds can also cause a hematoma.

A hematoma may occur in one or both ears. Initial signs include a sudden swelling, generally between the inner skin and the cartilage. Hematomas vary in size from small to half the size of the ear—or larger in a severe case.

The first thing to do is to restrain the dog from shaking his ear(s) any more, making the problem worse. Use adhesive tape or other porous tape, so that the dog does not sweat under the tape, to fasten the ear flaps to his head. Tape both ears as flat as possible over the top of the head, one on top of the other. Run the tape over the top of the head and under the neck, 'round and 'round. Don't worry about taping to the hair—it will help to hold the bandage securely until you can get the dog to the veterinarian. Just be sure the tape is loose enough under the jaw and neck areas that the dog can breathe easily, and eat and drink if necessary. This is not an "immediate" emergency. If it happens in the evening, take the dog to the veterinarian the next morning.

Your veterinarian may treat a small hematoma by removing the blood with a syringe and fine hypodermic needle, after thoroughly disinfecting the area with alcohol or another disinfectant. He will then either bandage the ear to the top of the head, or to a roll of gauze or cardboard. It is usually necessary to leave this in place for seven to 10 days. The pressure from the bandage holds the layers of the ear together so that the separation can heal.

A larger hematoma will usually require surgery. The clot of blood will be removed, usually through an "S"-shaped incision, which helps to reduce wrinkling of the ear due to scar tissue. A piece of plastic or other material is used to sandwich the ear. Then the ear is sutured through all the layers. This is to keep new bleeding from filling up the space between the layers again. Otherwise, all it would take is one more good shake of the dog's head, and the pocket would fill with blood. The sutures may be held with buttons, pieces of X-ray film or polyethylene tubing. These materials keep the sutures from pulling through the soft skin of the ear. The sutures are usually left in place for 10 to 14 days.

If there is a known cause of the hematoma, such as ear mites, an ear infection or a foreign body, it should be treated to prevent recurrence of the problem.

EAR INFECTIONS

Why and how do dogs get ear infections? Some begin with ear mites or other parasite infestations. These can often progress to chronic ear infections because of the irritation and debris from the parasites. Dogs can develop ear infections

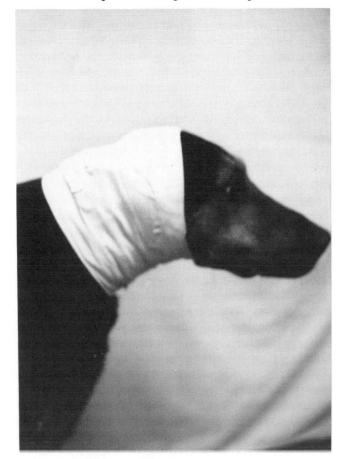

Bandage keeps dog from shaking his ears.

because of damage to the thin, tender skin of the ear canal from faulty cleaning. Hot, humid weather also increases the occurrence of ear infections by promoting moist conditions in the ear canal.

Many dogs, however, have ear infections because of the way humans have made them after generations of selective breeding. Most wild dogs have upstanding ears which have good ventilation. Think of the ears of a wolf or a fox. If a piece of grass or dirt gets into the ear, the dog simply shakes his head and it usually flies out. Domestic dogs with upright ears have far fewer ear infections than do the flop-eared dogs. Humans have bred many dogs which have hanging ear flaps, like the hounds and hunting breeds. This flap tends to hold in the ear objects which fall or blow into it. In addition, the flap keeps the ear canal warm and moist, a perfect environment for bacteria, fungi and parasites to live and thrive.

To add insult to this injury, many dogs which have a lot of hair on their bodies (such as Poodles) also have hair growing far down into their ear canals. This again helps to hold in pieces of grass and other objects, as well as making the ear canal even warmer and steamier than in a clean-eared dog like a Labrador. Dogs with allergic skin disease may be predisposed to ear infections, as are those with seborrheic skin disease. Polyps or tumors in the skin of the ear can also lead to ear infections.

In general, it can be said that a clean, dry ear canal is a healthy ear canal. ANYTHING that keeps dirt and moisture in the canal will, eventually, lead to infection.

Ear infections can be due to bacteria. These are perhaps the most common. Infection can start because of parasites such as ear mites. Or they can be yeast or fungus infections. One yeast, in particular, is especially happy with the waxy conditions found in the ear. Many times, two or three types of organisms live together in the mess of wax, bloody exudate, dirt and moisture which has accumulated in the ear. Ear infections may be secondary to other diseases such as allergies, hypothyroidism or seborrhea.

One sign of ear infection is scratching. The dog may paw and scratch at the side of his face until it is reddened, bloody and raw. He may sit down and attempt to stick a hind foot into his ear, while making groaning noises. He may shake his head violently enough to result in a hematoma. The hair on the underside of the ear and the side of the face may be sticky or wet with drainage. The whole mess may have a very unpleasant odor. If your dog has a greasy, "spoiled" odor, be sure to check his ears. Severe cases may have enough material accumulated on the eardrum that hearing may be impaired.

An ear infection may be acute, coming on suddenly. This may occur after an automobile ride in which the dog has hung his head out the window, or after a day in the woods when the cheat grass is ripening and he has gotten one of the seed heads in his ear. These infections are usually easily treated, especially after the cause has been removed.

An ear infection which has continued for a period of time may become chronic. At this point, several changes can occur. Early treatment may have eliminated all the susceptible bacteria, leaving only the more resistant ones. Yeast and fungi may have colonized an area where they do not ordinarily live. The lining of the ear canal responds by growing small nodules of skin. These are often called "cauliflowers," because the surface of the skin looks much the same as the surface of a head of that vegetable. The bacteria are now living down in the holes and hollows between the raised areas, where conditions are even warmer and damper and the organisms are more protected from treatment and medication. A chronic ear infection is a real challenge to treat.

TREATMENT OF EAR INFECTIONS

Ideally, treatment of an ear infection would begin by taking the dog to your veterinarian, who would then check to determine what factors are causing the problem. He would examine the ear thoroughly with an otoscope, allowing him to check the condition of the ear canal and eardrum. Dark-brownish waxy material, for instance, might indicate an infection with ear mites or yeast. Yeast infections may also show yellowish, more liquid drainage. A similar yellowish drainage may be seen with some bacterial infections. He might also include a microscopic examination of a sample of material taken from the ear canal to tell whether mites, other parasites or yeast organisms are present. He would then take a sterile sample from the ear canal to be sent to a laboratory to find out which bacteria are present, and to have a sensitivity test run to see what antibiotics are effective against those bacteria. This process, however, can be QUITE expensive, as well as time consuming. So, many veterinarians (and most owners) prefer to begin by cleansing the ear and treating the infection with antibiotics. The risk is that all the readily susceptible bacteria will be eliminated, leaving only those which are REALLY hard to eliminate, possibly leading to a chronic infection. The antibiotic sensitivity test is important because it will provide information to help eliminate all the bacteria—the first time.

Treating an ear infection begins with cleansing. If a grass awn is lodged in the ear, the dog's discomfort will have begun suddenly. If this is the case, and you cannot see the object to remove it, get him to your veterinarian THAT DAY (or the next morning if it occurs at night). In some cases, the foreign body may have been lodged in the ear for some time. Again, this will require veterinary care. If you do not have access to a veterinarian, try the cleansing method below. In some cases, it will wash out the grass awn and provide relief for your dog. If there is no relief, you have no choice but to find a veterinarian.

Whatever you do, DO NOT use cotton swabs to clean down into your dog's ears. It is OK to use them on the part that you can see, to gently remove wax and dirt from the surface. However, don't use the swab anywhere that you cannot SEE the end. This is because of the construction of the dog's ear canal. If you imagine the dog standing in a normal position with his head level, the ear canal runs downward almost vertically. After it has gone down an inch or two, depending on the size of the dog, it turns at a sharp right angle and goes inward. At this point, it is almost level with the ground. If you use a cotton swab, you can push dirt down toward the dog's

eardrum, packing it so firmly that your veterinarian will have to anesthetize the dog in order to reach in with a special instrument and remove the impacted material.

To clean the dog's ears you will need a soft-bulb syringe (ask your druggist for an "ear syringe"), a dish of lukewarm water, and pHisohex® or povidone-iodine, as well as some cotton or loose cotton balls. The cleaning can be done in the bathtub, or outdoors if the weather is good. Wear old clothes, because the dog will probably shake water and medication all over you.

You can do one step at a time on both ears, or do one ear completely before starting on the other one. If only one ear is infected, do just it. Be sure NOT to use the syringe (or any other grooming instrument, including your fingers) on the infected ear and then on the clean ear. This is a guaranteed way to have TWO infected ears! Clean and disinfect tools, instruments and hands between ears.

Begin by wiping as much of the greasy material as possible off the inside of each ear flap with a piece of cotton. Fill the syringe with the warm solution of pHisohex ® and lukewarm water (be SURE the water is not TOO hot!), and flush it VERY gently into the ear canal while holding the ear flap upright with your other hand. Do this two or three times. You are flushing the ear gently, not hosing it out with a fire hose. Too much pressure may cause the eardrum to rupture, or can even pack material deeper in the canal rather than removing it. After you have flushed the ear canal several times, gently massage the lower part of the ear canal. This will help to remove material which is crusted on and around the eardrum. Repeat the flushing several more times. Next rinse the syringe and dish and refill them with clear, lukewarm water. Flush the dog's ears until the water comes out completely clean—at least 20 to 30 times. Wipe the inside of the ears as far as you can reach with a cotton ball. Dry off the remainder of the ear flaps with a towel or rag. Put the dog in a place where he can shake, which he is sure to do.

Treat the dog's ears with whatever medication you have been given by your veterinarian for that purpose. Wait for an hour or two after you have flushed the dog's ears before treating them, to allow him to get rid of as much of the remaining water as possible. Wipe again with a cotton ball before putting in the medication.

Put the drops into the dog's ears. Most medications take around five to 10 drops per ear. You don't want to use so much that it gets shaken all over you and the furniture and walls and makes the hair of the ears all greasy. Nor do you want to use so little that it does not cover the ear surfaces. Aim for the happy medium, depending on the size and condition of your dog's ears. As with the washing, it's a good idea to do this with the dog in the shower or outdoors for the first few times, until you know how the dog is going to react.

Put drops into one ear at a time. Then massage the lower part of the ear canal, "mashing" it between your fingers. Do this gently for a very small dog, or vigorously for a large one. This massage accomplishes several things. It helps to break crusts and infected material loose from the inside of the ear. It also helps to "scratch" the inside of the ear, where the dog cannot reach (and you SHOULD not reach!). Most dogs really appreciate the rubbing after the first time or two. Be careful, though. If the ears are in very bad condition, you could cause a lot of pain. Repeat with the other ear.

Most ear infections will require treatment for at least a week. For most medications, two or three times a day are better than once. Follow the instructions on the label, or those given you by your veterinarian. The more regularly you treat the problem, the shorter the time needed to heal it. It is not uncommon for ear infections to require a month or more of treatment. They also are prone to recur. Early in the treatment, it may be useful to tape the ears up over the head on a dog who has hanging ears. This may be done for two to four days, until treatment can be seen to be working. It allows more air to get inside the ear canals and keep them dry. It also keeps the medication from soiling the ear flaps.

Many veterinarians treat a dog's first ear infection "generically," and don't test to find out exactly what bacteria or fungi are present in the ear. With a mild infection this often works well. However, if the infection goes on for some time, or recurs repeatedly, he may wish to send a sample of material to a laboratory for examination. This will allow treatment of the specific organisms present in the ears. As many as a half-dozen organisms may be involved at the same time, especially in long-standing infections.

Over a long course of treatment, the bacteria present in the dog's ears may change. This is because the antibiotics are working. They have killed off all the bacteria which are susceptible. But other bacteria were present, and without competition from the first batch they thrive and prosper. A second culture will often show a different kind of bacteria, with different susceptibilities, than did the first. Now the dog will be changed to a different medication. The process of test and change can take place several times in a tough case as, one by one, the bacteria are eliminated.

Dogs with drooping ears, like Spaniels, Poodles, etc., are prone to ear infection. They should have the hair plucked from their ears. This will help air to circulate into them, and to lessen the amount of moisture and wax that is trapped there. You can pluck the hair out, using your thumb and forefinger. Gently pull out a bit at a time. It is a good idea to treat the ears for two to three days after this is done. Use a corticosteroid and antibiotic combination ointment or drops. Tresaderm® and Panalog® are examples of this type of product. This treatment will help to prevent infection, and reduce the inflammation caused by the hair removal.

If your groomer plucks the hair from the dog's ears, find out if he is using any medication, and if so, which one. If not, you should treat your dog's ears as described above.

EAR MEDICATIONS

Many different ear medications are available. Some work well, and others are not so effective. Some will work well for a while, then lose their effectiveness because the types of bacteria present will have changed with treatment.

Some ear medications contain a number of different ingredients to combat different components of an ear infection. A corticosteroid (these drugs' names usually end in "-sone")

will help to soothe inflammation, and help to relieve the dog's scratching and irritation. Ear medications generally contain one or more antibiotics. Chloramphenicol, gentamycin and neomycin are some of the antibiotics which are most effective against ear infections. These drugs attack the bacteria which are causing the infection. One product also contains thiabendazole. This drug helps to control some of the fungus and yeast infections which affect many dogs' ears. Nystatin is included in some products for the same reason. Other medications include disinfectants such as chlorhexidine which help to kill bacteria and other organisms. Some ear medications are slightly acidic, which helps to make the ears less hospitable to infectious agents. Drugs which contain alcohol may be irritating and drying if the ears are severely inflamed. They may be helpful in ears which have little or no reddening and no opened or scratched areas.

Liquid ear medications often contain solvents called surfactants. These compounds help to dissolve the ear wax, bacteria and waste products which have accumulated in the ears, allowing them to be removed. Removing these materials cleans the ear canal, allowing the antibiotic or disinfectant to reach the surface skin where the infection is causing problems. Liquid ear solutions often do a better job of clearing up infections than do greasy or oily ointments which do not have any cleansing action.

Ear ointments are sometimes used. They often contain the same drugs and medications as do liquid products, but don't work as well. The main disadvantage is that they do not spread down into all the nooks and crannies as well as do liquid medications. They also do not have the beneficial solvent and rinsing effect that liquid preparations do.

Powders should not, in most cases, be used in the ears. They fluff down into the ear, but do not have a good way to get out, especially in dogs with ear flaps which hang down. They also do not get into the crevices and cracks which hold the harmful bacteria. Avoid powdered products for most ear infections. If you use them, about all you will do is add to the amount of junk in the ear canal.

Ear-wash solutions are available. One of these, for instance, contains solvents to remove accumulated wax and dirt, as well as a mild disinfectant (chlorhexidine). One product (Nolvasan® Otic Cleansing Solution), for example, helps to provide good cleansing. If the dog's ears are very dirty or infected, it may be necessary to use this type of product three or four times a day for two or three days, until the ears are clean. It can then be used once or twice a week to keep the ears clean. This will help to prevent infection.

If the dog's ears are very dirty, it may be helpful to put a dropperful of glycerine, baby oil or mineral oil, warmed to lukewarm, into each ear about thirty minutes before you are ready to clean them. Massage it in well. Do this outdoors, or where it won't matter if the dog shakes, because he probably will. Then when you wash out the ears, the dirt will come out much more easily, having already been softened.

After you are through cleansing the ears, you can use a product made for swimmer's ear in humans. This will help to dry out any remaining water.

Do not mix different ear medications together. There may be incompatibilities among the drugs or the carriers. For instance, a drug in an alcohol base would not work well in the same ear at the same time as an oil-based or solvent-based medication.

NOTE: Do NOT use ear medications in the eye. Some of them can cause severe damage, because they contain either medications or carriers which are caustic or irritating to the eye.

EAR CANAL SURGERY

Because of the construction of the dog's ear canal, many dogs will have ear infections for their entire lives. The cauliflowering will occur, and the dog will be under treatment most of the time. At some point, the treatments may no longer help. The bacteria which are present are no longer susceptible to commonly available antibiotics. The dog is scratching and shaking his head, and is miserable. He will often whine. If he is a working dog, he may have trouble paying attention to what he is supposed to be doing. Fungal and yeast infections, which are VERY resistant to treatment, often complicate the problem. If left alone long enough, and when they become severe enough, external ear infections may penetrate the eardrum, becoming middle ear infections.

The bad news is that a chronic ear infection probably won't go away. The good news is that there is a solution which helps almost all of the dogs who are treated. Surgery is performed to reduce the length of the ear canal. It opens it up so that it is more easily and effectively medicated. The shorter, more open canal will also remain dryer and cleaner. This surgery should be considered when the dog has been treated for a long period of time with little success, or when he has responded to treatment but the infection keeps coming back. Surgery is also the treatment of choice when the surface of the ear canal is so severely cauliflowered that medication will not penetrate to where the infection is occurring. It can also be done when the ear canal is narrowed or extremely hairy.

This type of surgery is called ablation ("removal") of the ear canal, ear canal resection, or the Lacroix operation. It involves removing part of the vertical, outside wall of the ear canal. Several good things happen as a result. Instead of a sweaty, damp, infected area, the ear canal is open to the air. The surgery ends up actually removing part of the infected skin, so it no longer causes trouble. And, with plenty of good ventilation, the remaining infection is usually cleared up quickly and easily. Surgery is not a cure-all for ear infection, but at least half the dogs on which surgery is done will have satisfactory results. Most of the other half will show at least some improvement compared to their condition before surgery.

Most dogs who are candidates for surgery will need it on both ears. Go ahead and have them both done at the same time. That way, the dog only has to go through anesthesia once. He will be glad to have ears that do not hurt or itch all the time. You will be happy not to have to treat him all the time. Everybody wins!

Removal of the entire ear canal all the way to the eardrum is done occasionally. This radical approach is usually reserved for cases where the ear canal is blocked by scar tissue, bony growth due to continuing infection, or tumors. It is usually a last resort. Facial nerve paralysis, which is usually temporary, may sometimes result from this surgery. It will cause one side of the dog's face to droop. His lips will sag, and his nose may pull to the opposite side. Most cases of facial paralysis after this surgery return to normal within a couple of weeks. However, some cases may be permanent.

MIDDLE AND INNER EAR INFECTIONS

Middle and inner ear infections have similar signs. In many cases, there may not be any external signs in the ear itself, such as you would expect with an ear canal infection. In other cases, the middle and inner ear infection may be due to an infection which has spread from the external ear canal through the eardrum. The dog with middle or inner ear infection may rotate his head with the affected ear held downward. He may circle to the affected side, fall or roll to that side, and show depression, fever and severe pain. In extreme cases, the dog may be unable to rise, and may not eat or drink. He may roll his eyes from side to side uncontrollably. The ear may be painful when touched. Severe cases may end with the animal dying because the disease has spread to the brain, causing meningitis or abscess formation.

If your dog is showing any combination of these signs, get him to your veterinarian as soon as possible. Antibiotics will certainly be needed to control the infection. Most animals will be treated for at least seven to 10 days, and some may require treatment for six weeks or more. Surgical drainage of either the eardrum or the tympanic bulla (the bulge of the skull below the ear canal) may be needed. The eardrum will heal in time, and the dog's hearing will sometimes return to normal if treatment is prompt and the infection has not destroyed the structures in the inner ear.

Middle ear infections have a better chance of complete recovery than do inner ear infections. A head tilt may persist for the rest of the dog's life, or it may go away after several months. Give your dog plenty of time to adapt to any problems which may remain after treatment of one of these ear infections.

EAR MITE INFESTATIONS

Ear mites (*Otodectes cynotis*) are small mite which live in the ear canals of dogs, cats, rabbits, ferrets and foxes. They are easily transmitted from one dog to another, especially among puppies. Ear mites live on the skin of the ear and ear canal. They feed by piercing the skin and sucking lymph. This results in inflammation and irritation. The exudate and crust formation which result provide an ideal growing medium for bacterial and fungal infections. Some of the itching and irritation which is seen with ear mites is due to an allergic response of the dog's body to them.

The dog with ear mites will usually show the same signs of head shaking and ear scratching as he would with an ear infection. There may be dark brown waxy or flaky exudate in the dog's ears. If you look closely with a magnifying glass, you may see tiny white or flesh-colored mites.

Ear drops can be used to get rid of the mites. They should contain an insecticide, such as dimethyl phthalate, rotenone or one of the pyrethrins. Thiabendazole products also seem to be effective against ear mites. Most products made to treat ear mites will also contain an antibiotic to help clear up the infection which accompanies the mites. A cleaning agent, included in the medication, will help to dissolve the exudate and allow it to be removed from the ear. In many cases, the insecticide product needs to be administered every three to four days for one to two months, MINIMUM. Ear mites are difficult to kill, which is why the prolonged treatment time is necessary.

At the same time, any other susceptible animals which you have should be closely examined. Make sure they do not have mites. If they do, they must be treated at the same time. Otherwise, the mites can still be transmitted (or may have already been) to the other dog, cat, rabbit or ferret. Just as you get the dog cleared up, the other animal comes down with a case of mites. With the animals passing the infection from one to the other, you can be treating them for years. So treat all of them at once and get it over with!

DEAFNESS

It may be difficult to detect that your dog is deaf. You may notice that he is not responding when you call him. Or you may find that you have to shout louder and louder to make yourself heard. Is the deafness a dispositional problem? A friend of mine contends that Dachshunds don't go deaf—they go stubborn!

Your veterinarian may detect deafness by measuring the electrical waves in the brain (an electroencephalogram, or EEG). The test is performed with the dog lightly anesthetized. Measured "clicks" are fed into the dog's ears. Brain waves showing responses to them are measured with the EEG (Knowles, 1988).

HEREDITARY DEAFNESS

Hereditary deafness is seen in several breeds of dog, including the Dalmatian, Rottweiler, some Foxhounds, Fox Terriers, Scottish Terriers and Boston Terriers. It is also seen in white Boxer dogs. It is present in Old English Sheepdogs, English Setters and Bull Terriers. The list of breeds which have the problem changes from time to time, as breeders become aware of the problem and eliminate it from their bloodlines.

Hereditary deafness also seems to be common in dogs of cattle-working heritage, including Collies, Australian Shepherd, Queenland Blue Heeler (and other Heelers from this heritage), and Shetland Sheepdogs. In these breeds, it is especially linked with white or blue merle coat color. Blue merle dogs may have varying degrees of deafness. One of my favorite dogs, a blue heeler, appeared to be deaf in one ear. She would react immediately when called, but was prone to go in the wrong direction if she had forgotten where she last saw me, or if I had moved while she was asleep. She could not tell where my voice was coming from. Deafness in these dogs may occur in one or both ears.

Blue-eyed white dogs are sometimes (but not always) deaf. Dogs from blue merle heritage who are born white may be both blind and deaf. These animals usually have internal problems associated with this genetic defect, including malformations within the digestive tract. Because of these hereditary defects which will not allow the animal to live a normal life, euthanasia as soon as the problem becomes apparent is the kindest course of action for these animals.

DEAFNESS IN OLDER DOGS

Old dogs commonly have diminished hearing. The hearing loss is usually gradual. As part of a geriatric checkup, the ears should be examined to see that an accumulation of wax or dirt in the ear canal is not causing the problem.

Diagnosis of deafness may be difficult. It's hard to tell the dog to raise his paw when he hears the noise! You, as the person who lives with the dog, may be the first to suspect that the dog has a problem. You may notice that he does not react to loud noises, such as a car backfiring in the street or a door slamming. He may not come back when you call him. Or you may have to shout louder and louder to make yourself heard. Sophisticated electrical testing (EEG) may be available in some very large clinics. Much of this is academic, anyway, as we don't yet fit dogs with hearing aids. The testing may be most valuable in determining that the nerves and their connection to the brain are normal.

When the dog goes deaf gradually, it is not usually a problem to him. He will still putter around the house and carry on his normal activities. It IS important, however, that YOU take over as his ears, compensating for his loss of hearing. This means keeping the dog strictly confined to your house or yard. Otherwise, he might be hit by a car or attacked by a dog that he did not hear or notice heading toward him. Because he cannot hear your commands, he should be walked on a leash. This will keep him from darting out into a street, and not hearing your commands to stop or return. Try not to startle him. If you walk up to him and he does not notice, he may snap at you. Try stamping hard on the floor a couple of steps before you reach him so that he can become aware of your presence by feeling the vibrations in the floor. Approach from the front when possible so he can see you. Small children who have not grown up with with an older dog should be kept away from him, as they may startle him and be bitten. An old dog who is deaf can still live a long and happy life.

ACQUIRED DEAFNESS

A dog may become deaf because he was injured, often by being hit in the side of the head or kicked by a horse. If both ear canals are blocked due to ear infection, or the middle or inner ear is destroyed because of an ear infection, deafness may occur. Loud noises may cause deafness—keep your dog out of the area when you are shooting, unless he is a sufficient distance away from the weapon. Noise pollution can affect your dog just like it affects you. Tumors in the brain or ear may cause deafness, as can excess or long-term administration of drugs which are toxic to the nerves of the ear, such as neomycin, gentamycin, streptomycin and salicylates.

EAR CROPPING

You do not HAVE to have your dog's ears cropped or trimmed. This is strictly cosmetic surgery, other than in cases where an injured portion of the ear must be removed. In some countries, Dobermans, Great Danes and other breeds are shown with long, natural ears. Do whatever looks best to you, and what you want to do. If you are showing the dog in shows, it may be necessary for him to have trimmed ears to compete successfully if this is a breed standard. Ear trimming is illegal in some states and countries.

The puppy who is going to have his ears cropped should have had all the immunizations which are appropriate to his age. He should be in good general health and not have any worms or external parasites. His ears should be clean and free of infection, ear mites or sores.

Veterinarians differ considerably on the age at which they prefer to trim puppies' ears. Also, this age differs from one breed to another. Some veterinarians will do larger dogs as young as six to seven weeks of age, and smaller dogs around eight to 10 weeks. Some breeders will have the ears cropped on their litters before they sell the puppies. This ensures that the surgery is done according to their preference for length of ear, and size and flare of the base. Consult with your veterinarian, either at the time you get the puppy or before you go to get it, to make sure that the ears can be done according to your preference (and the veterinarian's!).

Ear cropping is relatively simple surgery. However, there are so many variables—such as the genetic factors influencing the strength of the ear cartilage, the dog's temperament, the nutritional status of the dog, the dog's age, the aftercare, etc.— that there can be no guarantee that the finished product will meet your expectations. For instance, the surgery may be perfect, but the dog is shy, and does not "use" his ears by pricking them up and tracking the world around him. Nothing is as sour as an ear crop gone bad in a puppy that cost several hundred dollars! You pay your money and take your chances.

Chapter 16

HEART AND LUNG PROBLEMS

It is helpful to know what your dog's normal resting pulse rate is, and to be able to listen to his heart with a stethoscope. An occasional skipped beat is normal in resting dogs more than a month old. The heartbeat evens out if the dog is excited or exercised. Usually, heart rate speeds up as the dog breathes in, and slows down as he breathes out. In some dogs, this may be reversed.

While you're at it, note his normal resting respiration rate on your records. This may be helpful if the dog is ill at some time in the future.

CONGESTIVE HEART FAILURE

Congestive heart failure is common in older dogs, occurring in at least one-third of them. It can occur quite rapidly, as an acute problem. More commonly, however, the disease comes on gradually over a long period of time. Congestive heart failure begins when the heart cannot pump enough blood to meet the body's needs. Several body mechanisms initially take over to help boost cardiac output. As the disease progresses, however, these mechanisms cause more harm than good. As the attempts to compensate fail, symptoms of congestive heart failure are seen.

The body compensates for the congestive heart failure in three basic ways. First, the heart beats more rapidly. However, this rapid beating is less efficient at pumping blood than the normal slower rate. Digitalis and other drugs, are used to slow the heart and make it more efficient. This stabilization must be done at a veterinary clinic, and usually takes several days. You will then have to give a daily dose of medication to maintain this new-found stability.

Secondly, the dog with congestive heart failure tends to retain salt and water within his body. This can be treated with a special diet that restricts sodium intake. In some cases, diuretic drugs will be given to help remove fluid from the body.

Thirdly, the reduced output of blood from the heart stimulates blood vessels throughout the body to contract abnormally. This puts a further load on the weakened heart as it struggles to pump blood through the constricted vessels. Drugs may be given to relax these blood vessels, reducing the workload on the heart and helping the organs to get a better blood flow, which results in better function of the kidneys and other organs.

Obesity contributes to the development and severity of congestive heart failure. The dog's heart must pump blood through the mass of blubber, making it work extra hard. Large feedings containing lots of calories cause an immediate increase in the metabolic rate, necessitating an increase in heart and kidney output. These changes lower the blood flow to peripheral tissues (chiefly muscle), which may result in the loss of lean body mass. A crash diet is not the cure for this obesity, however, as such a diet may result in lowered resistance to infection and damage to the heart muscle. A reducing diet under these circumstances should be well-balanced and nutritious. It should result in a slow, steady loss of one to three percent of the dog's body weight per week.

With drugs and strict dietary control, most cases of congestive heart failure can be stabilized enough that the dog can live out his remaining years in comfort. A diet low in sodium will help to control the problem. Dogs do not seem to benefit from a diet low in cholesterol. Strict dietary control is necessary to keep from throwing the dog off his diet—no junk food or table scraps should be given! Low sodium and weight control are the dietary goals for a dog with congestive heart failure.

OTHER HEART PROBLEMS

In dogs, defective valves in the left side of the heart may cause problems. Inflammation within the heart muscle, tumors, and physical damage (trauma) as from being hit by a car or from other violent encounters with the world can cause heart disease. Heartworms can cause heart disease which may be fatal if untreated. Heartworms, however, can be cured if discovered early enough, and completely prevented if medication is begun early in the course of infection, or, better yet, before it occurs (see Internal Parasites Chapter).

Heart attacks such as those seen in humans are basically unknown in dogs. Veterinarians sometimes use the term "heart attack" to refer to sudden heart-related illnesses, because owners understand the term. Dogs do not get plaques of cholesterol in their arteries, so they do not have clots breaking off from the plaques and clogging the arteries supplying blood to the heart.

A form of heart disease called dilated cardiomyopathy is commonly seen in giant breeds of dogs such as Great Danes and Irish Wolfhounds. Its origin is unknown. Contraction of the ventricles (main or lower chambers of the heart) is weakened and dilatation occurs, usually in the left atrium (upper chamber of the heart). The heart lacks rhythm, and the atria do not beat, but just wiggle. Dogs with this problem may die suddenly.

Many dogs who have heart disease will not need treatment, unless they have weakness or fainting. If the dog is showing signs which are causing him trouble, or is in danger of sudden death, treatment will be needed. Medications will regulate an irregular heartbeat, improving the circulation and oxygenation of the blood. They will adjust fluid volumes so that the dog does not circulate too little blood throughout the body, nor have fluid pooling in the legs and tissues. In some cases, X-rays will be taken to determine the extent of damage to the heart. The dog may be given diuretic drugs to reduce fluid retention, as well as digitalis or a similar drug to stabilize and stengthen the heartbeat.

Slow heartbeats, as low as 40 beats per minute, may be seen in older Cocker Spaniels and other short-legged breeds. Cardiac pacemakers have been implanted to increase the heartbeat to a normal range. Medications may be given to increase the heart rate and stabilize it.

Kidney function may not be up to par in an older dog, especially if the dog has a weakened heart. Dogs with kidney or heart problems may have below-normal levels of potassium in the blood serum. This may result in a general muscle weakness. For this reason, a dog with heart problems will sometimes be given a potassium supplement, and may be put on a special diet to compensate for the reduced kidney function.

Many other heart problems occur in dogs. There are congenital abnormalities in which valves do not close properly, or the blood vessels are not attached to the proper parts of the heart. There are infections of both the heart valves (often secondary to kidney or gum disease) and of the heart muscle itself. There are a whole range of electrical disorders which may cause irregular or inefficient heart beats. Entire books, each several inches thick, have been written concerning heart problems in dogs. These problems are uncommon, but they do occur. Most of them cannot be diagnosed at home. Even your veterinarian may require an electrocardiogram, X-rays, and a number of laboratory tests to diagnose the problem. The good news is that supportive treatment can be given for many of these ailments, allowing the dog to live out a reasonably normal life in your company.

BLOOD PROBLEMS

HEMOPHILIA

Hemophilia in dogs, like that in humans, is an inherited lack of one or more factors which, in the normal animal, allow the blood to clot. The genetic defects are sex linked, and are reported almost entirely in male dogs. On rare occasions, hemophilia has been reported in female dogs. The mode of inheritance is recessive, meaning that each of the dog's parents must carry a gene for the disease before the offspring will have it. The disease is not transmitted directly from a male dog with hemophilia to his offspring. He transmits the trait to all his female offspring. Then, when his daughter is mated with a male with a similar genetic background, his grandsons will get hemophilia. The disease is seen in both purebred and mongrel dogs, with no particular breed predisposition.

Early signs of hemophilia may be seen with puppies whose blood does not clot normally when the umbilical cord is severed. Puppies may also bleed when they are teething. Perhaps the most common sign is the presence of "blood blisters" (hematomas) on the body surface where the dog has bumped into something and gotten a non-clotting bruise under the skin. Blood may also pool in the joints from very minor injuries, resulting in swollen, lame joints. Affected joints tend to be of normal temperature, in contrast to a joint filled with pus, which is generally quite warm to the touch. Some dogs may have nosebleeds. If surgery is required, the dog may continue to bleed severely after it is performed. Clipping the toenails of a dog with hemophilia can be a disaster if the nail is "quicked" and starts to bleed.

Special laboratory tests are needed to confirm that the dog has hemophilia and to tell exactly which clotting factor is involved. They may also differentiate hemophilia from warfarin poisoning and other causes of slow clotting. Treatment involves replacing the missing factor so the animal's blood will clot normally. Some drugs help to treat hemophilia on a temporary basis. For the most part, transfusions of fresh blood from another dog, or of normal plasma (fresh or frozen) are used to replace the missing clotting factors.

Your veterinarian may cauterize small hemorrhages on the skin or gums to stop their bleeding until the clotting factors can take effect. Rest and bandages may help to make the dog more comfortable until the blood in the joints and under the skin is reabsorbed. Hard biscuits or bones which might cause the gums to bleed should be avoided. Medications should be given orally if at all possible. Next best are subcutaneous or intravenous injections. Intramuscular injections may cause bleeding within the muscles, and should be avoided whenever possible. Hard exercise or training, which might cause bleeding into the joints, should be avoided. Dogs which are suspected of being carriers of hemophilia can be tested for clotting factor VIII activity and eliminated from the breeding program. Also, bloodlines may be traced to determine which dogs are carriers, and their offspring eliminated from the breeding population.

RESPIRATORY PROBLEMS

You should suspect canine distemper in any young dog who has not been vaccinated and who has a pus-filled, whitish or greenish nasal discharge. The dog's eyes may be filled with a similar material (see Vaccination Chapter).

Kennel cough (infectious tracheobronchitis) causes a constant, dry hacking cough (see Vaccination Chapter).

A persistent cough is one of the most prominent signs of congestive heart failure.

FOREIGN BODY IN THE NOSE

Dogs occasionally inhale grass awns, leaves or similar plant materials as they snuffle through the plants. The dog may have intermittent fits of sneezing. After the material has been lodged for a day or two, he may have a foul, odorous nasal discharge. This may look like pus, or it may have a little blood in it. Removal of one of these objects is a job for your veterinarian. He will sedate the dog and remove the offending object with a long, fine pair of forceps. The dog may need antibiotic treatment for a week or so to clean up the residual infection. Similar sneezing and discharge from the nose may be seen with nasal tumors, so prompt diagnosis is essential.

NOSEBLEED

Nosebleed (epistaxis) in the dog is commonly due to injury. The dog may have been hit by a car. Or he may not have been watching where he was going, and run into a tree or wall. Bleeding from the nose may occur with tumors or aspergillosis (see below). However, with these two conditions the blood is usually mixed with a pus-like drainage. Nosebleeds may also occur with disorders such as hemophilia or warfarin poisoning, which keep the blood from clotting normally.

Blood from a nosebleed usually comes from a small, ruptured vein. It is usually a darkish red and often falls in large, separate drops. This is in contrast to blood from the lungs, which is often bright, light red. Also, blood from the lungs is usually frothy from air being blown through it.

If the cause of the nosebleed is known, it must be removed. If it is unknown, an ice pack can be placed on the dog's nose. The ice pack should not be left in place long enough to cause frostbite! Keep the dog calm and quiet. If the nosebleed recurs, or if you cannot find an obvious reason for it, have the dog examined by your veterinarian.

NASAL TUMORS

Nasal tumors should be suspected whenever a dog over eight years of age shows persistent sneezing. The dog may also have a nasal discharge, which may be very slightly tinged with blood or even severely bloody in some cases. Similar signs may be seen with a foreign body in the nose, so it's worth having the dog checked to see if he's inhaled a grass awn before you assume that he has a tumor. Nasal tumors are more common in large, long-nosed breeds, especially German Shepherds and Collies.

The majority of nasal tumors are highly malignant. Surgical treatment is not usually successful. Radiation therapy may extend the dog's life in some cases. It is worth a try if you can afford it, or if you can get your dog into one of the special radiation therapy programs (see Tumor Chapter). Currently available forms of chemotherapy do not appear to be successful in treating nasal tumors.

NASAL ASPERGILLOSIS

Aspergillosis is an infection with a fungus of the genus *Aspergillus*. The disease is most common in younger dogs, but is occasionally seen in older dogs. It is most commonly seen in dogs of long-nosed breeds. The predisposing factor allowing the infection to start is not known. Occasionally, infection occurs following surgery on the facial bones or nasal cavity, or injury to the facial bones. In these cases, a small chip of bone may be left, unattached to its parent tissue. This fragment may die and provide a predisposing site for the infection to begin. Other cases, however, are seen that develop without surgery or trauma to the bones of the dog's face. Suppression of the immune system is often seen with aspergillosis. It is not known whether this allows the infection to occur, or is a result of it.

The dog may have a nasal discharge that persists for several months. At first, it may be clear. Later, the discharge becomes filled with pus, and, finally, with blood. One or both sides of the nose may be involved. The dog may or may not have nosebleeds. In some cases, the disease becomes gradually worse over several months. In others, the changes may occur within two or three weeks.

As the disease progresses, the fungi destroy the delicate turbinate bones within the nasal cavity, replacing them with masses of fungi. If not treated, they may continue to grow, moving into the skull or into the soft tissues around the eye. Your veterinarian may diagnose the disease by a combination of X-rays, laboratory examination of material draining from the nose, and, perhaps, serum tests for antibodies against the fungus.

Treatment of aspergillosis is generally long and involved. Systemic drug treatment may be needed for eight to 12 weeks and may be quite expensive, depending upon the drug that is used. A complication to treatment is that most of the drugs that are effective against the fungus tend to be somewhat toxic to the dog. As with treatment of many systemic fungus diseases, it's a race to kill off the fungi before you kill off the dog! Expect to pay for laboratory tests throughout the course of treatment to monitor the progress and safety of the therapy. In some cases, a tube may be surgically placed into the sinus above the eyes (the frontal sinus). The nasal passages may then be flushed with one or more drugs to try to get rid of the fungus. This technique may be used alone or in conjunction with systemic drug therapy.

TOOTH DISEASE

Infections involving the roots of the teeth in the upper jaw may form abscesses which can erode through the bone into the sinus cavity or the floor of the nasal area. The drainage which is produced will run out of the nose, giving signs much like foreign bodies in the nose, tumors and fungal infections: sneezing and an odorous discharge. Your veterinarian will fix the problem by extracting the diseased tooth. If the area is severely infected, he may wish to give antibiotics to the dog for several days before he does the surgery, as well as for a week or so afterward. Non-surgical treatment of abscessed teeth is not very successful. Pulling the tooth is a reasonable and permanent cure.

WARTS

Oral papillomatosis, also called warts, is a viral disease of young dogs. It is contagious from one dog to another, but not to humans or other animals. Warts may occur on the skin of the nose and face, as well as in the mouth and even on the tongue. The warts may range from pinhead size to an inch or more in diameter. They may be small pinkish or grayish bumps, or they may look like tiny cauliflowers on small stalks. Warts are most common in younger dogs. Older dogs who had the infection when they were young seem to have some degree of resistance to it.

The warts are unsightly, but do not cause any pain. If there are a large number of warts in the mouth, the dog may bite them as he tries to eat, and they may become infected. Your veterinarian can remove the warts by electrocautery or surgery. Or he may choose to freeze them off. If either of these procedures is performed, any warts which are not removed will usually disappear within a couple of weeks. This is probably due to stimulation of the body's immune reaction against the causative virus. If left untreated, the warts will go away by themselves, usually within a month or so. Meanwhile, keep the dog away from other dogs so he does not give them the disease.

COLLAPSED TRACHEA

Tracheal collapse may occur in older dogs of smaller breeds, especially Toy Poodles, Chihuahuas and Pomeranians. The rings of the trachea are not completely formed into circles of cartilage as they should be. Instead, the upper part of the ring is composed of a thin tissue membrane. The membrane collapses inward as the dog ages, especially if he is overweight and the fat is pressing inward against the trachea. The dog may have a chronic cough. He may have trouble breathing in or out, or both. Signs of this disease may be very similar to those of chronic heart failure or kennel cough. The dog may cough after he is exercised, or when he pulls on his leash. The cough becomes worse and worse over time until the dog is coughing almost continuously. Some dogs have a cough which has been described as a "goose honk."

Your veterinarian may give anti-cough drugs, as well as antibiotics to control bacteria which can complicate the problem. Drugs may be given to open up (dilate) the smaller airways (bronchi) in the lung. If medical treatment does not result in immediate and lasting relief, surgery should be done. Plastic material is usually used to make a stiff form. This is placed around the outside of the trachea (within the neck or chest), and the membrane which has collapsed is anchored to it.

TONSILLITIS

Tonsillitis is a common problem in the dog. It may occur by itself, or in addition to infection in the pharynx (back of the throat) or mouth. It seems to be especially common in small Poodles. It is also common in short-faced breeds of dogs such as English Bulldogs and Boston Terriers.

In some cases, grass awns or plant fibers may lodge in the tonsils, causing an abscess on one or both sides.

The tonsils are small oval pads of pinkish, spongy tissue in the back of the throat on each side of the mouth, just behind the lower rear teeth. They sit in small folds of tissue, called crypts or fossae. In most cases, if they are bulging out of their crypts, you may assume that they are enlarged and inflamed.

Early signs of tonsillitis include droopiness, lack of appetite, salivation and reluctance to swallow. The dog may have a soft cough. This is often followed by retching motions, as the dog spits out a bit of mucus. The dog may swallow more often than he normally does, while moving his head up and down. He may eat grass, and then spit parts of it back up. Although we will never know for sure, we think eating grass is an attempt to "scratch" these uncomfortable areas of the throat. The dog may paw at his ears. If you look at the tonsils, they may be of normal size, or may be so large that the dog has trouble swallowing. They may be reddened, or coated with pus or mucus.

If tonsillitis is allowed to continue for a long period of time, it may become chronic. The dog will have intermittent episodes of acute signs, as described above. In addition, he will have poor resistance to other diseases, and will be in generally poor health. Chronic tonsillitis may also shed bacteria into the bloodstream which carries them to the kidneys, much as occurs with dental disease.

Your veterinarian will treat tonsillitis with systemic antibiotics that will eliminate bacteria which are causing infection in the tonsils, as well as those which have been shed to other parts of the body. Treatment must be continued for a minimum of seven to 10 days. Be sure to finish all the medication, even if the dog is better within a few days. Otherwise, the tonsillitis may come right back. If you are willing to do it, swabbing the tonsils and their crypts with povidone-iodine solution may help the dog to heal faster. Give the dog a soft diet for a couple of days until his throat is less painful and he is better able to swallow. Remember when you had tonsillitis and your mother fed you ice cream? Well, we don't recommend ice cream for your dog. But he will appreciate having his dry dog food softened with water. Or you can feed him a canned food, similar in composition to his normal food, for a couple of days. The soft diet will also stimulate his appetite, which may be lacking.

If the dog continues to have attacks of tonsillitis, whether there are a lot of them or a few severe attacks, consider having his tonsils removed. Your veterinarian can do this relatively simply, and you can stop treating the dog. Your dog will also not be threatened by kidney disease resulting from the continued tonsillitis. Don't hesitate to have the surgery done. It provides real relief for many of the animals on which it is performed.

PHARYNGITIS

Pharyngitis is an inflammation or infection of the back of the throat (called the pharynx). Signs of it are much the same as tonsillitis, described above. In addition, the dog may cough if you squeeze gently on his throat. If you open his mouth and look at the throat area, it may be quite reddened, and it may be streaked with areas of pus. If you have ever had a severe "sore throat," you will have an idea of how your dog feels. It can occur in dogs who have had their tonsils removed. Treatment is similar to tonsillitis. Pharyngeal paralysis, with the dog unable to swallow his saliva, may be a sign of rabies.

ABNORMALLY LONG SOFT PALATE

The soft palate (the pad of soft tissue at the rear part of the roof of the dog's mouth) may be abnormally long in short-faced breeds of dogs, especially the English Bulldog and Boston Terrier. It is the result of selective breeding having shortened the facial bones of these breeds. However, the soft palate did not shorten as much as the bones. This leaves a thickened, fat pad of tissue hanging in the upper rear part of the mouth with nothing to do but cause problems.

On a day to day basis, most dogs learn to compensate for the extra tissue by breathing slowly and carefully so they do not choke themselves. When they are excited or exercise vigorously, this pad of tissue will flop back into the airway, choking the dog. He may gag, making a "snorting" or "oinking" noise. In severe cases, the dog may collapse from lack of air. This is a medical emergency. The dog should be taken to a veterinarian as soon as possible. It may be necessary for him to anesthetize the dog and put a tube down the animal's trachea. He will then administer oxygen until the dog is stabilized.

If the choking occurs often, or is life-threatening, surgery may be the best cure. A large amount of the extra soft palate is surgically removed. This gives the dog an enlarged airway and allows him to breathe with normal effort. The dog is a lot happier and more comfortable after surgery. And, you don't have to worry about him choking to death when he gets excited.

PNEUMONIA

Pneumonia refers to an inflammation of the lung tissue. This may be due to a bacterial or viral infection, fungal infection or smoke inhalation, among other causes. Pneumonia is common in dogs who are weakened by other diseases (such as distemper or tumors). It also occurs more frequently in dogs who have hormone imbalances, and in dogs who are very old or very young.

A dog with pneumonia may cough. Generally, the cough will be productive, clearing mucus and exudate from the lungs. He may have a fever and a nasal discharge. Because the lungs contain fluid and mucus and, perhaps, exudate (pus), the dog will have difficulty breathing. At the very least, the dog's rate of breathing may be faster than normal. In severe cases, he may actually be gasping for breath.

Severe cases of pneumonia may be accompanied by listlessness, depression, lack of appetite, weakness and dehydration. The dog may be cyanotic (have bluish membranes) because he can't breathe adequately. He may salivate and breathe with his mouth open.

If you suspect that your dog has pneumonia, it is important that you get him to your veterinarian as soon as possible so that an accurate diagnosis can be made and treatment started. Antibiotic treatment is the principal therapy. Many veterinarians will take a culture so that they can determine exactly which bacteria are causing the problem. Drugs such as amoxicillin, gentamycin and tetracycline are commonly used. He will often give the antibiotic intravenously or intramuscularly for the first couple of days, as it is poorly absorbed when the dog's respiration and circulation are abnormal. When the dog shows improvement, he can be switched to oral antibiotics. The dog will also be given intravenous fluids. These fluids will help to liquefy material deep within the lungs so that it can be coughed up. Dogs who have severe cases of pneumonia may need aerosol therapy (nebulization). Saline solutions and drugs to open the airways in the lungs are put into a nebulizer, which dispenses vapor into the air of the cage for the dog to inhale.

The dog should be encouraged to cough to help remove the material from his lungs. Chest percussion (tapping lightly on the rib cage) should be performed for 10 minutes, three or four times a day. This should be followed by a short walk on a leash. The vibrations from the percussion, combined with mild exertion, should stimulate a productive cough. The dog will usually swallow the material he coughs up. Also, a productive cough sounds "wet."

If pneumonia is treated early and aggressively, there is a good chance that the dog will recover with little damage to his lungs. However, if the case of pneumonia is especially severe, or has gone on for a period of time, the dog may never be quite normal again. He may have diminished lung capacity, and be unable to hunt or work hard. He may be more susceptible to respiratory infections and other pulmonary problems in the future because of the extensive lung damage.

MYCOTIC PNEUMONIAS

Mycotic pneumonia in small animals is caused by fungi that are found in the soil or in decaying plant materials. They are also called systemic mycoses, from the fact that they can spread throughout the animal's system. The dog usually becomes infected by inhaling spores or fragments of the fungi. These same organisms also infect humans, but seem to be more common in dogs, probably because their noses are closer to the ground than ours are. Because the dog's nose is usually the route of infection, the respiratory system is often the first to be affected. Signs of infection are similar in all mycotic diseases. A variety of fungi can cause the diseases. Fortunately, most occur in a rather specific, well-defined geographic area, which helps in their diagnosis. Some of these diseases show symptoms other than pneumonia, but pneumonia is common to all of them. For that reason, they are discussed in this section.

VALLEY FEVER (COCCIDIOIDOMYCOSIS)

This systemic fungus disease is found most commonly in the desert regions of the southwestern United States, especially the low deserts of Arizona and the San Joaquin Valley of California (where it received the name, "valley fever").

One of the most common signs of valley fever is that the dog has a chronic, dry cough. This cough may persist for months or even years. The dog may have a fever which either comes and goes, or persists. Either way, a temperature of 103 to 105 degrees F (39.4-40.6 degrees C) is not unusual. As the disease progresses, the dog may have trouble breathing and compensate by breathing rapidly. He may have a poor appetite, loss of weight and depression. "Cocci" commonly infects the lungs and the lymph nodes associated with them, along with lymph nodes in the abdominal cavity. The lymph nodes may be quite swollen and enlarged. Some cases will have involvement of the bones or spinal column, similar to tuberculosis in humans. These dogs may show odd lamenesses, enlarged joints or bony swellings on the long bones.

BLASTOMYCOSIS

North American blastomycosis is a fungus disease similar to valley fever. Signs are very similar with respect to lung involvement and general condition of the dog. In addition, the dog may have small draining pimples covered with yellow scabs, or have small nodules under the skin. The infection may involve the urinary tract—with blood in the urine, straining and difficult urination. The dog may have growths within the eyeball which may lead to blindness.

Blastomycosis is generally found in the Mississippi River area and around the Great Lakes. This disease should be considered if a dog has both respiratory signs and draining, nodular sores on the skin. This fungus does not respond well to treatment.

HISTOPLASMOSIS

Histoplasmosis is a systemic fungus, similar to that which causes valley fever. The fever may be as high as 106 degrees F (41.1 degrees C). Respiratory signs are about the same as those seen with valley fever. In addition, the dog may have diarrhea, leading to weight loss. The skin may have weeping, ulcerated nodules. This disease also occurs in an acute form, which progresses rapidly to death in 2-6 weeks. Histoplasmosis is mostly found in the Mississippi and Ohio River valleys, and the Appalachian Mountain Range.

CRYPTOCOCCOSIS

Cryptococcosis is a systemic fungus which produces respiratory signs similar to valley fever. In addition, slimy and ulcerated skin lesions may occur, especially on dogs' legs. If the brain is involved, the dog may show signs of staggering, circling, behavioral changes and, eventually, blindness. Cryptococcosis occurs occasionally in all parts of the United States, rather than in a particular geographic area. Treatment may not work well.

TREATMENT OF MYCOTIC PNEUMONIAS

Treatment of mycotic pneumonias and other systemic mycoses is complicated by misdiagnosis. These diseases often appear to be something else. Kennel cough or other respiratory diseases may be suspected at first. When the dog does not respond to treatment with antibiotics, further tests should be run to either confirm or rule out the presence of a mycotic disease. X-rays will often show masses in the lungs and/or abdominal lymph nodes. In some cases, X-rays may show lesions in the bones.

Antifungal drugs can be used to treat all of these diseases. The drugs have many side effects, and must be administered and monitored by a veterinarian. The course of treatment may run two or three months, or more. Laboratory tests are needed to monitor the kidneys, as some of these drugs are toxic to them. In many cases, it's a race to kill the fungus before you kill the dog, depending on how badly the dog is infected before treatment is begun. Surgery may be required to clean out lesions in the bone, or to remove some of the worst-involved lymph nodes. None of these diseases are easy to treat. Treatment is long, involved, expensive, and only successful perhaps half the time—depending on the infectious agent, the dog's overall condition and ability to resist, and other factors. The earlier treatment is started, the better the dog's chances are. There is no prevention for mycotic diseases, except good luck.

LUNG TUMORS

Primary lung tumors (those which start in the lung) are uncommon in dogs. Metastatic lung tumors are those which have spread from tumors in other parts of the body. These may originate as mammary tumors, bone tumors (osteosarcomas), melanomas on the skin or other parts of the body, or tumors of many other kinds and locations. Metastatic tumors start when groups of cells break off from the primary tumor. The cells are carried via the blood to the lungs and are trapped in the small blood vessels. There they grow and thrive, forming nodules which grow into larger masses. The prognosis for a dog with a primary tumor which has spread in this manner ("metastasized") is not good. Chemotherapy may be tried. It is more successful with some tumors than others. All in all, the dog's chances for long-term survival are not good, and the expense of treatment can be considerable.

Chapter 17

URINARY TRACT AND LIVER PROBLEMS

CYSTITIS (BLADDER INFECTION)

Cystitis is an infection of the urinary bladder. Bladder infections are usually caused by bacteria which have ascended through the urethra into the bladder. Because the urethra is shorter in the female, this type of infection is more common in bitches. Dogs who have malformations of the urinary tract or who have bladder stones are more likely to have cystitis. Dogs with cystitis or urethritis (inflammation or infection of the urethra), may urinate small amounts frequently. The urine may contain blood, especially at the end of urination. The dog may forget his or her housebreaking and urinate in the house.

The infection will be treated with antibiotics for as much as three weeks. If the problem recurs after treatment is stopped, the dog may be put on antibiotics for as much as four to six months. In some cases, the dog may have to stay on the treatment for the rest of his or her life, although this situation is more likely to occur in a female. Drugs may also be given to keep the urine acidic. The low pH (acidity) makes the urine a less hospitable place for bacteria to grow. Acidifiers may also be needed for the remainder of the animal's life. The dog may be put on a special food to reduce the load on the kidneys if they are already damaged.

KIDNEY INFECTION

Nephritis is the name given to inflammation or infection of the kidney. Chronic interstitial nephritis (CIN) is a disease which often occurs in older dogs, resulting eventually in kidney failure if it is not treated. Acute nephritis may occur with leptospirosis. This disease can be prevented by including "lepto" vaccine in your routine immunization program in areas where leptospirosis occurs, or if you are going to be traveling to dog shows where your dog(s) could pick up the infection.

In most cases, a kidney infection starts from a bladder infection which ascends through the ureters from the bladder to the kidneys. In some cases, the infective bacteria may have come from the roots of infected teeth, or through other infection in the body, and carried to the kidneys by the bloodsteam.

Dogs with kidney infections may have systemic signs such as lack of appetite, fever, vomiting and depression. If the infection is just starting, or is not severe, the signs may come and go.

If your dog shows signs of kidney problems, you should take him to your veterinarian for an examination. If you allow the infection to continue, it may progress to kidney failure and the dog could die. The examination will probably include taking a urine sample, which will be microscopically examined and cultured to see what kind of bacteria are present. Antibiotic sensitivity testing may also be done to find out what will work against the bacteria.

Treatment for kidney infection involves antibiotic therapy and, perhaps, a change of diet. Severe cases where the kidneys are nearly nonfunctional or not working at all may require heroic efforts to save the dog's life.

CHRONIC KIDNEY FAILURE

Kidney failure occurs when the kidneys can no longer perform their normal function of removing waste products from the blood. This may be due to reduced blood flow to the kidneys because of poor circulation from the heart (as with congestive heart failure), or problems with the blood vessels. Dehydration and shock can also cause kidney failure. Disease within the kidney tissue can cause kidney failure. Ruptures or tears in the urinary tract because of injury such as being hit by a car may cause kidney failure, as can obstruction to outlow of urine by tumors, bladder stones or blood clots.

Chronic kidney failure results from long-term, progressive loss of functional kidney tissue. It occurs when about three-fourths of the functional kidney tubules are damaged or lost. It usually occurs in older dogs. This is commonly due to infection (often from infected teeth or gums), or to tumors. This is often called chronic interstitial nephritis (CIN). In rare cases, it may be seen in dogs younger than one year of age.

Early clinical signs of chronic kidney failure include increased drinking of water, more frequent urination (in greater quantity than usual), and occasional vomiting. As the disease progresses over a period of weeks or months, the dog may lose appetite and weight, show fever, depression and dehydration, and have diarrhea. Ulcers may be seen on the gums and tongue, and the dog may have bad breath. Blindness, difficulty in breathing and coughing may be seen. The dog may accumulate fluid in the limbs and abdomen. Toward the end of the disease, vomiting may be continuous. The dog may be severely dehydrated, and progress to convulsions, coma and death.

If your dog shows signs of kidney problems, you should take him to your veterinarian for examination. He will usually perform blood and urine tests. These tests may show elevated BUN (blood urea nitrogen) and creatinine levels, meaning that the kidneys are not working normally to remove waste products from the body. These tests will also help him to separate this problem from diabetes, pyometra (infection in the uterus) and lack of hormones from the cortex of the adrenal gland, conditions that cause similar signs of illness. He may culture the urine to find out if bacteria are causing infection in the kidneys. In some cases, X-rays using injections of a special drug to provide radiographic contrast may be needed.

These tests also help to differentiate between chronic and acute kidney failure. Acute kidney failure, which occurs suddenly and is usually due to injury or infection, may be reversed if it is treated immediately and aggressively. Chronic kidney failure, on the other hand, has either caused more serious damage before it is discovered, or has been going on for a long period of time. All that can be done with chronic kidney failure is to manage it as best as possible.

Dogs can survive considerable loss of kidney tissue, and live for many years with only a small amount of normally functioning tissue. Dogs with mild cases of kidney failure and few signs, such as occasional vomiting, can be cared for at home. Clean, fresh drinking water should ALWAYS be available. Feeding a prescription dog food as recommended by your veterinarian can help to slow the progress of the disease. The diet will provide lower levels of protein and salt, and a careful balance of certain minerals.

Drugs may be given to help reduce stomach acidity and vomiting. Baking soda may be given to some dogs to help reduce excess acidity in the body. Anabolic steroids (the same ones that are bad for human athletes) may be given to help stimulate red blood cell production in dogs who are anemic. The steroids also help to rebuild muscle mass which has been depleted, and may enhance the deposition of calcium in the bones—in this situation, they're OK. Some dogs may require blood transfusions. Preparations of B-vitamins may be given to compensate for vitamin loss through the urine. The low-salt diet may help to reduce the elevation in blood pressure that is seen with kidney failure. Some dogs may need potassium supplementation, especially in later stages of the disease. It is especially important that these supplements be given only on the recommendation of your veterinarian. If they are given in the wrong kind or dosage, they could cause more harm than good.

Limiting the amount of protein in the diet may help to slow the progress of the disease. The bulk of the dog's caloric requirements should be be provided by carbohydrates, which most dogs like. Prescription diets may be necessary (and the easiest way) to balance the dog's diet and provide the proper nutrients. If the dog does not have a good appetite, it may be helpful to warm his dog food, or to feed frequent small meals to encourage him to eat. It may be helpful to flavor the dog's food with salt-free chicken broth, but check with your veterinarian before you use bouillon cubes or other products with any salt in them.

The kidneys normally remove large amounts of toxins from the body. With chronic kidney failure, high accumulations of toxic products may occur. Your veterinarian may need to give intravenous fluids to help remove these products from the body. If this does not help renal function and reduce the signs of intoxication, it may be necessary to euthanize the dog.

ACUTE KIDNEY FAILURE

Acute kidney failure occurs when the kidneys are damaged badly enough that they cannot regulate water and mineral balance in the body. Urine flow may be increased, normal or reduced. Antifreeze poisoning can cause acute kidney failure, as can excesses of certain antibiotics, poisoning by heavy metals and use of acetaminophen (aspirin-substitute products). Kidney infections such as leptospirosis, or those due to bacteria coming from heart or gum and tooth-root problems, can also cause acute kidney failure.

Signs are similar to those of chronic renal failure, and may include depression, lack of appetite, vomiting, diarrhea and a below-normal body temperature. Ulcers may be present in the mouth.

As with chronic renal failure, laboratory tests may be necessary to determine the exact problem. In some cases, it may be necessary to take a biopsy (small surgical sample) from the kidney to determine the exact problem.

If the cause of the acute kidney failure is known, treatment of the specific problem should begin immediately. Fluid therapy is very important. This is done either intravenously or by injecting fluids into the abdominal cavity, and is definitely a job for your veterinarian. Fluid therapy will have to be continued until the animal's kidney function improves and the dog stabilizes.

BLADDER STONES

Bladder stones (urinary calculi) are crystalline deposits which occur in the urinary bladder. Your veterinarian may use the term urolithiasis, which means "urine stones," and refers to stones occurring anywhere in the urinary tract, whether in the bladder, ureters or urethra. They vary from fine grains of sand to stones the size of a baseball. There may be one large stone, or a number of smaller ones that fit together like a puzzle, with flat sides toward each other and rounded sides facing outward to the bladder lining. Generally, they are smooth, but some can be jagged and sharp.

Some breeds are predisposed to stones in the urethra. Beagles, Terriers, Daschshunds, Pugs, English Bulldogs, Welsh Corgis and Basset Hounds are among them. Stones most frequently occur in dogs between two and 10 years of age. Between 10% and 75% of the dogs who have stones will have them recur after treatment. Different types of dogs have different kinds of stones, and some kinds are more prone to recur than others. German Shepherd dogs, for instance, have a higher incidence of silicate stones, while Dalmatians have a greater incidence of urate stones (referring to the material in the stones).

Bladder stones have many different origins. A bladder or kidney infection may provide small centers for formation of crystals. Decreased urinary production, whether caused by inadequate water intake or by lowered output by the kidneys, may cause bladder stones to to form. High levels of certain minerals in the diet may cause stone formation, as can situations in which the dog must hold his urine for excessive lengths of time. Some kinds of stones are more prone to occur in acid urine, others in alkaline urine. For still others, the urine pH makes no difference. In many cases, the cause is never determined.

Some dogs may have bladder stones without showing any symptoms. Usually, however, the dog will have blood in his urine. The urine may have a stronger, more ammonia-like odor than usual. Because the stones take up room in the bladder, the dog may urinate more frequently than usual, and may strain as he urinates. A dog who is normally housebroken may dribble urine or urinate in odd locations. The signs may begin abruptly, go away in a few days without treatment, and then come back again.

Urethral obstruction is uncommon in females due to the shorter, wider urethra. In males, bladder stones may completely shut off urine flow. The dog will show vomiting, weakness, loss of appetite, depression and pain. Repeated attempts to urinate may be unsuccessful. The dog will progress to coma, and usually will die within three days if not treated. IMMEDIATE veterinary care is needed. If the dog is not treated until he (or she) becomes comatose, chances for survival are slim.

If you get the dog to your veterinarian for treatment early in the disease, the outcome is usually good. X-rays may be needed to determine the location of the stone. Laboratory tests will often be used to determine the extent of damage to the kidneys, as well as to tell what type of stone is present. If an infection is suspected, a culture and antibiotic sensitivity tests may be run.

Large stones or those causing obstruction of urine flow will need surgical removal. If the stones are smaller, and the dog can still urinate, he may be treated with antibiotics to control the underlying infection. As with bladder infections, medications may be given to make the urine acidic. The lower pH also helps to dissolve some types of bladder stones.

Prescription foods which are lower in protein and certain minerals will help to dissolve some types of stones. These foods may also contain a higher level of salt to make the dog drink more water, thus producing less concentrated urine. Several kinds of prescription diets are available, depending on the type of stone which is diagnosed. If you are feeding one of these diets, it is VERY important NOT to supplement it with any human foods, any other dog food, or any vitamins and minerals except those prescribed by your veterinarian. Dissolving the stones by medical means will take from four to 28 weeks, if the treatment works at all with the type of stones in your dog. Dietary dissolution is only effective with ammonium urate or struvite stones. Diets to dissolve the stones are restricted in certain minerals, and for this reason should not be used in puppies or pregnant bitches. Also, because of their increased sodium content, these foods should not be used in dogs with congestive heart failure.

A dog with bladder stones may need lifelong management to prevent recurrence. In some areas, if your water is highly mineralized, your veterinarian may want you to give the dog distilled or demineralized water for the rest of his life. He may also need prescription food and acidifying drugs for the rest of his life. From time to time, the problem may recur, and further antibiotic treatment may be needed. Discuss with your veterinarian whether special diet and additional treatment will be needed to prevent recurrence. The need for these things will depend primarily on the type of stone and breed of dog involved.

KIDNEY STONES

Stones can sometimes form in the kidney, but this is far less common than stones in the bladder. Calculi in the kidney may not cause any signs at all, unless there is infection in the upper urinary tract, or unless the stone has produced enough damage to cause kidney failure. Signs are often similar to kidney infection. In humans, the passage of a small kidney stone through the ureter to the bladder is extremely painful. While this doesn't seem to happen very often in the dog, the signs would be those of severe abdominal pain. Unfortunately, other things can cause abdominal pain. Take the dog to a veterinarian immediately.

URINARY INCONTINENCE

Urinary incontinence (dribbling of urine or inability to control urination) is occasionally seen in younger dogs. This problem is usually noticed shortly after birth. The most common physical cause is ureters which do not attach to the appropriate sites in the urinary tract—a congenital defect. It is more common in females, especially Toy and Miniature Poodles, Siberian Huskies and Labrador Retrievers. The dog may drip urine constantly, or only when standing or lying in certain positions. X-rays and other examinations may be needed to diagnose the problem. Surgical correction may help in some cases and be useless in others—in which case euthanasia may be required.

Excitement or intimidation may cause a young dog to urinate when his owner comes home. Or he may do so when surprised. This usually goes away as the dog matures.

More commonly, urinary incontinence is seen in older dogs, rather than in the young. It is usually seen in dogs five years of age and older. It occurs in both males and females, but in elderly dogs is more common in females. Incontinence in the elderly dog is usually due to a lack of hormones—testosterone in the males and estrogen in the bitches.

Some older dogs may have a weak sphincter muscle (valve) which keeps the urine from flowing outward. This is common in elderly spayed females, but may be seen in both males and females which have not been neutered. The muscle works normally when the dog is awake. When she is sleeping or relaxed, dribbling or pooling of urine occurs as the muscle relaxes. The dog has no control over this, and may act quite ashamed of what has happened. Please don't scold the poor old dog anything more than mildly for the transgression! This is probably what is wrong if the dog wets its bed at night. The normal dog will not urinate in its bedding. If the urination occurs elsewhere, the dog is getting up and probably urinating voluntarily. In many dogs, treatment with male or female hormones will give considerable relief.

The dog may dribble as it walks (uncommon), or leave a pool of urine where it has been lying (very common). Hair around the prepuce or vulva may be wet, stained or odorous. Skin infection may be present from constant contact with urine. Incontinent animals will attempt to urinate frequently, but only pass small amounts.

Elderly dogs may forget some of their housetraining. This may be because of senility and absent-mindedness. The dog may not sleep well, wakes up during the night, and may not be willing or able to hold his urine until morning. Or he may not remember that he is supposed to do so. Old dogs with arthritis, hip dysplasia, pain, blindness or lack of energy may just not make it to the toilet area.

Diseases such as diabetes insipidus, kidney disease or failure, liver failure, pyometra, and excesses or deficiencies of adrenal cortical hormones may cause urinary incontinence. Dogs with bladder or kidney infections may be unable to control their urine flow and timing. Tumors in the kidney or bladder can cause urinary incontinence, but these are rare. Tumors are usually accompanied by difficulty in urination and blood in the urine. Male dogs with prostate problems will often dribble urine. Dogs who are receiving corticosteroid drugs to control itching skin in the summer may show urinary incontinence. This clears up in the winter when the medication is no longer used.

Urinary incontinence should be dealt with as soon as you become aware of it. In some cases, it is secondary to a much more serious problem. Delay in treatment may lead to expensive and life-threatening complications, such as urinary tract infections. Or the dog may get ulcers and sores on the skin because the hair has become soaked with urine. Electrolyte imbalances, stretching of the bladder from which it will never recover, and loss of muscle tone of the bladder are only a few of the possible complications, depending on the underlying cause. If urine backs up badly enough, the ureters or kidneys may be damaged by the resulting pressure, caused by a blockage. The dribbling urine associated with the blockage is from the pressure forcing a little bit of urine past the blockage. Also, the dog is miserable (and embarrassed!) when unable to control his urination, especially if he is normally well-trained.

To find the cause of urinary incontinence, your veterinarian will probably begin with a complete physical examination. A sample of the dog's urine may be examined to rule out infection in the urinary tract. X-rays of portions of the urinary tract may help to localize the problem.

Once the cause is found, it can usually be treated. If the dog is lacking in hormones, these can be appropriately replaced. Many veterinarians routinely evaluate and treat all incontinent dogs for urinary tract infections before placing them on hormones. Some dogs urinate excessively because they are drinking excessively (for no good reason). These dogs may do well when placed on a low-salt diet. CAUTION: The dog who is drinking excesively may have diabetes mellitus, diabetes insipidus, pyometra or another serious disease. Do

NOT restrict water intake without a veterinarian's evaluation. No matter which treatment is used, some dogs cannot be cured of incontinence. These animals can still be acceptable pets if you are willing to tolerate some inconvenience. The dog can be trained to wear diapers while in the house. Your veterinarian can show you how to express (squeeze out) the dog's bladder, helping him to urinate. Or he may teach you how to pass a catheter to drain out the urine, depending on the dog's problem and your inclination (Krawiec, 1988).

PROSTATE PROBLEMS

PROSTATIC ENLARGEMENT

Diseases of the prostate are common in dogs. The most common of these is prostatic enlargement, also called cystic hyperplasia or prostatic hypertrophy. As many as 60% of all male dogs over six years of age may have some degree of enlargement, although many of them will not show any signs. Prostatic enlargement develops over a long period of time. A general decline in body condition often occurs, along with weight loss. Because this occurs at the same time as the dog is aging, these signs may be noticed but attributed simply to the dog getting old. Other signs of prostatic enlargement look similar to those of chronic nephritis (kidney infection). The dog may dribble urine, or urine retention may cause the dog to strain to urinate. His attempts to urinate may be mistaken for attempts to defecate. If the bladder is distended for a period of time, it and the sphincter muscle may become limp, and urine may overflow without the dog being able to control it. Blood in the urine, with or without bladder infection, is often seen with prostatic enlargement.

The enlarged prostate gland may press on the rectum, causing the dog to feel the need to defecate. As he strains to defecate, the gland is pushed upward and backwards, somewhat blocking the passage of feces. This can lead to constipation. In some cases, hard feces may remain trapped in the rectum with fluid material flowing around the partial blockage, leading to a mistaken diagnosis of diarrhea. If the enlarged prostate is present long enough, the dog may have a changed gait, hind leg lameness or weakness in the hind end. Dogs with perineal hernia are likely to have prostatic enlargement as well.

In some cases, your veterinarian may diagnose this disease by a combination of rectal and abdominal palpation. In many cases, however, the only accurate way for him to determine the size of the gland is to take a series of X-rays. Some of these may be taken with either air or a contrasting material injected into the bladder. Or he may take a biopsy sample from the gland to determine if the problem is malignant or not.

Treatment of prostatic enlargement depends on the symptoms that are seen. If the dog is retaining urine, the bladder must be emptied for him three to four times a day. This can be done by compressing the bladder through the abdominal wall. Your veterinarian will show you where to press, approximately four to six inches (10 to 15 cm) ahead of the pelvis. Small dogs are easily emptied with one hand while being restrained with the other. Larger dogs often require someone with large or very strong hands who can push hard enough through the muscular abdominal wall to empty the bladder. This constant emptying of the bladder is very important. If it is not done, the bladder will become stretched and limp from being overfilled, and will never function normally again. It is also important to begin treatment before it reaches that point.

Your veterinarian may give a small amount of estrogen to suppress the overgrowth of prostatic tissue. This dose must be minimal to avoid the serious (or possibly fatal) side effect of bone marrow depression. If possible, it should not be given for more than a couple of weeks. After an interval of two or three weeks, the estrogen treatment can be repeated if necessary.

For most dogs, castration provides relief from signs of prostatic enlargement, without the side effects that may occur with estrogen therapy. The prostate gland will shrink noticeably within a week after surgery, and will continue to get smaller for two to three months after castration. Prostate surgery to remove the gland in the dog is not consistently effective.

PROSTATITIS

Prostatitis is an inflammation of the prostate gland, with the production of pus. Is is most commonly seen in older males, and often occurs along with prostatic enlargement. Prostatitis is more often seen in dogs who have been given estrogen to treat the enlargement, and in dogs with Sertoli cell tumors. The infective agent can come from several places. It may ascend up the urethra, it may come from the bladder, it may arrive in the blood, or it may travel from the rest of the reproductive tract via semen.

Signs are much like those of prostatic enlargement. In addition, the dog may be lethargic. He is more likely to show pain on palpation of the upper rear part of the abdomen. On rectal palpation by a veterinarian, the prostate will feel tender, warm and fluid-filled. During an acute episode, the dog will not eat, and will have an elevated temperature. Blood is usually seen in the urine. Some dogs will have a stiff, stilted gait due to the pain of movement.

Your veterinarian may run a laboratory examination of the dog's urine. He may also order a culture and sensitivity tests, to determine which antibiotic will effectively treat the bacteria causing the disease. X-rays are often needed for a positive diagnosis. Antibiotics may be given for two to three weeks to get the infection under control. Acute prostate infections easily become chronic. For this reason, your veterinarian may schedule a re-examination three to five days after the course of antibiotics is finished. This may include laboratory tests to make sure the infection is gone. As with prostatic enlargement, castration is helpful.

PROSTATIC ABSCESSES

Abscesses often occur in the prostate gland after a bout of prostatitis due to bacterial infection. The infection becomes localized in pockets filled with pus (abscesses). If the abscesses are very large, signs may be related to the dog's inability to defecate. He may strain without passing feces, or he may have difficulty in urinating. Urine dribbling may be seen.

A prostatic abscess may rupture, spilling pus into the abdominal cavity. If this occurs, vomiting, shock, and death usually follow within a few hours.

Surgical drainage may be the only possible treatment for a very large abscess. Or the entire prostate gland may be removed surgically. With either surgery, complications are common. In some cases, intensive care will be needed for several days after surgery. Castration is helpful if portions of the prostate gland have not been removed. A urinary tract infection may also be present, and will need treatment. In any case, antibiotics will be needed for a period of time. A few cases of prostatic abscessation have been treated with antibiotics only. The infection is controlled, not cured, by the antibiotics, and returns immediately when they are withdrawn. For that reason, surgical treatment is best.

PROSTATIC CYSTS

Large cysts are occasionally found within the prostate gland, or attached to it. Signs occur when the cyst becomes large enough to press on structures around it. They are similar to those of prostatic enlargement: difficult defecation, straining to urinate, etc. Total surgical removal of the cyst is the only treatment that seems to work well. Until that is done, a diet low in residue to reduce the volume of feces may help to ease the dog's discomfort. Estrogen therapy may be harmful to dogs with prostatic cysts. Castration alone does not seem to help, but may be helpful after the cyst or its contents are removed.

PROSTATIC TUMORS

Prostatic tumors are rare. Their signs are like those of other prostatic disease. The dog may show pain or weakness in the hind end, or stiffness. The dog may have weight loss over a long period of time. From the prostate, the tumor may spread (metastasize) to the lungs or heart, causing symptoms related to those organs. In most cases, the tumor has spread before signs become obvious enough that a diagnosis can be made. Small doses of estrogen may help the prostate temporarily, but do not cure the problem. Castration may be helpful in some dogs. Chemotherapy may work in a few dogs. If the tumor has already spread to other parts of the body, euthanasia is the most humane course of treatment.

LIVER PROBLEMS

The liver is one of the largest organs in the body and has a considerable reserve. It must be extensively damaged before signs of disease are seen. Because many of its functions are similar to those of other organs in the body, signs of liver disease may resemble disease signs of other organs or tissues. Liver disease may also accompany other disease processes. Since many diseases may be involved, it is difficult to describe specific symptoms of liver disease, or causes of it.

One which specifically affects the liver is infectious canine hepatitis (ICH). Ascarids, tapeworm cysts and flukes are among the parasites which may affect the liver. Canine herpesvirus infection affects it, as can diabetes mellitus and Cushing's syndrome (an excess of adrenal cortical hormone). Leptospirosis can also affect the liver. Toxins such as coal tars, cresols, dioxin, carbon tetrachloride and excess vitamin D can cause liver damage, as can congestive heart failure.

Because of its many functions, many signs are possible with liver disease. Icterus (also called jaundice) is one of the most common. This is a yellow coloration of the mucous membranes caused by an accumulation of toxins which are no longer removed from the blood by the damaged liver. This causes the "white" of the eye to appear yellow. The gums may also appear yellowish. Another sign of possible liver disease is fluid accumulation in the abdomen. This will be seen as a widening of the lower part of the abdomen. In some liver diseases, signs of brain and central nervous system abnormalities are seen. X-rays may be useful in determining the extent of liver disease. A liver biopsy may also be needed to confirm the diagnosis and determine the extent of the disease. Even this may not give a definite diagnosis of precisely what is wrong.

Liver disease is hard to diagnose, and still harder to treat. When it is caused by another disease or abnormality, treatment will be aimed at that cause. Very little therapy is available when the liver itself is involved. About all that can be done is to try to lessen its work load by providing a diet with high-quality protein, and carefully balanced vitamins and minerals. Drugs such as choline may be helpful in some cases.

Chapter 18

LAMENESS AND BACK PROBLEMS

LAMENESS EXAMINATION

Your dog is lame. Where do you begin? If there is an obvious cut or fracture, administer first aid (see the Emergency Chapter for what to do) and get the dog to your veterinarian.

If there is nothing immediately obvious, begin by observing the dog. Have someone walk him around the yard, on good footing. Is only one leg involved? Does he limp all the time, or just when he is turning to the right or to the left? Have them trot him. Watch for the dog to nod his head upward in time with picking up an affected front leg as he trots.

No obvious limp? Systematically examine the dog. If, for instance, the problem is in a front leg, check the apparently normal front leg first. And, bear in mind that both legs may be affected, with one being worse than the other, so that it is the more obvious. Go through the same routine with each leg (first the normal one, then the lame one), so that you can compare the two.

Begin at the foot. You can examine the dog's foot with the dog standing, or you can lay him on his side, with someone holding him for you. Move each joint of each toe, one at a time. Try to hold the rest of the foot still so that ONLY the joint you are examining moves. Move each joint slowly, through its whole range of motion, front to back. Check to see

if the joint moves sideways. Attempt to flex the foot backward toward the elbow. This motion is tolerated by most normal dogs. Some dogs with painful arthritis will show muscular "guarding" of the affected joint(s). They will stiffen the leg, attempting to prevent you from bending the painful joint. Also check to see if the joint can be flexed TOO much. This may occur when the ligaments or tendons around a joint are torn or damaged. Note any grating sensation (called crepitus or crepitation); this usually indicates a broken bone.

Is there a difference between the two legs? Does the dog show any pain? He may attempt to pull the foot away from you, move his head toward you, look at the problem area, or, in severe cases, may attempt to bite. Work your way up the leg, checking each joint in turn. Now go through the same routine with the painful leg.

Starting at the foot, palpate (feel) upward on each leg, checking the muscles and tendons. Do this gently and slowly. Palpate the length of each bone individually. Look for painful spots, lumps or improper alignment.

Examine each foot carefully. Check the nails to see that none are broken or worn down to the quick. Also look for abnormal wear (or lack of wear) on one or more nails. Examine the pads for cuts, cracks, spots that are worn through or excessive hardening. Now check the web between each of the toes. Look here for cuts, grass awns, pebbles, chewing gum, etc.

If your dog has a hind leg problem, check it as above for a front leg. The hock should have a normal range of motion of about 90 degrees. If it moves MORE than that, there may be a problem with the Achilles tendon. The tuberosity of the tibia (the portion which sticks out farthest forward on the upper end of the bone) is often fractured in young dogs. The tibia is the long bone between the knee and the hock.

Palpate the kneecap (patella) with your thumb and forefinger while you move the leg forward and backward. Attempt to push it toward the dog's body, and then away from it. Do this with the dog's leg held straight, and then with it bent. In a normal dog, you should not be able to push the kneecap out of its groove to either side, using moderate force.

Check the stifle joint (the one just behind the kneecap) for drawer motion. To do so, you hold the femur with one hand, and the tibia with the other hand. Then try to push the lower part of the leg straight forward or back in relationship to the upper part. If the leg has this motion, one of the ligaments within the joint is torn, and surgery will be needed to repair it. If you feel a "click," the dog may have a torn meniscus (cartilage) within the joint, much like a "football knee."

Check the range of motion of the hips. Dislocation of the hip is common in dogs who are hit by cars. Hold your hands on the dog's hips as someone leads him forward. You may be able to feel one of the hips popping or snapping in and out of place. Lay the dog on his back and pull both his legs out straight backward. Check to see that they are the same length. Do the same examination forward, with both legs straightened toward the dog's belly. If they are not the same length, your dog probably has a dislocated hip, and should be taken to a veterinarian to have it replaced. Before you decide that this is the case, make sure that both legs are relaxed and that the dog does not have a problem with one of the other joints which is not straightening out because it has a limited range of motion, or because it is being "guarded" due to pain. A dog who has hip dysplasia will often show pain when the legs are pulled backward in this manner. Push the leg upward and outward. This may cause it to pop in and out of joint.

Check for symmetry of the pelvis. Do this with the dog standing. Push inward on each set of points of the pelvis at the same time. If you feel any looseness or crepitation, the pelvis is probably broken. Take the dog in to have him checked. As with all lameness examinations, you must know the normal condition for your dog before you can determine what is abnormal.

FOOT PROBLEMS

Foot problems are perhaps the most common cause of lameness in dogs, much as in horses. If you do not do the entire lameness check, at least examine the foot VERY carefully before you take the dog to the veterinarian (unless there is an obvious cause of lameness, such as a fracture).

Grass awns are a common cause of lameness, especially in dogs with plenty of hair on their feet, such as Spaniels and Poodles. While these can occur at any time of the year, they are most common in late summer and early fall, when the seed heads of common annual grasses such as cheat grass (downey chess) and foxtail become ripe. The seeds become caught in the hair on the foot and then work their way through the dog's skin. They can cause pain just because they are there, or can cause an abscess to form. In either case, the dog may limp or otherwise show lameness. He may chew at his foot until it is soaked with saliva and foul-smelling.

You might feel the grass awn as you palpate the webs between the toes. Pull it out with tweezers or forceps. Now, clip the hair out from between ALL the toes. If you will always keep the dog's feet clipped clean, most of the grass awns which poke into this area will fall out, and your dog will have no further trouble with them. Clipping between the toes should be routine maintenance for ALL long-haired dogs— whether Saint Bernard, Poodle, Collie or mutt—on a year-round basis. It will save you a LOT of trouble and money and your dog a lot of pain in the long run. If the dog has an abscess, see below. Thorns may cause similar problems.

Glass may cause a cut pad in any dog at any time. Sharp pieces of ice in winter often cause cuts just like glass. These cuts should be treated promptly, as letting one go may result in considerable blood loss—foot pads tend to bleed severely. If the cut is fresh and sizeable (whether long or deep), put a gauze pad over the cut and a pressure bandage around the foot and take the dog to your veterinarian or emergency clinic as soon as possible. If it is small and you can get the bleeding stopped, seal it with cyanoacrylate glue (Super Glue®) and put a bandage over it. Keep the dog from licking it. If the cut is old, and you find it because the dog is licking it, pack it with nitrofurazone cream. Bandage it, and keep the dog from chewing at the bandage. Change the bandage every day or two until the cut is healed.

If the dog has an abscess between his toes, he will need treatment. If it has already broken, you can gently probe into the opening with a pair of forceps or tweezers to pull out the grass awn or other foreign body which caused the problem. The opening can be gently enlarged so that it will drain well and heal from the inside out. It can be swabbed out with povidone-iodine, used full-strength on a cotton swab. Do not worry about harming tissue which has already healed—dogs are put together better than that! You need to keep the hole open, or it will seal over and fill up with pus again, and you will be back where you started. Swab it out twice daily until it has healed.

If the abscess has not yet opened, you can wait to see if it will come to a "head." This is a weakened, thinned, often yellowish area at the top of the abscess, much like a pimple. At that point, it can be picked open with a blunt instrument, or a needle or pin. Then treat as described above. With any abscess, the feet should be cleanly clipped. It is often necessary to bandage the foot, not because the abscess needs it, but to keep the dog from licking and worrying at it. Licking is NOT helpful to healing. It just causes irritation, and often helps to keep a wound open.

Toes are sometimes fractured. This happens when they catch in brush or carpeting while the rest of the dog keeps going. Take the dog to your veterinarian to be X-rayed and splinted. If you cannot get the dog to a veterinarian, the fractured toe can be simply set in a spoon splint and bandaged. The healing may not be perfect, but the toe will usually be quite usable (see Emergency Chapter).

Ingrown or broken toenails can cause pain to the dog. Sometimes a broken toenail can be glued together to provide pain relief until it is healed. Chewing gum or a pebble caught between the toes can also be painful to the dog.

WORN PADS

A dog who is taken hiking or hunting in rocky terrain, or even for a walk on city pavement and is not in condition for it, may wear its pads and become totally lame. The pads may be worn completely through, to where they show rounded spots of wear into or through the outer layers of the pad. Ones which are less badly worn may merely show thinned areas, and will be sensitive when pressed.

You can use lightweight leather to protect the worn spots. Cut rounded pieces of leather to the approximate shape and size of the worn areas, allowing an extra 1/4 inch all the way around. Then shave the edges of the patch thin, from the suede (rough) side. In an emergency, leather cut from the outer layer of the top of your hiking boots can be used.

Have someone hold the dog upside down throughout the procedure. Apply a thin layer of cyanoacrylate glue (Super

Glue®) to the worn spots, and to the rough side of the leather pieces. Allow both glued surfaces to dry until the glue has a tacky consistency. (CAUTION: This glue will stick your fingers to themselves or to anything they touch. It won't help if your index finger is glued to your eyelid and you are fifty miles from town.) Now press the leather rounds firmly onto the worn spots and allow the repaired areas to dry. While they are drying, press back into place any areas where the leather tries to separate from the pad.

After the repairs are completely dry, apply more glue to the edges of any leather that has not adhered to the pad, to create as smooth an edge as possible where patch and pad join. When the second gluing has dried completely, you can allow the dog to stand. After a few tentative steps to try its new pads, the dog will generally walk freely, and can successfully complete a cattle drive or hike. This is a great reward for 20 minutes' work.

Check the repairs several times during the next few days. Occasionally you will need to glue new patches on the pads until they have healed well enough for the dog to walk without pain. Generally, by the time the leather has worn off he will be able to walk without pain, and will not need any further treatment. Dogs usually tolerate this repair well, without continuously licking at their feet, which often occurs when the feet are bandaged.

Small amounts of leather may be purchased at leathercraft shops. A piece the size of your hand will cost about $1 and will be enough to repair several dozen pads (James, 1986).

ELBOW AND HOCK CALLUSES

Calluses occur on the hocks and elbows, areas where the skin stretches tightly over bony prominences with little padding underneath. They are especially seen with bony, thin-skinned dogs with little hair, such as Dobermans and Great Danes, and other large dogs, such as Newfoundlands and St. Bernards, who are kept on hard floors or concrete runs or patios. The hair wears off and knobby, wrinkled calluses form. In some cases these may be filled with fluid. These are usually not functional problems, but may be cosmetic blemishes if you are showing the dog. They can be surgically removed, but may return if the original cause is not removed. These calluses are very rare in smaller dogs—they simply do not weigh enough to put the required pressure on the pointed spots when they sit or lay on hard surfaces.

Preventing these calluses depends on reducing wear and tear on the dog's bony areas. No, letting him get fat is not a way to cure it! Make sure that your dog has plenty of soft bedding. Clean, mildew-free carpet scraps can be used, building up several layers to make a thick pad. Or you can use a commercial pad filled with cedar shavings. An outdoor dog can have six or eight inches of clean, dust-free straw placed in his run or in a place where he likes to stay. If the dog runs loose, he may appreciate a couple of bales of clean straw placed together under a tree or porch—he can lie on top of them and look out over his domain from a comfortable perch.

ARTHRITIS

Arthritis (also called osteoarthritis or degenerative joint disease (DJD), similar to that in humans is also seen in dogs. As with humans, it is generally a wear-and-tear disease of the older animal. It may result from misaligned joints which do not function properly, or can be due to damage to the joint, as from being hit by a car. Arthritis from the two latter causes occurs more frequently in younger animals. Fractures which involve joint surfaces and do not heal properly may result in arthritis. Overweight dogs may damage their joints when they jump out of a pickup truck or from a high place.

Arthritis starts when the joint cartilage is damaged. It becomes rough and pitted. Eventually it wears away, exposing the bone underneath. The joint capsule and ligaments stretch, leaving the joint lax and less functional than before. Because the joint hurts and the animal uses the limb less than he normally would, the muscles in the area are often weakened. When the bones begin to move against each other within the joint, the dog will be in pain, and may visibly favor the leg. Arthritis may affect one joint or several. The dog may have several joints affected, but only show pain in the one which hurts worst.

A dog with arthritis is often reluctant to move. He reduces his normal activity, or stops altogether. The dog may not want to jump into a car or pickup truck, go for his walk or do his normal work. He may lie around, and have trouble getting up from a sitting or lying position. He may cry, whine or even snap at you if you handle the aching joint. You may notice that he is worse when the weather is changing or is cold and damp. The day after hard exercise, the dog may be unable to get up or move without help. After being helped to stand, he will move around and gradually warm out of the stiffness or lameness. When the arthritis has gone on for some time, the dog may have trouble getting up every morning, whether he worked the day before or not.

If the dog is young and has these symptoms, it is worth having him checked by your veterinarian as soon as possible. An elderly dog may be treated symptomatically. Have your old dog checked the next time you have him to your veterinarian for another reason, especially if the stiffness and reluctance to move comes and goes.

Aspirin will help to relieve the symptoms of pain for many dogs. A 75 lb (35 kg) dog can take three five-grain buffered aspirin twice a day. You can increase this to three times a day if necessary. As with humans, this drug may cause an upset stomach in sensitive dogs. If your dog has this problem, give him the medication with a bit of food. In addition to the analgesic effect, aspirin is also thought to reduce some of the inflammation in the joint and cartilages. Non-aspirin pain relievers (acetaminophen products) DO NOT work well in dogs, and do not seem to provide adequate pain relief. Drugs such as ibuprofen and indocin may be fatal to your dog. Don't use them!

Work with your dog to give the smallest amount of aspirin that will give adequate relief. In the beginning of the disease, it may be needed only after exercise or when the weather changes. Later, it may be needed daily to reduce the pain. The drug makes the animal more comfortable; it does not stop the progress of the disease. When the dog is feeling well, it is important not to allow him to over exercise.

Corticosteroids may be used in some cases, but dogs treated with these medications for a long time are at risk of developing Cushing's disease. Aspirin products are much safer when the drug must be given for the rest of the dog's life, if they will control the pain.

Moderate exercise is helpful for the arthritic dog. Slow walks can be used. Swimming is good exercise, and avoids impact on the joints. Make sure to dry the dog well, out of a draft, so he is not chilled, adding to his discomfort. Excessive exercise may increase damage to the joints. It may also cause the dog pain lasting for several days, and should be avoided.

The arthritic dog should be kept warm and dry. He should not be allowed to sleep on a cold concrete slab, in a basement, or in an unheated porch in winter. Flat plastic kennel heaters that the dog can lie on are available. These provide controlled, gentle warmth from below. It is not a good idea to use a drugstore-type heating pad designed for people. It may become too hot, and the dog may not move off it in time to avoid being burned. Or he may chew the cord, causing electric burns or electrocution. An extra-soft bed may ease the pain for some dogs, as will the warmth of a heated waterbed if your dog normally sleeps with you.

Vitamins and minerals do not stop the progress of the disease. They also do not help the joints return to normal. Unfortunately, at this point in our knowledge, arthritis is a one-way disease, going always toward "worse." As in humans, there is no cure for osteoarthritis in the dog.

SEPTIC ARTHRITIS

Septic arthritis is seen when infection occurs within a joint cavity. This may have been carried to the joint by the blood from an infection elsewhere in the body. It can occur because of a puncture wound to the joint, as by a bite or other injury. The joint becomes filled with pus. If the infection is not cured rather quickly, the pus may cause permanent degeneration of the joint cartilage and of the end of the bone, leaving the animal with a permanent arthritis. A dog with septic arthritis may show a joint that feels hot compared to the other joints, and which is very painful. Prompt treatment is necessary, and your veterinarian may have to inject antibiotics directly into the joint in order to save it.

Arthritis in more than one joint is a common sign of ehrlichiosis and Lyme disease. These diseases should be considered if you live in an area where they occur.

RHEUMATOID ARTHRITIS

Rheumatoid arthritis is a disease of the body's immune system. It is occasionally seen in dogs. The dog may show pain and swelling in one or more joints. It may begin with one joint and move on to others, but eventually several joints will become involved. The symptoms may be accompanied by fever, lack of appetite and swollen lymph nodes. Dogs of toy breeds are commonly affected, ranging in age from eight months to eight years (Mitzner, 1989). Systemic lupus erythematosus may have similar symptoms.

Signs of rheumatoid arthritis may include pain and soreness in one or more joints, along with swelling of the tissues around the joints. The joint may be puffy and swollen with fluid. These swellings may be symmetrical from one side to the other.

Dogs with signs of arthritis in one or more joints, accompanied by fever and lack of appetite, should be examined by a veterinarian. This is especially true if the disease comes on rather suddenly, or if the dog is young to middle-aged. Your veterinarian may run tests to check for rheumatoid factor, as well as examine the synovial fluid within the joint. He may also X-ray the joints, looking for characteristic signs of the disease. If the disease is recognized early, it can be treated, and may be slowed or even totally stopped.

BURSITIS

This is an inflammation of the bursae over the joints. These small, fluid-filled pockets are located between a bone and a tendon. They contain the same fluid that lubricates the joints. They can become hot, swollen and painful. The inflammation may go down with the use of ice packs. Be careful not to give the dog frostbite while treating him! Rest is also helpful, giving the area a chance to heal. In some cases, it may be necessary for your veterinarian to remove some of the excess fluid to relieve the pressure and to ease the animal's pain.

PATELLAR LUXATION (DISPLACED KNEECAP)

Patellar luxation refers to a kneecap which does not stay in its normal groove. Toy Poodles, Chihuahuas, Yorkshire Terriers, Papillons and other small dogs often have a very shallow groove on the end of the femur, which allows the patella to pop in and out of place. In the normal dog, the groove is deep and well-formed, holding the kneecap in place as if it were on railroad tracks.

Patellar luxation is most common in toy dogs less than one year of age. It may be seen in dogs as young as four months of age (Denny, 1985). A dog who has this problem often will hold up one hind leg or the other, often for only one or two steps at a time. Or he may carry one hind leg held up all the time. The problem often occurs in both hind legs, and the dog may hop along, first holding up one leg and then the other. The dog's gait will be affected, shifting from four legs to three and back again. Luxations to the inside (the most common) may cause the dog to look bow-legged. Those to the outside will cause him to look knock-kneed.

Check the dog by palpating the kneecap between your thumb and forefinger as you straighten and bend the leg. Try to push it out of the groove as you are moving the leg, first to the outside (away from his body) and then to the inside. In a normal dog, you should not be able to push the kneecap out of its groove. About three-quarters of dogs with patellar luxation will have a kneecap that can be moved to the inside, popping easily in and out of its groove. In almost all cases caused by injury, the kneecap will be able to be moved to the inside. The dog cannot straighten his leg while the kneecap is out of place. He must wait until it pops back into place by itself or until it is pushed back into place.

Luxations to the outside may be seen in dogs of smaller breeds later in life (5 to 9 years of age). When patellar luxations are seen in larger breeds, they are usually to the outside as well. Outside luxations are most common in dogs who are knock-kneed or cow-hocked.

Whether luxated to the inside or to the outside, this problem can be surgically repaired. The kneecap may be stabilized from one side or the other, depending on the side to which it displaces. The joint capsule is tightened to hold the kneecap in place. In some cases, the groove in which the kneecap rides may be deepened. Or the tibial crest, to which the ligament containing the kneecap is attached, may be cut loose and reattached in a more normal alignment. If the dog was born with patellar luxation, surgery should be done around four to five months of age, before the pull of the muscles permanently deforms the leg.

After surgery, the dog's activity must be quite restricted for about one month, until all the repaired areas have healed. Normal activity is gradually resumed. Most veterinarians allow about two months for the first leg to heal before doing the second leg when surgery must be done on both of them (Denny, 1985).

RUPTURED CRUCIATE LIGAMENTS

A dog may tear a cruciate ligament, either the anterior (front) or posterior (rear) one. These ligaments stabilize the stifle (knee) joint, crossing in an "X" within the joint. The front (anterior) ligament is torn much more often than the rear one. Tearing often occurs when the dog has a hard landing, such as jumping off a high place or out of a pickup.

The dog will show "drawer motion" when examined. Hold your dog's leg firmly with one hand above the stifle joint, with the leg bent at a normal angle. Hold the other hand firmly below the stifle joint. Now try to move the lower part back and forth (front to back) in relation to the upper portion. In some cases, your veterinarian may have to sedate or anesthetize the dog to feel this motion because the dog will try to hold the joint rigid to avoid pain.

The ligament will NOT heal by itself. In addition, other structures within the joint may be damaged and will need repair. However, surgery to replace the ligament has a high rate of success. The ligament will be replaced by a strip of tendon, fascia, skin or artificial material. Most dogs, after a period of recovery, return to normal activity, especially if the repair is done before arthritis develops.

DISPLACED HIP

Hip displacement may occur when a dog is injured. When the dog's legs are pulled either backward or forward, one leg may be shorter than the other. If you put your hands on the dog's hips as he walks, you may feel the hip popping in and out of the joint. Take the dog to your veterinarian. He will put the hip back into place, and either bandage it or stabilize it with a pin to keep it there while the damaged tissues heal.

HIP DYSPLASIA

Canine hip dysplasia (CHD) is a congenital condition in which the head of the femur does not fit well into its socket in the hip joint. Normally, the head of the femur is rounded, like a ball. The socket in the hip is well rounded and deep. The two fit closely and securely together. With hip dysplasia, the socket in the pelvis, instead of being nicely rounded to receive that ball, is flattened and shallow. The head of the femur is abnormally flattened, too. So instead of fitting tightly together and moving smoothly, the flattened "ball" slops around, in and out of the socket. Arthritic spurs develop around the edge of the joint, and both the ball part and the socket part become progressively more flattened. Inflammation occurs, and the joint becomes filled with an excessive amount of joint fluid. It becomes painful, and the dog has trouble moving. Eventually, because of the dog's unwillingness to move, the muscles of the hip area become weakened and shrunken. The dog may have difficulty moving at all at this stage.

Hip dysplasia is commonly seen in larger breeds of dogs, and has been most common in German Shepherds, Labrador Retrievers and other breeds of hunting dogs. Nearly half of all Saint Bernards, according to Orthopedic Foundation for Animals (OFA) figures, have hip dysplasia. It is occasionally seen in smaller dogs. A few cases may be due to injury, such as being hit by a car. Hip dysplasia occurs equally in male and female dogs.

Dogs with clinically normal hips may have puppies with hip dysplasia. Dogs with abnormal hips are almost certain to have puppies with hip dysplasia. Because of its strong hereditary basis, dogs who have hip dysplasia should not be used for breeding stock. Potential breeding dogs should be X-rayed after two years of age. The X-ray films may be submitted to the OFA, which certifies that the hips are acceptable, and that the dog has a good chance of producing puppies with normal hips. It will then issue an OFA registry number for the dog. Application cards and instructions are available from the Orthopedic Foundation for Animals, University of Missouri-Columbia, Columbia, Missouri, 65211.

Bitches who are in heat may show a degree of looseness in the hip joint, and may be diagnosed, falsely, as having hip dysplasia. Dogs who are in, or have just come out of, a prolonged period of inactivity may also look like they have hip dysplasia. If either of these conditions exist, wait until the dog is back to normal before you have the X-rays taken.

Imbalances among calcium, phosphorus and vitamin D may be contributing factors, as can excessive protein levels. However, the predominant cause of hip dysplasia is still considered to be genetic.

Occasionally, young puppies are involved. Their femurs may pull completely out of the sockets, and the puppies flounder around on their bellies like small frogs. It can occur as early as six or eight weeks of age. However, it may not occur in some dogs until they are around four to five months or one year of age. Less severe cases may show pain in the hind end, and be less active than you would expect for their age and breed.

The dog with hip dysplasia may shift his weight to his front legs, pulling the hind legs under his body. He may have an unsteady, swaying gait. After exercise, he may be severely lame. He may be unable to rise the next morning, and will need help to stand up. He will then totter off, painfully and unsteadily. He may have trouble climbing stairs. He may cry out or attempt to bite if you handle his hind legs or hip area. A long hike or run may show the presence of the disease in a dog which has been considered normal. The dog may be fine the day of the exercise, but be nearly unable to move the next morning.

Hip dysplasia is a progressive arthritic disease. The dog will never get "well." Some dogs, however, will still be able to move reasonably well despite severe arthritic changes in the hip joints, while others will get to the point of being unable to stand. These dogs drag themselves along by pulling with their front legs, hauling along their helpless, limp hind end.

You may suspect by the signs you see that your dog has hip dysplasia. It will need to be confirmed by your veterinarian, who will X-ray the hip joints. For the great majority of dogs, proper positioning of the hips and legs for this examination requires either deep sedation or complete anesthesia. A dog with hip dysplasia may feel considerable pain when his legs are pulled straight backward to position them for the X-rays. He will struggle and fight. Even a perfectly normal dog may resist having his legs pulled straight backwards, and may twist sideways, making it look like he has hip dysplasia. Especially if you are having the X-rays taken for OFA certification, perfect positioning is important to give your dog the most accurate evaluation possible. So don't argue. Let your veterinarian sedate or anesthetize the dog so the job can be done properly.

In the dysplastic dog, the X-rays will show the head of the femur to be flattened, and the socket joint shallower and flatter than it should be. Some dogs will not show definite changes until they are about two years of age. The severity of signs on X-rays does not always correlate with clinical signs. A dog with few changes in the bones may be quite lame and in severe pain. Another one, with a great deal of arthritis, may move much better than would be expected from the amount of damage present.

Perhaps the most heartbreaking part of hip dysplasia is that it generally does not show up until you are firmly attached to the dog. If you are buying a large-breed dog, or a hunting dog, it may be worthwhile having a purchase contract that says that the dog will be free of dysplasia or he can be returned. The only problem is giving up your pet after you have had him for a year or so, become attached to him, and put out the good money for vaccinations and, perhaps, spaying or neutering, and devoted some time to training him. It hurts to return the animal, who is by that time a good friend, so shop around in order to get a dog who has dysplasia-free parents, giving him a high probability of also being dysplasia-free.

If your dog has hip dysplasia, there is NO cure. Nothing will slow or stop the degeneration that is occurring within the joint.

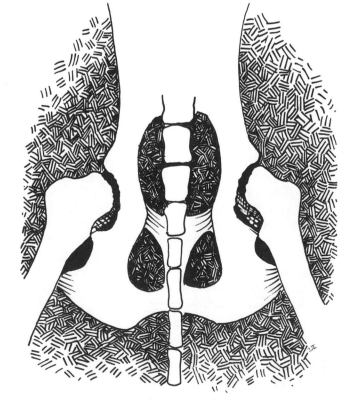

Normal hips with well-rounded ball and socket.   Severe hip dysplasia, with flattening of ball and socket.

The best that you can do is to make him comfortable and ease his pain. Giving him buffered aspirin when he is hurting will help. Vitamins and minerals do not seem to change the course of the disease. Moderate exercise such as walking or slow jogging may be helpful. Hard running, long runs and jumping should be avoided. Swimming is particularly good exercise, as it avoids impact on the painful hip joints.

Surgical procedures have been tried to help reduce the pain of hip dysplasia. They may work in some animals and be useless in others. Hip surgery is expensive, and its success rate varies so much that the possible benefits must be weighed against the cost, the pain which is caused the animal, and the probable years of life left to the animal.

One procedure to relieve the pain of hip dysplasia involves cutting a small muscle on the inside of the hind leg. This is thought to allow the head of the femur to pull outward from the socket, easing the pain which occurs when the ball grinds against the socket. Another surgical procedure involves removing the head of the femur. While this sounds quite radical, it actually can relieve much of the pain in some dogs, giving them a much happier life. It will not, however, fully restore the dog to function for hard work such as hunting, packing your grub while you are hiking (or even making it through a long day's hike, for that matter), or working cattle. Total hip replacement with an artificial joint has been used to treat hip dysplasia. Another surgical procedure builds a new shelf around the lip of the socket to hold the ball part of the joint into place. It's far better to spend more money for a puppy from good parents than to pay for expensive, "iffy" surgery later.

RUPTURED ACHILLES TENDON

A ruptured Achilles tendon may occur when a dog tears the back of his hind leg on a piece of wire, or his leg is cut by a mowing machine. It may be torn when the dog is hit by a car, or by extreme exertion on a hunt or race, as sometimes happens to Greyhounds.

The dog's hock will drop toward the ground while the stifle has a nearly normal angle. The dog will not be able to walk on the toes or stand on the injured leg. Many dogs will show little or no pain with this problem. There will not be any crepitus (crunchy or crackly feeling) when the leg is palpated or moved. This tells you that there are no broken bones.

These signs can also be seen with a ruptured gastrocnemius muscle, but that won't matter to you, the dog's owner. Surgery is the only treatment for either problem. So, take the dog to your veterinarian as soon as possible, and let him figure out which problem it is and fix it. Immediate treatment will give a better chance for healing. The leg will be placed in a cast or splint after surgery, for at least four to six weeks.

OSTEOCHONDRITIS DISSECANS (O.D. or OCD)

Osteochondritis dissecans is most often seen in the major joints of the limbs: shoulder, elbow, hock and knee (stifle). O.D. of the head of the humerus may show up as pain when the shoulder joint is extended or flexed. When you are ex-amining this area, be sure to limit the motion to the shoulder joint. Otherwise, you may pick up pain from the elbow and think it is coming from the shoulder. Shoulder joint problems show up most commonly when the joint is extended (the front leg is pulled forward). O.D. of the hock may show up as a swollen joint, with discomfort when the joint is palpated. In some cases, the elbow or stifle may be affected.

This disease comes on gradually and causes a persistent lameness. It usually begins between four and eight months of age. Some dogs may have several joints affected. Others will have only one involved, which may make you think that it has been injured. The dog may show stiffness after he has been resting. The lameness may become worse after the dog has been exercised, especially after he has run or worked hard. Crepitation may be felt when the joint is moved. Long-term cases may show shrinking of the muscles in the involved leg because the dog is not using it.

O.D. of the elbow joint may cause what is called elbow dysplasia. Elbow dysplasia also occurs with other problems which cause loose pieces of bone or cartilage to be present within the joint, such as an injury. These problems often occur before the dog is five months old, before the cartilage has grown firmly attached to the bone, although some may be seen as late as a year of age. The dog's elbow may sag to the outside and appear to be poorly aligned. The dog may show arthritis and swelling of the joint as it fills with fluid. Crepitus (a crackly sensation) may be felt when the joint is moved.

Osteochondritis occurs when the cartilage within a joint becomes excessively thickened. Small defects or separations develop between layers of the swollen cartilage. These defects may go into the bone below the cartilage. The separations allow the fluid from within the joint capsule to enter the bone, where it sets up an inflammatory reaction. The cartilage comes loose from the bone, and a partially attached plaque results. Continued movement of the joint keeps the plaque from reattaching, and causes pain. It is often torn completely loose by the movement of the joint. Some loose plaques will reattach to the joint surface, but may not be well aligned, causing a bony spur to form within the joint, which will cause continuing pain. Or it may continue to float loose within the joint, causing intermittent pain as the dog moves. A piece of cartilage or a bone chip free within the joint is sometimes called a "joint mouse."

The cause of O.D. is not known. In some cases, it is thought that damage to the joint surface may be involved. Some cases are thought to be hereditary, since littermates may also be affected. Offspring of animals who have had O.D. will often develop it. For this reason, affected dogs should not be bred. O.D. has been experimentally induced in foals who were fed diets low in copper. (Excess copper, by the way, can cause toxicity. As with many other trace minerals, proper balance is very important.) O.D. has also been found in horses with increased zinc levels, such as those living downwind from zinc smelters. These factors might also play a role in O.D. in the dog. We just don't know.

If the dog is not treated, the damage may become permanent because of the arthritis which occurs. X-rays will allow your veterinarian to diagnose the problem rather easily, although it may be necessary to take several views at different angles to demonstrate the defect in the cartilage. Hock and elbow lesions are often harder to find than are those in the shoulder joint.

Some cases may recover without any treatment other than rest. The dog can be confined to a kennel, run or playpen for four to six weeks. Exercise during this time should be confined to short walks several times a day, out to the yard so the dog can relieve himself. These weeks of strict rest may allow the loosened piece of cartilage to reattach to the bone.

Corticosteroids are not recommended, for several reasons. They relieve the pain, which encourages the dog to exercise excessively. Also, these drugs slow the growth of the bone and cartilage cells, possibly preventing reattachment of the loosened piece. For the same reason, aspirin and other painkillers should not be given. It is more important to limit the dog's exercise and use the pain to help keep him still. If he doesn't move, he doesn't hurt.

Surgery may be used to remove the loosened piece of cartilage and keep it from causing further pain and damage. This treatment is especially useful in shoulder joints with O.D. If it is performed shortly after the pain and lameness starts, results are often quite good. Your veterinarian will surgically remove the flap of cartilage and scrape the underlying bone clean. Hock, elbow and stifle joints may be treated in the same manner. However, the results are often not as good in these joints as in the shoulder. In some cases, if the clinic is extremely well equipped, the surgery may be done with arthroscopy, using a very small incision. This can promote rapid healing since the surgical trauma is slight.

OSTEOMYELITIS

The term "osteomyelitis," when properly used, refers to an inflammation of the bone marrow. However, most times it is used to refer to an inflammation or infection involving any part of the bone, especially if it is extensive or particularly invasive.

Osteomyelitis occurs when bone tissue dies in the presence of an infectious agent, usually a species of bacteria. In other cases, it may be a fungus or other infectious agent. Foreign bodies (such as porcupine quills, arrows or bullets) may also cause osteomyelitis, as can a metallic pin or other object which is left in contact with the bone for a period of time.

Most cases of osteomyelitis (bone infection) occur after accidents which cause penetrating injury to the bone, such as auto accidents, gunshot wounds, knife wounds, or punctures from the dog stepping on a nail or other metal object. Other cases occur after the bone is fractured, with or without bone fragments being separated from the main portion of the bone at the fracture. It may also occur after surgery, as well as after bite wounds which penetrate to or near the bone. It may be seen with long-term cases of dental disease, in which bacteria eat down around the roots of the teeth, into the root canals and into the surrounding bone.

Cases of osteomyelitis due to fungus infections are seen with coccidioidomycosis (valley fever, seen in Arizona, parts of California, Texas, and Central and South America). Osteomyelitis may also be seen with blastomycosis, which is found in the Central Atlantic states, the Ohio and Mississippi river basins, the northern border of Ontario and Manitoba, and parts of Africa.

One of the first signs of osteomyelitis is pain and swelling in the affected limb. The dog may be lame and reluctant to use his leg. He may have a fever, depression and lack of appetite.

Osteomyelitis is not a disease to treat at home. If you think that there might be infection involving the bone, it is important to take your dog to the veterinarian. His examination may involve X-raying the area to determine the extent of the damage. In many cases, he will wish to culture the lesion, and have an antibiotic sensitivity test performed to see which infectious agent is involved and what antibiotic will kill it. Further X-ray checks may be necessary to determine whether the treatment is working. Whatever you do, keep the dog on his antibiotics as regularly as you can. This is one of those diseases where quick and aggressive treatment may save you from having to treat it for a LONG period of time, at great expense. But, even if treatment is started early, a short period of antibiotic treatment may be one to two months, initially. A delay in starting treatment can extend that time to six to 10 or more months!

If a large piece of dead bone is present, removing it surgically may be the only way to allow the dog's recovery.

In other cases, it may be necessary to surgically drain and clean the area where the bone is infected. Bone grafts may be needed to fill in the area if a large amount of bone has to be removed. Sometimes, a drain is left in place, and you will need to flush a disinfectant or antibiotic solution into the area. In other cases, you will be instructed to swab out the wound with cotton swabs. Whichever is used, frequent treatment (often once or twice a day) is needed.

OSTEOSARCOMA

Osteosarcoma is a tumor which occurs in the leg bones. It occurs mostly in large breeds of dogs, especially Great Danes and St. Bernards. It spreads rapidly through the body, especially to the lungs. For many years, the only treatment was amputation of the affected leg. Even if the leg was removed, the dog usually died within six months, due to spread before amputation. Now some veterinary hospitals (usually located at veterinary schools) are using chemotherapy, with or without amputation. In some cases, the high cost of this treatment may be subsidized by the school or by a major grant for cancer research. It is worth looking into this, checking with one or more veterinary schools within driving distance, to see if such a program may be available to your animal. Perhaps the method which is currently most successful in controlling the cancer for the longest period of time is a combination of removing the affected limb and chemotherapy.

NUTRITIONAL OSTEODYSTROPHY

Nutritional osteodystrophy is a common skeletal disease in rapidly growing puppies and young dogs of larger breeds. The dog may show swollen carpal joints (the joints at the top of the foot in the front leg). These joints may bend backward as the foot sags toward the ground. The dog may have fever and lameness. Mild to severe bony changes may be noted around the joints on X-rays.

Veterinarians agree that osteodystrophy occurs because of nutritional imbalances. Very few, however, agree on just which imbalances cause it. Too high a caloric intake has been blamed, as has excess calcium intake and excessive vitamin supplementation. Genetic factors may be involved, because the disease is almost always seen in purebred dogs, and because breeds such as Great Danes and Irish Setters are particularly involved.

Almost all puppies of large or giant breeds who are being fed on a high nutritional plane will have enlarged joints, at least to a certain extent. These problems disappear when the dog is fed either less food or a less nutritionally dense brand of food. If you continue to push the dog to grow fast, permanent damage to the bones and joints may occur, leaving the dog blemished, disfigured with enlarged joints, or possibly with a permanent lameness as an adult.

NUTRITIONAL HYPERPARATHYROIDISM

Nutritional hyperparathyroidism can occur in dogs because of a calcium deficiency. The lack of calcium causes the parathyroid gland to secrete excess hormone. Dogs who are growing rapidly are most severely affected because of their need for calcium to build strong bones. It can occur when puppies (or even older dogs) are fed only meat or liver or other organ meats low in calcium. It is especially seen about six weeks after puppies are weaned and placed on that sort of diet.

The first signs may be lack of interest in the world around them and obscure lameness. The lameness quickly progresses to weakness in the hind end. The legs may sag and the joints may turn inward or outward at odd angles. All bones of the body are affected. If left on the deficient diet, the backbone may sag or turn to the side, the pelvis may become deformed, and fractures may occur. Several fractures may occur at a time as the weakened, demineralized bones collapse.

Treatment involves balancing the diet to supply enough, but not too much, calcium, and providing rest so that the bones may take up calcium without risk of fractures. Calcium carbonate is perhaps the cheapest way to supplement the diet to counter this disease. It can be added to meat at one part calcium carbonate to 200 parts meat, by weight. Meat may also be deficient in vitamins A and D and in iodine. Vitamin D supplementation by itself is not helpful, and may cause the problem to become worse. Feed a balanced, complete vitamin supplement along with the meat. Better yet, put the puppy on a complete, nutritionally balanced dog food and avoid the problem in the first place.

RENAL RICKETS

Renal rickets is also called osteodystrophy fibrosa, or renal secondary hyperparathyroidism. It is a disease of aged dogs with chronic kidney failure. The kidney damage causes the body to retain phosphorus. This raises the level of phosphorus in the blood serum, which lowers the level of calcium. The low blood calcium causes the parathyroid gland to put out excess hormone, which makes calcium dissolve from the bones.

Renal rickets is also called rubber jaw. This is because the calcium removed from the bones is replaced by fibrous connective tissue, leaving the jaw soft and rubbery. It may get to the point where you can easily bend it with your hand. The teeth are usually loose. The dog can fracture his jaw quite easily. He may also have a poor appetite and vomit frequently.

Examination and laboratory tests will show severe kidney disease. There is no good treatment which will make the calcium go back into the bones. Treatment with fluids and a special diet for kidney disease can only delay the dog's inevitable death.

FORELEG PARALYSIS

The nerves which supply the front legs are often injured when a dog is hit by a car. The dog may drag the entire leg, being unable to swing it forward normally with each stride. Or he may swing it forward, but not be able to pull the paw into place to take a step. The paw rolls under, and the dog puts his weight on his bent knuckles. If the injury is severe, the dog may not have any feeling in the leg. If the injury has been present for a period of time, the muscles of the leg will atrophy, leaving it thin and wasted when compared to the other leg. A few dogs with injury to the nerves will recover some use of the leg over a period of several months. Most dogs, however, will never regain any useful function of the leg. If the dog is dragging the foot, or chewing on it, amputation is the only course of treatment.

AMPUTATIONS

A dog may have a leg amputated for a number of reasons. He may have been hit by a car and the limb is damaged beyond repair. The accident may have damaged the blood supply to the point where the leg cannot be kept alive. The foot may have been caught in a trap, or a heavy object may have been dropped on it, causing a severe crushing injury. The dog may have an osteosarcoma, which is a bone tumor of the leg. In many cases, removing the leg may be the only way to save the dog's life. Do not hesitate to have the leg amputated if you love your dog and would like to have him around for years to come. This is especially true if the leg has been damaged from injury. Unfortunately, amputation may not save the dog with osteosarcoma.

Any one leg may be removed without causing the dog much long-term trouble. A hind leg is little problem at all, as each hind leg normally only bears about 20% of the dog's weight. A front leg is a little more of a problem, but the dog will still cope with it well. Given a bit of time, he will learn to hop easily on the remaining front leg.

Amputation of the leg is a relatively simple operation. Be sure that your veterinarian removes the leg as close to the body as possible, even if only the foot is damaged. It may seem kinder to leave as much as possible, but it is not! If a stub is left, the dog will attempt to walk on it—keeping it raw, sore, and bleeding. If the leg is taken off cleanly, near the body, the dog will learn do quite well without it.

So, you have brought your dog home from the veterinary clinic after his amputation. What can you expect? At first, he will probably be a bit tipsy, uncoordinated and unbalanced. He'll be like this for perhaps as much as two weeks. Give him love, attention, good nutrition, and let him find his balance by himself. Actually, he's having to learn to walk all over again. If you have a yard, let him spend plenty of time outside if the weather is good. Play gently with him. He will gradually become accustomed to not having the leg, and will walk around quite well without it. In time, most dogs will run, play and function much as they did before the accident. Do not worry if the dog falls occasionally. He will be much less bothered by it than you will. Try not to laugh at him—he will be embarrassed enough as it is by falling down.

It is especially important to keep your amputee at a normal weight. Excess weight can strain his remaining leg. After a while, this leg may break down and it will be necessary to euthanize the dog because of it.

BACK PROBLEMS

DEGENERATIVE DISK DISEASE

Intervertebral ("between the vertebrae") disks are rubbery cushions which fit between the bones of the spinal column. Think of them as jelly-filled doughnuts. They have a thick, fibrous outer covering with a soft center. They function as shock absorbers. Everything is fine as long as they hold together and cushion vertebral movement normally. Problems occur when the outer layer becomes torn or weakened. The jelly squeezes out. This is OK if it goes sideways or downward. Unfortunately, most of the time it goes upward, into the spinal canal, where the spinal cord lays. The material and the bleeding which accompanies the rupture can put pressure on the spinal cord. Worse, it causes an inflammatory reaction; tissue swelling causes even more pressure on the spinal cord. If the pressure is bad enough, the dog becomes paralyzed.

Because it is so common in Dachshunds, disk disease is often called "dachsie disease." It occurs, however, in other long-backed breeds such as Lhasa Apso and Pekingese, as well as in Toy Poodles, Beagles, Cocker Spaniels and others.

Signs vary with the location and severity of the damage. The dog may show pain, crying when he tries to move, and being snappish if you try to move him. One or both of the hind legs may be paralyzed or limp. The dog's entire hind end, including his tail, may be paralyzed, and he won't be able to move except by dragging himself. These dogs may also have either fecal and urinary retention or incontinence. Either they cannot void at all or they cannot stop.

The dog may hold his back arched, along with a tense abdomen. If you touch his back, he may show pain only over the damaged disk, or all up and down his back. He may not wish to go up or down stairs. He may show pain when he moves his head or neck if a disk in the neck is involved. He may even try to bite if you touch his head or neck. Front-leg weakness may be seen with a disk problem in the neck.

Your veterinarian will diagnose this disease by checking the dog's reflexes and the reaction of nerves in various areas to pain. He may also take X-rays. These may show the collapsed disk space quite well.

Treatment depends on the location and severity of the signs. If the paralysis is severe and getting worse, it may progress until the respiratory muscles are paralyzed and the dog dies. This paralysis can occur quite rapidly, and immediate surgery to relieve the pressure is usually necessary. The tops of one or more vertebrae are usually removed to reduce the pressure on the spinal cord. If done soon enough, the dog may return to normal with time. In other cases, surgery may be done from the underside of the spinal column to remove the offending pulpy disk material and get it out of the way. This surgery will also fuse two of the vertebrae together so that the problem cannot occur again at that location.

Mild cases respond to more conservative treatment. This mostly consists of good nursing care. The dog is confined to an area no larger than a playpen. He can be taken out two or three times a day to urinate and defecate, by carrying him very carefully, completely supported by your arms. The rest of the time, he should be kept completely quiet. He should especially not be allowed to stand up on his hind legs or jump around with excitement. If the dog cannot urinate by himself, you may need to squeeze out his bladder for him. You will need to do this about three times a day. Your veterinarian will show you how to put your hand up into the dog's abdomen about four inches ahead of the pelvis and press out the urine. If he cannot defecate by himself, enemas may be needed every day or two. Again, your veterinarian can show you what to use and how to give an enema. Good nutrition is essential for healing. Drugs may be given to reduce the inflammation around the spinal cord and to relieve some of the pain. It is VERY important not to let the dog become active before he is healed.

Strict rest may be prescribed for a week or more, depending on the dog's signs. Then physical therapy may be recommended. Swimming is often used as therapy for dogs who are recovering from disk problems. For example, your veterinarian might have you swim the dog in your bathtub. Fill the bathtub with lukewarm water, full enough that the dog cannot touch the bottom. Hold him by the chest or support him from underneath so that he has to paddle to stay afloat, but cannot try to climb out. Ten to 15 minutes once or twice a day can do wonders toward helping him to walk again. Dry the dog carefully, so that he does not become chilled. A whirlpool bath may be helpful. In some cases, ultrasound therapy may be used.

Recovery from one herniated disk, whether by surgery or by more conservative treatment, does not keep the dog from having another one rupture at a later date. In fact, the dog with a weakness or predisposition that contributed to the first disk rupture is quite likely to have another one or two of them rupture in his lifetime. Be aware that this may happen, and watch for signs so that you can get prompt treatment for it.

Try to keep the dog from doing things that involve violent bending activity with his back. No climbing steps, either up or down. No jumping on the bed or furniture or into or out of the car. No jumping on people's legs. Try to keep the long-backed dog, as much as possible, foursquare on the ground. Bend down to pet him only when he stays on the ground. Do not reward him for jumping up by petting him when he does so. Pick up the dog, supporting him carefully, when you want to move him up or down, as into a vehicle. Hold his back in as straight a line as possible. Try not to leave or forget him where he may wish to jump down, such as from the sofa. It is a good idea to train the dog to stay on the floor, and to not put him where he might try to jump down. If you are considering buying a puppy of a long-backed breed, you might think about teaching him to stay on the floor from the first day you bring him into your home and heart.

SPONDYLOSIS

This is a degenerative condition involving the vertebrae and the disks between them. It especially occurs in the lumbar (lower back) area. Small bony spurs grow outward, on the lower parts of the vertebrae and at the area between the joints. It is most common in older dogs, and seems to be a consequence of aging and wear and tear. It is especially seen in larger breeds of hunting and working dogs.

Many dogs will not have any clinical signs, although X-rays will show the bony spurs. Others will show pain as the bony spurs put pressure on the roots of the nerves where they branch from the spinal cord. The dog may move stiffly and appear as if his back is splinted. He may be reluctant to bend into any curved position. Aspirin (see Arthritis above) may give relief early in the disease. Later, your veterinarian may prescribe corticosteroids or phenylbutazone (Butazolidin®). These may relieve the inflammation and pain. There is no cure for the disease. Many dogs reach a point of such uncontrollable pain that they must be euthanized for humane reasons.

TAIL INJURIES

A dog may have his tail broken when it is slammed into a door, stepped on, or when he is hit by a car. The blood supply to the tail is not very good, and the bones are rather thin. It is very difficult to splint a tail without cutting off the blood supply. And if it is splinted, it probably will not heal well. The best treatment for a broken tail is amputation of the broken end. This merely shortens the dog's tail. The tail usually heals well following the surgery, and looks good cosmetically. It is the simplest, easiest and surest treatment.

If the dog is a show dog or you particularly value his tail, some veterinarians may attempt to use plates or screws to stabilize the fracture during the healing period. This some-times works, but does not work in all cases. Don't be surprised if this fails and amputation is necessary anyway.

MUSCULAR PROBLEMS

DIAPHRAGMATIC HERNIA

A diaphragmatic hernia is a tear in the diaphragm, through which abdominal organs bulge into the chest cavity. These are fairly common in dogs, and usually occur when they are hit by a vehicle. They can also occur if the dog falls from a height or is kicked. The diaphragm is ripped or torn. The tear may be small, or it may rip clear across the width or height of the dog's torso. Any of the organs of the forward part of the abdomen may bulge into, or completely move into, the chest—including the liver, spleen, stomach, or intestine. A sizable amount of abdominal contents may slowly be pulled through a small hole because of negative pressure in the chest. If the problem has gone on for a long time, adhesions between various organs are common, and fluid may be present in the chest.

The most common sign of diaphragmatic hernia is that the dog has trouble breathing. His membranes may or may not be bluish in color. Suspect this problem if you know the dog has been injured within the last few days. The dog may try to lie with his head and chest uphill to ease the pressure on his lungs.

Your veterinarian will diagnose the problem with a combination of history and X-rays. He will also listen with his stethoscope, hearing little or nothing in the way of lung or heart sounds in the chest. He may even hear intestinal sounds in the chest. Surgery is the only cure, as the problem does not heal itself. Surgery involves replacing the abdominal organs back where they belong, then suturing the torn areas together so that the barrier between the chest and abdomen, the diaphragm, is again complete. If the problem has not gone on for long, surgical repair is usually successful.

Pick up a long-backed dog carefully, keeping his back straight and well-supported.

Chapter 19

THE BRAIN AND NERVOUS SYSTEM

Convulsions
Epilepsy
Hydrocephalus
Head Injury
Stroke
Wobbler Syndrome

CONVULSIONS

Convulsion is a general term for a symptom which can be due to many causes. Seizure, fit and epilepsy are all names for the same problem, although epilepsy is a specific problem. A dog who is in convulsions will usually fall to the ground and twitch spasmodically. He may be conscious or unconscious. Convulsions may be due to epilepsy, toxins such as organophosphate or carbamate insecticides, strychnine poisoning, and a host of other toxins and tetanus. If you know that the dog is in convulsions because of a toxin, get him to a veterinarian as soon as possible.

EPILEPSY

Epilepsy is the general term for dysfunctioning within the brain which produces convulsions. These seizures typically occur with some regularity or pattern, and more than once. They are similar to epileptic convulsions in humans. In some cases, the cause of the epilepsy may be known. The dog may have recovered from distemper, or had a head injury. Heredity plays a role in epilepsy. Some breeds of dogs, including Poodles, St. Bernards and German Shepherds, are more likely to have epilepsy than are other breeds. Because of this, dogs with epilepsy should not be used for breeding stock. In many cases, a definite cause is never found.

Epileptic seizures seldom occur without warning. A preseizure stage is generally seen. In this stage, the dog may act peculiarly. He may be nervous, restless and look for affection. He may pace, salivate and whine. He may hide or show other odd behavior.

The first sign of onset of the seizure itself may be a loss of consciousness, followed by muscular rigidity. Or he may run in circles. The dog may fall over onto his side, throw his head back, and make twitching or paddling movements with his legs. He may whine, moan, or yelp, and may stare blankly, as if he has no idea where he is. He may urinate, defecate, vomit and salivate. This stage rarely lasts more than five minutes. After a few seconds or minutes, the dog will return to consciousness. He may be weak and panting, especially if the seizure has lasted for several minutes. Most seizures due to epilepsy are NOT life threatening. Dogs do not suffer strokes or swallow their tongues because of, or during, seizures.

Seizures which last more than 20 minutes may endanger the dog's life because of the severe exertion which is in-

volved. Seizures are hard physical work. If it continues, the dog may become so overheated that coma, brain damage or death may occur. Whenever a seizure lasts more than five minutes, take the dog to the nearest veterinarian.

What do you do if your dog has a seizure? Begin by doing nothing, if at all possible. If he is on the floor, move chairs or other objects out of his way. Make sure that he does not fall off a porch or down stairs. Do not move the dog if he is in a safe place, as he may bite you completely by accident as he involuntarily chomps or moves his jaws. Wait several minutes and allow him to come out of the convulsion gradually. Do NOT put your fingers in his mouth, unless he chokes completely. This is quite rare. Do not offer him water until he is completely back to normal, and withhold food for a few hours. Observe the signs which occur, and the strength and duration of the seizure. This will help your veterinarian to evaluate the problem.

An epileptic convulsion must be distinguished from poisoning, especially by strychnine or organophosphate insecticide. A dog poisoned by strychnine will have his front and hind legs pulled rigidly forward and back, like a sawhorse. His head will be pulled backward toward his back. He may turn blue as his throat chokes shut. And he will NOT come out of it in a couple of minutes. The dog who is affected by organophosphate poisoning will often have a strong insecticide odor from having drunk the product. Or he may have been recently dipped for ticks, lice, fleas or other parasites. If it looks like insecticide poisoning might be the problem, get the dog to a veterinarian IMMEDIATELY.

The dog who has come out of an epileptic convulsion may be tired from his exertions for the next day or two. Some dogs are uncoordinated and disoriented for a period of time afterward. Some seem to be temporarily blind. Many dogs quickly return to normal. What do you do now? Your choice. You may take him to a veterinarian, who will probably not be able to find anything wrong. Or you can choose to just wait and see what happens. The dog may have another seizure within a week or two, or it may be a year or more before the next one. It is a good idea to jot the date, time and duration of the seizure on your calendar, along with a description of how the dog acted before, during and after the event. This will give you a record to consult when you talk with your veterinarian.

There is no treatment which will cure epilepsy. The best that can be done is to control the seizures. Many veterinarians prefer not to treat the dog unless the seizures are causing problems. Seizures may be lasting for many minutes, leaving the dog drained and tired for several days afterward. Or they may be occurring more and more frequently. If one of these dogs is left untreated, the seizures may become increasingly frequent and violent. Mild seizures that do not last for more than a couple of minutes, or do not occur more than once every month or two may not need to be treated. A single seizure may be an isolated event that will never occur again, but there is no way to tell if it will or not.

A number of drugs are available to control epilepsy in dogs. No one single drug works well in all dogs. For many dogs, a combination of several drugs may be the most effective therapy. You must work with your veterinarian in finding the right combination and dosage for your individual animal. It may be necessary to try several different drugs until a workable program is found. "Control" of epilepsy can range from no more seizures, ever, to a longer time between them, or them being milder. Seldom do they go away completely.

The reason for not immediately putting every epileptic dog on medication is that once your dog is started on drugs to control epilepsy, it may not be possible to take him off them, and it will then be necessary to keep the animal on drugs for the rest of his life. For some reason, the brain seems to begin to depend on the medication. Then, if you stop giving the drug, the seizures may come back with a vengeance—stronger and more frequent than they were before medication. Also, medications for epilepsy can have some side effects, depending on the drug and dosage. These side effects generally include dopiness and sleepiness. For these reasons, many veterinarians prefer to wait until the seizures are causing problems for either the dog or the owner before prescribing durgs.

HYDROCEPHALUS

Also called "water on the brain," hydrocephalus is an accumulation of excess cerebrospinal fluid inside the inner spaces of the brain. It is often seen as a congenital defect, usually the result of some hereditary factor. Dogs of toy breeds, especially Chihuahuas and Toy Poodles, are frequently born with this disease. The puppy may have an unusually large, domed skull. As he grows, the eyes may turn outward. The brain becomes progressively smaller because of the fluid pressure on it. The dog may not behave normally and may appear to be retarded. He may stagger and fall or have trouble standing.

Dogs with hydrocephalus may be the "runts" of the litter, and may not grow normally. They often have other congenital defects. Eventually, epileptic seizures or convulsions are seen. Affected puppies usually die at an early age. Puppies may also have hydrocephalus due to infection with a virus or *Toxoplasma* organisms while they are in the uterus. There is speculation that Vitamin A deficiency during the bitch's pregnancy may also cause the problem. Puppies who only have 60 or 61 days gestation may be more prone to hydrocephalus than are those who spend the full 63 days in the uterus.

The same signs may be seen with acquired hydrocephalus, which can develop at any time during an animal's life. Hydrocephalus later in life is usually due to injury (as being hit by a car), tumors or infections involving the brain.

HEAD INJURY

Dogs who are running free or who escape from their owner's control are often injured by being hit by a car or kicked by a horse or human. They may be injured in a dog fight, fall from a high place or suffer from a gunshot wound. About a quarter of these animals will suffer some type of head injury.

The brain can suffer a concussion. This occurs when the head is hit hard on one side. The brain bounces within the skull, like a big, soft rubber ball. The brain is injured, bruised really, when it bounces off the side of its cavity opposite to the side of the blow. This is a common injury in dogs as well as in humans. The dog may be knocked unconscious for anywhere from a few seconds to several minutes. When he "comes to," he may be confused and disoriented. If there is no serious damage within the cranium, the dog will recover completely from the concussion. If the dog is unconscious for more than a few minutes, this may indicate more severe damage to the brain. Have him examined by a veterinarian.

Hemorrhage can occur within the cranial cavity. It may be within the brain tissue itself, or outside or inside the membranes which enclose the brain. A small amount of bleeding which stops by itself will not need surgical intervention. It may, however, cause the dog to have seizures after healing is complete and the scarred area contracts. More severe problems can occur when there is a large amount of bleeding. The blood pressing into the area leaves the brain caught between the proverbial "rock and a hard spot," and there is nowhere for the blood to go so that the pressure can be relieved. Surgery may be necessary to stop the bleeding and remove the blood clot which has formed. Surgically opening the skull also relieves the pressure, often with dramatic results. Clinical signs are usually more severe on one side of the body, and may become slowly worse over several hours or days after the injury has occurred. Hemorrhage into the brainstem area usually leaves the dog unconscious right after the accident. A coma (continued unconsciousness) may occur, from which the animal may not recover.

Skull fractures can occur with any of the traumas mentioned above. These can leave a portion of the skull caved in, usually requiring surgical treatment. Fractures which are not caved in usually are not treated, other than with rest and antibiotics. They usually do not result in much brain damage, and the bone fractures heal in place.

Compound fractures can occur when the scalp is torn open when the bone is fractured. These should be surgically repaired as soon as the dog's condition permits.

Skull fractures which occur at or near the eye, at the base of the ear, at the base of the skull, or those which penetrate the sinuses are much more serious. They can cause blindness or deafness, as well as damage to the cranial nerves which are coming directly from the brain. The openings where these nerves pass into the skull cavity may act to conduct infection into the brain if antibiotic treatment is not not begun promptly. (See Emergency Chapter for care of skull fractures.)

It is useful to administer oxygen in any case of skull trauma. It may significantly reduce damage to the brain.

STROKE

A stroke in a human is caused by a ruptured blood vessel in the brain. This causes various signs of personality change, uncoordination and paralysis, depending on the portion of the brain which is affected. True strokes are quite rare in dogs. However, a problem called geriatric vestibular disease looks quite similar to a human stroke. It is seen in old dogs. The problem occurs suddenly. The dog may have a head tilt, and will tend to roll or fall to the side to which the head is tilted. There is no apparent loss of strength, but the dog may be so disoriented that he is reluctant to move at all. The dog may roll his eyes, usually in a direction opposite to that of the head tilt. The dog may vomit during the first few days of the disease. There is no specific treatment for this disease. Fortunately, if you will provide careful nursing, the dog will probably recover much of his normal function within about three weeks. Occasionally, the disease will recur.

WOBBLER SYNDROME

Wobbler syndrome is a specific combination of signs sometimes seen in large dogs. It is due to caudal cervical spondylopathy. That mouthful means damage and deformity to the bones and disks in the lower neck. A similar syndrome is seen in horses. In dogs, the majority of cases occur in Dobermans and Great Danes. The cause is not known. Heredity has been suspected, as have improper nutrition and trauma.

A combination of damaged areas contribute to put pressure on the spinal cord as it passes through the spinal column in the neck. Some of the disks between the vertebrae may have degenerated. The ligaments which hold the vertebrae together may not be normal, allowing the vertebrae to shift around. Some dogs are born with malformed vertebrae which cause or contribute to the problem. The vertebrae may not be aligned normally, pinching the spinal cord.

The condition develops slowly as the dog gets older. Signs usually occur by one to two years of age in Great Danes. In Dobermans, signs usually occur later, sometime after two years of age. Some cases begin as late as six or seven years of age. Signs begin with slight uncoordination. All four legs are affected, but the uncoordination is usually worse in the hind legs. The legs may cross each other. In some dogs, the front legs may not have a normal range of motion, and may appear rigid. The dog may stumble on his front legs and knuckle over, with the carpal area hitting the ground. A minor injury may cause the dog to suddenly become much worse because the bones and other structures in the neck are not strong enough to sustain much damage.

A dog with an advanced case of wobbler syndrome may have trouble standing and walking. The dog may carry his neck bowed toward his chest. Your veterinarian will diagnose this disease by checking the dog's reflexes (called a neurologic examination). He may wish to do a series of X-rays of the dog's spinal column after injecting a contrast medium. This material will show where the cord is pinched or compressed.

Medical treatment can be tried. The dog will be strictly confined and rested. A neck brace may be used to attempt to stabilize the spine. Anti-inflammatory drugs will be used to reduce swelling and irritation in the spinal cord. This treatment is done for three weeks to a month. If the dog is better, he can be gradually returned to normal activity. He should not be allowed to move his head and neck excessively. In some cases, the dog may be put in a neck brace to help keep him from moving. If there is little or no reponse to the month's treatment, surgery should be considered.

Several surgical techniques have been used to correct wobbler syndrome. A portion of the top of one or more vertebrae may be removed to lessen the pressure on the spinal cord. Two or more vertebrae may be fused together so that their movement cannot continue to irritate the spinal cord. Or several vertebrae may be connected with steel plates so that all movement between them is stopped. Bone grafts may be used to connect the vertebrae, similar to using a steel plate. After surgery, the dog may be placed in a neck brace until the bones have healed. In some cases, physical therapy may be needed. Hydrotherapy may used to help the dog begin moving his muscles normally.

It is difficult to tell how well a dog will recover after surgery for wobbler syndrome. A lot depends on how much damage to the spinal cord has occurred before surgery was performed. If the dog has experienced complete paralysis and was unable to walk before surgery, his chances for recovery are poor. The spinal cord has sustained too much damage. Until more research is done on this disease, dogs who are wobblers should not be used as breeding stock.

Chapter 20

THE ENDOCRINE SYSTEM

The endocrine system consists of a number of glands throughout the body. These glands secrete hormones which are carried throughout the body via the blood. They regulate the action of various organs. For instance, the pituitary gland, which sits at the base of the brain, secretes hormones which help to regulate the ovaries or testicles. Other endocrine glands include the adrenal glands, the thyroid glands, and the pancreas. When there is either an excess or a deficiency of one of the endocrine hormones, disease may occur.

DIABETES MELLITUS

Diabetes mellitus occurs when the dog's pancreas does not produce enough insulin. This causes the dog's blood sugar to rise to excessively high levels (hyperglycemia). Diabetes mellitus may be caused by pancreatitis or other disease of the pancreas. This is the disease which comes to mind when someone says "diabetes." Most cases of diabetes mellitus occur in dogs over five years of age. It is about five times more common in female dogs. Samoyeds and Dachshunds are more at risk than other breeds (Merck, 1986, p. 266). Some Keeshond puppies are also affected. Many dogs who are diabetic are also very overweight.

The first sign that your dog has diabetes may be that he drinks more water than usual, and urinates frequently. He may also lose weight suddenly, while still eating as much (or more) than usual. The weight loss is especially obvious if the dog was previously obese. The dog may show abdominal pain and weakness. These may also be signs of other hormonal upsets, so the dog should be examined by a veterinarian. Some dogs may become suddenly blind due to the formation of cataracts in the lenses of the eyes.

Numerous laboratory tests may be needed to confirm the diagnosis of diabetes mellitus. The dog's blood glucose (sugar) level may be above 120 mg/dL (milligrams per deciliter). The test is performed after the animal has fasted for a period of time. Normal blood sugar is from 75 to 100 mg/dL. Diabetes may be complicated by urinary tract infections or disorders.

If the dog has had diabetes for a long time, you can smell an acetone odor on the breath. The dog may vomit continuously. If untreated, the dog may lapse into a diabetic coma, with death nor far behind. Long-term cases may have cataracts or cloudiness in the lenses or ulcers on the cornea of the eye.

If the dog is obese, on a poor diet or has other hormonal abnormalities, he may be at greater risk of developing diabetes. As with humans, some animals seem to have the disease occurring within their families. Some female dogs may develop diabetes. In some of these cases, spaying will completely reverse the disease.

Treating a dog for diabetes requires a long-term commitment from you, the owner. You will need to give the dog one or more injections of insulin at the same times every day for the rest of his life, as well as provide him a stable environment. Caring for a dog with diabetes may be difficult if you have irregular hours or travel a lot, unless you are willing to kennel the dog with a veterinarian who will treat the dog in your absence. If you kennel the dog, the amount of exercise he gets will change so that you will have to restabilize his insulin dosage when you take him home. The injections of insulin are given just under the skin (subcutaneously) with a fine needle, and cause little or no discomfort to the dog. You will need to check the level of glucose in your dog's urine at least once a day.

You will also be making a financial commitment, as the initial stabilization must be done by a veterinarian until a dosage is established which will work for your dog. This may take several days of hospitalization. The dog will need check-ups two or three times a year. If something occurs which upsets his program, he may need to be hospitalized to be restabilized. There is, of course, a continuing expense for needles, syringes, and insulin.

If you are not willing to make the commitment of time, effort and money that is needed, do yourself, your family and the dog a favor and euthanize him before you go through the cost and heartbreak of trying to save him. Oral insulin, as is used in humans, does not work in dogs.

Your veterinarian will stabilize the dog at his clinic, and determine the type of insulin and dosage which is most effective. The type and dosage have to be carefully tailored to the individual animal. The veterinarian will then show you how to give the insulin injections yourself, as well as how to test the dog's urine for glucose. You will be in close contact with the veterinarian when you take the animal home, as his food, activity level and environment will all be different than they were at the clinic. Every time the dog becomes unstable, whether because of dietary imbalances or other changes, he will need to go back to the clinic for several days to be stabilized again. This is a real incentive to keep everything on an even keel!

Dogs with diabetes must have strict dietary control. The time of insulin treatment from day to day should be as consistent as possible. Exercise should be of the same duration and intensity if at all possible. Food quantity and type should be the same every day. Food should be carefully measured. NO food or treats other than the dog's regular diet should be given. If the dog is at his normal weight (or above it), feed a high-fiber diet which is intended for weight reduction. It helps if the dog can be stabilized by the veterinarian on the diet he will have at home. A high-fiber diet helps to control the blood sugar level, reduces fluctuations in the blood sugar level which occur after meals, and may decrease the amount of insulin required. If you are not feeding a high-fiber diet, the dog should be given frequent, small meals, in order to help keep the blood sugar level as even as possible.

An overweight dog should gradually and carefully be brought down to his normal weight. If the dog is underweight, he should slowly be brought up to normal by feeding a high-quality diet designed for growth, containing high-quality protein and nutrients. The diet should have a low-to-moderate level of fat. Foods which are high in simple sugars should be avoided. Table scraps and pot lickings should be stricly avoided, as they may unbalance the dog's blood sugar level.

At home, you will want to watch for signs of unfavorable reactions. Low blood glucose may cause weakness, wobbling and incoordinated gait. The animal may appear to be drunken or dazed. These things are due to an excess of insulin excessively lowering the amount of sugar in the blood (hypoglycemia). Or a small dog may have missed one or more meals. If not treated, the hypoglycemia will progress to seizure or possibly to coma. If this occurs, you will give the dog one to two teaspoons of Karo Syrup, or an injection of glucagon, as per the instructions of your veterinarian.

When the dog is first stabilized and comes home, be sure your veterinarian has instructed you on what to watch for and how to deal with it. If no improvement is seen within 15 minutes, contact your veterinarian. THIS IS AN EMERGENCY.

Part of the weakness associated with diabetes has been found to be due to a lowered potassium level in the blood serum. Potassium supplementation, in carefully measured quantities, may be needed for some diabetic dogs (Willard, 1987).

Other signs of problems might be seen at home. These include changes in behavior, lack of appetite, depression or development of cataracts in the dog's eyes. Let your veterinarian know right away if there are any changes in the dog's normal urine glucose pattern. Over a period of time, the amount of insulin needed will probably change.

Hill's Pet Products Company has a superb booklet detailing treatment of the diabetic dog. Ask your veterinarian for a copy.

DIABETES INSIPIDUS

Diabetes insipidus (DI) is much less common in the dog than diabetes mellitus. It results in the dog producing large amounts of very dilute urine. The urine is otherwise normal.

It does not contain excessive amounts of sugar as in diabetes mellitus. The dog is, of course, driven to drink huge amounts of water to make up for the excessive urine output. If adequate water is not available, the dog may drink its own urine. He may need to get up during the night to urinate, and may be unable to contain the amount produced, resulting in frequent "accidents." Because the dog is constantly either looking for water or drinking, he may be restless, have a poor appetite and lose weight. Some cases of DI are caused by a tumor on the pituitary or hypothalamus glands. The dog may wander aimlessly, may not see normally, may stumble, or have seizures as a result of these tumors.

Your veterinarian will check the dog for the diabetes insipidus by depriving him of water for a period of time, under carefully controlled conditions. This test will show whether or not the dog is able to produce concentrated urine. If the urine produced is not concentrated, he will then administer anti-diuretic hormone (ADH) and check the dog's response to it. If the dog responds to the hormone, this confirms that the problem is DI.

Anti-diuretic hormone or a similar drug with the same function will be needed for the remainder of the dog's life. Some of these drugs are given by injection every one to four days, while others may be given as "nose drops." The dog should have an unlimited water supply available at all times.

Some owners choose not to treat their pets for diabetes insipidus. Some of these animals seem to survive well if water is always available. Life-threatening dehydration may occur if the dog should be without water for any reason for even a short time. A minor illness such as diarrhea or vomiting may cause severe dehydration. The "no treatment" plan works best with outdoor dogs who do not have to be let out to urinate. This approach does not work well for working dogs. They stop frequently to drink, and you will need to carry a lot of water for them.

HYPOTHYROIDISM

Hypothyroidism is a disease in which too little hormone is produced by the thyroid gland. It is common in some breeds such as Golden Retrievers and Doberman Pinschers, although it can occur in any dog. It does seem to be hereditary within some families. In many dogs, the underlying reason for the hypothyroidism is never determined.

Signs of hypothyroidism are those associated with a decrease in the dog's basal metabolic rate. The dog may gain weight without an increase in food intake. This weight gain may be slight, or the dog may become severely obese, with no change in appetite or change in diet. The dog may be less active than usual. He may work very hard at staying warm, because he is almost always cold. He may sit near a heat vent, or otherwise look for a warm place. The dog may shiver and his skin will usually feel cool when you touch it. The dog's coat may gradually become thinner and more sparse (which doesn't help the "cold" feeling a bit!). The coat becomes especially thin over wear spots, and may be dry, brittle and scaly. Hair loss may be symmetrical, and will occur on the tail, hind quarters or flank area. Hair on the legs is usually normal. Some dogs only lose hair on on the tail, giving a "rat-tailed" appearance. The dog may have blackheads and excessive pigmentation in the skin. He may have seborrhea or pyoderma. The dog's hair may not regrow after it is clipped for treatment or grooming.

A long-term case of hypothyroidism may show myxedema. Myxedema is an accumulation of mucoid material within and under the skin. The skin is severely thickened, especially around the head. The eyelids become thickened, producing a "sad" expression. The skin will feel doughy and thick, but a finger pushed into it does not show pitting as it would with "regular" edema. (There is no mark which remains for three to six seconds after you pull your finger out.) It is necessary to tell myxedema from a case of seborrhea which only affects the skin, and this is one of the ways in which it differs.

Dogs with long-term hypothyroidism may fail to reproduce. Males may lack interest in breeding, and will generally have a low sperm count. Females may have few or no heat cycles. Abortions about halfway through gestation and stillbirth may occur with hypothyroid females. Some cases of hypothyroidism in dogs are from hereditary problems within families. These dogs should be eliminated from a breeding program as soon as possible. The obesity associated with the disease can lead to behavior problems which also affect breeding. The dog might show changes in attitude—becoming dopey or dull, or, in some cases, grouchy or irritable. Some dogs will have joint pain and resent being handled or picked up. Constipation can occur, but in some cases diarrhea may be a prominent sign. The dog may have a lower than normal heart rate—you won't know this unless you have taken the time to find out what the normal heart rate is for your dog!

Your veterinarian will have laboratory tests done to check the thyroid gland. Some of these tests involve the injection of small amounts of radioactive material into the dog's bloodstream, and measuring how much is taken up by the thyroid gland. The amount of radioactivity is so small that it does not pose any danger to you, your dog or your family, so don't worry about it. Have the test done and find out what is wrong with your pet. Some veterinarians will repeat the test after a month to six weeks of treatment, to make sure the dosage of hormone is proper for your animal. Routine check-ups may be needed from time to time to keep your dog happy and healthy.

In some cases, your veterinarian may want to treat the animal for a trial period of four to eight weeks. The medication is then stopped to see if the original symptoms reappear. This procedure is also a legitimate test for hypothyroidism.

Hypothyroidism can be controlled by giving thyroid hormone. The hormone is given once or twice daily, in the form of a tablet. Replacement hormones come from sheep, cattle or hog thyroid glands. A synthetic thyroid hormone is also available. The dog's weight and mental attitude will quickly return to normal. Improvement may be seen in as little as two to four weeks.

When a hypothyroid dog is treated with thyroid hormone, he may begin to shed large quantities of hair. This is normal! It means that new hairs are growing. As they grow, they push the old hairs out of the way. This confirms that your veterinarian was correct and that the treatment is working. It may take up to six months for the hair coat to return to normal, as new hairs will have to regrow to their full length. The hair coat may never be quite as good as "new," but will definitely keep the cold out better than when the dog was hypothyroid. Thyroid hormone can cause the regrowth of hair in some diseases which are not related to thyroid deficiency.

While your pet is recovering, you can work at getting rid of the extra weight with his new-found energy. Treating the dog as if he has seborrhea (and maybe he does) will help the hair and skin improve while the dog himself is getting better. The dog will need "thyroid" pills for the rest of his life, but this is an easy treatment and a small price to pay for his health.

An excess of thyroid hormone from treatment may, on rare occasion, cause problems—hyperthroidism. Signs may include drinking excess quantities of water, urinating frequently and excessively, weight loss without loss of appetite, panting, nervousness and an increased heart rate. Consult your veterinarian if any of these symptoms occur.

HYPERTHYROIDISM

An excess of thyroid hormone is seen in dogs, but only rarely from natural causes. The excess is usually due to a tumor of the thyroid gland. The dog may show increased urine production and increased thirst. He may lose weight, yet have an increased appetite and be excitable. He may vomit and have diarrhea, plus produce an increased quantity of feces. Heart abnormalities may be seen, up to and including congestive heart failure. After a diagnosis is made, treatment with radioactive iodine is relatively simple. This treatment destroys some of the surplus thyroid tissue which is producing extra hormone, bringing the hormone level into line with the dog's needs. As another option, drugs can be used to block hormone production. Dogs on drug treatment may need occasional blood tests and monitoring to make sure that the dosage remains correct for the dog's needs.

Some owners give thyroid hormones indiscriminately to try to promote hair growth or improve the bitch's fertility. This is not a good idea, and can cause permanent damage to the animal.

HYPOGLYCEMIA

Hypoglycemia (low blood sugar) may be seen with lack of some endocrine hormones. Lack of hormones from the adrenal glands (Addison's disease, hypoadrenocorticism) may cause it. It can also be seen with a lack of hormones from the pituitary gland, as well as with an excess of insulin from the pancreas or from too much insulin used to treat diabetes. Some liver problems may cause hypoglycemia. Poor absorption of nutrients from the intestine can result in low blood sugar. Newborn or very young puppies which are not receiving adequate nutrition can be hypoglycemic.

Low blood sugar can occur in hunting dogs or cattle dogs who work very hard for much of the day. At first, the dog may appear to be disoriented. He will be weak and hungry. He might stagger, appear to be blind, and his muscles may twitch.

If he is not fed at this point, convulsions and coma may follow. Irreversible damage can take place. Death is due to depression of the centers in the brain which control breathing. The easiest treatment is to feed the dog. If your working dog has trouble getting through a day, be sure to give him a good breakfast, with an adequate protein content, an hour or so before work begins in the morning. Feed him small meals two or three more times during the day.

Low blood sugar is also seen in newborn puppies. Feeding and rewarming them will often strengthen them enough to allow them to be returned to their mother, accepted by her and enable them to nurse normally.

ADRENAL CORTICAL EXCESS (CUSHING'S DISEASE)

Also called "Cushing's syndrome" or hyperadrenocorticism, this condition is the result of overproduction of corticosteroid hormones (cortisol) by the adrenal cortex. The adrenal glands are small glands located above the kidneys. They produce numerous hormones which keep many of the body's systems in balance.

Cushing's disease is one of the most common endocrine (body hormone system) diseases in dogs. It may occur because of a tumor in the adrenal gland which causes overproduction of the hormone. An overgrowth of the gland so that it has extra hormone-producing tissue also results in the disease. Or it may occur because the dog has been given corticosteroid medications ("cortisones" or "corticosteroids") for a long period of time. These drugs are sometimes used for treatment of allergies or skin disease, as well as for a number of other medical problems. In moderate quantity and when used for a reasonable length of time, these drugs can relieve much pain and itching and save lives. When used for TOO long, or in TOO great a quantity, they suppress the adrenal cortex, causing the gland to produce less hormone than normal. Meanwhile, the excess drug quantity causes the symptoms of Cushing's syndrome. Therapy with corticosteroids is the most common cause of hypercorticism in dogs.

Cushing's disease comes on slowly and gradually over a long period of time, and is most common in older dogs (six years and up). It occurs in many breeds, with Dachshunds, Poodles, Boxers, and Boston Terriers, as well as other terrier breeds, being most commonly affected.

Some of the most common signs of Cushing's disease affect the dog's skin. Hair loss occurs, usually in a pattern which is symmetrical from one side of the body to the other. What little hair is left becomes rough and dry. Hair shafts pull from the follicles with little effort, or can be broken off easily. These changes in the hair coat are first seen over areas of wear such as the hips, neck and flanks. Eventually, the neck and trunk are most severely involved. Blackheads and pimples may be present.

After a period of time, mineral crystals may form in the skin. This does not occur with any other endocrine-type skin problems. Crystal deposition occurs most commonly in area of the lower abdomen, upper neck and inguinal area (rear part of the lower abdomen). These areas appear as whitish or grayish, raised plaques. A reaction to the mineral crystals may result in itching and reddening around the plaques. If the deposits are very large, they may push through the skin, which is already thinner than normal. Similar mineral deposits occur in the wall of the stomach, lungs and skeletal muscles.

Since the skin is weakened, it bruises easily, and hematomas (blood clots) will form under the skin wherever the dog bumps himself. Injection sites and places where blood tests are drawn are also prone to develop hematomas.

The corticosteroids change protein metabolism, leading to wasting away of skeletal muscle. The dog may have muscular trembling because of weakness. His back may sag, and the abdominal muscles weaken, leaving the dog with a sagging potbelly. As the dog becomes weaker, he will stand with his legs spread to keep his balance. His leg muscles may also be thinned, giving him a spindly appearance. Meanwhile, fat tissue is redeposited in many dogs. Some dogs will develop large fat pads in the neck area, making the neck and shoulders look thickened. The liver and abdominal tissues may accumulate fat, contributing to the pot-bellied look.

The increase in corticosteroid hormones reduces the animal's resistance to disease. Injuries or surgical wounds may heal more slowly than normal. Infections are likely in the conjunctivae (membranes) of the eyes, the urinary tract, the skin, the lungs and elsewhere. The dog can develop severe infection in the skin, or pneumonia. The susceptibility to infections is due to suppression of the dog's immune system. Since the animal is weak and less active than normal, he lies down more than he otherwise would. Pressure sores and death of skin over the bony areas such as the elbows can occur. These "bedsores" are slow to heal because of the susceptibility to infection, slower cellular reproduction to repair the defect, and a general lack of resistance.

Most dogs with Cushing's disease drink more than normal and urinate accordingly. The dog may eat ravenously. The hormone imbalance alters glucose metabolism, and signs of diabetes may accompany adrenal hormone excess.

To diagnose Cushing's disease, your veterinarian will examine the animal's history, looking especially for prolonged corticosteroid usage, for whatever reason. He may run several laboratory tests. One test involves the administration of ACTH (adrenocorticotropic hormone). He will take blood samples before and after administration of the drug to measure plasma levels of cortisol. Other similar tests may also be used.

Treatment may involve surgery to remove an adrenal gland affected by a tumor. Tumors may be present on both adrenal glands, so they both must be checked at the time of surgery. Unless both glands have tumors and are removed, administration of steroids is probably not necessary after the surgery. Other dogs may be treated with medication. As with any hormone-suppression therapy, close monitoring will be needed to make sure that a happy balance is reached.

ADRENAL CORTICAL INSUFFICIENCY (ADDISON'S DISEASE)

Also called hypoadrenocorticism or Addison's disease, this is the exact opposite of Cushing's disease, above. It is a deficiency of adrenal cortical hormone, and is most frequently seen in young and middle-aged dogs. It is far less common than Cushing's disease, and its causes are much less known. Most cases are thought to be due to autoimmune problems, in which the dog becomes immune to something within his own body—in this situation, the tissue of his adrenal cortex. Tumors, blood clots or bleeding within the adrenal glands may also lower production of cortisol. Sudden withdrawal of treatment with glucocorticoid drugs may cause Addison's disease. A dog who has taken corticosteroid drugs for more than a week or so, or in large quantity, should be tapered off them gradually rather than all at once. The drugs suppress the normal production of the hormone and it takes a while for it to recover.

Signs of Addison's disease often come and go, varying from one day to another over a long period of time. They are not so obvious and definite as those of Cushing's disease. Generally, the dog will have a poor appetite and lose weight. He may be weak, sluggish and disinterested in life. Diarrhea and/or vomiting can be present, accompanied by dehydration. In a few cases, acute symptoms may suddenly occur, with heart arrhythmia due to electrolyte imbalances. If this occurs and is not treated promptly, low blood pressure will be followed by shock and death.

Testing for Addison's disease is similar to that for Cushing's disease. Like Cushing's disease, the history and clinical signs will also be used to make a diagnosis of Addison's disease. An acute adrenal crisis, with heart failure and blood pressure problems, is a medical EMERGENCY. It will require hospitalization and immediate, intensive treatment. Long-term treatment will require supplementation with a carefully measured dosage of a mineralocorticoid drug. The dog's electrolyte balance must be carefully monitored until he is stabilized, and he may require salt tablets daily to regulate his fluid balance. He will need to be checked two to four times a year to make sure he stays in balance, and to adjust drug dosages as necessary to accommodate his changing body. When you and your veterinarian work together, Addison's disease can be controlled to give your dog long years of good life.

LACK OF GROWTH HORMONE

Hair loss in some dogs is due to a lack of growth hormone. This is most common in German Shepherd dwarfs, one to four years old (Smith, 1985). The dog may lose hair from the trunk, neck and upper part of the tail. The loss is symmetrical from one side to the other. The hair on the head and feet will be normal. There are none of the signs affecting the rest of the body which are seen with Cushing's disease. Tests to measure the amount of growth hormones are necessary to diagnose this disease. Thyroid and adrenal tests will be normal. This disease is treated by giving the dog growth hormone derived from cattle.

AUTOIMMUNE DISEASE

Autoimmune disease is a term referring to problems in which the dog's immune system reacts against tissues in his body. It means "self immunity." Autoimmunity is thought to be a major cause of Addison's disease. In addition, dogs can suffer an autoimmune hemolytic anemia. This condition may be part of systemic lupus erythematosus (which is also seen in humans). Rheumatoid arthritis is also considered to be an autoimmune disease. In many cases, the causes of these problems are not known. Maybe that's why all the the big words are used to describe them! How about some names like bullous pemphigoid, or pemphigus vulgaris? Sorry—there aren't any smaller words.

Another half-dozen conditions fall under the heading of autoimmune disease. Signs differ, depending on which tisues of the body are involved. The dog may be anemic, may be pale and weak, or may show icterus. Autoimmune diseases are all uncommon (but not exactly rare), and are very difficult to diagnose, EVEN for your veterinarian. If your dog has an unusual set of problems, which do not respond to simple or easy treatment, and they continue for a long time, it may be worth asking for a referral to a specialty clinic or taking your dog to a university hospital if you are close to one of the veterinary schools. The bad news is that most of these problems are also difficult to cure permanently. Corticosteroid medications are currently the most commonly used drugs for treating autoimmune problems. Early treatment seems to be more successful than if the problem has been going for a period of time.

Chapter 21

TUMORS

TUMORS IN GENERAL

Tumors (or cancers, as some people call them) can occur in any system of the body as cells mutate to abnormal forms, and multiply, "out of control." Dogs have many of the same types of tumors that humans do, and they occur in similar locations. Tumors in dogs and cats often serve as models for those in humans, and their successful treatment in these animals can advance the knowledge of treatment of tumors in humans. For instance, the same sunlight which causes skin cancer in humans causes similar tumors on the noses of some light-skinned dogs. Mammary tumors occur in female dogs at two to three times the rate that they do in humans. Our pets may possibly serve to warn us about environmentally induced cancers.

The most common tumors of old dogs are those which occur in the skin and in the mammary tissue (the equivalent of breast cancer in humans). If the dog is otherwise normal, treatment of most tumors can often be quite successful.

Before you decide to euthanize the animal, get a diagnosis of the problem. Take the dog to your veterinarian. A tumor affecting one or more mammary glands can often be removed completely. If caught early and if it has not spread to other parts of the animal's body, your dog may have several more happy, healthy years with you. Your veterinarian will give your dog a complete physical examination, and evaluate your dog's chances for a complete recovery. Then, you can make an informed decision.

If there is any question about whether the tumor has spread, your veterinarian may want to biopsy the tumor to find out exactly what kind it is. This will give him a better idea about whether it will spread or not, and if so, how rapidly. A biopsy is done by taking a small portion of tissue from the tumor and sending it to a laboratory. The sample may be obtained surgically, done with a needle, or done by swabbing some cells from it if it is open and draining. The same type of tumor tends to behave in much the same way, whether it occurs in animals or humans. If it spreads rapidly in an animals's body, it will also spread rapidly in a human's body.

A choice of treatment can be made, based on the biopsy results. If the disease is a local problem, such as a leg with osteosarcoma, local treatment (amputation) may offer the best chance for a cure. A localized mammary or skin tumor will be taken out. In general, surgical removal is the best therapy for most tumors.

If the disease has spread throughout the system, as is common with leukemias, it will require systemic treatment, such as chemotherapy. The goal of chemotherapy, please remember, is to control the cancerous cells. In most cases, it will NOT result in a complete cure. All anti-tumor drugs are extremely potent toxic agents. The reason for using them is that they are more poisonous to the tumor cells than they are to normal cells. With many of these drugs, there is a VERY fine line between the two. Bone marrow suppression is a common result of therapy. Chemotherapy will be stopped, either temporarily or permanently, to try to allow the bone marrow to recover, which it may not. Because of the bone marrow suppression, the dog may have little or no resistance to bacterial or yeast infections. Antibacterial therapy may be needed to control infections. Normal blood clotting can also be affected.

In some cases, cryotherapy (freezing) might be used to shrink or remove the tumor. Radiation therapy can be used for some tumors. Dogs who have radiation therapy often lose hair in the irradiated area. The hair will usually regrow, but may come in a different color. A moist dermatitis, similar to a sunburn, may occur. Hormones can be used to treat some tumors. Immune system stimulants are sometimes used to induce the animal's system to reject the tumor.

If surgery is the best choice for treatment, schedule it as soon as possible. More patients with tumors are cured by surgery than by any other method. Do not wait. If you are going to have it done, do so within a couple of days if at all possible. The longer you wait, the larger the tumor can grow, and the greater the chances are for spread, especially if it is of a rapidly spreading type. If you have decided not to have surgery done, doses of corticosteroid drugs may slow the development of the cancer. These drugs have side effects, and may make your dog a poor candidate for surgery at a later date.

Cancer patients are often in poor condition. Their wounds may heal slowly, if at all, and they are more susceptible to infection. The dog will need good nutrition and loving after-care to keep up his strength and to heal as fast as possible after surgery.

Your veterinarian will probably X-ray the lungs and other internal organs as a part of the examination. This will tell him if the tumor has already spread, and will also give him an idea of the dog's chances for survival or cure.

What if you can't afford to pay for treatment of your dog's tumor? Before you give up, check with your nearest veterinary college. Several of them have programs where family pets are treated to help develop and refine therapies for human cancers. Colorado State University, for example, has had a program comparing the results of chemotherapy plus radiation versus radiation therapy alone for canine osteosarcoma. Each treatment takes ten to thirty minutes, and the total program lasts 22 days or more. Surgery will usually be needed later to remove as much of the tumor as possible. Purdue has a similar program, as does the University of California at Davis. Other programs may become available, so it's worth a phone call before you make your final decision about what to do. These programs are done either at a reduced charge, or at no charge to the dog owner. If your dog is accepted for a program like this, make sure that you are willing to make a commitment to the entire program, as it may affect your funding if you do not show up for scheduled appointments and you may be charged for partial treatments. In most cases, you must also agree to submit the dog to a necropsy (autopsy) if the dog dies.

Whatever you decide, please make your decision within a couple of days. Don't decide not to treat the dog, let him go for several months, and then later decide to treat him. Later is almost always too late.

SKIN TUMORS

There are a number of kinds of skin tumors: lipomas, papillomas, melanomas, squamous cell carcinomas, and others. Lipomas are small, fatty tumors which occur in the skin. They are usually benign and only make the dog look "lumpy". Keep an eye on them. Papillomas occur as small nodules on the skin, especially on the face, and feet. They may occur singly or in groups. When you see a small nodule on the dog's skin, keep an eye on it. Have it checked the next time you take him to your veterinarian. If there is any change in the growth—if it changes colors, becomes larger, or becomes torn or bleeding, have it checked within a day or two. It should also be checked if it seems to be bothering the dog, shown by his chewing or worrying at it.

Melanomas occur on the skin and in the mouth. They are small raised nodules which may be noticeably black. They usually occur one at a time. These tumors are potentially malignant and should be removed reasonably soon, before they have time to spread to other parts of the body.

Squamous cell carcinomas are malignant skin tumors which are most commonly found at the edges of the mouth, eyes, or anus. These should be removed as soon as possible, as they spread quite easily to lymph nodes in the area. Once spread has occurred, treatment is not usually successful.

MAMMARY TUMORS

Mammary tumors account for more than half the tumors in female dogs. They account for only a tiny fraction of the tumors seen in male dogs, but they do occur. They are also a disease of older animals, being more common in bitches more than six years of age. There is no particular breed incidence associated with mammary tumors. The hindmost mammary glands are more often invovled than are those farther forward.

A tumor in a mammary gland may look like a hardened, misshapen mass involving one or more glands. Or, it may be a superficial, draining sore with only slight thickening under the surface. In some dogs, early detection may occur when you examine the dog and find that one gland is of a different consistency, whether harder or softer, than the others. Palpation of the mammary glands should be done once a month or so in female dogs over six years of age. Feel for the abnormalities and inconsistencies. If you find one, have your veterinarian check the dog immediately.

The involved gland or glands will be completely removed. Because dogs are not emotionally attached to their mammary glands, simple lump removal is not usually done. If the cancer has spread to lymph nodes in the armpit or groin, these will be removed, too. In any but the simplest cases, your veterinarian will probably X-ray the lungs to see if the tumor has spread to that area. If it has spread, the prognosis is much poorer than if it has not. Spread of these tumors to other organs such as the liver is quite rare in dogs. In some particular tumors, radiation therapy or chemotherapy may be appropriate follow-up to the mammary gland surgery.

It is always a good idea to let your veterinarian send the removed tumor to the laboratory for a microscopic examination if you can afford the charges. This will allow him to know exactly what kind of tumor he has removed, and what therapy and aftercare to use. It also gives him (and you) a better idea of the prognosis, and helps you to know where to watch for spread.

With prompt removal of the tumors, approximately half to three-quarters of the dogs which have surgery will be alive at the end of a year. Performing a complete ovariohysterectomy (spay) at the time the mammary gland surgery is done increases the chances of survival even more. Mammary gland tumors are much less common in bitches who have been spayed before they ever come into heat than in bitches who have had one or more litters or who have never been spayed.

LEUKEMIA AND LYMPHOMA

Leukemia and lymphoma are two related malignancies of the lymphatic system. Lymphoma generally refers to a growth of malignant cells in the lymph nodes throughout the body. Leukemia is a disease mostly of the white blood cell-forming tissues.

The most prominent sign of lymphoma is the swelling of lymph nodes throughout the body. These are especially noticeable behind the angle of the stifle joint (knee) in the hind leg. The nodes will feel like large, hard knots beneath the skin. These swellings are painless. Usually, they grow rather slowly as the disease progresses. If the lymph nodes in the intestine are involved, the dog may show lack of appetite, droopiness, vomiting, diarrhea, and weight loss. The mucous membranes can be pale, and the dog may have a fever. If the skin is involved, large raised plaques, or, maybe, ulcerated or reddened areas may be seen. If the lymph nodes in the chest are involved, the dog may have trouble breathing, and will have little energy or tolerance for exercise.

The signs of leukemia in the dog are vague, and can resemble many diseases. The dog may not have an appetite, and may show weight loss. He can have vomiting and diarrhea. He will probably lack energy, and in the later stages of the disease may become dehydrated. The dog may have nosebleeds, and hemorrhages might be present on the mucous membranes. The dog may have bruises under his skin. Anemia often develops, with the dog having pale mucous membranes. Fever and accompanying infection are not uncommon because the immune system is not working normally. Swollen lymph nodes are common. Depending on the particular animal, leukemia may progress very slowly or quite rapidly.

Of all the signs of leukemia, swollen lymph nodes throughout the body are the one most suggestive of this disease. Your veterinarian will diagnose the disease by using laboratory blood and chemical tests. He may also take X-rays of the chest and abdomen to see the extent of lymph node involvement in those locations. Ultrasound examinations may also be used. The dog's bone marrow will usually be checked to see how well it is functioning and how extensively it is involved in the disease. The veterinarian may take biopsy samples of cells from a lymph node, or from an organ such as the spleen or liver, to confirm the diagnosis. The biopsy will also give him a better information about the dog's chances for survival than he would otherwise be able to obtain.

Chemotherapy is currently the best treatment for lymphoma and leukemia. Surgery is not feasible because of the extensive spread of the cancer. A number of different drugs are used, depending on the stage of the disease and type of cells which are involved. These drugs are usually given every two to three weeks, for up to two years. They are given less and less frequently as the course of treatment progresses. The long term of treatment is necessary for complete suppression of the malignant cells.

Corticosteroids may be used early in the course of treatment. If a decision is made not to treat the dog with chemotherapy, corticosteroids may be continued as the only treatment, and may give the animal some relief for a period of time. Antibiotics may be needed if infection has occurred in the lymph nodes, or elsewhere in the dog's body due to his decreased resistance.

It is difficult to predict how well any one dog will do when affected by lymphoma or leukemia. The sooner the disease is diagnosed and the sooner treatment is begun, the better are his chances for survival. Less than half the animals suffering from acute leukemia will show remission, and many do not live more than six months after diagnosis. Perhaps less than 1 in 10 of the dogs treated for acute leukemia will live more than a year. In some cases, the dog's leukemia becomes better, but he dies because of hemorrhage, or because of infection due to his lowered resistance. Dogs with lymphoma (where the lymph nodes are much more involved than the bone marrow) have a better chance of survival. About 80% of those that are treated for lymphoma with show remission. About 30% of those that are treated will survive a year or more. However, only about 1 in 10 will live more than two years.

THYROID TUMORS

A dog with a thyroid tumor may show a swelling under where his neck meets his body. He may have problems breathing and eating. You may notice a change in the dog's bark. Thyroid tumors are seen in dogs between 4 and 18 years of age, with an average age of 10 years (Harai, 1985). Signs of hyperthyroidism may or may not be seen.

Treatment of thyroid tumors consists of surgical removal of the affected lobe(s) of the thyroid gland. Depending on how much of the gland is removed, the dog may or may not need supplementation with calcium, vitamin D, and/or thyroid hormone for the rest of his life. The future outlook for the dog after surgery depends on the type of tumor and how much of the thyroid gland is involved.

Chapter 22

THE ELDERLY DOG

THE "OLD" DOG

What is old? That depends on the breed and size of dog. In general, large dogs age much more rapidly than do smaller ones. A Saint Bernard, Great Dane, or Newfoundland is very old at perhaps seven years of age, and may die by 8 or 9 years of age, while a small Poodle or other toy dog who weighs eight or ten pounds, may easily live 15 to 17 years of age before death. Mixed breed dogs also tend to age according to their size. Most dogs begin aging around 6 to 8 years of age, and will be solidly into the geriatric set around 10. These ages are still relative to the dog's size. Most dogs are medium-sized, say between twenty and thirty-five pounds. For nutritional purposes, it is useful to consider dogs to be geriatric around 7 years of age. Giant breeds should be considered geriatric at five years of age. Dogs have been reported to live to 29 years of age.

As with humans, old age does not come on all at once. It may begin with a gradual slowing of activity. If you do not compensate by cutting his food intake, the dog may become obese. The hairs will become gray around the muzzle. The dog's attention span and mental facilities may become less acute, and bodily organs will begin to decline in function.

Much of the quality of your dog's life in old age will be determined by the care and nutrition he received in his earlier years. From the beginning of his life, good food, shelter from extremes of weather, and adequate exercise will contribute to a healthy "retirement." It is imperative that the dog NOT be overweight. Attention to his immunizations will help protect his body from the ravages of disease attacks in his earlier years and help him enter retirement with a healthier body.

PHYSICAL EXAMINATION

Annual veterinary check-ups are a good idea for the older dog. If the dog is not in good health, or has continuing health problems, the examinations should occur twice a year. This check-up should include a complete physical examination, including the eyes, ears, and mouth, and laboratory tests as needed. These tests may include a BUN (Blood Urea Nitrogen test) which makes sure that the dog's kidneys are functioning normally. As many as 80% of older dogs will have some degree of kidney disfunction. A CBC (Complete Blood Count) will tell your veterinarian that your dog's body is free of infections, that he is not anemic, and that his blood cells are normal. Liver tests, or other laboratory tests may be needed to check whether other systems of the body are functioning normally.

In some cases, your veterinarian may order or perform a panel of tests, or profile which includes a number of different tests. He may only be specifically interested in two or three of the included tests, but it is often less expensive to do them as a group of tests than to do a few individually. Also, having these test results on file will give him a baseline of values for your dog so that any changes can be noted as the dog becomes older. In some cases, the veterinarian may want to put your dog in a special cage in order to collect his urine for 24 hours to check protein and creatinine levels. The results from these two tests may at times detect early kidney disease even when the BUN is normal. In some cases, it may be advisable to run a thyroid hormone test. A chest radiograph also may be advisable, especially if you live in an area where valley fever (coccidioidomycosis) is present, or if your dog has been coughing or showing other signs of lung problems.

An electrocardiogram is often run. An electrocardiogram is an easy way to check for certain heart problems. If heart disease is detected and treated early, the dog can often be stabilized before permanent damage occurs. Heart and kidney disease are perhaps the most common problems detected on geriatric tests. And, their treatment is perhaps among the most gratifying in terms of healthy, long life for your pet.

The dog's teeth should be cleaned if necessary. Cleaning may be needed twice a year, especially for small dogs who are not prone to vigorously chew bones. A period of treatment with antibiotics may be necessary before the cleaning if the dog has severe gum disease, or infected tooth roots. It may be necessary to continue antibiotics for a week or two to get the infection under control before the dog's teeth can be safely cleaned. Teeth cleaning should be done with anesthesia in all but the very oldest or sickest dogs. It is difficult to get down under the gums and do an adequate job of cleaning without anesthetizing the dog. In human dentistry, this job is called "deep cleaning," and if you have ever had it done to your mouth, you know it hurts. Most veterinarians will use a small dose of a short-acting intravenous anesthetic, followed by a gas anesthetic agent, to make sure the dog wakes up as quickly and as smoothly as possible.

The dog's immunizations can be brought up to date at the same visit. Some people assume that when the dog becomes older, he gets some sort of permanent immunity. This is an old wives' tale that may be fatal to your dog. A disease such as distemper is likely to cause the death of a dog whose defenses are weakened by age. Keep his vaccinations current!

The dog's home environment and care are important to a long and comfortable life. Older dogs should have a cool (not necessarily chilled!) place available to them in hot weather. In cold climates, they should either be able to come into the house, or have a heated dog house. Hard plastic electric heating pads are available from dog-supply companies. These are not easily chewed by the dog, and can be purchased with a thermostat so that the heat can be controlled. Or, a light bulb (placed so that it cannot be broken) may add enough heat to keep the dog comfortable. Warm water should be provided in winter if the dog is kept outdoors, and the water should be available at all times. If you have no way to keep it continuously unfrozen, take warm water to the dog five or six (or more) times a day.

Your dog may have run freely in his younger years, but certainly should not be allowed to do so in his old age. His hearing and vision may not be very acute, and he may not notice an oncoming vehicle. Even if he does see or hear it, he may not be able to hustle out of the way. If he gets hit, his age makes him less able to recover from the injury. At times, an old dog may be confused, and if he wanders away he might not be able to find his way safely home. And, he is prone to attack by other dogs defending their territory. An old, arthritic, nearly blind, and maybe toothless dog is defenseless. Take care of him and protect him.

The older dog's household environment should also be made safe. An older dog who has a lessened awareness of the world around him should not have access to stairs. Block stairways with an accordion-style "kiddie gate." Any room into which he might stray and bump into objects which might fall on him should either have the doors closed, or have entry restricted by a gate. The dog who is dribbling urine or has reduced control of his bowels should be restricted to a room which can be easily cleaned and sanitized for your peace of mind and to protect the carpets in the rest of the house .

A heating pad (the kennel kind, not the drugstore kind) may help to make the indoor dog more comfortable, especially if he has arthritis. At the very least, he should have a thick, soft bed in a draft-free place. This will ease his aching joints and muscles. Or, you may choose to use old blankets, carpet, or rags which can be thrown away when they become soiled. If your dog has to climb stairs to reach his bed, it would be kind to make him a second bed downstairs for naps.

The aged dog is often a creature of habit. He will appreciate meals at much the same time each day. He may become confused and afraid if he is left alone in a kennel if he is not accustomed to it. For this reason, it is a good idea to board a dog from time to time in a kennel while he is younger. If you can't avoid change, try to make it as easy on him as possible.

The older dog may not defecate and and urinate as promptly as he did when he was young. Give him plenty of time to putter around and get into the mood. He may also have accidents in the house. Put down plenty of washable rugs and newspapers in places he is likely to soil. If he does have an accident, give him understanding. Don't scold him for forgetting his housebreaking or for being unable to wait any longer.

He is at least as distressed about his accident as you are, and probably more so. This period of his life is the time for you to be understanding and patient. The dog needs your attention and care more now than at any other time of his life.

GROOMING

Regular grooming will help to keep your dog's coat clean and shining, and will help to stimulate the skin. Many dogs enjoy the attention of being groomed, much as we enjoy a massage. Regular grooming will also help you to notice any parasites or growths on the skin. External parasites should be promptly treated. Small growths on the skin should be carefully observed. If they bleed, grow rapidly, or cause the dog discomfort, they should be examined soon by your veterinarian. If they remain much the same, just keep an eye on them, and have the veterinarian examine them the next time you are for a checkup or other examination. Two or three times a month, feel all over the dog's skin to check existing lumps and keep an eye out for new ones. This will help you to check for lumps that are not readily visible.

The dog's coat may begin to thin as he ages. The skin may become dry and scaly. Older dogs should need baths much less often than younger dogs, because they are less prone to get into dirt and things requiring a bath. Avoid bathing the older dog if at all possible, because it may lead to respiratory infections if the dog becomes chilled. If you need to bathe your dog, be sure to dry him carefully, and keep him a bit warmer than normal for a couple of hours after the bath.

Check the dog's toenails from time to time. As the dog is less active, the toenails may not be worn off as much as they were when he was younger. They may need trimming more often than usual. If you are unable to trim his nails, have it done by your veterinarian or groomer. Nails which become too long may cause twisted toes, difficulty in walking, and joint problems in the elderly dog.

Check the dog's ears once a month if he does not have a history of ear problems. Examine them every one to two weeks if he has had (or has) ear mites or is prone to ear infections. You can wrap a tissue around your finger and gently clean the outer parts of the ear.

At the same time, check the dog's mouth. Tartar deposits can accumulate any time from about five years of age onward, especially in dogs who get few or no bones to chew. Gum disease is found in perhaps 60% of dogs who are six years or older. Older dogs usually need their teeth cleaned once a year, and possibly twice, depending on the individual and how fast tartar builds up on his teeth. Tooth brushing, if you are willing to do it and have trained your dog to allow it, can significantly reduce the gum problems and infection.

WATER

Water should be available at all times, indoors and out. This is especially important for the older dog because kidney problems are so common in them, and it can be very hard for them to be without water. When you take the dog traveling, be sure to have water along and offer it in small quantities, frequently, especially when the weather is hot. Abrupt changes in the water quality may cause digestive upsets—take some water with you from home, and gradually change to new water as you travel.

EXERCISE

Regular, moderate exercise will help to keep the old dog's circulatory system in good condition. It will help keep arthritic joints from becoming stiff, and will keep the dog active and interested in life. It also helps burn off any extra calories that the dog may be getting. A bit of fresh air and activity is good for everyone, the old dog included! Unless in a safe area such as a park, the dog should be on a leash because he may not easily hear commands, especially if distracted and daydreaming. If he is hard of hearing, he may not hear you command him to stop or come, and get run over by a vehicle.

Remember that your dog may try to keep up with you, no matter what, and could severely fatigue himself, or injure himself doing so. Keep an eye on him and adjust your pace to what he can handle. Start any exercise program gradually—a trip or two around the block at a walk may be plenty for a beginning. Two or three short walks each day will be far more beneficial and less tiring than one long marathon. Being only a "weekend athlete" is as harmful for your dog as it is for his owner! Imagine yourself at the age of seventy or eighty, being invited to play a game of football or tennis, especially without a chance to build up to it.

Extremes of heat and cold are very hard on the older dog. Exercising him in the middle of a hot day may cause severe stress, or could even be fatal. During the hottest part of the day, keep the dog indoors or in a cool, shady spot in your yard. Keep plenty of fresh, clean water is available. Take the dog for a walk during the cooler part of the morning or evening. During extremely cold or windy winter weather, keep the walks very short. You may wish to put a coat on the dog to help keep him comfortable while he is outdoors. If the dog has become wet from rain or snow, be sure to dry him off well with a towel when you get home. If it is really wet and cold outside, turn around and come home. You can "tough it out"—he can't. A hair dryer, on low heat, may also be used to help dry your dog's hair. Wipe his feet with a damp rag to help remove salt or other chemicals used to melt ice. Otherwise, the grains and chemicals may irritate the dog's feet.

TRAVEL

If your dog is accustomed to travel when he is young, traveling should not be a problem when he is old, especially if he is in good health. He will need more frequent stops to relieve himself and to unbend and limber up his aching joints. Offer him a bit of the water you have brought from home each time you stop. Take along some of his regular food if you are going to be gone over a mealtime. Keep him from being overheated or chilled. And NEVER leave him alone in a car. Even a sunny winter day can heat the inside of a car enough to severely stress him. A hot summer day may be fatal. This book is about dogs, but I will mention that several children die each summer from being left in cars in the sun.

If your dog is not accustomed to travel, it may be better to leave him at home. If you can find a reliable friend or neighbor to come in once a day (or twice if possible) to feed and water him, he will appreciate not having to go to a kennel. If the person likes the dog and can spend a few minutes talking and playing with him, that is even better. If you can't find someone to care for the dog at home, try to find a kennel that will give him a bit of personalized attention. This service may cost more, but will be worth it in terms of comfort for your dog and peace of mind for you.

SPECIAL DIET

The elderly dog needs basically the same nutrients as his younger counterpart, but in lesser quantities. He will need between 10% and 30% fewer calories than the younger, more active dog. The dog's metabolism is usually slower than it was in his younger years. Reducing his caloric intake can be accomplished by feeding less of a regular dog food, or by feeding one of the "diet" dog foods. The food should be of a high quality so that it is easily digested. Dogs with kidney or heart problems may need prescription diets tailored to those problems.

The elderly dog will also need more fiber to help compensate for his lack of activity. More fiber helps keep the food material moving through the intestinal tract, and avoids constipation. Constipation occurs in the older dog because there is a less-active dog wrapped around a less-active digestive tract.

Excess protein can harm the kidneys. A lower level of protein in the feed will help prevent kidney failure, or slow its development if it has already started. The protein in the diet, however, should be of high quality so that it is easily digested by the less-efficient digestive system.

Lower levels of phosphorus in the feed also help to prevent kidney disease. The kidney is one of the first organs to reduce function with aging.

A reduced sodium level in the dog food helps to prevent congestive heart disease and high blood pressure, much as it does in humans. With some kinds of kidney disease or kidney stones, the dog may need to drink more water than usual. If this is the case, the dog may need more sodium than normal to stimulate thirst so he will drink more. If there is any question about high or low sodium in the diet, consult your veterinarian. If you're just betting the probabilities, low-sodium is the way to go.

Higher levels of water-soluble vitamins are needed for the older dog, because they are excreted faster when the dog drinks larger amounts of water and and urinates more than he did when he was younger.

OBESITY

Because the dog is less active, and his metabolism has slowed, he will probably become obese if fed the same amount of the same food as earlier in his life. Obesity is a serious problem in the elderly dog. Extra pounds of fat put an extra burden on the heart, lungs and other organs of the body. In some cases, extra fat can cause severe respiratory distress, partly because of pressure on the lungs and trachea, and partly because of the need to "aerate" a lot of fat. Coughing may accompany the respiratory distress. Extra weight can severely stress the joints and muscles. In some cases, it may result in total collapse of ligaments and tendons, with the joints no longer able to support the weight of the animal. In these cases, it is usually necessary to euthanize the dog for humane reasons, as it is not generally possible to keep the dog alive and comfortable long enough for him to lose weight and stand again. The obese dog will have less resistance to stress and disease. He is a poor risk for surgery, and his life expectancy may be reduced as much as 30 to 50 percent.

YOU have to be your dog's weight watcher. Start BEFORE the problem becomes severe—at the first sign of bulges or weight gain (see Obesity in Canine Gourrmet Chapter).

WATCHING YOUR DOG

It is very important to observe your dog carefully in his old age. Small changes occur from day to day, so subtle that they are not easily noticed. At this stage of his life, noticing small signs of trouble can prevent illness from becoming serious. Note how much he eats and drinks, how much and how often he urinates, and whether his bowel movements are normal. Changes in weight may signal problems, as can changes in the eyes, ears, and haircoat. Old dogs have good days and bad days, so do not worry if he is different on one day. You are looking for trends and large changes.

A sudden increase in the frequency and quantity of urination may signal kidney problems, which are common in older dogs. Or, it may indicate diabetes or adrenal problems. A check for urinary function should be a standard part of a veterinary examination at least once a year for all older dogs. Some degree of kidney disease is found in nearly all dogs over eight years of age.

Many dogs retain their normal personalities as they go into old age. Others may become cranky, or stubborn at times. Be as patient as you can, but do not allow the dog to get away with things that make you feel uncomfortable or that you really don't want the dog to do. The dog who has never been allowed on the sofa need not be there now. He should still be a pet and not the homeowner. He may come to you more often for love and touching and reassurance. Give it as long and as often as you can.

In some cases, buying a puppy will do an old dog a world of good. At first, the old dog will grump around, defending his territory and resenting the attention that the intruder is receiving. If the dog is not extremely old or crippled, he will eventually begin to interact with the new dog. Soon, he may actively play with the puppy, responding to teasing and tugging. He may begin to sleep less and take more interest in life. An additional advantage is that you, who may be contemplating the upcoming loss of your old and faithful friend, will have another to help soften the loss when it inevitably comes. Of course, if your kids are grown and gone from home and you are looking forward to fewer responsibilities, a new puppy may not be a good idea.

Urinary incontinence can be a problem in the older dog, whether male or female.

EUTHANASIA

Your dog is a pet, and as such is meant to be a comfort and a pleasure. As he goes into old age, he will slow and no longer be the bouncing companion he was in his earlier years. He will sleep more and become gradually less active. He will still, however, be a loving and grateful friend.

As he goes through the years, he may no longer be a comfortable pet. He may have urinary incontinence, or be unable to control his bowel movements. His needs and care may have truly become a burden. If you have had him examined by your veterinarian and you know that his problems cannot be fixed, it may be time to consider whether he is still a good pet. If he is making a mess of your house, and is making a mess of himself to where he is always uncomfortable because he is soiled, it may be time to ask if he should be kept alive. A pet is supposed to be a pleasure, not a burden. If the animal has become a burden to you, it is time to consider euthanasia.

You may feel guilty about even considering "putting your pet to sleep." And other people may try to make you feel guilty. But, one of the advantages of a pet is that we CAN put him to sleep. We DO NOT HAVE TO keep him alive, in pain and misery and discomfort, totally without dignity at the end of his life. I try not to preach about it, but ask yourself: is that the way to reward your pet for being a good friend and companion all those years? We can give him the ultimate kindness, that of helping him to die comfortably, kindly, and with dignity. It is not a selfishness for you to wish to euthanize the animal because he is causing you to have an hour's cleaning to do each night when you come home from work. The animal has become a burden, a job of work, not of pleasure. You will come to resent him—and he will know it.

It's not a matter, either, of "replacing" the pet. There WILL NEVER BE ANOTHER pet just like the one you are losing. He was his own individual self, just as you are different from your sister or brother or friend. While you may have another pet, you will never have another JUST LIKE this one. Even if you have another of the same breed, he will not be the same. And, if you are worried about comparing your new dog to your old one, wishing the new were the old, change breeds. I tried, unsuccessfully, to replace a once-in-a-lifetime Doberman with others who never quite measured up. Then, I went without a dog for quite some time until I decided to change breeds so that I would not be hanging the same expectations on the new dog.

When is euthanasia appropriate?

1) When the dog is unable to enjoy life. He is so arthritic that he is not able to move well, or to stand up by himself. When he has urinary or bowel incontinence so that he is always soiled, or cannot wait until he is taken outside, or he forgets to go to a permissible place to do those jobs. When he is blind or deaf or both, and seems unaware of the world

around him, or where he is and who he is with. When he has an advanced tumor or other disease process which makes him miserable, and with or no hope of cure. When the dog is in enough pain or discomfort that is unkind or even inhumane to keep him alive.

2) When the owner is no longer able to enjoy the dog. Again, when the cleaning or upkeep is more than the owner can handle, or wishes to handle.

3) When a dog is vicious, whether toward humans or toward other animals. Dogs of any age who are dispositionally or temperamentally unsuited to being kept alive should be euthanized for the protection of those around them, whether family or people in the neighborhood. Some dogs are NOT suitable pets, no matter what is done with them or who their owner is. They do not work out for the family who currently owns them, and they will not work out for another family, no matter how well-meaning these people are.

4) When the dog, such as some Dachshunds, refuses to be housebroken. If you have a situation where the dog has to be kept in the house, even part of the time, a dog like this would not be a suitable pet. While some people may hope that this animal might make a good pet for someone else, the dog's disposition often makes him unsuitable for anything other than as a completely outdoor dog.

In many cases, it is much kinder to a dog with a bad temperament or bad habit simply to put him to sleep rather than to turn him in to a humane society, and have him placed with one or more other owners, during which he gets nuttier and nuttier, until he finally goes completely crazy. Giving him to a humane society to be placed may NOT be a kindness. It may in fact be a real cruelty. Some veterinarians refuse to euthanize dogs which they judge to be "normal" (i.e., not old or terminally diseased). I totally disagree with this—it is YOUR dog, and it is YOUR right to have him put to sleep if you wish. If your veterinarian refuses to put a temperamentally unsuitable dog to sleep, find another veterinarian. Keep shopping until you find one that will do as you ask. And, ask to see the body after the job is done (even if you are leaving the body with the veterinarian for disposal) to confirm that it has been handled as you wish. Don't let the veterinarian make you feel guilty about putting your dog to sleep.

5) When it is an economic decision. In some cases, people are unable to keep a perfectly suitable pet for economic reasons. Try to find a home for the pet with someone who can afford to keep him. It is often better to give the dog away than to try to sell him. You'll be more successful in finding a good home for him. If worst comes to worst, give the animal to a humane society so that they can try to place him. If he is registered, take his papers along—they may help him to find a home. Also take along records of health care, immunizations, and any other information that may be helpful in placing him. Be honest with the people who will be placing the dog. Tell them if the dog is grouchy with children, or prefers a quiet home. You need to know that if the dog is not adopted by someone, he will be put to sleep.

What is the procedure for euthanasia? Call to make sure that your veterinarian will be there when you want to take in the dog. If the dog is vicious or otherwise hard to handle, go by the veterinary clinic in advance and get some tranquilizers which can be fed to the dog an hour to an hour and a half before you leave home with him. Take the dog to the veterinary clinic. A receptionist who is sensitive to your needs should take you to an examination room as soon as possible. Or, if you choose, you can leave the dog at the clinic, for the veterinarian to euthanize when he has time. You may want to have someone go along with you to drive you home, as you may be too upset to drive (it happens to all of us, me included).

In most cases, you will be asked to sign a release form. This gives the veterinarian permission to euthanize the dog, and is a legal formalilty in most states. It is also routine, and should not make you feel like you are being singled out for something that no one else has to do. Read it through, and sign it. The same form, or another form may give the veterinarian permission to dispose of the body. You may choose to dispose of the body yourself (check into the legality of this, depending on the state or city you live in), by burying it in your yard, or another place which has meaning to you. You can to take the body to a pet cemetery, or, you have the veterinarian dispose of it, by burial, cremation, or whatever his normal method of disposal is. If you do not specify or discuss what is to be done with the body, the animal might end up in the daily trash. In fact, in most cities you may assume this to be the norm. If this bothers you, be sure to ask about other arrangements, or be prepared to make them yourself.

If you are leaving the dog for euthanasia and disposal, your job is done. If you are going to have the veterinarian euthanize the dog while you are present, you will be waiting with the dog. The veterinarian may ask you a few questions about why you are euthanizing the dog if he does not know you and the reason is not readily obvious. He will then either have an assistant hold the vein on the dog's leg, or may put a tourniquet around it. He will place a needle into the dog's vein, and begin to inject the euthanasia solution. The dog may stiffen slightly, but in most cases, he will just relax and lie over to one side like he is going to sleep (which he is). Euthanasia performed by most veterinarians is done by an overdose of an anesthetic agent. The dog feels no more than if he were being prepared for surgery. He may sigh once or twice, and then be gone— quickly, quietly, and kindly. An occasional dog may howl briefly, but that's all (this is a reflex, not a sign of pain). The veterinarian will usually check him with the stethoscope to make sure that his heart has stopped. Be prepared for the dog to possibly defecate and urinate after death. These are normal, and are due to the anal and urinary sphincter muscles relaxing. If you are leaving the body at the clinic, you may wish to spend a few minutes alone with your pet before you leave. Just ask the veterinarian to close the door and leave you alone for a bit.

If you are taking the dog with you, bring in a box or bag if you have one. Otherwise, the veterinarian will place the dog in whatever he has handy. Take him home and bury him, and remember how he was your friend.

THE MOURNING PROCESS

Don't be surprised if you enter a period of grieving, particularly if the dog was an old companion and friend. This can occur whether the dog died or was euthanized. It is normal to grieve for your pet, whether you are young or old, male or female. You have suffered the loss of an old friend, one who may have been with you longer than your children or friends or mate. It is normal to feel guilt, to feel that perhaps you should have done more for him, or taken him to a veterinarian sooner, that you SHOULD have done something else to make him well. Chances are that you did all you could have done. Death is a reality of life, and for most of us, whether animal or human, it should be a blessed relief, an ending to the pain and suffering of old age or disease which have been plaguing us.

The first stage of grief includes denial that the pet is gone. You may be depressed. You may feel pain, and be angry. The anger is particularly difficult to handle, as we tend to lash out at those around us in our helplessness, our inability to do anything about a terminal illness or death of our beloved animal.

It is hard to believe while experiencing it, but the pain WILL go away in time. For some people who have had the pet for many years, the difficult period may last three to four months. If you have been extremely attached to the pet, or he was central to your life, the mourning may last longer. A sign that you are recovering from the loss of your pet is often a flood of pleasant memories about the pet, and an appreciation of the time the animal was able to spend with you. You may find yourself smiling quietly when you remember a long forgotten antic by your pet when he was a puppy.

For some people, it is helpful to get another pet right away. Some will want another "little yellow Cocker just like Buffy."

Others who are concerned that they will expect the new pet to BE another "Buffy," will choose a different color or sex of dog within the same breed. Yet other people will choose a completely different breed, or even a different pet: a cat or bird for a change. Get another pet right away ONLY if it is right for you.

Some people wait weeks, months, or even years until the time is right. Most people feel better waiting to get another animal until they have resolved their grief and are completely at peace with the loss of the former pet. There will NEVER be another dog JUST like the one you have lost. But, there may be another (or several more) pet(s) in your life who will give you pleasure and share your company, each in his own way.

Please, if you are having trouble coping with your pet's death, get professional help. Some veterinarians offer bereavement or grief counseling. Help may be available through a psychiatrist or local mental health center. In some larger cities, grieving classes are held. It is sometimes easier to deal with the process if you know something about it and can share your experiences with others. Occasionally, some professionals may pooh-pooh your concern. If this occurs, keep looking until you find one who is sympathetic and sensitive to your feelings. Be aware that some of your friends and co-workers who have never lost a pet will not understand your feelings. Go to a friend or counselor who does. Cry a few tears. And, remember that the love you have given is never lost, whether for an animal or another human being. I have come to believe that our ability to grieve, like our ability to love, is one of the things that makes us human.

MEDICATION NOTES

ASPIRIN

Aspirin can be used to reduce fever, as well as to relieve pain in the muscles and joints. It should be given with a bit of food. Discontinue it if the dog vomits. Do not give it to dogs with kidney problems. Check with your veterinarian before giving aspirin with other medications. Do not give aspirin to a cat without consulting your veterinarian first—it is easy to kill a cat with aspirin.

Dosages of aspirin for the dog are:
For fever: 5 mg/lb body weight (10 mg/kg) twice a day.
For muscle and joint pain: 5-12 mg/lb (10-25 mg/kg) twice a day.
Standard aspirin are 325 mg, but read the label on the product that you have to make sure.

PENICILLIN

One of the most common injectible antibiotics is penicillin-streptomycin combination. This usually comes as 200,000 Units of penicillin and 250 mg of streptomycin per cc (ml). This is given intramuscularly at the rate of 1 cc per 20 lb body weight (1 cc per 9 kg) per day. Half of the dosage should be given in the morning and half at night. If the bottle has directions or a package insert, follow them.

Rule for using antibiotics: Anything worth treating is worth treating for three days. If you don't feel that three days' treatment are needed, the animal probably doesn't need antibiotics.

Note all warnings and cautions appearing on drug labels. Observe all local laws and regulations regarding drug usage.

Chapter 23

TRAVELING WITH YOUR DOG

Traveling with your dog can be a pleasant experience if the dog is accustomed to it. If not, it can be a miserable, unpleasant experience for all concerned. Begin with the dog when he is a puppy. Take him on short trips for a start, and not JUST to the veterinary clinic. Also take a few trips where you get out at the end of the trip and play—to the park or into the woods. A treat before and after the trip will help to put a pleasant memory in the puppy's mind. Make the trips gradually longer. If you begin when the puppy is young, he will probably never have a problem with motion sickness. Many dogs become eager travelers.

Dogs, especially in farm and ranch country, are often carried in the back of a pickup truck. If you tie the dog in the pickup, make SURE that the chain or leash is SHORT enough that the dog cannot get his body out over the side. Otherwise, he may hang there until dead. Or, if the rope is very long, he may jump overboard while you are driving along, and be dragged—these accidents range from expensive to fatal.

If you haul the dog loose in the pickup, train him not to jump over the side to get out. If he is only allowed to get out when you drop the tailgate, he will be much less likely to bail out as you drive down the road. Start by training him to "Stay" in the pickup while it is parked. Repeat this training for short periods of time until you are sure he understands. Then, take a few short drives with him until he can keep his balance and will not dive out.

You can teach the dog not to put his feet on the side of the box by having a passenger watch the dog. When the dog places his feet on the box edge, hit your brakes lightly. The dog will roll forward in the box. Most dogs quickly learn that when they put their feet on the edge of the box, they "cause" the pickup to stop sharply, rolling them over. Do this, of course, without any shovels or sharp objects in the box, and on a deserted road where you will not cause an accident. A dog trained in this way will not be nearly so likely to fall out as one who learns to jump on the edge.

If you find that your dog is not a good traveler, plan on kenneling him or having a friend come in to care for him while you are gone. If you are moving, it will be necessary for the dog to travel. You can either get a quantity of tranquilizers or sedatives to help him to travel without being upset. Or, you can send him ahead by plane—he will still need to be sedated.

Consider your dog when you are heading off on vacation. If he is adaptable and happy, he will probably enjoy the trip. If your vacation includes a lot of sunbathing or sightseeing, your dog's "vacation" may mean many hours locked in a vehicle or abandoned in a motel room, which may not be pleasant for him. If you have a female who is in heat, both you and she will probably have a better vacation if she stays at home in a kennel. If you are visiting someone who has a dog, do the two animals get along well? If not, you may end up driving 1000 miles, then kenneling your dog in a strange city when you arrive. He would have been better off left in a kennel at home.

Make sure that your dog has a collar and identification tags with your name, address, and phone number. Do NOT put the dog's name on the tag. Calling the dog by name may be the only positive way to prove your ownership if he is lost and his tags are removed. For positive identification, you can have your veterinarian tattoo numbers or letters on the inside of the dog's ear flap, or on the skin inside the thigh. This can be done very easily at the time that the dog is anesthetized for any other surgery such as a spay, or it can be done separately.

If you are getting ready for a longer trip, pack for your dog as well as for yourself. Take his food dish, water bowl, and bed or blanket. If he has a delicate digestive system, take some of the water that he normally drinks. Also take his regular food—this is NOT the time to change diets. It's a good idea to have two leashes: one 6-8 feet long for walking around town, and a longer piece of rope (20-25 feet) for runs in the country or rest stops. If you're going to be gone for some time, take his brush or comb, shampoo and a toy or two, and perhaps a rawhide bone. Flea powder or spray is useful, too. Your dog may never have had a flea, but if he picks up some on the trip, a quick dusting helps to avoid bringing them home. It's also helpful to have a pooper scooper, plastic bags, and lots of paper towels.

DO NOT feed the dog for about six hours before you leave. Plan for stops for your dog to exercise, relieve himself, and get a drink of water. Feed him at the last stop of the day, or after you are through traveling for the day. Walk him a half-hour or so later, and again before bedtime. Remember that these are not normal surroundings for your pet. Make sure that he is on a leash. Otherwise, if he panics and bolts, he might not be able to find his way back to you. Please don't walk your pet on lawns, paths, or flower beds. It may take a little effort to find a vacant lot to relieve him, but you will be welcome next time.

Car safety includes teaching the dog to stay in a given area (for instance, on his bed in the back seat). Give him a comfortable, roomy place and train him to stay there so that he is not roaming all over the car. Otherwise, you may be paying attention to his gyrations rather than the road, with fatal possibilities for both of you. Do not leave a leash on the dog in a vehicle. He may become caught on a door handle and strangle himself. If your dog has a regular crate at home, this can also be his "home away from home" in the vehicle, and in motels. Pet harnesses are available that attach to a seat belt to keep the dog safely restrained.

Do not allow the dog to stick his head out an open window. This is an open invitation to get insects and flying objects in his eyes, and may also cause ear infections. They can lodge in the nose, or get sucked into the windpipe. Leaving a rear window open in a station wagon may allow exhaust fumes into the vehicle, which could poison the dog (and you!). Never put a dog in the trunk of a car, even for a short period of time. Becoming too hot may quickly kill him, and the danger of carbon monoxide poisoning is considerable.

DO NOT leave the dog in a vehicle in hot weather, even with a window open. In some cities, it is legal to shatter your car window if a passerby feels that the dog is in danger of suffocation. And, do not underestimate the effects of the "greenhouse" effect in a closed vehicle. A day of only 70 degrees F (22 degrees C) can still give a temperature over 100 degrees F (37.8 degrees C) within the car. If you are leaving the dog, try to park in the shade if at all possible. Remember that the angle of the sun changes. If your dog's "place" is on the side of the car where the sun is shining, either put something over the window for shade, or allow him to move to the other side of the car. A few cases of heat prostration are seen when the car is relatively cool inside but the sun is shining directly on the dog. Adequate ventilation WHILE you are traveling will make the trip more comfortable for the dog, as well as helping him to avoid motion sickness. A damp towel laid out on the seat or floor may help to cool the dog. Carry cool (but NOT ice-cold) water for the dog to drink, and offer small amounts frequently.

Airline travel can be a convenient way to send your dog elsewhere, or to take him with you. Call the airline WELL in advance of when you want to travel. Some airlines allow a dog to be carried in lieu of baggage if you are traveling at the same time. It may be much more expensive to send the dog by himself. There may be a limit on how many pets are allowed on a given flight. Very small (and quiet!) dogs may sometimes be taken as carry-on luggage. Be sure to check in EARLY. Some airlines allow one pet to a cabin on a first-come, first-served basis. Many airlines require a reservation for the dog much as they do for yourself. Airliner cargo areas are pressurized but not air-conditioned or heated. Federal regulations prohibit shipping pets if the outside temperature is below 45 degrees F (7.2 degrees C) or above 80 degrees F (26.7 degrees C). In most cases, dogs must be at least eight weeks old for shipment. If you are flying during the summer, try to fly at night or early in the morning.

Do not feed your dog for 6 to 12 hours before the flight. And, do not muzzle the dog—this risks suffocation.

Most airlines require a health certificate from your veterinarian, assuring them that the animal is in good health at the time of shipment. Most airlines require a current rabies immunization. While you are at the veterinarian's, have the rest of the dog's vaccinations brought up to date if they are not current (but not within a day or two of shipment if you can avoid it, in case your dog has a reaction to the vaccine).

Discuss airline connections if the dog will transfer from one plane to another. Avoid peak travel periods when delays are longer. Animals usually sleep during the flight, but may be upset during layovers. They may also be left in the sun or rain, depending on airport facilities. Some airports, such as JFK in New York, and Los Angeles International have kennel facilities, where the dog can be fed, and exercised.

Most airlines require an approved shipping crate. It should have sloping sides (wider at the middle than the top or bottom). This helps to keep baggage from being stuffed around the dog and suffocating him. Take the dog along when buying the crate so that you can try it on him for size. If you buy it a couple of weeks before the trip, your dog will have a chance to become accustomed to it. Attach copies of the health and rabies certificates, and destination instructions to the crate, but do not send originals if you can avoid it. They may be ripped off by other pieces of luggage and lost. Make sure that someone can meet the dog on the other end. If you are moving, someone from a veterinary clinic or kennel could meet the dog at the plane, and take him to the kennel to await your arrival. Use rags or disposable bedding. If the trip is long, pack food and water dishes, as well as feed, and instructions. If the dog is vicious, or bluffs well, don't bother to pack feed, as no one will try to feed him.

If your dog is prone to motion sickness, or is excitable, obtain tranquilizers or a motion-sickness drug well before the trip. Some people seem to feel that it is wrong to tranquilize a dog for travel. But, if he does not travel well, or is sick all the time, it far kinder to sedate him. The dog may have a "hangover" or be less than lively for several days after the trip. This is partly due to the drugs and partly due to fatigue and letdown after so much excitement. As long as he is not showing other signs of illness, just let him sleep it off.

Interstate bus lines do not allow dogs except guide dogs for the blind. If you are traveling a short distance, it may be possible to do so on local bus lines, but the bus driver may make the decision as to whether or not the dog is allowed.

Amtrak trains do not allow animals other than Seeing Eye dogs, either in the passenger compartment or the baggage area. Other rail lines may allow the dog to travel in the baggage compartment. Baggage compartments are not heated or air-conditioned. Some oceangoing ships do allow dogs in special kennel areas. Pets are not allowed in cabin areas.

If you are traveling internationally with your dog, whether by plane or by vehicle, check with that nation's consulate WELL in advance to find out the current requirements are. It doesn't hurt to call the State Veterinarian in your state (generally located in the state capitol), and ask for the information THEY have on the country where you are going. In some cases, you have to get an international health certificate form, and allow time for it to go to both the state veterinarian's office and the consulate, to be countersigned. Some countries do not allow any pets at all (such as Ecuador and the Soviet Union). England and some Caribbean countries have six-month quarantine periods. Hawaii has a 120-day quarantine period. In general, these countries are free of rabies and want to be sure that it, as well as other diseases, are not introduced. And, some quarantine facilities are not of high quality. Of course, boarding during the quarantine period is at YOUR expense. Also, make sure what the requirements are for bringing the dog back into the United States (if you are bringing him back), AND for the state to which you are returning. Bon voyage!

NOSE BLOTS

Fat, jolly love-cat,
Apple-headed cat,
Sits on sofa back
Faces sightless eyes to the sunset
Sniffs the west-washed breezes
Dredging sagebrush scents
Blowing across sand prairies
Hauling meadowlark songs
Taking his world beyond four walls
Presses his nose to the screen.

Another day, window closed,
He reaches to feel
Wishing it to open,
Widen his world
Small damp spot on the glass,
One, many, multitude,
Nose blots on the pane.

There after he is gone,
I cannot wash the glass
Reminder of his love of life.
House rented
I come back
Window clean.
I cry.

Plump speckled heeler
Rides shotgun on the toolbox
Behind my pickup seat.
Vet calls, long trips,
Wet nose on my ear
Or pushed to window glass
Watches world outside
Through bright brown eyes.

Two years she's gone
Must wash the window.
Traces vanish
Leave another hole
In my heart.

To Kitter,
To Gina Lolibrigidog,
To Christy of Birchmeadow,
To these and all the animals I have loved,
In memoriam.

Ruth B. James, D.V.M.

REFERENCES AND NOTES

Ackerman, Lowell, Medical and immunotherapeutic options for treating atopic dogs, Veterinary Medicine (Vet Med), August, 1988, p. 790-796.

ALPO Pet Center, Canine Nutrition and Feeding Management, Allentown, Pa., 18001, 1984.

Bradley, Richard E., Brewer's yeast for flea control: fact or fiction, Veterinary Medicine/Small Animal Clinician (VM/SAC), July 1983, p. 1042-1051.

Brown, Jenaay M., Use of prostagland in F2 alpha in treatment of uterine diseases in the bitch, Modern Veterinary Practice (MVP), June 1985, p. 381-382.

Buck, William B., and Paula M. Bratich, Activated charcoal: preventing unnecessary death by poisoning, Vet Med, January 1986, p. 73-77.

Budsberg, Steven C., and Jack D. Robinette, R. Keith Farrell, Cryotherapy performed on perianal fistulas in dogs, VM/SAC, May 1981, P. 667-669.

Campbell, Karen L., and Donna S. Vicini, Dermatology Reports, Solvay Veterinary, Inc., Vol. 4., No. 3., Veterinary Learning Systems Inc., Princeton, N.J., 1985.

Denny, H.R., The canine stifle. I. Developmental lesions, British Veterinary Journal (BVJ), 1985, Vol. 141, p. 109-113.

Edwards, W.C., and J.C. Remer, Nettle poisoning in dogs, VM/SAC, March 1983, p. 347.

Fleming, Edward J., and Brian Hill, Nursing the patient thru canine tetanus, Vet Med, November 1984, p. 1357-1361.

Fraser, Clarence M., et. al., The Merck Veterinary Manual, Merck & Co., Inc., Rahway, N.J., 1986. The Merck Manual is a classic in the veterinary field. It is basically a bible that few veterinarians will practice without. Very technical.

Greiner, T.P., Surgical treatment of canine perianal fistulas, VM/SAC, May 1981, p. 663-4.

Greene, Craig E., Rocky Mountain spotted fever, Journal of The American Veterinary Medical Association (JAVMA), Vol. 191, No. 6, September 15, 1987, p. 666-671.

Gunther, Roland, Lawrence J. Felice, Robin K. Nelson, Anita M. Franson, Toxicity of a vitamin D3 rodenticide to dogs, JAVMA, Vol. 193, No. 1, July 1, 1988, p. 211-214.

Halliwell, R.E.W., Ineffectiveness of thiamine as a flea repellent in dogs, Journal of the American Animal Hospital Association (JAAHA), 1982. Vol. 18, p. 423.

Harai, Joseph, Thyroid tumors in dogs, MVP, November 1985, p. 862-866.

Hornfeldt, Carl S., Chocolate toxicity in dogs, MVP, December, 1987, p. 552-553.

Hornfeldt, Carl S., Poisonings in animals, MVP, January, 1987, p. 25-27.

James, Ruth B., A quick fix for injured footpads, Vet Med, June, 1986, p. 542.

Jenkins, Suzanne R., et.al., Compendium of Animal Rabies Control, 1989 (Prepared by the National Association of State Public Health Veterinarians, Inc), JAVMA, Vol. 194, No. 2, January 15, l989, p. 188-192.

Kirk, Robert W., ed., Current Veterinary Therapy X: Small Animal Practice, W.B. Saunders Co., Philadelphia, 1989. This is a superb collection of articles covering the latest in veterinary medical thinking. Its topical range from the practical to extremely technical. Its very high price will keep it off the shelves of most dog owners.

Kirk, Robert W., and Stephen I. Bistner, Handbook of Veterinary Procedures and Emergency Treatment, 2nd. Ed., W.B. Saunders Co., Philadelphia, 1975.

Kirk, Robert W., and Stephen I. Bistner, Handbook of Veterinary Procedures and Emergency Treatment, 4th. Ed., W.B. Saunders Co., Philadelphia, 1985. This handbook is a concise compilation of emergencies and their treatment. As technical medical books go, it's more readable than most. It's chock full of useful information on poisonings and injuries and their treatment. It is also useful for understanding tests which your veterinarian might run.

Knowles, Kim E., Walter C. Cash, Bruce S. Blauch, Auditory-evoked responses with dogs of different hearing abilities, Canadian Journal of Veterinary Research, 1988, Vol. 52, p. 394-397.

Krawiec, Donald R., Urinary incontinence in dogs and cats, MVP, January 1988, p. 17-23.

Kronfeld, D.S., and Downey, R.L., Nutritional strategies for stamina in dogs and horses, Proceedings of the Nutritional Society of Australia 6, 21-29, 1981.

Kronfeld, D.S., Hammel, E.P., Ramberg, C.F., and Dunlap, H.L., Hematologic and metabolic responses to training in racing sled dogs fed diets containing medium, low, or zero carbohydrate, American Journal of Clinical Nutrition 30, 419-430, 1977.

Knapp, Ken, Deadly pennies, Reader's Digest (excerpted from Medical Times), February 1989, p. 124.

Leighton, R.L., Chronic ulcer of the olecranon treated by skin graft, Vet Med, January 1984, p. 55-57.

Lloyd, S., and E.J.L. Soulsby, Prenatal and transmammary infections of *Toxocara canis* in dogs: Effects of benzimidazole-carbamate anthelmintics on various developmlental stages of the paraiste. Journal of Small Animal Practice, Vol. 24, p. 763-768, 1983.

Mitzner, Barry T., Simple test kits can enhance your veterinary diagnostic skills, DVM, January 1989, p. 36.

Morgan, Rhea, Manual of Small Animal Emergencies, Churchill Livingstone, New York, 1985. This is a very good emergency handbook. It is, however, quite technical in its presentation and terminology.

Moses, D.L., and V.M. Shille, Induction of estrus in Greyhound bitches with prolonged idiopathic anestrus or with suppression of estrus after testosterone adminstration. JAVMA, Vol. 192, P. 1541-1545.

Newsletter, American Academy of Veterinary Dermatology, Business Meeting, Atlanta, 1981, JAVMA, Vol. 182, P. 1048, 1983.

Scott, Danny W., and Donna K. Walton, Clinical evaluation of a topical treatment for canine acral lick dermatitis, JAAHA, Vol. 20, July/August 1984, p. 565-570.

Shirk, Marianne E., Offer services for older pets, Veterinary Forum, August 1988, p. 34.

Sibley, K.W., Diagnosis and management of the overweight dog, BVJ, 1984, Vol. 140, p. 124.

Siegmund, O.H., et. al., The Merck Veterinary Manual, Merck & Co., Inc., Rahway, N.J., 1973, p. 1520.

Smith, Ernest K., Diagnosing growth hormone responsive alopecia in adult dogs. Vet Med, August 1985, p. 48-52.

Smith, Ernest K., How to detect common skin mites through skin scrapings, Vet Med, February 1988, p. 165-170.

Swango, Larry, and Ted Rude, Jonas Salk, and Ron Schultz, Measles vaccination: a different perspective, DVM, January 1989, p. 33-51.

van Ee, Rene, and Anthony Palminteri, Tail amputation for treatment of perianal fistulas in dogs, JAAHA, Vol. 23, January-February 1987, p. 95-100.

Walsh, J.H., Grossman, M.I., Gastrin, New England Journal of Medicine, 292:1324-1384, 1975.

Willard, M.D., C.A. Zerbe, W.D. Schall, C. Johnson, S.E. Crow, R. Jones, Severe hypophosphatemia associated with diabetes mellitus in six dogs and one cat, JAVMA, Vol. 190, No. 8, 1987, p. 1007-1010.

Williams, Leslie P., Jr., Campylobacteriosis, JAVMA, Vol. 193, No. 1, July 1, 1988, p. 52-3.

Wright, Roy P., Identification of zinc responsive dermatoses, Vet Med, August 1985, p. 37-40.

While doing the research for this book, I came across a couple of articles of special interest. They were not used in this book, but may be useful to people with dogs who have special problems. They are:

Ettelson, Richard, White canes for blind dogs, MVP, March 1987, p. 165-166. This fellow made a cane apparatus to fit on his blind dog's collar which greatly aided the animal's movement and comfort.

Vaughan, Richard W., and K.D. Kirkland, Construction of a cart and sling for rehabilitation of immobile dogs, VM/SAC, February 1983, p. 191-194. This describes relatively simple construction of a cart for dogs who are paralyzed or otherwise unable to move, made from materials from the hardware store.

INDEX

About The Author

Ruth B. James, DVM

Dr. James took her preveterinary training at the
University of Denver and graduated from the College
of Veterinary Medicine at Colorado State University.
She replaced veterinarians who were on vacation,
working for over fifty veterinarians in five western states.
During this time, her work included dogs, cats, horses,
and numerous farm animals. Later, she established
a successful equine practice in Casper, Wyoming.
She has emphasized preventive medicine for her
clients, preferring to prevent problems rather than to
treat them, and has given horse health clinics and
seminars for horsemen, as well as for 4-H members.
Dr. James pilots a Super Cub airplane, and currently
divides her time between Arizona in the winter
and Wyoming in the summer. Her other interests include
hiking and backpacking, tracking, jogging, riding cutting
and trail horses, aikido (a martial art somewhat resembling
judo), snorkeling and scuba diving, and travel.

A Do-It-Yourself
VETERINARY GUIDE FOR HORSEMEN!

100%
Money-Back Guarantee for One Full Year!

If, for ANY reason, you are not satisfied with this book, return it within 1 year from date of purchase for a full, courteous refund.

FREE
postage and handling!

Also available at better feed stores, tack shops, and bookstores.

H OW TO BE YOUR OWN VETERINARIAN
(sometimes)

A Do-It-Yourself Guide for the Horseman

Ruth B. James DVM

TOPICS INCLUDE:

Medications

Bandages and Bandaging

Treatment Methods

Lameness and Soundness

Back Problems

Restraint and Safety

Common Sense Horse Feeding

Equine Management to Avoid Illness and Injury

Reproduction and Foaling

Skin Problems

Eye Problems

. . . and MORE!

with Dr. Ruth B. James

Dr. James, a respected equine practitioner, has written this book in the same easy-to-read style as her many articles in the Vet's Corner of *WESTERN HORSEMAN*. This book's 352 pages cover the latest breakthroughs and newest treatments, as well as tried-and-true remedies that really work! You'll know how to give your own injections, saving time and money. Most importantly, you'll know when you should call your vet, and when you can take care of a problem yourself. This book contains 21 chapters, with over 125 photos, diagrams and drawings. A quality, stitched binding and tough plastic-coated cover make this a durable addition to your tack room or library.   Dealer Inquiries Invited.

A Wealth of Money-Saving Information for only $19.95. SEND TODAY!

Each book is shipped in a custom mailing package.
Please send:

_____ How To Be Your Own Veterinarian
[Sometimes] at $19.95 each $ _____

[Canadian and foreign orders payable in U.S. funds.]

Wyoming residents only, add 3% sales tax. $ _____

Total Enclosed $ _____

☐ Check Enclosed   ☐ MasterCard   ☐ VISA

Card No. _____ Exp. Date _____

Card Holder's Signature _____

SHIPPING LABEL
SPECIAL 4th CLASS BOOK RATE

FROM: *ALPINE PRESS*
P.O. Box 1930, Dept. F-9
Mills, WY 82644

TO:

Name _____

Address _____

City _____

State _____ Zip _____

We Hope...
You've enjoyed reading this book as much as we've enjoyed writing and publishing it.

Please...
Help us to help others keep their dogs healthy and save money on dog care.
Give this page to a neighbor or friend, or use it to order a copy for a gift.
Remember, the postage is FREE on all shipments!

Please complete and include the following if this book is a gift or institutional purchase:

Shall we enclose a gift card? ☐ Yes.

Occasion_____

     (Christmas, Birthday, Graduation, Mothers' or
     Fathers' Day, Valentines, etc.)

Schools or Libraries:
     Purchase Order Number_____

Person sending gift:

Name_____

Address_____

City_____

State_____Zip_____

Each book is shipped promptly in a custom mailing
package:

Please send, postage paid:

____The Dog Repair Book at $16.95   _____

____How to Be Your Own Veterinarian
(Sometimes) A Do-It-Yourself Guide
for the Horseman at $19.95   _____

(Canadian and foreign orders payable in
U.S. funds)

Wyoming residents only add 3% sales tax _____

            Total Enclosed _____

☐ Check Enclosed   ☐ MasterCard   ☐ VISA
Card No._____
Expiration Date_____

Card Holder's Signature_____

SHIPPING LABEL
Special 4th Class Book Rate

_____

From: ALPINE PRESS
       PO Box 1930
       Mills, Wyo. 82644

TO:

Name_____

Address_____ Apt._____

City_____

State_____ Zip _____

Our Guarantee

We are convinced that this book will help you to care for your dog(s), and that the information contained in it will help you avoid problems and save money.

If, for any reason, during ONE YEAR following the date of purchase, you are not satisfied with this book, you may return it for a full, courteous refund. Send it, with the receipt with purchase price circled, to:

Alpine Press
P.O. Box 1930
Mills, Wyoming 82644

Sincerely,

Lynn Wilson

Lynn Wilson
Production Assistant